The Sociology
of Development

PRAEGER SPECIAL STUDIES IN
INTERNATIONAL ECONOMICS AND DEVELOPMENT

The Sociology of Development

IRAN AS AN ASIAN CASE STUDY

Norman Jacobs

FREDERICK A. PRAEGER, Publishers
New York • Washington • London

The purpose of the Praeger Special Studies is to make specialized research monographs in U.S. and international economics and politics available to the academic, business, and government communities. For further information, write to the Special Projects Division, Frederick A. Praeger, Publishers, 111 Fourth Avenue, New York, N.Y. 10003.

FREDERICK A. PRAEGER, PUBLISHERS
111 Fourth Avenue, New York, N.Y. 10003, U.S.A.
77-79 Charlotte Street, London W.1, England

Published in the United States of America in 1966
by Frederick A. Praeger, Inc., Publishers

Second printing, 1967

Library of Congress Catalog Card Number: 66-15743

Printed in the United States of America

CONTENTS

The Sociology of Development

CHAPTER **1** INTRODUCTION

THE PROBLEM OF ASIAN DEVELOPMENT AND THE IRANIAN CASE

Why have European and Japanese societies successfully developed economically while other societies--
especially continental Asian societies, despite the
considerable economic and political aid they have
often received--have not? And, more important, how
can the situation be improved?

The present study is an attempt to provide one
possible answer to these two vital development questions, through means of a case study of one such
problem Asian society, Iran.*

The author has selected an Asian society for
the case study because he wishes to limit the implications of the present study to Asia. For it is
among Asian societies that his first-hand field experience and research has been carried on these past
two decades. And hence, it is only among Asian societies that he believes he can make comparative observations and draw conclusions that will have any
degree of validity. It may be that the kinds of
things he talks about in this study have applicabi-
lity elsewhere in the economically underdeveloped
areas of the world, specifically Africa and South

---

* In presenting the Iranian case study as a
"typical" example of underdevelopment problems
in an Asian society, the author does not wish
to imply that he believes that all (continental)
Asian societies have identical development problems, let alone that all these societies are
alike. But he does believe, based upon his own
experiences and those of other specialists, that
these societies do share certain similar characteristics which are significant for the study
of development in those societies; at least he
wishes to use this assertion as a working hypothesis in the present study. See also below,
Section Five and Chapter Ten.

America, and that the approach and conclusions of the
present study, certainly with certain necessary modifications, may be useful both for understanding and
for action in these areas. But such consideration
cannot be a part of his goal due to his ignorance of
development problems in non-Asian societies.

The author has selected Iran as the specific
subject of the case study on Asian development for
the following reasons. From the personal standpoint,
first, Iran happens to be the Asian society in which
he resided most recently for an extended period,
1959-61 to be exact. This residence coincided with
the time when the underdevelopment problem in the
society was uppermost in everyone's mind, thus affording a very favorable opportunity both to observe
and discuss the problem and also to reconsider earlier views and consider new views on the subject.

He hastens to add, however, that the case
study does not offer any "inside" or official information, either American or Iranian. And although
the data are supplemented by some documentary printed
material of others, either books or newspapers, the
case study primarily represents what the author observed and was told by Iranians, predominantly but
not exclusively, in provincial south-central Iran
during the two years of 1959-61. The study, therefore, quite obviously is incomplete and heavily
biased by the author's point of view, the views of
the Iranians with whom he came in contact, and that
part of Iran and that level of development to which
the author was exposed. But, at the same time, by
virtue of these very limitations, the author believes he is justified in presenting the present
study. For what he records and interprets is a
first-hand account of at least one phase of the
Iranian development program, and to the author's
best knowledge that account has not been recorded
before. Although he hopes that he is presenting
new facts, at the least, he believes that his observations, based upon two decades of field work and
research on Asia, will sufficiently be novel to warrant the reader's attention.

Second, from the scientific standpoint, a study
of Iranian society offers certain advantages. For
one, Iran has not been occupied formally as a colonial
possession. Nor has Iran been a "neo-colonial" society; that is, a nominally independent political entity

but a country which is an agricultural raw material
producer run by and for outsiders. And, finally,
Iran, unlike, for example, the societies of Southeast
Asia, has not been a "plural society"; that is, a society in which minorities, directly or through agents,
hold the pre-eminent economic positions—although
Iranian minorities do play an important role in the
economy, for reasons that will be discussed subsequently.[1] Had any or all of these situations existed in
Iran, this fact would have created certain peculiar
developmental problems and raised theoretical issues
which only would have befuddled the basic concerns of
the present study. In addition, Iran is blessed with
certain natural resources, particularly oil, to help
finance development. And finally, Iran is a recipient
of major outside economic aid and technical assistance
that have excited the envy of most other Asian societies, although Iran has claimed that this aid and
assistance have been inadequate. Yet, in spite of all
these advantages, Iran seems unable to develop. Consequently, asking why Iran has not developed, this
author believes, does strike at the very essence of
the development problem, stripped of all those atypi-
cal considerations and technical disadvantages that
allegedly bedevil the process of development in other
Asian societies.

THE SPECIFIC RATIONALE OF THE PRESENT STUDY

On theoretical grounds, the author has been
prompted to write this study because, based upon his
research and practical experience, especially in
Iran, he believes that certain significant aspects
of the problem of economic development have not been
adequately treated in the literature. First, he believes that foreigners or foreign aid will not make
or break the prospects of any development programs,
certainly not the prospects of economic development
in Iranian society. Rather, he fully supports the
conviction that the basic problems of development
are endemic to the underdeveloped societies themselves, and consequently, that primary accountability
for underdevelopment and primary responsibility for
development must rest with these societies. Or to
use an overworked cliche in this field, outside assistance, technical or material, can only "help
those who want, do, and can help themselves."

Second, he believes that the impediments to development not only arise out of social maladjustments engendered by a process of change, or the fear of change, but also are consequences of the interests and values of the people, or particular people, of the underdeveloped societies, and that these interests and values very well may be incompatible with the goals of a developed society. Or, at the least, he believes that the values of a developed society are considered by the members of an underdeveloped society as too high a price to pay for developing their society.

This study does not propose to be a systematic compilation and critical review of concepts and practices in existing development literature. Nevertheless, the author believes, third, that the existing literature not only does not touch upon some of the key problems of underdevelopment, but also that it contains certain presuppositions which he thinks, at the least, require re-examination and "reconsideration." (Hence the title of Chapter Eleven). One might say that existing development studies provide many necessary but, in some cases, insufficient considerations of what all concerned know to be a most difficult problem that has yet defied solution, logically and on the practical level.

Finally, the author believes that it is now apparent to students of underdevelopment that an underdeveloped society, no matter how it is conceived, needs changing before economic development is feasible. But making this assertion alone does not solve the problem because not even each discipline that concerns itself with the study of society, let alone each scientist within each of those disciplines, can agree on what are the necessary social changes, when the changes must or can take place (as, for example, before, along with, or as the result of the development process) and last, but far from least, how to bring about these desired changes once they are agreed upon. Obviously, not everything can be changed, nor is it logically necessary to do so. And, certainly, it is not advisable needlessly to cause disruption and dislocation merely for the sake of change in the hopes that change of a particular kind, that is economic development, will take place. For conceivably, change alone very well may not produce economic development, and only produce "change." At the risk of further muddying the already turgid

water of conflicting suggestions in this area, the
author will present his version of what he believes
the order of change should be.

MODEL ANALYSIS

In the present study, certain technical, theoretical, and methodological assumptions will be employed. Since on the one hand, the author believes
that it is a good idea to avoid any technical discussions in the body of the study; yet on the other
hand, he believes that some of these technical considerations transcend purely abstract, pedantic considerations and are requisite to understanding what
he is trying to do, and the way he is attempting to
do it, he believes it is in order to discuss briefly
and clearly for those who are interested, some of
these considerations in this and the next sections
of this chapter. For those who are not interested,
immediate progression to Chapter Two is suggested.

For those who are interested, first, the
characteristics of model analysis, the particular
kind of analysis employed in the present study will
be discussed. A model is a series of logically
interrelated statements (or assumptions) about
reality. This series of statements serves as the
particular pattern or blueprint for the analysis of
that reality, termed model analysis. It is most important to realize immediately that although a model
is a blueprint for reality, it is not "real," in the
sense that it is an attempt to reproduce the reality
to which it refers. Rather, it is an artificial construction of what an observer believes he sees happening, and is made up as a blueprint-summary to
represent these observations. Since it has been recorded by a human being, it is based upon the observer's notions of what in all the infinite variety of
reality or experience he believes it is important
(that is, relevant) to include in the blueprint
model. And this selection process, in turn, is based
upon all the observer's previous experience as to
what, by the time of observation, he has come to
believe is important to the kinds of problems with
which he is trying to deal and for which he has drawn
up the blueprint model. Since the selection process,
by definition, is so intimately tied to each individual observer, logically, it will vary from observer
to observer, even observers of the same "reality."

Consequently, at first blush, it would appear
perhaps, as if models are imperfect tools, and hence,
that model analysis is an imperfect analysis to use.
But, as far as science is concerned, quite the contrary is true. For it not only is a basic premise of
science that logically it is pointless to argue that
model analysis is inadequate because it leaves something out, and because it varies from observer to
observer, but that, quite the contrary, the whole
purpose and virtue of building and using models is
the fact that this is so. For models enable one to
see the forest in spite of the trees, and to see
that forest from many different vantage points; vantage points which are based upon what individual observers believe are relevant and significant for explaining the particular reality under observation.
Consequently, science (and the author likes to believe that the present study is in accord with science)
is convinced that it is a virtue that models can be
built up which are not overly complex and which do not
attempt to reproduce reality in total, but only to
approximate it by representing a part of it and in a
particular way. For this reason, it is hoped that
models can be used to clarify the essentials of reality;
essentials, that is, according to the model builder.

But although, with all its limitations, models
still are legitimate and useful at the same time,
because, by definition, models select from reality,
conceivably, a particular model may not necessarily
be the best means to describe that reality to which
it applies under all situations. This is a plea not
for dropping model analysis, but rather a plea for
devising and using other models. Consequently, one
need not accept any model, not only as the guide to
"everything possible" about a particular reality,
but also even as the best guide to view and analyze
that reality. For whether or not it is the best
guide depends on how much understanding it provides,
and to the practical individual, how useful it is in
solving the kinds of problems with which he must deal
in the world of reality.[2] It is on this basis that
the author wishes to justify the particular models
he is going to use in the present study to describe
and analyze the process of economic development in
the Asian society, Iran, in contrast to selection of
similar models which now are used to study the same
phenomena in the same geographic area.

In the present study, the author is going to use
a particular kind of model, termed a "postulational model." A postulational model is a model in which all the
statements of the model are worked out completely before any attempt is made to use the statements to observe and analyze "reality." These model statements
are divided into two categories. The first category
consists of the few general statements of the model
which are called "postulates"; whence comes the name of
the method. From these broad, and somewhat abstract
statements are derived, by purely logical implication
and reimplication, other statements. When these
derived statements are completed, formulated, and,
hence, when the model is completed, any or all of
these statements may be used (selectively) to observe
and order the "reality," for which the model was devised. The statements in this second category, not
surprisingly, are called "derivative statements."3
In the present study the author proposes a postulational model of an underdeveloped society which has
been derived from his earlier experience in Asia, and
which will serve to organize and interpret his observations of Iranian society. It is believed that although obviously by definition, the proposed postulational model cannot claim logically and empirically
to be the only way to interpret the Iranian development problem, it is hoped that it will be a more
useful tool for analyzing and proposing action and
economic development problems in Iran, and by implication, elsewhere in Asia than at least some of the
existing models used to the same end.

SOME TECHNICAL DEFINITIONS

In the present study an attempt has been made
to eliminate all professional jargon, especially
sociological and economic jargon. Nevertheless, the
use of certain key technical terms and/or concepts
is unavoidable, unless one wishes to repeat the same
descriptions and explanations at length over and over
again. Consequently, the author prefers to state,
define, and to discuss briefly at this point a few
key concepts that are used many times over in the
study.

The first and most important concept to be discussed, since much of the study hinges upon it, is
the concept of economic development in a society, or
as it is sometimes termed, of an economically developed society. An economically developed society is

a society that has (a) a rational, (b) self-generating,
economic system. "Rational" connotes the acceptance of
the goal of economic profit as being primary in the
economy. A self-generating economic system connotes a
system of continuous productive investment and action
which enables the economy to breed upon itself not only
to sustain the economic system, but also to expand it.
In this view, a fully developed, rational, self-
generating economy then, is an economic system which is
self-sufficient through its own efforts, and (or because
it) maximizes the economically relevant potential of the
society. A developed society is a society in which this
has been accomplished and a developing society is one
in which this actually is happening.

        An underdeveloped (or less romantically, an undevel-
oped) economic system, in contrast, is a system that does
not treat rational profit as the primary goal of the
economic system; precisely what it does treat as the goal
of the system will be the subject of much discussion in
the present study. It also is a system that does not,
or cannot, maximize the economic potential of the system
and, as a matter of fact, consciously or not, is not
seriously attempting to do so.

        These views of developed and un(der)developed
economies or societies are model analyses. For, as
far as is known, no economic system ever is completely
"rational," nor completely self-generating, for no
other reason than since human beings operate the economic system and since human beings want to eat better
than the barest minimum total rationality and the absolute needs of total self-generation require, both maximum rationality and maximum self-generation are bound
to suffer. But in spite of this fact, economists have
maintained that still a clear enough distinction can
be made, even by the untrained observer, between a
(model) system that is developed and a (model) system
that is not, if one accepts as guide the qualitatively
distinctive criteria which have been suggested above;
especially the criteria of what the society is doing
with its existing economic resources. Consequently,
even though drawing the line at the meeting between
the two (model) extremes of development and underdevelopment might become blurred, and might result in some
controversy as to whether or not a particular developing society already is developed, no problem exists in
using a model analysis in the case of a society such as
Iran, which, it will be demonstrated, does not fulfill
the criteria of either a developed or developing society,
and hence, clearly is underdeveloped (or undeveloped).

The second concept to discuss is one aspect of the
functional approach which will be used extensively in
the present study, although it will not be referred to
by name under the already mentioned canon of eliminating technical jargon. That aspect of the functional
approach that is of particular importance to this study
is the premise that the evaluation of any observation,
or characteristic, made about a social phenomenon
should be in terms of the contribution that that observation makes to the operation of the society, rather
than merely be a description of the particular form
that the characteristic takes. In this interpretation,
it is logically possible for a particular form to have
any number of functions, depending on the number of
social situations in which the characteristic is observed. And conversely, it is possible for a particular function to have any number of forms, again depending on the number of social situations in which
the function is observed. For example, to quote an
old Iranian proverb, "Locust (the form) is a curse
to those with land but a blessing to those without
food (the two functions); and conversely, a misfortune
(the function) may come from locust or man but not
from God (the three forms)."

This conceptual distinction between form and
function is important. For one, it has become obvious that the mere imitation of the forms of development as found in economically developed societies
have not produced development in the economically underdeveloped societies, such as Iran; possibly, this is
because these forms do not have the same function in
economically underdeveloped societies that they do in
the economically developed societies. And so, it is
one of the principal purposes of the present study to
try to find out not only how these formal patterns
function in economically underdeveloped Iranian society,
but also why this is so, and what are the implications
for development theory and practice.

Third, and finally, the present study is an institutional sociological analysis of development. This
implies, first, that the present study does not accept
as primary the concepts and method of either the anthropologists or the human-relations sociologists. This
does not mean that the author believes that these other
approaches are "wrong" or "inferior" to what he is
trying to do. But it does mean that he believes, for
the kinds of problems that will be discussed in the
present study, that those approaches are not sufficient

by themselves, certainly as presently formulated, to
exhaust the possible avenues of development analysis
and action. This conviction is founded, in part, on
his own discipline bias and interest, (and he freely
admits that the present study is a special plea for
the role of the institutional sociologist in development theory and action), and in part upon "hard-
nosed" field experience in Asian economically underdeveloped societies for many years prior to residence
in Iran.

     Specifically, the institutional sociological
analysis of development implies that it is important
in development analysis and action to emphasize social as well as cultural considerations (the anthropological approach) and institutional-structural as
well as interactional, problems (the human relations
sociological approach). The term "social" denotes the
relationships that exist between human beings, as
such, or in organized associations, termed societies.
The term "cultural" denotes the learned and transmitted
ideas and behavior patterns or the products of man
in those societies. Certainly the social cannot exist in reality without the cultural. But a distinction can be made logically, and that distinction is
worth making in the present study.

     It is further suggested that this (logical)
distinction between the social and cultural be combined with the functional approach previously discussed, to draw a second order of distinction;
namely between cultural and social forms on the one
hand, and the functional (contributory) aspects of
social relationships on the other hand. In this
manner, it is possible to maintain that regardless
of cultural similarities between economically developed and underdeveloped societies (models of these
societies, of course), as far as either specific
patterns of behavior or ideological systems are
concerned, and regardless of similarities as far
as the social forms of the interrelationships of
the human beings in those societies are concerned,
it still is possible to maintain that certain fundamental differences in the functions of these
social relationships may exist. As concrete examples
of this abstract possibility it may be cited that, as
more than one observer has noted, Iranian culture resembles Western culture much more than it does
Japanese culture; yet Japanese society and Western
society have economically developed, and Iranian has not.

It is the conviction of the present study and it will
be argued so, that this phenomenon can be better explained in terms of social rather than cultural considerations. At the same time, from the point of
view of social forms, Japanese and Iranian societies
have more in common than they do with the economically
developed Western societies; but once again, Iran has
not economically developed while Japanese and Western
societies have. In this instance, it will be argued
that these social considerations are better related
to the functional contributions of the social institutions of the various societies than to the forms
of the social interrelationships.

THE SOCIAL INSTITUTIONAL ANALYSIS OF ECONOMIC
DEVELOPMENT

It is now in order to review briefly the specifics
of the social, institutional analysis of the present
study. Social institutions may be defined as those
crucial problems in all social units (here societies)
that all social systems must solve if they are to survive. One such crucial problem would be, for example,
how to produce, consume, and distribute the scarce
economic resources of the society (termed the "institution" of the economy).

It is assumed in this approach, first, that although the particular way in which each society attempts to solve these crucial problems may differ,
all societies must face up to the same series of
problems. It also is assumed, second, that the specific ways in which the crucial problems are solved,
although they may be of infinite variety at the same
time, are not unique. Especially do we expect overlap if focus is not upon the specific forms that
the solutions take, but is upon potentially identical
contributions (function) that any number of differing
forms may make to the solution of these crucial problems (in the same spirit as described in the discussion of form and function in the previous section).

Or to view the same matter from another point
of view, it might be said that each society takes
the available patterns of its social or cultural
baggage (that is, its social and cultural patterns
or forms) and tries to adapt them in ways that they
will contribute to solving the institutional problems of the social system. We may term the adaptation

of the social or cultural forms, the "adaptive mechanisms," and the needs to which these adaptations
hopefully contribute, the "goals" of the institution.
Conceivably, these adaptative mechanisms and goals
may be repeated again and again in any number of
societies, even though simultaneously the related
social and cultural forms that are used may differ
radically from society to society (or from culture
to culture, if one prefers). It is the belief of
the author that this is true of Asian societies,
regardless of the fantastic differences in the
formal aspects of those societies.

Another observation (a third assumption?):
Institutional problems, adaptive mechanisms, and
goals, may be viewed not only as the concern of
particular institutions, but in the larger view,
as the concern of a particular group of institutions in a specific society, and finally, in the
model spirit, as the problem of particular institutions in specific kinds of societies, such as
underdeveloped societies and developed societies
(again, as in the same spirit as the descriptions
of both the model and function discussions of
previous sections.)

In this context, the goals and adaptive mechanisms
are but the postulates and derived statements of the
model of development and underdevelopment, while the
specific cultural or social patterns and forms are
the reality with which the model identifies in specific societies. It is for this reason that the goals
and adaptive mechanisms of the proposed models of
economically underdeveloped and developed societies
constitute the signal quest of the present study.
For, it is possible, that an understanding of these
key contributory adaptive mechanisms and goals will
shed light as to why the introduction of the social
and cultural formal patterns of the developed societies do not seem to work out in an economically
underdeveloped society such as Iran. For it may be
that there is nothing wrong with the patterns or
forms themselves, but that it is the ground rules
as determined by the goals and the ways in which
these patterns are being adapted, that are the root
causes of the problem of economic underdevelopment
in these societies. This is the reason for the
author choosing the social institutional framework
for his analysis of the problem of economic development.

What specifically are these social institutions? For the present study, the author believes the following seven are necessary and sufficient. It is freely conceded that, for another observer who sees the same problem in a different light, or is concerned with a different problem, another total and another list may be a much better choice. These seven institutions, along with some of the kinds of questions to be asked about them in the present study, are:

(1) Authority refers to the legitimate exercise of will and power. Pertinent questions: What is political legitimacy? On what basis is power legitimized to become authority? Who determines this? How is authority exercised and by whom?

(2) The economy refers to the production, distribution, and consumption of the society's subsistence.* Pertinent questions: Who controls the operation of the economy, and on what basis is this justified? What does control of the economy imply? Is the maximum pursuit of economic profit (the maximum accumulation of subsistence surpluses) legitimate, and who in the society makes such a determination?

(3) Occupation is the mode of specialization of those seeking profit in the society. Pertinent questions: Who determines the number and composition of occupations in the society, and upon what basis is this done? What is occupational profit? What is the relationship between occupational profit and economic profit?

---

* By treating the economy as a social institution in the present study, the author accepts the sociological premise that the economy is but one part of a social system, and that economic behavior is only a particular kind of social behavior. This probably is heresy to some economists, but then that is why we have economists and sociologists. See Talcott Parsons and N.J. Smelser, Economy and Society, Free Press, Glencoe, 1956, passim.

(4) Stratification is the evaluation and relative ranking of individuals into a hierarchy which
determines relative access to the privileges (profit)
of the society. Pertinent questions: On what basis
is evaluation and ranking made? Who makes the evalu-
ative and ranking judgments? What is the significance
of the ranking for the acquisition of profit?

(5) Kinship: Descent. "Kinship" refers to biologically relatedness in man's social relationships.
"Descent" refers to the terms upon which property is
transferred in time from one generation to the next.
Pertinent questions: What consequence does descent
have for determining the nature and end use of the
economic profit of the society?

(6) Religion. In the present study, religion
refers to (1) the role (or function) of religious
beliefs in determining the legitimacy of social relationships and social actions in the society, and
(2) the role of religious practitioners in the
social order. Pertinent questions: What are the
consequences of dogma, in contrast to the content
and patterns or forms of specific dogma, upon the
relationship of religion to the social and economic
order? Who are the religious practitioners of the
society, and what is their role in determining the
legitimacy of the social order?

(7) An Integrated and Stable Social Order and
Legitimate Change refers to the society's values
(that is, assumptions) of what constitutes an integrated and stable social order and what constitutes
legitimate change, and to whom in the society the
task of making such a determination is entrusted.
Merely because every society strives for stability,
and what it thinks of as stability, does not imply
that a society does not account for change. But
societies do differentiate between legitimate expected change and illegitimate change, both from
within or without. Pertinent questions: What kind
of change is legitimate, and from which quarter does
legitimate change come? (To note, what is being
changed is not being asked). What is the relationship between social and economic change?

In the treatment of each institution in the case
study, primary concern will be upon the consequences
of the structure of the institution for the economic
development process, especially whether or not the
structure of the institution impedes, facilitates or
is neutral in the process of economic development.

THE SPECIFIC FORMAT OF THE PRESENT STUDY

There remains only the need to provide a brief
resume of the specific format of the present study.

The first part of the study, save for the present chapter (that is, Chapters Two to Nine), is a
case study of an economically underdeveloped Asian
society, specifically Iran. Fundamentally, to repeat an earlier observation, it is a view of that
society during the author's residence there in the
years 1959-61. Whenever the present tense is used
in any statement in the case study, the readers
should take it to mean that it is that period and
the judgments of that period that is intended. If,
for any reason, other than these years are referred
to, insofar as possible, all those observations and
judgements are tied down to a specific date or some
specific historical context.

This case study is divided up into seven institutional categories along the lines suggested in the
previous section, with each institutional discussion
accounting for a single chapter. This has made certain chapters inordinately long, but this format does
have the virtue of maintaining the institutional
framework of the study before the eye of the reader.
In addition there is a chapter (that is, Chapter Nine)
which is concerned with Iranian interpersonal relations.
The inclusion of such a chapter might be considered
logically as superfluous afterthought of an institutional analysis (as is the present study), but it is
a useful addition because it serves to tie down the
discussions of the previous discrete, seven chapters
to a coherent presentation of the effect of those institutions on the "typical" individual Iranian with
whom the author came in contact, in the former's
everyday struggle for existence within (the institutional structure of) Iranian society.

The second part of the present study, that is,
chapters Ten to Twelve, is the analytic consequences
of the Iranian case study. In Chapter Ten, a postulational model of an economically underdeveloped Asian
society is presented, followed by a discussion of the
consequences of the model for an understanding of
Iranian society. Finally, an alternative model of a
developed society is posed as example of what, in the
author's estimation, must be done in Iran if the society ever is to develop. As will be explained again

in the introduction to Chapter Ten, logically speaking, the model and model discussions should have been
presented before the case study, since strictly speaking, postulational models cannot be inductive sum-
maries of case materials. It can only be stated that
the logical requisites of formulating the postulational model have been met, since the postulational model
is the result of the author's experience in Asian
economically underdeveloped societies previous to his
residence in Iran. But in preparing the format of
the study, the conclusion was reached that if the
model was presented first, it would have little meaning for an audience with little familiarity with
Asian materials. Hence, the practical, if not the
logical interests of the present study might best be
served if the model discussions stand as the bridge
between the case study and the analysis which follows.
But of course, one is free to follow the logical,
albeit, more difficult, procedure, if one so chooses,
of reading Chapter Ten before reading Chapters Two
through Nine.

Chapters Eleven and Twelve represent final observations on the problem of economic development;
what these problems are, why they have come about,
and what may be a way to overcome at least some of
them in Iranian society, and by extension, in other
economically underdeveloped Asian societies. Specifically, Chapter Eleven, termed the "Myths of Underdevelopment," is a special plea to reopen the question
of the validity of some pet, prevailing notions concerning the analysis and process of economic development. Chapter Twelve contains specific proposals
for the analysis of Asian economically underdeveloped
societies and suggestions for productive action, to
initiate and maintain economic development in these
societies.

2

SOME FUNDAMENTAL PRINCIPLES OF IRANIAN POLITICAL AUTHORITY

The Goal of Political Authority: Service for the People

According to a 1950 survey of responsible Iranians who were reasonably sophisticated in modern politics, who in some cases, were trained in the West, and who were then undergoing in-service training in modern public administration, the primary responsibility of a good political authority was to do good things (not only political things) for the people (as determined by the political authority). In return, the people would appreciate what that authority did for them, and in consequence would support the political authority. In order to carry out this political responsibility, political authority must lead the people and clarify the public will, providing the people with supervised guidance and outlining popular duties.[1]

It may be said, then, that the Iranian political system is conceived of as one of interlocking service by the ruler and loyalty by the people. For if the people truly are convinced that political authority, as represented by a particular polity, is serving their interests, then the people actively will support the policies of that polity. If, however, the people are not convinced that a polity is serving their interests, then they will engage in the Iranian national pastime of blaming a government for every social ill, real or fantastic, and will respond to the policies of the polity with cynicism, apathy, and even passive resistance.[2]

Under these circumstances, political authority does not have an easy time trying to satisfy various interests while maintaining the loyalty of all. Consequently, first, a polity may be forced to equivocate. For an action (or lack of action) might be praised or condemned simultaneously by different interests, so that no matter what the decision is, the polity is "damned if it does--damned if it doesn't."

For example, during the electoral difficulties of
1960-61, the government found that if it did "supervise" the elections, as it volunteered to do in order to fulfill its responsibility of political service - political guidance, it would face charges
by the political opposition that the election was
not free. If it did not supervise, on the other
hand, local landlord interference would play a
paramount role in the elections and the elections
likewise would not be considered free.[3]

And second, since the role of government
action is assumed in all politics, political authority frequently is forced to disown responsibility
for consequences in those cases where it has been
unable to carry out effectively an expected mandate
in order to preserve its position from criticism.
This especially is true in remote areas of the
country where political effectiveness is nebulous.[4]

Yet in spite of these difficulties, and potential failures, political authority is assumed by its
members and by the people to have the responsibility
for initiating and accomplishing the primary functions of the society, and is measured by itself and
the people against its ability to satisfy this mandate. This not only is the essential Iranian political value but is one of the essential values of
Iranian society.

The Meaning of Political Strength:
International Implications

Why must an Iranian political authority always
be a strong political authority? One possible answer is that a strong authority creates attention
and respect, especially in the eyes of the foreigner.
For the Iranian believes that the reason the foreigner in general but especially the more advanced
European, American, or Japanese foreigner has become
respected is that it has a strong authority which
warrants respect. And, in order to be respected,
the Iranian authority too must be strong.

And so, whatever the political authority does
externally or internally to increase its strength,
and, hence, its respect by the foreigner, is worthwhile and consequently justifiable motivation for
selecting the kinds of activities, including economic
activities, with which the Iranian political authority

busies itself. Consequently, the authority gives
priority to those activities which add to international respect and prestige because it is believed that international prestige implies acceptance of political strength. For example, sports
receive serious political attention in Iran because it is assumed that successful athletes abroad,
by demonstrating that Iran can compete on an equal
basis among the nations of the world, will enhance
the prestige of the nation, and the strength of
political authority.[5]

The Meaning of Political Strength:
National Implications

Internally, a strong authority is considered
essential in order to carry out the necessary political role of service for the people. To Iranians, a
strong authority implies the necessity of a strong
leader. A strong leader is a man capable and willing
to force his will on others. If and only if this
will of the strong leader is effective, then will
things get done; and if this will is useful socially,
useful things will get done. Conversely, if the pos-
sessor of the strong will is absent, nothing much is
expected to be accomplished politically or otherwise.
The success of enforcing such a political will then
is capricious, for it depends on particular individuals (capable of enforcing will) for implementation.[6]

Too often, unfortunately, this will operate
as follows.*

Office "X" had been without a chief for some
time. The previous chief has been transferred after
effectively demonstrating his administrative inefficiency, and procrastination, and with rumors of

---

* The method as employed here and in certain other
  instances in the study is that of a composite
  model drawn from the author's direct personal experiences. This technique is used not only to focus
  upon social situations, rather than upon particular
  personalities, but also to protect those individuals
  who are the sources of observation or information.
  In no case is any source, either Iranian or non-
  Iranian, "official" or "privileged."

corruption surrounding his departure. The staff
under him had become demoralized completely and
eagerly had concurred in the chief's removal. An
acting-chief now was on the scene, but the staff was
aware, in accordance with Iranian tradition, that
this individual would not receive a formal appointment as chief. Consequently, this period is viewed
as an interregnum, and the staff is insecure and
apathetic. Routine housekeeping chores are stressed.
One day, without advance warning, the new chief ar-
rives from the capital, Teheran. As expected, the
individual is a member of what the Iranians term
"a good family." This is a man whose family has
some degree of social status, locally or in the
national society. The chief considers his superior
family position as automatic justification for
forcing his will on the socially inferior staff.
To do this the staff must be convinced that the
chief has a "strong personality"; that is, that he
is an aggressive individual who will not submit to
anyone else's will and who will expect others to
submit to his will. The chief considers the easiest
way to make his policy and determination clear is to
shout out commands, demand respect (as for example,
to force those speaking to him to stand at attention),
to denounce loudly what appears to be the potential
opposition, and to demand that his orders no matter
how dubious be carried out forthwith and to the letter. To show he means business the chief has some
of the staff transferred from one sub-office to
another, and grumblers and malingerers are publicly
dressed down before the entire staff on the grounds
that they lack respect for his authority.

At first, the staff is very impressed. In the
new chief, as the chief has anticipated, the staff
sees the strong Iranian political leader who by
force of will will overcome all political obstacles
and accomplish the national and personal good. Consequently, there is a noticeable positive reaction:
an increase in morale, and an increase in office
activity. Within a short period of time, however,
a noticeable change occurs. As the chief insists
on enforcing his will, right or wrong, and often
merely only to enforce that will on underlings whose
own personality needs for security are being ignored
or threatened (out of the sincere conviction that
this is the only way to accomplish anything), the
staff becomes increasingly restless. But since the
chief is considered to be powerful in his own right
or because of good connections associated with member-

in a good family, the staff is fearful of him. Consequently, a direct frontal assault on the chief is impossible. Rather, the staff turns to passive resistance and even sabotage, by forming cliques in the
office to impede the chief's efforts. In addition,
the staff seeks support outside the office by complaining about the chief to those having official
business with the office, in the hope that the word
will come to the attention of the chief's superiors
that he is weak and ineffective before his underlings.
The staff also considers going over the head of the
chief to a higher authority, if and when the occasion
presents itself, as for example, when a staff member
"happens to be" on leave in the capital. However,
when one opportunistic individual leaks the plot to
the chief, the erstwhile rebellion is crushed. The
conflict is now in the open. At this point two actions
are possible for the chief. Either he can back down
and lighten the enforcement of his will at his initiative and thus not lose prestige, or he can continue
to repress the staff, trusting that his superiors
will support him. Since his position in the total
structure of authority seems secure at this point,
the chief decides to suppress the staff. The chief's
will prevails, although passive resistance continues.
In time, however, due to changes above him beyond
his control, the chief's secure position erodes.
The staff now does everything possible to destroy the
chief's prestige without fear of reprisal. The chief
fights valiantly against his enemies, external and
internal, who in the final phase combine openly
against him. However, subsequently, since he does
come from a good family, the chief is allowed to seek
a position elsewhere in the organization, more fitting
his prestige and abilities. At this time, there is
talk of an interim chief, perhaps a member of the existing office staff, who will preside until such time
as a new chief can be selected. The staff expects
that the new chief will be a man with strong personality, capable of forcing them to work steadily and
effectively, but they hope that he would have a
lighter touch in his enforcement procedures. They
have heard indirectly that their ex-chief once again
strongly is asserting his authority in his new position.
This is to be expected, for in a new situation, it is
important to impress on the staff that one is a man
of strength, for without a strong leader what ever
can be accomplished? And so the cycle begins anew.

THE STRUCTURE OF AUTHORITY: THE TITULAR RULER

The strong leader principle in Iranian political theory crystallizes in the person of the titular ruler, traditionally the Shah. The titular ruler is a particular kind of strong leader; a strong leader whose strength is based on wisdom and consequently, whose actions (or guidance) theoretically should not be wrong.[7] The ruler's political wisdom and guidance, therefore, is useful and, at times, even necessary for political action. For example, it is claimed that during the time of Mossadegh's ministership, in the earliest period when Mossadegh subjected himself to the Shah's guidance, the former was successful, but when the premier went off on his own and even counteracted the wishes of the Shah, it was a foregone conclusion that Mossadegh would be unable to accomplish anything. It is for this reason, also, that it is important to prevent ambitious individuals from seeking to usurp the guidance positions in the structure of political authority to which they are not entitled.[8]

Although the titular ruler is a vital part of the political order, at the same time he is not responsible for his political actions, especially those political actions that fail. This is based on a sanction dating back to ancient times[9] which states that it is the political apparatus which executes but does not indicate; that is, that it is a government, or polity, in contrast to political authority in general, which is responsible. This is so because the ruler's superior wisdom is constant but is not enough to insure perfection in others. And, since, by definition, that wisdom does not extend automatically to those about him, it is in this gap between constant wisdom and mortal political men who cannot, and do not understand the ruler's wishes, or who serve their own interests (that is, when guidance is not being followed), that political evil and error arises.[10]

It is at this point, when the ruler's guidance is not being followed, and hence when his wishes are not being carried out, intentionally or otherwise, that the ruler may intervene (if he so chooses) to protect the people and to show that he makes good on his promises even if the government cannot fulfill its mandate.[11] For example, during the period of British and Russian occupation of Iran during World War II, had it not been solely for incompetent ministers about the then (reza) Shah, the regrettable state of Iranian political affairs at that time would never have occurred.[12] It was only

after this period, when the present Shah was able to
step forth, purge the incompetent, and once more take
the responsibility for guidance in tackling the nation's problems that the situation was reversed.[13]
Yet in doing so, since from the point of view of actual fact the titular ruler has the right and often
does intervene politically, the titular ruler, and
the polity, regardless of theory as to responsibility
and blamelessness, are very much involved with each
other. For this reason, the ruler always is faced
with the prospect that his enemies will not always
be kind enough to disassociate him from political
responsibility especially political failure and that
the "people" (mostly politicians) might accept this
position.[14] Consequently, for example, the political
authority always must be alert to disclaim responsibility for Iran's difficulty, regardless of what
either the so-called anti-Shah "foreign agents" or
those politicians in the government who have failed
to carry out the Shah's mandate and seek to avoid
retribution for their failures might claim.[15]

Although without the formal sanction surrounding the titular ruler the principle of guiltlessness
of a political superior before an incompetent and
venal inferior has extended by usage to the titular
ruler's subordinates. For example, a prime minister
may claim to be plagued by ignorant advisors volun-
teering bad advice in spite of his firm desire to do
what is correct.[16] This principle, in effect one of
always passing responsibility down, goes all the way
down the line through the whole political apparatus
to the lowly tea lackey.

THE STRUCTURE OF AUTHORITY: RULE BY MODEL

It has been suggested in the previous section
that, in Iranian political theory, it is possible
for someone who is involved constantly and directly
in political decisions, especially decisions which
lead to political failure, still to remain wise and
free of political sin. This is possible through
evocation of the principle of "rule by model."

"Rule by model" connotes a system of political
relationships in which an individual, or a group of
individuals, is vested with primary responsibility
for initiating political action for others, through

declarations of pious political intent, in the hope
that political action will be consummated by the
others as the direct result of the personal and moral
qualities of the initiators, above and beyond all considerations of the possible technical, impersonal demands of the specific situation and of any evaluation
of the empirical results of the initiated action.
The term "model" as used in this context has two separate, but related meanings; namely, first, that the
initiator is an idealized but personalized representa-
tation of the perfect political symbols of morality
and wisdom, and second, that political action is carried on not by enforced, defined rules but by imitation through telepathic personal magnetism (or
charisms), which is the moral equivalent of the
"dominant personality" described in section "The
Meaning of Political Strength: National Implications"
above.

What are some of the qualities of this political
(initiator) model? He is an individual of good reputation, he is truthful, he keeps his promises, he
talks and thinks "well," he is sociable, and he is
wise.

In short, he has those qualities in his personal
life that the Iranians believe justifies his being
considered as a superior (political) man, and hence
worthy of emulation. And conversely, if the initiator
is found wanting of these personal, moral qualities,
he will not be considered a real political leader;
and, thus, he is not expected to accomplish anything,
regardless of the specific technical demands of the
situation, or of his technical ability to meet the
technical challenges.

Good models, obviously, are desirable throughout
the political apparatus, but in one position a good
model is essential. This position is the apex position, the position of titular ruler which by definition is the model for all positions in the political
apparatus. The nature of the wisdom of the titular
ruler already has been discussed in the previous
section. This wisdom is considered to be an endless
model fountainhead of inspiration and valuable information to all politicians for solving hitherto in-
soluble problems which range from the international
(such as in recent history the means to reincorporate
Azerbaijan Province into Iran in 1946) to the domestic
(such as how to introduce local self-government).[17]

But how is the titular ruler's model guidance
precisely to be translated into action? For, logically, under the second rule by model, it is left to
the members of the political apparatus to take up the
leader's advice and to translate it into effective
political action, for the superior's political responsibility ends with guidance. Thus, if the Shah acts,
as when he distributes his lands to the landless
peasants, and creates model (sic) villages on his
estates, this is intended to be only a source of
guidance to his fellow countrymen and not to be considered as political interference (that is, political
action) into the actual, mundane political affairs
of the society. And consequently, it is important to
realize that, in the Iranian context, beyond guidance
even political initiation "backed by the titular
ruler," although it may include direct political action legitimately may be only pious hope, even when
formal laws requiring action may be, and almost always are, on the political books.[18]

For this reason, the old pragmatic Western political truism that the proof of the pudding is in the
tasting conspicuously is avoided in Iranian political
thinking, and hence, it is the implementation phase
that rule by model is weakest, perhaps fatally weak.[19]
Consequently, exhortations to rule by model to implement are frequent. The Minister of Justice calls on
judges to pay attention to their court responsibilities
and also to campaign against political evil in the
society.[20] On the other hand, the opposition party
can always accuse the government of not enforcing the
laws of the books.[21] Or worse, it can accuse the
government of never putting anything on the books at
all and resorting only to empty promises, knowing full
well beforehand that the charges regardless of whether
or not they can be proven, by model definition, always
must be true.[22]

Political evil, then, results from the model instrument's (the government's) not employing either men
wise enough to understand the wishes of the titular
ruler and those in whom he can place his trust, or men,
who, out of ignorance or venality do not carry out his
wishes.[23] To work at maximum effectiveness, or even to
work at all, rule by model depends on political servants
who are honest, diligent, capable, and sincere individuals who personally will be motivated to carry out the
good programs proposed by the titular ruler.[24] Consequently, the Iranian politician can, and does argue that

cynicism among the electorate can be overcome by putting up honest men for election,[25] that the standard
of education can be raised and parents guided (the
model again) by selecting a number of well educated
individuals and enthusiastic teachers,[26] that the
people eventually will provide good men who are needed
to create an honest and reliable government,[27] and
that if more good people like "X" would come forth and
loyally serve the (model) Shah effective political
action somehow would take care of itself, regardless
or in spite of existing rules on the books.[28]

Yet the Iranian political theorists must still
concede that even with good, loyal men coming forth,
it may still be possible for something to go wrong
with the system of political model implementation.
Why? For one, the model's orders, as model guide,
of necessity, may be too general and open to too
many interpretations by those who may not share the
model's superior wisdom.[29] Perhaps more important,
implementation of the model guide, no matter how
clearly and specifically drawn up, requires an independently conceived system of implementary "solutions."
These implementary solutions, drawn up by ordinary
politicians, may be of unequal utility. And even if
this was not so because many solutions may be offered,
the solutions may be improperly coordinated. This
can but result in inaction or failure through the
presence of incompatible and contradictory solutions.[30]

It is to be noted that in all discussion of the
failure of rule by model the question of whether that
failure might be due to failure in the principle of
rule by model rather than to failure in particular
situations never is raised. For it is argued that,
although Iran is one of the most advanced countries
in the world, as far as its formal system of laws are
concerned, it does not have proper implementation
of these perfect laws.[31] And the problem of proper
implementation always is assumed to be dependent on
whether or not individuals will live up to model responsibility, not upon clear definitions of rights
and responsibilities of politicians. Thus, evil
(or failure) is always due to factors outside the
model principle for the possibility that the good
model alone may not be an automatic magnet to attracting and motivating good men and repelling evil men is
not admissible in terms of the Iranian theory of moral
politics.

A final observation. Since the titular ruler
does not logically enter into that concrete political reality with which the average individual must
contend, what the titular ruler does or does not
do has scant practical consequence on the implementary phases of political action, which is all that
concerns most people as they go about their daily
activities, including their economic activities.

THE STRUCTURE OF AUTHORITY: RULE BY PERSON

Political action in Iran is personal; that is,
the personal inclinations of particular individuals
rather than the prescribed rules and regulations
serve as guides to political action. As one perceptive individual has observed, Iranians prefer to
accommodate organization to people rather than vice-
versa, as is preferred, for example, by Americans.[32]
Consequently, a man in a position of authority is
expected to make of that position what he wills, too
often regardless of what the rules say he should or
should not do; and what he does, or does not do, is
considered to be that individual's prerogative. For
this reason, it might be said that Iranian officials
are not really public servants, but rather are individuals who serve particular individuals or interests.[33]
Examining the activities of any organization over a
period of time that includes the tenure of two or
more individuals in authority confirms this. A rural
program conceivably might shift from building roads
(economically lucrative) to village improvement
(politically lucrative), reflecting the different
interests and desires of two different programs
directors; one, the program of a man concerned with
increasing his wealth; the other the program of an
already wealthy man attempting to advance a political
career to enhance his social prestige.

Since political action may be a matter of individual prerogative, unhindered by administrative rules,
it often is the quality of the personal relationship
of the individuals involved in potential political
action rather than consideration of the abstract
merits of the action itself that determines whether
or not the action will be consummated. The previous
discussion concerning rule by model is applicable in
this context, because it may be "respect for a man of
a good family," for example, that solely determines
the willingness of someone else to act, although to

the non-Iranian observer the attributes of coming
from a good family necessarily may not have any rele-
vance.

Since action is so much a product of particular
individuals, it is conceivable, and too often it
happens, that disgruntled individuals can sabotage an
entire program purely out of personal considerations.
Characteristically, criticism of programs rather than
individuals are rare, even in those cases in which
principles and not personalities obviously are involved. In such cases individuals are expected to
avoid attacking policies directly and rather to build
up their case in personal terms, hoping to have the
individual(s) fired or transferred in the hopes that
the individual's departure will be accompanied by the
program's departure. Consequently, differences between individuals are never assumed to be differences
of principle, but rather to be differences of personality, caused by jealousy and expressed by a lack of
cooperation. For example, the Shah has interpreted
his differences with Premier Mossadegh not as a matter of principle (which may be true) but as motivated,
at least in part, by the fact that Mossadegh is related to the previous dynasty, and thus, he wished
to destroy the new dynasty in any way he could, using
differences of "principle" as cover for his real
motives. If this is not sufficient and conclusive
evidence of bad faith, then there is the fact that
Mossadegh betrayed a man (that is, the Shah), who
had earlier saved his life; and this should convince
even the most dubious of the ex-premier's unprincipled,
personal motivations.[34] Consequently, when a subordinate is being reprimanded, the question of the right-
ness or the wrongness of the act never may come up
for discussion, only the alleged personal reasons
for acting against the superior. And the reprimanded
individual will base his defence on such grounds as
(in order of retreat) that he was uninvolved, that
the situation was beyond his capabilities to affect,
and finally that the discipliner would not punish a
personal friend or retainer, all personal grounds to
note.

We may conclude then, first, that political action cannot be predicted rationally with reasonable
probability, since all the determinants of the action
are "non-rational" from the point of view of either
prior knowledge or any accepted administrative procedures.[35] Second, we may conclude that since neither

knowledge nor efficiency as such determines security
in a work situation, a work situation arouses continued uncertainty and even fear among all office
personnel. It is hardly surprising, therefore, that
the Iranian, if he is to survive, has had to become
an expert primarily in landing always on his feet,
rather than striving to become an expert in productive work. He is in effect an expert in forming
and reforming office cliques with every change in
the political wind. Although this is an uncertain
preoccupation, it is a full-time preoccupation.

But cliques are of nebulous value to the insecure because, by definition, no individual with any
degree of political security normally would be involved. A more effective tactic is to seek out
such an individual in a position of political security as patron, who, in return for personal service and loyalty, will support one in any situation
of personal difficulty. With such a patron, regardless of the formal rules of an organization, a man
can obtain and hold on to a good position regardless
of personal qualification, and regardless of the
empirical situation in the informal office (clique)
situation. This is because for the the patron not
to support what in truth are his personal retainers
would be an admission of personal political weakness.[36] And materially, the system is reinforcing
to the patron since by accepting retainers, he gains
support to entrench his position vis-a-vis those
about him, laterally, superiorly, and inferiorly.
This patron-client relationship, although it offers
some degrees of security to both patron and client,
as any relationship which depends on specific individuals and not upon defined rules of the game, by
definition must be uncertain. Too close association
of the client with certain important individuals as
patrons, although affording maximum security for
the moment, may suddenly backfire to create maximum
insecurity, for the client, if the patron suddenly
is out of political favor, most probably because
his patron further up the line in turn is out of
political favor.

THE NATURE OF IRANIAN PERSONNEL
AND PERSONNEL POLICIES

Crucial to an understanding of the structure and operation of political authority in Iran, is the fact that the political arena is looked upon as the major, and to most, the only source of potential employment for Iranian male youth.*

To all Asian political authorities the great political nightmare is that educated and allegedly educated youth who always are clamoring for prestigeful government positions will join extremist organizations who promise them such employment. The Iranian political authority is very conscious of the possibility of this nightmare coming to Iran.[37] The political authority also is very much aware of the fact that when students among these youth become restless, it is because primarily they are anxious about the possibility of obtaining after graduation prestigeful government employment and that their restlessness does not derive from any altruistic motives to change the social system.

And hence, for all youth, but especially for university graduates, since they are politically the most sophisticated, the Iranian political authority is determined to offer suitable government employment lest they take to the streets in frustration.[38] Not surprisingly, the bureaucracy steadily has swollen starting with the period of World War II and has continued to enlarge ever since,[39] regardless of rational need for these positions. In addition to the large regular staff there are also "temporary" employees who are striving to obtain regular staff status. A recent (1960) estimate puts their number at 23,000.[40] The temporary employees, however,

---

* More will be said on this key topic later (see Chapter Four below). The discussion in this section will be concerned primarily with the question of political principles as they directly affect the structure of political authority, whereas in Chapter Four, the discussion will be centered directly upon the economic implications of this situation.

for all practical purposes, are regular employees as
far as staff patterning is concerned, for although
they do not have the formal security of regular employees which entitles them to such privileges as
retirement benefits, their right to be fired is only
theoretical considering the fact that they would be
as dangerous on the streets as would be fired unemployed government personnel. Consequently, once in
a government position, a man, in effect, is assured
of a position regardless of need, and by implication,
personal ability. At worse an individual may be
transferred.

By implication, then, on both theoretical and
practical grounds, the basic premise of Iranian
personnel policy is that all existing personnel are
necessary and that the basic personnel problem is
that of finding sufficient activities to keep those
already in positions reasonably occupied if they so
desire or to justify the constant hiring of ever-
eager new recruits. Unfortunately for the system,
there never seems to be enough for the bureaucrats
to do in spite of the political authority's preoccupation with political (and economic) service
and in spite of all the problems facing Iran. So
reluctantly all agencies when pressed admit that
they are overstaffed, although as good bureaucrats
they tend to underestimate the problem.[41] Consequently, although an admitted estimate of 50 per
cent overstaffing in the Ministry of Education
which has been made is high indeed, since this
comes from a political source, it is probably very
conservative.[42] And any such figures of overstaffing, of course, will not include the wastage
of man hours by a mal-distribution of work levied
alike on the personnel who are needed and those
who are superfluous.

Along with the problem of overstaffing is the
problem of finding efficient, well trained, and
highly motivated individuals to serve in the political apparatus.[43] For example, good teachers and
efficient agricultural technicians always are in
short supply. Consequently, paradoxically, both
shortages (quality) and oversupply (quantity) exist
simultaneously in the Iranian bureaucracy.

To appreciate the full measure of this problem,
one must understand another tenet of the structure

of Iranian authority; namely, that all political servants solely by virtue of the fact that they are
associated with the political order are considered
to be possessed of some special, general moral competence. And this moral competence exists regardless
of the field of specialization of the civil servants
or, practically speaking, to what degree individuals
have mastered specialized subject matter, not to
speak of an ability to put it into practice.

Some implications of this line of argument for
purposes of the present study are as follows:

First, there is no bona fide technically, spe-
cifically-oriented career civil service (bureaucracy)
in the generally accepted administrative meaning of
the term. The job security discussed earlier in
this section refers exclusively to government retention in general, and not to retention in a specific
position. For if all personnel equally are competent in the eyes of the government in terms of association with a generalized political morality, all
equally are competent to fill any kind of position
in the civil service. Consequently, personnel
movement, geographically and technically (that is,
between ministries or agencies) creates no administrative problem regardless of the technical background of the individuals involved and regardless
of the alleged technical demands of the positions
involved. For this reason, for example, when the
Minister of Health became the Minister of Education,
no one raised an eyebrow, since both positions were
on the same (prestige) level of seniority; and that
is all that mattered.[44]

Second, length of service and training rather
than the kind or quality of service is important,
and hence, more education and/or service is believed
to entitle one automatically to a more important
position in the bureaucracy in relation to those who
have less education and/or service. Personnel conflict may occur when, of two individuals with the
same amount of service and/or education, one receives a better position than the other. Rather
than lose prestige before his fellows, the loser
will demand a transfer or will decline the employment, and this is considered justified by colleagues.

Third, individuals try to avoid having to solve
operational problems for which they have no training.

They rather prefer to carry on tried and tested, and
often operatively meaningless administrative routine
in order to insure the perpetuation of a non-technical
"moral" political apparatus as well as to guarantee
their own ability to fill positions within such a political system. When pressed for suggestions to problems, suggestions abound, but of course, any association between these suggestions and technically sound
solutions may be purely coincidental.[45] But normally,
when faced with technical problems, a staff prefers
to play it safe and procrastinate. The problem is
compounded daily as novel and specifically-technical
(including economically technical) problems arise;
problems which cannot be solved by government servants who fall back on an internalized, generalized
morality.[46]

     Fourth, since personnel are not oriented to the
solving of technical problems, criticism or praise
of an individual by a superior usually does not
refer to the inferior's technical knowledge or work
performance, but rather to his personal attributes,
even to such aspects as whether or not he uses the
proper dress befitting a member of the superior
moral political order.

     Fifth, since, once again, personnel are not
oriented to the solving of technical problems, preference is given to the employment of generalist-
administrators rather than to technicians. When
funds are tight, which often has been true in the
last decade, the technician is the first to be
"transferred" or even dismissed.

     What happens, then, to the technician in ad-
ministration, or as some have termed him, the techni-
cally-trained public administrator? If the administrator is considered to be so crucial to the operation of the Iranian bureaucracy, why is there so
much difficulty in obtaining trained and efficient
ones? Since there is no guarantee that the trained
administrator will have any advantage over his moral
competitor, and since quite the contrary, he probably will be at a disadvantage, there is little or
no incentive to take technical training seriously
when an educational program is being considered.
Once on the job, neither the man nor his superior
is very sympathetic to technical "in-service training,"
since the superior sees little benefit to be derived
from such training as against the loss of a retainer

in a potential intra-office battle. And the individual himself, in turn, may not wish to "lose time"
in the seniority system by removing himself for
training. Also, he could be replaced in his position
while in training by a non-technician due solely to
the results of interoffice politics.

The measure of the successful bureaucrat, then,
is a man who, first, is a master of human relations
and, second, is a man who has the ability to maneu-
ver and to survive. In the absence of a contest
for technical mastery which pits man against man as
in Iran, mastery of human relations demands an ability
to accommodate to people. Such accommodation implies
acceptance of a conservative philosophy that men's
relationships to each other, and, even that the world
situation itself, are unchanging, and that, consequently, those who are senior (that is, those who
have arrived further up the ladder by seniority) in
the bureaucracy have, by the very fact that they are
there (that is, that they have maintained good accommodations with their fellow workers), validated the
right to hold the positions.[47] The new men at the
bottom of the ladder are expected to realize that,
if they merely hang on long enough, eventually they
too, will get to the top. The significance of this
is that this can be maintained regardless of any
potential change in technology.

But on the other hand, given the ever present
danger that a clique will destroy one's chances
orderly to move up the status ladder to the top,
proficiency in survivalship is equally important
(the second dimension of the hypothetical successful bureaucrat). Consequently, coupled with the
principle of accommodation just described, survivalship is achieved best not by activity but by
inactivity. For only in this way is it possible
for no one (deliberately) to be antagonized. Also,
trying to accomplish anything requires some responsibility and leaves one open potentially to the
charge of ineffectiveness, most probably on personal,
rather than upon technical, ("neutral") grounds.
So unless one is absolutely sure of the outcome of
one's action, and who ever can be under these circumstances, he avoids a commitment of any kind
wherever and whenever possible. Consequently, passive resistance is a better measure of valor, especially if one suspects that pressure is being
put on him to commit and fail by a clique intent

upon undermining one's position. Variously, whenever commitment seems inevitable, yet is undesirable,
one must deliberate; one is busy with paperwork on
the subject; one goes into conference (the bigger
the better to spend the time); one shifts the responsibility to others; one makes minor errors in a report so that it must be returned for revision and
thus may never see the light of day again; one refuses to fill out forms or routes the forms back
and forth between bureaus so that routing will substitute for action; one refuses to answer mail
(especially from the top where key decisions are
expected); one plans to transfer to a better job
and spends one's time preparing for it; one complains about the lack of cooperation in others; and
mostly, one reports out sick or just disappears temporarily from the office where the going particularly
is rough.[48] Because of all of this busy work the
outsider can understand readily why although apparently a great deal of activity in various Iranian
offices seems to go on, very little seems to be
accomplished. In spite of this fact, or because of
it, the man of action, the man who is devoted to duty,
the man who does not have empty promises, the man who
accomplishes free of ballyhoo, hoping to gain the confidence of the ordinary people (rule by model) is ad-
mired, most probably in the abstract, or at least in
the concrete, in someone else's office. Admittedly,
these individuals are rare, and thus so is commitment and activity in any Iranian organization.[49]
Consequently, for so many reasons, the Iranian bureaucracy is overstaffed in quantity yet understaffed in
quality in terms of contemporary bureaucratic tasks
and demands.

POLITICAL ACTION: FORM OVER SUBSTANCE

The earlier discussion of rule by model now may
be carried one step further, by combining that concept with the gist of the observations of the last
few sections. Simply, rule by model emphasizes formal, often only verbal commitment without any implication that a commitment need be implemented. As
the Shah himself has stated so well, Iran has among
the best laws in the world on the books, but proper
enforcement is another matter.[50]

Consequently, not surprisingly, little wrangling
on formalizing proposals exists, probably because it
is understood that little thought ever need be given
to the implications of the proposals, and even less
attention need be shown to implementing them. This
wide discrepancy between interest in what is proposed
and what is implemented suggests that, in Iran, it is
accepted that political promises that are made will
soon be forgotten on the basis of one excuse or another.[51] Yet, since optimism for a better record
burns eternally in political hearts around the world,
especially in Iran where all acknowledge something
should and must be done to alter the present political situation, plans appear eternally, or at least
what are called plans. Since it is known that it
will be debatable whether or not any of these plans
ever will be implemented with the best of intentions,
or whether or not they can be or are intended to be
implemented with the worst of intentions, a cursory
examination of most of these plans demonstrates
very quickly that conveniently there is little substance, consistency, or reality to any of them. In
consequence such plans might best be labeled
"proposals" or even the pious declarations of the
wishful; in brief, another illustration of rule by
model.

To carry the argument one step further, since,
in Iran, the areas of formal law and legal implementation have merged in the concept of rule by model,
whenever difficulties in implementing existing laws
arise, rather than consider searching for adequate
means to enforce existing laws, it is assumed that
changing some existing law will solve the implementation problem. This may be contrasted with Greek
legal theory that has come down into our own tradition that law is inanimate in the hands of man
and, consequently, it is the execution that is
important.[52]

It may be useful to present now, by way of illustration, the life cycle of a "typical" administrative
problem.* Problem "X" has been discussed for some

---

* As before, this case study is a composite of a
  number of specific, concrete situations brought
  to the attention of the author.

time now, possibly for the last two or three decades,
without success in solving it. The new premier, as
usual, is a "reform premier." He has the full,
conditional confidence of the Shah to clean up the
mess left by the last premier and implement a new
imaginative program that will be the country's salvation.[53] The people, it is said, want constructive political action. They have not yet lost hope
in Iran, but their confidence in a new government,
in fact in political authority in general, may very
well depend upon how the new premier handles Iran's
problems, including problem "X".[54] But this time
they are heartened by the prospects for the future,
and why not? With the backing of the Shah and a
definite, bold program in hand, imagination has
been fired among the populace and the extremists
of right and left once again have been frustrated
in their nefarious attempts to set up an "unnatural",
"un-Iranian" political authority.[55] Yes, here and
there, there is grumbling, which usually is overemphasized in the foreign press, that the premier's
proposal is not really a plan, that one should
talk of what is being done and not what will be done[56]
so that there will not have to be denials tomorrow,[57]
and that as much attention should be paid to execution
as to programming.[58] But by and large, however, optimism prevails as feverish preparations are made to
carry out the new mandate, for has not the Shah himself this time made a strong plea for doing something
constructive?

       Conferences are called to discuss the premier's
new proposals. Since solving problem "X" is considered very important, because of the Shah's interest
in it, some very important people attend the initial
conferences. Great attention is given to the presence of these visitors, who are encouraged to speak
well and extoll the virtues of holding such conferences, and the importance to Iran of the challenge
of solving problem "X". Photographers everywhere
are present to record for posterity the inevitable
pictures both of the speakers and the enraptured
audience, carried away by the intoxicating quality
of the Iranian language. Duly inspired by contact
with such notables and such fine oratory, the conference body eventually gets down to hard work. The
members of the conference meet and meet, and talk
and talk. Since the Iranian politician prides himself on being long on ideas (the more abstract, the
better), and no one wants to be considered indiffer-

ent to problem "X", with the Shah's backing and all,
not surprisingly, everyone has a novel solution to
offer, or a comment on someone else's solution.

But as the conference drags on, the more important people lose interest in the conference, for no
other reason than that there are various duties,
perhaps of a similar nature in another newly formed
program, that demand their attention elsewhere.
And after all, they have made evident their suggestions for solving problem "X" and it is now up to
others (inferiors) to implement them (under the
principle of rule by model). More frequently now,
meetings must be called off because certain of the
very important people scheduled to participate in
a particular discussion or plan do not appear at
the conference table. In some cases this is acknowledged to be a blessing in disguise, for then
the workers (that is, those responsible for trans-
lating ideas into concrete proposals) can turn
their attention to their responsibilities.

The proposals for solving problem "X" which
have come out of these conferences may be anything
from grandiose sweeping proposals for social change,
to meaningless declarations which imply, in fact,
that no action ever will be taken. It all depends
upon how seriously the proposers expect their proposals to be taken. In part, this is the result
of how serious the proposers consider the Shah and
his ministers really are about the proposals; and,
in part, how ugly a mood they believe the populace
is in as far as its own political security is
concerned. If anything materializes concretely
from these conferences, which is the case with
problem "X" because of its importance, the proposals are sent along with a commendation for implementation to the appropriate parties, usually the
chief(s) upon whose shoulders responsibility has
been placed by the prime minister. If the chief,
as the prime minister, also is a new appointee
and is interested in making a splash to enhance
his prestige before his superiors, he may promise
spectacular results from the proposals, much to the
possible embarrassment of those who may be responsible for making good on the promises. This is especially so in the case of problem "X" because in
spite of past unfavorable experience with proposals
for solving problem "X", some of the public still
have hope that something will happen. Out of serious

concern, some people even have come to the office, in
order to find out why the promises have not been implemented, and even have become annoyed if they are
brushed aside. Hence, frequent proclamations are issued that "red tape" must be cut and that the people
should not be kept waiting when they come to government offices with inquiries.

Even if there is a sincere effort to implement
the proposal, and particularly with limited funds
in the case of over-ambitious plans as with the
proposal to solve problem "X", the staff and the
chief will come to the conclusion that it is best
to play it safe and do nothing that will bring dis-
grace upon themselves should their efforts fail as
has happened with past attempts to solve problem
"X". And so all malinger, blaming the planners for
such things as not forwarding the proper orders
(that is, assuming the responsibility in case of
failure) or not supporting the proposal with "adequate"
funds (that is, in case of failure making it personally worthwhile by building up a retainer-staff
or opening the door to personal gain). If the imple-
mental body is working on the local level, this body
is apt to point out that even in Teheran, the capital,
proposals can't always be implemented, so why do the
planners expect perfection out in the provinces where
it is more difficult to implement projects?[59] In
turn, the planners will blame the implementers for
inactivity. The planners argue that if only the administrative staff would do its duty and put the
public welfare before its personal interest and gain,
and would weed out the useless employees, then their
noble solutions to problem "X" easily could be implemented.[60] If the groundswell for action is considered
important enough (that is, if it would react unfavorably politically if nothing was done) as in the case
of problem "X", some responsible official will be
forced to take the initiative to break this deadlock
of charges and countercharges between planners and
executors and will commission a high level study group
to look into the matter. In fact if the issue particularly is volatile politically, the Shah himself may
issue a royal patent (farman) for this purpose,[61] and
in this case, the program effectively will be put in
limbo until such time as it is considered necessary
or useful to bring the proposal up again (which may be
never). Alternately, as the excuse for inaction, it
may be hinted about that certain "evil interests" have
thwarted the will of the people as represented by the

Shah (the model), the prime minister or some other
noble public official. These same officials will
in turn appeal for some action (rule by model)
against these enemies of Iran in the name of the
public good, to at least keep up appearances in the
eyes of the people that political authority sincerely
is interested in solving problem "X".[62] The "public"
may be pacified by either of these two maneuvers,
believing that something eventually may be done,
(and to wait for it), or that it may not be done
(and to ignore it). In the latter case, the political authority then is forced to admit that nothing
has been or can be accomplished--"at present." Yet
the proposal to solve problem "X" still may be defended as "useful," because, even if nothing tangible
has been accomplished to date through all this interest and activity, some progress is being made in
paving the way "eventually" for a solution,[63] or,
when there are such difficulties, it should convince
the people to take a more active interest in implementing their own affairs.[64]

     Since, sooner or later, the prime minister, or
the official made responsible for solving problem
"X" is on the way out of the government or being
reassigned (perhaps in the civil service), at that
time of confusion, as a final gesture of defense
of the proposal to solve problem "X" and as vindication of the regime, the proposal may be defended
as fundamentally sound and on the verge of accomplishment; only due to present political vicissi-
tudes and insufficient time it has not been possible
properly to implement it.[65] Or, if the outgoing
prime minister now is being pillored, and outgoing
officials usually are, lack of funds due to the
corruption of the prime minister or of individuals
associated with him rather than any defect in the
proposal itself, can be blamed for non-implementation.
In any case, if it has not been implemented, why be
concerned with the existing proposal for solution of
problem "X"? A new prime minister is in the wings
with a new program. Since problem "X" is important,
probably it will be brought to the new prime minister's attention. Being a "reform" prime minister,
he certainly will have a plan to meet Iran's significant challenges, such as problem "X", and hence,
will be interested in having a committee draw up a
proposal to solve problem "X". The political apparatus already has been alerted to support a new program including a possible proposal to solve problem
"X"; and the cycle begins anew.

In conclusion it must be observed that the difficulties in handling administrative problems in Iran
cannot be attributed solely to the inadequacies of
the existing specific government or polity. Rather
they are the result of the inadequacies of the fundamental goals of Iranian political authority which
justifies behavior ill-adapted to contemporary bureaucratic tasks which the Iranians have chosen, or claim
to have chosen, to undertake.

POLITICAL ACTION: ADMINISTRATIVE CONFUSION

The Iranian penchant for ritual procrastination
rather than constructive action is accompanied by
tolerance of, and even encouragement of administrative confusion and instability. It is extremely important to understand that this confusion and instability is the norm and not the exception in all
Iranian organization, and that Iranian administration,
consequently, cannot accomplish any administrative
task quickly and effectively.66*

First, a great deal of staff overlap and duplication of function exist. Many individuals on many
levels in the same organization, and even in different agencies, may be responsible for an identical
task. This is because, since, to recall an earlier
discussion (see the section "The Meaning of Political
Strength: National Implications" above), an individual can mold a position to serve his personal desires, and since therefore no one is responsible
absolutely for any specific task, or tasks, officials
may not be content to do the task or tasks ostensibly assigned to them. Rather they will try to do
the tasks of others, or claim to be doing these tasks,
simply because these tasks are associated with greater prestige than the assigned task(s). For example,
the two major health agencies operating in Iran,
one emanating from the Ministry of Health (Behdari)

---

* Many aspects of this problem already have been
   discussed in previous sections. In this section we concentrate upon those elements of
   organization which contribute directly to
   confusion.

and the other from Public Health (Behdasht), each run
parallel programs with overlapping jurisdiction and
responsibility. Disputes often only can be resolved
by the personal (and temporary) whim of the particular current prime minister. And conversely, under
the same line of argument, there are situations in
which nobody has jurisdiction because no one wants
to bother, regardless of any formal placement of individuals in particular bureaucratic slots.

Second, no distinction is made between policy
functions and administrative functions. Rather, the
chief of any section usually combines both functions
and by traditional practice or personal choice (or
both) spends most of his time in routine housekeeping
administration and in endless paperwork, without any
purpose (or policy) to guide his efforts. For this
reason not only is no attention paid to systematic
policy planning in Iranian administrative thinking,
no incentive exists to develop it. Consequently,
when money becomes available, impulsive spending
backed by ex-post facto justification and not by
prior planning is the rule.

Third, there is no requisite horizontal administrative cooperation, inter-agency or intra-agency.

Fourth, confusion exists in the apparently contradictory administrative responses of rigidity and
formalism, on the one hand, and impulsive action without formal sanction, on the other hand. "Formalism "
may be defined as negative response to requests for
action justified on grounds of formal technical
violation in order to save the bureaucrat the time,
the effort, and the commitment he may not wish to,
or cannot adequately assume; as for example, hospitals which refuse to accept patients because they
do not follow certain regulations, usually by in-
conveniently not being able to come to the hospital
in an ambulance.[67] Impulsive action without formal
sanction implies using one's rank or general prestige to harass others to act or force action without
legal sanction or jurisdiction, justified only by
the right to mold one's job to one's wishes. Such
individuals doing this not only are resentful but
are amazed when regulations are cited to contradict
their self-asserted prerogatives. And more significantly, they are as amazed as are the formalists
when it is suggested that perhaps it is better to
uphold the spirit and intent of the regulations and

to hold to that <u>consistently</u>, rather than to espouse
alternately rigid conformity or total flouting of
the regulations as it suits the varying, personal
fancy of individuals, even the same individuals on
different occasions. For this can but lead to confusions.

<u>Fifth</u>, there is poor communication <u>vertically</u>
and horizontally to and from the point of reference
in the administrative system. Communication perpetually is slow and inaccurate. Individuals prefer
to avoid reporting of any kind, lest even something
noted in innocence be used against the reporter.
But when communication occurs, it emphasizes only the
positive, even if the resultant virtue must be fic-
tionalized completely. For anything that might enable a superior or colleague to place blame for misfortune or inaction is completely avoided. Consequently, empirical data are unreliable, especially
so-called "activities reports," which misrepresent
inaction as action. The inept glorify themselves
and the competent are forced to cover for the incompetent, lest the competent be pillored for being
weak over an incompetent staff or out of fear that
worse incompetents will be transferred to replace
the existing useless ones.[68] Since, to re-iterate,
the Iranian tends to see every problem as arising
out of difficulties of <u>individual</u> personalities,
what little realistic or consciously adverse information that flows up, or laterally, tends to be restricted to complaints about personalities.

<u>Another kind of communication</u> problem. The fear
of an administrative chief that some information
may escape his attention too often reaches paranoid
proportions. No incident is so trivial that the
chief must not be made aware of it, preferably
as soon as it happens, or even before it happens.
An underling may be pillored in a public staff
meeting because he had neglected to report the
absence of a "sick" colleague to the chief. The
assistant had reported the matter only to the
accountant since the only consideration was to have
the colleague's regular salary payments stopped as
prescribed by administrative decree. But the chief
was not mollified. What if there was an unexpected
administrative investigation at that very time the
man was absent, and the chief had had to admit that
something in the office routine was not known to
him? Would not the investigator be suspicious that

the chief was trying to cover up some sort of hanky-
panky?

Yet, in spite of all of this fear of being
caught unawares, offices are notoriously careless
with records. The filing system is a nightmare.
Papers are filed chronologically and not by classification, no distinction is made between the dead
and the live files, papers removed from the file
can be misfiled if they ever are returned to file,
and most seriously, not everything in an office
gets filed in the first instance. Part of the
problem certainly is that efficient, motivated,
and not merely "educated," clerks are in critically
short supply in Iran. The so-called secretaries
usually are not competent at filing anything be-
sides their lunch or movie magazines. They look
after papers in the office by piling them willy-
nilly in large folders. One result is that the
chief and others must keep their own files and records of papers they consider important to insure
that these papers will not be lost, and that they
can lay their hands on them immediately whenever
they need to do so. In addition, or perhaps because of this, individuals are not adverse to
making off with documents whose contents they
prefer to keep hidden from their office colleagues
because they contain either unfavorable or personally useful information. After a man has been
transferred, it is not unusual for the staff to
find in his hitherto locked desk, office items
that have never been filed or have been removed
from the file without record. Consequently, significant documents frequently are "lost" and unavail-
able for conference or project action, and "follow
through" requests from other administrative levels
may go unanswered not always out of wilful neglect
but because the original material is no longer
available for any number of reasons, innocent or
deliberate.[69]

Sixth, when new political problems occur, the
standard procedure is not to work through existing
organs of administration but to fabricate new ones.
This device is supposed to avoid the red tape of
existing confusions, which is certainly true enough;
but unfortunately the choice only compounds the confusion. The bongah, or autonomous administrative
organ outside the old-line technical administrative
agencies, is a familiar case of this. But the exact

administrative status of bongah never has been defined and consequently the bongah is out on an administrative limb. It not only runs into all the problems of the old-line agencies, but, at the same time,
it has to contend with the new one of relating itself
to the established administrative structure without
any comparable status enjoyed by the old-line agencies.

The political authority, to be sure, is well
aware of all these problems. Periodically, attempts
have been made by leaders to enforce administrative
discipline, to strive for regularity of all office
routine, and to improve administrative communication.
With ferment from above, there may be a sudden hum of
activity. And if a chief is persistent, something
constructive may be accomplished, and then a chief
can say, with justification, that he is managing his
department the way it should operate. However,
regardless of whether or not anything specific is accomplished, the built-in confusions discussed in this
section, inevitably will overtake any tightening-up
in administrative disciplines, since the tightening-
up had not changed anything of substance as far as
the causes of the original difficulties were concerned.
Thus, any discipline campaign is sure to be relaxed,
if not ground to an absolute halt, and the staff operates at its normal pace until the next campaign starts.[70]

SELECTIVE BUT EFFECTIVE CONTROL

It must not be assumed from the discussion so far
that the Iranian political structure may be characterized solely as an amorphous mass of ill-fitting, independent segments working at cross purposes, although
this certainly is true to some extent. In spite of
the only too apparent confusion in structure and operations, it is important to grasp that, in addition,
significant, effective channels of control within the
system do exist. These channels of control deliberately are highly selective and underplayed, but nevertheless, they are there and are available when, and if
required and must not be ignored.

These channels or sources of selective control
are six in number. The first source may be entitled
supervisory-inspection. This order of control is a
logical extension of the previously discussed rule by
model. (See above section, "The Structure of Authority:
Rule By Model.") Rather than directly and openly

assuming "titular" responsibility (and receive judgment) for the actual administration of the apparatus
of political structure, those in control of the apparatus prefer rather to control by means of watching
("supervising," as it is termed in Iran), or threatening to watch all administrative operations, intervening only whenever and wherever considered necessary
on the arbitrary initiative of, and on the terms personally established by the controllers. Such selective control is justified on the grounds that the
correct (model) leadership is located at the center,
inspiring and supervising all work and spreading
good relations between the center and any or all
organs at any level of its jurisdiction.* For only
in this way can the desires of the many diverse elements below the center suitably be presented at the
center which is the only proper authority for handling such matters.

In this system of selective control, the "correct"
supervisor referred to primarily is an inspector,
rather than an individual charged with the many familiar responsibilities of supervisory leadership in
which inspection plays an important but merely one
of many possible roles.[71] Significantly, rarely do
inspectors consult the technicians or attempt to
examine the actual operations of an organization. But
this is not surprising, for due to the pervading principle of training bureaucrats in generalized moral
education, the inspector very rarely is able to understand the problems of a technician.

Since criticism in Iran, as stated previously,
is often aimed at individuals and not necessarily
at performance, investigators in reality judge people--
especially their opinions and associations. Thus, all
inspecting criticism is considered to be, and most
probably is, a personal attack. Consequently, all
signs point to the fact that constructive criticism
by supervisors (that is, inspectors) aimed at improving
work performance without the intrusion of personal considerations, objectively speaking, is impossible.

---

* Note the implication of the absence of responsibility and coordination below the top level.
  This allied problem of political centralization
  will be discussed in the next section.

Rather, the supervisor-inspector is considered to be
a lurking spy, ready to pounce upon his victim(s)
when least expected. And unless the transgressor
can mollify the inspector, by dint of the former's
social position or by some monetary consideration,
the trapped individual may face serious sanctions.
But this may not be significant since it is doubtful whether what is being done, or how it is being
done, truly is the prime purpose of the inspections.
To wit, the inspector is an agent of supervision,
an agent of threatening supervision, or in some
cases, an agent of actual interference; all in order
to insure the center's control of local political
action.[72]

The most interesting supervisory-investigative
agent of selective control in the country is the
Special Inspection Department of the Shah (Sazemane
Bazrasi Shahanshahi). The department was established in 1957 with definite, but sweeping rights
to investigate (inspect) the workings of any and
all government organizations, and frankly in order
to control their activities.[73] The department is
an independent agency responsible solely to the
Shah.[74] Its primary specific duties are to prevent
the cover up of abuse and corruption by means of
investigating any (even anonymous) complaints,
with the possibility of interference of any order
into organizational activities during the course
of any investigation.[75] The power of the department may be appreciated by the fact that during
perennial anti-corruption campaigns, it is expected
formally to charge some prominent politicians with
corruption and abuse of official position in order
to serve as moral lessons to others (rule by model
again) and to demonstrate that the political authority means business this time concerning political
reform.[76] However, on a more modest level of
operations, representatives of the department can,
and do, show up anywhere, at any time, since if the
department receives a complaint it is to travel and
investigate it.[77] This is supposed to show that
the Shah is interested in all his people regardless
of differences in political power. Although some
see a danger in the method of its operations, most
individuals accept the department and its activities
since it affords an opportunity for the ordinary
official to backbite by making trouble even if charges are never substantiated. But for purposes of
the present study, the department is important be-

cause it offers the Shah and his close allies an
unpaid public opinion poll, the right to claim that
it is doing something to protect the noble and
punish the evil, and most significantly, a means to
intervene-control or not as it chooses in the structure of political authority.

The second means of selective control is derived from the Iranian political premise that although responsibility is delegated, authority
rarely is. Decisions are expected to be made by
those at the top, and to be passed on for implementation to those below. Since, as previously discussed (see section "The Meaning of Political
Strength: National Implications" above), a program
on any particular level of political authority is
assumed to be that chief's program, this really is
not strange. Consequently, authority implies that
the chief, often without formal written sanction,
will make decisions as he sees fit, and those below will disobey at their own risk.[78] The chief,
then, is not a true leader but an autocrat (the
"boss"), and those below are not staff members
but patrimonial retainers of the chief. The operational control implications of this kind of relationship are as follows:

First, initiative from below automatically is
frustrated. No one dares to do anything to which
he is not specifically and completely assigned.
For example, if the lowly storekeeper is away for
a long period, he may take the only key to the
store with him, and consequently, office supplies
will not be available until his return.

Second, since all decisions must be referred
to the chief, offices are overstaffed with personal
aides ("yes-men") and other supernumeraries with
low level education, instead of being staffed with
real assistants with defined responsibilities and
authority to support definitive programs.

Third, all manner of decision making, no
matter how trivial and routine, must be referred
to the chief for implementation. It is literally
impossible for anyone to hold an uninterrupted conference with the chief as he constantly is being
interrupted either at his initiative or on the
initiative of the retainers, often over matters of
no consequence whatever, other than the fact that

regardless of importance, the chief must make the decisions.

Fourth, since all retainers regardless of hierarchial grade, individually are directly responsible
to the chief as the sole source of office authority,
office cooperation horizontally or vertically is
discouraged. This is prompted, in part, out of the
same motives as all control in Iran (out of fear to
trust potential rivals) and, in part, to discourage
"troublemakers." Rather what is encouraged is that
cooperation of a sort which is the temporary, disrupting backbiting of cliques seeking the temporary,
specific favors of the chief and on grounds of personal rather than impersonal technical merit. This
is guaranteed only to further the chief's control
as he can play "divide and rule," in the office,
and thus can destroy any opposition to his position
or policies.

A third source of control is a system of geographic rotation of political personnel, from lord-
ly provincial governors on down to petty office
clerks. Nominally, almost all positions, certainly
those of political consequence, are appointments
for specified and short periods; for example, pro-
vincial-governors are appointed for two years.
The actual period of appointment, however, is up
to the powers that be at the center and in no case
is any appointment ever to be considered permanent
or even final, and the appointee must accept this.
Hence men who have gained experience in one location, constantly are being relocated into positions
in which they must learn a new task, or new local
conditions.

Regardless of this sacrifice of rational political efficiency, this system assures the center of
the more important considerations of subservience
of the appointee, who is only too eager to please
his superiors in order to hold on to an existing
appointment or to insure further and more desirable
appointments in the future. The system also assures
the center that popular or powerful appointees will
not build up a permanent base from which to harass
the center. This is very important because, to
recall, individuals mold programs to their own
liking and when influential individuals move, they
often take their pet programs with them to try them
out elsewhere. And if these individuals have personal connections at the center, and hence have cer-

tain significant decision making power, this might
be rotated also. Obviously, it is in the interest
of the center to keep this potential power on the
move. An ordinary individual is expected to be
alert to this system if he wants to get anything done,
for regardless of the formal specifications of any position, he must locate the powerful individuals who
are constantly being sent on their travels. Consequently, in a process of rotation, when, say, "X" is
transferred to location "a" and "Y" formerly in "a"
now is located in "b", while "Z" who was in "b" turns
up in location "c", the practical solution may be
that, since "Y" in contrast with "X" and "Z" is in
favor with the center one may now have to go to location "b" and seek out "Y" rather than be content
with dealing with "X" and "Z" in order to get something attended to, even though one lives in "a" and
works in "c".

On the level of the lowly office worker, the
rotation system offers a possible way out of what
he believes is an intolerable office situation.
He believes that a transfer always will solve his
interpersonal problems or promotion frustrations.
For in Iranian terms, such problems can be rationalized, with considerable justification, as the product of interpersonal problems, and in another location these problems may not exist. Since flight
from any office situation always is possible, there
is little incentive for individuals on any administrative level either realistically to come to terms
with the existing situation or to improve the existing situation. Consequently, there is no stability
among the rank and file, who, consciously or not, by
seeking transfers, often secretly through friends
at the center, are undercutting any opportunity for
their chief to build up a stable personal empire of
loyal retainers to counteract the actions of the
center. And once again the center profits. It is
the program which is the major victim of all these
arrivals and departures. But this is a secondary
consideration to the security needs of the center.
This conclusion is of utmost importance to the present study.

The fourth source of selective control is the
enforced "coordination" of mass social organizations.
Although private organizations, especially charitable
and social uplift organizations, actively are encouraged by the political authority, at the same time
all organizations are encouraged to, and if need be,

are forced to, submit to the supervision of the political authority. This especially is true of those
organizations capable of the possibility of concentrating opposition to the political authority and with
the economic or political wherewithal to translate
possibility into action.

The fifth source of selective but effective control is the presence of a national police force, responsible to the center. The rural force, (gendar-
merie) is the only daily contact that 80% of the
population, the peasants of Iran, ever have with political authority. In addition, there is a secret
security police (Savak) which carries out national
objectives, especially the suppression of any dangerous opposition, internal or external. The threat of
secret police intervention often is enough to discourage all but the most dedicated opposition to any
political policy of the center.

SELECTIVE CENTRALIZATION

The sixth, and perhaps the major source of selective control in Iran, is the selective centralization of political authority. Selective centralization arose out of the circumstance that, although
the Iranian political authority very early in its
history was able to establish an absolute, centralized
state in undisputed mastery of the military and financial resources of the society--and this order became
the basic ideal of Iranian political theory--con-
stant invasion, conquest and foreign intervention
too often in Iranian history destroyed that order in
fact.[79] Consequently, an equivalent political form
had to be devised which would preserve the theory of
centralized control, and which would serve the same
end as centralized control, but which would be feasible and consistent with political reality whenever
centralized autocracy was impossible and until such
time as the center would be in a position to reassert
centralized control. This equivalent system of political control is limited, or selective centralization.

Selective centralization, then, may be defined
as the autocratic but rationed exercise of control
over a political order by a political center which
has limited effective resources of control at its
disposal. The center hopes that this limited control
will be (minimally) effective because it is known

that control is potentially available for concentrated exercise anywhere in the political order at
the option of the center.*

Selective centralization, when it is effective,
may be as useful to the political authority as total
autocratic centralization, for the following reasons:
First, its exercise seems lighter in terms of the
total structure of authority, and hence it is less
likely to create suspicion and effective united opposition. Second, because it is limited in scope,
and therefore, because it operates with a smaller
staff than does a total autocracy, greater probability exists that it can obtain loyal and effective
retainers to carry out its control program. Consequently, third, it does not offer retainers the same
opportunities as in the case of larger staffs to
build up potential islands of significant political
independent power that may one day challenge the
center. Fourth, because its exercise is dependent
upon the option of the center and operates in a way
that no one ever is certain in the belief that the
full, albeit limited, weight of the existing machinery of control will not be concentrated against him,
it can be just as effective as total centralization
in deterring undesirable political action against
the center. And most significantly, for all these
reasons, it is extremely difficult to work out effective methods to combat positively what amounts to
nebulous opposition regardless of the relative empirical balance or power between center and periphery.

---

* When this control cannot be readily exercised
  because of the empirical political situation,
  but the right of the center to intervene has not
  been surrendered, this may be defined as localization of authority. Localization is to be contrasted with decentralization, a situation in
  which local political control, even if greatly
  circumscribed, is legitimately recognized by the
  center, and in which reciprocal rights, privileges,
  and obligations between center and local authority
  may be established. Localization, in contrast,
  does not recognize the legitimacy of local control,
  only the empirical political fact that the center,
  at a particular time, cannot exercise what it considers its legitimate control over local power.
  For a further discussion of this, see below,
  section "The Structure of Local Authority: The
  Absence of Local Countervailing Power to the
  Center".

Selective centralization operates as follows:
First, the center reserves the right at any time to
pass judgment on any or all of the activities of its
subordinates. For example, in many Iranian agencies,
but especially in the key Ministry of Interior, local
officials are expected to report directly on demand
to the center, ignoring any formal hierarchy and
channels of control that may exist on paper. This
violation of the nominal channels of political communication assures the center that its local agents
will not combine against it. For in this manner
the center offers each of its local agents individually the possibility of an alliance with itself
against possible competition from any other local
agents.

This situation is repeated in miniature in each
of its own center levels. At any level local chiefs
have a penchant for relying upon centralized control
rather than upon delegated responsibility and relying
upon assistants who in effect are personal retainers
rather than upon subordinates with defined duties and
responsibilities. Yet simultaneously the structure
also hierarchially is established and maintained from
top to bottom. Consequently, although individuals
may report to the center directly if the center or
the individuals desire it, nominally each individual
on each rank level also is made responsible to the
center indirectly through his immediate superiors.
And this pattern is repeated throughout the structure.
Consequently, at any level, that particular center
will receive the reports of the next lower hierarchial level, and, in addition, may receive the direct reports of any individual at any lower level.
At the ultimate center, any and all reports from
individuals at any level may be made directly, in
addition to the report from the second level in the
hierarchy. In this way, the hierarchy principle is
preserved but at the same time the center can violate it as it sees fit, providing a center with the
advantages of both systems of selective centralization out of channels and of hierarchy. This works
to the disadvantage of any and all lower levels in
the hierarchy, and, due to the pyramid principle,
an increasing disadvantage as one descends in the
hierarchy.

This, in effect, is the second principle of
selective centralization; that is, the encouraged
right of an individual in or outside the political

apparatus, at any level of the hierarchy, to complain
directly to the center without consideration of the
formal channels of communication in that hierarchy.
In this way the center is assured of a universal spy
network. In return, the center pledges to pass along
all reports and suggestions to the appropriate office.
Not surprisingly, complaints pour in. For example,
the Prime Minister stated in 1959 that approximately
750,000 such reports (letters) are received in an
average year by his office alone.[80] Letters and reports, however, do not exhaust this channel of communication. Many private and public individuals
voluntarily come to the center in person, especially
on annual leave, to see which way the political wind
in a particular office is blowing and to entrench a
position with the current powers to be.

The third principle of selective centralization
is the reserved right of the leadership at the center
physically to present itself and intervene selectively
whenever it wishes, at any level of the political apparatus right down to the lowest echelon of administration. This right has sometimes been justified by
quoting the old Middle East political concept that
administrative affairs should be carried on by local
or circuit officials before petitioners and observers
in the presence of a ruler who traveled about on circuit.[81] This administrative device, of course, has
ceremonial significance. For in this way the political leaders, including the titular ruler, have been
able to display to public view their personal political charisma, omnipresent and available to high and
low alike.[82] In Iran, it is the Shah who has assumed
much of this ceremonial burden, although cabinet members, especially the Prime Minister, normally participate, and all ordinary government agents are encouraged to get out of the office.[83]

But much more than ceremonial motives are involved. The practice, first, serves to reinforce
the superiority of the center over the periphery by
demonstrating that the remote, omnipotent center is
concerned about the problems of all the Iranian
people, especially the humble people in remote areas.
And when action is taken, it demonstrates empirically
the ability of the superior center to solve local
political problems, in spite of all the built-in
confusion in the administrative structure.

(2)   Second, the grand tour of center notables is an
independent, direct source of information from the
periphery that is able to bypass the normal hierarchial channels.

(3)   Third, the practice is but another means by
which the center demonstrates its ability to humble
the periphery politically. By cutting administrative red tape and reducing the hierarchial barriers
between government and public, the center is encouraging out-of-channels, direct contact between
center and public. Through this device, in instances of popular dissatisfaction with the political
order in general, only too frequent in Iran, the
center hopes to obtain for itself whatever residual
popularity still exists for the political order and
redirect political aggression and frustration away
from the leadership toward the remaining segment of
the political apparatus.[84]

(4)   Fourth, the practice hopes to motivate local
political action to the leader's liking by the mere
threat of outside political intervention from the
top.

(5)   Fifth, by concentrating political effort the
center can confront the opposition directly with
overwhelming prestige and potential power behind
it, "refuting error" and nipping potentially dangerous political unrest in the bud. The center has
used this again and again against rebellious students.[85]

In employing any or all five devices successfully to the rusty mechanism of Iranian political
administration, of course, only particular problems in the system at particular times are solved,
while the general pattern of selecting centralization, problem-solving in the system is not touched.
And in fact, willful or not, the devices maintain
the general pattern of selective centralization problem solving in the system. For doing something contrary to some formal regulation, no matter how admirable, does not preclude the same problem from
turning up again, and at a time when the weight of
the center is not available for this kind of intervention, which very well may be most of the time.
Yet the political authority does not consider changing the regulation, but only encourages appeals for
more selective intervention.

(4)   The fourth principle of selective centralization
is the total predominance of the citadel of the center, the capital city, Teheran, in the geographic
structure of political authority. This predominance
is based upon primacy in wealth, population and most
significantly, power.[86] For example, 30 per cent of
administrative expenses, 50 per cent of the educational budget, [87] and 50 per cent of the representation
in both the Senate and the House of Parliament are
reserved for Teheran.[88]

    The singular implication to be drawn from this
state of affairs is that the ambitious, especially
the politically ambitious, hope to be located or to
remain located in Teheran. For consequently, any
position in the provinces at best is considered only
a chance to make good in the eyes of the center,
with the hope of being transferred to a "better"
position, which can but mean ultimately a position
in the capital city. The provinces tend to receive
either transients or secondary talent, and perhaps
more significantly, receive only secondary interest
by both the personnel working there and in the center. The capital then, truly, may be viewed as an
obstacle to provincial development, because locals
either passively accept the situation as inevitable,
and, consequently, accept the fact that decisions
to their disfavor will be made for them by the center, neutrally accept the situation in the hopes
that direct intervention of the center, even on a
personal basis, will serve local interests, or finally,
actively accept the situation in the hopes of using[89]
it to facilitate their own migration to the center.
Consequently, through apathy, neutrality or hope, the
accepted predominance of the center dissipates all
resentment against selective centralization.

(5)   The fifth, and final, principle of selective
centralization is that the power and the services of
the center are ready and able to appear on any local
level with great speed whenever the center feels its
interests are served by such intervention. This may
be dramatized by an amusing but characteristic incident. The villagers of a certain village near
Isfahan had been convinced of the necessity of being
inocculated and vaccinated for a long time, but requests for this service through normal local channels,
not surprisingly, went unheeded. Why should superior
politicians worry about mere stupid peasants, especially since villagers and not politicians thought up

the idea? The impatient but clever villagers then
fabricated an epidemic, listing fictitious deaths
and making a dramatic appeal for aid. At this point
the wheels of the political apparatus moved quickly.
For which politician would want to be blamed for an
unfavorable incident sure to come to the attention
of the center? Serum was hurriedly brought in from
Isfahan and all the villagers were treated before
the panicked bureaucrats were any the wiser.[90]

THE STRUCTURE OF LOCAL AUTHORITY: THE ABSENCE OF LOCAL COUNTERVAILING POWER TO THE CENTER

It is to be observed, first, that the pattern
of relationship that exists between center and
periphery as far as the administrative system is
concerned is repeated in the pattern of relationship that exists between center and periphery as
far as the formal structure of political authority
is concerned. For localized political authority,
as such, is not inconsistent necessarily with the
right of selective, centralized control; but the
acceptance of localized centers of political authority based on legitimately established political
rights which are not reversible is inconsistent with
this right. It cannot be repeated too often that
the absence of a pragmatic ability by the center to
enforce its authority locally, including, as usually
observed, against the powerful tribal chiefs (khans)
in areas remote from the center, especially at times
when communication is difficult, is not evidence for
the existence of a decentralization principle in
Iranian political authority. This is so because the
center during periods of localization of power never
relinquished the legitimate residual right and moral
obligation to re-establish centralized authority, or
selective centralized authority whenever it was able
to do so and/or empirically considered it expedient
to do so.[91] The center, under certain circumstances,
in fact, deliberately prefers to tolerate localization of power, resorting at most to limited, selective centralization. This is especially true when
the center believes it is wiser not to attempt to
force its will and face possible determined concerted
resistance and an outcome in which it might have to
recognize formally the independence of local authority.
Rather, it contents itself to tolerate temporarily a
power situation which may not be much to its liking
and to its disadvantage as the lesser of two evils,

until such time as it is confident it can reverse the
situation. And for the same reason, the center acts
with caution or refuses to act, when in asserting its
authority against one source of localized power, it
would have to depend upon building up counter-sources
of localized power which in time might be strong
enough to challenge the authority of the center,
placing the center in a new situation of political
challenge of its own making. With this in mind, it
is easier to understand and appreciate the traditional,
deliberate tolerance of local political confusion, even
anarchy, by the center which outside observers, have
mistakenly taken for formal, institutionalized rights
and not temporary expediency.92 Total centralization
in fact, is not different operationally from this order of anarchy, since both work against the formal
acceptance of independent local authority. Thus, it
cannot be argued that the centralization trend in Iran
in the twentieth century is a reversal of fundamental
political principles. Rather it is a change of possible formal alternatives which achieve the same fundamental end; namely, to prevent the emergence of
truly independent, autonomous, local authority in
Iran.

Consequently, so-called traditional self-
government of Iranian villages is not significant
because nothing significant is left for villagers
to decide and villages were not able to band together
to challenge the center's political prerogatives.
Likewise, the independent tribal chiefs were protected from encroachment by the center through foreign
alliances, and not through acceptance of any localized rights.93 For increasingly, as more "modern"
systems of control from the west came to the attention of the center, and the changing political situation made it feasible for the center to enforce
its will once again, especially under Reza Shah, the
autonomous tribes no longer protected by the foreigner
were reduced to subservience. By this action two ends
were served at the same time. For in the name of
"nationalism" not only was tribal power broken, but
also simultaneously center power was established over
the people in the former tribal areas.94

Second, the question of centralization or decentralization as a principle never enters into the process of asserting or reasserting recognition of the
center's pre-eminence over local power. Rather, decentralization is denied by default; by the failure

to prepare personnel on the lower echelons to handle
their own affairs, by denial of the autonomous right
of financing or budgeting, by the subtle refusal to
lend support, by the avoidance of answering inquiries
or appeals for aid to the center, by the interference
in local affairs often on the basis of a trivial
excuse (as for example through "visits" of the Shah's
Investigation Department, consequent to anonymous,
back-biting complaints), by the use of non-local
people in important local administrative positions,
and finally, by the insistence that the concept of
true localization of authority cannot work in Iran
on "practical" grounds because of the Iranian cultural
tradition.

The third major observation concerning Iranian
localization is that the appointment and removal by
the center of all officials, which in Iran means
down to and including the county officials, and of
the vast majority of personnel who work in the local
bureaucracy, insures that local political interests
will be subordinated to center political interests.
Quite obviously in a system of appointments and re-
movals routed in tours of duty of uncertain duration,
and in which the development of local ties and interests between officials and office staffs necessarily
are weak, individuals can maintain their security
only by placating their employer, the center.[95]

The fourth and final aspect of the problem of
localization of political authority in Iran concerns
the nature of the urban political environment. It
is important to appreciate that in Iran, as elsewhere
in Asia, the urban center primarily is a political
center, save for the occasional Holy City, which, in
fact, is associated with the political order. For
unlike in the pre-modern West, the primary political
forces of the society reside in urban centers and
make of the urban centers their stronghold. And in
so doing, the Iranian political lords brought with
them their particular political and social interests
and allegiances and made these interests and allegiance to them paramount. Especially, they have
maintained their dominance in urban affairs against
any tendency to develop a generalized ("civic") spirit and community of interests which would represent
all the diverse elements of the urban center, as
developed in the Western urban centers. Consequently,
in Iran, politically peripheral and especially non-
political organizations such as guilds politically

always have been weak. This is so because in Iran,
unlike in the West, it was not possible for strong,
commercial interests to band together in units of
their own choosing to oppose politicizing of their
interests of political encroachment on their prerogatives. For example, guilds were forced to include
both employers and employees in one organization
and consequently the element that was comparable to
the patrician element in the Western guild was
weakened and unable to challenge the political order
as it was in the West. By dominating the urban centers through domination of local political power,
through all the means described in this section and
in previous sections, the center also insures its
domination over all the non-political forces of the
urban centers, especially the economic forces of the
urban center.[96]

THE STRUCTURE OF AUTHORITY: THE MEANING
OF POLITICAL FREEDOM

Iranian political freedom has been defined of-
ficially as action under certain restrictions, so
that freedom will not disturb the basic peace of
Iran. These restrictions require that political
actions be coordinated with government policy or
at the least be submitted for approval by the authorities if the political authority so decides.[97] To
note, the definitions of "coordinate" and "approve"
are not formally incorporated in legal codes, but
are open to varied individual interpretations by
particular officials as they believe the occasion
warrants.

Although diversity of political action is
accepted in principle, standing above diversity
must be the "unity of the society," as symbolized by
and enforced by the titular political authority (the
Shah), who intervenes in cases of individual freedom
of action in the name of the good of the (united)
general society.[98] The crucial terms of reference
(e.g., "unity") are defined exclusively by the political authority and without any formal restrictions
on the process of definition.

The term "public opinion" has at least three distinct references in Iranian political thought. The
first reference is to that body of individual complaint against the political authority by the popu-

lace for not creating a paradise on earth for each
and every Iranian. Since this order of complaint
is endemic, negative, and unorganized, it normally
is considered harmless, by both the populace and
the political authority. However, the political
authority is fearful of the collective effect of
these individual reactions on morale in times of
political instability, as at the present. Consequently, the authorities have attempted to direct
aggression away from themselves and toward the
"imperialists" or, alternately, convert negative dissatisfaction about a present situation into positive
support for their programs.[99]

The second reference of public opinion is to a
reaction to political self-interest, which, often
as not, is assumed to be selfish. As soon as a new
government (or regime) is formed in Iran, it is assumed that a coalition of those deprived of power
will be formed to overturn the new regime in order
to re-install themselves in power.[100] At this point
public opinion is supposed to create mass support
for members of the existing regime, especially the
Prime Minister, in order to enable the new regime
to survive at least long enough to be tested.[101]
But in no case does public opinion operate to select,
or control, the specific actions of officials in any
particular regime.

The third reference to public opinion is a
familiar political concept in so-called "underdeveloped democracies" as is Iran. The concept can best
be described as one in which the members of the political authority, by the very nature of being members
of a political authority, are sensitized peculiarly
to the needs of the people in a way that any or all
members of the political authority can understand
the true needs of the people even if the people do
not understand these needs themselves. For this
reason, these individuals associated with the political authority can act correctly and wisely even
when the people themselves only dimly are aware or
are aware incorrectly of their own best interests,
not alone ready and capable as yet to carry out these
interests.[102] The titular ruler, and by extension,
all members of the political authority, have used
this concept as one basis for the political intervention in the name of the people's interests (as noted
previously in this chapter).

Individual political freedom in Iran, then, although accepted as a _formal_ abstraction (it is sus-
pected in part, to satisfy the critical foreigner)
is denied in actuality. In its contemporary setting,
to be sure, the political authority talks pragmatically of a period of political tutelage and of a
guided democracy, leading "ultimately" to popular
sovereignty when the people are ready, and this may
be both necessary and feasible. Certainly one cannot
overlook the empirical facts of life, vis-a-vis the
Russians, and the potential subversive underground in
the country in casting a political stone at the political authority. But, in turn, the political authority cannot overlook the fact that denial of personal
freedom is justified on value grounds not unfamiliar
in Iranian history; especially that individuals left
to their own devices morally and technically are incompetent and selfish, and that, in consequence,
guidance from the morally and technically superior
political authority (and ultimately, from the apex
model position) is essential if the political order
is to function properly.

THE FORMAL STRUCTURE OF POLITICAL AUTHORITY: LAW AND CORRUPTION

Law may be interpreted as those formalized
rules established by a political structure to relate
individuals in a society to each other and to the
political structure. In Iran the legal role, qualitatively, has been different from the Western legal
role, and it is important for purposes of the present study to appreciate that difference. First,
although Iranian law is flexible on Middle Eastern
standards, it stresses formalism and places greater
emphasis on appearance than on substance. This formalism, historically has been attributed to those
juridicial innovators of the Iranian Middle Ages,
who, in order to preserve the illusion of an idealized past-age, ignored the existing imperfect world
and formulated systems of model standards of life
that conceivably no one ever expected would be enforced.[103]

Second, because in Iran the distinction between
public and private jurisdictions of political authority have been blurred, if not merged, a clear distinction between public and private law has not developed
as it has in the West. For this reason, the political

authority has molded the legal system to suit its own
purposes.   Not surprisingly, the punishment of political transgression, such as rebellion, conspiracy,
counterfeiting, theft, and regulation of the political authority's political rivals, has become the major
concern of the legal system.[104]

③   Third, the principle of analytic, deductive law
has not developed. Consequently, rather than a system of abstract law, which includes the principle of
abstract defined rights, Iranian law has emphasized
the resolution of conflict by examining the exegesis
of each individual case. Iranian law then neither
is the true code-law of western Europe, nor is it
comparable to Anglo-Saxon law. For although it is
based on precedents in analogy, Iranian law does
not have the same flexibility to handle radically
new solutions as does Anglo-Saxon law, in that it
does not incorporate the principle of abstract
rights within its system. For this reason, the
Iranian legal case book could not hold its own as the
old society began to give way, creating a dangerous
vacuum in legal institutions. And consequently, nowadays, although the citizen respects the old hallowed
legal tradition, vaguely associated with the religious
tradition, "in principle," he forever ignores the law
in particular. This is in contrast to the Westerner
who might break the law in principle, but upholds the
law in general.[105]

④   Fourth, equality before the law, although, admittedly an ideal in the Western tradition, has not been
seriously attempted in Iran. Rather, the existing
social and religious diversity in Iranian society has
been recognized formally and accepted as the basis
for legal diversity, with each community enjoying its
own legal system and rights, under a nominal symbol
of unity, the Shah. Law, then, has not been used as
the medium for social, moral, and political cohesion
to the extent that it often has in the West. What
unity has existed in Iranian society has existed only
at the top in the substance of the titular ruler (the
Shah) as intervener and coordinator of the diverse
society.[106]

Modern Iran has inherited the spirit of this tradition. Especially, as the Shah claims, whereas formal modern Iranian law (note the singular) very well
may be at the "level" of all "progressive" countries
(presumably the West), on the operative level, admit-

tedly laws (in the plural) are neither abstractly satisfactory nor administered properly.[107] This raises
two fundamental legal issues of interest to the present study.

First, how can Iranian law be considered so advanced, and yet the legal system be considered so unsatisfactory? For one, Iranian law and legal institutions are abstract (model) principles that a priori
are suitable and sacred for Iran, but specific imple-
mental laws (as devised by other than the model) may
be both defective and obsolete. Again, even if laws
might be perfect in theory, they still may not be enforceable or seriously considered for enforcement.
In addition there is the practical consideration that,
perhaps, after much procrastination, a law might suddenly appear as the result of a new official coming
to power, and, thus, represent only that official's
pet project for "reform." In that case, the law
seriously is considered only while that official is
in office, or is ignored if it is expected that that
official's days are numbered. In truth, it could be
argued that, since sooner or later, the days of all
officials are numbered, legal change in Iran is not
uncommon; in fact quite the contrary. Laws may be
piled haphazardly one upon another so rapidly that
no one is aware of which particular laws are current.
And so, it is not unusual to have complaints of legal
inaction in one area matched simultaneously by complaints of too much action in another area in which
adjustments are said to be too rapid to have any effect.[108] The result of both action and inaction, is
the same: the existing laws are meaningless since
they either are obsolete or transitory, so why take
seriously any law?

The second legal issue concerns the problem of
the mal-administration of existing laws. The heart
of this problem lies both in the confusion and uncertainty about the validity and permanency of existing laws, as just discussed, and in the Iranian
preference for changing forms rather than for devising an efficient system to administer the forms
when dissatisfaction arises with the forms. For
either or both reasons, Iranians take diabolical
pride in not following existing regulations.

Such legal evasions are aided and abetted by the
partiality in enforcing the law. Partiality is prevalent because the legal administrators, first, are

not technically trained for their jobs, second, are
harassed constantly by extra-legal pressures for
favorable treatment by "influentials," and third,
are tempted to use their position for personal advantage based upon the principle (often discussed
in this study) that each man is expected to seek
his self-interest whenever he can.[109] Because of
such partiality, law enforcement tends to be concerned primarily with the un-privileged, and consequently, the legal machinery tends to be concerned
primarily with trivia. For example, three unsophis-
ticates were charged with a one-time offense of
using cancelled stamps on their first-class corres-
pondence. The dossiers of these three cases, contained over 300 pages of details.[110] Since the
Iranian preference for inaction, especially in conflict situations, implies that litigation will be
ignored in so far as possible, unresolved cases pile
up on the docket in the hopes that somehow they will
disappear by being ignored or being bribed into settlement. This by itself would not be of much consequence considering the mass of legal trivia, but the
occasionally important case also dies, and most significant, general faith in the ability of the wheels
of justice to move when necessary also dies. Justice
also moves slowly because there always is the possibility of intervening partiality from above; as, for
example, from the gracious forgiveness of the Shah.
This tempts the judicial machinery to wait for outside resolutions of the occasional important cases,
and even of the not so important cases, such as possible exemptions from draft status, in order to
avoid any possible negative personal reaction against
an unfavorable decision affecting influentials.[112]
And the final cause of legal partiality lies in the
fact that litigation for the ordinary citizen is expensive. Beyond the usual consideration of legal
fees, account must be taken of the wages that are
forfeited when an individual has his day in court
and the numerous procedural rituals overseen by legal
clerks, each seeking a gratuity for services rendered.[113]

The average Iranian, not surprisingly then, is
somewhat less than enthusiastic about the efficiency
of the legal machinery in his society. Consequently,
for the individual who has no personal influence with
the formal legal system to make it work favorably for
him, the only alternative is avoidance of the system
whenever possible. This the individual does by re-
dressing his grievances informally, on his own or

through utilization of an intermediary, if necessary,
to arbitrate a thorny controversy; that is, by ignoring or circumventing the law to carry on what most
often are legitimate activities, that should be handled in formal, legal channels.

But there may come a time when one must use the
legal system and be assured that the legal system
will work for one. Due to the partisanship of the
legal machinery, this assurance can be made only
through bribery. In this line of reasoning, what
to the West is corruption, and hence a deviation
from the norm, in fact, in Iran, is an integral part
of the system by the very nature of the way the system must operate.

Corruption may be classified as passive and active. Passive corruption is apathy: apathy in using
the legal machinery unless one is sure one can see
profit by it; apathy about the possibility of changing the situation; and apathy about corruption as an
evil. From the standpoint of the average (that is,
the non-politically involved) individual in Iranian
society, apathy toward the legal machinery is but a
logical deduction from the slowness and capricious-
ness of justice.[114]

Active corruption, on the other hand, is the
conscious taking advantage of the situation of litigation or legal doubt for one's own political or
economic profit, from the petty official who expects
a bribe to do his simple duty,[115] on the one side, to
the big-time operator (the "influential") who ignores
or bribes the weak judiciary and the highly placed
government official to make the cumbersome political
machinery work in his interest, on the other side.[116]
The influential assumes, quite correctly, that the
legal system (as the political system) is an integral
part of the society as a whole, and that the political structure, as the society, is not set up to encourage action without personal advantage and self-
interest as long as it can operate at all with it,
and, hence, that bribery and corruption are but the
material means to facilitate the expression of that
self-interest.

For this reason, officials often are evaluated
primarily and overwhelmingly on the basis of honesty
and only peripherally on the basis of such other
qualities as efficiency. This does not mean that

honesty is its own reward in Iranian political thinking. Rather, it is argued that if a man is honest,
he will probably be courageous, since it is individual
weakness (and never the system) that leads to corruption and allows the corrupt to operate. And if a man
is courageous, he is strong; and if a man is strong,
he maintains the welfare of the people against the
influentials. Consequently, by implication, an honest
man is interested and can serve the people, and conversely, a corrupt man neither wishes to, nor can,
serve the people. Consequently, although both honesty
and efficiency politically are desirable, it is honesty,
rather than efficiency, that has become over the ages,
the overriding political consideration. If pressed,
the Iranian will argue that there cannot be any basic
logical separation between the concepts of efficiency
and incorruptibility, in that the incorrupt, by definition, are efficient (since they "serve" the people).
and the corrupt must be inefficient. And conversely,
the inefficient can but be the corrupt.117 (See section
"The Goal of Political Authority: Service for the
People" above.)

THE MEANING OF ECONOMIC DEVELOPMENT

This section will discuss how Iranians view the role of economic development in their society, and why they select the kinds of projects they do to carry out that economic development.

The first role assigned to economic development is that of serving as vindication of the Iranian's belief that his country is, or can be, the equal of the foreigner, especially the European foreigner. For, since the country of the foreigner is developed economically, Iran also must be developed economically. Although, at the present time, Iran is not developed, she is making great "progress" toward that development, and so can claim to have demonstrated, at the least, that she <u>potentially</u> is the equal of the foreigner.[1]

This need to validate a doctrine of an innate Iranian <u>natural</u> capacity at least the equal of the foreigner, has played an important role in many contemporary Iranian <u>economic</u> decisions, whereas, the purely monetary economic implications of the decision, have been dismissed as of secondary importance.[2] For this reason, Iranians have been very incensed at the doctrine that they should "learn to walk before they run" economically, which they believe is but a plot of the foreigner to keep them in an inferior economic position by not allowing their innate ability to demonstrate their economic capacity to gain equality with the developed countries.[3] Consequently, when it is suggested, for example, that a simple, home-made, casting furnace, that will serve the present economic needs of Iran, rather than an imported, complex furnace, obtainable only at many times the cost of the home-made object, should be used, Iranians object.[4]

The second role of economic development is to convince the (European) foreigner of the equal worth of the Iranian, so that the <u>foreigner</u> will acknowledge <u>psychological</u> equality between himself and the Iranian. It has been noted that, in relationships between locals

and foreigners in underdeveloped societies, contrary
to Marxist ideology, the local quest for psychological worth--that is, to be treated as human beings
worthy of respect and dignity on an emotional level
--far outweighs concern over the presence or absence
of physical or economic domination by the foreigners.[5]
In order to earn this equality, Iran must prove to
the world that it is a modern land. Since a modern
land is an economically developed land, Iran must
develop, or alternately, convince the foreigner that
it is developed or developing. Consequently, for
example, if the foreigner claims that the land-
holding system is "medieval," then Iran must reverse
it, or failing that, deny that the system is medieval.[6]

   A third role for development, closely related to,
but categorically distinct from the second role, is
that of serving to squelch foreign criticism of Iran.
Pass the land reform bill, it was argued, so that the
vexatious foreigners will not keep harping on this
matter and using it to make light of the prestige of
the country.[7]

   Fourth, development serves as vindication of the
efficacy of the Iranian system of political authority,
and in particular, of the Shah and the Iranian monar-
chy. Especially, the development process demonstrates
that the regime is changing the face of the country,
and consequently, that something is being done to fulfill the primary moral-service responsibility of Iranian political authority (see above, Chapter Two,
section "The Goal of Political Authority: Service for
the People").[8]

   Fifth, development serves to attract foreign aid,
especially foreign financial aid. It is true that
some foreign economic support, from the West in particular, will come to Iran because of its pivitol geographic position, but much more aid will come if the
donor believes that the Iranian political authority
is efficient, stable, and has the ability to run its
own economic affairs satisfactorily.[9] And a successfully run development program is the means to make
the foreigner believe this, for, it is claimed, it
was previous mal-administrations in the development
programs that convinced the foreigner that it was unwise to invest in Iran. The situation has been reversed in recent times, however, and the foreigner has
been led to appreciate Iran's use, or potential use,
of foreign funds for productive development purposes,
and that conviction must be maintained at all costs.[10]

Sixth, development serves as a spur to action throughout the economy and throughout the society. The argument is that if the ordinary people are convinced that development is being implemented, then they will overcome their skepticism and will give more support to the other goals of the political authority.[11] This is but an economic consequence of political rule by model; namely, the belief that if a proper impression or "sincerity" can be made by the model (the political authority), then the Iranian people operating in the larger arena of economic and social action will be inspired to accomplish wonderous deeds. Since the problem of development in Iran is an inspirational problem, development must stress spectacular changes in the spirit of Aladdin and the jin.[12] The ideal model development project is one that does not call upon skills which are not available in Iran and "shows" something physically to vindicate the model developer, who is, ultimately, the political authority.[13] But, since the Iranian political authority sincerely is interested in development, and consequently, by (model) definition, the people are overcoming their skepticism and are ready and capable to act, the obstacles to development must be grounded in some other source. Most probably, it is the outstripping of available resources which has resulted from the great Iranian urge to build and create in the present liberating climate. And in failing to accept this interpretation and blaming the difficulty, in contradiction, erroneously on an alleged Iranian reluctance to react vigorously to the challenge of economic development on existing funds, and reducing foreign aid accordingly, in fact, it is the hard-hearted foreigner himself who has caused the present difficulties and discouragement. For it is the international bankers, who, by withdrawing the funds, have discouraged the very effort whose discouragement they claim is the cause of fund withdrawal, and, who, consequently, have directly caused the very difficulties to which they claim to be responding.[14]

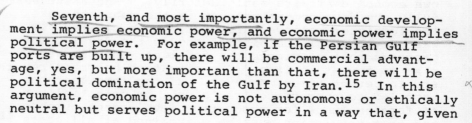

Seventh, and most importantly, economic development implies economic power, and economic power implies political power. For example, if the Persian Gulf ports are built up, there will be commercial advantage, yes, but more important than that, there will be political domination of the Gulf by Iran.[15] In this argument, economic power is not autonomous or ethically neutral but serves political power in a way that, given the choice, concern for the former is subordinated to concern for the latter.

It is worthwhile, by way of summation of this section, to present a case study which demonstrates the interrelationship of the seven roles of economic development described above.* This case study concerns a proposal to build a steel smelting plant in Iran. The plant originally had been proposed by Reza Shah, but his efforts had been thwarted by World War II. Since Reza Shah is the inspirational father of "modern" Iran, the steel plant has to be completed to vindicate the ideas of this model political ruler (fourth role).[16] But economically speaking, it would satisfy a national need for an essential product (fourth and seventh roles),[17] it would employ many people (fourth role), and it would replace foreign imports (first role).[18] Steel, moreover, is the very backbone of a developed country (seventh role), and Iran must be a developed country (second role).[19] Certainly, Iran has the natural resources for a steel industry (fourth role) and the proper utilization and successful operation of a steel mill will be a source of economic inspiration to the nation (sixth role), and a demonstration to the world of Iranian economic and technical ability (second role).[20] If properly planned, it is sure to attract foreign capital to participate (fifth role), and if successful, it will lead to further economic assistance (fifth role),[21] because of the renewed confidence of the foreigner in Iranian economic abilities (second role). It is true, the cost will be high, that the exact location of Iran deposits, and, hence, the exact location of the plant have yet to be determined, that based upon Iranian needs, the exact steel or steels to be smeltered have yet to be determined; but these are mere "details" (sixth role) against the personal conviction and economic necessity to have the plant completed (third role).[22] Surely, those against the plant only are foreign saboteurs who wish to keep Iran

---

* This statement does not imply that "purely" developmental economic considerations also have not entered into discussion or that the project may not be useful to the Iranian economy. But it does suggest that non-economic considerations play a significant role and that these considerations are of an order that they may, in fact, be at the heart of the problem of achieving the goal of economic development.

from her rightful place as an industrialized nation,
and to serve their own economic advantage (second
and sixth roles).[23] So hopes are that the study
concerning the plant will not be too prolonged,
and that the consulting (foreign) engineers will come
up with positive and hopeful indications to satisfy
the Iranian national interest (sixth role).[24]

THE EDIFICE COMPLEX, OR THE PRINCIPLE
OF CONSPICUOUS CONSTRUCTION*

In the previous section it was suggested that
certain projects, which, for various reasons, seem
to vindicate the belief that economic development,
in fact, has taken place or is taking place in Iran,
have been emphasized in development programs. These
projects have been termed "show projects." The
prime Iranian show projects are "bricks and mortar"
projects. The Iranian mania for building brick and
mortar anything, so striking to an outsider, has
been termed by some the "Iranian Edifice Complex."
This appellation summarizes very well one of the
basic problems of economic development in Iran;
namely, the conviction that a building program is
equivalent to an economic development program, and
that if sufficient natural real estate is covered
with brick and mortar projects of some sort, Iran
will be developed.

Although monument building, especially monument
building by the political authority is nothing new
to Iran,[25] the modern mania for construction, as
with so much of modern Iran, usually is attributed
to the desires and efforts of Reza Shah. In his
attempt to modernize Iran, and in a hurry, Reza Shah
attempted to introduce modern construction en masse,
all the way from model (sic!) towns to statues of himself.[26] Many of these projects were inoperative or
not maintained once built; hence, the attribution of
"monuments" to them.[27] The tragic lesson of this

---

* Edifice Complex: This flippant parody on Freud's
  Oedipus Complex saw print in a syndicated weekly
  news magazine in 1960, but it had circulated a-
  mong American residents in Iran even before the
  author's arrival in 1959. Conspicuous construction: the author's apologies to Thorstein
  Veblen.

program has never been taken to heart in Iran, no
matter how many times the disaster has been repeated
subsequently, which has been often.

Ironically, as strong as is the interest in construction, as strong is the disinterest in the proper maintenance of what has been constructed. The
belief is that, somehow, what has been constructed
will maintain itself, or that it is more important
to build than to use what has been built. It is for
this reason, that construction budgets are drawn up,
primarily, to expand into new facilities, with little
or no funds allocated for the operational expenses of
existing structures.[28] Given the choice, most Iranians would rather build a new version of the same
structure, rather than allocate sufficient, and considerably less funds to maintain the existing structure in good working order. For example, in many
villages in Iran, villagers have built communal bath
houses through their own efforts, under conditions of
major financial sacrifice and great physical hardship.
They justly are proud of their efforts. Yet when repairs became necessary, such as replacing blown out
windows or breakage, which often have occurred through
negligence, for some reason, the villagers are "unable"
to find the nominal price to make such repairs.
Rather, as the bath houses deteriorate step by step,
they become interested more and more in new bath
houses, sometimes at somewhat greater expense than
the cost for the original structure, but certainly
always at a much greater expense than the cost of the
repairs. Suggestions that it might be better to re-
pair the existing facility, even at any stage of de-
terioration, since it would cost much less than the
construction of a new bath house, are met with blank
stares.

In building, what kinds of projects are, as the
Iranians say, "good projects"? In general, preference
is for (1) spectacular show projects of possible
rational economic value; (2) spectacular, but economically useless projects, the so-called "embellishment
projects"; (3) the extraneous containers and embellishments for economically useful projects.

Spectacular show projects include, for example,
the steel plant discussed in the previous section of
this chapter. These projects aim to impress either
the Iranian, or the foreigner, or both, although sub-
sidiarily, they also have some economic justification.

Such projects have been attacked on many rational
economic grounds. For they offer no major economic
return, are of no basic short-range need at the
present stage of the Iranian economy,[29] are over-
capitalized,[30] are lavish and have needless high
cost operations,[31] are indifferent to the primary
economic needs of the mass of the population, even
if the construction increases government revenue
(as for example, new oil refineries),[32] often are
located in areas of maximum visibility, especially
the capital, rather than in the economically feasible or desirable areas (as for example, the many
proposed locations of the steel plant),[33] and drain
capital from possible use in smaller innumerable
projects which are better able to increase the total
economic output by multiplier effect.[34] But, of
course, it is fruitless to attack these spectacular
show projects on rational economic grounds, when,
as implied, rational economic grounds are not the
prime motives for selecting the projects in the
first instance, although it very well may be that
rational economic grounds might be involved subsi-
diarily in justifying the decision.

Embellishment projects, second, do not claim
to have any rational economic justification, but
frankly, are aimed at having the ruling authority
impress the local population.*

Certainly, such endeavors are not unknown in
economically developed societies, but in underdeveloped Iran, funding these projects competes
with scarce capital needed for projects more valuable to the goals of development. The beautification
campaigns in most of the Iranian towns as, for example,
park embellishments, are prime examples of this order
of projects. Although such projects impress villagers
coming to the urban centers on weekend holidays, or
ex-villagers now residing in the urban centers, something more spectacular is required to impress the sophisticated foreigners, and those worldly Iranians
who have been abroad. Consequently, the embellishment
program has been extended to include elaborate airports, luxury hotels (even if the accommodations out-

---

*   It must be appreciated that the populace, for
    aesthetic and other psychological reasons, which
    are more significant to the Iranian than are crass
    (that is, rational) economic considerations so dear
    to the Westerner, is impressed.

strip the demand), and palaces to receive foreign
dignitaries in pomp and circumstance.[35] Not too
strangely, these spectaculars are concentrated in
the larger urban centers, particularly, in the capital city of Teheran. And abroad, the Iranian government has been busy constructing new embassies and
consulates; as, for example, in Washington, D.C.[36]

Also in this category, are the pure monuments,
the statues. Their role is to keep the memory of
certain (especially political) individuals alive,
to encourage citizens to pay homage to Iranian
national heroes, and to express gratitude for what
these (service) individuals have done for the country.[37]
Significantly, while the economic problems that then
were clouding the scene in Azar, 1339 (December, 1960)
were being bemoaned in one column of a prominent newspaper, the importation from Italy of a huge and costly
monument to the historical conqueror (and strong model)
Nadar Shah was being reported in another column of
that newspaper, without any suggestion that the two
events might be interrelated.[38]

The third and final category of conspicuous construction is a potentially rational-economic
form (a construction) which in and of itself, or
through needless embellishment, is made to serve a
non-rational economic end, and which then is cited
as a sample of economic development, unfortunately
has escaped the attention of most observers. In
this instance, great attention is paid to elaborately
furnishing economically necessary construction, e.g.,
a polytechnical institute, based not upon actual
space or operational requirements but as befitting
the social position to which the organization would
prefer to be evaluated. All Iranian organizations,
but especially government organizations, are guilty
as they are forever clamoring for "new," (that is,
larger, and more elaborate) quarters, solely to improve their prestige, vis-a-vis their competitors.[39]
In this way, never-ending pressures exist to encourage
the economically wasteful, vicious circle of ever expanding jealousy, frustration, and conspicuous aspiration.[40] One perceptive Iranian observer has noted
the discrepancy between the modest buildings of the
old British operated, Anglo-Iranian Oil Company, and
the fantastically elaborate displays of the national
Iranian Oil Company, particularly as measured against
the inverse economic efficiency of the two operations.[41]

The question of these elaborate expenditures for

embellishments in connection with bona fide, economically justified construction becomes critical and not
merely undesirable, when, in the allocation of funds,
the conspicuous aspect shown to outsiders becomes so
important, that adequate funds cannot be provided for
those basic building and maintenance requirements
which supposedly justify the fancy display package.
Iran then has another of its economic white elephants;
as, for example, the health centers all over Iran for
which funds have been used for construction and office
beautification, while staff, and vital equipment are
either short in supply, or in some cases, non-existent.

This tremendous concern for embellishment construction has direct bearing on the question of the
economic necessity of constantly building new construction (see above section "The Meaning of Economic
Development"). Economically speaking, most existing
facilities can be utilized much more adequately than
they are now, merely by using existing, wasted space
and/or by eliminating the elaborate reception rooms,
corridors, and other display areas, and converting
these areas to operational use. But this, an economically rational, suggestion violates a non-economically rational consideration, namely, prestige, which
is judged to be more important. For example, if "X"
now was quartered with "Y" in order to utilize wasted
space, this action would be interpreted by "X" (and
others) as that "X" now works for "Y". Consequently,
regardless of technical economic necessity, or cost,
"X" must have his own building, teaboy retainers,
vehicles, and other non-economic prestige trappings,
regardless of cost, so that "X" will not be humiliated
before "Y" and his friends. That this is not merely
a bureaucratic vice of political authority (and this
point is of utmost importance to the present study)
may be seen from the fact that each village in Iran,
yearns for a new school; very admirable indeed, but
often too costly for the smaller villages to maintain. When it is suggested that, because of limited
funds, perhaps priority might be given to securing
a teacher (textbooks often are supplied free) or that
perhaps until sufficient funds are raised for the
building, it might be wiser to go ahead and hold
classes in the open, the suggestion, politely, but
firmly, is ignored.

JUSTIFICATION FOR POLITICAL INTERVENTION
INTO THE ECONOMY

At present, the intervention of the Iranian political authority into the economy is sweeping. It
would be both erroneous and misleading, however, to
assume that this policy is recent or that it has
arisen in response to contemporary economic development challenges. Rather, it is based upon a relationship between political authority and economy,
established in the very earliest days of the first
Persian Empire thousands of years ago, which or-
dained that the economy supply the power, especially
manual power and that the political authority supply
the organization and concentrated monetary wherewithal, in order to construct large-scale enterprises, especially the politically important monuments. With the introduction into Iran of modern
Western economic enterprises and techniques of production, especially in the politically significant
sector of the economy, as for example, the modern
armament industry, in the Nineteenth and Twentieth
centuries, the political authority either arrogated
control directly for itself, or reserved the right
to intervene or "supervise" at its discretion in
any and all activities which were left in private
hands.[42]

Iranian political authority has justified this
policy on many grounds. First, and foremost, is the
authority's moral right and duty to be concerned
with all the activities of Iranian society, especially
those activities which create problems and dissensions
in the society. For, it is argued, in that economic
activities if left to their own devices, often give
rise to social, even political "distinctions," and
dissensions,the political authority as the guardian
of society, must be concerned with economic affairs
to insure preservation of harmony.[43] It is economic
harmony which assures economic peace, and economic
peace which assures economic and social development.
For these reasons economic and social development are
evidence of the moral fitness of a political authority.
The present polity has determined that it shall be
judged fit, especially since it justified overthrowing
the previous dynasty, the Oajars, on grounds that it
was devoid of moral responsibility for the welfare of
the Iranian people and hence, was morally accountable
for the economic dissension and economic and social
decadence in Iranian society prior to the present
regime.[44]

Second, the political authority must intervene
to stimulate the Iranian people to economic action.
The people, because they appreciate this interest
and encouragement by the (model) political authority
cannot but be fired with the necessary incentives to
advance the economic interests of the society.

Third, the political authority also may have to
intervene more directly into the economy to guide
the Iranian people in their economic action. For,
although, as Iranians, they have superior, natural
intelligence, still at the present time, they are
backward technically. Consequently, without proper
guidance from the political authority, there might
very well be an unwise selection of economic activities, over-or under-production, mal-administrative,
and waning enthusiasm for vital economic development.[45]

Fourth, the political authority must intervene
whenever and wherever necessary to insure the ade-
quacy of certain economic facilities which, historically, have come to be associated with the largess
of Iranian political authority; as for example,
insurance of the minimum, winter requirements of
food and fuel.[46]

Fifth, the political authority has the right
to intervene in economic activities which involve
"nation-wide" problems. This assumption is based
on the conviction that, in Iran, nation-wide problems are national problems, (that is, that they
have a singular national etiology). Hence, as the
only force able to serve national interests, the
central political authority has the right and responsibility of intervention. For example, since
a sufficiency of charcoal is a widespread and
chronic problem in Iran, in Iranian thinking this
makes it a national problem, and consequently, it
is assumed that it is up to the national polity to
decide on the best method and means of insuring
proper supply and distribution.[47]

Sixth, the political authority in the name of
public welfare, must intervene into the economic
market to suppress the powerful and the selfish
few and protect the helpless many.[48] For example,
when prices of commodities rise, creating an intolerable condition for the little man living on a
fixed income, the political authority is expected
to institute price control in order to thwart the
evil speculators.[49]

7 Seventh, when what is termed "economic confusion
in the market" arises, it is believed that the political authority alone can respond firmly enough to lay
down uniform and fair economic policies that will be
acceptable to all, terminate needless haggling, and
get the economy moving forward once again.[50]

8 Eighth, in cases of "economic discord," the political authority will intervene to restore economic
peace. For example, during delay in the payment of
salaries to workers in the Isfahan mills, a chronic
problem, the political authority intervenes by taking
control of a factory or factories and appointing its
own management and administrative staff, so that
worker "dissatisfaction" (potentially disruptive to
the political authority, to note), will not occur.[51]

9 Ninth, the political authority must intervene
to thwart foreign economic imperialism. This order   ? joke ?
of intervention, in the past, led to the nationalization of certain foreign enterprises, especially the
confiscation of the properties of the Anglo-Iranian
Oil Company. Less spectacular, but perhaps of more
importance to the present study, is the intervention
into the activities of foreign-managed Iranian enterprises. Iran encourages joint foreign-Iranian economic operations, to be sure. But foreign govern-
ments must not be allowed to dominate vital sections
of the Iranian economy by "sneaking" their own
nationals into key policy positions in important
enterprises whose ownership they jointly share with
the Iranian polity, under the economic guise of insuring the proper management of these enterprises.
For foreigners must assume that Iran is as interested
as is the foreigner in the efficiency of these enterprises.[52]

10 Tenth, and finally, the political authority
must intervene whenever and wherever private forces
in the economy hesitate to venture, regardless of
the reasons for this lack of entrepreneurial spirit.
Even pertaining to economic development, this policy
is not very recent; certainly, it had crystalized
before the reign of the late Reza Shah who used it
quite liberally. Justification for the policy is
based upon a fundamental assumption concerning the
nature of the Iranian economy; namely, that the private sector naturally is timid and that the technicians and managers required for economic action
(here economic development) are not available or

going to be available in the private sector. Therefore, it is the public sector, because it is assumed
to be vigorous and dedicated to Iran's general progress, that must take up the burden of Iranian economic development. It is not that Iranian political
authority is against "private enterprise" as such,
for it has, through its model, the Shah, "advised"
the private sector to live up to its economic responsibilities. But, because the leaders of the private
economic sector are not trained in economics, they
seek only high profits.* And so, the political
authority, by default must concentrate on providing
the necessary investments and managements not to be
found in the private sector.[53]

The general reaction of those outside the political authority toward this intervention is as follows: As suggested in the previous chapter, the
average Iranian yearns for the charismatic political
leader who will assume the initiative and the responsibility for extending protection to the helpless,
who will somehow get the impossible but desirable
accomplished, and who will get the possible and desirable accomplished without any undue effort on
the part of followers.[54] To the average Iranian,
then, the sins of political authority, primarily,
are the sins of omission, not commission.[55] In consequence, the individual waits and expects, and the
political authority reciprocates these expectancies
as best it can, in part by its policy of intervention into the economy.

POLITICAL INTERVENTION INTO THE ECONOMY:
THE BASIC CHANNELS OF INTERVENTION

Intervention by the political authority into
the economy takes the following forms:

First, the political authority, on its own
initiative, and on its own terms, dispenses social
and economic service. The major service is that
offered by the Red Lion and Sun Society (RLSS)

---

* Presumably this might refer to the choice of
  speculative "high" profit rather than "low"
  long-range productive investment profit. But,
  as readily, it might refer to the choice of
  economic profit rather than political or social
  profit.

which operates in every area of the country, administering a tremendous government welfare program from
disaster relief to maternal care.[56] The Paklavi
Foundation, whose revenue originally came from the
Shah's landed estates, but which now is assisted by
the revenue of various government commercial and industrial enterprises, offers widespread educational
and cultural services; as for example, scholarships
to worthy students.* But the most significant government service is the general budgetary welfare program,
which includes inexpensive or free housing for teachers and regular government servants, and social insurance for civil servants and laborers.[57] But this
service often can, and does go beyond that; as for
example, when the former Premier Eqbal promised
workers not only better facilities, but even government intervention into private enterprise operations
whenever and wherever necessary to insure "satisfactory" wages.[58]

It is obvious to the political authority that
with limited resources and extensive demands, welfare programs, of necessity, often may be thin indeed. Consequently, rather than circumvent cover-
age, a polity whenever possible, tries to establish
models which it hopes will be emulated by others in
the society; as for example, the "model" villages
established by the RLSS.[59] But often this is not
feasible, and the services must be ignored, although
the principle never is surrendered, and recipients
are encouraged to believe that the service may be
resumed at any time, but, of course, at the sole
option of the polity. Significantly, in these
cases, political considerations often determine who
profits by the dispensation, the form that it takes,
the concrete benefits, and the efficacy of the service.[60] For example, although beneficial projects
always are being considered to ameliorate the admittedly bad conditions in south Teheran, this program
has secondary priority, as against projects in the
volatile Kurdish tribal area adjacent to Iraq.[61]

A second form of intervention by the political
authority into the economy is direct intervention
against "vested" economic interests. A prime example

---

* An interesting sidelight, of value to the present
   study, is that justification for the continuance
   of government ownership and operation of these
   enterprises is based upon the need to continue
   the Foundation's work.

exists in the area of rising prices on basic commodities. Apparently, manipulation of the price market, followed by government intervention, successful or not, has been characteristic of Iran since ancient times. But the problem has appeared with increasing frequency in the last decade. This is the result of the average individual, especially the civil servant on a fixed salary, being caught in a tighter and tighter price squeeze resulting from the galloping inflation. From the standpoint of the political authority, this politically is a very dangerous situation, because under the principle of political service, a polity is expected to do something constructive about this, a basic problem concerning the welfare of the people.[62]

Consequently, recent regimes have made a major effort to meet this challenge by various devices, such as;

(1) by offering subsidies to middlemen who guarantee that an adequate supply of the commodity will be made available at specified times when hoarding is most likely to take place;[63]

(2) by approaching the middlemen directly and demanding that a further supply of a commodity be made available or the middlemen may suffer the political consequences;[64]

(3) by cutting off the credit of those who use loans to hoard merchandise of limited availability in order to force up prices;[65]

(4) by setting up rival production centers to force price-fixing monopolists to heel;[66]

(5) by taking over or regulating the distribution of a commodity;[67]

(6) by negotiating with the culprits and together working out a compromise, negotiated price;[68]

(7) by increasing the bonuses of the civil servants to equalize the rise in basic commodity prices;[69]

(8) by instituting price control on basic commodities;[70]

(9) by competing actively with the middlemen, forcing them to reduce prices to those established by itself;[71] and finally, and most interestingly,

(10) by establishing an "ever-normal agency" to buy basic commodities when readily available and cheap in price, store them in government warehouses, and then release them in times of alleged scarcity to undo the price speculators.[72]

But in spite of all these levers to affect the price level, the policies of the political authority in the contemporary situation, as in the ancient past, never have been especially successful. In reaction, a polity has attempted to place the responsibility for failure on others; as for example, by accusing the middlemen of betraying the model (in this case, the Shah). But it also has had to admit that its intervention programs are not well organized and are not part of a stable, economic policy,[73] but rather are an ad hoc, political reaction to a political conviction that, in Iran, political authority, stands to lose or gain in political prestige on the basis of how it reacts to the economic needs of the people, but as those economic needs are conceived of by a political authority.[74] Quite obviously, what are missing are well-planned, well-sustained and economically motivated efforts, requiring a type of attitude toward an economy that the Iranian political authority is unwilling, or is unable, to formulate and execute.[75] Yet in spite of this painful demonstration of ineptness, or disinterest, or both, the right to, or the actual exercise of, this kind of intervention into the economy has not been, yet cannot be, abandoned--for political reasons.

3   The third pattern of intervention into the economy by the political authority is the system of government monopolies or near-monopolies. Government monopolies include control of basic commodities such as tea, tobacco, and salt; of economic operations such as grain marketing; of processing, such as the licensing of bakeries; of commodity transportation, such as the state railroads whose operations put truckers at a disadvantage; and of huge modern industrial enterprises, such as the oil industry.[76] Through these monopolies, directly or indirectly, the political authority is involved at some point in all components of the national economy; as operator, as regulator, as watchdog, or as imperfect competitor (that is, as a competitor with special privileges that in effect make the political authority an unfair competitor) with the private sector. And in its roles as deter-

miner of the prices and of the subsidies that are to
be paid to farmers for producing certain key commodities, and as the controller of the oil industry and
of its revenue, the government, in effect, has the
key level to the economic structure of the entire
country, and by implication, to the whole process
of economic development in Iran.[77]

These government monopolies have been challenged on a number of technical grounds; as for example,
that the prices the government pays are too little
and the prices at which it sells are too high, discouraging production on the buying hand, and encouraging private merchants and service contractors to
raise their prices exorbitantly on the selling hand;
while on the other hand, its policies serve the material interests of the polity.[78] But it appears
that the government monopoly system, not only continues to hold its own, but most probably will expand,
especially as new opportunities present themselves
in the Iranian economy.[79]

The fourth form of intervention into the economy
is the government purchase and distribution system
for its own personnel. In this system, the political
authority purchases commodities at favorable prices,
and then distributes them, on a coupon-rationing
basis, at fixed, lower-than-market prices outside
normal market distribution channels, most particularly in a government "cooperative" store. These commodities usually are basic commodity items, such as
coal, but they may include even such items as artificial teeth.[80] The system purports to alleviate the
effects of the spiraling inflation on the average
government worker who is on a fixed salary, and, hence,
by implication, to relieve the constant pressures on
the political authority to increase salaries which it
is not capable of putting into effect.[81] It also has
not been overlooked by the political authority that
the program serves to benefit the farmer, assuming
that the government will provide the farmer with a
fair price for his products, and to hurt the inevitable villain, the middleman and hoarder.[82]

In spite of all these potential benefits, the
program has not met general success or approval; for
one, because the government worker-recipients prefer
that they be paid the desired bonus in cash and not
in coupons which are good only in a canteen that offers a limited variety of products. Significantly,

government stores do not pay any duty on imported
articles or internal taxes on domestic products, thus
automatically creating for themselves an artificial
advantage over the private sector, no matter how inefficient is the administrator of the stores and no
matter how efficient is the administrator of the private sector. This further encourages economic inefficiency and inflation in the general (that is, in
both the public and private) commodity market.[83]*

    . A fifth avenue of intervention into the economy
is the latent consequence of having to depend upon
sales to the political authority in order to dispose
of the lion's share of the productive forces of the
society. For example, it has been estimated by one
source that 35 per cent of the national income is absorbed by government institutions, and servicing
those institutions cannot but provide the political
authority with a powerful lever into the operation
of the economy.[84]

    A sixth means of intervention by the political
authority into the economy is through joint government-
private enterprises. In such endeavors, the political
authority, obviously, is the more powerful senior part-
ner, and it takes advantage of this to dominate management decisions, even to the point of disrupting
operations for its own economic or political advantage.
The supermarket and the (joint Iranian) "German" department store, both in Teheran, suffered from such
extensive, erratic interference by the political authority.[85]

    The seventh, and final, channel of intervention
is the political authority's ambiguous policy toward
the structure and operation of private economic organization. For example, all "legitimate" private businesses are required to register with the authorities,
entitling them to a charter to carry on their economic
activities. Yet registered businesses are not required
to file profit-loss statements for taxation purposes
nor are they otherwise forced to rationalize their
operations in any way. Again, the political authority
has recognized formally the traditional guilds, not
as corporate economic units with defined rights and
privileges, but as amorphous intermediaries (the ba-

---

*   This will not be the only reference in the study to
    a policy of the public sector which harms both the
    public and the private sector of the economy.

zaar merchants) to haggle with over taxes and price
policies. Quite obviously, government policy is not
aimed at "modernization," let alone rationalization,
of private economic organization.

By way of summary of this section, it may be observed that, regardless of the specific channel of
intervention selected by the political authority, and
only seven have been described, the result on the economy always is much the same. It is apparent that,
consciously or not, government intervention has not
led to any increase in the economic efficiency of
either the private sector or the public sector of the
economy; in fact, in most instances it has led possi-
tively to the economic inefficiency of both sectors
of the economy. But, from the vantage point of political profit, the channels of intervention are most
effective in validating the service role of political
authority and thus, validating the perpetuation of
the existing kind of political authority in Iran, and
in subordinating the economy to the whims and benefit
of political authority.*

POLITICAL INTERVENTION INTO THE ECONOMY:
THE TAXATION SYSTEM

The structure and operation of the Iranian system is a typical example of intervention by the political authority into the economic order.

---

* It must not be assumed that the study is arguing
  that all defects in the Iranian economy (or in
  any economy) are to be attributed to government
  intervention, and hence that the absence of such
  intervention would cure the ills of this economy.
  This more general problem of the relationship
  between a political authority and an economy will
  be explored theoretically later--to some extent
  in the section "Political Intervention Into The
  Economy: The Taxation System" below, but especially
  in the concluding chapters of the study. All that
  is being argued at this point is that, contrary to
  an axiomatic assertion in Iran and among certain
  outside observers, the intervention of a particular
  kind of political authority with particular kinds
  of goals in the economy, characteristic of Iranian
  authority in general, regardless of the specific
  policies of specific regimes, is not conducive to
  the economic development of that society.

The tax system has the following characteristics:

First, the tax system is both centralized and non-centralized, without any clear-cut jurisdictional division between the two authorities. The tax system is <u>centralized</u> in that, although a number of tax offices do exist formally on the local level, these offices are independent of local authority and respond directly, and exclusively, to directives of the national Ministry of Finance in the capital city, Teheran. The tax system is <u>non-centralized</u> because, throughout the system, a division of responsibility exists between those who set the tax rates and levy the taxes, on the one hand, and those who operate the system and actually collect the money, on the other hand. Yet, the spheres of jurisdiction between nationally-determined "local" and truly-local, taxation are not clearly differentiated. Consequently, much overlap and duplication exists in taxation rules, rates, and jurisdiction.[86]

Because of this duplication and overlap, second, the administration of taxation in Iran is characterized more by individual personal negotiation, based upon skill and influence between tax administrator and taxpayer, than by the application and enforcement of impersonal, universally determined, established tax rules and rates. Moreover, no clear-cut and effective penalties exist for delinquency, and the penalties themselves are subject to negotiation. This is why, when an Iranian tax specialist talks about improving tax collection, he may mean only improving the negotiating facilities, in the belief that the more negotiating mediums that are made available, the more taxes that can be collected.[87] The average taxpayer, therefore, cannot calculate with assurance from one tax assessment period to the next what taxes he must pay.[88]

The tax assessment and collection on guilds is a prime example of this order of tax negotiation. Instead of taxing individuals, the political authority approaches the guilds as fiscal units, and suggests the total amount of revenue which it would like to collect. This is then subject to negotiation. When the amount is settled, and this may drag on for years, the guild is made responsible for collecting the tax from its members and delivering the total amount to the tax office. It is up to the guild itself to determine how much of the assessment each of its members will pay, and which members will be taxed

and which members will be untaxed. These decisions
are very much the product of particular members'
personal relationships to the particular designated
guild tax assessor; and, hence, once again, are subject to negotiation and maneuvering on a personal
basis.[89] In return for agreeing to be assessed and
to collect the taxes in this form, the guild exacts,
in return, certain concessions from the political
authority. For example, the Teheran brick kiln owners, in return for agreeing to accept a higher tax
rate in a particular year, were promised by the political authority in return, as a bonus, a new road
to the kiln.[90]

     Third, the principle of negotiation and inde-
cision operates not only to determine the amount
but also to determine the time of the tax payment.
For attached to most tax laws, are such provisions
as a grace period for payment and whether or not
the assessment is acceptable in installments (both
often of undetermined negotiable duration), and
how much of a rebate may be forthcoming for prompt
payment (prorated according to the speed of negotiation and payment). At any time, the political
authority may issue reprieves of deadlines, including liability periods for auditing tax reports.
The political authority claims that this policy
has been established to ameliorate sluggish business conditions by increasing the amount of capital in circulation. But, willful or not, the
policy does increase possibilities for negotiation
for delinquent tax payers. However, lest the taxpayer believe that he can stall endlessly, and
therefore, that the time factor works solely to
his advantage, the political authority, on the
other hand, may suddenly decide to enforce payment
(immediately) prior to when the statute of limitations expires. The taxpayer, then, is forced into
negotiations under circumstances of acute disadvantage to himself. But this possibility does not
seem to have had any influence on the prevailing
pattern of deferring payment as long as possible in
the hopes of a favorable negotiated settlement.[91]

     Consequently, fourth, tax delinquency is fre-
quent, with the threat of punitive enforcement ever
present, but uncertain. For the taxpayer knows
full well that tax legislation may be meaningless
not only because members of the Ministry of Finance
are willing to negotiate every assessment, but also

because they have the authority to waive completely
the tax assessment. With the possibility of total
fiscal amnesty present, the taxpayer stalls his
payment, negotiating and renegotiating, appealing
and re-appealing a decision. However, to re-iterate,
the threat of sudden enforcement always is present,
especially on the occasion that a newly appointed
political officer, as for example, a mayor, may decide to collect taxes as a means to demonstrate and
validate his power.[92]

Fifth, uncertainty further is intensified by
impulsively changed tax laws. Changes in schedules
are frequent, perhaps yearly. Since the negotiation
over taxes may go on from one year to the next, and
pile up one on another, neither the assessor nor the
assessed knows with certainty which schedule actually
is in effect for purposes of final negotiation, or
whether, by the time that a negotiation is finalized,
which assessment legally will be applicable. For
surprisingly, once again, these uncertainties are
resolved only by negotiation between assessor and
assessed.

Sixth, basic uncertainty exists that a tax
settlement, once negotiated, is final. This is due,
in part, to the fact that tax records in Iran, are
maintained very incompetently, and, hence, are unreliable as records of anything. Dead and live
cases often are filed together, so that it is hard
to say what cases are out-standing. Losses and mis-
filing of individual documents occur so that the
many parts of an individual's records may be filed
in any number of different places, or merely filed
chronologically. Consequently, if a negotiation is
considered on the basis of incomplete evidence,
which is only too likely, the political authority
reserves the right to re-open the case if unfiled
papers suddenly appear. The uncertainty of settlement also is intensified by the fact that the
authority for settlement of claims is diffused
among a number of different agencies, three bodies
and a higher tribunal, to be exact,[93] with doubt as
to whose word is to be taken as final proof of
authority of settlement of a tax claim. Finally,
negotiations once made, may be reversed, not because there is a question of the substantive contents of the tax report, but because of some hair-
splitting violation in the formalities of filling
out the tax forms themselves.[94] And in cases in
which the files are re-opened for negotiations on

any grounds, if the tax laws have changed meanwhile, which is very possible, negotiations very well might have to begin all over again.

The seventh characteristic of the Iranian tax system is that the tax schedules and their enforcement are grossly inequitable. Taxes are high on the poor and enforced, while in contrast, taxes are low on the rich and more easily evaded. Landlords pay very little or no taxes, especially since the time of Reza Shah when they were exempted from direct taxation (taxes on crops are passed on to the peasants).[95] Real property, which is the largest potential source of revenue in any society, in Iran, appears not to be taxed at all. All government personnel, who in Iran constitute a considerable portion of the higher salaried group, are permanently exempt from taxation, as are many foreigners who earn among the highest salaries. In addition to these preferences determined by membership in particular groupings, there are the so-called general "exemptions" which cut across group lines. These exemptions may be temporary or permanent, and may refer to a total or a fraction of the monies due, without any stipulation that tax exemptions are to be granted on the basis of pecuniary need.

Who then, pays taxes, in Iran? Such direct taxes that do exist fall heaviest on business men. Indirect taxes fall predominantly on the consuming population. Theoretically, in a good tax program, the revenue from indirect taxes should be minor as compared to the revenue derived from direct taxes. But in Iran, indirect consumption taxes are not minor; in fact, they make up 90 per cent to 95 per cent of the tax revenue.[96] And from the standpoint of the taxpayer, they are not inconsequential, because they fall heaviest on the middle and lower income groups.[97] Interestingly, the political authority goes out of its way to publicize the importance of direct taxation, although, revenue-wise, it is of very minor significance as compared with indirect taxation. In fact, some have argued if it was eliminated from the tax system, there would be no substantial change in the country's budgetary situation.[98] For, by definition, the tax must fall predominantly on those petty business men who do not have the economic wherewithal to induce particular officials to formally exempt or otherwise ignore the business men as taxable subjects

of the realm. These taxable business men are the
ones least worth the trouble of taxing, and when it
is considered that given the inefficiency of Iranian
administration, it is most probable that almost all,
if not all, of the modest taxes actually turned in
(less the usual slippage, that is) must go out immediately to pay the salaries of collectors and for
administrative purposes, the fiscal benefits of the
tax become even more doubtful. Direct taxation,
then, perhaps is a means to justify the need for collectors who are representatives of the moral-service
authority, an additional source of "something extra"
for officials, and a means of harassment on the evil
middlemen-business men as proof that the political
authority is doing something about the economic problems of the society.

The eighth observation on the tax system is that
the distinction between a tax levy and a private fee-
levy rarely is made, and when it is, the distinction
carelessly is drawn so that the two levies are applied arbitrarily and capriciously. Historically,
the distinction between forced "gifts" to officials
and legitimate "taxes" was blurred. Many an official
of old often was both a tax-farmer and the local political authority personified, who had to be supported
in the style to which he preferred to be accustomed.*

----

* Historically, the tax-farmer was an individual
  who had won, by successful bid or influence, the
  exclusive right to collect "taxes" in a particular
  area. For this privilege he guaranteed either a
  fixed sum, or a percentage of the money he collected, to the local authority, usually the provincial
  governor, who supported his collections with force,
  if necessary. All these officials used the money
  they collected indiscriminately for both their
  personal and public needs, sending a percentage
  of the collection up the line to their superiors,
  who in turn, did the same at each stage of the
  political hierarchy until the funds reached the
  apex of central authority, the Shah. For these
  reasons, the lines between the fiscal and political rights of officials and between public and
  private revenue were blurred.[99]

From the taxpayer's standpoint, any distinction between this appropriation of state funds for personal
use or for enhancing personal prestige (through
conspicuous construction) and stealing was a fine
distinction to make, indeed, and more a decision
based upon the official's personal relationship
with his superiors than upon any formal legal definition.[100] These high-living local governors eventually gave way to landowner-potentates, and finally
with Reza Shah, to the direct appointees of the central political authority.[101] But, in spite of these
changes, tributary taxation did not abate; quite the
contrary. In fact, Reza Shah was most famous for
his arbitrary cash-or in-kind levies often to his
personal advantage, on local sources of wealth; as
for example, his appropriation of many huge estates
all over Iran. These confiscations were approved of
by the common people who felt that, at last, they
had a champion against the "big names" whose property
or wealth, probably was either stolen or embezzled
from them in the first place.[102]

The tradition of fiscal confiscation in the
name of taxation, has persisted. Only now, with the
growth of commerce and industry, the sources of con-
fiscatory wealth have been extended. For example,
when the Governor-General of Fars, in September,
1960, required money for his edifice program, he
tried to raise the sum simply by taxing, or fining,
one Rajab 'Ali Havai, a serraf (that is, a money-
changer and check-cash of the Shiraz Bazaar), one
million rials (approximately U.S. $13,000). And
he collected it; much to the surprise and gratifi-
cation of the Shirazi who probably were short
changed by this man at one time and were pleased
that morality once again had triumphed over immorality.

The ninth characteristic of the tax system is
that temporary tax laws drawn up for special purposes remain on the books long after their original
purposes have disappeared. As for example, the
special (national) tax to establish throughout the
country work-camps for indigents entered the permanent, regular budget, although such work-camps long
since had been abandoned.[103]

The tenth, final, and summary observation, is
that the tax system does not operate to facilitate
or encourage productive economic activity or the

development of a rational, economic system. At first
blush, the system appears to be ideally designed to
extort the most revenue feasible from those who, under the existing politically determined ground rules,
are taxed, without regard to the consequences of the
taxation policy on the economy. However, this tax
system, as any tax system, does influence significantly the structure and operation of the Iranian
economy; but unfortunately, the consequences are negative for the developmental process. This is because,
simply stated, the system does not tax the few with
high (luxury) demand who do not invest, but it does
tax heavily (relatively speaking, of course) those
in the lower, especially, the lowest, economic bracket
who are least able to pay and who constitute the element out of which the potential productive forces of
the society might come.[104] Moreover, the tax laws,
since they prey on the weak who cannot resist, discourage the accumulation of scattered small capital
by the fiscal harassment of the small enterprises
(as noted in the seventh observation). And, in return for such harassment, little economic benefit is
offered in return; for example, truckers must pay
toll after toll on the roads, but who that has tra-
velled in provincial Iran, can dare to claim that
roads are properly maintained?

The Iranians hardly are unaware of all these
problems in their tax system. Certainly, fiscal
experts have been in Iran working on the problems
for almost a century, and, as in other areas of
Iranian administration, there is no shortage of
useful proposals.[105] Most recently, some isolated
constructive changes have been made. For example,
if the tax forms submitted by payees are not approved
by a certain prescribed date, the payee can consider
his form approved,[106] the graft-ridden "inspectors"
in the Tax Department have been abolished,[107] and
new tax legislation ever is in the hopper to cut
the red tape in both the assessment and collection
process.[108]

But significantly, as useful as these isolated
technical reforms are or may be, it is the basic
fiscal relationship between political authority and
taxpayer that has not been changed nor seems likely
to be altered. Especially unchanged is that aspect
of the relationship between economic actor and the
political authority which introduces perpetual uncertainty in the former's activities. This uncertainty arises out of the economic actor's inability

to know, with certainty, what the tax rate and tax
regulations will be immediately hence, let alone a
year or so hence.

Because of this, the economic actor cannot be
assured that any evasion tactic, no matter how successful, will truly avoid fiscal disability. For,
first, although evasion exists, at best it successfully can only postpone potentially punitive action,
which is held in abeyance while negotiation goes on.
Second, evasion and negotiation operate in that
"twilight zone" of political legality where success
is dependent not on abstract right or privilege, but
rather upon favorable, specific personal ties to specific influentials, and at specific times. Even if
successful, because of the dubious legality of these
relationships, the actions may be subject to sudden
repudiation by the political authority without legal
recourse. Third, because negotiations depend upon
relationships between specific individuals, and
these individuals may and do change, the terms of
negotiation may and do change, always to the disadvantage of the economic actors who must start anew
finding and making suitable contacts and stimulating
them financially.

A final observation on uncertainty. In the
developed West, although taxes are high, the rate
and the probability of enforcement reasonably are
certain. Consequently, although economic actors
often grumble over the rate, the principle of taxation and the rate are accepted, are anticipated
and, hence, are calculable in any of the actor's
economic plans. In contrast, in Iran, although
taxes often are low or even non-existent, rates and
enforcement are uncertain. Human beings, being
human beings, the principle of taxation and the tax
rate are not accepted, because the possibility of
evasion exists. Hence, the tax structure is not,
nor can it be anticipated in any economic calculation.
Consequently, although perhaps of immediate advantage
to the economic actor, this kind of tax system is
detrimental to long-range, calculable economic action,
the touchstone of potential economic development.

THE BUDGETARY AND FINANCIAL POLICY AND OPERATIONS
OF THE POLITICAL AUTHORITY*

As in other societies, an important key to the
economic policy of the Iranian political authority
is to be found in its budgetary and financial policies and operations. Briefly stated, the political
authority, because of its overriding non-economic
interest in the economy, accepts--willingly or
grudgingly, but accepts--working within the existing
economically non-rational structure. It diverts and
wastefully consumes on economically non-rational,
politically motivated projects, funds in short supply
that should go elsewhere in the economy into productive channels; even though on the surface and after-
the-fact, the projects it sponsors may be rationalized as economically justifiable. Worse, whenever
it runs out of funds, it borrows (especially oil
revenue) funds which are earmarked exclusively for
national economic development, and uses these funds
for non-productive purposes (termed, "budget support").109

Specifically, first, the Iranian budget suffers
from the nature of suggestions which pour into it
for funds. Funds are requested primarily for salaries. Project funds are apt to reflect the whim of
the influential official who wants to make a conspicuous impression but who may not be around to implement the project. But this is of minor consequence
against the fact that little or no attention is
given to the economic or technical feasibility of
many projects, or, to the proper utilization of
funds that are appropriated. Requests often arrive
late, and sometimes, anticipated requests do not
arrive at all, perhaps in the hope that last year's
request may be repeated with an appropriate increase.

---

*   What is said in this section (specifically those
     observations without references) has been gleaned
     from accounts--rather complaints--of business-
     men who have had to contend with these problems
     in their fiscal relations with various government
     bureaus. Since the sources have proven to be
     straightforward and reliable on other matters,
     the author believes he is presenting a true pic-
     ture, but the reader is warned accordingly.

Upon such raw material, a budget is drawn up and reviewed in the Ministry of Finance. The budget then
is sent to the Majlis (parliament), whose members
pass judgment on it without any clear notion of what
policy the budget is supposed to be carrying out,
save perhaps the one of continuing to spend money to
support the bureaucracy. The extent of current revenue, whether or not it can support the budget, and
if not, whether a deficit budget can be justified,
are all apt to be ignored.[110]

The administration of the budget also creates
difficulties. For one, although in theory it is the
lower echelons which determine their own operational
budgets, the center feels free to force the lower
echelons fiscally to support out of their budgets
any ad-hoc decisions concerning local operations
that the center may care to make at any time during
the fiscal year. At the least, this causes problems
during the year; at the most, radical re-adjustment
of operations must be made to avert potential fiscal
disaster late in a year. Again, budget approval can,
and does, take place after the year's operations must
begin; that is, after the fiscal year has begun. Consequently, operations have to move along for a considerable time under the cloud of not knowing whether
or not requests have been approved at all, let alone
how much has been approved.

Disbursement also follows this pattern. The
Minister of France assures the public of fiscal
plenty and promises both a balanced budget and a
budget that will satisfy all of Iran's "needs."[111]
When these promises come to naught, which is always,
a substitute promise to economize and, thus, to
increase the revenue is made.[112] When this, too,
falls short of promise, the polity borrows heavily
from the Bank Melli.[113] It also stalls on paying
its debts to contractors or even its own personnel,
especially outside the capital. In this case, employees must borrow or dig into existing savings to
meet personal expenses, and operations may close
down for want of funds. This happens often enough
that a feeling arises in the bureaucracy that the
government chronically is short of funds. This
not only affects morale, but affects the budget
adversely, since personnel are reluctant to waste
time working up budgets which they feel have little
relation to operational reality. Finally, when the
personnel are most restless and discouraged, but
never discouraged enough to quit the bureaucracy,

from one source or another, funds are obtained.
Then the machinery of administration grinds on once
again, until the New Year approaches when funds run
out again and the cycle begins anew.[114]

Considering the specific disbursement of funds,
it may be observed first, that all initial disburse-
ments are under the control of the Minister of Finance.
This minister jealously and zealously guards his prerogatives to use what can only be generously described
as a flexible system of fund allocation, enabling him
to disperse the available funds on the occasion, and
on the terms, that he alone sees fit regardless of
the directives of the formal budget (which, to repeat,
often is meaningless in its own right). Second, in
Iran, revolving funds are common and operate in a
way that a disbursement agency, such as a treasury,
cannot ascertain, if it ever wants to, at any one
time, precisely what funds are at hand at any of its
constituent agencies. Third, the funds of one section, regardless of the regulations, can be and are
"transferred" ("borrowed" in Iranian terms) by other
sections, in horizontal or vertical relationship to
the original section, according to the whims of section "chiefs" powerful enough to do so, and, although
this supposedly is very illegal, funds authorized for
one project are transferred for use on another project. Fourth, on the operational level, no attempt
is made to relate directly authorizations and expenditures. Specifically, once a budget has been authorized, provided money is still available in the till,
there is no requirement to know, and not much interest in knowing, precisely what has been, or is currently being obligated and spent.

Fifth, and finally, inflated expenditures.
These are two distinct but interrelated problems;
namely, the problem of unnecessary expenditures,
and the problem of loose expenditures. As to the
former problem, it is a truism that if all the admittedly non-rational, economic expenditures were
eliminated from the Iranian budget, the budget easily
could be balanced.[115] But the Iranian budgetary principle is that, at the minimum, last year's level of
expenditure must be maintained, and that, if at all
possible, that level should be increased, presumably
to demonstrate the expansion in the moral concern of
the political authority through expansion of fiscal
benefices.[116] Consequently, since these specific
purposes for which the expenditures are to be used
are of minor consideration, save as later rational-

ization for the amount, the concept of unnecessary
expenditures is meaningless, and even preposterous
if it implies pruning, rather than, at the least,
maintaining the existing level of expenditures.
Occasionally, when the economic situation worsens
and approaches the brink of disaster, the political
authority reluctantly concedes that retrenchment,
temporarily, might be in order. Retrenchment implies
only that such minor expenditures as additional bonuses for personnel should be rescinded. The cutting of
major wasteful government expenditures, such as the
padded bureaucracy or conspicuous construction are
not considered.

     Because of these basically, economically, non-
rational policy decisions, expenditures cannot be
brought into line with rational economic needs in
spite of Iran's constant economical difficulties.
But theoretically it still is possible to insure
that all these admittedly unwise expenditures will
be dispersed efficiently so that expenditures will
not be unnecessarily inflated further. Theoretically, (that is, technically speaking), this is so;
but actually this is not feasible, not only because
of the Iranian's preference for looseness in the
allocation of funds, already discussed, but also,
more significantly, because policy (that is, the
Iranian value system) is involved in what at first
blush seems only a technical economic problem. For
it is the act of making the expenditure and not the
efficiency of the expenditure, as against the results, that has primacy in Iranian economic thinking.
And, it is the total expenditure as such, and to
whom it goes, rather than the rational economic justification of the total budget, or of any individual
items in that budget, that is the key to determining
whether or not the allocations will be made. It is
for this reason, that Iranians are unconcerned when
some items are incorrectly estimated in a budget.
For such estimates always can be reworked, especially
backward from an arbitrary total, which remains firm.
This is possible because the total has been determined
on other than an economically rational basis and the
singular items of the budget subsequently have been
drawn up to justify the expenditure. This is why
projects drawn up under particular authorizations
tend to end up requesting expenditures for the same
amount as the authorizations. For in Iran, for a
polity to admit an inability to send to the maximum
is to admit an inability to govern out of incompe-

tence or out of indifference to playing the vital
role of benefactor of the society.

POLITICAL INTERVENTION INTO THE ECONOMY:
THE CREDIT SYSTEM*

The Iranian credit system offers still a
further clue to understanding the interrelationship
of polity and economy in Iranian society, particularly
the subordination of economic interests to political
interests in a way that is not conducive to economic
development.

The primary characteristic of the Iranian credit
system, and the first observation, is that the Iranian
commercial and industrial economy is capitalized primarily through loans and credits and not through savings, and that the primary source for these loans and
credits is the political authority through the medium
of the Iranian National Bank (Bank Melli Iran).[117]
In general the Bank has attempted to award these loans
on a first-come first-serve basis without any reference to priorities, and as long as money is available.[118]
Consequently, loans are decreased whenever money is
scarce (and, incidentally, when most desirable).   In
this way the loan policy feeds inflation in good times
and helps to keep up the open market interest rates in
bad times.[119] Moreover, since loans cannot be granted
when funds run out, the existing loans, of necessity,
must be terminated, regardless of the economic value
of the projects the loans are supporting.[120]   It is
for this reason that the spurts of Iranian economic
activity, which sometimes are very impressive, cannot
be sustained, because the projects are financed from
loans, whose source by definition, cannot be reliable.[121]

With capital becoming scarce in comparison to
the expanding fiscal obligations of the political
authority in the most recent years, the government
has had to resort to considerable belt-tightening.
A Coordinative Council has been established to bring
the government loan policy more closely in line with
general Iranian development policy.[122] Since the

------

*   This section considers the urban-commercial and
    industrial credit system, leaving the question of
    rural credit for later discussion (see section
    "The Structure of the Rural Economy" below).

government Bank dominates the loan market, this turn-
about in liberal credit policy, regardless of the
merits of the situation, generates a climate of credit insecurity throughout commercial and industrial
circles, forcing businessmen to turn to the traditional, but highly unsatisfactory, Iranian source
for raising capital; namely, to the bazaar moneylenders.[123] This is so, historically, because there
is a chronic shortage of large scale (that is, mobilized) funds from non-banking, non-bazaar sources.
For, although 75 per cent of Iranian capital is
"free-floating" (that is, outside the banks), it cannot be mobilized readily in the open market. This
is because Iranians, due to the general climate of
capital insecurity, prefer to invest separately,
rather than to pool resources. Thus, capital needlessly is scattered, and large amounts of capital
are very hard to accumulate. At best, access to
free-floating, pooled capital is limited to closely
related individuals, especially blood relatives
which sources, of course, individuals seeking capital would already have tapped, not only before coming to the bank in the first instance.[124]

The bazaar, the only source of non-bank mobilized capital, has adequate credit available, but at
a price and on terms few are able to underwrite.
As to price, in contrast to the United States, for
example, where 8 per cent is the low and reasonably
standard loan rate, the Iranian loan rate is both
high and unpredictable.[125] One source has characterized bazaar loan rates at 15-19 per cent for
prime loans, 19-21 per cent for second class loans,
and 21-24 per cent for third class loans, with 20
per cent about par. It should be noted that this
classification of loan rates is based not upon the
purposes of the loans but on the reliability of
the guarantors.[126] Because the interest rate on a
loan is high in any case, the profit margin can be,
and must be, high enough to pay off the loan to
make the endeavor worth the bother. Under these
circumstances, the anticipated American 6 per cent
profit margin can but be looked upon with amazement.
As to terms, as in the case of bank-credit, there
always is the threat that the loan will be called
in whenever credit is scarce, which is likely to be
the same time that the business man is in difficulty
and has even greater need for capital. Since effective insurance against bankruptcy largely is unknown
in Iran, the consequences for the average business
man may be grim indeed.[127]

The effect of this unreliable and costly system
of short-term, high-interest investment-credit, whether that credit is derived from government or private,
principally bazaar, sources, is that capital is invested speculatively in internal or external commerce
rather than in productive industry, for it is only
through speculation that potentially high profits can
be made to overcome the burden of high interest rates
and to maintain operational costs at a minimum.[128]
A true security market and a government bond market,
essential to long term, low interest productive credit, characteristic of Western (public-cum-private)
finance, is unknown.

The problem is not unappreciated in either
business or political circles. The comparison of
the Iranian with the Austrian credit system and
economic development, for example, has been cited as
evidence of what should and could be done.[129] One
attempt to meet this challenge has been the establishment of the Industrial and Mining Development
Bank (IMDB) whose initial capital came from a currency devaluation, termed "rial revaluation" in
Iran, and American loan support.[130] This bank has
attempted to finance sound and worthwhile projects,
especially small projects, of an industrial and
mining nature, in order to encourage interest both
in initiating and in operating successfully such
enterprises.[131] The Bank's operations have compared
very favorably with other investment sections of the
Iranian economy. For example, it has funds when
other prime sources do not, which indicates at the
minimum, that its loans are being paid back--out of
productive and not speculative profits, it is hoped.[132]

The Bank Melli from time to time carries out a
very admirable government policy of credit stabili-
zation in the open market,[133]*but, at the same time,
it supplies the central and local political authority
with non-productive credits for administrative expenses, and subsidizing such pet projects as the
Mortgage Bank of Iran, which, it has been charged, is
supported for political rather than for rational economic profit.[134] The consequence is that in commercial circles credit becomes scarce; interest rates

---

*   It must be stated that subsequent to the time of
    the present study, a Central Bank has been estab-
    lished. Its policies have successfully amelior-
    ated some of the problems discussed in this para-
    graph.

are upped, and a general business recession occurs;
for to re-iterate, economic activity thrives on credit and not on savings.[135] Because of such spending
programs of the political authority, which alone has
access to substantial credit, while all private sources of credit have been dried up, at the same time
that a business recession exists, a general inflation
(due to government spending) exists in the economy,
further squeezing the hard-pressed private sector.
The credit-hungry commercial and industrial sectors
of the economy are now at the complete mercy of the
political authority, failure is inevitable. The political authority is not unaware of its power for
it can, in fact, hasten the ruin of the private sector simply by refusing such vital credits. It has
done so; for example, in the case of the private
Teheran Electric Company which was squeezed out
simply by denying it improvement credits under justification that the private sector in electricity
was only "temporary," because new grids, then being
built by the municipality, would be the future
source of Teheran's electrical power.[136] But the
political authority, to be sure, has no intention
of allowing "worthy" merchants or industrialists,
who are in difficulties because of such circumstances beyond their control, to suffer. Consequently, some merchants or industrialists, the so-
called "exceptions," are offered monetary aid
regardless of the specific regulations prevailing
in a credit austerity program.[137]

It is to be noted, for purposes of the present
study, first, that this right of the Iranian political authority, as an abstract right, to make what
amounts to moral, economically non-rational decisions
of life and death over one phase of the economy, in
such instances, never is questioned. What is questioned only is whether or not specific credit
choices are fair, or are profiting political favorites of the regime; which, of course, admittedly is a
legitimate question, but hardly is the vital one.[138]
And, second, when the political authority does re-
lent and extend a loan, it does so on its own terms,
at its own pace, and selectively to whom it wishes;
that is, upon criteria it alone determines and follows. Since the political authority alone is privy
to the criteria, and the criteria are changeable by
their very nature, the criteria cannot be predicted
beforehand by the business community. Consequently,
although individuals of the business community who
profit by a credit windfall (economic grace) are

grateful to the political authority for its generosity, at the same time, they must remain nervous
over the possibility and probability that a reversal
of policy (a loss of political grace) may occur at
any time, again, on terms which cannot be predicted
by that business community.[139]

Hence, such a credit system, characterized by
indecision, instability, and uncertainty, can but
imply that systematic and planned long-range economic action, so necessary for economic development,
if it is dependent on financial credit, is not feasible in Iranian society.

PLANNING: THE QUINTESSENCE OF THE RELATIONSHIP BETWEEN THE ECONOMY AND THE POLITICAL AUTHORITY

Economic planning has captured the imagination
of the Iranian political authority, as it has the
imagination of political authoties elsewhere in the
underdeveloped world. Planning, it is argued, is
natural and basic to man, and has been used since
time began to insure man's welfare and happiness.
Originally, when society was less complex, planning
was carried on within the circle of the family,[140]
but in modern times, to be effective, planning must
be carried out on a national scale. This is true
because modern problems are complex and require the
dynamic, integrated approach, which only national
planning can effect.[141] In national planning, economic planning is the most important aspect, for
although economics is not the sole determinant of
human behavior, it is the most important determinant.[142]

National economic planning hopes, first, to
eliminate waste.[143] Second, it insures that a
nation will be successful. When the backward
countries, as Iran, look to the forward countries
for the clue to success, they see economic planning.
Third, planning is a means to redistribute wealth.
Consequently, planning can solve Iran's twin problems of social maladjustment and economic stagnation
in its subsistence economy.[144] Fourth, planning encourages foreign investment because it convinces the
foreigner of Iran's interest in positive economic
action. Fifth, it provides economic independence
for Iran, and places her eventually among the world
powers.[145] Sixth, it fires national political unity,

injecting new blood into the body politic, especially
the administrative structure. Seventh, and finally,
it is the best way to convince the citizenry that the
political authority sincerely is interested in organizing itself properly to ameliorate the people's ills
and improve their social status.[146]

Although economic considerations certainly are
of importance in these seven rationalizations, political objectives are not underplayed, and hence, the
role of economic planning in Iranian society is no
different from the role of political economy in Iranian society. Consequently, economic planning in an
economically underdeveloped Asian society such as
Iran, as any type of systematic, rational planning,
faces certain prime difficulties which are but reflections of the general difficulties in productive
(economic) action in the society at large.

These difficulties may be described under eighteen headings, as follows:*

First, the Iranian attitude is "to get the cash
and let the credit go";[147] that is, to treat preliminary planning as a waste of time and as an unnecessary delay in getting on with "essentials." For example, much is made of the necessity of having an effective vocational education training program in Iran.
Yet, very few vocational surveys ever have been made
to ascertain what specific vocations are required
for Iran's future economic roads, and hence, what
kind of training programs must be established. And
even these few surveys are inadequate. At the most,
they are based on the superficial impressions of
some Teheran administrators who interview local officials who have no facts to back up their opinions
and are not about to admit their ignorance before
superiors. Field technicians who are working on vocational problems and businessmen who will be the
ones to employ the trainees are ignored. At the

---

*   It is to be noted that some of the behavior dis-
    cussed under two or more "difficulties" appears
    to be contradictory. Certainly this is not
    unusual in any system of behavior in any society.
    But in Iranian society, in particular, the ten-
    dency to ignore rather than to resolve behavioral
    conflict is very pronounced and aids positively
    the persistence of many of the difficulties.

least, the surveys often represent only the not-too-
educated guesses of officials who have never left
Teheran and rely on the usual, admittedly inadequate,
and falsified reports from the periphery.

Second, since Iranians hate to be tied down and
associated with firm, precise decisions, for which
they may be held responsible if anything goes wrong,
planning documents tend to be vague and imprecise to
avoid possible future culpability. The Iranian language admirably serves this end. It is rich, imprecise, and flowery, and its phrases are a most useful
substitute for the concrete data that true planning
requires. Such items as budgets, work plans, maintenance provisions, and economic justification for
projects tend to be subordinated, or even crowded
off the document, by clarion calls to action and inspiring quotations from the works of medieval Iranian poets. When the necessary data are included in
the project, they are deliberately made vague, although planners are well aware of what is required
and can obtain the information readily when it becomes a matter of rejecting a project if the required information is not included. But unfortunately, project reviewers act on the same premise
as project proposers; that is, that one must avoid
potential accountability if at all possible, seldom
require such hard economic information.

Third, rather than face the possibility of
failing in striking out on new ground, planners, in
order to protect political prestige and self-respect,
are apt to concern themselves only with time-tested
projects. Unfortunately, in Iran, time-tested projects are trivial projects. And for this reason,
the major problems of the economy go on being ignored. For example, when the possibility of total
bankruptcy faced Iran in 1960-61, and bold, creative
economic action was demanded, many in the political
authority were conspicuously busy with such political trivia as setting a new price on non-alcoholic
beverages.[148]

Fourth, perhaps out of this fear of failure,
but certainly out of faith in rule by model, a paper plan too often is confused with plan accomplishment. If only the right plan can be found, the
Iranian argues, somehow, the accomplishment will take
care of itself. And by extension, if only the right
people, presumably, the executors in the political
authority in particular, can be motivated to asso-

ciate themselves with a plan, somehow, great things automatically will be accomplished.[149]

Fifth, a plan, as a moral model, once devised, is adhered to tenaciously, whether or not that plan turns out to be adaptable to the situation. The problem is compounded when it is recalled (the second observation) that plans too often have been devised without proper preparation. And, consequently, a plan right from origin may not be adaptable. The problem further is compounded if the situation changes during the life of the plan, which is very possible. It is because of this rigidity, that organizations perpetually complain about the shortages of funds to meet planned obligations, instead of adapting and modifying plans according to the current resources and changing circumstances.

Sixth, at the same time that plans are adhered to rigidly, (and this is one of those apparent behavioral contradictions), Iranians may reverse the principle and use the sum total of available resources as point of departure, drawing up a plan to justify the maximum expenditure, often after the expenditure has been made. For this reason, planners prefer to avoid working up a plan until the full extent and nature of available resources are made known.[150] But since in Iran it is assumed that resources will be allocated on a personal basis rather than upon such an impersonal, rational basis as a "plan," the Iranians, in ignoring a plan, at the least until after the allocation is known, only are responding to reality; but, of course, it is a reality totally unrelated to considerations of rational planning.

The contradiction between this and the previous discussion only is an apparent contradiction because both approaches to planning simply are the contraries of one basic principle; namely, that available resources and planning are not coordinated rationally, that resources are expended wastefully on personal whim, and, hence, that any plan can be used to rationalize, either before or after resources are expended, the prevailing pattern of Iranian economic action.

Seventh, the planning process is unstable and capricious. Since a plan is considered to be the pet of the man responsible for requesting it, a plan serves more as a means for personal (monetary, or particularly, social) advancement than as response

to a rational economic challenge. Since plans are
personal, little chance exists that a plan will outlive a sponsor's tenure of office, for each new planner will want to devise his own plan to enhance his
monetary or social status. And hence, any new plan,
conceivably, may be motivated more by the desire to
innovate for innovation's sake, than by forethought
of what the situation demands. And, finally, since
a new plan will have to be devised soon after the
arrival of a new planner, at a time when that individual has very little prior knowledge of the existing situation, still another negative influence is
introduced into the planning process.

Eighth, considerations of economic feasibility
rarely enter into plan formulation. If the planner
is pressured, certainly, technical details can be
devised for any plan. But, quite obviously, then,
such details are rationalization, (the sixth point
above) and significantly, these details cannot be
said to demonstrate the economic feasibility of the
plan. As example, the case of the steel mill plan,
so much in the news for so many years, may be cited.
Certain influential individuals, including the Shah,
"wanted" the project, particularly for non-economic
reasons, and that decided the matter. Technical details piled up upon technical details as to how to
carry out the plan, and some attempts were made to
justify the necessity of the plant, but on political
or social grounds (e.g., prestige). But on grounds
of economic feasibility, the desirability of constructing the mill in the first instance always was
open to doubt and hotly debated in Iranian economic
circles. The expressions of these doubts at first
were ignored by the planners, and, then, finally,
were attacked as an imperialist or traiterous plot
to deprive Iran of its rightful place in the world.

Ninth, in Iran, (as elsewhere), too often it
is believed that planning automatically will lead
to economic and social change. Consequently, Iranians are convinced that if a "good " plan can be
devised, it will insure that an enterprise constructed to its specifications will force individuals
associated with that enterprise to run it successfully, and that this success, in turn, will trigger
dramatic social and ideological reorientations,
even possibly leading to the dream of the economically developed society.[151] For example, under
both the previous and present Shahs, a great amount

of time and effort has been expended in the attempt
to devise a satisfactory plan for settling permanently Iran's tribal people. The hope has been that
through such a plan the tribes will become an economic and political asset to the political authority,
instead of the present economic and political liability. The program has been a miserable failure, in
spite of the use of force at some times, and the
active sponsorship of the project by both Shahs at
all times. Monuments of deteriorated and deterior-
ating empty houses are to be found all over tribal
Iran, especially in south Iran. In brief, the plan
had no effect whatever on the abortive tribal settlement policy simply because, sociologically, the
tribes were not interested in living in houses, and
economically, the tribes could not support their
flock in permanent settlements. At best, the tribes
used the houses for storage while on migration.
And obviously, in this and in similar cases, certainly the mere physical presence of these enterprises did not provide any incentive to change existing modes of behavior.[152]

As in such cases, tenth, the Iranian is apt
to turn to a scapegoat whenever his plans do not
work out as anticipated. This is because in these
instances, he is more interested in settling blame
on someone else rather than trying to learn from
his mistakes as a possible guide to improve future
planning and performance.

Eleventh, instead of accepting planning as a
matter of routine and hence approaching each new
problem as it arises with measured, careful forethought, the Iranian usually acts on a plan only
when pressured, and, then, in a state of near-
panic. It is not so surprising, then, that so
many planning efforts end in failure, further discouraging interest in planning.[153]

Twelfth, there is little cooperative action in
Iran. Consequently, many plans go awry for no other
reason than individuals other than the planners,
whose cooperation may be necessary for success of
the plan, are not consulted in formulating the plans.
For example, irrigation projects have been built
where the soil is salty, and a sugar beet factory
has been built where the supply of sugar beets is
inadequate for the size of the plant and the supply
is not apt to expand; in both cases for no other
reason than that planners and technicians did not

consult "stupid"farmers who lived and worked in the
area (and who eagerly pass on these stories to any
visitor).

Thirteenth, planning discussions are valued far
beyond their potential. Certainly, it is true that
prior discussion can eliminate a number of the dozen
problems that have been reviewed so far.[154] However,
discussions do not lead necessarily to action and
surely this is the case in Iran. In Iran, in particular, verbalization too easily becomes the substitute for action, creating an illusion that something
positive is being accomplished simply through the
process of discussing a problem.

Fourteenth, bold proposals, properly conceived,
are essential to creative planning. But, if such
bold proposals cannot be carried out, then any planning effort connected with the proposal is a waste
of time and effort. Unfortunately, this is very
much the situation in Iran. It is for this reason
that in Iran plans emanating from the political
authority, although they appear at first blush to
be very impressive and sophisticated to the outsider,
are skeptically treated to the point of indifference
by the very Iranians themselves who must carry them
out.[155]

Consequently, fifteenth, even once committed to
action, the Iranian still is indecisive. For the
Iranian, on the one hand, is entreated not to be
inactive, yet on the other hand, he is also cautioned
about acting rashly. He is entreated not to talk
only, but to act; yet he is told to take advantage
of the experiences of the last half century of failure, for otherwise there would be only compounded
failure, more frustration, and pessimism. The Iranian solution to such a conflict of pressures is not
a true solution, in that it is not a resolution of
the conflict. Rather, the Iranian will drift until
one or another alternative is made both evident and
inevitable; for in that case, fate can be blamed for
the result, especially if the result is unfavorable.[156]
Such an order of problem solving hardly is conducive
to positive creative planning; in fact, it is a major
contributor to Iran's worsening economic and social
malaise.

To extend this argument as a sixteenth observation, the Iranian is not convinced that tomorrow will

be any better, or even the same, as today. In fact,
tomorrow may very well be, and probably will be worse.
And as far as the average Iranian is concerned, unfortunately, there is enough empirical evidence about
him to demonstrate the truth of this belief. And so,
he argues, why should I go through the agonizing experience of having to devise or submit to rational
plans which depend on the conviction that it is worthwhile to think of, and scheme for a better tomorrow,
which as far as I can see, is more a dream than a possibility?

And so, in Iran, seventeenth, for various reasons,
no one is committed on a long term basis to anything,
least of all, to long range, rational planning. This
is especially true of the political authority, which
as has already been suggested, plays so vital a role
in the society (see above Chapter "Political Authority")
And since the average Iranian certainly has no control
over political policy, and that policy is apt to change
readily and without warning, the political authority
only reinforces its own doubts, confusions, and indecisions everywhere in the society. Since rational
planning depends on security, planning in such an atmosphere is extremely difficult.[157]

Eighteenth, and finally, the political authority
has failed to clarify precisely the objectives of any
of its plans. In consequence, it has failed either
to inspire popular participation in its own plans,
or alternately, to inspire private planning. And,
thus, it has failed to involve positively in the planning process, the human resources so necessary to
carry out the plans themselves.[158]

Given these eighteen general difficulties to
any kind of successful planning in Iran, and especially the last two observations, the question presents
itself as to whether or not the Iranian political
authority is capable or willing to carry out rational
economic planning. Certainly, there is a Plan Organization in Iran and there has been a series of planned
programs. In 1962, the second plan was to be completed
and a third plan was to be inaugurated. The political
authority, then, is committed to planning, and, in fact
has been committed to planning since the Iranian year,
1325 (1946-47). In that year, the existing government
development projects, which, often as not had been
earlier conceived hastily, and operated predominantly
on an ad-hoc basis, especially under direct intervention and inspiration from Reza Shah, were placed under

the aegis of a comprehensive development plan. The
1325 Act established an Industrial and Mining Bank
to operate and finance all existing government enterprises, except oil, tobacco, and railroads. More
significantly, the act established a Planning Board,
to plan all future government enterprises. The
First Seven-Year Plan, which grew out of the 1325
act and was approved in the year 1327 (1948-49), was
an Iranian reworking of a foreign consultant report
originally prepared for review by the International
Bank who supplied 32% of the capital for the Plan.
Coincident to the establishment of the First Seven
Year Plan, a new Plan Organization was set up to
plan and to operate all government owned enterprises.
In keeping with this mandate, Plan Organization was
authorized the major share of Iran's oil income as
capital. Its first act was to take over the enterprises of the former Industrial and Mining Bank.

        The First Plan was doomed before it really got
off the ground by the nationalization of oil in the
year 1330 (1951-52) which cut off its revenues.
But the First Plan was not suspended formally until
the year 1334 (1955-56), when, after a new oil agreement was signed with a foreign consortium, a
Second Plan was inaugurated. The Second Plan was
much more ambitious than its predecessor. It consistently ran into financial difficulties, in part
because of a steady inflation, and in part because
the political authority had cut its share of the
oil revenue from 80 per cent to 60 per cent in 1336
(1957-58), and again to 55 per cent in 1337
(1958-59) and had placed other restrictions on its
use of the oil revenue. But beyond this question of
funding, there have been serious shortcomings in the
planning and in the operations of many of its enterprises (which is to be discussed shortly). But the
new Third Plan hopes to correct these shortcomings.
It has emerged from a careful and frank study of
past failures, and has been devised with the active
participation of an international group of competent
advisors, who have worked on the spot in close cooperation with top caliber Iranian economic and social planning talent.[159] In addition, the Shah has
endorsed publicly the philosophy and objectives of
Plan Organization and had defended it vehemently
against its critics.

        Plan Organization, through the medium of the
Third Plan, now is, and will be, increasingly invol-

ved in the vital sectors of the Iranian economy--in
communications, in industry, in social affairs, and
in agriculture--to the extent that success or failure
of the organization's endeavors very well may determine the future economic prospects of Iran. Consequently, although technical economic problems as such
do not concern the present study, according to the
task set forth in the Introduction (See above,
chapter "Introduction"), it still is most worthwhile
to review systematically certain of Plan Organization's
difficulties as these selected problems are concerned
with the non-material (social) problems of economic
development.*

The first source of difficulty for Plan Organization is that it has never been able to gain the
active cooperation of the old-line, technical-
service agencies for its policies. The first and
most obvious source of strain has been that it is
Plan Organization, through the oil revenue, that in
most cases has had project money, and Plan Organization has refused to release these funds to the agencies until those agencies have submitted project
details in advance in a (rational economic) form
that Plan Organization is willing to approve. The
agencies have rebelled against what they consider
usurpation of their policy prerogatives and alien-
ation of their moral right and privilege to funds.
This conflict has arisen, in part, from the already
discussed Iranian political assumption that individual agencies have the right to direct their own
affairs according to the personal dictates of their
chiefs, certainly as far as the use of money is concerned. And, in accordance with an additional political principle, the relationship between Plan
Organization and the agencies has never been precisely defined, nor has the basis for acceptance or

---

* Some of these problems, to be sure, are only
  extensions of the same general planning problems
  discussed above, and so focus will be upon those
  problems peculiar to Plan Organization. Many,
  but not all, of these problems are well described
  in the Plan Organization's "Review of the Second
  Seven-Year Plan Program of Iran," issued on March
  10, 1960. The work is called to the attention of
  the reader, for a fuller account of much of what
  is about to be discussed.

rejection of agency projects by Plan Organization
ever been carefully defined for the benefit of the
agencies. Consequently, the agencies have never had
any clear idea as to how an agreement could be reached on a regularized basis so that they would have
reasonable assurance that funds would be forthcoming,
if certain established procedures were followed.
Logically, it could only be on the basis of such a
consensus that the agencies effectively could draw
up projects and make their own long-range plans;
and presumably Plan Organization is a tool of economic rationality in Iranian society.160 But, in
typical Iranian response, the old-line agencies
quibble with Plan Organization over each and every
project, in the hopes that this will (in descending
order of hope) destroy Plan Organization, absorb
Plan Organization's function into old-line agency
functions, limit Plan Organization's power, eliminate Plan Organization's supervisory power over
agency projects, or finally, establish a principle
of personal negotiation with specific individuals
within Plan Organization and within the old-line
agencies to assure approval of pet projects of
"influentials."161

A second source of conflict between the agencies and Plan Organization is that, save for the
education program, Plan Organization in spite of
its name, is very much involved in operations as
well as in planning.162

And, need it be repeated again, there is no
easier way to get an Iranian bureaucrat agitated
negatively than to challenge his right to run his
own show as he sees fit. Especially in those projects which are apt to receive good publicity, particularly abroad, and/or please influential superiors in the political hierarchy, especially the
Shah, the rivalry for control of operations between
Plan Organization and the agencies is very keen.163

A third source of agency-Plan Organization conflict, is that Plan Organization specializes in intellectual talent, while the old-line agencies spe-
cialize in political-administrative talent. The two
groups, as elsewhere in the world, have mutual contempt and suspicion of each other. This conflict is
reflected in the bickering and in the behind-the-
scenes maneuvering discussed just above. Moreover,
it is no secret that certain ex-Tudeh (that is,
Communist) Party members are in Plan Organization.

The Shah even has boasted of this as an example of
his clemency.[164] Be that as it may, these individuals and certain other non-communists in Plan Organization are committed to planning as a means of introducing social change in Iran in a way and form
likely to antagonize the non-rational political conservative to be found in the old-line agencies, and
thus further to intensify the intellectual-adminis-
trative antagonism in the Iranian political authority.

A second general source of difficulty for Plan
Organization stems from the unreliability of its
funding. It has been mentioned already that Plan
Organization funds come primarily from a percentage
of the oil revenues, but that Plan Organization
never has received all the oil money which it has
been promised.[165] Second, each time the foreign
dominated Oil Consortium meets, Plan Organization
is thrown into panic lest its revenue sources be cut
again by an unfavorable price adjustment.[166] And
finally, the specter of another Mossadegh, threatening to cut off the flow of oil and oil revenue, is
not an empty joke at Plan Organization any more than
it is elsewhere in the political authority. If, for
any of these reasons, Plan Organization's revenue is
diminished, unless foreign loans are made available
on an emergency basis to bail it out, the Organization must suspend operations pending a further allocation of funds from the political authority. This
latter support is not likely to come readily in that,
at such a time, the political authority is apt to be
in similar fiscal difficulty and seeking financial
support for its own politically motivated projects
and not at all sympathetic to the rational-economic
needs of Plan Organization. And Plan Organization's
reaction to this admittedly difficult situation only
has compounded the problem. As other Iranian planners, the Organization has tended to select its projects and guide its operations in ad-hoc response to
the varying amount of revenue it receives, rather
than draw up economically rational, but realistic
objectives, appraising the financial needs of the
objectives, and carrying out selected objectives at
specific times.[167] In sum, long-range, rational
economic planning is impeded both by the nature of
Plan Organization funding and the typical Iranian
reaction to such difficulty.

A third source of difficulty for Plan Organization is that its projects have not been selected
to fulfill any coherent, consistent rational economic

policy drawn up to achieve economic development.
Even with a chronic problem of having to work with
limited financial resources, the Organization never
developed a system of rational economic priorities.
Rather, Plan Organization has attempted to satisfy
too many diverse interests, and on a first-come,
first-served or personal influence basis, competing
with the old-line agencies in the political game of
beneficial one-upmanship.[168] Consequently, although
many projects of political as well as rational economic importance, as for example, roads, were approved, others as vital, or even more vital, from
the rational economic standpoint, especially in agriculture, were slighted or ignored, because they lost
in political competition.[169] Projects were said to
be chosen for "impact." Iranian "impact projects"
are those large and impressive projects with only
economically marginal utility in terms of construction costs, construction time, maintenance costs,
and market utility. For example, regional programs
in depressed areas, given Iran's level of economic
development, cannot be justified on grounds of
rational economic priority; that is, given other,
more pressing general economic demands on Iran's
resources. But the programs may be justified on
non-economic, specifically political "impact"
grounds, and this is why they have been selected.
This has been the case in Sistan-Baluchistan in
eastern Iran, where the attraction to Muslim India
(now Pakistan) has been traditional, and in
Kuzistan in western Iran, where association with
the Arab world is strong.[170]

Another principle which contributes to the difficulties in project choice may be termed the "vindication principle." The choices of many projects,
at the time that they are chosen, very well may be
justified on rational-economic grounds. However,
in time, as rational-economic considerations change,
especially in response to development tempo and
technological development, the projects, perhaps no
longer can be justified as useful from the rational,
economic standpoint; yet, the projects are continued.
For example, even though oil now can be piped, and
trucking is more economical in many areas, the expensive and difficult railroad building program goes
on, because Reza Shah built railroads, and the wisdom of Reza Shah, the "model of modern Iran" must
be vindicated.[171] Significantly, although many of
these vindication projects have been judged as less
than successful, the polity goes on building them.

Rationally, this would suggest that the political
authority only is demonstrating failure, but since
the projects are meant to serve primarily non-rational
(model) ends, and since rule by model never has been
challenged by failure of its operational arm, the projects a priori are vindicated.[172]

A fourth problem area for Plan Organization is
that project operative and maintenance costs and difficulties are ignored, or at the least slighted, once
the actual construction has been completed. In
theory, Plan Organization should provide the initial
capital budget for building the projects, and the
old-line agencies, then, should underwrite the operation and maintenance of the projects. In practice,
however, since no integrated relationship between
Plan Organization and these agencies exist, in turn,
no clear-cut division of responsibility exists.
Rather, both Plan Organization and the agencies compete for the right to construct, since this is where
the political prestige lies, and largely ignore the
operations and maintenance of what is constructed.[173]
Yet the more that is built, the more that has to be
maintained.

Unfortunately, it is often difficult to tell
until it is too late, if a project is operating successfully, since capitalization and not operating
costs, often is the only consideration, and, since,
for reasons of "prestige," managers tend to cover
up difficulties as long as possible.[174] But, in
those cases in which the situation in either operations or maintenance has become so desperate that
it no longer can be covered up or ignored, since
no funds have been allocated for such a contingency,
a frantic search ensues to find the necessary funds
to keep the project from collapsing. Even so, a
sudden infusion of money cannot always save a project. This is so, because, in addition, since in
Iran, little thought is given to the human factor
in operations and maintenance, the managerial problems of maintaining the project also have been
slighted in relation to the attention lavished on
the construction.[175] In part this is based on the
not unusual belief that it is much more comforting
to believe that by changing the construction, which
is easy, rather than by changing people, which is
difficult, somehow project problems can be solved.[176]
But it is also reflected in the often ridiculous
conditions of employment and low salaries that

trained technicians receive as compared with the
economically superfluous, but politically necessary
"administrators." A final observation: By slight-
ing upkeep, especially the need to provide for trained humans to insure upkeep, construction easily out-
paces the capacity of people to operate and maintain
it. Consequently, regardless of the original
rational-economic value of any construction, this
situation certainly will pervert what originally was
a good idea.[177]

The fifth source of difficulty for Plan Organization is that delays in completing its projects,
even those delays which can be justified on rational
economic grounds, are used to discredit Plan Organization, as an organization and as the symbol of a
principle. The critics have been aided by the fact
that, by the very nature of Plan Organization's
operations, delays have been inevitable. For many
in the organization, from the planners right down
to the contractors, are inexperienced in the kinds
of economic actions for which Plan Organization has
been made responsible. Also, Plan Organization has
been plagued with shortages and delays in capital
and in trained personnel at many critical moments.[178]
But these problems are hard to explain to the unsophisticated, egged on by the jealous who stand
to lose if Plan Organization, or its ideas, succeed.

Common are such criticisms as that Plan Organization is but another Iranian talker, not an actor.
In Reza Shah's time, some have observed, things
didn't take so long to do. To the economically unsophisticated, such questions as how good were Reza
Shah's plans in rational economic terms, or what
happened to them, once completed, are of no concern,
for if Reza Shah did something, it must be sound
morally and empirically.[179]

Criticism of Plan Organization, especially by
Iran's traditional, politically sophisticated elite,
to speed up "visible development" has not been lost
on the political authority. For the polity is
aware that an obvious inability to deliver "service,"
in Iranian political terms, implies weakness and indecision, vices of the order no polity wants to be
accused of.[180] The consequent pressures for "action"
upon the Organization have had a desultory effect on
its operations, since such pressures push for the
type of ad-hoc decisions without careful prior pre-

paration to serve _political_ rather than _rational-economic_ ends which, presumably, Plan Organization had been set up to avoid.

A sixth source of travail, is that Plan Organization has not fired the imagination of the average Iranian in a way that he feels he is a part of the planning venture, or in fact, that economic planning is something worth getting excited about at all.[181] For one, projects of importance to over-all rational-economic development, as, for example, the industrial infrastructure, might not be "visible" to the man in the street, especially in a way that they are reflected in an increase in his _consumption_ capacity _at this stage_ of Iran's economic growth. Again, although the Shah has given his blessing to Plan Organization, he has not seen fit to take an active part in the work, (perhaps wisely out of consideration of rule by model) as has, for example, the former Prime Minister Nehru in India's plans. Although some observers have not been impressed with the extent of mass enthusiasm for planning in India, no one questions the benefit of having the (titular) leader of the nation take an _operational_ interest in so important an endeavor as national economic development.[182]

The sixth difficulty, and the one that probably lies at the heart of the problem of instituting rational economic action in Iran is that rational planning is too alien and too (politically) dangerous to be taken seriously, even though the empirical economic situation has become desperate and this is obvious to all. Consequently, people who know better pretend to view Plan Organization as only another government agency and to attribute to it all the disabilities of inaction and failure associated with the old-line agencies.[183] And these individuals have compounded the problem by publicizing the failures of the First and Second Plans in a way that the average man on the street has become disillusioned, not only with Plan Organization, but with planning in general.[184]

A seventh source of difficulty has been that Plan Organization has accepted, either forced or voluntarily, the traditional Iranian political preference of serving the center to the neglect of the hinterland. Those local projects that have been authorized have been sanctioned on a piecemeal basis, according to the political pressures of the moment, and, as such, have not excited any continuous local

interest. The apparent exceptions have been the
regional programs in Khuzistan and Sistan-
Baluchistan. But those two programs, although
regional geographically, serve purely national and
not local objectives (and at that, not economic, but
political objectives), at the same time that they
are not part of an integrated national development
plan.[185]

The eighth problem is that the best laid plans
of Plan Organization easily go astray once they have
to be implemented on the local level. Given the
political premises of Iranian society, projects,
once they leave Teheran, usually are "reorganized"
by those on the local level who are responsible for
carrying out the project so that the projects serve
primarily personal benefit; at the least, political
benefit in return for dispensing economic "service"
in particular localities or to particular individuals.
Plan Organization has tried to circumvent these
tactics by requesting concrete, pre-planning suggestions for local projects, especially from the principal culprits, the provincial governors-general.
But the suggestions Plan Organization receives, not
surprisingly, reflect only rationalizations for
funds which the locals expect to use at their own
discretion rather than plans, or even programs, in
the technical economic sense;[186] and the governors-
general believe they have the political "connections"
to get their way, which too often is true. Another
source of difficulty is that jealousy between old-
line agencies which are made responsible jointly
for carrying out specific projects locally may
create more problems than existed before the project
got under way. For example, while the Khuzistan
Development Service may be most successful in building huge irrigation complexes in that area, if the
local Ministry of Health is not "cooperative" with
the service, Bilharzia can spread in the irrigation
channels and the local people will be worse off than
they were when they lacked water, and further tempted
to curse the evils of Plan Organization and of planning in Iran.[187]

A ninth source of difficulty for Plan Organization is that even if its projects become operational,
there is no way to avoid the often accompanying waste
of manpower and financial resources which diminishes
and even nullifies the effectiveness of the projects.
This problem has arisen from both technical-economic
and non-technical sources. Some of the non-economic

sources include first, the rivalry between Plan
Organization and the old-line agencies, on the one
hand, and among the old-line agencies themselves, on
the other hand, which has given rise to an unnecessary duplication of projects, and in the process, to
a wastage of talent perpetually in short supply.[188]
Second, non-economic considerations in project decisions bids up economic costs dangerously. For
example, the weight limitation on trucks using Plan
Organization-built roads was set at thirteen tons,
and the roads constructed accordingly; this, in
spite of the fact that international limits are set
at eight tons and that building roads able to withstand the punishment of thirteen ton vehicles is
far more difficult and costly than building roads
to withstand the weight of eight ton vehicles.[189]
This was decided solely to enable the Iranian truck
drivers to overload their vehicles as they wished
to do, and solely because truck drivers are infiltrated with radical political ideas and the government is cognizant that drivers, by the very nature
of their occupation, are in a position to make political trouble. Third, when changes in projects have
to be made because funds are short, a chronic problem in Iran, the changes are not made on the basis
of a coherent rational-economic system of priorities,
but rather made on an ad-hoc basis according to the
strength of individual political pressures being
placed on the Organization. Consequently, a near-
completed and economically vital project may be,
and often is, sacked in order to provide support
for a project either still on the drawing board,
or a project of dubious economic utility, only because the selected project is the pet of a political
influential. Fourth, an honest reporting of operational problems is rare, indeed. For in Iran, always,
one strives to give the best impression and, hence,
only a fool would admit an inadequacy which conceivably could be covered up. Consequently, serious
mistakes often are discovered only when the situation
is so hopeless it can no longer be concealed, and
hence, it is too late to save the project.[190] And,
if this was not bad enough, meanwhile, funds and personnel have been expended fruitlessly merely to save
someone's "prestige." Fifth, the members of Plan
Organization, as Iranians in general, tend to ignore
the human institutional problems in project planning,
believing rather that if some miraculously-perfect
plan that is technologically feasible at the same time
can be conjured up, automatically it is operationally

feasible and it is assured of success. For example,
supporting an identical, technologically feasible,
improved agricultural seed program for tenants in a
landlord-owned village and for freeholders, ignores
the question of differential cost and benefits, and
even the question of differential incentives between
the two groups.[191] Sixth, because of varying political pressures placed upon it, Plan Organization as
other political groups, at times, becomes over-
cautious, lest it make a mistake that will bring
down upon it the wrath of some influential official.
In the process of malingering, needless funds are
spent in investigating and re-investigating the
problem without any decision to fish or cut bait
being taken; as for example, the steel mill.[192]
But, in general, it can be said that it is the lack
of efficient investment and not the rate of investment that is being slighted in Plan Organization
activities, for as in all Iranian organizations, the
desire to spend and create always is more important
than rational economic feasibility and any purely
economic benefits to be derived from specific projects.[193] In consequence, Plan Organization's
enemies have argued that Plan Organization is a
luxury Iran cannot afford, and former Plan Organization heads have been interrogated by the government for alleged excess costs and political favor-
itism. That the very critics may practice what
they charge, or because they do and assume it goes
on in Plan Organization as it must in all government
organizations, is ignored; for in this line of thinking, Plan Organization is a luxury, but old-line
agencies are not.[194]

     The tenth source of difficulty for Plan Organi-
zation is that the private sector of the economy has
all but been ignored in Plan Organization calculations. In consequence, first, a vital sector of the
economy that could be mobilized to contribute to
development arbitrarily has been excluded. Second,
some needless duplication has occurred between the
public and private sectors of the economy. Third,
since the private sector <u>relatively</u> is more efficient
in certain areas, for no other reason than that it is
not saddled with the inflated labor force that is
found in all public enterprises, it might very well
be given responsibility for implementing certain
projects.[195] For Plan Organization to support the
activities of the private sector, need not, and does
not, imply that the public sector in Iran does not

have a vital role to play in providing capital support, and more important, in creating a favorable
climate for long term, productive private industrial
investment.[196] Although "obviously" this is an economic decision, and a decision to Plan Organization's
as well as to the economy's benefit, the decision
to support the private economy adequately still has
not been made, because such decisions are <u>political</u>,
and the Iranian political authority does not see
such a decision as being in its <u>political</u> interests,
for no other reason than this would reduce its
"service" role in the society.

An eleventh area of difficulty lies in reliance
on foreign technicians. At the least, these foreigners, though technically more efficient and productive than Iranians, because they often fill positions
in <u>operations</u>, do not build up Iranian experience
and confidence in making difficult decisions. Hence,
when they leave, the vital know-how that they have
introduced into Iranian operations leaves with them.
More important, since by definition they are removed
from the political situation, or as Iranians like to
put it, "not allowed to interfere in administration,"
the foreign technicians cannot operate in such vital
areas as "coordination" with old-line agencies.
Thus they reinforce rather than reform existing
operational procedures.[197] Again, and perhaps most
significant, the foreigners serve as scapegoats, inside and outside Plan Organization, for any situation
in which Iranians desire to refuse to face the inadequacies of their own planning and operations.
Consequently, foreign technicians, ironically, have
enabled Iranians to perpetuate their problems under
the rationalization that when the imperialist vul-
tures finally go home and give up their fat salaries,
when they stop making decisions which "sell out Iran
for their own interests", when they stop their attention to detail and "slow methods" which they use to
keep Iran backward,* and when they stop paper-
planning, knowing full well that some poor Iranian
must put their impractical schemes into action, then,
and only then will Iran be able to develop.[198]

---

*   Apparently this is a reference to insistence on
    economically feasible projects which can operate
    on the basis of local cooperation and understand-
    ing rather than on political service projects
    run by authoritarian methods.

The twelfth order of difficulty, and which, in fact, is a summary of all the difficulties discussed to this point, is that Plan Organization lacks as its guide a coordinated, comprehensive plan, that comprises consistent and clearly defined rational-economic objectives, and that takes into account, and hopes to mobilize, the total resources of the country.[199] Presumably, the Third Plan is to be such a plan; a true plan, and not the ad hoc collection of projects of the First and Second Plans.[200] This Third Plan, then, is supposed to provide both for a preliminary appraisal of Iran's resources, both social and economic, and of market opportunities before any project is approved. No longer will influentials be able to send their pet proposals up to Plan Organization whenever it suits their fancy.[201] And instead of, as now, automatically authorizing new equipment for each new project in the interest of "conspicuous construction," the organization will consider whether existing equipment and present projects might be re-utilized.[202]

But comprehensive planning of this order implies that institutional change must be supported whenever it is needed, even changes which are painful and step on influential toes. For example, increased agricultural productivity must be accompanied by marketing rights for peasants, even though usurers find that this cuts into their fiscal tribute.[203] Another significant change is that rational economic considerations must be paramount in making project decisions, otherwise the economically trained staff will be wasted and whatever enthusiasm for economic development the plan ought to encourage will soon be dissipated. In addition, rational-economic considerations must tighten up costs, so that costs can be anticipated and projects completed, regardless of which "influential" suffers, economically, socially, or politically.[204]

Certainly, few economists can quarrel with the Third Plan's spirit. The issues and the peculiar problems of planning in Iran are clearly and frankly set forth. But unfortunately, although the appreciation of the necessity to have this kind of a plan and the formulation of such a plan is a good first step in a society such as Iran, the mere appreciation for, and formulation of such a plan does not guarantee that it ever will be carried out. For Iranian political considerations too often subordinate

rational economic considerations, and it is unfortunate, but true, that such political considerations
can enter into the Third Plan all the way from the
choice of basic projects to the vital process of how
plans ought to be implemented and by whom. If this
is so, first, this plan, as previous plans, may be
used primarily to build more monuments. And, even
if this is not so, and the intent is there to carry
out the spirit, as well as the letter of the Third
Plan, the question remains whether that Plan can be
nurtured in the particular kind of politically-
oriented, economic environment of Iranian society.

POLITICS AND ECONOMICS:
SOME FURTHER CONSIDERATIONS

Urbanization

From the economic standpoint, as well as from
the political standpoint, Iran is dominated by its
few large urban centers; now especially by its one
paramount urban center, the capital city of Teheran,
where 25 per cent of the total population of this
"agricultural" society is concentrated.[205]

In this city the significant elements of economic action--credit, supporting services, labor,
and managerial talent--are concentrated.[206] In
part this has resulted from the preference shown
by the "service" political authority in the allocation of its economic benefices. For example, of
the total number of "development" loans approved
by the National Bank (Bank Melli), approximately
half have been awarded to Teheran.[207] Even on the
basis of rational-economic considerations alone, then,
economic action can be expected to concentrate in
Teheran where it is cheaper and easier to initiate;
in brief, where previous economic action has been
most successful and active.[208] In this manner, economic concentration in Iran feeds upon economic concentration in a vicious circle. In consequence, on
the one hand, the hinterland increasingly is depressed
by the diversion to Teheran of those necessities, material and human, which would enable it to escape from
the dilemma of backwardness breeding more backwardness.
While in Teheran, on the other hand, productive economic action breeds increasingly productive economic
action.[209] Simultaneously, Teheran has the negative
influence of attracting existing local resources, human
and material, from the periphery, thus denuding both

the small towns and the rural countryside of available talent and funds.[210] For to establish oneself in Teheran is the ultimate ambition of all
those who strive to better their economic status,
as it is the ultimate ambition for those who strive
to better their political status. A private survey
conducted in June, 1960, in Azerbaijan, concluded
that 85 per cent of those with primary school education leave the villages for the nearby market
towns, (where they serve as semi-skilled, or even
unskilled, workers), but that the majority of these
individuals have as their ultimate goal, even if
they are never able to achieve it, migration to
Teheran.

Significantly, for all these reasons, although
it must live off the productivity of rural Iran,
this order of urbanization does not prosper or even
change the countryside. It is for this reason that
one observer has termed Asian urbanization a para-
site, for it is not productive of itself, nor does
it help to increase the productive capacities of
the countryside; in fact, quite the contrary.[211]

Significantly, Teheran, the capital city, has
become the economic magnet that it has in the first
instance, in part at least, ironically, because
that city is not and never has been primarily an
economic center, certainly not an industrial center,
nor has it grown to such eminence because primarily
it offers economic opportunities and advantages that
the remainder of Iran does not. Rather, Teheran, as
other paramount Asian urban centers, owes its growth
to its eminence as a political center, as the center
of Iranian political power and authority. Since, in
Iran, as far as the general society is concerned,
economy must be intimately associated with polity
in order to thrive or even survive, Teheran offers
economic actors the maximum and most secure political
protection, on the one hand, and the maximum opportunity through association with the maximum political
influence, on the other hand. The periphery, because
it does not have the most important and influential
officials residing there, or in fact, below a certain
administrative level, because the administrative apparatus does not have any representatives present,
cannot offer this political protection and influence
that is to be found in the capital city. For this
reason, the economic actors, as their fields of
operation widen and increase in volume, gravitate to

Teheran. In the process, as these actors leave the
periphery and concentrate in Teheran, an increasing
discrepancy arises between the capital and the periphery, and as long as true, and not merely formal
decentralization of political authority does not
exist in Iran, there will continue to be this attraction to Teheran.[212]

This order of close relationship between economy
and polity also helps to explain why in Iran, as
elsewhere in economically underdeveloped Asia, the
economic roots of urbanization necessarily may not
be associated with industrialization. Rather, because the political apparatus concentrates in the
paramount urban center, great numbers of economic
actors are needed to service that apparatus. Urban
employment opportunities other than in bureaucratic
"service," then, predominantly are in servicing
politicians, would-be politicians, and the economic
actors themselves; and industry, such as it is, may
only concentrate on construction. The city, for
this reason, attracts not only the economically and
politically sophisticated, but also the impoverished
ruralite and small town laborer, who swell the unskilled labor pools, especially in construction.
Many such migrants are unemployed, under-employed,
or only occasionally employed. Yet the migration
does not cease; quite the contrary. Some retain
their village roots to the periphery and in time
may return only to be replaced by others. But those
with some limited talent wait it out regardless of
opportunity, and this provides one source for the
tremendous increase in the capital's population.[213]

The Legal System and Economic Action

The fact that a judicial system which provides
a series of coherent legal rules and legal protec-
tions by which an actor can plan his activities with
reasonable assurance that certain actions (that is,
means) will lead to certain results (that is, ends)
does not exist in Iran, already has been cited
(Chapter Two, "The Formal Structure of Political
Authority: Law and Corruption"). Consequently, the
Iranian economic actor, even if he is so inclined,
cannot be assured that rational economic calculation
over specified lengths of time will be provided with
judicial security. For in Iran, from the economic
standpoint certainly, the wheels of justice grind
slowly, and when they do grind, they grind inadequately

and poorly so that the results are uncertain. An
Iranian judiciary that both can cut red-tape and
provide security for financial transactions, as yet,
is an idle dream.[214]

Consequently, the Iranian economic actor pro-
tects his economic interests by seeking to obtain
legal protection and security in the same way as
does anyone else in Iranian society. He either
seeks out an influential political patron who will
be in a position to go to others to move things
along in the right direction, or that actor attempts
to influence directly the individual official(s)
responsible formally for the decision-making process
that affects his economic interests, whether those
individuals be judges or lowly policemen on the beat.
In return, the economic actor provides economic benefit for services rendered.[215] However, all such
officials, including ordinary policemen, forever
are being changed, ostensibly to prevent such personal relationships of influence from developing.
This policy further increases both the uncertainty
and the cost of legal security for the economic actor. For the economic actor normally only can hope
to solve his security problems by establishing a
good personal relationship with each and every
specific individual that comes to fill the particular political positions of vital interest to him, no
matter how frequent the turnover. And, since by definition, each case is a novel situation involving
particular individuals, the economic actor has no
way of knowing beforehand whether or not he will be
successful. For the new official may be too greedy
to make economic effort worthwhile, or the new official may want to aid a relative or friend who is
in economic competition with the economic actor. The
primary significance of this kind of legal system,
however, is not how often or how expensive the achievement of a satisfactory relationship of legal-political
influence for economic action may be, which surely is
important enough, but the fact that the relationship
is <u>uncertain</u> and as such, cannot be calculated <u>ration-
ally</u> by the economic actors.

Another implication. If the formal judicial system is not the real basis for establishing the rules
of legal constraint, which it is not, then, in effect,
formal assurance of legal enforcement does not exist
in Iran. This thought is beyond the additional consideration, as observed in the previous chapter, that

even if the political authority is serious about formal laws, it is ever ready to change those laws, on
its own initiative, whenever it suits its fancy (especially after a political shake-up), on the premise
that if criticism of laws exists, it is easier to
change them than to enforce them properly.[216] Consequently, for all these reasons, belief persists that
if one tries hard enough or long enough, one may be
able to avoid any legal imposition. This explains
the Iranian propensity to treat with irreverence
existing statutes, and if pressured, to procrastinate
in the hope that unpopular laws will be voided if one
can only hold out long enough. For example, as discussed in the previous section, when with rational
economic justification, the political authority decided to bear down upon the use of overweight trucks
on newly paved, provincial roads, the truckers resisted and denounced the political authority for not
protecting the trucker's economic interests. They
threatened to bring to a halt this most vital sector
of the transport system, unless the political authority, ever fearful of antagonizing this group on political grounds, relented by not enforcing the road
rules.[217] Consequently, to draw one conclusion, it
must be observed that the elaborate formal Iranian
legal codes and regulations do not and cannot have
the same role to play in the operation of the Iranian
economy as they do, say, in the western European,
Japanese, and American economic context.[218]

     Ineffective laws do not profit the economic
actor in the long run, and in general, although they
may appear to be to his benefit in the short run,
and in a particular instance. In the previous example,
the ineffective road law was not repealed, it was only
not enforced; it was there to enforce or to use to
harass the economic actor another time, on such occasion as it suited the personal whim of a particular
official. Ineffective laws, potentially favorable or
unfavorable to economic action, in and of themselves,
because they do not establish a code of legal precedents, do not establish a basic, general code of expectancies that can be used as rational, calculable
guides in economic action. For every time the economic actor "gets away with something," ironically, he
is in fact, undermining his own position. For even
if he obtains an economic advantage, whatever he
gains, neither has he obtained it legitimately (since,
nominally, it is counter to a law) nor is he assured
of a successful repetition of his performance. This

is why, although it may sound strange at first reading, restrictive regulations strictly and impartial-
ly enforced, which are accepted and calcuable, are
superior from the standpoint of rational economics
to favorable regulations which are not accepted and
not enforced. It is worth noting in passing, that
the speculative economic actors alone stand to gain
by the ineffective Iranian legal system and that the
political authority by its inability or refusal to
reform the judicial system, regardless of its formal
statements to the contrary, discourages rational
economic action and encourages speculation.

Certainly, from the standpoint of the economic
actor, viewing the existing judiciary system, it
seems that the political authority supervises in a
way that its activities are a positive obstacle to
rational economic calculation, while it absents itself in those cases in which it could serve positively
by creating a climate of calcuable economic confidence.
For example, appropriate ministries seem particularly
unable to enforce adequately existing laws concerning
standardization and quality control of export products to insure foreign sales.[219] Yet, on the other
hand, the political authority never seems incapable
of passing (and forgetting to repeal in most cases),
new and conflicting tax legislation and of attempting
to enforce petty harassing taxes on the use of public
facilities.[220] In the same spirit, major economic
conflict of interests, as for example, the perpetual
transportation war between the government railroads
and the private truckers, are not settled by clear-
cut decision, but by periodic concession to one side
or another side, which by the very nature, varies
from occasion to occasion, and hence is not calcuable
or considered a final decision by either side.[221]
And, finally, it must be observed that too often,
when the political authority acts, even when that
action is useful from the rational economic standpoint,
it is apt to be hasty, ill-conceived, and personally
motivated by the material or prestigeful interests of
particular officials.

And so, obviously, contrary to classic Iranian
political theory, it is the actions of the political
authority in these cases, specifically the way it enforces the laws, and not the inert laws themselves,
that are at the heart of the problem. For the legal
actions of the political authority, quite clearly,
create confusion and doubt which can but lead to eco-

nomic indecision, inaction, and attempts to outwit
the legal system, regardless of whether the laws
themselves are "favorable" or "unfavorable" to rational economic action.[222] In contrast, in the economically developed societies, even "unfavorable" economic decisions, clearly formulated and enforced, can
be calculated and accounted for in productive, rational economic decision making.

THE STRUCTURE OF THE RURAL ECONOMY

In Iranian economic philosophy, agricultural
surpluses are measures of the wealth of a society,
and the revenue derived from such surpluses provide
the fiscal foundation of political authority. But,
as in the case with commercial economic actors, left
to their own devices and "interests," the agricultural actors may not fulfill satisfactorily their
responsibility to produce and make available to the
society in general, and to the political authority
in particular, the required surpluses. Consequently,
in order to insure compliance with this, a moral-
material obligation of the agricultural actors of
the society, the political authority, in its capacity as the arbiter of the society, has the right
and the duty to supervise, and if necessary intervene, into the agricultural economy.

Although these agricultural surpluses are
considered to be essential to the society, and
even morally desirable in their own right (in that
they support the political order), since the supervisory role of political authority in Iran primarily
is to spread morality in the society, given the
necessity of a choice, morality must take primacy
over crass material (i.e., rational) considerations
of maximizing agricultural surpluses. Hence, ironically, although in Iranian economic theory much is
made of maximizing productivity to maximize surpluses,
so that the political authority will be able to
spread morality in the society, consideration of
maximizing productivity must compete at a disadvantage with certain other considerations in the operation of the Iranian rural economy. And significantly,
in the same spirit, conversely, less than maximum
agricultural productivity can not be considered criticism of a political authority in that, although
surpluses are most desirable, even on grounds of morality, the overriding (moral) consideration of re-

inforcing the existing rural social structure, if
need be, might have to take primacy over any rational-economic considerations of maximizing agricultural productivity.[223]

This, perhaps, is one reason why, although
every responsible official and lay economist in
Iran appreciates the fact that agricultural development is a necessity in itself, and certainly in the
process of economic development, yet not too much
concrete has been accomplished along these lines.[224]
In fact, it even might be argued on the basis of
examination of its rural programs, that the political
authority is determined that the contrary should prevail. For, although the political apparatus ever is
present on the rural scene whenever it is time to
collect the surpluses, "to show the flag" on ceremonial political occasions, or to pick up recruits
for the army or police, generally it is conspicuously
absent, day after day, whenever vital services are
needed to maximize productivity. And it is acknowledged, that, in allocation of funds, the first two
Seven Year Plans for economic development slighted
agriculture for conspicuous construction (especially
urban construction at that), although the Third
Plan promises to remedy this gross inbalance.[225]

And so, as in other economically underdeveloped
societies, Iranian agriculture is characterized by
low yields, and the employment of mass, underdeveloped
labor, utilizing primitive and inefficient equipment.
This is why, ironically, although Iran primarily is
an agricultural country, in that 80 per cent of her
population is engaged in agriculture, food often has
to be imported. For increasing the food area economically is impractical because per capita and per acre
yields are so low that foreign foods often can be
grown, shipped, and imported more cheaply than home
grown products.[226] Yet (or because of this), ironically, although only one-third of Iran is arable,
only four per cent of that one-third actually is in
use; and of the four per cent, forty per cent must
be irrigated to be usable. And it is this low yield
four per cent that supports the Iranian population
of close to twenty million people.[227]

It is often asked how the Iranian economy, especially an economy that claims to be able to support an economic development program including industrialization, operates on such little potential.
One way of answering the question, of course, is to

state the obvious; Iran can't, it is underdeveloped,
and its general per capita income is very low.   But
another possible answer more useful for the present
study, is that today, as yesterday, the agricultural sector of the economy is organized primarily to
support a largely unproductive, parasitic, but
"morally" superior, urban population and political
apparatus, by placing a very disproportionate share
of its surpluses at the disposal of those people who
are not the people who produce the surpluses.[228]
This is accomplished through means of a system of
land ownership, crop marketing, and general rural
financing on terms unfavorable to the peasant, but
favorable to those who do not work the land.

First, the question of land ownership.*   The
exact pattern of land ownership in Iran never has
been known accurately.   Traditionally, land ownership is not registered by specific individuals associated with large indefinitely surveyed tracts.
It is on this admittedly inaccurate basis that one
estimate has it that only 20 per cent of the land
is in freeheld ownership, and that all the best
land is in larger landlord holdings.   The distinction between free-holder and tenant, however, is
formal at best, for the free-holder is not much
better off than is the tenant, in that the former
always is subject to foreclosure for debt.[229]
Consequently, it is not the fact that widespread
tenancy exists in Iran that is the heart of the
Iranian land-ownership problem, although this has
become a political bug-a-boo in some quarters.
Rather, it is the terms of tenancy that create
the difficulty for the tenant.   For the tenant is
a sharecropper, working on a five-category, equal-
share system, consisting of land, water, power
(typically, animal power), seed, and labor.   Since
all shares are equal, labor is equal to only one
share.   So if the landlord supplies all but labor,
theoretically, by custom, he is entitled to 80 per
cent of the crop.[230]   This is not even all of the
difficulty, since if the landlord does not supply

---

*   Subsequent to the period of time to which this
    study refers (1959-61), in early 1963 to be exact,
    the Shah announced his intention to move more dras-
    tically to obtain conformity for his land reform
    program.   What this policy implies, for purposes
    of the present study, is suggested by the con-
    cluding remarks to this section.

seed or animal power, and he usually does not, there
is no guarantee that the farmer will be able to obtain these on the open market on terms equivalent to
a 1/5 share ratio of his costs. Moreover, in localities where it is scarce, yet vitally needed, water,
in fact, may be valued at far more than the theoretical 1/5 share by the landlord who supplies it, and
a mere peasant is in no position politically or morally to object to such a decision made by his superiors.

It is, therefore, the inability of the peasant
to affect the terms of his tenancy that is at the
source of one of the major rural difficulties; namely,
that the landlord can do much as he pleases with his
land and with "his" villages, and in truth, also with
the peasants in "his" villages. This is symbolized
by the usual lack of a written contract between landlord and peasant. In fact, the lack of security for
a tenant reaches the extent that a tenant even does
not know if he will be alloted the same tract of
land to farm from one year to the next. Rather, in
most villages, there is an annual lottery immediately
prior to the farming season to decide which peasants
will get how much of what land to farm. Through
this annual accounting, of course, the landlord can
reward those who are tractable and punish those a-
gainst whom he holds a grudge. And since, in effect,
a landlord obtains control over people when he obtains control over the land they cultivate, a landlord has the right to, and does, expel villagers
from his villages, or force "his" peasants to work
in other than their own villages, as punishment or
simply to demonstrate by such a show of control and
forced humiliation who it is who is the master of
rural Iran. If still a landlord has difficulty with
"his" peasants, the landlord can count on local official support. In fact, the landlord may be the
local official, but certainly, at the least, he has
access to officialdom through personal or family
relationships. In this way, the landlord can call
upon the gendarmarie and even the army to "keep the
peace" in the name of enforcing the collection of
surpluses from the peasants; surpluses from which,
to recall, the lion's share of the tax revenue of
the moral political authority comes.

As bad as direct landlord-tenant relations may
be, and, as in other aspects of Iranian life, this
is a personal matter between a specific landlord and
specific tenants, and not a defined, contractual re-

lationship under certain acknowledged general rules
of tenancy, there is greater probability of pain for
the tenant if the landlord uses an intermediary to
carry out his impositions. The landlord's usual
intermediary in the village is the village headman
(khakhoda). The headman is an "unofficial" official.
That is, on the one hand, he is unofficial in that
he is a village notable, selected, perhaps reluctantly, by landlords (and approved by the local political authority) who consider him reliable. He
is official, on the other hand, in that, although
he is not recognized formally as an official, the
political authority uses him as a channel of official communication into the village. The headman
serves as buffer and go-between the villagers, on
the one hand and the landlord and officials, on the
other hand. Although obviously, a headman will not
oppose a landlord directly, he can smooth over difficulties; and that is his prime function. In this
capacity, the headman can be of some service to the
tenant, even if it is only in the negative role of
alleviating some onerous landlord or official policy;
although, as always in Iran, this will depend upon
the specific headman and the specific landlords and
officials in question. Unfortunately for many tenants, when the landlord is an (urban-) absentee landlord, and the larger landlords who own a whole village or many villages are apt to be absentee landlords, in addition to the headman, the landlord may
appoint an agent to take care of his personal affairs and be his personal representative in the vil-
lage(s). In such instances, the landlord and his
children and their children may never see the villages owned.231 Consequently, the landlord will
have little, if any, personal interest in what goes
on in the villages or in the villagers provided he
receives his surpluses as expected. For this reason,
and since the agent either gets a percentage of the
landlord's share or what he can squeeze out of the
tenants on the side in addition to a salary (illegal
but acceptable since the tenant has no one to whom he
can complain), the agent is apt to be less willing to
be reasonable than a landlord; certainly less reasonable than a resident landowner who must live among
his tenants. But as bad as this situation is, still
more irksome to the tenant is the landlord practice
of renting out a village. In this case, the rentee
pays a set fee, usually high, in return for the share
normally received by the landlord. A few rentees are
trained agricultural engineers who rely on increasing
productivity in the village in order to increase

their profit margin. In this case, everyone, including the tenants, profit. But in most instances,
the rentees are but ruthless men who make their profit margin out of their ability to squeeze the last
possible drop of economic blood from hapless tenants.

In addition to this crop-sharing system, which
is disadvantageous enough, the tenant also is beset
by additional hidden levies upon his own meager
share; such as "presents" to landlords on festive
occasions, (public festivals or, say, the marriage
of the landlord's son), enforced "hospitality" for
itinerant gendarmes or visiting dignitaries to the
village, bribery of officials, (particularly of
gendarmes, to keep sons out of the army), legitimate
levies (as for example, the 6 per cent levy for village improvement) which are pocketed by landlords
without providing the services for which they are
levied, the khadkhoda's salary (that is, 4 per cent
of the crop) which, legally, the landlord is supposed to pay, and illegal escalation in the landlord's legitimate share of the crop, (especially on
water which the tenant is unable to monitor, for no
other reason than that the tenant cannot read or
write, and consequently, the landlord, by default,
keeps the account books).

A particularly insidious form of levy, characteristic of Asian societies in general, is labor
service (bigari). The introduction of labor service into Iran has been attributed to the Safavids,
but probably it existed earlier. Unlike the military service of feudalism, the traditional Iranian
labor service was service in kind exacted by the
political authority upon its local retainers -
officials, in return for grants of land. The retainers simply passed this exaction on down the
line to their tenants. In addition to this basic
levy, the local officials also could and did demand
laborers for "public purposes." It was in this way
that the political authority not only was able to
create the monuments of conspicuous construction,
but also was able to build and maintain the public
projects (e.g., roads and irrigation) that validated
its moral service role in the rural areas. Nominally,
labor service died out when this kind of land grant
no longer was awarded, and rural construction programs were taken over by regular salaried officials.[232]
However, labor service remains, in spirit, in the
form of landlord "guarantees of so many peasants as

free laborers for so many days whenever monetary or
material support is needed for government-sponsored
village improvement projects in the interest of the
landlord or his agent.

        In addition to the problem of land ownership,
which now may be in process of resolution, the farmer, also second, is at a tremendous disadvantage
with respect to his credit and marketing situation,
which is not necessarily resolved in the process of
a land redistribution program. The average farmer
chronically is in debt because his subsistence farming does not provide for any savings margin, and
because his lack of understanding how to budget insures that he will not know what to do with any surplus capital, if he ever is able to accumulate any.
Normally, the debt-ridden farmer, in order to obtain
the seed, clothing, and so forth he requires to tide
himself over from one harvest to the next, can avail
himself of credit from (a nearby) market town merchant, a market town money lender, relatives, government sponsored cooperatives, or his landlord. Not
all of these facilities are to be found in any one
area, nor does local practice suggest that the
tenant will attempt to obtain credit from all sources, even if theoretically they all are available.
For example, cooperatives are found in only a fraction of the villages and normally require security
the peasant cannot offer. Landlords, for one, although ubiquitous, do not extend credit readily, but
normally grant it only in cases of dire emergency
when it is clearly to the landlord's interest to
keep the peasant from going under (and consequently,
it usually is extended at the very reasonable rates
of interest on Iranian standards). It is the market
town merchant who is the most usual source of credit
for the peasant. Credit normally is extended by the
peasant "forward selling" his crop to the merchant,
usually at one half, or less, of the true harvest
value; a value which normally is unknown to the unsophisticated peasant. In addition, as part of the
understanding, the peasant usually is forced to pledge
to buy all his needs from the same merchant who extends the credit, thus further insuring that the pocket of the naive peasant will be well picked.[233]

        Not surprisingly, incentives to increase produc-
tion, either by tenants or landlords, under these
existing ground rules of land ownership and crop disposal, are extremely limited. It has been reasoned

that if a cultivator receives only one half of his
crop, he will not intensify if his returns are less
than twice the cost of input (assuming he bears all
operating costs), and it is not certain that most
Iranian peasants ever receive even this much of the
crop.[234] Consequently, the peasants have shrewdly
sized up their situation, and have argued that it
is ridiculous to increase production at all since
this only attracts the attention of the parasites.
For the parasites (including the tax collector)
can be counted on not to take a set amount of the
crop, or even a predictable, calculable share of
the crop, but the total of what they think the traffic will bear beyond the peasant's subsistence level.
Consequently, if the peasant increases his productivity, the reapers only will take a greater percentage of the total, leaving the peasant with the same
amount, or even conceivably less, since, now, many
peasants are able to appear too poor to even bother
with. Unlike the petty official who stands to gain
by conspicuous consumption, the peasant stands to
gain by inconspicuous poverty, fancied or real. And
the typical landowner, on his part, sees no more to
be gained by increasing the productivity of his property than does the tenant who farms it. This is
because most landowners, through political pressure
or violence, legally or illegally, can obtain the
revenue they desire with a minimum productive investment in their land. To be sure, beside such
landlords stand those who are among the most forward-
looking element in Iran (on society), men who have
done much to change for the better villages and villagers. But, unfortunately, it must be added that,
since these improvements have been made by the personal initiation of specific landlords on the grace
of these landlords, they have not grown out of a
feeling that tenants, in general, have an abstract
"right" to a better economic arrangement with landowners in general. Consequently, individual, benevolent landowners, no matter how numerous, and no
matter how admirable, are not forming the basis for
building a qualitatively new relationship between
tenant and landlord of a regularized, generalized,
and defined nature. And certainly, empirically speaking, these enlightened landlords have not had much
influence on their less enlightened colleagues, who
have destroyed property improvements made by their
tenants out of malice and fear.

Because of this general indifference to land improvement, and because of a lack of interest in capi-

tal investment in land, the productive returns on
existing land can be said to be adequate, and is so
regarded by the rural population. Consequently, for
these reasons, and because it is assumed by landowners that it is economically infeasible to open
new areas of cultivation, migration by tenants from
one farm area to another in order to improve themselves economically, is not considered justifiable,
although such migration does exist to a limited
extent. Rather, the predominant choice of tenants
interested in bettering themselves is to desert
agriculture and the rural areas for the market towns,
and, ultimately for the urban centers. Consequently,
in spite of an apparently low population to land
ratio on world standards, rural Iran may be considered
over-populated.235

Because mass desertion of the rural areas would
open grave economic and political consequences for
political authority, various polities have not been
immune to the tenant and his problems, although rural
interests have tended to be slighted as compared with
urban interests. Certainly, the Agriculture Ministry
runs an elaborate program of technical aid, rural
education, and a government cooperative credit program under the Ministry of Interior, at least in
theory, actively stimulates and subsidizes self-help
programs in the villages. But all of these programs
have been in serious difficulty. For one, as all
political programs in Iran, they are long on theory
and short on practice. And, too often, paternalistic,
morally superior, but economically ignorant, urban
bureaucrats are placed in positions of authority over
rural peasants pontificating about matters the former know nothing about, merely to validate the political authority's "service" interest in "his" people.
Second, no coordination exists among the agencies
involved in the programs. Typically, each agency
tries to outdo the other in "prestige-service,"
rather than in utility-service. Too often contradictory information is disseminated by two or more agencies to the confused and easily disillusioned peasantry. Third, in general, field staffs are inadequately
trained, ill-motivated (that is, concerned only with
the prestige of their government position), and are
reluctant to go into the rural areas to become ritually
polluted by association with morally inferior peasants
(especially if they have come recently from peasant
ranks). And finally, little cooperation, if not downright sabotage, exists on the part of many landowners
to any programs that are aimed at improving the economic control of the environment of "their" peasants.

The agricultural loan and credit program, in addition to these more general problems, also suffers from the fact that those least needing credit are apt to be granted loans. For, as is not unusual in the case of credit everywhere, those who receive the money often are the ones who can offer security. And in rural Iran this implies that it is landowners, or local political notables, who are the preferred credit risks and who receive the credit. As bad as this is, and admittedly it is not for the best, it would not be the major calamity that it is, if it were not for the fact that, since landowners, in general, are not interested in capital improvement of their land, the credit which is received is not used for productive purposes. Rather, credit is used, as is usual in Iran, for conspicuous consumption, such as, for example, the building of "impressive" (urban-style) houses among the mud huts or lean-to's of the village. Such houses even may remain perpetually empty to become the typically Iranian monuments, since the landlords, if they are absentee landlords, never may visit the village. And certainly they would not consider allowing mere tenants to contaminate these status symbols by living in them or using them for community centers. At best, these houses may be used to store the landlord's share of the crop until they or their agents are ready to come and claim it.

The credit that is received by those who can obtain it is lent out at usurious rates of interest to those very hapless peasants who theoretically should have received the loans at the lower credit rate in the first instance.[236] However, it is most important to realize that, even if the peasants were able to receive all the loans they need and to which, presumably, they are entitled, under the present ground rules of economic action in rural Iran, the loans are apt to make them worse off economically than they would be without the loans. This is so because of the peasants' ignorance of what to do with capital, of the ignorance of the ill-prepared, but often sincere, credit teachers from the Agricultural Bank to advise the peasants what to do,[237] and most significantly, of the Iranian peasants' inability to control their economic environment, or even to be able rationally to calculate the obstacles to productive economic action that exist within it. All this implies that any loan granted to peasants soon foolishly (that is, non-rationally) will be spent probably on consumption, and the peasants only will end up deeper in debt than they were before, which was bad enough.[238]

Although land in Iran is so unproductive, and likely to remain so under present conditions, yet competition exists for control over it and the hapless tenants who cultivate it. Moreover, peasants are forced to compete for ownership and control of land with those who not only do not have any interest in cultivating it themselves, but also who are less interested in improving the productivity of the land than are those who do cultivate it. This situation exists for both social and economic reasons. From the social standpoint, land ownership, as elsewhere in many societies, is prestigeful, conjuring up association with the leisured gentry of Iran's past. In particular, for the nouveau riche with profits earned in "immoral" speculative commerce, and for the nouveau politique with sub-rosa profits earned in "servicing" the nouveau riche, land is the most rapid and secure means to establish social ties with Iran's ancient traditions. But from the purely economic standpoint, there are two major attractions to ownership of land. First, land is secure. It cannot be stolen in the same sense that it can be removed. At best, it only can be usurped, which may be a temporary situation. It can be desecrated and despoiled, say by raiding tribesmen, but it cannot be destroyed and it can be recultivated. If one has land, one always can sell it and raise cash, which if hoarded can depreciate through inflation or can be lost or stolen. Second, by neglecting the rational interests of peasants and land, and in contrast, by depending on the grinding of tenants who cultivate the land, through means of intermediaries, land can offer a reasonable return to an absentee landowner with little or no further personal investment of money, time or effort, beyond that of the original decision to own the property. This is why although improvements on land could pay off generously--as for example, one estimate has it that up to 20 per cent improvement return on citrus in semi-arid Fars Province is possible--upkeep and improvement investment on land almost is unknown. Improvement investment in land also is rare because capital accumulations built up through ownership in land can be let out at much more lucrative rates of return in speculative economic action elsewhere in the economy. Consequently, money earned in agriculture, instead of being plowed back into the land,

often is drained off to the urban centers and for
non-productive purposes at that.[239] A most typical
use of the capital derived from rural landownership
is for urban land speculation. This fever has produced a wild orgy of soaring profits, on the one
hand, or sometimes profit, sometimes ruin, on the
other hand.[240] Finally, the little man without
either the sizable concentrations of capital, or
the ready access to important political connections,
so necessary for large-scale lucrative investment,
also has discovered that land purchase, on a modest
scale, is a good channel of investment for surplus
capital. Especially has this been true of the
petty, village merchant, who, through clever manipulation of the advance sale of crops from those marginal peasant-proprietors, who own small tracts of
land, sooner or later can foreclose for debt, reducing the peasants to tenants.

     In sum, in addition to impeding the material
agricultural base for economic development, the
rural pattern of ownership and rural system of
economic action, impedes economic development in
general by offering the monetary wherewithal for
alternative competitives to productive investment
in both rural and urban environments. It is in
this context that the equity land policy, especially the Shah's much-publicized land reform program, must be placed. First, as far as the Shah's
own property is concerned, the ruler's motivation
seems to be to rid himself of an economic and non-
economic albatross from around his neck. From the
economic standpoint, private interests who have
leased government lands have abused the soil, over-
grazed, usurped portions and forced extra dues from
peasants to allow them to cultivate at all; and
hence, have lowered the potential future income from
these estates. Consequently, it is to the Shah's
economic advantage to prevent further erosion of his
personal funds on amtak (the personal estates of the
ruler) or the economic resources of the political
authority on the khaliseh (government land).[241]
Moreover, since this land is to be sold, revenue
will flow into the coffers of the political authority
(the Development Bank) to be used, at the least, for
enhancing the "service" role of the political authority (dispensing credits) in the rural areas.[242] Non-
economically, first, the Iranian land system has
given Iran a bad press abroad, and the Shah is very
sensitive about the international prestige of his

country.[243] Second, those landowners who stand to
lose the most by land redistribution are the very
wealthy and powerful, but are few in number; and, to
reiterate, private economic power automatically is
suspect in Iran. And the small landowners, who make
up the bulk of the landowners if not the landowning
area, repeatedly have expressed a willingness to sell
out to the tenants if they can get a "fair price";
that is, if they can obtain a suitable capital base
from which to take advantage of the new urban speculative environment. Obviously then, favoring land
redistribution is a socially advantageous position
for the Shah to take, and he has stated so. The
Shah firmly believes that the present land system is
doomed as a relic of an agrarian past, and hence, if
the landowners are not forced by him to give in now,
they will be forced to give in by others, who, in
the process, will destroy the present political authority with it, and obviously, this is something
the Shah is determined will not happen. Very significantly, the Shah, by his refusal to sell off certain of his non-agricultural property to support
the charity and service functions of the Pahlavi
Foundation now dependent predominantly on the income
of the rural estates, has given sanction (by model)
to the decision that rather than landownership,
"investment" in the urban centers is the future
source of wealth and social status in Iran; hence,
its support in many quarters, as suggested above.[245]

Land redistribution in both public and private
estates, then, in spite of opposition to it in certain quarters, seems definitely in the offing. Yet,
if land distribution programs elsewhere are any
guide, it can be said, without a moment's hesitation,
that unless the social framework in which the peasants
now must operate is altered drastically, the new peasant proprietors do not stand to gain very much economically from land redistribution. This is so because,
as discussed in this section, peasants still will be
at the mercy of those forces, who are able to operate as effectively to bleed peasants of their livelihood, whether peasants are independent proprietors
or tenants. For, unless the former tenants, in their
relationships with their former landlords and with
their marketing contacts, and even with the political
authority itself, have clearly defined rights backed
by enforceable sanctions--such as written rights to
land, regularized schedules of peasant fees and taxes,
the proscription of arbitrary levies, definitions of
debt and the obligations thereof, and access to

grazing and orchard lands--then, they do not stand
to gain by being set adrift on their own, still subject to the same capricious, arbitrary abuse by former antagonists, who soon will have them once again
in bondage in spirit, if not in name. The mere redistribution of land, **therefore,** although undoubtedly it has immediate psychological impact on the
landless peasants, and provides political dividends
for the existing regime, necessarily will not bring
with it permanent economic benefit, unless, as with
many other formal changes in Iran, it is accompanied
by signficant changes in the institutional ground
rules in which the forms must operate. Unfortunately, it does not appear probable that these changes
are about to take place. And on the other hand, it
is unlikely that ex-landlords will as hoped for, invest the capital derived from the sale of their land
to tenants productively in economic development projects. For low return, long-term productive development projects which forever are under the threat
of capricious, arbitrary supervision and intervention of a political authority in the name of moral
service, cannot compete with money lending and speculation, unless once again, drastic changes in the
urban economic investment environment accompany
land reform.

ECONOMIC OPERATIONS:
SOME GENERAL GUIDING PRINCIPLES

Discussed here are those basic principles underlying the operation of economic enterprise in Iran,
whether public or private, which have not been explored elsewhere in this chapter.

The first basic principle is that considerations
of personnel take precedence over considerations of
operations. That is, when funds for an enterprise
are allocated, personnel is satisfied first, even, if
need be, to the detriment of successful operation of
the enterprise. The rationalization is frankly non-
economic (political). It is argued that those who
have a position, especially, but not necessarily a
governmental position, with income and status, even
if they make no operational contribution from the
rational economic standpoint to the enterprise, if
dissatisfied, will not be tempted to take to the
streets in violence, but only will grumble about
(that is, verbalize) their discontent. Also, with

each sign of political tension, along with promises
to increase the number of government retainers in
the enterprises, promises are made to increase existing salaries, admittedly low, without much thought
as to where the funds will come from. If these promises are kept, unless new financial sources are
discovered, as for example, foreign loans, operational funds suffer.[246]

A second characteristic of economic operations
in Iran is that, from the rational economic standpoint, tremendous waste occurs. Some of this certainly stems from the political necessity of maintaining large, superfluous staff of possibly ill-
trained, indifferent personnel who have job security,
but who have little or nothing constructive to do,
while the motivated and talented few carry the work
load and justify the existence of the operation.[247]
But beyond this consideration is the fact that operations themselves may be characterized as conspicuously wasteful. Funds, which always seem to be in
short supply for (rationally determined) essential
operations, somehow, always are found for ceremonial
observances; as for example, for the visits of dignitaries.[248] Architectural adornments abound, while
funds for spare parts, if enterprise machinery
breaks down, are scarce.[249] While the political
authority talked austerity, the Treasury was empty,
and economic enterprise was threatened with disaster
because of the lack of operational capital, in 1960-
61, high-priced belly-dancers were being imported
for Teheran night life and the new luxury swimming
pool in Teheran Pars was opened with great fanfare.[250]

Perhaps, one explanation for this lies in both
inside and outside the political authority, to prove
that Iran is the equal of any society, especially
the equal of the developed societies who apparently
can afford to squander and still develop. Certainly
the western-sponsored fundamentalist notion that
waste as such is evil or a "sin," or at the least,
undesirable, on rational economic grounds, is incom-
prehensible; unfortunately, especially to those Iranians who have access to the larger accumulations of
operational capital.[251]

But perhaps another explanation, and the one
most significant for the present study, lies in the
fact that, although it is admitted readily in Iran
that expenditures for conspicuous consumption reduce

the amount of funds available for productive investment, it also is pointed out that productive investment basically is insecure and unrewarding. And so, the Iranian argues, by conspicuous waste, one, at least can get something tangible out of one's (temporary and ever insecure) monetary accumulation.[252]

Conspicuous waste also exists, third, because to reiterate, enterprise capital is obtained primarily by borrowed credit and not by internal generation. It is the political authority who is the major source of this credit, in the form of specie or in the form of tarriff subsidation against the competition of cheaper, imported foreign manufacturers.[253] And that political authority, since, it has a political vested interest in perpetuating certainly the large, "show" enterprises, even at a capital loss, in order to insure the availability of employment for people who might otherwise join the radical-left in desperation, and in order to impress its people and the world with its ability to industrialize, at least quantitatively, is most cooperative. Hence, enterprisers (the author deliberately chooses not to say entrepreneurs) know that they probably can blackmail the political authority whenever the chips are down and financial disaster threatens; certainly if they have picked the (politically, if not rationally economic) right kind of enterprise.[254] Most enterprises, then, are assured of being able to continue operations, even if the political authority formally has to replace the management and run the plants itself in a show of punishment toward the economically inefficient.[255] It is for this reason that private enterprise, then, has little incentive to rationalize operations. It is for this reason that management can afford to be based on seniority and social position. It is for this reason that the work force may be made up of semi-literates or illiterates and industrial education ignored. It is for this reason that the expensive and ill-developed marketing system operated through the traditional brokers and not through salesmen can persist. It is for this reason that more modern and efficient machinery and new techniques may be ignored unless they are offered as a gift, probably by the only rationally-economically concerned, the foreigner. And, finally, in sum, it is for this reason that overstaffing, indifference to waste, and conspicuous expenditures, can operate with equal indifference both in private as well as in government enterprise.[256]

The third feature of Iranian economic operations is that enterprise, public and private, including productive enterprise, exists to be plundered, but plundered legally and with finesse. This is especially facilitated by the director's ability to manipulate people and funds fraudulently. If the director, particularly, is clever, the enterprise always will be at the brink of, but not actually in, bankruptcy. For, in this way, the monetary desires of the director and his allies, if not that of the enterprise, can be served indefinitely. Even if the director miscalculates and takes too much at a particular time, if he has been reasonable about it, the enterprise can be saved from outright bankruptcy through the potentially ever-available government loans, or through special privileges such as preferential purchases of the enterprise's products by the government and sales subsidies (especially export subsidies). In Shiraz these individuals are termed "business foxes." In one case the members of a whole family received this honorary appellation, having become famous for their ability to make off with the funds of many enterprises while simultaneously staying out of jail through either cleverness, or through bribery of officials, thus gaining the undying respect of their more envious "business" colleagues.

Although the most typical directoral tactic is this outright embezzlement of funds, more significant for purposes of the present study is the malappropriation of company funds for one's personal advantage. This includes such actions as loaning out company funds to speculators at high interest rates, the purchase of raw materials used in one's firm through oneself as a dummy supplier, the padding of payrolls with one's friends or relatives who provide kickbacks, the use of false invoices for fictitious purchases, the supply of inferior substitutes for claimed purchases, the entry of fictitious costs, and the use of enterprise property and labor for personal advantage.[257] With all this the norm and not the exception, not too strangely, almost daily, the newspapers are filled with accounts of plant failures accompanied by absconding directors, in such diverse enterprise areas as mills, transportation, power plants, meat packing, and retail sales.[258] And because of a fear that this kind of hanky-panky is going on in any enterprise, even a so-called solvent enterprise, enterprise shares have few ready buyers, and when they are traded, they usually are traded at 10 per cent to 20 per cent below par value.

Significantly, the problem is not characteristic of
either the public or private sector of the Iranian
enterprise, even so-called productive enterprise,
in general.[259]

The fourth principle of Iranian economic operations is that operations favor expansion in the means
of ostentatious consumption, or the accumulation of
capital to be used eventually for expansion in the
means of ostentatious consumption.* This may be attributed in part to the overriding desire for conspicuous consumption as previously described. But it
may be attributed, further, to the fact that rational
economic operations (which conceivably may have to go
on over a period of generations before the material
payoff in consumer goods or in capital to obtain consumer goods is realized, given the Iranian economic
environment) appear less desirable if material advantage can be obtained more easily, more quickly, more
directly, and more assuredly in trade and speculation.[261] It is for this reason that when capital investment does take place, which is rare in comparison
to direct consumption purchasing, it is apt to be
(over-)investment in the same consumption channels,
especially in the speculative importation of high-
priced foreign luxuries.[262] Significantly, in spite
of the consequent flood in imports, no serious consideration ever is given to changing over the primary pattern of investment to productive channels.[263]
For the only consequence of glut seems to be a more
fervent search for new kinds of imports to insure new
avenues of speculative profit.

----

* It must be observed that we here are not considering the Marxist vs. non-Marxist controversy as to
  whether capital should be invested, respectively,
  primarily in industrial equipment or primarily in
  consumer goods. Rather, discussion is upon
  whether capital should be invested in rational
  economic productive enterprises of either the industrial or consumer type, or both types, on the
  one hand, or whether, on the other hand, as in
  Iran, capital should be used primarily to import
  consumer goods from abroad to be paid for out of
  speculative commercial profits derived from government loans. As if this were not bad enough, in
  Iran, only 16.5 per cent of capital ever is invested at all for any purpose, including speculation, while the remaining 83.5 per cent is used
  for direct consumption purchase.[260]

Consequently, even if funds were to be made
available for productive consumption investment,
from no source, public or private, does incentive
exist for productive investment.[264] Particularly,
those who have wealth, even if that wealth is more
than adequate to support the conspicuous display of
consumer possessions, will not invest the surplus
productively. Rather they will use it for such
activities as expanding the number of their prestigeful, but economically useless retainers, building
monuments, and lavishly entertaining friends. And,
not to be ignored, is the fact that, in rural areas,
the income of the vast majority of not so affluent
Iranians that is not used for consumption, goes into
petty money lending, and into buying land.[265] Unfortunately, it is these individuals who are successful
in getting rich quick (and painlessly) and who use
their wealth to validate prestige by wasteful consumption, who are the economic heroes of the less
fortunate.

The fifth and final characteristic of Iranian
economic operations is the absence of what might
be called "business ethics," and of a sense of
ethical responsibility beyond oneself in one's economic transactions. "To get while the getting is
good without thought of tomorrow," and to convert
what is obtained into hard cash immediately is the
overriding consideration in all Iranian economic
enterprise. One acute Iranian observer described
this phenomenon as derived from a passion for
money alone and as a recent introduction into
Iranian society.[266] It cannot be denied that this
is true, as far as it goes, but the problem may be
interpreted further as the consequence of a justified lack of faith in long-term political and economic security and in long-range economic action,
which requires the kinds of "trust"-transactions
that encourage customers to return. As such, this
state of affairs is not especially new to Iranian
society.

It is most important to appreciate that this
lack of ethics is found both in the public and private sectors of the economy. In the private sector
it is characterized by such acts as cheating customers with short-weight, or with inferior or falsely
represented merchandise (as too many purchasers have
discovered when they have bought goods under "foreign"
labels).[267] In the public sector, on the other hand,
it is characterized by the willingness to condone any

economic hanky-panky for a price (that is, for a
bribe) and by the willingness to use almost any
official position in any way possible to increase
one's monetary wealth, regardless of the situation
of trust, and regardless of the detrimental effect
of such actions on the potential (that is, future)
development of rational interpersonal economic
relations in Iran.[268]

We now turn to consideration of the effects of
these five guiding principles on the operation of
potentially rational economic productive (especially
industrial) enterprise in Iran. Considering the
level of Iranian development, industrial enterprise
is not inconsiderable in Iran.[269] Modern enterprise
received its initial impetus through the efforts of
Reza Shah, who, primarily for nationalistic (that is,
political) reasons, lavished funds in order to introduce the physical manifestations of economic growth
from abroad. Enterprises were built especially in
the northern capital city, Teheran, and to some extent also in Isfahan, in central Iran. Although
many enterprises, as, for example, the wool and cotton
mills of Isfahan, operated on a very modest level,
yet, because of modern machinery, tariff protection
and very significantly, the disinterest of speculators at this time due to limited profit opportunities, the enterprises made a respectable profit
and were operated at reasonable rational-economic
efficiency.

World War II, however, had a regressive effect
on Iran's efforts to establish a productive industrial development program. Although the maintenance of existing enterprise and the replacement of
parts from abroad became increasingly difficult,
the enterprises still were able to make fantastic
profits because of military demand, wartime inflation, and the lack of competition from abroad.
Most unfortunately, this chance for quick profits
on modest capital outlay soon caught the attention
of the speculators, already bloated with surplus
capital derived from wartime generated profits in
the general economy,[270] and when devaluation of the
rial and the influx of foreign capital as loans and
gifts occurred in the 1950's, although all this
additional revenue was earmarked for industrial
enterprise, inevitably, it was the enterprise specu-
lator, aided and abetted by the five operating principles of economic enterprise described above,[271]
and not the true industrial entrepreneur, who was able
to take maximum advantage of the situation.

Consequently, it is not the quantitative insignificance of productive industrial enterprise in Iran (as important as this may be) that has been at the heart of the Iranian economic development problem. Rather, it is the qualitative way in which the industrial enterprise that does exist is operated. Hence, the acquisition of capital in and of itself, although a problem in Iran as in all economically underdeveloped societies, is not the (capital) problem of economic development in Iran. Rather, Iran's (capital) problem lies in the way existing capital (and by implication, further capital) is employed in the operation of Iranian enterprise, especially in potentially productive industrial enterprise. The political authority is always pleading poverty, especially to foreign sources of capital. The claim is valid enough, for capital by definition, quantitatively always is short, in an economically underdeveloped society. But the claim is valid in terms of the present study, only if it is accepted that the guiding assumptions concerning the allocations and expenditures of capital as described in this section are also valid. In that case, the need for funds would obviously be limitless, to note, without any necessary emergence of self-generating, rational economic development. For with each increase in population more funds would be needed to bribe would-be trouble-makers by providing employment opportunities for them; and with each new, even apparently productive enterprise established, new opportunities would arise to embezzle or wastefully mis-appropriate available capital. There is no evidence, for example, that capital ever is short for such "essential" purposes as social, religious, ceremonial, or other special functions, or for "influential individuals" to spend as they see fit. In a frank moment, one Prime Minister admitted that it is the lack of administrative skill (i.e., in the use of capital) and not the quantity of capital itself that is the prime Iranian development problem.[272] In this context, capital-short Iran even may be said to be even over-invested at the same time, since obviously it is unable to use what capital it does have in a rationally economic way or to rational economic ends.[273]

CHAPTER **4** OCCUPATION

THE EDUCATED MAN: THE BUREAUCRAT

   In a society, historically to a great extent illiterate, the educated came to be accepted as an inevitable minority. Since literacy was so unusual
and to be prized, an education, in and of itself, regardless of content or level of proficiency, has become the basis upon which individuals have been allocated to membership in a distinct occupational grouping; namely, the grouping of the educated man. By
implication, by virtue of being educated, whether
the educated man was at work or at leisure, and no
matter what specifically he contributed to the general division of labor, he remained a member of the
educated grouping. And by sole virtue of being educated, he was considered as productive as any member
of any occupational grouping in the society. This
was so because, regardless of other occupational
responsibilities, the primary role of the educated
in the division of labor was to preserve the cultural heritage, especially the "sacred literature," of
Iran by mere knowledge of that heritage, and to
carry out those duties in the division of labor associated with the preservation of that heritage,
most typically public service for the uneducated.
And these roles, to this day have been considered
as the crucial roles, since they are believed to
insure, respectively, the successful preservation
and operation of Iranian society.*

   The educated man, therefore, is a generalized
educated man; that is, he is a man who, based on his
general mastery of the Iranian literary heritage, is
considered to be equally the master of the Iranian
spirit, on the one hand, and capable of mastering

---

* In the present chapter the discussion is restricted to that of the secular occupations. Certainly,
  the members of the clergy are educated and are a
  repository of at least one phase of the Iranian
  cultural tradition; see Chapter Seven below.

the practical arts, especially public service (statecraft), on the other hand. Consequently, the educated man, through mastery of the Iranian literary
heritage, gains mastery of the Iranian spirit, <u>and</u>
the capability of mastering the practical arts. And
conversely, mastery of the practical arts (especially,
of public service-statecraft) implies prior mastery of
the Iranian heritage; and by implication, mastery of
the Iranian spirit. In this way, the separation of
mastery of the Iranian spirit and the mastery of the
practical arts has been, at best, an intellectual
exercise. However, if the distinction has to be made,
the Iranian spirit was to be accepted unequivocably
as paramount and fundamental, because its mastery provided the knowledge of Iranian human relations that
enables all the activities of Iranian society to be
carried out successfully. Consequently, the essential
problems of Iranian society, including public service-
statecraft, have been considered as dependent on mastery of the Iranian spirit.

Or to look at it another way, the Iranian spirit, dependent on the Iranian tradition, although it
constitutes knowledge (that is, tradition) has to be
more than rational knowledge, because it is the
<u>Iranian</u> tradition. That additional element is the
fundamental ethical system of Iranian society, which
for want of a better term, has been called "moral(ity)"
in the present study. Since morality and knowledge
come from the same source, namely, the Iranian tradition, morality and knowledge are intertwined inevitably, so that mastery of the Iranian traditional
knowledge has come to imply, automatically, an association with morality and an association with morality has come to imply, automatically, mastery of the
Iranian traditional knowledge.

In sum, the educated man is a man who is exposed
properly to the Iranian literary heritage, and in so
doing, automatically has become moral. The Western,
Stoic, Greek-Christian tradition that the pure (that
is, the moral) are, not even may be, as likely to be
found among the uneducated as among the educated, is
not repeated in the Iranian philosophical tradition.[1]
To draw a conclusion, the signal importance of this
Iranian combination of knowledge and morality lies
in the fact that (1) the bearers of knowledge consider themselves as constituting a distinct occupational grouping, whose occupational distinctiveness
must be employed primarily for perfecting morality

in the society; and that (2) all potential occupational activities which may arise in any future division of labor unless they are integrated into the
traditional framework of knowledge and morality may
very well be ignored by the educated as not befitting their attention.[2]

This occupational orientation has had the following effect on the Iranian educational system,
including the modern and apparently "Western" rational and practical, morally-neutral educational
system: First, since Iranian knowledge primarily
is concerned with morality, and the ultimate practical application of knowledge is politics, the
educational system primarily is the training ground
for morally-oriented statesmen. Consequently,
those who are certified by the educational system,
expect, automatically to be entitled to a political
position, whose significance is in proportion to
the achieved educational level. Consequently, those
who are university graduates consider themselves to
be the ones entitled to the command positions in the
apparatus of the political authority.[3] And step by
step down the line, the level of aspiration descends
until it reaches the men who barely are literate,
but still associated with literacy, who expect,
still as a right, a position in the political apparatus, even if it is only the right to serve in the
more menial positions, such as that of storekeeper.[4]

Second, since the role aspiration of the educated is statecraft, and since mastery of the Iranian tradition is considered as primary preparation
for this role, not surprisingly, the university
curriculum stresses Iranian literature, poetry and
morality, with a mere smattering of mathematics and
dialectics.* The secondary schools teach some history, geography, and general science, but here as
well, great stress is placed upon mastery of the
Iranian language and the essence of Iranian culture
as expressed in its literature and poetry.[5] And so,
as one observer has put it, traditional Iranian
education trains people to read and write in general, but to do nothing much in particular.[6]

---

* Professional education, including medical education, is to be discussed in the next section;
  see below.

The introduction of so-called modern, Western
education into Iran has not altered materially this
pattern, for no other reason than that the basic
values of the society have not altered. For, the
same order of political aspirants are flocking to
the newly established "modern" higher education
facilities as traditionally have flocked to the
older facilities. This has been true, for example,
of the recently built higher education facilities
of Shiraz and Abwaz which have tried to provide
facilities for the 20,000 politically-aspiring secondary school graduates turned out yearly who cannot
get into the University of Teheran. Alternately,
most of those who go abroad (and 15,000 students now
are abroad) seek the same kind of education that
they would have pursued had they remained in Iran;
namely, education in law and political science, for
alternative to Iranian literature, these are the pre-
paratory courses for careers in statecraft.[7]

(3)   Third, technical education is resisted because
it is considered that this education runs counter
to the basic spiritual training of the educated individual man, the man who, most probably, will associate with statecraft. Practically speaking, it
must be admitted that the positions taken by the
students and the faculty are defensible, from their
point of view, although not from the standpoint of
the rational economic needs of the society. The
students argue that it is better to take a chance
upon graduation of becoming unemployed intellectuals
than becoming possibly employed technicians, for,
since no felt need exists for a large number of technicians in Iranian society, but a felt need does
exist for a large political authority, sufficient
pressure on the existing regime, or a change of regime, conceivably might create job opportunities in
the political apparatus; while a basic change in the
whole fabric of Iranian society would be necessary
to provide sufficient employment for technicians.

(4)   Consequently, fourth, for the same reasons,
potentially rational technical education, wilfully
or through passive resistance, becomes non-rational
technical education. On the one hand, technical
courses, as the traditional humanities courses, rely
heavily on lectures rather than upon practical demonstrations. This provides unlimited opportunities
for teachers to express their ability to use the
Iranian language, and thus prove the moral worth of

themselves and the program; but certainly, this is
of dubious rational-technical value.[8] And, on the
other hand, even in those cases in which training
time critically is very short, such courses as
"Writing Good Persian," manage to creep into the
curriculum to the detriment of practical, technical,
pre-service experience. As far as the teacher,
student, and even the future employer (most probably,
the political authority) are concerned, none of this
is either strange or diabolical. For, armed with
the essentials of the Iranian tradition through its
literature, the educated individual certainly, at
least, must be the equal, if not the superior, of
the narrow technical specialist who cannot be an
educated man in the Iranian sense. At best, the
technical man has mastered only facts and has not
mastered morality-knowledge. And morality-knowledge
is essential for the accomplishment of tasks in Iran,
in which the manipulation of human beings is more important than the manipulation of the environment.[9]

(5)   Fifth, since non-technical, non-rational (non-
functional) education is the education to pursue,
and the substance of that education is morality-
knowledge, and since all morality-knowledge by definition is of equal worth, and since, consequently,
the more exposure one has to it, the more educated
one becomes, then the problem of education is a
cumulative problem. And since absorption of morality-
knowledge is the essence of learning (for who is to
question morality?), then memorization is both more
legitimate and more economical than is analysis in
the mastery of education.[10] And so, in consequence,
historically, education has been learned by rote,
and what has been learned rarely has been challenged
by either teacher or student. Modern education and
modern educational practice have not altered nor are
likely to alter this pattern, simply because the
role of education in Iranian society has not been
altered nor is it likely to be altered under existing
ground rules.

Since education primarily is concerned with the
acquisition of Iranian morality, and, thus, quantitative considerations predominate in the acquisition
of an education, then, sixth, the extent and not the
intrinsic caliber of the education is considered as
significant. Consequently, it is the certified
level of exposure that is of primary importance in
determining how one's education will be evaluated.
And by extension, it is the degree and not the sub-

ject matter or efficiency of one's performance that
makes or breaks one's career. For example, when it
was suggested that a roster of Iranian "experts" be
compiled, the roster was limited to a listing of
those with Bachelor's Degrees, or higher, without
any reference to the quality of performance, and
with the obvious omission of those competent individuals without formal, academic qualifications.[11]

Since all employers, especially the political
authority who is the prime employer in Iran, evalu-
ate the potential position and entering salary of
candidates for employment on the basis of diploma
or certificate of highest academic level achieved,
and failures are more common than ambitions will
tolerate, students are ever striving to insure
this achievement.[12] Bribery is not uncommon, although corrupt teachers face the danger of exposure,
often by frustrated students. Unbearable pressure
is exerted on a hapless teacher, especially from
students of "good families" with a social position
of continued association with the political authority to uphold. Constant pressures exist on the
political authority to lower educational standards
to make it easier for students to pass. In some
cases, failure to do so, or the threat of raising
academic standards has led to open rebellion, so
incendiary is the diploma issue in Iran.[13] But,
perhaps most interesting, since of the 22 1/2 per
cent of the male and 7 1/2 per cent of the female
population who can read and write to some extent,
some estimated 400,000, mostly on the lower level,
do not hold formal academic certification,[14] and
since that piece of paper is so important, certification is made with false credentials, or merely
claims to certification. Few in Iran dare to challenge certification for few in Iran are in a position
to throw academic stones.

Finally, no attempt is made to train for responsibility, for independence, or for truth searching.[15] A tug-of-war exists perpetually between teacher and student, with the student learning very quickly
to resent a teacher's "dominant personality" in a position of authority, and the teacher, in turn, resent-
ing the student's attempts to embarrass him by questioning his judgment or by asking even pertinent
questions not in the prepared notes (which, perhaps,
were compiled fifty years previously during the teacher's student days abroad). Students, even on the university level, are not expected to do any original

work on general principles, mainly because the library
normally is not available to them. Nor do professors
do true research. Their work out of class consists
usually of translations or "compilations" of the work
of others, usually without credit. And if a professor is hard up for a publication, he might even pub-
lish those old foreign notes as his own creation.
The university itself has few, if any, outside-Iran
contacts and its administrative staff, faculty, and
students have a fantastically unrealistic view of
Iran and its place in the world.

Although this academic environment sounds grim
on the basis of abstract educational theory, it is
no different from the environment or society into
which the student will have to enter after he leaves
school. Consequently, the educational system may
be said to be well-adapted to preparing the students
to live and work effectively in their society, and
as such, the Iranian educational system may be said
to be a success. It only is a failure if, it is
argued, its role is to change and not to adapt to
the occupational environment that the student enters.*
For the system incubates the "educated man" who primarily, although not exclusively, is a political
animal, who is a good memorizer, who speaks well,
but not concretely, who is quick to copy and serve
those in authority, who tends to talk rather than
to act, who hates to make decisions, who is not
utilitarian, who is not objective, who cannot operate effectively in a critical environment, who does
not necessarily understand what he accepts, who cannot analyze his responsibilities, who is not adaptable as far as the work and the positive environment
are concerned (but only as far as maneuvering people
is concerned), and finally, who basically is insecure
and maladjusted to any of his occupational demands
and consequently, unproductive--in brief, an individual who is the very antithesis of the kind of educated or sophisticated individual required to participate in, let alone create and develop, a rational,
self-generating economic system.[16]

---

* This has already been discussed in the previous
  two chapters and need not be repeated here.

THE OCCUPATION OF THE EDUCATED MAN:
THE PROFESSIONAL

Professionals, although nominally members of
the occupational grouping of the educated, deserve
separate treatment for they may be employed as readily outside the political authority as within it,
and they may train and work in an occupational environment conceivably different from the one discussed in the previous section.

Historically professionals included the clergy,
lawyers, and physicians.* In spite of the fact that
at the time of Reza Shah, the subject matter of law
was said to have been secularized and modernized,
and the jurisdictional scope of the (secular) lawyer
was enlarged, the modern lawyer continues to be
trained as he always has. Magistrates still dispense
justice, not on the basis of a rational code composed
of a series of predictable precedents, but rather on
the basis of personal judgment and interpretation in
specific cases which are treated as unique situations
(so-called "qadi justice"). Lawyers, as in the past,
still are not noted for being above temptation or
political pressure. And finally, contrary to pious
regulations on the books, an insufficiency of lawyers,
and hence an insufficiency in the administration of
justice, continues to exist, especially in the rural
areas. In brief, lawyers, by choice and circumstance
are not potential contributors to the development of
rational (professional) behavior and standards in
Iran.17

Medicine, because of its honored and prestigeful
role in the Iranian division of labor, recruits its
trainees automatically from the academically most
proficient stratum in the secondary schools.** Consequently, candidates for medicine, as other candidates on the university level, are selected not so
much on the basis of individual desire to pursue a

---

* As suggested earlier, the clergy will be discussed elsewhere; see below, Chapter Seven.

** Members from the next proficient academic stra-
tus generally major in liberal arts, including
politics. And finally, the practical professions,
such as agriculture, must be content to recruit
from the bottom stratum of the secondary schools.

particular profession, as on the basis of academic
standing. By itself, this might be an important but
not a vital problem, but for the fact that academic
rating can be, and is heavily influenced by pressures from "good families," irrespective of the abilities of the students, and once accepted, medical
students as candidates do not take their work very
seriously.* For, since entering medical school is
considered to be the primary problem of occupational
achievement, students expect to be graduated, as
they earlier expected to enter school, if need be,
through family and political pressure on the medical
school authorities. Both teachers and administrators
are reasonably cooperative, so that favorites, or
relatives of favorites, receive degrees. And, obviously, examinations can be made up, and certainly
can be graded or "adjusted" to an arbitrarily passing standard, in order to assure that certain favored
individuals one day will have the social position of,
if not the professional mastery of physicians. The
medical faculty, on the other hand as the faculty
elsewhere in the educational system, is strong on
lectures and weak on demonstrations and training for
practical experience. The staff has the option of
showing up or not for instruction, and students simi-
larly may be as casual. Instructors are not held to
the published curricula. The faculty may even repeat
the same course for extra credit, "on demand" or
voluntarily, if it is financially advantageous. Consequently, in brief, although buildings and even
equipment may be up to expectancy and exacting professional standards, the medical training program is
not rationally oriented and is not scientifically
autonomous of those social-institutional pressures
that impede the learning process elsewhere in the
educational system.

After five years of such "training" the new
physicians are released upon the Iranian public, and
true or not, physicians have developed the reputation
for fleecing the public by charging exorbitant fees,
or by prescribing or using themselves unneeded, ex-

----

* Of course, significant exceptions do exist, as
  exceptions do exist throughout the characteriza-
  tions drawn in the present study. But exceptions
  are exceptions, and no society can be characterized by its exceptions, nor, significantly for
  the present study, are exceptions necessarily a
  catalyst for change.

pensive, and even fraudulent, diluted drugs in col-
lusion with pharmacists.[18] This certainly, in part,
is a consequence of the psychological insecurities
of the average Iranian (patient). Patients come to
physicians frequently with such imagined illness as
sterility and impotence, and various psychosomatic
disorders. Yet, unless they receive advice and a
prescription, they believe the doctor is ignorant
or is attempting to cheat them. And even if patients receive advice and a prescription, since they
distrust doctors both on objective, professional
grounds, and on general Iranian subjective grounds
that no one ever is to be trusted, they may go from
doctor to doctor collecting prescriptions, which
they may never use. Physicians, then, are forced
to prescribe whether they can diagnose or not, since
the chances are that illnesses are not true illnesses,
and perhaps, more important, because their reputation
is at stake, and a defense of one's reputation is considered more important than is the defense of the
rational-technical demands of medical professionalism.

And so "modern science" is adjusted to the traditional non-scientific way of life. And so a traditional occupation is "modernized" but without
radically altering its occupational role. And so
in turn, Iranian society is not altered by"modern"
professionalism. And so, it can be suggested, the
notion that societies can be rationalized through
means of the introduction of "modern" technology,
is open to serious doubt.

The (female) nurse, however, is not a traditional
occupational role in Iranian society as is the physician's role. It is an alien role associated exclusively with rational, scientific behavior. Hence,
the occupational actions of the nurse conceivably
might be used to "break through" non-scientific traditionalism, and thus serve, at least, indirectly,
to aid the process of rationalization in Iranian
society. On the one hand, nursing, because the role
is associated occupationally and prestigewise with
that of the physician, and because of the general
restriction of movement of other than "emancipated"
women in Islamic tradition, has tended to recruit
candidates from girls of "good families" with a certain standard of education and a certain degree of
personal freedom. Consequently, many nursing candidates have much the same motivations and attitudes
as do their physician counterparts. However, on the
other hand, unlike the medical schools, which have

resisted the influence of Western technical imperatives on grounds of "cultural imperialism," the
nursing schools, as admittedly an alien element,
have been able to enforce high standards of training;
in fact, so high that many candidates from "good
families" have dropped out when it became obvious
that the schools were not an easy and cheap way to
get a prestigeful Western-type finishing school education.* To fill this placement gap, girls from
other than Islamic "good families," and in certain
training centers, girls from minority groups such as
the Bahai'i and Jews have been accepted; girls who
are not committed to Iranian traditions to the same
extent as are the Islamic girls of "good families."
Consequently, in some cases, nurses even know more
medicine than do physicians, but, certainly, they
are more highly motivated in learning to use it properly. However, after graduation, regardless of personal interest or ability, nurses work for doctors
and follow doctors' instructions. And, regardless
either of the competence of the physician, or of
the medical necessities of the situation, no physician is likely to allow a social inferior such as a
nurse to demonstrate his incompetence before another
(the patient). Consequently, as in the case of the
traditional profession of medicine, the behavior and
values of the new profession of nursing, regardless
of the auspicious promise of nurse training, also
is subordinated to Iranian professional behavior
and values.

Finally, conceivably there may be a difference
in the behavior and value system of those physicians
and nurses who have received all or most of their
training in the developed societies. Without question their knowledge, competence, and dedication to
medicine all are radically superior to the local products. But, unfortunately, these individuals at the
least, must serve under administrators who, themselves, even though they may have been trained in the
developed societies, are forced to accept traditional
Iranian behavioral rules, for no other reason than
they must operate in Iranian society or in a microcosm

---

* Ironically, but significantly, some of these failures then have applied for entrance to medical
  school, have been accepted and have been graduated.

of Iranian society (that is, a hospital). And so,
not strangely, in "Western"hospitals, as readily as
in Iranian hospitals, technical scientific demands
are subordinated to the interests of prestige, the
usual difficulties in Iranian interpersonal relationships effectively impede rational technical
operations, (see below, Chapter Nine), and non-
technical considerations determine what should be
professionally autonomous, technical (rational)
decision making. For those few who object to this
perversion of rational scientific medicine, voluntary or involuntary removal into private practice
normally is the only alternative available. In the
extreme case, exile from Iran is forced on the most
adamant, through personal conviction or by colleagues
who fear the threat to existing norms.[19]

THE OCCUPATIONS OF THE EDUCATED AND THE UNEDUCATED IN RURAL IRAN

Two interrelated occupational roles developed
about agriculture. The first role was that of the
educated, which, associated with the structure of political authority, served the land with the mind by
providing such administrative and technical service
as assuring peace and overseeing rural road and irrigation construction. The second role was that of
the uneducated which served the land with the hands
and produced the vital economic surpluses to support
the educated in particular and the larger society in
general.

Since both roles were considered necessary for
the proper utilization of the land, both roles were
considered essential and productive. In spite of
the fact that the cultivator role was essential, unfortunately, this essentiality offered nothing substantial necessarily to the cultivators themselves.
The idealization of agriculture, then, was tenden-
tious, being more appreciation of the benefits ac-
cruing to the political authority and his occupational allies from the surpluses of agriculture than
appreciation of the occupational best interests of
the cultivators themselves. For the educated, always have taken from the cultivators all that the
traffic could bear, to the point that the occupational
fortunes of the greedy, as well as those whom they
grinded unmercifully, declined.

The basic occupational characteristics
peasant already have been discussed in the
chapter and need not be repeated here (see
"The Structure of the Rural Economy" above
suffice to observe in the present context
peasants have occupational security in the sense tha
they can count upon farming to provide sufficient
earnings to sustain themselves. Often they must work
as day laborers, carrying produce from farm to nearby
market town, building and maintaining the metal, un-
surfaced rural roads or serving as unskilled manual
labor, especially truck coolies, in the nearby market
towns. If even this will not ameliorate their economic burdens, and often it does not, they may be forced
to leave the land to seek non-cultivator occupational
roles in the nearby urban center. Significantly, even
if these migrants remain in the urban centers for an
extended period, they may not consider themselves as
permanent urban laborers, for they are determined not
to lose contact with the land or family members left
behind. They return to their village from time to
time, especially when occupational opportunities in
the urban centers are worse then, or even are equal
to, opportunities in the countryside. This is so
because a right to land ownership, or a cultivator
right for tenants, is coveted even though the farmer
no longer physically is present in the village (see
below, Chapter Six).[20]

In its relationship with the rural occupational
structure, the political authority acts much as it
does in its relationship with the urban structure.
As the pre-eminent service force in the society, the
political authority does not offer the occupational
security and benefits the farmers desire, but rather
offers only what it thinks farmers deserve and need.[21]
A good example of this is to be found in the role of
the government agricultural engineer or extension
advisor who is long on theory, short on research and
practical experience, and with a low level of learning motivation. Not only may this individual be ill-
prepared to assume his responsibility, he may even
have little interest in doing so, because, to recall
an observation of the last section, he probably has
been recruited on the basis of a minimum acceptable
academic standard for advanced education, and not on
the basis of vocational choice. And certainly, as an
educated man, with a degree title in addition, he may
not be overly anxious to spend too much time in an
uneducated environment and in intimate association
with mere farmers. He is apt to be a young urbanite

who cannot find other employment and is willing to
accept his position as a "fill-in" that will provide
some social prestige while he attempts to improve
his prospects elsewhere. When he goes into the
field, he may take an untrained aide (that is, servant)
to do the actual work that he supervises. As an educated man, by definition, he obviously knows more
than the farmers, so that if he takes a position contrary to that of the farmers, obviously his must be
the correct one. Consequently, as a product of an
authoritarian educational system, and as a city boy
intent on covering his insecurities by attempting
to be someone of importance before the uneducated
peasants, an advisor will be misunderstood and resented by farmers who will look upon the advisors'
often wrong advice as more unwarranted bureaucratic
interference into what they consider should be farmers' occupation prerogatives.

This situation most likely will occur when the
so-called engineer has forged credentials and, hence,
has not completed his education or, perhaps, even
never has attended a technical institute or an agricultural college. Significantly, failure, no matter
how often repeated, has not shaken the belief of the
educated, especially the politically associated educated, in its claimed superiority over the uneducated
peasantry. And so, the educated are not even willing
to listen to the questions and tentative proposals
of the peasants, who although they lack the techniques
of modern agricultural science more fully to satisfy
their own conceived occupational aspirations, obviously are closer to their own problems, and know better
than the engineers at least what they want to know.
This view is totally alien to the Iranian educated,
and in fact to the Asian educated in general. It is
for this reason that the peasant often resists change
from above, as an acute observer once put it, not
because he is stupid, but because he is wise and cautious. At his level of subsistence agriculture, the
peasant can not afford the luxury of the dubious services forced upon him if and when he gets to see the
technical advisor. And the advisor, frustrated and
disgusted, in turn, will find every excuse to stay
in the office behind the physical and emotional security of the desk; and another pattern of distrust,
inaction and incompetence has been established in
Iranian society.22

THE OCCUPATION OF THE MILITARY

The military always has held a special position of esteem in the hearts of Iranians. As any visitor can attest, Iranians never tire of extolling the grandeur of the great conquerors Darius and Xerxes, and in the most recent period of the exploits of Reza Shah, the founder of the present dynasty, who came forth from the ranks of the military to conquer Iran's foreign enemies on Iranian soil.

As Iran basically is an agricultural society in general and the political authority in particular, the military, in the service of political authority, has had the occupational responsibility of protecting the fields from the depredation of spoilers, external or internal. Although the military , during many periods of Iran's history, has not been eminently successful in fulfilling this responsibility, the right of the political authority to assert this responsibility never has been withdrawn. At present, on the strength of foreign assistance, the political authority has asserted the traditional occupational role of the military with renewed vigor. Since most of the population is rural, the military is symbolized to most Iranians, not by the line soldier, but by the gendarmarie, which, in fact, may be the only contact the villagers have with political authority. The political authority is very conscious of the proverb "a good gendarme is the sign of a good government, and a bad gendarme is a sign of a bad government," and has tried to popularize the gendarme force in the rural areas. In this way the polity hopes to encourage a sense of political security and trust in the existing regime, and in turn, a sense of economic security so that farmers will continue to produce the agricultural surpluses for the political authority and the society.[23]

It is important for purposes of the present study to appreciate that the intimate association of polity and military in Iran always has been predicated on the assumption that the military is under the direct control of the polity and, consequently, that the military must carry out political policies, rather than military occupational interests. For most significantly, unlike in the feudal system of Medieval Europe, the Iranian military never developed its own independent occupational grouping with a distinctive military code of rights and obligations, but rather always has been one of the patrimonial re-

tainers of one or another political force subordinated to a political will and a political occupational ethos. This was true even in periods of disunity,
which were frequent, when the military occupational
role obviously was more significant socially than
that of the ineffective civil authorities. For even
in those instances, the military served local political predators, especially in the rural areas,
where they extorted and bullied the peasants for the
benefit of local politicians.[24]

This intimate association of a military servant
and a political master helps to explain why it has
not been uncommon, especially these days, for the
military to be allowed to engage also in bureaucratic
service as a privilege granted by its political master. Especially is this true of on-duty, high-
ranking military officers, or of old army officers
who have been retired after serving well the political authority, both of whom, not surprisingly, owe
their position more to loyalty to the political
authority than to a military prowess which has never
been tested.[25] This service has proved as economically rewarding as has service in the regular bureaucracy. For example, three high-ranking officers were
accused of fantastic graft and corruption at the time
of Amini's take-over of the prime ministership in
1961. But, save for such upper-echelon officers who
stand to gain substantially from their position,
less and less enthusiasm for military service appears
as one goes down in the ranks, although admittedly,
the military, for political reasons, is pampered and
lives much better than civilian counterparts. The
deprivileged enlisted men, traditionally, are drafted
reluctantly from villages in a system notorious for
dishonesty and corruption.

Military service has been viewed by some as a
potential source of change in Iran. Certainly, since
it has expanded literacy and a knowledge of the outside world for the average peasant-enlisted man, and
as well for many of the younger officers who do not
come from influential families (for if they were of
influential families, they probably would not have
had to serve in the military), it has aroused both
a sense of social awareness and aspirations for a
better future among a wide spectrum of the populace.
But the measure of the possibility of the military
becoming a catalyst for qualitative change must depend on the military seeing itself in other than its
historical role of the palace guard of the political

authority in return for economic privilege. Thus,
even if the lower officers, in particular, were to
play the role that their counterparts have played in
other lands by seizing _political_ power, a radical
change in the assumed relationships between polity
and military must accompany such action. Otherwise,
the military would only be covering a familiar political role in the society with a mantel of military
form; which indeed is what has happened in military
coups elsewhere in Asia.

THE OCCUPATION OF LABOR

Laborers, without the formal moral and literary
training of the educated, and manually oriented without the alleged restraining and stabilizing influence
of the agrarian community, could but be looked upon
as marginal in the traditional Iranian society.
Most typically, labor was considered as suitable for
servants and casual employees for the educated wealthy.
The wealthy filled their homes with such personal retainers who served no rational economic need, but who
demonstrated the wealth and charity of those who employed them.[26]

This historical attitude toward labor has persisted in the modern Iranian occupational structure;
as, for example, in the already discussed strong
desire for the non-manual desk job over manual employment, regardless of relative rewards in income.

It is perhaps amusing for the outsider to watch
the many devious ways in which Iranians strive to
avoid manual contact, or, failing this, strive to
associate their roles with non-manual roles. For
example, a driver will not load the vehicle he drives,
a doorman must have a desk even if he cannot read
(he not only must have it, but it must be high with
official-looking papers), and a storekeeper will not
carry parcels to a car but rather, has a "boy" to do
this. Foreigners, especially those who readily use
their hands, if need be, to accomplish tasks, are
viewed with amusement and even contempt.

Quite understandably, this attitude toward
manual labor has had a detrimental effect on developing a pool of motivated and skilled workers so
necessary for economic development. The political
authority, in response, for example, has attempted
to shift the emphasis of the secondary educational

system from one of liberal arts grinding out future
desk jockeys or unemployable experts in Iranian
literature and culture to one of vocational instruction, training low-level technicians to serve Iran's
economic development needs; but resistance, not unexpected, is great.[27] For the students who attend
vocational schools do not want true vocational training. They desire, rather watered-down science and
engineering courses, whose completion, duly entered
in their documents, conceivably might be used as
stepping stones to more advanced training, even to
university education. In this way, they hope to use
vocational education to up-grade themselves occupationally to the ranks of the educated chair-warmers.

In-service vocational training for ordinary
laborers also suffers from the same primary difficulty. Especially is this true on the middle level
of worker competence; that is, the very same level
for which vocational school graduates supposedly
are being trained to fill, up-grade, and expand.
For it is on this level that the desire to delegate
hard work to inferiors or to abandon a labor role
for a desk role is most intense.[28] Consequently,
most of those capable, but untrained individuals
who are removed from an enterprise for special
training, especially for foreign training, desert
their labor occupational role after completion of
training. Hence, knowledge gained on a training
mission will not be returned, necessarily, to the
enterprise. Conceivably, in sum, then, enterprises
may not only not profit from vocational educational
programs, they might even be hurt by them. Finally,
laborers on all levels of competence also resist
technical or vocational improvement because the less
efficient the enterprise, the more jobs that are available, especially for the average, low-level worker.
The laborers, in this instance, are not any different
from their bureaucratic cousins, for both are responding to the realistic demands of the society in which
they are involved occupationally.

Consequently, for all these reasons, labor is
highly unproductive, and, consequently, labor costs
in Iran are much too high. It is one of those curious
misconceptions that in underdeveloped areas, labor is
cheap. This may be true on an absolute basis, (that
is, on the basis of wage costs per worker,) but when
the fact that many more workers are needed to do a
similar job, then, say, in the United States, even
on a lower level of quality, is taken into consider-

ation, quite a different picture emerges. Since,
given the best of intentions, it is not possible (on
a rational economic basis) to raise wages under existing circumstances, and because high costs by themselves cut the market for Iranian goods among its
own producers, this lack of purchasing power further
bids up costs by impeding the development of mass
production for a mass market. This problem is compounded for the worker by the fact that trade unions
are not concerned with serving or protecting the occupational interests of workers. Rather, unions, as
other Iranian organizations, are made up of retainers
who follow patrons ("strong personalities") who promise favors and protection. These so-called labor
leaders ignore true labor occupational interests,
for they use the strike not to bargain with management, but as a political weapon to exact many concessions as better working conditions and wages for
their followers and material benefits for themselves,
from a political authority ever fearful of political
unrest. In return, the polity then will put pressure on management, in the public and private sector,
to conform to its desires.[29] This probably is realistic, given the ground rules of social action in
Iran (see above, Chapter Two), but it does not serve
the role of establishing labor occupational rights
and interests in the Iranian occupational structure.

     Finally, the question of women labor. Women
labor has not contributed to productive, industrial
enterprise, since most women in the labor market
come from moderately well-to-do families and compete
with men in an already overstaffed desk-job labor
market. Mass women labor power in Iran is not playing the role it did in the early industrialization
of the West, in which women's work in the home was
replaced by more efficient mass machinery, thus
liberating women for work elsewhere in the economy,
because Iran's male labor considers such work, even
aided by machines, as beneath dignity. Add to this,
the Iranian male's belief that women who work among
men are probably jaded, and one does not have the
basis for establishing the kind of women's labor
force that has been so important in supplementing the
male labor force of the developed countries.

THE OCCUPATION OF THE MERCHANT
AND THE INDUSTRIALIST

Perhaps the easiest way to sum up the traditional Iranian view toward (urban) craftsmen and merchants is to state that the market place always has
been considered to be the one place in the society
where the lie was paramount. Hence, schools, dedicated to propagating truth and the symbol of the
moral and the enlightened, could not be established
in such an evil place![30] This association of commerce with illiteracy, in a land in which virtue and
knowledge have been so intimately intertwined--with
occupational activities alien to the ideal occupa-
tional-structure consisting of politician and aides,
(that is, priests and warriors) on the one hand, and
an inert and tax-productive peasantry on the other
hand; with activities encouraging usury and engaged
in by unbelievers, such as Jews and Christians;
with activities employing trickery and selfishness,
in an Islamic society dedicated to fair dealing and
brotherhood--all, certainly were most successful in
relegating independent, unsupervised, commercial
activity well beyond the pale of the honorable, respectable, occupational roles of Iranian society.
Significantly, this attitude persisted in spite of
(or because of) the tremendous monetization and com-
mercialization of the whole Muslim world in the
medieval period, and in spite of the vital role
that commerce played in helping to provide the ruling authority with the economic surpluses, here,
hard cash and critical materials from afar, that it
used to enhance its prestige and power. For, as in
the case of farmers, a vital occupational contribution to Iranian society did not lead necessarily to
occupational reward, unfortunately for itself and
for Western sociology which too often has assumed
this to be the case. Consequently, although often
wealthy, and sometimes wielding individual power
and prestige, merchants, as merchants, were never
able to develop occupational worth or prestige to
the extent that they were able to establish their
occupational independence from the occupational interests of the ruling authority. Rather, political
authority, as the arm of the moral force in the society, insisted on "supervising" the intrinsically
immoral activities of merchantry. Traditionally,
this has been symbolized by a moral judge (muhtasib)
who patrolled the bazaar in the name of Islamic
virtue.[31]

The modern merchant, and his successor the industrialist, have inherited these traditional occupational disabilities. For example, a slang word for "crafty" in the Iranian language is isfahani. Literally this term means only "one who comes from Isfahan"; but Isfahan is the traditional home of commerce and "crafty" craftsmanship, and now is one of the key centers of Iran's burgeoning industrial growth. For, as was the craftsman and traditional merchant before them, the modern merchant and industrialist are looked upon as necessary, but basically immoral intermediaries between producer and consumer, more apt to cheat both than to serve the larger interest of Iranian society.

Objectively, as observed in the previous chapter, the conclusion more often than not is correct. But whether this is true because of some basic moral or psychological fallability of Iranian merchants and industrialists, or because the society is so organized that merchants and industrialists are responding to the occupational demands of that structure, is one of the key questions posed by the present study. In any case, both the practices of merchants-industrialists, and the traditional attitude toward them have served to justify continued political interference into their occupational activities. This policy is justified on grounds that representatives of the political authority a priori, are more honorable and selfless than merchants and industrialists. And significantly, if evidence to the contrary appears, it must be dismissed in the same spirit as all such charges against political authority must be dismissed. For political failure is due to the personal failings of specific individuals, who are enforcing the model virtues of the political authority (see above, Chapter Two). Consequently, given the operating assumptions of the Iranian occupational structure, even if merchants and industrialists developed fully the virtues of competence, honesty, or any of the other behavioral characteristics that have come to be associated with carrying on a developed rational-economic system, merchants and industrialists still would not be able to justify either their own occupational independence or to protect their occupational ranks from infiltration of the personnel or behavioral values of non-economically oriented politicians. And so, merchants-industrialists, as other occupational groupings outside the pale of political authority (as laborers and farmers, for example), have had to accept the basic ground rules

of the existing occupational structure and have
tried to make them serve their occupational interests as best they can. It is for this reason, for
example, that Iranian Chambers of Commerce essentially are an intermediary between merchants and the
political authority, bargaining for tax benefits and
warding off anti-commercial legislation as best they
can, rather than being the private businessman's association that they are in the West. Also, it is
for this reason that local booster clubs, as for
example, the Lions, are more apt to be prestigeful
social clubs or political wards used by the political
authority to drum up support for the municipal "prestige" projects of primary interest to the local authorities, than to be business booster clubs catering to
businessman's occupational interests, which they are
in the West. Certainly, at the very least, all these
organizations are neither motivated by, nor operated
in the service of independent, commercial or industrial occupational interests, for private economic
interest groups seeking independent occupational advantage immediately would be morally suspect by the
political authority.

     The significance of the discussions in this
section may now be stated. True entrepreneurship,
in contrast to traditional bazaar-type speculation,
absconding directorships, or political, moral eco-
nomizing, so typical of Iran's enterprise in both
the public and private sectors, cannot but be a
marginal oddity in the Iranian occupational structure. The Iranian political authority and Iran's
economic critics forever are shedding "crocodile
tears" over the great deficiency in entrepreneurship, which, it is felt, if it can be remedied, will
somehow save the society. However, these critics
never have considered that the Iranian occupational
structure, including the political relationship to
merchants-industrialists, perhaps, might have as
much to do with the problem as does the spirit and
behavior of the hapless merchants and industrialists
it is employing as scapegoats for Iran's entrepreneural
ills.

     And the significance of the discussions of the
entire chapter, in like tone, is that from no occupational quarter has come, or is coming, the spirit
and occupational behavior conducive to the development of a self-generating, rational economic system
in Iran, and that this is at least as much a product
of the ground rules (fundamental assumptions, or

values) of the Iranian occupational structure as it
is a product of the failings of <u>individuals</u> to "break"
out" of existing values and behavior.

THE BASIC PRINCIPLES OF SOCIAL STRATIFICATION:
THE ROLES OF LEADERS AND FOLLOWERS

The fundamental organizing principle of the Iranian system of social stratification is that of differentiation of leaders and followers. Leaders have the following responsibilities:

First, leaders provide from their ranks the functionaries necessary to administer the political apparatus of Iranian society. Although individuals can be trained technically in the means of leadership for present day needs, those who can be, and have the right to be trained so are those who possess the natural qualities of leadership, such as courage and forcefulness (termed a "dominant personality"). Although all Iranians share some of these qualities in relation to foreigners, significantly, all these qualities are not distributed at random in the population but are to be found together almost exlusively among the members of the educated and morally superior "good families."[1]

Second, leaders coordinate an Iranian society in which the various occupational groupings, as for example, merchants and farmers, are arranged in discreet, self-contained vertical compartments, with assumed conflicting occupational interests. It is the leaders, who as the sole leaders of all the society, are the members of the sole occupational grouping in the society that can stand above these conflicting interests. And it is the leaders, who, as the bureaucrats of the society, alone have the organization to put these desires into effect. Therefore, it is the leaders alone who can coordinate these occupational groupings of the society in a way that inter-group conflict in the society will be minimized or eliminated. Without such coordinated harmony, occupational (in effect, class) feuds will break out and the cohesion of Iranian society will be threatened.[2] This is especially true in periods of rapid social change, as at present.

Third, leaders are the equalizers of society. This is because the inter-group harmony and cooperation, so essential to the social order, must be based upon an equitable distribution of wealth and social privilege in the society. And only leaders, as the leaders of all the society, can determine, and can achieve what is equitable through supervision and direction of the economic, social, and political actions of the society.

Fourth, leaders provide public service benefits for the others in the society. Significantly, the leaders alone determine when and on what terms service will be offered. But since this right also is a duty, leaders should never be obstinate, refuse to face reality, and become stiff-necked to the needs of their followers. For when this is so, the service relationship between leaders and followers breaks down, and with it the chance to maintain the harmony and equalization so necessary for the well-being of the society.[3] Such has been the case again and again in Iran's past.

Fifth, in order to achieve harmony, and in order (in turn) to provide satisfactory service to the society, leaders must insure the absence of disorder in the society, even if such absence of disorder has to, and often does mean diminished, active and positive social action by other than leaders. Conversely, because of the natural fear and suspicion to be found among social groupings, or classes, leaders also must stimulate and enforce whatever group inter-group responsibility and cooperation they consider necessary to carry out their service activities in the society, rather than leaving such action to voluntary, or what is termed "hit-or-miss" initiative.[4]

Sixth, leaders provide guidance. Guidance is both moral and technical. Its goals are the adjustment of the individual to his social grouping, and the adjustment of the social grouping to the general social order, so that individuals, by themselves, and as members of social groupings, will accept roles and assume responsibilities toward the society which have been defined (that is, guided) by leaders. Such leaders must be sincere leaders. It is believed that, regardless of apparent, temporary success, no element can contribute more to the eventual defeat of Iran-type leadership than insincerity and falsehood.[5] For the good leader, although he is to be strong and decisive, and is respected for this, (see above, first observation) can never gain the confidence and support of the followers without sincerity. Given the choice between a technically competent leader and a sincere leader, the Iranian prefers the sincere leader. For, the Iranian argues, technical shortcoming can be remedied, but sincerity cannot be rectified.[6] The sincere leader forgives insincere individuals, even those who have transgressed morally by rising against him. For the sincere leader, unlike followers and corrupt leaders, is not revengeful, and is interested solely in spreading sincerity in the land. He attempts to win over opportunists to his point of view, by a social rule by model, which demonstrates the sincerity and good intentions of true leadership.[7]

We now turn to discussion of the responsibility of followers. First, followers acknowledge subservience to leaders. Second, followers must be disciplined by leaders, for without such discipline, followers are apathetic, and thwart the service roles of the leaders. Third, followers do not criticize leaders. Criticism is not necessary because leaders, by virtue of being leaders, can ascertain best the desires of followers and put into action the followers' true wishes. Fourth, and finally, followers are patient and passively accepting, while they wait for the actions of leaders, at such times and on such terms, and for whom the leaders decide to act. Since leaders a priori are superior, morally and intellectually, this is both inevitable and just for followers to accept.

It is the contention of the present study that these views of leadership and followership are basic to Iranian society, and are upheld both by those now in positions of leadership and those contending for positions of leadership. Consequently, although those who aspire for positions of leadership criticize either the existing leaders as individuals unworthy to be leaders, or perhaps, even the specific pattern (form) of existing leadership, refusing to have themselves relegated to the role of followers, they do not challenge the basic relationship between leaders and followers, since they expect to assert that relationship themselves once they attain leadership positions.

LEADERSHIP: SECURITY THAT IS NOT SECURITY

In the preceding section, reference was made to certain political concepts, such as rule by model. This was done because, in Iran, (social) leadership and followership, essentially, but not exclusively, is considered to be <u>political</u> leadership and followership, and the highest <u>social</u> prestige has been accorded to those individuals who have associated with <u>political</u> leadership, whether those individuals are associated with the established order or in opposition to it. This is why, although political leadership may provide substantial economic benefit for its members, it would be misleading to overemphasize economic motives in the intense desire of Iranians to seek public office in the existing polity or in an alternative polity. Many already wealthy men have considered it an obligation, and a privilege, to offer themselves for public service in order to obtain <u>social</u> merit for themselves and for their family. And conversely, office seekers have considered that it is the obligation of the existing, or opposition political order to provide sufficient positions of service in its apparatus for themselves to validate or improve their <u>social</u> prestige. Selection of candidates for public office in Iran, then, may be characterized as a process which provides, as a right, prizes to certain individuals who are concerned with expressing or enhancing prestige, rather than necessarily being a response to either technical need or individual merit.[8]

These aspirants to leadership, as described in the previous section, are the educated men. No matter how (well?) this arrangement worked out in the past, in the more recent period, this assumed necessary association of the educated with leadership positions and the structure of political authority, has caused a great deal of anxiety and insecurity in Iranian society. Succinctly, at present, far more educated men are seeking political positions as a traditional right than the political apparatus has either the need or economic wherewithal to support. This problem usually is attributed to the educational laws of Reza Shah. Reza Shah was intent on breaking the education monopoly of the rich and the clergy who were associated closely with the regime of his predecessor and enemy, the Qajars. By expanding the education system, Reza Shah first hoped to develop a class of educated-politically oriented youth, who would be loyal to the new Pahlavi Dynasty. Second, he hoped to obtain a class of patrimonial aides who

would provide the leaders he required to expand the
service political apparatus he needed to modernize
Iran. Individuals were encouraged to go abroad to
study, until today there are 15,000 overseas students, of which 5,000 are government supported. A
Teheran University was created. And most significantly, a secular secondary school system was established. All or most of the graduates of all these
institutions were encouraged to enter political
service in the new bureaucracy, which kept on expanding in proportion to the number of graduates,
long after rational need and the educational preparation of the individuals involved seemed to justify additional recruitment, simply because Reza
Shah's need for loyal followers did not diminish.
And so it has continued until the present day.

        At first blush this policy seems to work well.
The overwhelming majority of the educated, especially
the university educated, accept the existing political and social system, and look forward to their
future roles as leaders within the system. For certain obvious advantages exist for the educated, especially for the university educated, in return for
support of the existing system. For example, although never enforced completely, laws drawn up in
1923 and 1930 guarantee equal pay for equal education
in the bureaucracy, regardless of rational need, or
of technical competence.[9] Consequently, when talk
arises of raising salaries in the bureaucracy, and
it always arises, it is the educated man who stands
to gain the most; and the educated man who stands
to gain the most, of course, is the university graduate.[10] Again, it is the educated who not only will
obtain positions when others will not, regardless of
relative abilities to do specific tasks, but also
will enjoy the benefits of a system which promotes
on the basis of seniority and education, rather than
on the basis of merit, and which never demotes on
the basis of incompetence.[11]

        Even outside the formal bureaucracy, the educated
have privileges if they accept the social system.
For example, although the draft status of the educated
varies from time to time, nevertheless the educated
are assured of favored consideration. Especially is
this true of teachers, who, of course, are government
employees.[12] In a land where morality and knowledge
go together, the educated, because they are assumed
to be more honest than the uneducated who may serve

their own or other's selfish interests, often believe that they stand beyond the pale of popular criticism by the less educated element in the society
(the followers). For example, doctors have objected
to attacks by officials that they are not as quali-
fied or as conscientious as foreign physicians, on
the grounds that as educated men, such attacks are
unwarranted.[13]

But most recently the political authority has
had to admit that not all is well with this system
of education and politics. For it has become obvious that the Iranian education system has not
been turning out the <u>kinds</u> of graduates critically
needed for the development process to which Iran
supposedly is committed, no matter how well the
system may have served other needs and ends in the
past. But, perhaps, more significant, the more the
political authority feels itself compelled to expand educational facilities, out of pressure to increase the <u>means</u> to obtain favorable social prestige
for potentially politically restless youth, the more
apparent is its pecuniary inability to provide sufficient political positions, even socially meaningless political positions with low salaries for all
the new graduates.[14] The question of who gets into
school, especially who gets into the university, and
who goes abroad, then, has become more critical recently as the political authority reluctantly is
beginning to toy with the idea of limiting educational opportunities. For the political authority
believes it is too dangerous politically to admit
that it cannot take care of all graduates who want
bureaucratic positions, because even now it is
spending too much of its budget for personnel purposes. And so, in order to solve the problems of
quality and quantity simultaneously, the present
regime has hit upon the idea that it is wiser to
reduce the pressure at the source by reducing the
potential number of prestige-oriented candidates.[15]
But, unfortunately for the polity, the students have
become aware of this. It is obvious to the students
that the attempt of the political authority to divert
educational interest from liberal arts to vocational
training is but a clumsy effort to lower the prestige
of the educated and dissuade aspirants from becoming
low-level bureaucrats. Raising the pass mark, or
any measure to raise educational standards, is considered so dangerous a threat that mere suggestion
has led to student rioting.[16]

In response, the political authority, because
it fears that a potentially dangerous political problem may develop among the insecure volitile students,
has attempted to regulate even further academic activities, especially on the level of higher education
where the potential leaders of the bureaucracy are
molded and where the students are most sophisticated
and apt to cause the most trouble. The polity has
not been able to carry this out without a demonstration of overt force, including closure of universities. But more importantly, the polity promises,
first, that those who conform and do not make trouble
for the regime, and who accept the social system will
not have any major difficulties in finding prestigeful positions worthy of their bureaucratic aspirations. And to remedy a situation in which only two
or three thousand openings existed to serve 20,000
secondary school graduates, the polity has had to
pledge, second, that the university system would be
expanded; thus simultaneously, increasing the social
prestige of youth,[17] diminishing subversion among
both students and teachers,[18] and cutting the ground
from under potential political agitation.[19] In sum,
the political authority, whenever the political
threat to itself becomes paramount, capitulates to
the educated and the educator-to-be and further expands both the educational system and the educated
political leadership class, regardless of rational
need or the availability of economic resources to
support the policy. Both the political authority
and the students are well aware of the difficulties
which have arisen over an ever increasing horde of
students seeking political careers and the security
of such careers, which obviously are not very secure.
Yet, in spite of such awareness, neither side is willing to take the steps necessary to alter the existing pattern of bureaucratic training, recruitment,
and employment; steps that will both rationalize the
bureaucracy and encourage the educated to seek employment in other than the bureaucracy, or even to seek
in greater numbers, non-administrative positions in
the bureaucracy.

For as far as the political authority and the
students are concerned, it is a truism that an educated man with a government position, any government
position, no matter how unrewarding, is not a political subversive, and conversely, that an educated man
without a government position is apt to be a subversive in the hopes of reversing a political situation
unfavorable to himself. Such doctrines as "neutral-
ism" provide comforting ideological support for the

political opposition, but the insecure student opposition, on the one hand, and the political authority, on the other hand, realize full well that abstract principles are not at the heart of the political matter; positions are. For example, in a two and a half hour interview between the Minister of Education and students at Shiraz University on August 30th and August 31st, 1960, much to the chagrin and surprise of the minister, (for some strange reason) all the questions presented to him by the students were on politics, and not on educational policies.

Appreciation of this basic premise, goes a long way to explain why, contrary to certain development theories, the Western trained professional students of Iran do not necessarily provide an opportunity to "break through" this unrewarding vicious circle of unrewarding education reinforcing a non-rational bureaucracy and vice-versa. The political authority, to be sure, verbally has encouraged students, especially students abroad, to interest themselves in such careers as engineering and medicine, rather than law and literature. And returnees from abroad are encouraged to establish themselves in technical fields, and even quite radically, it is suggested that they serve their occupational interests outside the bureaucracy.[20] Logically, such individuals could be a stimulus to change in Iran. But this has not come to pass, because first, the returning technicians are not used necessarily in the capacity for which they have been trained. For technicians, regardless of training or ability, automatically are considered socially inferior to administrative bureaucrats. By pressure or choice (that is, for prestige reasons) most technicians succumb and become administrators. In fairness to technicians it must be stated that making the "rational" decision to remain technicians would not facilitate the rational accomplishment of technical tasks. For in Iran, lowering one's social position for any reason is an admission of inferiority, and this alone would be enough to alienate the necessary support of others to accomplish any tasks, let alone, rational, technical tasks.

Second, technicians are not received favorably by many employers. For one, technicians face competition from bogus-titled technicians who infest Iran.[21] Since these "technicians" obviously are incompetent when faced with responsibility, employers

have become very sceptical of technical knowledge.
Again, since it is the amount of education, real or
claimed, and not the quality or kind of education
that matters in Iran, technicians do not seem to
offer anything special to employers. And if they
do, employers are afraid of them, as they might
rationalize the work situation and show up existing
incompetence.

Third, technicians have been led to expect,
often by foreigners, that they will be able to
accomplish much more than they are able to accomplish without experience, especially in the hostile
social environment in which they must work. Consequently, both they and those they serve, often become
impatient and distrustful of the efficacy of these
new skills.

Consequently, in sum, Iranian technicians do
not have the same favorable social environment that
technicians in the West now enjoy, and did enjoy at
the time technical knowledge first was being appreciated, which may be more meaningful in terms of the
contemporary Iranian situation. For Iranian political authority, that is, all authority--the present
regime or its opponents--is well aware of the fact
that if technical autonomy and a technical educational
system are allowed to "break through" the existing
environment, the system of leadership by experts
educated in the moral tenets of Iranian culture
will be destroyed. Consequently, although the political authority admits that the world is moving on,
and that technicians are needed to insure Iran's
survival, it seems determined that technicians never
will be allowed to gain positions of leadership so
that they will be able to spread their doctrines in
the society at large independent of (political)
"supervision."22 The irony of this policy, of course,
lies in the fact that, although in the short run,
such political expediency cannot but be reasonable
in terms of the Iranian system of values, in the long
run, the political authority may be digging its own
grave by favoring old-line administrators over technicians. For old-line administrators, and their system of training, selection, motivation, and lack of
abstract loyalty (that is, loyalty only if employed)
are not apt to be very useful to the political authority in times of crises.

Technicians, of course, may reject this role so

carefully defined for them; and some technicians do.
But in such cases they go into exile to practice
their convictions; much to the distaste of the political authority who somehow believes that technicians should accept the existing system and "work
out" what is termed their "personal problems" in
Iran.[23]   But, not too surprising, most technicians
accept the system, as almost all the other educated
do.   For the favorable position in the Iranian system of social stratification afforded the educated,
and the security that comes with acceptance of the
values of any society, are incentives enough to conform.   Certainly this is true in this case, since
for the Iranian educated, what security and social
position is available is obtained from the grace of
the political authority who dispenses or denies favors (that is, jobs in the bureaucracy).   And so
most technicians, as the "traditionally" educated,
cannot be counted upon any more than the traditionally educated can be to "break through" the existing
pattern of non-rational employment of the educated
in Iranian society.

FOLLOWERS: INSECURITY

As superordination and security (such as exists
in Iran) associated with political authority, characterizes leaders, so dependence upon leaders and insecurity disassociated from political authority,
characterizes followers.   This is true of all followers, regardless of the possible relative ranking
of the discrete occupational groupings among them.
We turn now to discuss the characteristics of
each of these various follower groupings in turn.

The rural classes.   The negative evaluation of
agriculturists has been attributed by some to the
Iranian traditional contempt of horsemen for farmers.
But this attitude was not markedly different in those
periods when Iranian society essentially was peaceful
and sedentary.[24]   For the insecurity of the general
rural population--the insecurity of both the landowner and the peasant as against the political authority, the insecurity of the peasant as against the political authority, and the insecurity of the peasant
as against the political authority allied with the
landowners--always existed in Iran.   And, in the
most recent period, commencing with the reign of Reza
Shah, when bureaucrats replaced the remaining inde-

pendent tribal leaders and local potentates as potential rival superordinates over the farmers, this certainly has been true.[25]

First, in the case of the relationship of the
insecure peasant to the (relatively) secure political
authority, rural law, if it ever was defined, was
never enforced in an impartial, regularized, predictable manner. Rather, it was carried out according
to the arbitrary desires and abilities of particular
local or national officials.[26] Again, whenever the
political authority wished to do so, and it usually
wished to do so, it was the peasants who, by forced
draft ("taxes"), were forced to glorify the political authority in the cities by supplying the capital
to build edifices the peasants rarely, if ever, saw,
but certainly never used. Peasants also have had to
support the impressive urban bureaucracy of leaders,
who, in return for that support, do not even have
the common decency to stay out of the villages and
away from the peasants, but insist on making life
more intolerable for them by interfering in their
lives and wasting the peasants' potential capital
by providing "service" they do not need or want,
while denying them the basic social, economic, and
political security they do need and want.[27] Although
obviously economically relevant considerations exist
for this policy (that is, to insure the flow of the
vital surpluses), the motivation may be, as readily,
social. For the right and duty of the educated
(moral) leadership is to control the uneducated,
much as they see fit. This is only to be expected
because the uneducated cannot understand what is in
their own best interests, and, hence, the educated
have the right and the moral obligation, to do what
they believe is right and in the best interest of
the uneducated, whether it be ramming unwanted "service" down their throats, or "disciplining" them.
A very important consequence of a policy which
creates insecurity and a sense of degredation for
the average peasant is that those of intelligence
and potential "natural" leadership among the peasants
do not become true peasant leaders, but flee the land,
hoping to obtain somehow the precious education that
will remove them, physically and socially, from association with the soil, and thus open some measure of
prestigeful social status and security to them.
Most migrants only go on to neighboring market town
where they do not obtain enough education to accomplish either of these goals.[28] For it is soon obvious

to a peasant that, whether he stays on the farm, or
whether he goes into the urban centers to seek his
fame and fortune, that his social future and his security very much depend on the largess of the political authority. And it is obvious to the political
authority, in turn, that the peasants are helpless,
and hence, that the political authority can offer or
withdraw security as it sees fit and on its own
terms. In sum, no formalized channel exists for
peasants to protect their interests as <u>they</u> conceive
their interests to be. And in turn, since as inferiors, peasants are powerless, pragmatically and
ethically, to establish such a channel, the peasants'
situation is one of a vicious circle of hopelessness
feeding on hopelessness.[29] For example, Iranian agrarian legislation that reads so well in print, such
as the law empowering Village Councils to raise
and use 5 per cent of a village's crop for development purposes, is meaningless, if those who make decisions for the peasants are opposed to concrete
group action by peasants who alone may be sincerely
interested in true rural development. Hence, not
surprisingly, the law is circumvented easily, by
not allowing the councils to meet, on the grounds
that the councils separate peasants (the illiterate
inferiors) from either the landlords or the political authority (the literate superiors) who are solely
responsible for initiating (productive?) social action in the society--in this case, rural development.

     The Iranian landlord's social position is com-
plex. On the one hand, first, since he may be educated but certainly, at the least, does not use his
hands, as compared to the peasant, he has a long
standing position of <u>social</u> superiority. Social
superiority does not necessarily imply <u>economic</u> superiority. This is so because it is mere ownership,
and not the income derived from the land, that is
the measure of membership in the landlord grouping.
This is why the Iranian landlord has little incentive
to invest economically in his land; especially when
in consequence of the social value of land, the price
is raised out of all proportion to its yield and
scarce capital can be invested more profitably elsewhere in the economy, especially in urban commodity
speculation. For these reasons, particularly in the
case of the smaller landlord, a landlord only may be
<u>comparatively</u> better off than his own tenant peas-
ants, but there is no confusing the <u>social</u> composition of the two groups.[30]

It is important to realize also, on the other
hand, that the landlord has social and not necessarily political superiority. Consequently, it is only
when landlordism is associated with political authority, that social prestige and (political) security
go together. In general, then, as in the case of
peasants, landlords must protect their interests
against the depredations of the underpaid members
of the political authority, especially local bureaucrats, who use their position to acquire some of
the landlords' surplus in order to supplement meager salaries. This tradition apparently goes far
back into Iranian history.[31] The landowner, then,
because of his relative political disadvantage vis-
a-vis political authority, regardless of his relative
economic and social advantage over "his" peasants,
is, for example, saddled with forced gifts and expenses for entertainment and comfort of all order
of officials on the local level. He even may be
forced, if the extent of his domain and his predilections warrant, to maintain an agent in the capital,
Teheran, to protect these interests at the vital
center where political policy is formulated.[32]

In brief, the landlord is as dependent on the
whim of the political authority for what (political)
security may be offered him on grace, as is the
peasant, who in turn, is insecure in relation to
him, and to the political authority. The difference,
however, is that the landowner, unlike the peasant,
may have the economic wherewithal to acquire political security by associating himself with the political authority, either by paying for it (not necessarily completely out of land revenue if he is an
urban "absentee" landowner busy in urban speculation), or by protecting his interest directly by
virtue of becoming an official himself or having a
relative who is an official. It is for this reason
that landlords, normally, are associated with or
become officials; and vice-versa (although it is
cautioned, again, that the two roles are distinct
and not always are associated). For the only source
of predictable security such as it exists in Iran
is by association with political authority, and, it
is only when political security is assured, that it
is worthwhile to consider how to exploit that security for economic and social benefit. Consequently,
not surprisingly, many members of Parliament, traditionally, have been landlords,[33] and most of the important bureaucrats also are landowners. Most of
these individuals have acquired their property subse-

quent to their acquisition of a position of security
in the structure of political authority from which
to insure and protect their holdings. Or to restate
the observation, they have used political office for
economic and social benefit, which, traditionally,
both is legitimate and is encouraged in Iran. But
the opposite process, that is, first the acquisition
of property, and then, the acquisition of political
security, certainly is the case for some. But,
which came first, the political chicken or the landed egg, is not of major consequence; what is significant, is that, in either case, without association
with political authority, the acquisition of land
would not and could not be attractive.[34]

     Finally, a word about the formal village leader
(khadkhoda) and the rural class structure. This individual, although normally he is the representative
of the peasants in village-owned villages, or the
intermediary between landlord and peasant in landlord-
owned villages, in the peasant context, may be considered as a tool of local political authority, because he settles disputes that would otherwise have
to go into the local courts and he helps collect
local taxes and other dues from the peasants. Yet,
in return for these invaluable services, he does not
attempt to stand on his own politically. Rather, he
is content to support the local political order in
return for local political acceptance, and support
if need be, for whatever economic and social benefits
accrue to him from his role in the village. Consequently, he is of inestimable value to the political
authority, for he is a source of enhancing the security of the political authority, without at the same
time striving himself to become an element of (political) security, and in so doing pose as a possible
threat to the security enjoyed by the political authority on the village level.[35]

     The military. Historically, the Iranian mili-
tary has been bureaucratized; that is to say, the
military has been considered not as an independent
class with potential individual class interests, but
rather as the patrimonial security arm of the political authority. In return, many military leaders
have received a share of the bureaucratic spoils
through appointment to civilian posts which offers
social and economic benefits. But the security of
such privileges are dependent on the grace of the political authority, for what office the political

authority grants, it also may take away. To wit, in
the anti-corruption campaign in 1960-61, it was high
army officers in civilian posts who were singled out
and denounced for taking advantage of positions of
trust to squeeze the people illegally (see above,
Chapter Four).[36]

Labor. Although the political authority is well
aware that labor is a potential source of political
unrest because of constant intrigue in its ranks, especially from Iran's northern neighbor, the political
authority has calculated correctly that it has little
to fear positively from it. This is so, not only because labor now lacks independent organization, but
also because labor has not developed any abstract
right to create such organization, if it was so inclined; a situation which the political authority,
by the very nature of political authority in Iran,
has fostered. For typically, the political authority
perpetually offers the bait of economic benefit on
grace and not as a right (the carrot of the security
that is not security, once again) in return for assured political quiescence on the part of labor; a
quiescence, incidentally which, the political authority is not adverse to assuring forcefully, if need
be (the stick). And labor is well aware that it is
this grace from the political authority, rather than
such unpredictable "rights," as the excellent labor
codes which are not enforced, that is the primary
source of such social and economic benefit that it
obtains. Consequently, labor unions, as most organizations in Iran, when they seek either occupational
or class privileges, are political and not economic
action groupings. The unions reason: why bother to
waste time fighting economic battles over economic
issues to be sure, when, if one can make the proper
political connections, simply by demonstrating
"political loyalty," one is assured that the political authority will "harmonize" employer-employee
relations in the public or private sector not to
labor's disadvantage.[37] And certainly, why do anything politically foolish. For this might anger the
political authority who will refuse to support the
interests of labor, when, for example, absconding and
embezzling employers or overproduction might close
down plants and throw men out of work unless the political authority is willing to intervene. And most
significantly, with the chronic, superfluous labor
supply in Iran, it is debatable how many laborers
could ever be put on private sector payrolls without
government pressure on employers. Strikes, to be

sure, are not unknown in Iran; but significantly,
they are politically motivated. Even communist-
infiltrated strikes are concerned with putting pressure on authorities to conform to the pattern of dispensing favors in return for labor peace. And so,
to conclude, when it is recalled that the political
authority so often is the employer himself, it can
be appreciated how much labor is at the mercy of the
political authority, for its very security.

    <u>Commercial Groupings</u>. The thesis that wealth,
not associated with politics, is morally suspect, implies, in the present context, that, for the moral
good of society, those associated primarily with the
accumulation of wealth cannot be allowed to pursue
those class interests and to obtain security for
those class interests without political association
of some sort. And so, for example, the guilds of
Iran, unlike those of medieval Western Europe, traditionally have been placed under the supervision of
the political authority who work through the guild
head (<u>sheikh</u>) to insure that the members of the
guilds would be responsive to the "interests of the
society," as defined by the political authority.
To achieve this goal, the guild head serves primarily
as a political intermediary who enforces the politically inspired guild regulations. These regulations,
unlike those in medieval Western Europe, are not
defined, detailed, and predictable rules offering
security to the guilds, but rather are the changeable
interpretations of moral-supervision as conceived of
by the political authority. And the onus that commerce somehow is unclean, and that political-economic
pressure by such commercial organizations as guilds
somehow was unworthy, has encouraged the guilds to
become, primarily, religious and social-fraternal organizations. Even today, a close relationship exists
between religion and the artisan-commercial bazaar,
for the bazaar usually is located adjacent to, or
close to the mosque, and, as shall be seen, religious
leaders are active in guild affairs (see Chapter
Seven, below).[38]

    Although modern commerce has outgrown the guild
and even left the bazaar physically, it is not evident that the social position and prerogatives of
modern commerce have been improved thereby. For as
much as in the past, commerce is dependent on the
good will of the political authority. Through its
control of commercial credit and marketing, and as

the tax collector (see above, Chapter Three), the
political authority is ever ready and able to delay,
and otherwise harass those who are not cooperative
and willing to submit to political supervision of
their class sections. And so, once again, a class
must make the inevitable political connections to
obtain whatever security and privileges may be offered to it, on grace, not as a right. In this case
such favors include the coveted government loans
without which much of the commercial activity would
be impossible.

Finally, industrialists. Independent entrepreneurs are not held in high esteem in Iran, any more
than in any other economically underdeveloped society, although, because of their novelty, their
life story might warrant a column or two in a Western oriented newspaper.[39] For the question asked
in Iran, as elsewhere, is why should such a person
not take a responsible government position and run
an enterprise for the social good, instead of serving his own selfish interests? Consequently, on
moral grounds, independent industrialists can and
are denied access to the security necessary to translate their class interests into effective independent class actions by a political authority who always is tempted to discourage independent enterprise
often only in the name of social morality. Industrialists, especially the large industrialists,
accept this situation even more readily than do the
commercialists, because alliance with the political
authority is often necessary to insure sufficient
investment capital, purchases of overstock production,
and a share in the spoils of foreign technical and
material aid.[40] Hence, the large industrialists in
particular, who have most to gain through political
cooperation, "encourage" the investments of members
of the top echelon of the political authority in
their enterprises, in return for political protection
of class interests, and in some instances, for the
favor of being accepted socially by members of the
political grouping.

And so, in sum, security (protection) for all
followers in Iranian society is individual and subject to reversible decisions by the leader (political
authority), who alone has access to whatever security
exists in Iranian society; and since even this security is not firm, it is termed "the security that is
not security."

SOME INTERPRETATIONS OF THE IRANIAN
SYSTEM OF SOCIAL STRATIFICATION

The Iranian system of social stratification,
then, may be characterized as one in which all its
component groupings, save possibly for one grouping,
the leadership grouping, suffer a high degree of
social insecurity. What security exists for the
non-leadership groupings, is obtained solely through
association with the leadership grouping. Association is achieved and maintained only between specific
individuals in the leadership grouping and specific
individuals in any of the other groupings, rather
than between the leadership grouping as a unit, and
(all members of) any other grouping, as an unit.
The association also is achieved and maintained on
the grace of individuals in the leadership grouping
alone, and not on terms of reciprocal rights and
obligations among the individuals involved. As such,
any security enjoyed by any member of a follower
grouping is tenuous and reversible at the initiative
of individuals in the leadership grouping.

The leadership grouping is the political grouping. Although this grouping, as a unit, possesses
a measure of security, as compared to the other
groupings in the system, within the leadership
grouping itself, it is only the segment found in
the very apex position of that grouping that can be
considered as possessing any degree of persistent,
calculable, security. Traditionally, this apex
position has been filled by the titular ruler, the
Shah, and the few individuals that constitute his
trusted inner circle of personal patrimonial retainers. Although politically committed, that inner
circle may very well be heterogeneous, in the sense
that it is not representative of the interests of
any one occupation grouping, because it is derived
potentially from individuals from any occupational
source who are willing to accept the class values of
the grouping (that is, intellect-morality). Certainly
this is true in the contemporary society, for the
apex-leadership grouping of the present dynasty has
been built up by selection from among those personal
patrimonial retainers who flocked to the ban   of
Reza Shah from many occupational sources to
the bureaucratic wealth and prestige derive
novel military, agrarian, commercial, and i
programs.

It is now in order to discuss whether or not,
in the light of these principles, the Iranian system
of social stratification is a mobile system. At
first blush, and certainly from the standpoint of
interpreting mobility in terms of individual mobility, Iran does have a highly mobile society. For in
a society characterized primarily by social insecurity, almost everyone in the system is subject to
radical changes of fortune, up and down. Even within the political apparatus itself, for almost all,
security is only relative, for this security can
and does change rapidly as positions of individuals
in the political hierarchy change.[41] Likewise, the
Iranian system of social stratification is highly
mobile, when viewed from the standpoint of individuals moving among social groupings. For, as even
the Shah properly has noted, rigid caste or class
distinctions have never existed in Iran, even though
Iran has been more autocratic than democratic.[42]

But it is important to realize that because
all this is true, the channels of mobility that do
exist are open for use of individuals, but not
necessarily for the use of groupings. That is to
say, individuals who move up and down in the status
hierarchy may move solely as individuals and not as
representatives of their occupation or class groupings, no matter how many individuals of particular
groupings are involved in such movement. Consequently, in any movement of individuals, groupings
do not necessarily improve or diminish their position in the status hierarchy, especially with respect to the crucial element of security. At the
most, when individuals move, families move.*

Second, and even more significantly, regardless of the quantitative extent of upward mobility
in Iranian society, the legitimate channels for
upward mobility qualitatively are restricted. For
sooner or later, in the process of upward mobility,
one must either enter into, or ally one's self
with the apparatus of political authority as representative of the leadership grouping. Conse-

---

* In general, "family mobility," especially in the
  upper reaches of the status hierarchy, refers
  to upward mobility, because, in cases of down-
  ward mobility, especially at that level, "black
  sheep" can be protected by family economic or
  social protection.

quently, in upward social mobility, only the status
of the political grouping is strengthened, because,
logically, individuals must abandon primary loyalty
to (former) individual groupings, even to the extent
of becoming actual members of the political grouping,
in order to improve their relative position in the
status hierarchy. It is for this reason also that
potential leadership and talent among all non-political groupings are seduced into becoming allies of,
and even members of the political grouping. For, by
(Iranian) definition, legitimate leadership can only
be associated with political authority, although not
necessarily within an existing regime. Consequently,
in conclusion, because only a small elite at the
apex of the hierarchy of social stratification holds
what real leadership prerogatives and class security
that do exist in Iranian society, because those
others, who, due to education and bureaucratic employment in the service of this elite, hold more
limited prerogatives and security (but much more
than those outside the charmed circle of political
authority), and because only one approved channel
is available to validate superior social status
and access to leadership prerogatives and class security (bureaucratic employment, that is), it cannot be said that the Iranian system of social stratification is mobile in the same sense that the concept of "mobile" is used in western social stratification theory.[43]

A further implication of this discussion: At
the same time that mobility exists in Iran, (mobile
insecurity would be a better characterization),
rigid class distinctions also exist. The distinctions especially are obvious between peasants and
non-peasants, and between those who are politically
associated, and those who are not. But it also is
apparent to any enterprising youth "on the way up,"
perhaps already in the bureaucracy, that in general,
the pre-eminent positions of security in the hierarchy are reserved for those members of "good families," especially for former retainers of Reza Shah
and his relatives or their offspring. This is not
a contradiction to the basic thesis that individual
mobility is great in Iran, provided one is willing
to abandon the desire for group mobility and aspire
to become a member of the political grouping. As
elsewhere under similar circumstances, and especially
because of the insecurity inherent in the Iranian
system of social stratification, those (temporarily)
in positions of (relative) security hope to hold on
to whatever security they have at any cost.

Frantically striving to enforce social rigidity
and class distinctions in order to escape the consequences of the inevitable Iranian mobile insecurity,
much as King Canute once tried to turn back the sea,
has had a significant effect on Iranian social behavior of interest to the present study. On the
one hand, rigidity tends to make superfluous success
or failure in job performance, since neither directly affects one's status.[44] On the other hand, mobile
insecurity has the very same effect on performance,
because it is only one's political connections or
membership in the polity that provides whatever
status security can exist in Iranian society. Consequently, because the (apparent) contradictions of
rigidity and mobility (or mobile insecurity) contribute alike to a lack of interest in work performance,
substantively speaking, these contradictions are only
apparent and not real.

Another way of looking at the same problem: It
is a behavioral maxim that it is security, ironically,
that enables risk to take place. For in a social system, such as the Iranian, characterized by general
insecurity, individuals are reluctant to risk what
little security they have. An adverse decision which
appears, at worst, a slight depreciation to those in
a position of basic security can but be a threat of
total disaster to the insecure. Consequently, it is
the Iranian insecurity that encourages Iranian rigidity, save for those few at the bottom who have
nothing to lose and are prepared to risk all impru-
dently. It is for this reason that Iranian political authority has determined that some minimum of
"service" will be provided to all, especially at
the bottom of the status hierarchy, so that the desire to overturn the system of social stratification,
and by implication, the social order, will not ma-
terialize.[45]

DOES IRAN HAVE A MIDDLE CLASS?

It is now possible to discuss the prime question
of this chapter; namely, whether or not Iranian society has a middle class, and if so or not, what the
implications are for Iranian economic development.

It is possible to delineate and rank relatively
certain obviously discrete groupings in Iranian society; namely, farmers (peasants) who are ranked at
the bottom, and the key political leaders from "old

families" or "good (Reza Shah related) families" who
are ranked above them. But beyond this, one runs
into certain manifest difficulties in attempting to
allocate other groupings in the society. Some of
those observers who have been influenced by western
sociological concepts have insisted upon the existence of a middle class or middle stratum between the
two strata which represent these obvious extremes of
upper and lower. They have variously included in
their calculations such groupings as middle-level
bureaucrats, university students, business men of
varied economic resources, skilled (and sometimes
semi-skilled) labor, professionals, politicians
(including Communist Tudeh members), middle level
military offers, petty landlords, and finally, landlord agents, or, in brief, the middle reaches of all
the possible social groupings of the society.[46]

It would be pointless, as well as logically fal-
lacious, to get into a hassle over whether or not
this analysis is "true" or "false." It is worthwhile,
however, to question whether or not the objective
purposes of all stratification analysis is served
necessarily by lumping together arbitrarily, and in
every case, what purports to be the middle strata of
all social groupings in a society and labeling this
collectivity as a "middle class." To be meaningful
and useful, the mark of class identification must be
some identity of interests, similar style of life,
and intimacy of social interaction.[47] Consequently,
it is possible that a social stratification analysis,
that assumes that inclusion of a "middle class" is
mandatory, may not be necessarily the most rewarding
way to treat the material at hand. This very well
may be the case in the present study. For, if any
identity of interests exists among the members of
all the elements of the suggested so-called middle
stratum of Iranian society, as listed above, it is a
negative one. Most of these individuals do not consider themselves as constituting a distinctive layer,
but rather consider themselves as potentially upper
status members who have not, as yet, made the grade.
For this reason, the individuals have strived, as
best as they are able, to imitate the material and
non-material attributes of their betters. This is
so, first, because positions in the upper reaches
of the status hierarchy represent security of status,
or the nearest to security of status, as is possible
in Iran. By attempting to associate and be associated
with, in any way possible, this security, the indivi-

duals in these segments hope that some of this security will rub off on them. And, in order to achieve
security, the members of these segments have learned
that they must abandon any attempt to use their potential leadership talent in an effort to legitimize
themselves as an independent, distinct grouping (or
class) with their own class interests, and their own
style of life (that is, their own concept of what is
social prestige). They must concede that they are
not, and will not become, potential rivals to the
class interests (and style of life) of those in position to offer them security; namely, the members
of the political authority-leadership grouping.
Also, since this so-called middle stratum must differentiate itself from the lower (peasant) stratum,
the middle stratum places great emphasis upon literacy. This, of course, is an attribute it shares
with the upper stratum. This further intensifies
the middle stratum's association with the interests
and the style of life of the upper stratum. Significant for purposes of the present study is the fact
that most of the members of Iranian commercial and
industrial groupings are included in this middle
stratum.

There still is a second reason why the so-
called middle stratum identifies with the upper
stratum. Many of the occupational skills of the
members of the middle stratum have come to them
originally from the upper stratum, and not out of
the resources of its own stratum. Yet, almost by
definition, access to these skills are less available to them than they are to the upper stratum.
Consequently, although the members of the middle
stratum often command an income and social prestige
based on scarcity due primarily to education (which
is an upper stratum attribute), still, the access
to commanding resources (as for example, overseas
education) generally is not available to them.[48]
Moreover, since the skills of education in Iran
are associated primarily with bureaucratic activities, access to and use of these skills have become associated almost exclusively with the upper
stratum - leadership grouping. Consequently, for
those who aspire to better themselves socially, this
can mean only upward mobility into the leadership
stratum, which means at the least, abandonment of
any pretense to the desirability of creating distinctive class interests, values, and a distinctive style
of life by those in the middle stratum. This is well-
known and is accepted by those in the middle stratum,

including the commercial and industrial segments.
This is of great significance to the present study
in so far as it concerns the possibility that the
commercial-industrial segments of the middle stratum
might "break through" and help to form a new system
of social stratification in which their alleged distinctive class interests would be represented, if
not established as significant. These asserted distinctive interests do not exist in Iranian society.

Finally, since in what way one is associated
with the political apparatus, and with whom one is
associated in the political apparatus, determines
social position in Iran, no necessary correlation
exists between one's economic ranking and one's
social class ranking in Iranian society. For example,
a rich landowner without bureaucratic connections
conceivably could be ranked lower than another landowner of more modest economic circumstances, but
with political affiliation. Consequently, economic
success necessarily does not determine social status,
for unless economic action becomes associated with
politics, it does not stand much chance of being
used to improve social status.

For all these reasons, although it is logically
possible to devise a system of social stratification
applicable to Iranian society in which rank is determined by relative access to income, (or other material resources), and which is hierarchically arranged
into three horizontal layers of upper, middle, and
lower, and this may be useful for some purposes, it
is suggested that for purposes of the present study,
it may be better to divide up the hierarchial pie
into two layers or classes, differentiated by direct
access to security (leaders) on the upper layer, and
lack of security (followers) on the lower level.
The leadership class is a political class; and consequently, may be differentiated internally by relative
access to maximum political security. At present the
Shah at the top holds maximum security and the petty
bureaucrats at the bottom can rely upon only minimum
security. The follower class, in contrast, is highly
differentiated internally on the basis of occupational
roles and economic gradations. But regardless of
these internal differentiations (which may be useful
to point out for certain purposes), all the members
of the various segments of this follower class share
in common the single characteristic that they, as
individuals, in each instance, again and again, must

obtain class security on grace from individuals in
the leadership class in order to carry out class
interests.

The significance of this interpretation of the
Iranian system of social stratification is that it
does not assume that certain members of segments in
the follower class, particularly commercialists and
industrialists, who, conceivably might develop singular interests and style of life, and distinctive
class aspirations, automatically will develop such
distinctive interests compared with other groupings
(or segments) in the society; that they will strive
to form their own independent grouping (distinctive
class) to facilitate the pursuit of distinctive
class interests as conceived by the members themselves; and that in so doing, they will try to obtain, through their own efforts, legitimate recognition of those interests and as favorable a position as possible for themselves in the status hierarchy, as was the case with the commercialists and
industrialists in the developed societies at a particular historical moment in their development process. Rather, these commercialists-industrialists,
as certain other members of the follower class, have
the same class attitudes and aspirations as the
leader class, although the economic resources of
some of them may often preclude similar class behavior. These class attitudes and aspirations include
the purchase of land or speculative activities to
extend wealth, the retention of, or search for public office to protect (or extend further) that
wealth, and the conspicuous consumption of wealth.
Significantly, throughout the status hierarchy,
neither class nor any segment within either class,
including the commercialist-industrialists segments,
espouses thrift and productive investment.[49] For
this reason, an increase in income among commercialists-industrialists in the follower class, any more
than an increase in the leader class, need not lead,
and has not led to the development of those attitudes, aspirations, and style of life associated
with entrepreneurship in the developed societies.
Consequently, increasing the income of the follower
class, especially in its upper reaches among
commercialists-industrialists, may only create a
rising tide of expectations to imitate the leader
class, in the hopes that conspicuous spenders and
constructors will be (mis-)taken for members of the
leader class. That the leader class is not unwilling

to support these class attitudes and aspirations in both the private sector, as well as in the public sector of the economy, for its own political reasons, is obvious. In sum, whether among the political-leadership class representing the public sector, or among the commercialists and industrialists in the followership class representing the private sector, no class basis exists in Iranian society for the development of an entrepreneurial "spirit" or an entrepreneurial industrial class.

6

INHERITANCE IN LAND AND ITS MODIFICATIONS

The Iranian system of inheritance in land is derived from the general Islamic Shia principles of inheritance. These principles require a series of fixed, but unequal inheritable shares: Males receive shares twice that of females. The inheritance normally goes to the male and female children of the predecessor, but other relatives may share in diminishing amounts, according to the distance of their relationship to the benefactor. The wife does not inherit landed property, but only movable property and a fair valuation in cash of orchards and buildings; but if the heirs refuse to accept the valuation, then the orchards and buildings may be possessed by the wife. If the individual has no heirs, the state can claim the property.[1]

In this system of inheritance, regardless of the number of heirs or the nature of the inheritance, unless the individual has but one heir, which is a very unusual case, indeed, in Iran, no one heir possibly can inherit anywhere near the amount of landed property held by the predecessor. However, this normal course of inheritance in land may be offset by a number of measures; namely,

(1) A gift may be made of the property or part of the property during the owner's lifetime. Gifts are revokable under certain conditions, unless the recipient is either the child or the parent of the benefactor.

(2) Unless it can be proved that force or duress is involved, a non-revokable transfer (sulh)

---

* This chapter arbitrarily is concerned solely with the question of descent as it **affects** the question of (landed) property. See above, Chapter One, for discussion of the methodology of the study. Certain other aspects of kinship, particularly family relationships, are discussed in Chapter Nine, **below.**

may be made of property, which, if subject to the
regular laws of inheritance at the donor's death,
will create a major and dangerous intra-familial dispute. To recompense those who stand to lose by the
transfer, stipulation normally is made in the agreement that those who are disinherited are entitled to
some compensation, which is inherited at the donor's
death. This stipulation likewise, is non-revokable.[2]

(3) Property can be donated to the Shia "church"
(vaqf property). In this instance, the administration and/or the benefits derived from the property
may be returned to the donor, or to his designated
heir, who serves as trustee (mutavalli).

(4) The property may be retained intact and dis-
posed of collectively by all the heirs who subsequently divide up the profits on a fixed share basis.
Or the heirs may hold on to the property and appoint
one of their numbers as administrator of the property,
claiming their fixed share of the property's income,
less certain additional benefits which accrue to the
administrator for his services in caring for the property.[3]

(5) The land may be retained intact by the heirs
and leased to tenant farmers with the proceeds (that
is, the rent and other perquisites) divided among the
heirs. In this system, occupancy rights and ownership
rights are differentiated, so that the heirs are assured both of the income and the social prestige to be
derived from ownership of the land without having to
be bound occupationally to the soil. In such instances,
the tenant occupancy rights and the ownership rights
over the same piece of property are subject to the same
general law of landed inheritance, although the specific
forms of inheritance, dependent upon the number and kinds
of heirs, vary as between the two kinds of rights.[4]

THE ROLE OF THE IRANIAN INHERITANCE
SYSTEM OF LANDED PROPERTY

The Iranian inheritance system of landed property
guarantees a successive dimunition of landed property
in time. For although certain heirs, especially sons,
may inherit a greater share of the property than any
other relatives, no one heir possibly can inherit,
free and clear, anywhere near the holdings of the donor. And to look at the problem conversely, regard-

less of the ability of an individual to add physically to his holdings during his lifetime, his holdings are subject to diminution at his death, or the
loss of primary control by transfer prior to his
death. Consequently, it is conceivable that any one
heir, including a son, might succeed in increasing
the area of land under his ownership or tenancy
right, and yet not equal the holding of his donor.
And it is conceivable, further, that even if one
succeeded in accumulating the same amount of landed
property of one's predecessor, or even surpassing
it, through one's own effort, one could not hope to
pass along anywhere near the same amount of land
accumulated or even equal the holdings of the first
generation at the time of inheritance. As Alice in
Wonderland, one has to run to allow one's successors
even to maintain one's very place in the inheritance
system.

For too many landowners and tenants, especially
in the lower rungs of the economic ladder, the effects of the inheritance system are such that the
amount of inherited land is too small to insure a
minimal satisfactory livelihood. This certainly is
one of the major reasons that rural youth are leaving the farm and going into the urban centers, or at
least to the nearest market towns, to seek fame and
fortune, either as landless "lumpen-proletariat," or
as owners of landed property too small to insure an
adequate income, in the hope of supplementing the
landed income in some way. Most of these people normally retain their contact with their rural relations
back home, either sending remittances back to these
dependent relatives, or returning from time to time
to obtain the income from their landed holdings.[5]
These itinerant landholders may become the source of
a major social problem, if they obtain sufficient
capital in the urban centers to enable them to increase their absentee land holdings by taking advantage of credit-short independent proprietors in
their native villages. These individuals are one
example of those petty absentee landowners who live
and spend their income primarily outside the rural
area but who derive a good part or all of their
income from the rural population, and who in doing
so, take capital from the rural areas while offering
little or nothing in return.[6]

Although ownership of land, traditionally, is
considered a stable source for social status in Iran,
this is but a relative stability. Certainly, there

has never been a stable landed aristocracy in Iran.[7]
And part of the reason for this, undoubtedly, has
been the inheritance system. For any sharp, social
divisions of wealth and power based on ownership of
land can only be maintained for short periods of
time, perhaps only for a single generation. At the
most, a particular landed aristocracy survives only
during a particular dynasty. Once again, then, only
political patronage makes it possible to protect
and enlarge economic interests, in this case, the
accumulation of landed holdings, against the iron
law of diminishing inheritance returns. Most typically a new dynasty confiscates the landed holdings
of those considered to be members of the old regime,
usually the allies of the previous dynasty, and
then distributes the property to its personal retainers, who have aided in the establishment of the
new political order. After this initial act of
generosity, the dynastic elite has but to sit back
and watch the successive diminution of the landed
power and relative wealth of its new potential
rivals, through the workings of the inheritance
system--<u>unless</u> the political authority chooses to
intervene and provide opportunities directly (through
wealth) to once again increase the accumulations in
land. In this way, the political authority either
is assured of political support and economic benefices for itself, or the destruction of the economic
potential of its enemies. This further contributes
to the fluidity and insecurity of Iranian society,
and the inability without political association to
protect potential economic power. Consequently, the
possibility of being able to accumulate and use
landed wealth outside the "moral" supervision of political authority, as a possible basis for financing,
say, a productive, self-generating economic system,
is impossible.

THE MEANING OF LAND REFORM

Although land reform has been explored in another context (see above, Chapter Three), it seems
appropriate to discuss it once again in the light
of the previous discussions of this chapter. The
inheritance system which provides some piece of
landed property, albeit even an economically inadequate piece of property, to all legitimate heirs,
has the dual role of impoverishing the rural population, while at the same time offering an inducement
to continue some association with the land.

This fact too often is overlooked in the many proposals that make up a land reform program. First, removing the absentee landlords from the rural scene, no doubt, materially will aid the hapless tenants, by providing them with land free of rent (but of course, not free of taxes). But since removal of landowners will not alter the inheritance system, at best, this measure will only delay the inevitable decline in holdings, and thus assure only a more equitable and more orderly procession of the new procession of the new proprietors into poverty.[8] For the same reason, technical aid, and readily available development capital, coupled with land redistribution, although certainly providing for improvement in the economic situation of the average Iranian peasant, and providing him with incentives to shake off traditional apathy and to work for a better future, can not "solve" the land problem.[9]

Nor can these measures even ease the path into industrialization. Certainly, radical changes in land organization and production are vital prerequisites to progress in the industrial sector of the economy, as Communists have learned to their sorrow. And certainly, the termination of a system of wide-spread tenancy will terminate, or at least diminish, the desirability and the ability to invest surplus capital in land instead of elsewhere in the economy. But such a land reform, without an accompanying inheritance reform, contains within it the seeds of a countervailing tendency actually to encourage the mass of the rural population to remain on their land. For if it is true, under present circumstances, that, even with the rural society so unfavorably organized for the average peasant, the dream of owning a suitable piece of property exists, even to the point that if dispossessed physically from the land, former peasants dream of returning one day to the land, then, surely, the dream will be even stronger in a situation in which the possibility of ownership is enhanced under a land redistribution and land reform program. Presumably, land reform, regardless of political persuasion, is supposed to aid economic (including industrial) development by increasing the productivity of the rural areas so that a "surplus" of farmers will arise. These individuals then will move to the urban centers and contribute directly to the industrial process, while they are being supported by the increasing surpluses of those who remain on the land.[10] But in Iran, with its inheritance system, this change is apt to happen

only on the basis of forced migration and forced
levies on the remaining farmers, or alternately,
under the age-old condition of rural impoverishment,
which follows land reform in due time, as it has in
the past.* In contrast, land reform <u>cum</u> industrial
development has been successful in Japan, because
of a unilinear inheritance system (in this case,
primo-geniture) which has encouraged both the permanent rural migration of all but the eldest son.
Hence a successful land reform without inheritance
"reform," as the Taiwanese case, although of immediate benefit to the rural economy, cannot have
the lasting effect on economic (especially industrial) development that land reform has had in
Japan.[11]

     To conclude, it may be said that once again,
it is the particular social (that is, institutional
value) rules of the game in Iran, that may be the
crucial element of what, at first blush, purports
to be but a technical problem of economic development.

---

* The question of whether forced migration and forced
  levies familiar to the Communist "solution to the
  agrarian problem" is an inevitable result of the
  inheritance system found in Iran, and in Asia, is
  an interesting query, but does not concern us here.

RELIGION AND POLITICAL AUTHORITY

General Principles

Since Muhammed, the founder of Islam, was both
a religious prophet and a political innovator, Islam,
from its inception, was both a religious movement
and a political movement.[1] Although this close association between religion and political authority
was not to be challenged from the time immediately
subsequent to the death of Muhammed, controversy
always has arisen as to the exact relationship between the two elements.[2] One religious faction,
which came to be called Sunni, maintained that legitimate succession to the polity went to those who
were able to obtain it, provided they maintained
general peace and upheld the faith. The Shia faction,
in contrast, maintained that political succession was
based on a hereditary lineage; specifically the lineage
through Ali who was the husband of the Prophet's
daughter, Fatima.

Although Ali and his descendents were Arabs, as
was Muhammed, the original followers who espoused
the Shia cause were generally, but not exclusively
Iranians, who resided predominantly in what is present day Iraq. Although loyal followers of Islam,
as non-Arabs, the Shia resented the attempts of the
Arabs, who had conquered their land, to rule them
politically from the Arab citadel of Medina.[3] In
addition, the Shia believed that the wife of Husain,
the maternal grandson of Muhammed, had married the
daughter of Yezdegird, the last Iranian Sassanian
king. Both the Sassanian dynasty and Husain were
overthrown by the Arabs who represented the Sunni
faction. For all these reasons, the Iranians developed simultaneously, political, national, and reli-
geous animosity toward the opposite Sunni faction.[4]

---

* Some of the remarks in this chapter are an adaptation and amplification of the author's paper entitled, "The Social Basis of Capitalism: The Case
of Iran," which was read before the Fifth World
Congress of Sociology in Washington, D.C., in September, 1962, and subsequently was published in a
French version in Archives de Sociologie Des
Religions, No. 15, Paris, 1963.

By emphasizing religious and political separateness
from the Sunni, who were to become the dominant
force of the Islamic world, the Shia also developed
a distinctive political-religious community, in
which submission to the (shia) religion came to
imply submission to (Iranian) political authority
and vice versa, and conversely, a challenge to the
(Shia) religion implied challenge to (Iranian) political authority, and vice versa.

Consequently, on the positive side, for example,
it can be argued that to submit to the social and
political teachings of the early religious leaders
will insure that Iran will become a developed nation.[5]
And, on the negative side, for example, religious
heterodoxy can be associated with political heterodoxy. For example, the religion of the Bab and of
the Bahai'i, when it arose in the nineteenth century,
because it denied the role of the Islamic religious
leader, the mullah, and the primacy of Islamic law,
so antagonized the Islamic religious community that
it sought political support against its nominally
religious enemy. The political authority, however,
was not reticent to support the religious suppression of the Bahai'i, because of a claimed indifference of the Bahai'i to the political loyalties of
nationalism and patriotism.[6] Even today, the Bahai'i
is evil because it is supposed to be both a political
as well as a religious Trojan horse, encouraging
both religious and political dissension within Iran,
in the hopes of continuing foreign domination to
thwart Iran's moving forward to the status of an
advanced, developed nation.

At the same time that it can be said that
religion and political authority are interlocked
very closely in Iran, in the actual dynamic relationship between the two forces, for all practical reasons, it can be said also that political authority
dominates religion. The Shia religion in Iran, then,
may be said to be a national religion. Historically,
the religious sanction of secular authority was derived only from the assumption that the religious
order had delegated, indefinitely, certain of its
prerogatives to the political authority in order to
carry out the vital responsibility of protecting the
theocratic religious order and interests in the society.[7] But in time, this idea of indefinite delegation of responsibility was transformed into the
concept that the religious order provided the religious sanction for the (religiously approved) activi-

ties of the political order. In this way, the growing Iranian national, political absolutism was sanctioned by the national religion of the Shia. Steadily, the political order gained in dominance over
the religious order, although the religious were to
be found everywhere in any polity. As the power of
the religious community (ulama) steadily weakened
in the more recent decades, the absolutist concept
of political authority grew, so that, by the time
that the Pahlavi dynasty replaced the Qajars in the
third decade of the 20th century, the religious order agreed to the change without too much fuss,
even though the change meant a sharp curtailment of
its prerogatives and policies under the so-called
"reform movement" of Reza Shah.[8]

The dominance of political authority over the
religious community does not signify that the religious order is unable to assert itself and make
trouble for the political order. Certainly, even
the modern, secular political order wisely has de-
ferred to, and even supported the religious order
on all such matters of vital importance to the
clergy that do not challenge key political prerogatives. For example, the polity solemnly supports
the fasting rules in public restaurants during the
holy Ramazan fasting period. It also is not lost
on political authority that religion can serve as
a useful excuse for the political order to avoid
unpleasant political decisions. For example, in
1891, the religious order opposed the tobacco concession given to a foreigner, on grounds that
believers should not be encouraged to use tobacco.
The government was "forced" to withdraw the concession. Although the clergy obviously was the
most active, overt party in pressing the matter,
some historians are convinced that the political
order was the covert, inspirational party in the
campaign, because it was unable on its own politically to resist the encroachment of the imperialist
foreigners.[9]

The practical consequences of this particular
association of authority and religion are as follows:
First, in accord with Islamic law, all land theoretically belongs to the religious community in general.
Consequently, no absolute right to private ownership
of land exists in Iran. However, along with the delegation by the religious order of certain of its prerogatives to the political authority went delegation
of ownership over land.[10] Included in this delegation

was not only church property, but also secular land
that had been confiscated from non-believers and
which now reverted to the ruler as crown land
(khaliseh),[11] and religious trust property (vaqf).[12]
Although the trust property nominally was to continue to be administered directly by the religious
order, political authority, under the delegation
principle, "reserved" the right to exercise control
and supervision over the church's administration of
the property, if and when it so wished.[13] It was
this reserved right of control of even church administered property that, for example, was used by
Reza Shah in the 1920's to bring under his political
control the major religious shrine of the non-
political urban center of Mashed in northeast Iran.
He assumed control of the ecclesiastical property
and turned over the revenue derived from pilgrimage
activities to the National Bank of Persia to be
used for municipal, especially (secular) educational
activities in Mashed. By cutting off the money that
would have constituted their stipends, he also reduced the number of religious personnel in Mashed.[14]
Consequently, in sum, the political authority has
gained, at the least, the significant theoretical
right of supervisory control over all private property in land in Iran, including church property,
a right that could be backed by the moral sanction
of the religious order; if need be, even over religious property!

Religious service and obligations connected
with land also have reverted to political authority.
Corvee, or unpaid obligatory public service labor,
originally was a religious obligation. It was used
for irrigation purposes, and for the maintenance of
nominally religious owned property, in those cases
in which finances of a polity were not adequate to
pay for what was otherwise obligatory, but paid-for,
public service labor. Under terms of the delegation
concept, the political order inherited this right to
recruit corvee labor for its own political purposes
while claiming religious sanction for its enforcement.[15]
Again, political authority gained a significant means
of support for its secular political prerogatives,
for although corvee itself has all but disappeared,
the derived principle of the right to supervise and
control (now secular) service projects in the rural
areas has not.

The intimate interrelationship of religion and
authority in Iran, second, has affected the legal

system. Although secular laws existed even from the
beginnings of the Islamic period, and a secular
civil court has superseded much of religious law in
contemporary Iran, the secular court has claimed always to be in conformity with Shi religious law.
Thus, even the modern civil code is not the body of
coherent, abstract doctrine that has come to be associated with codified law in the developed societies, but, rather, is a body of specific, discrete,
consequences which are left to individual judges,
who are generalist-moralists, to interpret and apply in each instance as they see fit.[16] For although the Iranian judge supposedly is bound by
local custom, since no set guide or binding body of
precedents exists, save the very principle that justice must be done, specific interpretations by specific judges in specific cases can but be the basis
for judicial decision. For this reason, a settlement in any one case cannot necessarily be a guide
for future decisions in similar cases, even by the
same judge![17] Consequently, law enforcement, in
the sense that law will prevent by example, as well
as punish, is extremely difficult. Rather, law enforcement in Iran accords with the Islamic, especially Shia Islamic, propensity for pious declarations
of moral rectitude which either are unenforceable
because of the nature of the declarations, or are un-
enforced, because of the nature of secular (rule by
model) authority.[18]*

In sum, no calculable, logical relationship exists between the judicial system and the social action in a way that judicial consequences necessarily
can be predicted beforehand as the inevitable result
of particular behavior. This is in keeping with the
kind of judicial process so prevalent in Asian justice, which the sociologist Max Weber termed "qadi-
justice" in honor of the Islamic religious judge,
the qadi.[19]**

---

*   More will be said on this below.

** Importantly, the equivalent of the qadi already
    was an honored member of pre-Islamic Iranian con-
    cepts of justice. He was incorporated into the
    Shia Islamic traditions in a way that the qadi,
    although nominally a religious officer, was sub-
    ject to political authority, and, not surprisingly,
    became a political judge.[20]

The Shah And The Religious Order

A third, and highly significant consequence of the association of religion and political authority in Iran, arises from the relationship between the titular political leader (the Shah) and the religious order, understanding of which is dependent on appreciation of the Imam principle of Shia Islam. The Shia branch of Islam is made up of a number of sub-branches, but the one branch that is directly associated with Iranian political authority is the Ja'fari sub-branch, named in honor of Imam Ja'fari of the eighth century who established certain important tenets of the Iranian principle of the Imamate. In this principle, twelve Messianic leaders, called Imam, are recognized. These leaders are directly related to the prophet of God, Muhammed, through his son-in-law, Ali, the first Imam, from whom they claim the source of the legitimacy of their power and knowledge. For, according to the Ibn Saba doctrine, Ali not only is Muhammed's son-in-law, he is his executor and transmittor (Wasi), and each Imam, commencing with Ali, has transmitted his legitimacy and knowledge to the next Imam, without interruption, generation after generation.[21]

"Imamic knowledge" refers to a divine light or cosmic force, because it includes not only the revelations of Muhammed, but also the special revelations attributed to Ali, as recorded in his personal copy of the Koran (the jafr)*, which was passed along from Imam to Iman.[22] This knowledge is the key to salvation and it requires the intercessor to God, who is the Imam, as transmittor. Consequently, there must always be an Imam, for without one, the end of the world (Judgement Day) will come. At present we are, and have been for about a millennium, in the age of the twelfth Imam, who has been in hiding almost all this time. But on Judgement Day, an Imam, the Mahdi, will return to establish the Kingdom of God in place of the present imperfect social order.

The Ja'fari Imam, then, first, is not the social convention that the Imam often is in the Sunni tradition; he is a religious necessity. Second, since the Imamate comes from God, the Imam is free of sin. Evil is the result of the acts of ordinary me[n] cially when they fail to heed the commands of [the] Imam, which in effect, are the commands of Go[d]

---

* Jafr is not to be confused with (Imam) Ja[']

Third, as direct representative of the authority of God, the legitimacy and prerogatives of the Imamate are not dependent on whether or not the people accept the Imamate. This is so because only God can determine who is free of sin, which is the qualification for Imamhood, while ordinary men, in contrast, tend to judge authority according to their personal advantage, possibly and probably bringing to power those who are unworthy in the eyes of God. But, it is assumed, nevertheless, that because selection of the Imam is attributed indirectly to God, ordinary men will follow and accept the decisions of the Imam, and by extension, of the Shia religious order.[23]

The significance of the Imam doctrine for purposes of the present study lies in the long standing intimate relationship between the Imamate and Iranian political authority. Specifically, in 1502, the Iranian Safavid dynasty formally established the Ja'fari version of Shia Islam as the Iranian state religion. But long before this date the two concepts had in essence been interlocked. At this time of origin, in general Islamic thinking, the Imam was both the religious and political leader of the faithful. However, it soon became apparent that the activities of the Islamic community increasingly were running counter to orthodox religious prescription, and that secular political leaders were not adverse to pushing aside or even murdering Imams who stood in their way. If the Imam was of divine support and free of sin, why was it possible evil could so easily triumph, many asked. The first answer was for the twelfth Imam to disappear without naming a successor. This preserved the sin-free nature of the office, but did little to preserve the theocratic role from political upstarts. So, a second solution was attempted. The Imamate claimed that it was temporarily delegating its temporal authority to its moral inferior, the secular political order which already was exercising these political prerogatives. The accommodation of 1502, in effect, traded political recognition of the Imamate for religious legitimization of political authority of an absolute state. It established the principle that until the return of the missing Imam, the people were to be absolutely loyal to the Iranian political authority. For although the secular political order, a priori, was morally inferior to the perfect Imamate, because of its particular relationship to the Imamate, a priori as an institution, it was superior to the ordinary people. Consequently, rebellion in any form

could be interpreted also as religious sin, and for
the people, or ordinary men, to assume that they had
certain reserved political rights of dissent, ultimately implied that the Imamate's authority which
was now represented by political authority, could be
overturned by popular disapproval, which, as has
been previously discussed, was inadmissible.

A further step in the general argument: Since
Iran is an absolutist state, ruled by the Shah, the
temporary delegation of the prerogatives and the
association of legitimacy of the Imamate with Iranian political authority in general came to imply de-
facto, if not de-jure, delegation of the prerogatives and legitimacy of the Imam to the Shah himself. In this way the delegation was personalized
completely, for now de-facto delegation of legitimacy and prerogatives went not only from religious
order (the Imamate) to secular political order
(Iranian political authority), but also from religious leader (Imam) to secular leader (Shah). The
significance of this step is that, in time, the
Shah, once again de-facto if not de-jure, came to
take on, in the political sphere, of course, the
very attributes of the religious leader (Imam)
whose prerogatives and legitimacy had been delegated de-facto to him. Specifically, both superior political wisdom and possession of superior political virtue became associated with Shahs, even if
certain Shahs did not live up to expectations.[24]
For this reason, Shahs, although they cannot claim
to be Imams incarnate, do maintain that, through
a line traced back to Ali, and even to Muhammed himself, they are at least associated with the
Imamate-cosmic divine force and that they have the
right to expect the same loyalty from their subjects as would the twelfth Imam, if he was to appear. Isma'il, the founder of the Safavid dynasty
often expressed himself in this way,[25] and the present Shah has described certain visions in which he
came in contact with certain Shia religious leaders
as proof that the Imamic force still is to be found
in the personage of a Shah, even in so secular a
Shah and in the secular present age.[26] For such
a leader so blessed, especially if, in addition,
he has the Iranian secular virtues of strength
and dominant personality and character, nothing is
impossible, for no other reason than in Iranian
thinking, under such conditions, ordinary men are

expected to follow unquestionably.[27]*

The doctrine of charismatic absolutism does not exhaust the implication of de-facto delegated Imamic authority. For, second, if the Shah has been delegated, de-facto, certain leadership prerogatives by the Imam, then the Shah, in turn, as far as these prerogatives are concerned, is free of sin. As a secular leader he claims to be free, not of religious sin, of course, but of secular political sin, which is more than sufficient for purposes of political authority. For according to the Shia doctrine, although God has commanded mortals not to commit sin by providing them with reason, revelation, and prescriptions for conduct through the Koran, mortals can commit sin. Sin arises because man is a free agent, and is not perfect as is God who cannot be tempted by man's greed, envy, anger, or lust. The Imams, although not God, at the same time are not mere mortals. Hence, they are not subject to the temptations and banality of ordinary men.[29] In the de-facto delegation of the Imam's prerogatives to the Shah, the Shah receives the same state of grace as does the Imam, but since this is a political mission, he receives only a political state of grace. This thesis, of course, is a sacred version of rule by model; for whenever the question of (secular) reform arises and individual, ordinary men are considered replaceable, but not the titular ruler, and, more important, by extension, neither is the political and social order he defends, this may be interpreted theologically as purging the sin of mortals while defending the authority of the Imam and the Imamate.

A third implication of the doctrine of de-facto delegated Imamic authority, and of more far reaching consequence to the present study, is that the political authority has used the doctrine to justify political intervention, supervision, or control over certain aspects of the social order, particularly the economic order, as discussed in Chapter Three. As morally inferior to the Imamate, but as morally and

---

* A similar concept of charismatic political leadership is accepted throughout the Islamic world, but in accord with Sunni principles, the concept envisions random, individual political charisma for as long as one can hold on to a charismatic position, rather than the hereditary charisma peculiar to Iran.[28]

intellectually superior to other elements in the society, political authority, presently personified by
the Shah, has assumed that it not only has the moral
right, but has the moral duty to intercede on its
own terms and on occasions of its own choosing into
the society in the name of protecting the political
and moral rectitude of the society as decreed by the
Imamate. In this way, intervention and supervision
into the society could, and often has been, justified
by a political authority on purely religious grounds.
Of major concern to the present study, for example,
political authority historically has claimed the
right to intercede into the affairs of the bazaar in
order to protect the pious and "cooperative" merchants
against the evil speculators who violate the religious
prohibitions against usury.

By similar reasoning, it is possible to suggest
that many of the previous observations concerning political authority and the Shah (especially in Chapter
Two) may be interpreted in religious terms. For example, the assumption that automatically the political order is superior morally and intellectually to
the economic order, especially to the private sector
of the economy, may be said to be justified on the
grounds that the Shah and his arm, the polity, have
access, albeit de-facto and inferior access, to the
higher morality and knowledge of the Imamate which
is not approachable by merely ordinary men. Likewise,
anyone working for the political authority must carry
some of the superior-intellectual and moral Imamic
charismatic qualities delegated de-facto to political
authority as a whole, regardless of the civil servant's prior experience, training or present status.
Finally, on the basis of the same argument, the expressed desires of ordinary people, especially the
lowly peasants, need be given little attention, since,
being politically superior, the members of the political authority, as the Imams, must know better what
the people need than do the people themselves.

It must be appreciated that to oppose this a
priori religious moral authority on purely secular
political grounds, or even on such technical grounds
as "efficiency," also is to oppose it automatically
on religious-moral grounds. It is perhaps this fact
which explains, to some extent, the apparent weakness
and hesitation of all political opposition in Iran,
and the devious means that those outside an existing
polity use to serve their interests without incurring

the wrath of the polity. Another point to recall:
the Imamate of old, although it never was in the position to carry out its mandate from God to control
successfully Iranian society, never gave up formally
its right to assert absolutist control. In a final
act of desperation it only delegated de-facto its
political powers. The political authority, in turn,
even when it has not been in a position to enforce
its political will, which has been often enough,
likewise in the same spirit, never has surrendered
its right to absolutist political control of the
society. It has been this threat of possibility
and probability of enforcement of such a moral-
political will, backed by such a religious sanction
which, by definition cannot be competitive, that is
most desponding to rational economic (developmental)
action, since it is not calculable and is not normally legitimately opposable.*

The Clergy and the Political Authority

   To reiterate, although not all members of Shia
Islam are Iranian, the majority of the followers
of Shia Islam are to be found in Iran. In consequence, in Iran, religion and political authority
are interlocked in a way that Shia Islam is considered to be a national religion, and religious
practitioners (the clergy), although obviously they
perform religious roles in the social order, also may
have (religious) roles in support of political roles,
especially if the political authority so wishes. In

---

*   The following observations are suggested by cer-
    tain comments brought to the author's attention
    by an anonymous reader. Since the Imamic author-
    ity is delegated to the political authority only
    de-facto, no polity has unlimited moral sanction
    for its actions. The learned religious ones
    (mujtahids) as representatives of the Imam, at
    least verbally, can oppose the secular authority,
    and for that matter, so can, and has the more tra-
    dition-minded in the society, whenever their moral
    sensibilities have been offended. Most signifi-
    cant, because it is secular, all authority, no
    matter what its character, is imperfect, and hence,
    always may be criticized on moral grounds (real
    or rationalized). These observations have direct
    bearing on the discussions of the following sec-
    tion "Orthodoxy and Heterodoxy in Iran" and Chapter
    Nine.

return for performing these roles, the clergy are
considered government servants and are supported directly and individually by the political authority.

The rationale for religious support of political roles by the clergy is, as follows: During the
time that the last Imam remains in hiding, and consequently, the Imamate is dormant, the learned religious ones (mujtahids)are responsible for guiding
the people in moral rectitude. But since certain
roles of the Imamate have been delegated de-facto
to the political authority, the mujtahids have certain religious responsibilities in the political
sphere.[30] By extension, these responsibilities
have come to be assumed by all the clergy, from the
leaders of the Shia faith (ayatollah)on down to the
ordinary cleric (mullah), although, to be sure, the
nature and extent of these responsibilities vary
with the differential religious roles and statuses
of the clerics themselves, and the specific relationship between the clergy and a specific polity at a
specific historical moment.

Religious support for high state policy, domes-
tic or international, is expected of the upper clergy.
On the foreign policy level, for example, in the con-
duct of Iran's cold war with Russia, religious lead-
ers play an active part in denouncing the "Godless"
Soviet Union, and have been called upon to denounce
Iran's (Sunni) Moslem neighbors, such as Iraq and
Egypt.[31]

The lesser clergy, as represented by the individual mullah, on the other hand, although politically involved, certainly has a more ambiguously
defined relationship to political action than does
the other clergy, partly because the attitude of
political authority toward it has been more ambiguous. On the one hand, the present polity has de-
ferred to "religious opinion" (as in the case of
enforcement of religious rituals during religious
holidays) and has subsidized the clergy as paid
civil servants in order to mollify it. But on the
other hand, the polity has circumscribed or competed
with some of the clerical prerogatives, such as
education and bureaucratic service in the rural
areas. The clergy, not surprisingly, has reacted
to the polity with the same degree of ambiguity,
both supporting and opposing policies of the polity
according to the way those policies affect its prerogatives and privileges.

A prime example of this ambiguous relationship
is the case of a recent urban political movement,
the National Front, in which the lesser clergy is
participating. Historically, the bazaar and the
mosque often have been contiguous. The traditional
merchant, craftsman, and laborer, who live and work
in the bazaar are organized into individual guilds,
in which members of the clergy play significant
roles as moral, intellectual, and especially political leaders. The bazaari never have developed
the occupational rights and privileges associated
with the Western guilds. Consequently, rather than
positive measures to protect and expand occupational
interests, the bazaari, came to rely upon such negative policies as strike and riot to redress grievances, and upon the lesser clergy who associate with
them to whip up guild members to religious zealous-
ness and to sanctify such conduct. At present, the
lower ranked bazaar elements have fallen upon evil
days. On the one hand, first, no longer are people
interested in buying the wares of the bazaar craftsmen when foreign-made goods are readily available
at cheap prices. Also, second, the petty bazaar
merchants do not have the proper political connections to obtain large loans so that they can import
luxury goods for speculative profits, but must depend upon a market catering to the lower-income
groups, a market which too often is sluggish. And
finally, third, the lesser clergy, especially in
the recent decades, has seen its roles successfully
whittled down or made obsolete by the Western education and secular interests of the political authority in particular, and of the society in general.

All three groups attribute their ills to the
modern, foreign innovations introduced into Iran
starting with the policies of Reza Shah in the
1920's, which threatened to make obsolete traditional
economic services and religious messages. And so the
bazaari have made common cause with other groups such
as shopkeepers, students, low-level civil servants,
and semi-skilled workers, who, although they do not
share the reactionary social and economic designs of
the bazaari, still agree on eliminating the foreigner
because they believe he is supporting those elements
in the society whose policies will not allow Iran to
develop in the way that these groups will be the major beneficiaries. For, with the foreigner's departure, all the members of the Front believe that the
present social order will be shaken up enough that
certain selected changes in the social structure will

take place. They envision that the development programs will be speeded up and carried on in a way
that will profit them specifically (this satisfies
the progressive faction), but that all social changes
will be made by Iranian methods and will serve Iranian values (this satisfies the reactionary faction).

In addition to providing leadership for its own
faction, as in earlier days, the lesser urban clergy,
then, now provides religious sanction for the activities of those secularists in the National Front, who
seek that sanction. For, in the minds of many of
the secular members of the Front, no contradiction
exists between traditional religious values and the
potential changes they envision for Iran. In the
economic sphere in particular, they view religion as
a necessity because they claim that current economic
problems have been due to the substitution of foreign
ideas for traditional religious values. They see a
religious revival, often on a very high intellectual
level, as the gateway to a national soul-searching
and cleansing movement that will purge Iran of those
foreign sins that they believe are at the root of all
Iran's ills. As nationalists, they do not look upon
the traditions of the past as practices and ideas to
overcome, but rather as a source of inspiration and
instruction in the world of today. Certainly, a
strong element of modern nationalism is secular, but
it would be a grave error to ignore the religious element in the nationalism, even the secular nationalism,
which is to be found among all segments of Iranian
society. An example of the last point may be noted as
an interesting combination of ideologies. In the investigation following the attempted assassination of
the Shah some fifteen years ago, it was discovered
that the youth involved was on intimate terms with
both religious zealots at the same time that he was
an avid reader of Communist literature.

What may be termed the "middle clergy," or
"locally-powered clergy," for want of better terms,
also, has created concern for the political authority,
although, as the upper clergy it tends to associate
less ambiguously and more closely with the political
order than does the lesser clergy. However, there
are notable exceptions, especially when a particular
polity is weak and must temporarily tread carefully,
so as not to antagonize the religiously faithful
(see above, Chapter Two, Section "The Structure of
Local Authority: the Absence of Local Counter-

vailing Power to the Center"). One such exception
was Seyed Nuradin of Shiraz who was, for many years
before his death in 1958, a power in local and even
national politics. He used his pulpit not only to
express his religious views, but also to support or
denounce political leaders. He sponsored political
petitions in support of secular aspirants for seats
in the Parliament, significantly, not out of abstract
principle, but in return for the usual monetary considerations. He became the bitter enemy of Reza Shah,
who attempted to arrest him. When the Shah came to
Shiraz, Nuradin closed the bazaar and kept it closed,
forcing Reza Shah to release him under an understanding of mutual disregard of each other's political prerogatives and domains.

    The rural clergy, unlike the urban clergy, has
few of its previously significant prerogatives remaining. Such traditional religious services as marriage now can be performed in the town under civil
auspices, and the registration of vital statistics
and the rural educational system now are in civil
hands. However, it is questionable how much religious depth, and hence, how much clerical power, ever
existed in Iranian villages. In Islam, traditionally,
clerics are not required for prayer, and certain nominal religious services, such as the washing of the
dead, can be performed by relatives or close friends.
In addition, Islamic policy in Iran, in any case, has
been to accept nominal conversion for true conversion
among the rural illiterates who affiliated with Islam
mostly in order to legitimize their own land holdings,
which would have been confiscated from "unbelievers,"
or to obtain the confiscated holdings of non-Muslims.
It is not unfair, therefore, to characterize Iranian
rural Islam as a thin veneer of orthodox Islamic doctrine, overlying and sanctioning pre-Islamic religious
practices. It is because of this, that the rural
cleric (mullah), to survive, has specialized in those
pre-Islamic practices that cater to the peasants' uncertainty and frustration. For a price from those
ill-able to afford it, the mullah offers services
that will cure, foretell the future, or destroy enemies, real or imagined. It is not surprising, then,
that mullahs and other religious, and alleged-
religious practitioners have come to be looked upon
by the peasants as parasites, the spoilers of village
women, and troublemakers for their own purposes. Although individual mullahs can be, and are found in
the forefront of the rural reconstruction and community development programs in Iran, these individuals

are rare indeed. Consequently, the average peasant
associates the rural clerics with the old political
order, as a force to be tolerated grudgingly along
with the tax collector.

By way of conclusion to this section, then, it
may be said that regardless of whether or not the
clergy is urban or rural, is upper or lower, is
powerless or is powerful, supports or opposes the
present polity, is for or against productive change
in the abstract, that clergy, with some notable exceptions, does not represent a force in Iranian society that can be supported or opposed by a potential element representing the introduction of a
rational economic system in Iranian society. For,
first, members of the clergy either are panderers
to sentiment for a continuation of the non-rational
features of the present society, or, if they are in
opposition to the present society, certainly, are
not opposed to it in a way that an opposition committed to rationalization of the existing society
can use their support constructively.

For, second, the clergy when it goes into opposition to the existing order, does not attack
rationally, nor does it seek to institutionalize
its power as a countervailing element in the political realm (political authority), as did the medieval western Christian clergy. The weapons of
the Iranian clergy are emotions which lead only to
rioting. Also, as other Iranians in a position of
potential power, albeit only irresponsible trouble-
making power, too often it is only too willing to
be paid off to keep the peace. For example, industrialists, on the one hand, by supporting the
clergy, have discovered that workers will not strike
or break discipline, and that their products will be
sponsored in religious sermons. Especially members
of religious minority groups who are merchants, not
unusual in Iran, have found bribery satisfactory
insurance against possible "religious trouble" during
the passion holidays of Ramazan and Moharram. For
the polity, on the other hand, support of the clergy
has meant support of the polity, especially support
of the general peace whose violation the polity so
rightly fears.

RELIGION AND SOCIETY: DIFFUSED
RELIGIOUS VALUES*

Islam and Certain Iranian Social Values

In Islam, theoretically, faith in God is primary and fulfillment of the rituals prescribed in
the Koran is secondary. But in Iranian Islam, as
actually practiced, religious prescriptions are very
significant; in fact, they are supposed to be the
very blueprints for all facets of daily life. Thus,
the religious order and the social order must be
interrelated, for both are concerned with the moral
ordering of man's social behavior. Because of this
duality, a basic paradox exists in what appears to
be religiously motivated social behavior in Iran, a
paradox so striking to outside observers. On the
one hand, the Iranian is non-committal as far as
conforming to behavioral norms and rules are concerned, preferring rather, speculation and conformity to abstractions; for faith is paramount. But
on the other hand, the Iranian often retreats into
legalisms, justified by alleged citations from the
Koran, whenever pressured into accepting, or even
considering, innovations which are distasteful; for
religious prescriptions of the social order are
crucial. For example, on the latter hand, a sani-
tary village water system in a village is rejected
on the basis that it is unnecessary because the
Koran states that water clean enough to wash in is
clean enough to drink, and that in any case, water
purifies itself every six feet at the least. (Incidentally, reference to such "facts" are not to be
found in the Koran.) On the former hand, to argue
for the necessity of the same water system on the
basis of specific, technical, social and health considerations equally may be fruitless. For no matter
what the argument advanced, no Iranian ever seems at
a loss for a reason why he cannot or should not do
something. Answering one argument only precipitates
another argument. Sometimes, these arguments con-

---

*   Diffused religious values are those norms of so-
    cial behavior found in the general secular society,
    which, although not religious norms, may be de-
    rived from religious norms, or are logically com-
    patible with, or derivable from, contemporary or
    historical religious norms.

form to both phases of the paradox, when they appeal
to tradition and pseudo-rational abstractions at the
same time, and hence, are impossible to answer on
the meaningful, concrete (rational) level.

This paradox in Iranian thinking may be attributed further to the historical development of Islam. Islam spread very quickly from an Arabic base
with its characteristic set of religious ideas and
prescriptions derived from Arabic social challenges,
into non-Arabic societies, whose peoples claimed
allegiance to the universal ideology of Islam, but
were indifferent to Arab social prescriptions.[32]
Consequently, very soon after the establishment of
the Islamic faith in Iran, in part the result of a
very rapid conquest of the country, it became evident that there were wide discrepancies between the
Arabic-Islamic religious prescriptions and daily
social reality in Iran, and that that gap, not only
was not disappearing, it also was widening. The
religious leaders came to believe that the only way
to salvage the truth and efficacy of the faith, and
at the same time salvage something of an Islamic
social message, was by retreat from and not mastery
of worldly affairs. One may say that through this
action, the religion remained in and of this world,
but not subject directly to its effects. This conflict has remained to the present day, and, may be
cited, in part, as the religious origin and/or
rationalization for the "rule by model" described
in Chapter Two above.

This conflict and paradox also may be used to
explain why, when pressed with the ugliness of contemporary Iran or himself, the Iranian prefers passi-
vity or a retreat into what an outsider would consider the world of non-reality, a non-reality that is
rationalized in religious terms as the only external
"true" reality. Since, as elaborated earlier in this
chapter, in the absence of the Imamate, this world is
morally wanting, man and man-made rules of this world
of alleged reality cannot be trusted. Certainly,
when the chips are down, perhaps only one man in a
thousand will be a faithful and true friend. Hence,
man and society, that is, reality, cannot be trusted.
All except God is an illusion. For the Iranian argues that since everyone he meets may want something
of him, that he does not want to, or cannot surrender,
social relationships which cause loss of (social)
respect in the eyes of the people have to be refused.

In this way, society becomes the source of perpetual evil and conflict. In contrast, God can be trusted, for he does not need favors, and he will give without asking for anything in return, save submission to him as prescribed by Islam. This is not without practical significance, for through faith in Him and not in man directly, one can be favored through men as His instrument. Consequently, it is not man or a relationship to man that determines anything of importance, _even_ anything of importance related to man. What one thinks he sees that is important in the real social world, is but an illusion, that will only mislead one, take one from God, and in effect, defeat the very mastery of the social environment one foolishly believes one can obtain by turning attention to man and man-created society instead of to God and His will.

This fear and reluctance to accept the area of interpersonal relationships among men in society as the primary working arena, even of the desires of this world, have had many significant consequences on the way in which the average Iranian conceives of his general social privileges and responsibilities. First, the Iranian rationalizes a social situation that is not to his liking as either a challenge that doesn't matter very much anyway because it relates to man, or as some punishment visited upon him impersonally because of the irreconcilable discrepancy between ideal religious prescription and social reality. Consequently, even if he complains about his plight, he doesn't expect the situation to change. And, hence, in turn, he does not consider it worthwhile for him, personally, to bother to change the situation, since this will only create human conflict without accomplishing anything.

Second, since true honesty and integrity cannot be expected to exist in society, trying to develop a public, generalized social morality is considered fruitless.[33] The Iranian's ability to exaggerate and his lack of veracity are notorious.[34] It can be argued with justification that much of this is self-protective and not premeditatedly vicious, but whether or not a defensive aggression is any the less destructive on positive, rewarding, social interaction, is a mute question. Islam and the Koran, cannot be blamed directly for this. Rationalization, however, can be found directly in the words of the medieval poet, Sa'adi, and indirectly in the doctrine of religious dissimulation (_takiya_) for the Shia

during a period of Sunni supremacy, which was supposed to serve as a self-protective device and not
as a means actively to take advantage of others.[35]

Third, in the face of temptation, isolation
and retreat are considered more feasible than the
cultivation of either individual discipline or positive social relationships. Traditionally, this attitude has been used to justify separation of non-
familial related males from contact with women
(through isolation of women in haram or behind the
veil), as the only sure protection against the un-
restrainable actions of men (i.e., society). For,
it is assumed that the individual, male or female,
cannot be trained to resist temptation. This time
the legalistic argument that action is supported by
the Koran is true, although whether the implications
concerning the natural inferiority of women usually
associated with this argument are also in the Koran
are open to question.[36] And not surprisingly, when
the prescription of retreat is ignored, no general
positive public morality exists to self-regulate
social interaction. For example, among the so-
called moderns of the upper stratum, who practice
non-familial social intercourse between the sexes
to some degree, this sociality can be rationalized
as moral only on the claim that the individuals are
following "modern," that is, foreign, moral social
prescriptions.

Fourth, since basic insecurity exists in the
sphere of daily social activities and social interrelationships, positive, rational control of the
future environment is fruitless. This may be attributed in part to inferences to be drawn from the
second observation above, and in part to the fact
that the religion, because of its concern with its
sin-free mission, may not, or cannot be concerned
with the arena of social reality. Under such circumstances, the Iranians argue, there is little hope
that tomorrow will be better than today; in fact, it
very likely may even be worse. The poet Sa'adi sum-
med up the Iranian attitude on time when he wrote,
"Forget the past, ignore the future, and enjoy the
present."* To the Iranian, then, the future, because it is at best uncertain, is something to be
treated with trepidation, rather than as a new opportunity to overcome adversity. The future is
feared also because it is within the realm of the
uncontrollable, except by God, who necessarily is

---

*   A thought usually and erroneously associated in
    the west with the name of Omar Khayyam.

not responsible to the needs of the socially-based
world. When speaking of the future, then, even one
moment hence, Iranians say, "En shah Allah" (that is,
"If God be willing"). As one observer has put it,
"en shah Allah" is the future tense in the Iranian
language.

If the future is what God wills, then the future cannot be handled positively and rationally by
mere men. Consequently, whenever man acts, he must
act on a short term basis, step by step, for too
many undecided elements subject to God may enter
in to destroy the calculations of the best of men.
Under these circumstances, certainly it is perhaps
wiser and certainly perhaps even more moral religiously, to try to adjust to the existing order of
things (that is, to accept God's will) rather than
attempt to change circumstance.

By the same line of reasoning, the Iranian
never blames himself for error or even inaction.
He always has ready an excuse as to why something
cannot be done, before he even considers how it
might be done.[37] For what God does not do, and to
repeat, God is under no moral obligation to serve
man as man is obligated to serve Him, is rationalization why something has not been done, for it cannot be done. If he has any faith in the future,
it is the belief that, in spite of all the reasons
why it should not, Iranian society probably will go
on; certainly no better than it is today, but with
hopes that it will not be any worse. And, if Iranian society does continue, in any case, it will go
on subject to a will beyond man's ability to affect its course; hence, the Iranian will be, at
best, a passive bystander.[38]

Fifth, reliance on religious "fate" reinforces
(or gives rise to) the Iranian predisposition to
general social dependency. Social life is conceived
of as an onerous burden, to be borne both as inevitable and as a burden of this world, which isn't of
major religious importance anyway. For those few
individuals who seem to be able to accomplish something, then, obviously that is their fate. They are
favored by God, and one can only hope that one will
be able to profit spiritually and materially from
association with such individuals. Consequently,
following the will of a patron, any patron, is justified. And most significantly, supporting those in
control of the social order is justified because

those individuals must be in those positions because
God has favored them; for otherwise, they would not
be able to hold on to these positions.

By way of summation, we might conclude that the
Iranian religious heritage, not abstractly in its
own right, but in so far as can be related to social
behavior by inference, has coincided with a pessi-
mistic view of this world and this life, and with a
feeling of hopelessness or at least insecurity before a destiny the individual never feels competent
he can control. For Iranian individualism is a sign
of distrust, even fear, of one's fellowmen in society, and is not a sign of a self-discipline born
of confidence in one's ability to act successfully
and rewardingly in social relationships. Consequently, society primarily is of negative interest
to the Iranian and its prescriptions are more to be
avoided than to be manipulated positively or challenged to serve one's rational interests. The
Iranian, then, is other-worldly, but in the sense
that he cannot rely on, and hence must retreat in
so far as possible, from this world. He is not
other-worldy in the sense that he has a transcen-
dental value system which he can use to justify and
provide strength to manipulate or challenge positively
the social environment. For the only discernible positive doctrine is the one which suggests that some
moderating limitation should exist on individual
"temptation." But this is dwarfed by a dogma which
suggests passive acceptance of the existing evil
social order as undesirable but as inevitable "fate"
rather than by a doctrine which suggests that the
existing social order might be the root cause of the
evil that produced the unfavorable fate in the first
instance.[39] This social world view, buttressed by
diffused but still discernible religious values which
give it moral sanction, hardly is conducive to either
the introduction or sustenance of the behavior patterns required to support an autonomous, self-
generating, rational, economic system.

Religion and Education

According to the tenets of Shia Islam, religion
and education are very intimately associated. For
in Shia Islam, since knowledge is one of the prime
means to achieve religious perfectibility, religion
has stressed learning and the acquisition of knowledge. But since that learning must aid man to acquire (religious) perfectibility, religious education,

not surprisingly, stressed the acquisition of morality. Consequently, first, whatever learning was associated with the acquisition of religious perfectibility, was considered desirable and proper for
study; and conversely, what was not so associated,
if not morally inferior and misleading, at the least
was considered to be of secondary interest. This
association between moral knowledge and education
persisted, even after education formally was disassociated from religion; that is, at the time when
religious values came to affect education only in
diffused form. The pre-eminent tract of moral
learning, is the Koran. The Koran is the complete
path to perfectibility, since to the faithful, it
is God's revelation in its final, most perfect form.
Since it is perfect, mastery of each verse, step by
step, brings its master closer and closer to perfection. Religious education, then, save for the very
few, fashioned the learning process into one of
obedience and concern for the acquisition of rules
and prescriptions as exemplified by the Koran. In
turn, the Iranian educational system in general,
which primarily was religious until most recently,
came to associate these methods with the acquisition
of all learning.

    Second, when secular education was introduced
in the curriculum of the religious schools, and
even when secular schools were established in the
twentieth century, no qualitative change was made in
this learning process. It is for this reason that
some observers have claimed that Islamic learning
has not been conducive to the expansion of experimental, creative science. This is not to say that
experimental, creative science has not appeared in
the Islamic world, for it certainly has. But such
science, unfortunately, has represented the efforts
of particular individuals isolated from the mainstream of learning, who sometimes have pursued that
learning at the risk of their lives. In the thoughts
of Bertrand Russell, creative Islamic science and
thought was only a spark and an end unto itself, and
not the beginning that the identical learning represented to the mainstream of Western thought when it
was introduced into Western science during the European Renaissance.[40]

    Third, the secularization of religious education
did not imply any change in the belief that the education process was to concern itself primarily with

the acquisition of morality. For, it was argued
that, since the Koran contained the prescriptions
necessary to insure religious perfectibility in this
world (that is, in society), and these prescriptions
were acquired by learning, then learning implies
mastery of morality as well as mastery of mere facts.
And when education became secularized in Iran, the
association between morality and "fact" learning was
not severed, rather, both morality and "fact" learning were secularized simultaneously. This was facilitated, in part, by the fact that morality now referred to the Iranian cultural tradition, a tradition
which, as discussed earlier in this chapter, has been
associated with (at least the Shia branch) of Islam.

Fourth, since as suggested in the initial discussions of this chapter, religion was associated
so intimately with statecraft, education, first as
religious education, and then as secularized education, has been associated with preparation for statecraft. And in consequence, the educated have looked
to statecraft to provide empirical application of
that education. And since, as suggested in the
third observation, this education is concerned with
morality, so statecraft has been concerned with the
spread of morality in the society.[41]

And by further implication, fifth, due to its
common heritage with religion and religious values,
secular education which, in fact, is secularized
religious training, has come to be looked upon primarily not as the means to acquire empirical skills
and other objective "ethically-neutral" information,
but rather primarily as the means to acquire access
to the religious-political-national Iranian spirit.
For the educated, this validates an assumed political and social superiority, and for the uneducated
masses, this validates the right of the moral political authority to demand obedience from them.[42]
For political authority, as the de-facto, delegated
representative of the Imamate in Iranian society,
stands to gain by the spread of morality in the society; and political authority, as the delegated representative of the defender of the interests of the
Imamate in Iranian society, has the sanction to insure that it stands to gain by the spread of morality
in the society. Because an intimate association of
political authority with morality, and by implication,
with (morally oriented) learning exists in Iran, learning might be thought of as a political (diffused reli-

gious) ideological system, in which a good educational system is one that reinforces political authority,
and a bad educational system is not only one that
weakens political authority, but also is one that ignores or subordinates the positive role of reinforcing political decisions to other considerations.
Such an educational system may be termed a system
of (political) moral guidance.

Teachers, who not coincidentally, are members
of the political apparatus, have the prime operational responsibility for enforcing moral guidance,
because they alone can reach that vital audience,
which, in the opinion of the political authority, requires moral guidance; namely the literate youth,
who, properly guided, will support the political authority, and who, not properly guided, will go into
the political opposition. Hence, the Iranian teacher
is much more than a source of rational, ethically-
neutral "materialistic facts," which are of secondary
importance in the educational system.[43] And for
those adults and others outside the jurisdiction of
the formal education system, the informational media
are the prime source of moral guidance. The polity
has conceded that radio, for example, is maintained
primarily for political reasons, and not to edify the
masses with "mere facts."[44] The moral guidance system has not been without its critics. But, characteristically, this criticism has not been concerned with
whether or not moral guidance is useful for the present educational needs of Iran, but rather has been
concerned with whether or not the present system is
attracting and adequately training sufficient and
effective moral guides; that is, future teachers and
bureaucrats specializing in informational media.[45]

It is obvious to political authority, however,
that even though the system of moral guidance and the
moral guides themselves are satisfactory, if the
source material of moral guidance is not satisfactory,
then, a model guidance program will not be satisfactory. It is for this reason that the political authority maintains that academic text control is most crucial to the success of moral guidance, and malingers
on much needed curriculum revision and up-dating.
Especially, Iranian literature and history, subjects
most vital and readily susceptible to guidance principles, are held to their present form with great
tenacity, even in cases in which they obviously are
maladjusted to the rational, empirical requirements

of a developing society. And significantly, educational moralists even have suggested that technical education should be brought within the scope of traditional educational philosophy. For example, these moralists have suggested that a list of Farsi (Iranian language) technical and scientific terms be compiled, and that teachers use these terms alone.[46] In this way, it is argued, foreign technical knowhow will be absorbed through the medium of the moral Iranian language and literature rather than through the morally indifferent and alien ideological medium of the foreigner.[47] Thus, even though the Koran states, and as many Iranians are quick to quote, "a man who amasses knowledge without knowing how to apply it resembles a donkey burdened with a heavy load of books,"[48] yet, in Iran, because of overriding considerations of moral (political) guidance, generalized, non-specific, literary, non-technical, and non-utilitarian education is considered by many as sufficient as, and even superior to autonomous, rational, technical education, even, at times, for the accomplishment of specific technical tasks. Consequently, purely technical, and even more significantly, purely scientific education, has a great negative moral-religious obstacle to overcome, if it ever is to be accepted as legitimate education in its own right in Iran. For, unlike in the "traditional" West, the indigenous education is not considered merely ethically-neutral-"traditional," but it is considered to be a positive, integral part of a timeless moral order.[49]

Insuring ideological purity is not the sole means at the disposal of political authority to insure that the educational system serves the primary interest of extending religious-political moral rectitude in Iranian society. For the political authority also controls directly both the administration of the system and, because they are civil servants, the personnel. It is for this reason, first, that the problem of establishing a de-centralized educational system in Iran, acknowledged by all to be necessary on technical grounds, is so difficult to solve. Also, second, since schools are so necessary for ideological training,[50] the Ministry of Education cannot allow the private institutions to become "incompetent" (i.e., ideologically incompetent).[51] Thus, at the minimum, private schools including technical institutes, must be licensed to assure that they will fill the roles defined for them by the

Ministry of Education which is, in this context, the administrative arm of the political authority's ideological control.[52]

The ideological control of Iranian students overseas is considered a special problem by the political authority. For such students may leave Iran to study abroad at too early an age; that is, at an age when they morally are vulnerable to a way of life that is radically different from that to be found in Iran, and at an age before they have interiorized the Iranian religious, social, and cultural traditions to the extent that they forever will be bound to Iran and the Iranian way of doing things.[53] Also, as returnees, they may not adjust to the realities of Iranian society. For they (too often) expect as a right, prestigeful occupational opportunities (usually in the political apparatus, of course) comparable to what they have become accustomed abroad, which do not exist in Iran. And when they do not receive these opportunities, they grumble and create dissatisfaction and political unrest in the society. However, these individuals are not the threat they often are made out to be by Iranians and foreigners. For, first, as long as these individuals stay abroad, and it is freely admitted that Iran has the highest national rate of loss of students sent abroad,[54] at best they are but a nuisance. And, second, when they return to Iran, whether they support or oppose an existing polity, they are not necessarily a potential major ideological threat to Iranian political authority in general, because their education probably will seduce them back into the traditional Iranian political system of gentlemanly, bureaucratic "service." Consequently, regardless of the negative trouble certain students have created, and it has been considerable, yet, it must not be thought that these students are necessarily agents of positive change that many over-enthusiastic economists, political scientists, and sociologists have made them out to be. This premise does not preclude the fact that these students are, or may be, agents of "modernization" and other innovations, as described in Chapter Four, which do not challenge the essentials of the basic Iranian institutional structure. This, in essence, is the significance for the present study of the Iranian education system viewed as an ideological system.

Orthodoxy and Heterodoxy in Iran

As Islam expanded from its original Arabic cultural and social milieu, it encountered many beliefs
and practices which either were not treated in, or
were at variance with, Koranic prescriptions. Consequently, even though Islam, in theory, remained an
"absolute" faith, on the practical level, a decision was soon made to avoid formulating hard and
fast rules of stricture on local beliefs and customs, so as to administer the new followers with a
minimum of friction. Rather, Islam strived to sup-
plant, but not to abolish the religions that pre-
ceded it, by either ignoring or considering as ir-
relevant to the core essentials of the Islamic
faith, many or most local non-Islamic practices.
In time, many of the surviving practices became associated with Islam, or at least with "popular" Islam,
in a particular locality; as for example, the use of
the blue stone for good luck and good health in Iran.
But in cases of obvious dispute, some customs were
accepted and some were not, again dependent on the
locality.[55] For example, consumption of intoxicating
beverages is tolerated in Iran, but consumption of
pork is not, although wild boar, or "nightingale" as
it euphemistically is termed, is eaten by some villagers and tribesmen. This selective, tolerant attitude on matters of custom, and even belief, has earned
for Islam, particularly Shia Islam, as for (continental) Asian religion in general, a reputation of religious toleration not shared by western religion. For
nowhere in (continental) Asian religion did the
western religious concept of radical evil in an all-
inclusive moral system develop. Likewise, selective
tolerance has earned for Asian religion the reputation for accepting easy compromise with the hard
facts of the empirical world, so that inactivity and
passive indifference to the social order takes primacy over positive action in improving the social order (including the economic order). This is in marked
contrast to (western) Christian attitudes on social
reform and economic development.[56]

It is important to appreciate, however, that
Shia Islam and Asian religion in general, religiously
is tolerant as to belief and practice only so far as
belief and practice do not affect the ideological
foundations of the social order as determined by political authority. The Iranian political authority
tolerates such minority religious beliefs as those
of the Jews because Jews and their belief system do

not threaten the structure of Iranian political authority. But that authority is intolerant of the
beliefs and practices of the Bahai'i whose beliefs
political authority believes do threaten its position. It is significant to note that political
authority does not attack the Bahai'i as a _reli-
gious_ movement but as an alleged _political_ cat's
paw of outside conspirators, particularly of the
British, who, the Iranians argue, hope to use the
Bahai'i movement to divide Iranian from Iranian.
Therefore, it must be suppressed as any other _poli-
cally_ subversive movement. Significantly, this
honor of being _the_ politically subversive religion
in Iran is reserved for a group whose membership is
native Iranian. Perhaps this is so because, regardless of its later "universal" dogma, the Bahai'i
grew out of Islam as an Islamic "reform" movement,
and many of its tenets are challenges to Islamic dogma (as, for example, to the Imamte described earlier
in this chapter), which political authority finds
most useful. Consequently, it may be concluded that
the question of orthodoxy and heterodoxy, although
couched in religious (moral) terms, is answered on
the basis of hard, practical, _political_ considerations.

The converse of this conclusion also is of interest; namely, that all (including secular) beliefs
and practices considered to be positive and beneficial to the interests of the political order, automatically have positive religious connotations and
that all (including secular) beliefs and practices
considered to be negative and against the interests
of the political order automatically have negative
religious connotations. For in its "diffused" form,
"general morality" may be substituted for "religion"
in the previous proposition. As concrete illustration of the positive relationship of authority and
general religiously diffused morality, the example
of the relationship of authority to the press may be
cited, and as concrete illustration of the negative
relationship, the example of the relationship of political authority to rumors may be cited.

Because it is assumed that the Iranian press
has a vital positive contribution to make in helping to uphold the moral, political order, the concept of a free press committed to the _objective_ reporting of all _available_ news information is beyond
the comprehension of the Iranian political authority.

For it is reasoned, on the one hand, the press has a
definite moral role to play in society by building
closer contact and trust between the political order
and the people, and, on the other hand, the press
should never allow the political order to look bad
before its own people and Iranian society to look
bad before the world.57 In order to "help" the
press properly to carry out these responsibilities,
the political authority has instituted a series of
press regulations, whose enforcement is very difficult to gauge. Certainly few printers dare print
even a commercial handbill without prior approval of
the police. Yet, newspapers apparently do get too
far out of line, at least as far as the opinion of
the government is concerned, for occasionally issues
are suppressed, sometimes to the protesting surprise
of editors who have considered themselves "cooperative." It was to avert this kind of embarrassment
on both sides that a Press Association also was established. The Association is supposed to align more
closely press staffs with political authority in what
is termed a "logical relationship," in which the press
will know what is expected of it, and consequently,
no deviations from certain standards of conduct established by the political authority are apt to occur.58
It is generally assumed, but obviously never documented, that the polity in order to be doubly sure
of its position, also subsidizes the press and journa-
lists to insure compliance with its wishes regardless
of whether or not a "logical relationship" can be established between the two parties.

Second, the political attitude toward rumors:
That all Iranians are rumor-mongers is widely acknowledged and accepted both by outsiders and by Iranians
themselves. In fact, rumor-mongering has been termed
by some nameless Iranian as the Iranian national pastime. The reason for its prevalence has been variously
attributed, but to the political authority the cause
is obvious and simple: too many Iranians are impatient
with the polity and expect service benefits the polity
cannot offer, especially in these days of economic
"progress" and rising expectations. Consequently,
people are willing to accept all sorts of unfounded
stories as to why those benefits are not forthcoming.59
Rumor-mongering, then, is assumed by the political
authority to be concerned, directly or indirectly,
with discouraging action associated with the policies
of political authority, and hence, in effect, to be
concerned with negative political action. Consequently,

rumor-mongering is not politically innocent, even
though not all rumor mongerings are considered to be
direct agents of some nameless non-orthodox subversive political force, operating either inside or outside Iran. Rumors, then, are considered to be a
dangerous (political) ideology that must be stamped
out with the full weight of political authority. For,
at the least, if authority is successful in suppressing rumors, and thus in suppressing one form of opposition to itself on the ideological level, the
Iranian people will be encouraged to believe, or left
to believe through uncompetitive "news," that the political authority truly is a moral authority and is
meeting its responsibilities properly.[60] And if
the Iranian people are convinced, in consequence,
they will be encouraged to support political authority and will do what is expected of them to build a
strong and prosperous Iran.[61]

The significance of the concepts of religiously
diffused orthodoxy and heterodoxy now may be simply
stated. If a social movement espousing doctrines
that may be contrary to the values of the institutional order, including political authority, were to
appear in Iran, a priori, the movement could be denied access to the legal (that is, the open) channels of communication, including the educational
system, on the grounds that it is morally wanting,
or at least amoral. Its message even could be attacked as rumor-mongering and the movement could be
suppressed as both religiously (or morally) heterodox and politically dangerous. Such was the case
in the nominally religious Bahai'i movement of the
nineteenth century.* But of more immediate concern
to the present study, it is suggested that such would
also be the case with a social movement espousing the
institutionalization of a rational, self-generating
economic system. This, of course, would not insure
the failure of such a movement, but it would make
it immeasurably more difficult for it to succeed.

_____

* For a fuller discussion, see the author's "The
  Bahai'i of Iran and Pariah Entrepreneurship, an
  exploratory paper," reproduced for limited circu-
  lation by the Study Group on Entrepreneurship,
  International Development Research Center, Indiana
  University, 1964.

THE CONCEPT OF "LIMITATIONS" IN LEGITIMATE CHANGE

It is assumed that there must be a distinctive Iranian way to consummate (social) change. Each society, it is argued, has its own distinctive rules for the initiation of change that cannot be transgressed or otherwise the entire social structure will be destroyed. As desirable as a change may be, therefore, if the rules of change are transgressed and, hence, the social order inevitably destroyed in the process, then that change must be rejected. For like Humpty-Dumpty of nursery rhyme fame, once the social order is destroyed, little, if anything, can be done to put the social order together again. However, the rules of change are not intended to discourage change in general; quite the contrary. For reform in Iran, especially today, must go on. The rules, however, establish necessary <u>limitations</u> on change (the limits) under which reform (change) is possible and assured of probable success, while simultaneously avoiding the destruction of the basic fabric of Iranian society in the process.[1]

The specific limits of change are two in number. First, the fundamental <u>morally</u> superior tenets of Iranian society must be preserved at all costs. Significantly, <u>social</u> change must never undermine the social institutions and values which support the peculiar position and role of Iranian <u>political</u> <u>authority</u>, otherwise, it is argued, Iranians will lose their fundamental mooring, and social chaos inevitably will occur.[2] Second, social change must be within the limitations determined by a(ny) morally superior political authority as suitable for the social order at that particular time. Hence, the people should never become impatient, because what change is introduced into Iran by political authority must be in accord with existing social circumstances.

Productive social change may be, first, "mild reform." "Mild reform" implies that regardless of the

exaggerated claims of "dominant personalities," because social change in Iran is extremely difficult
and does not lend itself easily to consummation, when
the time for action occurs, it is best to follow a
more moderate policy, which does not violate the basic
Iranian institutional structure, which must prevail.[4]
But, more drastic social change may be necessary, and
therefore, second, there may have to be a revolution.
Regardless of whether that revolution is violent or
mild (the so-called "white revolution" of the present
polity), and regardless of specifically who directs
that revolution (that is, whether by supporters or
opposers of the existing regime), significantly, it
is some polity that defines the terms of the revolution, decides when it will start, and is involved in
--nay, even directs--all phases of the action. Consequently, a social revolution must depend upon political inspiration and support, and even if drastic
changes are brought about, they must be channeled in
a direction approved by some political order.

The Iranian view of the possible role of outsiders in this process of limited social change is
worth noting. Hanging over the head of every foreign
innovator in Iran is the Iranian's belief that no
foreigner possibly can have any basic sympathy for
or understanding of Iran.[5]* For, the foreigner,
unaware of the Iranian theory of "limited" change,
along with, or instead of the desired material aid
to Iran, forever is providing unsolicited gratuitous
advice of dubious value in the Iranian milieu. And,
also the advice might be motivated very well out of
pretended sympathy for Iran, while its true purpose
is to attempt to use Iran for the foreigners' own
ends, willfully or not, destroying the existing
Iranian social order in the process.[6]

CORRUPTION AND THE CATHARTIC POLITICAL REVOLUTION

The primary cause of social malfunction in Iran
is assumed to be due primarily to the nefarious personal interests of those selfish individuals who manage
to obtain key positions in the structure of political

----

*   If this were true, why this was so would be of
    interest for the Iranians to stop to consider;
    but this is another question.

authority. That is, <u>social</u> problems are the result
of the (a) <u>political</u> (b) <u>corruption</u> of (c) <u>specific
individuals</u>. Consequently, political corruption
must be the prime obstacle to the social change or
social progress which all concede is so necessary in
contemporary Iran. For example, the failure of the
American aid program has been attributed to the
charge that the money has come into the hands of the
politically corrupt. If only the Americans had
listened to the good Iranians, and had taken the
trouble to find out who were the honest, incorrupt-
ible officials in Iran and given them the money,
then the program surely would have succeeded.[7]

Because of this assumed intimate connection between political rectitude and productive social action, it behooves the political authority periodically to ferret out the corrupt and to thwart the
corruption that is holding up the process of productive social change in Iran; an action to which each
specific Iranian government or aspiring government
must be, and nominally is committed. Each new
government, especially, with great fanfare, turns
its initial attention to sweeping out the rot which
is alleged to have permeated the very fiber of the
previous government; otherwise, why would that
regime have had to be overturned?[8] For, unless this
is done, it is assumed that little or nothing much
productively can be accomplished by a new regime,
regardless of the sincerity of the convictions, or,
significantly, of the technical competence of the
new leaders.[9] The corruption of a predecessor
regime may be extended to predecessor regimes in the
indefinite past, if need be, to justify the fact
that nothing much now can be promised in the way of
change; for, since long-standing cancerous corruption exists in the body politic, it will take a long
time to cut it out.[10]

All this concern primarily with the elimination
of corruption as a means to facilitate social change
has been characterized by one observer as a "cathartic revolution," since it seeks solutions to problems by purging decay, rather than by considering
basic institutional reform.[11] Although such a predisposition toward the problem of social change has
certain obvious advantages to Iranian political
authority concerned with preserving a "limits"
theory of social change, it also has created certain
interesting dilemmas. For, by constantly harping on
corruption as <u>the</u> reason for inaction, or inability,

a polity is goaded into purging and purging in order
to save popularity and legitimacy. And, in doing so,
regardless of the merits of each case, wide-spread
purging raises the specter that corruption is widespread, and if so, that it might have institutional
roots. To the thoughtful, this might reflect not
only upon the acceptability of a particular government or regime, but upon the acceptability of the
tenets of Iranian political authority in general,
and even of the Iranian institutional structure as
well. And this attitude, in the Iranian concept of
"limited" legitimate social change, cannot be allowed
to happen.[12] Yet, for the political authority, on
the other hand, to attempt to suppress and contain
anti-corruption, would not only alienate the population on general principles, but in turn, would also
suggest that the polity itself, perhaps, is corrupt,
is not interested in productive social change, and
does not believe its own propaganda that corruption
indeed is at the root of all social evil; which, of
course, would be an admission that it is no longer
worthy to lead Iranian society.

THE CHANNELS OF LEGITIMATE CHANGE

Iranian political authority not only is responsible for defining what constitutes legitimate change,
it also determines the acceptable channels for consummating that change.

These channels have the following characteristics:
first, change in personnel has priority over change
in social structure and process.[13] The reason for
this is given as follows: The signal for the periodic
anti-corruption campaign is the signal for the rolling
of those significant political heads which are associated intimately with the regime (the "cathartic
revolution" of the previous section). In purging the
political ranks of individuals, along with the elimination of the corrupt, it is assumed that all the
corruption associated with the regime also will be
removed. And since political corruption is the source
of social evil, the elimination of the corrupt implies,
in turn, the elimination of inefficiency and procrastination in a government, on the one hand, and popular
dissatisfaction with that polity, and, (it is hoped)
by extension, with political authority and the entire
social structure, on the other hand. By dint of the
same line of argument, in converse, whenever the political apparatus seems to be bogging down with ineffi-

ciency, it is assumed that this is due to corruption.
And the way to eliminate corruption is to eliminate
the corrupt. The corrupt are the individuals now in
public office.

It must be noted that in these arguments no assumption is made that a corrupt free administration
can exist. This notion has practical support among
those Iranian politicians and civil servants who are
ever ready to allege the existence of widespread corruption to justify their own weaknesses and the necessity for frequent changes in personnel to provide
jobs for themselves and for other eager office-
seekers.14 For this reason, it is suggested that it
is the very system of purging the corrupt which encourages and condones the corruption the channel is
supposed to eliminate. For, since no regime is
assumed to be free of corruption and hence is inevitably doomed, and since it is the personnel of the
regime who are personally responsible for the corruption, and, hence who periodically must be purged,
and since those interested in political positions
(and the public at large) are ever eager to assume
that this is true in order to help the purging process along, corruption, and its companions, inefficiency, indifference and indolence are "built into"
political office as officials attempt to take advantage of the assumed temporary nature of the assumed
corruptibility of their office.

(2)   For all these reasons, second, social change in
Iran is assumed to be cyclical and not necessarily
progressive. A new political regime is formed on
the assumption that sufficient members of the corrupt
who have been associated with a previous regime have
been driven from the political temple. Through this
channel at least a diminution, if not an elimination,
of corruption has occurred. Hence, by implication,
an increase in political interest, activity, and
efficiency now can be anticipated. The government
gains the confidence of the people and the social
order properly is served. In time, however, the
members of the new government, in turn, inevitably
are weighed down with personal failings. These failings, of course, are not due to any intrinsic defects
in the political system or the social system, but are
due, rather, to individual weakness and cupidity,
especially, perhaps, among the corrupt left over
from the previous regime(s) who somehow have escaped
detection in the opening ceremonial purge. Unless

all these newly discovered rotten apples are cast
from the political barrel, the regime will become so
bogged down in efficiency that a loss in the momen-
tum of productive political action can be expected.
But the corrupt individuals are not, and cannot be
eliminated. This causes a rise in dissatisfaction
both inside and outside the government. Interest,
activity, and efficiency flag as the corrupt come
more and more to dominate the regime. The government, more and more, loses prestige and confidence
in its ability to serve the interests of political
authority and of the society. The question of
whether or not a new regime, with a change in faces
to ones free of the taint of corruption is necessary,
is raised. The political authority "responds" by
changing the regime. The process begins anew.[15]

Significantly, the alternative implication that,
since all become corrupt in time, then it does not
make any difference who comes to power, cycle after
cycle, and, hence, that institutional, rather than
cathartic change may be needed to remedy Iran's
difficulty, rarely is drawn; apparently not especially by those in the present struggle for social
change. This is because support for the existing
presuppositions concerning social change is aided
and abetted by the hordes of overeager office-
seekers, who, even when they are working to establish a novel polity of their own choosing, do not
desire to change the ground rules of social (including political) action. These political aspirants
justify their position on the grounds that they are
selflessly attempting to replace the corrupt (and by
implication, the inefficient) with the uncorrupt and
efficient--namely, themselves--and that is all that
is needed for productive social change to occur in
Iran.[16] Consequently, political authority (in
possible contrast to a specific polity) need only
worry about finding places for the articulate and
dangerous few (that is, for the potential leaders of
institutional change in the society), inducing them
to serve in apparently influential positions, and
then, isolating and frustrating them. In this way,
in time, inevitably, inefficiency and corruption
surely will be attributed to even the most selfless,
by aspiring officeholders. Then, these potential
sources of non-cathartic change and their doctrines
can be discredited and (cathartically) purged (see
above, Chapter Two).

THE PROCESS OF LEGITIMATE SOCIAL CHANGE

The process of legitimate social change in Iran, as the other aspects of legitimate social change, follows certain predetermined, predescribed rules. These rules may be described as follows:

First, legitimate social change neither is initiated, nor is consummated by the actions of mass social movements. Rather, legitimate social change is the exclusive responsibility of the political authority, who has the exclusive moral right to determine when, and in what way, all legitimate social change will be undertaken. This is so, because the true pulse of the people may not and often is not, known to the people themselves. For only the political authority, by dint of its assumed superior moral and intellectual qualities, is aware of the mass pulse.[17] And hence, only political authority is able to initiate and consummate successfully what is in the best interest of the non-political groupings of the society. For, logically, if these non-politicians know what to do, they wouldn't be in the ranks of the ordinary, but would be members of the political authority.[18]

The political monopoly of initiating and consummating legitimate social change, of course, does not preclude popular participation in the process of social change; in fact, quite the contrary. Often mass participation is considered essential to assure social solidarity and to whip up enthusiasm for the social change policies initiated by political authority. But, at the most, the role of those outside the administrative apparatus, is to pressure the authorities to act wisely in their interest, but the decision as to what is in their interest is not left to non-political initiative.

Consequently, and this is the second process rule of legitimate social change, outside pressure must never "force" political authority to do anything "rash" that it does not want to do or is alternative to what it already had decided to do, before it turned its attention to the masses.[19] For if the masses ever were allowed to pressure for what they wanted, at the least, they would transfer the initiative for social action from the political authority to themselves, and this might open channels to legitimate social change outside approved cathartic

channels. In truth, this is the definition of the
"spontaneous demonstration," so popular in Asian
social action, in which the masses demonstrate on
cue from a political authority, who wishes to drama-
tize impending changes already decided upon. This
type of protest has been termed by certain observers,
"tame criticism," for these demonstrations primarily
are a safety valve for social discontent to insure
that popular resentment for change does not crystal-
lize in non-approved, non-cathartic channels.[20]

A third rule of the process of legitimate social
change in Iran is that individuals, once they have
repented for their social (which to the political
authority are political) sins of attempting to initiate and consummate novel legitimate social change,
are to be accepted fully once again within the pale
of the Iranian society.[21] Such is the case with
those previously mentioned ex-Tudeh (Communists)
rebels who now busily are dream-planning in Plan
Organization (see above, Chapter Three). By avoiding such Western moralisms as radical evil and absolute irrevocable judgements based upon universal
ethical standards, and by concentrating rather upon
judgements of specific individual transgressions of
approved specific rules, the carrot always can be
held out to individuals who are willing to shift
sides. Although this horrifies Westerners, in Iran
this is accepted without malice and as a fact of
life. Since it is the political authority who has
the most inviting carrots in the form of job opportunities and the social and economic benefits attached thereto, desertions of individual causes for
the cause of political authority are not unusual.
Nor is it considered immoral; for what could be more
moral than supporting the most moral force in Iranian
society, the Iranian political authority? It is to
be expected, therefore, or at least political authority hopes so, that sooner or later those who have
attempted to induce change outside of the politically
approved cathartic channels will repent and once
again will be willing to work for change, even change
of the existing regime, within the prescribed channels. And so, as added inducement, the door always
is open to those who repent and recross the threshold
into the circle of the approved.

Those who stand to gain by the existing presuppositions of social change, especially, but not
exclusively, the political authority, are well aware
that all these elaborately constructed rules for the

containment of the process of social change in cathartic channels may go astray. But this kind of
soul searching, unfortunately, is limited to disagreement over specifics, especially whether or not
the existing social order and the existing polity
should or should not be replaced, rather than over
such potentially more crucial questions, such as who,
classwise, initiates social change and the legitimacy
of non-cathartic (that is, institutional) change in
Iranian society.

The conclusion of this chapter now may be stated.
In general, even those Iranians who oppose the existing specific social order, including the existing
specific political order, and intend to overturn
that social (and political) order, and replace it
with a novel social (and political) order, support
the existing ground rules of social change in Iranian
society as much as do those who support the existing
social (and political) order. Hence, those who, potentially, aspire to introduce a rational, self-
generating economic system in Iranian society cannot
hope to be served by either those who support the
existing social order or those who (currently) are in
opposition to it. For they require support for altering the existing ground rules of initiating and consummating social change, before they can hope to
alter the (other) institutions themselves--a formidable task, indeed.

CHAPTER **9** INTERPERSONAL
RELATIONS

INTRODUCTION: THE IRANIAN UNDERDEVELOPED MAN

    To this point, the study has been discussing
Iranian society from the point of view of its institutional structure, or more accurately, from the
point of view of the structure and operation of each
of its social institutions. The author believes that
this discussion is all that is both necessary and
sufficient for purposes of the theoretical analysis
which will follow. However, before entering into
that analysis, it is useful also, first, to consider
Iranian society as a whole (that is, as a single
operating unit) from the vantage point of Iranian
interpersonal social relations which underlie all
the social institutions of Iranian society simultaneously. In doing so, the author wishes to answer
the question of how the social coincidence of being
a member of Iranian society (in general) affects the
social outlook of the "average" or modal Iranian,
whether that Iranian is a lowly peasant or a self-
styled superior bureaucrat, as a flesh and blood
human being interacting with other human beings in
Iranian society.* The quest then may be considered
to be an attempt to define the Iranian social personality; that is, personality as the institutional
sociologist views personality and not as either the
psychologist or the culture-personality anthropolo-

_____

*   The questions of the validity of the concept
    "national character" and of defining the aver-
    age (or modal) individual in a society, are too
    complex to be discussed here; see for example,
    Kluckhohn, C., Marray, and Schneider,
    Personality in Society, Nature, and Culture,
    various editions. Suffice to state here, im-
    portantly, the discussions of this chapter do
    not purport to say something of the social
    personalities of all Iranians.

gist views personality. For the question to be
answered is, what is it in the web of accepted interpersonal social relationships in Iranian society
that produces the probability that Iranians will
interact with other Iranians in certain characteristic social patterns rather than in other characteristic social patterns, and of what consequence are
these patterns for social action, including potential economic developmental action?

By way of introduction it is to be said, first,
that from the point of view of the social scientist,
it is assumed that Iranians potentially are capable
of creating and using any interpersonal relationship
patterns ever devised, including creating and using
those interpersonal relationship patterns conducive
to doing the kinds of things the Iranians claim they
want to do; especially, to develop a self-generating
economic system in the society. But it is obvious
to both outside observers and to the Iranians themselves, that the interpersonal relationship patterns
now being generally employed in Iranian social action
are not adequate to service constructive ends.
Although Iran certainly has the material resources
and other economic advantages in developing a self-
generating economic system, and even though the
"need" exists, and rapid changes are being made in
the material, and to some extent, the non-material
cultural aspects of Iranian life, yet, its people
do not now have available the interpersonal social
relations necessary to accomplish productive economic goals. To explain why this is so in terms of
the principles of interpersonal relations underlying Iranian society in general, is in fact, to
describe the man of the economically underdeveloped
society that is Iranian society. Or to rephrase,
it is to describe the Iranian underdeveloped man; a
man who is forced by the imperatives of the institutional structure to carry on his interpersonal
relations under a mandate that is personally,
socially, and economically unrewarding.

Briefly, this chapter will strive to demonstrate
the following thesis. Economic development in Iran
is not possible without social development; that is,
economic development is not feasible without the
maximization of the productive potential of the
relationships between human beings in Iranian society.
Hence, activation of psychological motivations con
ducive to economic development are not feasible wi
out the development of structures of interpersonal

relations and of supporting institutions that facilitate rather than impede such motivations. For, to
expect individuals to be motivated "rationally" in
Iranian society, so that they, and their motivations,
will change Iranian society, as the argument goes to
some, is to ignore the dynamics of the ground rules
of Iranian society. For, in one sense, Iranians are
responding rationally, and perhaps in the only way
feasible, to the existing ground rules, and
they would be responding irrationally, or at least,
non-rationally, if they followed what is rational in
terms of a developed or developing society. When the
fact is faced that it is these social ground rules
that must be changed, the acceptance of motivations
conducive to the development of a self-generating
economic system among the broad spectrum of Iranians
certainly will not be as difficult to achieve as is
now the case.

THE BASIC INSECURITY OF THE INDIVIDUAL

The Iranian individual, regardless of his
specific position in the hierarchy of social stratification, save possibly for those few at the very
apex of that hierarchy, constantly is reacting or
responding to a social environment in overwhelming
and continuous crisis, and no relief exists from the
pressure of this. This has resulted in the lack of
stable, coherent acknowledged patterns by which individuals can assuredly anticipate the behavior of
others. Consequently, any individual is not provided
with any reasonable assurance that if he behaves in a
particular way toward a particular individual or
toward a particular object, that he can expect a particular reaction in turn, save that the reaction will
be unanticipated and unpredictable, and probably to
his disadvantage. The Iranians' personal adjustments
to the social environment, then, are very poor.
Individuals cling desperately to patterns of behavior
which are acknowledged to be inadequate at the least,
and which at the most succeed only in generating
more insecurity with similar counteraction in a syndrome of accelerating rigid, inadequate, and frustrating behavior.[1] A self-generating system of economic development may not exist in Iran, but certainly
few deny that a self-generating system of personal
insecurity in all interpersonal relations does exist.

Consequently, self-reinforcement looms large in the motivational design of Iranians. Yet, because the Iranian understands how hollow and false this praise must be, he feels he must reject as insincere what he most seeks to hear, in order to protect himself from what he believes will be an inevitable dissolutionment when others reject him. The Iranian, then, to be on the safe side, either readily accepts the worst possible interpretation of the actions of others or anticipates the worst from possible, not even probable actions of others. In this line of reasoning, others always are guilty, unless proven innocent.

Consequently, Iranians are very susceptible to rumors and are notorious rumor-mongers. This is so, Iranians claim, because in spite of the oft spoken assertion that intellectually they are too clever to be taken in by anyone, they must be sure not to be caught napping since the worst might occur.[2] Rumor-mongering is a powerful and well used counter-means in Iran to create social situations for one's personal advantage; as for example, to gain economic advantage in the market place.[3] The probable success of such action is predicted on the assumption that any story, no matter how ridiculous, might be believed if it is at all possible, and to the average Iranian, anything, expecially anything bad, is possible. Fears of the possible, and not even the probable, lead but to preventive counter moves. For example, "X" who doesn't want "Y" to affect situation "Z", may move first to thwart "Y" before he has a chance (to note, often only the feared chance) to affect "Z".[4] Since "Y" never may have intended, or been able to affect "Z" in the first instance, "X" can always feel that it has been his actions that were responsible for the fact that nothing devastating occured; that, indeed, "X" is as clever as Iranians are supposed to be.

The significance of the discussion is as follows: Iranians attempt to seek solutions to their problems of security within the system, (that is, by outsmarting the other fellow), no matter how impossible logically this is to accomplish; and most Iranians admit that it is impossible. Both the basic insecurity of Iranian interpersonal relations and the way in which Iranians attempt to satisfy the problem are inconsistent with the calculable, interpersonal relationships and positive mastery of problems so necessary for the formation of a rational, self-generating economic system in Iran.

THE ISOLATION OF THE INDIVIDUAL

Iranian individualistic behavior is legendary.
There is a famous tale about Kosrovi, the medieval
author-philosopher. Kosrovi had raised the ire of
the clergy for certain anti-religious sentiments in
his writings, and the religious leaders organized a
party to kill him. When the party came to his house,
Kosrovi offered to submit if the party would nomi-
nate a single individual to kill him. Each member
of the party, eager for the prestige to be gained
by killing the famous Kosrovi, disputed who would
be the one to carry out the decision. In the anticipated confusion, the clever Kosrovi escaped. The
story may be apocryphal, but the moral is authenti-
cally Iranian, for it has many attested modern
counterparts; as for example, when, some would-be
"inventors" dreaming of success, become bitter
enemies over a conflict as to how to share future,
imaginary, profits.[5]

Quite clearly, Iranian individualism contrasts
with the individualism of the developed societies in
which autonomy coexists with a sense of responsibility to others. In the case of Iran, rather,
autonomy coexists with irresponsibility and with an
attempt to avoid any possible entrapping personal
commitment to others. This is because each man is
assumed to have "personal interests" which justifiably
can be and probably are, indifferent if not hostile
to the interests of those about him, even in those
cases in which individuals claim to be committed to
cooperative effort. Individualism, then, is license
for striving for one's interest in any way possible,
and for as long as one can serve those interests.[6]
Consequently, in any group action, betrayal or at
least the fear of betrayal is commonplace. Consequently, individual self-seeking, more often than not
is self-defeating, for no other reason than that,
logically, few can gain in a jungle where all must
claw for a place at the precipitous ledge of the
illusionary security (discussed in the previous section). Iranian interpersonal relations, then, operate
in a way that potentially each individual will be
isolated. For Iranian individualism deprives anyone
of the security of knowing that, when the chips are
down, colleagues will be ready to defend the potentially isolated. It is for this reason that no one

shares any phase of his work or of his true self, especially his weaknesses, for such knowledge readily could be used against one in the individualistic showdown that inevitably will come to all men. In such an atmosphere, of physical and psychological isolation and precarious security, the individual is convinced he stands alone and must be out for what he can get, when, or so long as, he can get away with it. For, indeed, in Iran one must do in others before they can do one in. For example, villagers will strive to rush their crops to market before other villagers (even from their own village) are able to do so, in the hopes of obtaining an early, most favorable price; even though in the ensuing scramble, the majority inevitably must lose out by selling at depressed prices (which, ironically, may be the case for the favored villagers the next time around).

Consequently, in sum, social action which depends on good cooperative interpersonal relations is extremely difficult to consummate in Iran. Constant confusion exists in organizations as individuals get in each other's way and panic in any crisis. This was reported at Lar, after the 1960 earthquake, when the supply of relief clothing which was made available in adequate quantities for all, was ripped to pieces in the mad scramble to serve oneself no matter what, out of the fear that since someone usually profits to another's disadvantage, it had better be oneself who profits. And so, not without good reason, the Iranian has come to believe that if it is at all possible it is best to try to accomplish what he wants to do alone, and in isolation. For, since an individual may pursue his own interests as he sees fit, any task necessarily is complicated by supposed joint effort. Or, to quote a local proverb, "one Iranian is worth eight foreigners, but two Iranians are worth only four foreigners."

It is worthwhile to discuss the interpersonal relations of the Iranian family since the topic has direct bearing on the question of the isolation of the individual in Iranian society. The Iranian family is represented by many Iranians as the sole surviving source of security, cooperative mutuality, succor, and selfless social action in Iranian society; in contrast to the general society in which more and more, the universal (that is, treat-all-alike) values of self-interest in interpersonal

relations are becoming the rule. It cannot be denied that, if forced to make the choice, Iranians
will prefer to work within the kinship unit, for no
other reason than that to Iranians, interpersonal
relations appear more secure when carried on among
those whose behavior is known. However, it must be
appreciated that the security offered in inter-
familial interpersonal relations, in contrast to
that offered outside the family, is relative only.
For, if such claimed security exists at all, it
exists in individual, specific cases and not as the
general rule of behavior. Even a cursory survey of
the actual state of affairs in inter-familial relations in Iran demonstrates that the same pattern of
values holding in the general society, by which individuals treat everyone, stranger or kin, alike, as
it suits their own selfish purposes, holds as well
within the family. For both inside as well as outside the family, the Iranian attempts to impose on
others or to escape impositions on himself in the
very same way. And when the individual is rebuffed
or out-maneuvered within the family, in the same
manner as he is outside the family, he cannot but
consider his family circle as of the same order as
his circle of "friends," or as the circle of strangers, with whom he comes into contact in his attempts, in the larger society, to influence others
or avoid the influence of others on himself in turn.
In his family circle, then, the Iranian must learn
to live in a world, which, although it is one of
intimacy, also is one of duplicity. Consequently,
he also must anticipate potential disaster before
it happens within the family, and to protect himself
materially and psychologically in much the same way
as he does in the general social environment. Some
typical instances of family problems, which reflect
the same order of interpersonal counter-moves in the
larger society, follow, by way of examples of this
thesis.

(1) The Marriage of Convenience, in which the
husband tries to force a divorce on terms that he
will not have to return the dowry (mahar), which
leads to bitter inter-family squabbling.[7]

(2) The Attempt to Exploit Other Members of
One's Family for One's Own Ends, in which a man with
three good-looking married sisters, believes he is
entitled to economic support by his brothers-in-law.[8]

(3) <u>Indifference to the Individual Needs of</u> <u>Others in the Family</u>, in which a relative, even a parent, is willing to accept payment from another suitor of a girl to break an existing engagement to marry.[9]

(4) <u>Mistrust Within the Family</u>, in which the family patriarch is slandered in an inter-family land feud.[10]

(5) <u>Indifference to Family Sentiment</u>, in which a critically ill man in the hospital, who, learning of his wife's death, comes home to secure her belongings against possible other claimants, and then returns to his hospital bed.[11]

(6) <u>Revenge for the Loss of Family Honor</u>, and <u>Indifference to the Personal Interests of the Alleged</u> <u>Offenders, who Even May be Killed to Wipe Clean the</u> <u>Disgrace</u>, in which a mother who tries to find a missing virginal daughter on the night of her disappearance is indifferent to her when she is found three months later deserted by her male betrayer; that is, at a time when no cash value is attached to her because of her loss of virginity.[12]

(7) <u>Material Betrayal</u>, in which children attempt to steal a will out of the fear, and not the fact, that they will be disinherited by a father who has taken a new wife.[13]

Undoubtedly, all these problems exist in all societies, perhaps in some societies even to a greater degree than in Iran; and conversely, undoubtedly, many Iranian families are free of most, if not all, of these problems. But these caveats certainly do not preclude the fact that the Iranian family is not a universal, solidary front of social and psychological security for the individual; and, in fact, is the contrary. Consequently, because fundamentally the Iranian is isolated within the family, in much the same way as he is without the family in the larger society, it can be maintained as a general principle, that the individual Iranian stands alone. And, to be sure, even if he is fortunate enough not to have to stand alone, either within or without the family, he has learned through bitter experience to expect that this might happen at any time; again, either within or without the family. Hence, as far as the average Iranian is concerned,

to depend on one's family any more than to depend on
any other solidary relationship in the society for
one's security is to build on sand. And, by implication, for the Iranian to be able to count on his
interpersonal relationships within or without the
family with any calculable degree of security save
probability that those relationships are, or can
become insecure at any time, likewise is to build
(here economically) on sand.

THE AUTHORITARIAN RELATIONSHIP BETWEEN INDIVIDUALS

Given the isolation of individuals and the
lack of cooperative, responsible interpersonal
relations in the society, Iranians argue that only
an authoritarian relation between strong leaders
and unwilling followers, who resist discipline, can
accomplish anything.

Consequently, although all Iranians prefer to
believe that they are born leaders, they concede
that it often is necessary to accept a pattern of
servility to superiors in return for the obligation
of these superiors to care for dependent inferiors.[14]
As in the case with other patterns of Iranian interpersonal relations, however, this faith in authoritarianism is misplaced and often is betrayed, for
superiors fail to care for dependents, and dependents fail to live up to obligations to superiors
whenever possible. But quite typically, as chronic
complainers, who do not, or cannot do anything
positive to solve their interpersonal problems,
Iranians maintain these unrewarding patterns with
great rigidity, although simultaneously they have
widespread resentment against authority, all authority, just below the surface. It is for this reason
that although Iranians always are grumbling against
those in authority, at the same time, they formally
are servile to them. It is doubtful that those on
any particular level of the hierarchial ladder are
impressed by these formal acts of obsequiousness,
for they too are carrying out the same formal ritual
with their own superiors. And, consequently, since
Iranians believe with good reason, that formal,
surface conformity cannot be trusted, they conclude
that authoritarian control is the only reliable
means to insure compliance, which completes the
vicious circle. For although authoritarianism is
accepted as the best of a bad situation because of

the prevailing suspicion and lack of cooperation and
responsibility of Iranians, the possibility seems to
have escaped Iranians that these very conditions
also are encouraged by authoritarianism which frustrates "individualistic" subordinates, and obtains
at best only surface conformity to superiors. Also
outside the range of possibility is that the willingness of superiors to accept surface conformity as
true conformity from followers, regardless of the
true state of interpersonal relations between leader
and followers, can but encourage the continuation of
non-conformity and irresponsibility among subordinates.[15]

The validity of these observations may be demonstrated by the ubiquitous office conference. The
average Iranian soon learns to appreciate that decisions will be made and enforced exclusively by those
in position of superiority in spite of the possible
existence of formal conferences or meetings to discuss interpersonal actions.* Consequently, in conferences, the kinds of topics discussed are limited
and basic policy never is decided. Yet conferences
are held because, it is claimed, the decision-makers
in the group must always have a chance to act on
"alternatives," even though ridiculous alternatives
are suggested. In this game of proposing mock
solutions, the illusion of authoritarian infallibi-
lity by the decision-making superior is reinforced.
The ordinary participants, because their "suggestions"
have not been accepted, once again, ceremonially are
removed from the area of responsibility and the
alleged decision-makers are excused from responsibility, because they may not receive the proper
information (the "good alternatives") upon which to
act. All this is true, for in accord with the principle of surface conformity, long-winded and pointless speeches take the place of true discussion.
But, once again, the justification, in reality, is
the cause of the problem; for it is argued by

---

*   The word "conference" in the Iranian language was
    introduced from the French and not the English
    language. Consequently, it has both French mean-
    ings of a formal consultation (also its English
    meaning) and a lecture (its exclusive French mean-
    ing). Within the authoritarian frame of reference
    discussed here, it has especially the latter mean-
    ing.

inferiors that it is pointless to make positive suggestions which only will be ignored.

Two implications. First, Iranians tend to avoid contracting interpersonal obligations of any sort, since such obligations only increase the possibility of being required to act without any opportunity to participate in the formulation of the terms of the actions. In general, Iranians try to accept commitment only for obvious, immediate gain with the expressed privilege of withdrawing whenever self-interest no longer is served. In this sense, Iranians may be said to be speculators with human beings as much as they are with objects, for they will refuse to fulfill obligations with people, whenever better opportunities arise, as readily as they will with objects in the market place.

Second, since an individual has no choice in formulating the essential features of his enforced (authoritarian) obligations, he tends to choose rather how effectively he will carry out these obligations. Usually this means trying to maintain a minimum of personal responsibility in order to extricate quickly if the situation becomes unusually odius. "Why should I bother, it is not my job," the Iranian pleads. He parries with the phrase, "If God is willing"; perhaps tomorrow it will be possible to accomplish the task, he says. But in effect, he means, perhaps tomorrow it will be possible that you either will forget about the task or be too discouraged to ask again about it.[16] Whenever accountability for inaction is inevitable,[17] the Iranian tries to hide in collective responsibility which diffuses the punishment and perhaps also the chance to find the responsible party. He clothes himself in technicalities; for example, an injured person is rejected from the hospital on the pretext that the patient has not appeared at the hospital in the proper vehicle.[18] He talks aimlessly and avoids a direct answer; for to be obscure is to be ignored, or to cover one's inaction in advance.[19] He simply runs away to less onerous action whenever possible. And, finally, he claims not to "understand" instructions from a superior. In this tactic, accountability remains with the decision-maker, because if the instructions are carried out, but fail for any reason, failure can be attributed to the bad instructions of the decision-maker. In the authoritarian situation, obviously, followers are not asked to accept or reject, but only to conform, and the only

way out of onerous obligations is through incapacity.
To admit one cannot implement reflects on the inferior, not on the superior. But not to understand
what has to be done reflects not upon the inferior,
who claims to be eager to carry out commands, but
upon the superior, who is unable to understand and
communicate what the problem is. This is effective
because, especially in Iran, being a poor communicator is a sign of inferiority, whereas "good
speakers," even those who never have anything concrete to offer, are held in high prestige.*

To conclude, Iranian authoritarian interpersonal relationships work effectively, if at all,
only for very limited goals, involving limited numbers of people, under direct "supervision," and
most significantly, for only limited periods of
time. A developed economy, dependent upon a hierarchy of individual responsibility and authority,
for long periods of time, cannot work successfully
with such ground rules.[20] Although this problem is
one of the most crucial problems of Iranian economic
development, no serious consideration is given to
the possibility that it might be the patterns of
interpersonal social relationships themselves,
rather than sporadic individual failing, that is at
fault. Consequently, most Iranians, rather, forever
are attempting to justify continuing the existing
unrewarding authoritarian interpersonal relationships,
on the grounds that Iranian inferiors never cooperate
and only malinger, especially in those cases in which
their support is a necessity to consummate those
social and economic actions required to develop Iran.

---

*   That being labeled a "poor communicator," consequently, might not have any basis in reality
often is lost on foreign advisors in Iran, who
accept the Iranian suggestion at face value that
many operational difficulties are due to "poor
communication" with locals. The foreigners fail
to see that they are not working in the same
situation as "back home," where it is assumed
that subordinates will be motivated profession-
wise, or money-wise, to carry out the suggestions
of superiors, once they understand what their
obligations are, and why the job has to be done.

THE ROLE OF IRANIAN INTELLECT AND PERSONAL
ADVANTAGE IN INTERPERSONAL RELATIONS

In Iran, each individual is very much on his own in a society which has not been able to provide for individual security and in which loyalty and responsibility are absent. And so, individuals do not see merit in acting with "other-interest" as well as "self-interest" in anticipation that such actions toward others most probably will be reciprocated. In consequence, (and in consequence of the implications of the discussion of authoritarianism of the previous section as well) no individual, internalized norms of responsibility have developed in Iran. For example, to recall, instead of encouraging the development of personal responsibility and individual ethics to prevent sex abuse, Iranian society has relied rather upon the surveillance of women. For it is assumed that all individuals will seek their own sexual "self-interests" if at all given the physical opportunity.[21]

For all these reasons, Iranians claim that it is not that they basically are distrustful or that they prefer the interpersonal relations to be the way they are, but that since no basis for altruistic trust exists in Iranian society, they can but respond accordingly to protect themselves; or, as more than one Iranian has expressed himself on the matter, "If I am trustful, I will only be taken advantage of by others." And the Iranians can always cite instances in which the trusting, not only have not been appreciated, but have been made out to be the unwilling dupes by the selfishly clever. For example, the kind shopkeeper who goes to buy some medicine for an ill customer, returns to find his store robbed.[22] No wonder Iranians are trained, if only by experience, to be skeptical of all claims,[23] to look for deviousness and deception behind all action, and especially to mistrust those who claim to be "sincere,"[24] to be cynical of all "neutrals" who serve as go-betweens,[25] never to expect others in an interpersonal situation to reveal true motives, lest they become vulnerable to manipulation; in brief, to expect that others always will act to gain advantage of one and that if one attempts to ignore this basic pattern, and act selflessly, the results only can be useless, pointless, and even downright dangerous to one's precarious security.

And so, with full justification as far as the
Iranians are concerned, intellect must be employed
in the service of personal advantage and in the
service of plotting and counter-plotting to thwart
the actual and anticipated plots of others. Iranians
always have been famous for their quick intellect,
especially their ability to survive by their wits.
But too often, the plotters are "too clever" and outsmart only themselves. For example, a young man who
kills another in a dispute, buys a fake birth certificate to try to prove he is underage in the hopes
of cheating the law; but the fraud is discovered and
the youth is punished.[26] To Iranians such stories
are not examples of an irony of fate, but of the
tragedy of the Iranian man in the Greek sense. For
Iranians believe that, no matter how hard they try,
they never will be able to extricate themselves from
this fatal web of unrewarding social relationships
that is their social heritage.

Under such conditions, the Iranian can but
believe that the ends always justify the means,
since it is his security, even his survival, that is
at stake in every interpersonal confrontation.
Piling up virtuous acts, by foregoing personal advantage, is for those privileged to be Imams, (that
is, saints) who are acknowledged to be far removed
from the world of Iranian social reality.[27] Even
more, to be moral in situations of potential personal advantage is but to court disaster. For the
Iranians argue that an opponent is unlikely not to
take advantage, especially if one is foolish enough
to trust and forego personal advantage in such a
situation. This is so because it is clear to an
Iranian that if an individual does not act to serve
his own advantages, he will not act to serve his own
vital security interests.

From this point of view, it is only one step
in Iranian thinking to expect personal advantage in
all social action, and to reason that unless personal
advantage can be realized, considering the risks to
one's security involved in any social act, a particular act probably is not worth the effort. For
example, two drivers whose vehicles collide are busy
trying to outfox each other on damage claims until
they realize that they both are driving government
vehicles, and hence, are not personally liable for
damage. Immediately, passionate interest in responsibility dies.[28] And further, if an action has been
suggested by another, the suggester probably is

desirous of action solely because it is to his personal advantage. For example, it turns out that a
teacher who generously volunteers to tutor his weak
students, expects a good "fee" for his services. As
further inducement to receive a satisfactory fee, he
suggests that the tutoring will "insure" that the
more backward students will be brought up to the
pass grade.[29]

This basic insecurity of Iranian interpersonal
relations which enables the man of intellect to seek
to serve his personal advance, gives rise to endless
haggling. If one is clever enough, the Iranian believes, one may be able to obtain advantage, upon
advantage until the ultimate is reached. And in
Iranian society, where the opportunities of tomorrow,
to say the least, are uncertain, one must frantically
press the opportunities of today.[30]

One of the most interesting of Iranian responses
to the nexus of personal insecurity and anticipated
personal advantage seeking by others is the preventive counter-thrust, or initial, successful strike,
before an enemy, or alleged enemy, has his chance.
It is accepted that he who strikes first, regardless
of the merits of the attack, puts his opponent at a
decided disadvantage. This is so because truth is
assumed to be on the side of the attacker. For, the
Iranian reasons that, if, in like token, the opposition had a potentially believable case, it probably
would have attacked first.[31] This view is held by
most Iranians, even in the face of situations in
which the counter-thrust demonstrably is ridiculous and easily disproved, placing the accuser in an
even more vulnerable position than perhaps he was in
previously (the Iranian tragedy once again), and in
which clearly, the new difficulty would not have
occurred if the individual had not tried to be overly
clever and take advantage of someone else in the
first instance. For example, a wife accuses her
husband of insanity in order to get hold of his money
for her lover, a charge easily disproved, and leading
to a divorce.[32]

Confidence rackets thrive in situations in which
people believe that they are too intelligent to be
fooled, yet that they are intelligent enough and
eager to outsmart others; and all Iranians believe
that they are such individuals, more out of necessity
than out of arrogance. And so, even "sophisticated"

students complain of fraudulent employment agencies who promise to send them abroad or otherwise cut employment corners for them. Significantly, the confidence man demonstrates the absence of trust in interpersonal relations. As a famous American comic once stated, "You can't cheat an honest man." The "honest man," to be sure, is a man with a basic trust in his fellow inter-actors, living in a society whose institutions reinforce and encourage interpersonal relations of trust; hardly Iranian society.[33]

To draw the basic conclusion of this section, in sum, given the fundamental institutional nature of Iranian society, no basis exists for establishing reasonable trust and reciprocal, calculable self-interest in social action--that is, the confidence that self-interest and other-interest operating in the same direction are productive. Consequently, Iranians are convinced that they can insure minimum security and reciprocal expectancy in interpersonal relations only through bribery, blackmail, or especially guile. When hardy individuals attempt to "break through" this vicious circle of mutual distrust and personal advantage-seeking by attempting to introduce reasonable trust into their interpersonal relations, these individuals are treated with suspicion, scorn, and even taken advantage of, until they become disillusioned in turn, and succumb to the accepted patterns of social behavior.

RIGIDITY IN INTERPERSONAL RELATIONS

The isolation of the individual and the basic insecurities inherent in the pattern of social interaction in Iranian society, to reiterate, have made the Iranian extremely cautious about committing himself to any social action. For action, any action, conceivably may lead one into difficulties and even disaster. A favorite proverb reads, "The water-trench (jube) is a better source of water than is the river, because it is slower and more reliable than the river; in consequence, the water-trench is more useful. The river, on the other hand, is fast, yes; but it gives out quicker than the water-trench; hence is less reliable, and thus is less useful." Risk in Iran, then, is associated with rashness. And within the Iranian social context, this, undoubtedly, is true. The individual from the developed society, who loses his patience with the Iranian,

often forgets that his risk taking is both feasible
and often rewarding only because that risk taking
can take advantage of a social framework in which
reasonable assurance of interpersonal relations
exists, and hence, calculable odds of the probable
success of social action can be made. But in Iran,
such reasonable, calculable assurance does not
exist. Hence, to place one's trust in one's interpersonal relations in the process of social action,
not only courts betrayal, it courts failure. And,
consequently, to volunteer to act, that is, to risk,
certainly is to court disaster deliberately. Initiative, then, is associated with rashness, and is
the philosophy of the foolhardy. And, once again,
the Iranian can point to evidence in the operation
of his society to support his position.[34]

This fear to commit one's self voluntarily
(to risk), implies that the Iranian is inflexible
and rigid in his social action. Normally, he prefers to follow time-tested routines which, he hopes,
even if they are not effective, certainly will help
keep him out of unnecessary trouble with his fellow
men. But in situations of social stress, when
these routines may be denied to him, he is at a
loss as to what to do. This is true not always
because he is unable to solve his social action
problems, but because he deliberately prefers,
rather, not to try to solve the problems, in the
conviction that improvised solutions only will get
him further into difficulty. This especially is the
case at present, in which social and economic challenges have shaken and even terrorized the unpre-
pared Iranian because they demand flexible, adaptable responses to a novel and rapidly changing
social environment. Often heard nowadays is the
remark that life is moving too quickly for the
Iranian to handle.[35] Such turmoil to the Iranian
cannot be the challenge of wonderful potentiality
that it is to the individual in the developed society;
to the Iranian such challenges are but a beacon from
the pit of disaster. And so often in panic, the
Iranian retreats into the mechanical repetition of
those familiar social action and interpersonal relationship patterns which, even though obviously ill-
adapted to the novel problems of the changing environment, at the least, can be counted upon not to get
him further in difficulty. These reactions, then,
may be best thought of as a form of magical manipulation, or ritual, which, although they no longer have

any empirical validity (if they ever had), at least, extricate the Iranian from the charge, of the foreigner in particular, that he is doing nothing to solve his problems.[36] To challenge these ill-adapted, rigid patterns, as outsiders have learned, results in displaced aggression against the challenger, whom it is said fails to understand Iran and Iranian ways. And certainly this is true insofar as the outsider is unaware of the insecure system of interpersonal relations which the Iranian must employ in his social acts.

Another facet of the problem of social rigidity: Rigidity also is reflected in the Iranian's inability to understand that intellect is more than the cultivation of rote mastery of the concrete, and that intellect is not nurtured only through the accumulative, additive knowledge of age and experience in human interpersonal relations. This has two major implications. First, the Iranian concept of human relations has been developed to enable the individual to be a success, or at least to get by, in a stable society in which social action primarily is the manipulation of beings in interpersonal relationships. All outsiders agree that the Iranians are masters in their own diabolical, non-constructive way of handling interpersonal relations. But in a society committed to the development of an ever changing, self-generating economic system, based on trust and flexibility in interpersonal relations, this kind of intellect not only is useless but also is an obstacle. Second, the Iranian's cognitive belief that the concrete only, in and of itself, is what really matters, tends to associate whatever absolute values the Iranian has inevitably with (existing) concrete ways of doing things. Under such circumstances, it is extremely difficult to persuade him to adjust his existing interpersonal relations and social actions, simply on the basis of responding to new challenges in the environment. For the Iranian is apt to see principles, especially principles of his "sacred culture" involved in every new challenge in the environment, when in fact principles are not involved at all, only the need to devise new concrete ways of doing things.[37] At the same time, second, because of this same association of absolute standards with the existing concrete ways of doing things, the Iranian has no generalized absolute standard with which to justify beforehand and automatically respond to novel, and as yet unforeseen chal-

lenges of an ever changing environment. The Iranian's only generalization, perhaps, is that the new
involves new chances for something to go wrong, or
someone bad to confront, and within the Iranian
social frame of reference, he is not far wrong.
This brings us full circle to the opening remarks
of this section.

FANTASY, REALITY, AND FAITH IN INTERPERSONAL RELATIONS

The individual Iranian, isolated, insecure,
rigid, and subject to the whims of authoritarian
interpersonal relationships, has developed a series
of mechanisms to protect himself. The mechanisms,
at best, make life bearable, but they do not engender
either satisfactory or personally rewarding interpersonal relationships, or, more significantly perhaps, dissatisfaction enough, and of an order, to
encourage challenge of the existing patterns of
interpersonal relations.

The first mechanism to be discussed is that of
the lack of separation of radical reality and radical fantasy, so that the two concepts are combined
into a grey area in which neither pure reality nor
pure fantasy exists (in the Iranian language,
"dastan").[38] In this way, the Iranian can talk in
terms of lofty ideals, while at the same time his
interpersonal relations and social actions may be
considerably less than ideal, and he does not have
to worry about reconciling the two. And he is very
resentful of those who do point out any such discrepancies, for as the Iranian proverb has put it,
"If you know it, why talk about it."

But, at the same time, to recall, the Iranian,
of necessity, must be "realistic" as safeguard
against the "realistic" conduct of others. For he
must be ever ready to anticipate and expect evil
from others or face the practical consequences of
betrayal. Under such conditions, the Iranian recon-
ciles what is, and what he would like to be, by
simply accepting reality (hypocrisy) in others, yet
insisting that he himself be judged on the basis of
his superior moral, internal intent.[39] It is for
this reason, for example, that although highly moral-
istic pronouncements are expected (moral intent),
they are discounted immediately as nonsense by any
audience (reality).[40] Thus, the Iranian is a "cynic"

(in our frame of reference) because he attributes
hypocrisy to every noble pronouncement and nobly
enshrouded act of others. And, in truth, since
views give rise to reality, as readily as views reflect reality, it must be conceded that the very
noblest of Iranian sentiments often are apt to be
evoked for the most dastardly of interpersonal conduct; and, in this sense the Iranian is a realist.[41]
In turn, the Iranian reacts to the (probably true)
charge of others that he is guilty of the same kind
of high-minded talk and low-minded action that he
denounces in others, yet still preserves his belief
in his moral intent, simply by separating his inner-
self and his outer-self. In this way, he maintains
the absolute integrity of his inner world of morally
pure motives, while he is permitted to respond
realistically to the crass, material world of empirical, inter-personal relations and social actions
(a sort of personal, moral, rule by model or
Imamate).[42] For, the Iranian argues, Iranian society
being what it is, rarely is it possible for one to
express one's inner ideal motives. Rather, one can
only hope to fulfill one's high-minded (inner)
desires only if and whenever the situation presents
itself, which may be rare, if ever, in Iran. On
second thought, probably it is not even wise to
verbalize such inner thoughts, lest others abuse
one's moral sense and corrupt it, or at least use
it for nefarious advantage.

        The Iranian, then, thinks and acts in two
worlds, a world of absolute ethical standards (the
inner-self) and a world of no ethical standards
(the outer-self) which is subject to an empirical
test of power and wits. But he must protect the
outer-self in this social jungle of all against all.
For it is realized that unless the outer-self is
protected satisfactorily, the wall around the inner-
self may be breached and, that breach may evade the
last stronghold of individual security. Iranian
society, being Iranian society, protection of outer-
self cannot be absolute, but certain ground rules
can and have been developed so that individuals can
get along with each other without creating unnecessary friction among themselves in the outer world;
and especially so that the inner-self, the true-
self, will never be placed on the attacking block
of the realistic world. These rules make up the
world of the outer-self, a world of formalized
interpersonal relations, completely devoid of those

ethical considerations associated (solely) with the
inner-self. In this way, on the one hand, since
ethics are not involved in any social act, the morality of the inner-self is not an issue in the empirical world. And, on the other hand, the self involved
in interpersonal relations and social actions in the
real world, in effect, is but an actor in a formalized social game of ritualized rules which are judged
proper or improper, but not morally good or bad.
And, in this formalized game, the actor wears a protective mask for his hidden, true-inner self, which
may be termed his "face."

The significance of face, for purposes of the
present study, is, first, that face emphasizes form
over substance. For, doing something properly according to the accepted rules takes precedence over
such inner-self ethical considerations as the intent
and the meaning of one's actions. Talk of motives
and principles in the real world only bore, if not
irritate most Iranians who prefer to relegate these
considerations to the inner-self world of fantasy,
which is expressed, most typically, as poetry.
Consequently, in economic action programs, for example, Iranians are interested primarily in what
is going to be done and especially in formal blue
prints. Such considerations as what the project
may mean in terms of generating economic development
in general, in terms of teaching generalized principles of organization, and in terms of new social-
interpersonal relations, are considered out of bounds,
for no other reason than that such considerations
refer to the arena of the inner-self. Also relegated
to the preserve of the inner-self is concern as to
how well a project has been carried out. For, the
Iranian argues, if the project formally is certified
and some action has been taken, then that is sufficient to satisfy the formal prescriptions. Hence,
according to the rule of live and let live, preserve
face for those involved and ignore efficiency. This
is why, for example, education programs in Iran
emphasize real estate (buildings and furniture) and
the number of teachers, rather than what is taught
and how well it is taught.[43]

Conversely, for those intent on discrediting
others, causing a loss of face is considered much
more efficacious than moralizing, for moralizing is
considered a breach of the ground rules, and apt to
be discounted. The usual means to cause a loss of
face, not surprisingly, is to charge failure to

fulfill formal prescription, especially to demonstrate that promises which were made in fulfillment
of formal prescription were never kept. For, as one
Iranian put it, "Iran is a land of (unfulfilled)
promises, though those in power call it a land of
promise." Such economically relevant questions as
why difficulties may have occured in fulfilling
promises, and more importantly, what is the quality
of what has been accomplished will never be raised
in such a numbers game between defender and critic
of how many promises (formally) have been fulfilled.

Face, second, stresses reputation over creativity. For personal evaluations, involving ethical
judgments, belong to the world of the inner-self.
Consequently, Iranians behave for effect on others
in this real world of formalized interpersonal relations and social action and reaction, rather than
out of conviction, which it is assumed, rarely, if
ever, is pertinent outside the inner-world of one's
self. It is for this reason that to outsiders,
Iranians seem superficial, although Iranians are
convinced that the formalized world of the outer-
self is difficult enough to operate in, and one must
be very clever to work in it, without unnecessarily
complicating the problem with ethical considerations.[44] Of practical economic concern here is the
fact that this outlook might be said to have impeded
critical evaluation of what actually has been done
in Iran, for it has encouraged formalized "impact"
performance which is to be accepted at "face" value.
And many an economic decision has been defended long
after the intrinsic economic uselessness of the
decision has been demonstrated, solely because it
protected and enhanced face. The hodge-podge of
"show projects" in Iran, as in most economically
underdeveloped societies, such as ultra-modern industrial plants running at under-capacity, or not at
all, amidst a sea of stagnation kept from view in
the back rural areas, merely to "show face" and
bolster up outer-self ego to the participants, and,
it is hoped, to outsiders as well, also may be attributed to this outlook.[45]

Since outer-self prestige (face) is so important in the Iranian system of interpersonal relations and social action, and ethical considerations
are not involved necessarily in the acquisition of
such prestige (since ethics belong to the world of
inner-self), it is not surprising that, third, Iran
abounds with individuals with fake credentials that

few are ready to challenge, lest their own credentials be challenged in turn.[46] On the one hand,
these false faces are the ubiquitous, fraudulent,
"doctors," medical or liberal, and the fraudulent
"engineers," who either are outright fictions of the
imagination, or are holders of degrees from diploma-
mills abroad.[47] But on a more modest scale, but
more widespread in the society, are such individuals in the tradition of the Iranian tragedy, as
the boy who appeared for a job on the basis of his
honesty, whose six-grade diploma was forged.[48]
The consequences for economic action can but be
obvious; for who will be willing to acquire, painfully, the attributes necessary for economic action
in a developing society when so easily (falsely) one
can acquire the face of these attributes?

Regardless of the acknowledgment of widespread
facial fraud, face, fourth, places great stress upon
the superficial achievement of merely possessing
face. For example, obtaining a diploma (outer-self
face achievement) rather than the education itself
(which may have merit for inner-self satisfaction or
cultivation) is what is important.[49] An obvious
consequence of this is that since formal achievement
in Iran has no necessary correlation to "real"
(inner-self) achievement, no confidence exists in
existing standards (titles). But, then, if all
potentially are assumed equally competent (or incompetent), on what basis can judgments be made? It
is in this rare instance that the Iranian may be
tempted to dare to express his inner-self or what
he believes is his inner-self in the outer world.
For each Iranian believes that based on his inner-
self convictions, he personally can fill or not fill
to the same extent any role in the society. It is
only fate, the fate of the outer world, by denying
him the lack of the superficial achievement of the
face (that is, the title) that has robbed him of
this opportunity. But such a commitment as any commitment of inner-self to the outer world, is fraught
with danger. For one, the individual may not be
able to keep his inner-self fantasy role and outer-
self reality roles logically apart. He may carry
out the cherished role of his fantasy in the real
world. This is the case of the individual who may
bluff his way into a position of responsibility, but
then cannot deliver, and in order to save face, forever is finding excuses for his constant inaction,
indecision, and random behavior. This situation can

lead to serious psychological consequences if pushed
far enough. The individual may be forced to combine
his world of fantasy (what he thinks he is) and
reality (what he really is) in a way that it inter-
feres with even a minimum adjustment to the demands
of his "real" interpersonal relations and social
actions. Or he may be forced to retreat, more and
more, for self-protection, into the world of his
inner-self alone where he can be what he thinks he
is, or should be regardless of reality.[50] It is
for these good reasons that Iranians have learned,
through bitter experience, if at all possible, not
to pass this threshold of harassment where the mark
of face has to be dropped and the whole system of
interacting faces disintegrates with potential personal disaster for all concerned. An individual,
therefore, must never be backed into that corner
where his face cannot be retrieved. Ideally, then,
backbite if you must, for whatever reasons, but never
call a bluff directly, lest you put someone in the
embarrassing position of having to admit inadequacies. And never displease anyone to the extent
that it forces such drastic face-saving actions and
reactions that will cause dangerous friction within,
and possible disintegration of, the web of interpersonal face relations.[51]

Deliberate extreme violations, consequently, are
rare, but ideals are often hard to keep in practice.
For frictions, sometimes dangerous frictions leading to violence, do exist in Iranian society. This
is true for no other reason than that, once again,
in Iran no expectation exists that if one is consi-
derate of the face needs of others, one necessarily
can expect the same consideration in return; unless
such a reciprocal action serves the self-interest of
the other party. Being made a fool of, that is,
losing face, then, is a constant and acute problem
to the Iranian. It is most important to him, because
having surrendered his inner-self to the realm of a
never-never land, if his formalized world of face is
not satisfactory, the Iranian will be naked and without any protection in this world. To prevent this
from taking place, the Iranian must ever be ready to
defend his face honor. Hence, even only the fear of
losing face may be enough to motivate a defence of
one's face. For example, a man murders his young
niece so she will not, in future, possibly follow a
path of dishonor.[52]

In such a system of formalized face, fifth,

interpersonal social actions are interpreted as measures motivated by <u>personal</u> desires to enhance or attack the face of other <u>actors</u>, rather than as measures motivated by <u>abstract judgements</u> of the merits
or demerits of the <u>actions</u> themselves. And conversely,
"issues" are used in the attempt to enhance or reduce
the face of others, without the necessity of a direct
confrontation among individuals, which could be dangerous to all involved. The Iranian, then, for still
another reason, is skeptical of moralisms. Consequently, it is extremely difficult to get any Iranian
to view criticism of actions, especially of his own
actions, as being criticism of rational judgement
and not of personality. And so, no rational basis
upon which to decide when an issue really is an
issue exists in Iran.

     Concern with formalized face also implies, sixth,
that individuals are apt to make judgements of others
in stereotypical categories, determined solely by
outer-self considerations. In such a system, individuals who do not fit the preconceived stereotypes are
stereotyped just the same, but as poor adjustors to
a particular category. If this is not possible, especially under changing role demands as at present,
the stereotyper often finds that he cannot categor-
ize and, consequently that he cannot respond successfully to the interpersonal situation. He becomes
aggressive and non-cooperative in the defensive hope
that the strange individual will be destroyed, or,
at the least, removed from the situation, so that
interpersonal relations will return to normal. Such
is the fate of those who attempt to "innovate" in
the Iranian system of interpersonal relations; especially those few individuals trained abroad or those
foreigners who, as obvious strangers without an
acceptable stereotype, are attempting to introduce a
self-generating rational economic system into the
society.

     In addition to specific conclusions drawn under
each of the above individual aspects of face, it is
worthwhile also to draw certain general implications
concerning the question of face. First, prime concern with face implies that rational considerations
are subordinated to considerations of social prestige (face-enhancing) in social action (including
economic action). For example, a servant who complains of his or her work load does not anticipate
being replaced for incapacity, but expects to be supplemented with another servant. For this enhances

the face of the employer as well as that of the servant, in that both are associated with a "big-face"
household which now is able to afford two, instead
of one, retainer. The biggest culprit, of course,
is the political authority which believes that it
has to maintain the biggest face in the society, and
which, in consequence, is not adverse to spending
recklessly without rational consideration in both
the public and private sectors of the economy to
enhance face.[53] And so Iranian investment wealth,
made available in proportion to one's face, is expended ostentatiously on luxuries, which primarily
have prestige value.

Second, face impedes the development of a
realistic (that is, rational) appraisal both of self
and of the patterns of interpersonal relationships
employed in social (including economic) action.
Consequently, face has impeded the Iranian's desire
and ability to confront the hard facts of Iranian
economic reality with a rational-critical and not a
frustration-critical (backbiting) eye. In truth,
it has provided support for the Iranian's image
fantasy that he, and his society, are in the process
of introducing a rational, self-generating economic
system into Iran.

Finally, face, by dividing the world of the
inner-self of moral conviction from the world of the
outer-self of crass (here, economic) materialism supports the traditional Iranian view that economic
activity, in and of itself, is morally inferior and,
hence, that "anything goes in the market" unless it
is checked by non-economic moral supervision. This
is to be contrasted with the likewise crassly-
material world of economic action of certain of the
developed societies which at least theoretically, is
morally supervised primarily by the individual's
personal inner-worldly convictions (the business
ethic"). And, since in Iranian thinking, the world
of the inner-self man should not be contaminated with
the crass (here, economic) material world, to concern
one's self primarily with risk-taking productive economic action is to tempt fate, for potentially such
a view may harm one's inner-self. Such a view is
not very conducive to the development in Iranian
thinking of a favorable view toward entrepreneurship.
In contrast, in Western economic thought, economic
autonomy did not bifurcate the worlds of the inner
and outer man, as in Iran, so that economic action

was not "evil," it either was ethical or neutral. This interpretation is most conducive to the development of a <u>rational</u> economic system.

THE NEGATIVE REACTION: ESCAPISM

Concern with face does not exhaust the category of fantasy in Iranian interpersonal relations. The Iranian also reacts more directly both to the web of interpersonal social relationships and to the real world of social action which he would prefer to avoid if at all possible, by escapism. These escape mechanisms demonstrate some consideration for the demands of the existing social order, while some illustrate total withdrawal from social situations.

First, self-deception: Unfavorable facts (especially mistakes) or hard reality about one-self are ignored, and any minor favorable signs, often only verbal fantasy signs and not hard inductions, are magnified out of proportion to enhance the self-worth of the individual.[54] This lack of personal frankness is not the product of some basic inner duplicity of the Iranian, but simply is the mechanism by which he can refuse to admit even the possibility of personal inadequacy. To protect himself the Iranian also will use this same mechanism in reverse, to "expose" the faults of others, even, not unusually, if those "exposed" faults completely are false. For the Iranian argues: if I cannot build up by self-esteem because I dare not look at myself realistically, or if I cannot succeed when I practice personal self-deception, then, all that is left to me to make myself look good to myself and to others, is to tear down the esteem (face) of others, so that I will look better <u>in comparison</u>, although both of us, on an absolute scale of perfection, appear as poor examples, indeed.[55]

Second, the Iranian comforts himself in the belief that an individual does not have to accept responsibility for action, because he is but a "tool of fate."[56] Certainly this appears valid in Iranian society, where problems are so overwhelming, that the lonely, isolated individual cannot do much to alter the course of events, and hence, where the difficulty of acting and interacting successfully is almost insurmountable. In consequence, the Iranian believes that all he can do is to complain against a society characterized by corruption, poor adminis-

tration, insincerity, insecurity, injustice and slowness to protect individual action.[57] He may shift
the responsibility to act to the mystical Shah (rule
by model). In such a case the Iranian argues, if
even the Shah, who is most favored by fate, cannot
act successfully, how can he, a mere ordinary individual do anything?[58] The fact that the ordinary
individual would have to interact positively with
his fellows no matter what the Shah's decision might
be, conveniently is ignored. Here it may be suggested that the Iranian is not being realistic. For
although his view of the social situation may be
realistic, this view is not used either for a realistic appraisal of the causes of Iran's difficulties,
or, in turn, for rational, realistic positive action
to ameliorate these realistic complaints. For while
he is complaining about his society, especially to
the wide-eyed outsider, much to the consternation of
the political authority, he also is busy drinking
tea and bemoaning his inability to act and his bad
fate in being born in contemporary Iran.

Third, Iranians believe that a problem probably
will go away of its own accord if it is ignored per-
sistently. Since, as has been indicated previously,
Iranians tend to avoid frontal, interpersonal con-
frontations that might involve them in situations
in which realistic appraisals of themselves will
cause them to lose face, they back away from open
conflict by hopefully seeing interpersonal consensus
and fellowship when, in fact, it does not exist.
But such consensus, at the most, is but a truce in
which the antagonists have agreed not to bother each
other, preferably forever, in the belief that if
conflict arises, for no other reason than that reality may have to be faced, one may win, but all may
lose. And so, to recall the proverb, "If you know
about it, don't talk about it." Unfortunately, this
attempt to avoid conflict not only has not reduced
interpersonal problems, ironically it has increased
them. For although such a stand avoids personal
difficulties with one's colleagues, it does lead to
personal isolation, as individuals withdraw from the
arena of each other's interpersonal relationships;
at times into individual (inner-self) fantasy worlds
where personal esteem is inviolate. This can but
cut all meaningful communication among individuals
and lead increasingly to the atomization, isolation,
and mutual incomprehension and intolerance of the
actions and desires of others. The social system in
Iran is a prime example of this. Villages which

consist of few families, or even one family, exist,
because people have "moved down the road" after an
intra-village, unresolved, conflict. And with each
new village born out of such conflict, appear social
islands unto themselves, harboring against former
neighbors suspicions whose origins may long since
have been forgotten. For, because of the failure to
resolve conflict realistically and positively at one
time, these communities have drifted into unresolved
hostility; each to live in a fantasy-world in which
enemies outside the village are unseen, but are all
about to threaten constantly.

A fourth mechanism of escape is to rename un-
desired phenomena in the world of reality so that
they have a more favorable, or at least, less unfavorable, connotation when brought to mind. Or in
the extreme case, one can deny, simply, the existence of the unwanted in a world that becomes neither
real nor unreal (the "dastan" of the previous section's discussion). For example, beggars are "eliminated" from a city simply by not listing them in the
census, prohibiting any pictures of them, or teaching
them new trades in rehabilitation centers and arbitrarily assuming that they will never go back to
their old trades (which of course they will often
do because of the lucrative return of begging).[59]

The fifth step toward total escapism into non-
reality is to approach this troublesome world with
a deviousness and obscurity that enables one to live
physically in this world, but, simultaneously, to
communicate with and live in a world beyond reality.
In this case, the inner-self, the true ultimate
reality, is supreme and the frustrating world of the
outer-self is unimportant. It is for this reason
that the mystical Sufi movement which is concerned
specifically with this problem has always been strong
in Iran. Very significantly, for purposes of the
present study, the Sufi movement has attracted many
influential intellectuals, who, although they are
disgusted with Iranian society on realistic grounds,
seek relief only through a mystical escape from a
distasteful reality.

Sixth, retreat from this realistic world of
pain and frustration, albeit for a limited period,
is possible through narcotics, especially opium.
The political authority has made a tremendous effort
to eliminate the production and use of narcotics in

Iran, but frequent reference in the press to the apprehension of smugglers and narcotic dens, and the impounding of illegal caches attest to the use of drugs throughout the society. Be that as it may, it is worth noting for our purposes, that attacking the use of drugs, noble in itself, medically and socially only is treating the symptom and not the cause of the problem.

Seventh, and most drastically, insanity or suicide will remove one from this painful world. Obvious psychological maladjustment and aberrant behavior are not unusual in Iran, and are found as readily in urban environments as in isolated villages, and among individuals in all walks of life. Known cases of suicide appear to be caused by the inability to carry out desires or to predict the actions of others in a society in which no unambiguous standards of right or wrong exist; as for example, a parent who commits suicide because her children refuse to listen to her advice.[60] That is, Iranian suicide predominantly is the type that the sociologist, Durkheim, termed anomic suicide.[61]

By way of summation, it may be said that the Iranian, regardless of the particular retreat he chooses, is responding to the challenges of his social environment negatively and to protect himself, rather than positively and to improve the society. This can but have a detrimental effect on the possibility of introducing a rational, self-generating economic system which depends on the positive resolution of difficulties in the social (including economic) environment.

THE NEGATIVE REACTION: RESIGNATION TO THE EXISTING SYSTEM OF INTERPERSONAL RELATIONS

It always is fascinating for the outsider to observe that, although existing patterns of interpersonal relations and social interaction in Iran do not appear to offer any individual, personal satisfaction, personal security, or an effective means to respond to the challenges of his environment, these patterns, nevertheless, are accepted as the inevitable and only legitimate "Iranian Way" by most every member of Iranian society, regardless of his walk of life. For interestingly, those who control the social order, and who obviously profit by their retention; those who attack those in control

because they want to control the social order themselves; and those who constitute the vast majority
in-between who believe they must accept and adjust
--all acknowledge the same ground rules of social
action, even though they may differ among themselves as to what the consequences of those ground
rules ought to be. Consequently, either by design
or by default, these three elements of Iranian
society, that is, controller, attacker, and mass
accepter, all seem committed to the perpetuation
of existing patterns of interaction regardless of
the inadequacies of these patterns in (rational)
sociological terms. The relationship of each of
these three groups to the existing patterns will
be discussed in turn.

A common technique of the ruling authority
and its allies to insure continuation of the
existing patterns of interpersonal relationships
is to cry foul, or "cultural imperialism," any
time the question of pattern change is broached.
If this cry of "wolf" does not work, especially
in achieving necessary desired material changes
in Iran, the political authority, most typically
waxes eloquently about the need to solve a problem
without offering the opportunity to introduce any
interpersonal means to remedy it. This approach
is effective because human resources are hard to
develop in comparison to non-human resources, such
as machines which can be imported from the foreigner
to use.62 Or if someone insists in introducing
novel interpersonal relationship patterns, the political authority insists on adding on these new channels of interpersonal relationships to existing
channels, rather than rationalizing the existing
channels. For this is sure to increase jealousy,
the atomization of individuals, conflict, non-
cooperation, and withdrawal in the face of confusion.63
It is for this reason, that the many formal changes
in Iran to which many Iranians point with pride, lack
substance. But this play at change discourages more
pressure building up in the system, for it satisfies
the unsophisticated that something important, in
fact, has been accomplished, and it frustrates the
sophisticated that anything much, really, can be
accomplished.

None of these protective maneuverings are novel
to societies which have decided to face similar problems with similar solutions, often with the same
disastrous prospects that now confront Iran.64 But,

if the <u>preservation</u> of the patterns and not the
<u>utility</u> of the patterns is the measure of success,
then, by and large, the forces in control of the
social order have been successful. The effort particularly is successful because those few who oppose
those in control have been made to accept the same
pattern of interpersonal relations in their proposals of change for Iran. The issue between polity
and opposition, then, is not one over a difference
in attitude toward existing interpersonal relations,
but rather is one over who will control the plums of
face and power in the society. It is for this reason, that the political authority believes it always
can adjust to existing threats to its position
through bribery, by dispensing favors, or by giving
a little, quantitatively but not qualitatively, when
the political chips really are down, and by and
large this has been true and successful. The Iranian
opposition then, is what the social psychologist,
David Reisman, has termed an "adjusted opposition,"
that is, an opposition that appears to be maladjusted
in terms of what is expected as loyal supporters of
the existing social order, but whose socio-
psychological character structure is one of adjustment, because it is but a reflection of but a segment
of the existing society. And in this case, certainly,
that segment shares the same ground rules of wants,
of social action, <u>and</u> significantly in the present
context, of the interpersonal relations as that of
the "in's" of power.[65] The Iranian opposition, which
primarily is a <u>political</u> opposition, then, cannot be
counted on to change the existing <u>social</u> interpersonal
patterns, since it is resigned to serving its own
interests by supporting those patterns. Thus, whatever changes the opposition might introduce, if it
came to power, necessarily would not be conducive to
the possibility of developing a rational economic
system in Iranian society.

The vast majority of Iranians, since sociologically speaking they are outside both the arena of
political power and the arena of potential political
power, and hence, in Iranian terms, not in a position
to change the social patterns of interpersonal relations, can but be committed to the perpetuation of
the existing patterns.[66] Consequently, most individuals in Iranian society do not waste time trying to
reform the system, even if this might cross their
minds, which is unlikely. For without the more than
reasonable prospect of the introduction of a defined

better alternative to what now exists (which
neither those in power or the opposition suggest, to
recall) Iranians believe it is more satisfactory to
stick with what they know (and this is the attested
lesson of the problem of innovation everywhere).[68]
Consequently, at best, individuals hope to make the
existing system of patterns work for him by being
as clever as is possible. But such action at best,
only conquers the existing system by evading it.
And this, in turn, perpetuates the existing inadequate patterns of interpersonal relations (to complete a vicious circle), so that the "breakthrough"
to establishing those positive, productive interpersonal relations, useful in rational economic
action, remains so difficult to achieve.

THE POSITIVE REACTION: AGGRESSION AND VIOLENCE

Resignation and withdrawal do not exhaust the
reactions of Iranians to the frustrations of the
existing patterns of interpersonal relations, much
as those in control of the social order would like
this to be so. These frustrations also lead to
aggression, open hostility, and even violence.

Iranians are famous for their quick tempers
and their willingness to give battle for the
slightest provocation, and rightly so. Some of
this, undoubtedly, is bluster; a show of face and
formalized anger which impresses the uninitiated,
especially the foreigner. But this kind of anger
does no harm to interpersonal relationships, for
the feuding individuals soon make up once the steam
of such innocent aggression is let out of the
chamber of frustration.

But much of aggression is not sham, because it
represents deep-seated frustrations which can be
triggered to sudden flashes of violence as the
breaking point is reached, often over an apparently
trivial incident. Some cases of aggression are
tragic in the Greek sense, for they highlight the
hopelessness of attempting to act rewardingly in
the frustrating web of Iranian interpersonal relations. For example, a betrayed woman who learns
that her husband has taken a second wife in secret
can only do violence to the couple to express her
frustrations.[69] Violence often is committed out of
spiteful vindictiveness, in situations in which it

is obvious to the individual that he has nothing
rationally to gain by violence, and even in which
the principle sufferer in the violence very well may
be the instigator himself. For example, the father
whose neighbor refuses to marry his daughter later
claims that the neighbor raped his daughter. After
an inspection showed her to be still a virgin, the
father is handed over to the courts for action.[70]
Significantly, and in sum, violence is both a
personalized (that is, random) and irrational attack upon the obvious frustrations of Iranian
society; consequently, violence does not offer any
constructive, positive solutions to the interpersonal problems which provoked the violence in the
first instance. Moreover, the pattern of the
violence itself is a dramatic indication of the inefficiency, and even of the failure of existing channels available to adjudicate violent conflicts in
interpersonal relations when they do arise. Consequently, the achievement of personally rewarding,
positive, cooperative, interpersonal relations in
times of social flux and conflict, so essential to
the consummation of a rational, self-generating
economic system are most difficult to introduce into
Iranian society.

A CONCLUSION: THE ABSENCE OF LONG-RANGE COMMITMENT
       IN IRANIAN INTERPERSONAL RELATIONS

        Considered here are those characteristics of
Iranian interpersonal relations which have inhibited
the development of a commitment or "calling" to
long-range, productive social, and by implication,
economic action. These characteristics are as follows:

        First, in response to the harsh realities of
Iranian society and especially to the unrewarding
consequences of most all interpersonal relations,
the Iranian prefers to talk, rather than to act.
In doing so, the Iranian hopes that his verbal
incantations, as if by magic, either will accomplish
the task, or, if employed long enough, will outlive
the task challenge. For, even if he does know what
to do, the Iranian balks at doing it, for somehow,
something may go wrong. And if he does not commit
himself, he cannot be held responsible for a non-
existent mistake.

        But, second, it could be said more often that

the Iranians do not seem to know what to do even when
they wish to act and do act. For since the Iranian
normally is not conditioned to seek positive, active
mastery of his environment as a means to solve his
problems, he has not devoted much time and thought
to either the processes or the organization of human
beings necessary to insure successful action. Considering the fact that one success does not encourage the Iranian to try to find out rationally why he
succeeded, and then to try to repeat that success
again and again, so that successful action, especially
productive economic action, becomes a matter of
predictable routine, successful action, even if
repeated, is lucky (that is, fortuitous) action; and
the Iranian's interpretation is correct.[71]

Third, the Iranian especially is wary of productive (including economic) action since this requires long-range and long-term dependence on others.
For he has learned through bitter experience that
dependence on others can cause personal disaster for
those who are rash enough to assume that a commitment
to others commits others in return. And so, by
force of circumstance, he will choose short-term
opportunity rather than long-range commitment, even
though he may be convinced logically that his interests could better be served by long-run commitment.
It is for this reason that otherwise (long-range)
good work collapses whenever it appears that this
work no longer serves immediate advantage. And it
is for this reason, that schedules of work in Iran
often have to be fitted to personal convenience
instead of individuals fitting themselves to rational,
economic work needs. For example, health centers in
Iran have had significant, operational difficulties
arising out of the fact that work schedules must be
restricted to half-days only. For even if overtime
is paid as an inducement to personnel to return
"after lunch," personnel only will pocket the overtime, and on one pretext or another, will fail to
appear for work in the afternoons.

Fourth, since long-range commitment has little
positive value to the Iranian, the personal qualities
associated with long-range commitment, such as depend-
ability, efficiency, persistence, patience, and
accuracy, likewise, have little positive value in
Iranian interpersonal relations and social (including
economic) action. In fact, contrariwise, they are
apt to be considered as vices by Iranians, since they

impede the chance to react quickly to changes in
opportunity. Likewise, such personal disciplines
as punctuality, honesty, and cooperation indeed are
admirable qualities for Imam and for the moral,
inner-self. But in this cruel world of the outer-
self, only a foolish man who is sure to be swept
aside would accept them as his values.[72]

Fifth, and finally, as has been noted many
times, to the Iranian, personal security if it
exists at all, is limited to the here and now, and
subject to drastic change on short-term notice. A
man, therefore, in order to survive, must take advantage of _present_ opportunities rather to reshape
positively the social environment so that _in future_
perhaps he, among all Iranians, might be able to
live in a better world. This is why, although
nominally committed to an everlasting Islamic spiritu-
ality, the Iranian also has treasured the words of
Sa'adi who has offered justification for enjoying
the here and now, "for who knows what tomorrow may
bring." And so, in order to preserve his spirit-
uality (the world of the inner-self), and yet take
advantage of the opportunities of this world of the
outer-self, as has been suggested elsewhere in this
chapter, the Iranian has accepted the notion that
these two selves operate in two independent realms
which must maintain their separate identities. And
so, the Iranian has developed a separate ethic for
this world, which is materialistic, opportunistic,
and which stresses _immediate_ goals, even when, to
repeat, these short-range goals appear to defeat a
long-range potential advantage. It is for this
reason, that to the outside observer, the Iranian
forever seems to be cutting off his (economic) nose
(that is, short-range, this-world ethic) to spite
his face (that is, long-range, universal ethic);
for, to the Iranian, perhaps tomorrow may not be
around to worry about noses. For example, the egg
salesman who hard-boils his rotten eggs, and, in
doing so, loses his customers, rationalizes his
actions on the basis of the this-world ethic that
individuals must profit as they can here and now,
for who can control the vague possibility that opportunities may exist tomorrow; to wit, customers may
die or move away. Ironically, acceptance of a this-
worldly ethic of opportunism has not prevented the
Iranian tragic element of cleverness outwitting itself once again to creep in and to thwart _even_ the
chance to maximize the opportunities of today; thus

leaving the Iranian with nothing to look forward to,
since he has no hope that tomorrow will offer him
anything. Example: The ambitious parent who breaks
up a marriage to take advantage of a better offer
and then finds it cannot be consummated because the
man of promise welches. The girl becomes a suicide,
or the girl is killed by her offended ex-husband.[73]

By way of summation, it may be said, then, that,
to the Iranian, with the chance of disaster ever
present in the here and now, long-term commitment
is unthinkable. And more significantly, so is the
belief that anyone in Iran is about to reshape his
environment in a way that long-range commitment ever
will be feasible. Hence, too many Iranians are convinced that long-range sacrificial commitment can
realize the utopia of development only in heaven as
far as Iran is concerned, although it may exist on
earth in other societies. And thus, to conclude,
although one validly can argue that, unless, and
until the Iranian accepts the psychological Freudian
"reality principle" in the sphere of economic action;
that is, the willingness to forsake the "consumption"
pleasures of today to insure the development benefits
of tomorrow, a self-generating, rational economic
system in Iranian society is not feasible. It must
also be appreciated that, until the institutional
ground rules of the social order (in this chapter,
the assumptions underlying the unrewarding Iranian
interpersonal relations) are altered, the Iranian's
refusal to accept long-range commitment, logically
and feasibly, can be expected.

CHAPTER **10** THE DEVELOPMENT MODEL
AND
IRANIAN SOCIETY

GENERAL INTRODUCTION

It was stated in Chapter One that the nature of
the case study would be guided by a particular framework, or model, which not only would determine the
kind of questions to be asked, but also would determine the selection, classification, and ultimately,
the significance (or interpretation) of the data
which would be examined in the process of answering
the questions. That model now will be presented.

At first blush, it would seem as if the model
is but a summary of the discussions and interpretations of the case study; that is, that the model is
the boiling of the case data down to certain generalizations which still are specific enough to explain
meaningfully how and why Iranians now act, and
probably will continue to respond, in certain ways
rather than in other ways to the challenge of economic development. However, as suggested in Chapter
One, this is not so, because the decision was made
to present the model _after_ the discussions which the
model was supposed to have been used to examine,
only to serve the interest of clarity and ease in
comprehension. Consequently, even though the logical
sequence of model and case study apparently has been
reversed in the format of the present study, in
actually preparing the study, the author adhered to
the logical requisite that he first determine a set
of general principles or postulates (the model) and
subsequently use the model to select, order, and
draw conclusions concerning the case material.

This statement is made not to affirm loyalty
before the altar of science, in the face of possible
criticism from pedants, but to highlight what the
author believes is an important corollary implication
of the present study. In some of the footnotes in
the text, and in the general observations of the
chapters to follow, the author draws upon the data
of Asian societies other than Iran. These data are
a part of his theoretical effort and practical ex-

perience in those societies <u>prior</u> to his exposure to
Iranian society and his writing the present study.
It was during this period that the author began to
develop a model of a hypothetical Asian society* and
it was this model that he used as a working framework when he collected his Iranian data.** And when
the data which he collected were critically evaluated, before he drew certain conclusions concerning
the process of economic development, the results
were compared against an alternative model of a
developed society. This alternate model is the
concluding section of this chapter. It is this
more "logical" format that the author proposes be
kept in mind, as the material of the present chapter is reviewed.

THE BASIC MODEL

Political Authority

The basic postulate:

Political authority is characterized by the assumptions that the right to authority is determined
primarily by moral-intellectual considerations,
that that right is monopolized by a self-asserted
elite, and that that right is validated by the

----

* This was presented in its initial form in the
  1958 work, <u>Origins of Modern Capitalism and</u>
  <u>Eastern Asia</u>. The theoretical sources of the
  model and those who have contributed to its
  development are discussed in this study.

** It should be mentioned, therefore, that the
   model, because it represents a hypothetical
   "Asian Society," or social typology, at a more
   generalized level of view than would be the case
   with a model of one specific society on the Asian
   mainland, requires that certain distinctions (or
   variations)--say, between Chinese and Iranian
   societies--must be accounted for when one or more
   concrete societies are discussed in detail in
   terms of the model. This is <u>one</u> of the purposes
   served by section "The Model and Iranian Society
   Relative to the Problem of Development" of the
   present chapter, which examines the essentials of
   the case material of the study (that is, Chapters
   Two - Nine, above) in terms of the model.

dissemination of morally-based service in the society, through political means, by that elite and
on terms defined by that elite.

Derivative statements:

The legitimacy of political authority is based
on pre-eminent mastery of morality* and of intellect.
These elements are combined in a way that mastery of
either element necessarily implies mastery of the
other; for morality is achieved solely through knowledge, and mastery of knowledge implies mastery of
morality. The morality of morality-intellect is not
composed of a series of abstract universal principles
guiding social conduct in general, and the intellect
of morality-intellect is not mastery of pragmatic
knowledge. Rather, morality-intellect is mastery of
the essential rules (morality) of the basic cultural
heritage of the society as expressed in its sacred
literature (intellect), which is applied specifically
to specific situations by specific masters of morality-
intellect. The substance of morality-intellect, then,
is constant, even though the pragmatic (here political)
circumstances to which intellect-morality apply very
well may change.

---

* Morality and legitimacy must be differentiated.
  All political authority, by definition, is legitimate; for authority is defined as the legitimate
  exercise of control or power. In this context,
  any authority is moral (or is a moral order), as
  contrasted to power alone, which is the probability that a determination will be carried out,
  despite resistance (or the doctrine that non-
  violent might is right). However, morality, as
  used in the present study, contrasts with empirical, coordinate and administrative ability,
  which is characteristic of an alternative kind
  (or model) of authority, to be discussed in
  Section "The Alternative Model" of this chapter.
  In this context, morality is but one of a number
  of possible sources accepted as fundamental for
  the establishment of a (moral-) legitimate authority. The author can only apologize for the use
  of a term likely to cause confusion, but he is at
  a loss to provide a better one, save perhaps
  "virtue," which was used in his 1958 work, but
  which is tied closely to the Chinese language
  (teh), and the Chinese case.

Morality-intellect not only is sufficient to
legitimize political authority, it is necessary to
legitimize it. And conversely, the legitimization
of political authority is both the necessary and
sufficient role of morality-intellect. Consequently,
intellect-morality not only entitles its bearers to
intimate association with the political authority,
it also makes it mandatory that they establish this
intimate association.

For the primary role of political authority is
to insure that morality exists in the society.
Hence, those who master intellect-morality are expected under moral compunction to serve political
authority to enable that authority to make maximum
use of their talents of intellect-morality. By
definition, those who are divorced from the right
of association with political authority, must submit to the prerogatives of those associated with
political authority, who are charged with spreading
morality among them.

Since the primary concern of political authority is to insure that morality exists in the society, the mere association of men who are masters
of intellect-morality with the political authority
is considered to be what is sufficient and necessary
to make satisfactory political decisions in the
society. And since it is assumed that masters of
intellect-morality will become associated with political authority, that authority is assured of the
necessary and sufficient talent to fulfill most effi-
caciously its responsibilities of operating the apparatus of political authority, regardless of possible technical considerations arising out of any
specific political decisions. Since technicians
necessarily are not masters of morality-intellect,
but only masters in the preserve of non-moral-
intellect, technicians must be subordinated to those
who are the masters of morality-intellect and never
must be placed in positions of decision making.

But political decisions which are based upon
considerations of morality-intellect are hard to
define and measure. For it is most difficult to
translate intellect-morality into concrete, yet
generalized arbitrary, standards and rules for administrative decision. For who can anticipate with
reasonable assurance what the meaning of morality-
intellect will be from one specific situation to the

next? For this reason all administrative decisions,
including law, rarely are defined, codified, administered, and enforced on a generalized, yet concrete
level. It is argued that such a system not only
would place the political emphasis in the wrong
place (that is, on ethically-neutral standards which
may be insufficient and even superfluous to morality)
but it also positively would lead to evil, since
those experts in "law" may not have morality to
accompany their knowledge and hence, would use law
to their own ends, which only can produce evil.

     In order to insure morality, therefore, it is
better to leave administrative action to specific
negotiation between specific individuals. Especially is this true between the (constantly) moral
members of the political authority and the non-moral,
non-political outsiders who seek decisions as to the
morality of their right to pursue their individual
political interests in the society. In return for
this decision, those who make the decision are entitled to a legal fee; either political control of
the social actions of the outsiders or economic
benefits. Such economic benefit sometimes, and by
some, is considered to be corruption; if this is so,
it means that corruption logically is built into the
very nature of the structure of political authority.

     It is reasonable to assume that in the name of
its responsibility to extend morality throughout the
society, the political authority must protect the
society from the non-moral and the actions of the
non-moral. This is believed to be best achieved by
central political control of the whole social order.
This is so, because, since the possession of intellect-morality presumably radiates out in decreasing
intensity as one descends the hierarchy of political
authority, then those who are at the vital center of
the structure of political authority, presumably,
are the most intimately associated with morality and
intellect. Consequently, although each level of the
political apparatus is responsible for the protection
of morality in the society at large, since each level
is inferior in morality-intellect to ascending levels
in rank, and especially to the center, each level
must expect any and all the members of levels above
it to protect morality in its own level as well.
Also, since justification for decisions is based upon
superior mastery of morality-intellect, and not upon
defined technical principle, those inferior in the

hierarchy, because their mastery of moral-intellect
is either less or nil, cannot challenge or even question the decisions of those above them in rank, especially the decisions of the center. Hence, political
decisions, characteristically, are centralized, hierarchial, and arbitrary.

Although the political authority, especially
the central political authority, not always is successful in enforcing its claim to pre-eminent political decision making in the society on grounds of
intellect-morality, the political authority never
renounces the right to assert its claim, which a
priori, cannot be challenged. For no matter what
the empirical situation may be, those outside the
orbit of political authority are not possessed of
the same intellect-morality as are the politicians,
and only can fulfill their moral responsibilities by
being the loyal followers of the masters of intellect-
morality.

Opposition to the existing political order, then,
faces not only the problem of establishing its own
point of view against the existing political ways of
doing things (against so-called "tradition") and
against the "vested interests" of those committed to
perpetuating that existing political way of doing
things, but also against the sanction that any opposition, automatically, is political rebellion against
the constant intellect-morality of the political
order, and, by extension, of the whole social order.

The Economy

Basic postulate:

The economy is characterized by the assumption
that it is to be manipulated in the name of public
service morality and that that morality has primacy
over economic rationality.

Derivative statements:

The social order must be a moral order, that is,
an order characterized by intellect-morality. For
this reason, the economy cannot be considered as an
autonomous sector of the society because if it were
autonomous, such materialistic considerations as non-
moral profit would dominate the economy and would
threaten to spread materialism and non-morality

(although not necessarily, immorality) throughout the social order.

The political authority, as the prime repository of the intellect-morality of the society, has the responsibility for enforcing morality in the economy, in order to insure the triumph of morality in the society. Although the political authority does not believe that such an economic policy necessarily will harm the maximum development of the economy (as we shall soon see), even if it does, this policy is justifiable because of the assumed necessity for the primacy of morality in the society.

In order to carry out its mandate, the political authority may exercise the right to ownership of the means of the economy, but this is not essential to achieve its responsibility. For it can achieve the same objective by intervening into the economy whenever it chooses and on terms of its own choosing. And since the intervention always is done in the name of protecting and extending morality in the society, and not for purposes of selfish material profit, who is there in the society to challenge such a policy?

It should not be thought that profitable economic activity is considered undesirable; quite the contrary. For the society in general, and the political authority in particular, are most vitally concerned with insuring economic surpluses in the society. And by dint of the political authority's pre-eminent intellect, the success of accumulating surpluses is assured, and by virtue of its pre-eminent morality, the use of the surpluses in the moral interest of the society also is assured.

To insure that the surpluses will be used in the moral interest of the society, the political order reserves the right to place varying amounts (even the pre-eminent amount if need be) of the surpluses at its disposal and to utilize these surpluses to provide (social) service for all the people, and to enhance the prestige and material resources of the political authority, for as the repository of pre-eminent morality and intellect in the society, this act enhances intellect-morality in the general society. The economic surpluses also are to be used to support materially those individuals associated with the apparatus of political authority; that is,

the politicians and administrative bureaucrats who
are the superior men of intellect and morality. For
these individuals are entitled to material privilege
for supporting and spreading intellect-morality in
the society.

In the private sector of the economy (if a
private sector exists in the economy), individuals
of material wealth are expected to associate themselves and their wealth with the political authority,
in the name of morality, both in order to insure
that their economic actions will be morally acceptable, and in order to help to support materially the
morality of the whole social order. This, once
again, normally is accomplished on a basis of an
association between morally acceptable individual
economic actors and individual politicians imbued
with intellect-morality, since if this were accomplished on a collective basis between political
authority and economy, certain regularized, generalized principles and rules might arise which would
imply that morality could be extended to the general
economy. But because of the intrinsic potential immorality of the economy, and the responsibility of
the political authority ever to watch for breaches
of morality in the society, such a state of affairs
never could be accepted. Thus it is considered
proper that the members of the political authority
also receive certain personal economic benefices in
return for their public service of morally supervising individual economic actors. In return, the
individual economic actors avoid the moral-intellectual threat of sanction against their materialistic
economic action which if successful, prima facie
could be considered as perfection in evil. Such
association between politics and economic cannot be
considered as corruption, since it is morally justified in terms of the system.

Those individual economic actors in the private
sector of the economy who are cooperative with the
political authority also may receive political favors,
such as politically associated loans and contract
privileges. For the political authority, in the name
of service morality, is justified in rewarding the
moral and punishing, albeit often by omission, the
non-moral, in order to insure the spread of morality
in the economy and in the society.

It is upon the peasants, who because they are
not allied or associated with the political authority,

and who, because they are illiterate, are by definition the moral and intellectual inferiors in the society, that the major burden falls of providing the surpluses for the political authority and its allies. In what way these surpluses are collected, and what percentage of the total production of the producers these surpluses represent, are not as important as is the fact that they must be collected, since by right they belong where pre-eminent intellect-morality lies. Periodically there are political and economic crises when the political authority or his allies become too greedy and ruthless. This is the traditional signal for rural, usually land, reform to redistribute more equitably the burden of taxation and forced economic draft.

A modern economy is expected to conform to the same "constant" goal of subordinating economic action to political action in the name of intellect-morality. Since, economic support of political aims, including the material economic support for members of the political authority, is prime, the rational economic aims of a modern economy have to be subordinate to these considerations, even if this will interfere, admittedly unfortunately, with the maximum utilization of economic potential.

Occupation

Basic postulate:

Occupation is characterized by a division of labor which qualitatively distinguishes between a role which is associated with intellect-morality and other roles which are not.

Derivative statements:

The men of intellect-morality are considered to be the guardians of the moral aspects of the social order. In this capacity they are considered to be members of a singular occupational grouping which qualitatively is distinct from other occupational groupings in the division of labor. Because the presence of intellect-morality is considered essential to the proper operation of the social order, this grouping both is judged to be essential to the occupational structure, and is judged as productive as any other grouping in the occupational structure. This is so regardless of the specific roles particular members of the grouping assume in the empirical

division of labor. But, since the guardianship of
intellect-morality is associated with political
authority, these individuals normally hold public
office either as politicians or as administrators-
bureaucrats. Because these individuals are motivated primarily by consideration of intellect-
morality, they cannot be expected to be concerned
with, or be judged by, the same considerations of
role specificity as, say, would be the (modern)
professional or technician. And given the choice
between morality and technical professionalism,
morality is to be preferred, for the men who fill
the positions of primary responsibility in the
division of labor must be men of intellect-
morality to insure that morality predominates in
the society. And, for the same reason, if need be,
mastery of morality is supposed to compensate for
any alleged deficiency in technically-specific
professionalism among these individuals.

     Farming also is an essential occupation in the
division of labor because it insures that economic
surpluses will be made available to the men of
intellect-morality to enable them both to sustain
themselves and to spread morality in the social
order (especially through their roles in the political apparatus). It is, therefore, most important that farmers not be diverted from their occupational responsibilities, since this would undermine the maximization of the surpluses of the
society. But since it is important that the surpluses be made available to the men of intellect-
morality, the production of these surpluses may
not profit the farmer, because of a possible high
rate of confiscation in the name of serving the
cause of a higher social morality.

     Although, in an agrarian society, labor is
viewed as occupationally peripheral, in a more
modern society, labor is considered essential because it further contributes to the creation of economic surpluses for the men of intellect-morality.
As in the case of the farmer, however, the vitality
of labor's role in the division of labor does not
imply, necessarily, that the occupational welfare
of laborers will be of primary concern to the men of
intellect-morality. However, as in the case of the
farmer, this attitude may be reversed if the surpluses are threatened by too zealous a disregard of
the occupational well-being of the producers in the
process of confiscation.

Commerce, and now industry, also are considered useful in producing surpluses for the men of intellect-morality to consume or use to spread morality in the society. But the members of this occupational grouping must never be allowed to control independently the pursuit of their own occupational interests. For commercial and industrial occupational interests are based upon maximizing material profit, even if, in the process, moral profit is disregarded. Hence, if left to their own devices, these groupings might undermine the very necessary moral foundation of the social order. Such devices might include, for example, diverting surpluses unnecessarily into non-moral channels and for non-moral purposes, tempting farmers to desert their vital occupational role for commercial or industrial roles, and tempting the men of intellect-morality to be concerned primarily with material advantage rather than morality.

For much the same reasons, the occupational interests of the military must be subordinated to those of intellect-morality. For the military must never become the forceful tool of the non-moral, especially of the non-moral commercial and industrial occupational groupings, who forever are tempted to destroy the intellect-moral basis of the social order in their own selfish occupational interests.

Stratification

Basic postulate:

Stratification is characterized by the assumption that the intellect-moral occupational role alone is entitled to formal recognition and protection of its independent occupational rights and privileges.

Derivative statements:

Evaluation of the occupational roles in the division of labor is a constant evaluation. For the men of intellect-morality, a priori, are evaluated as superior and as the leaders of the social order, whereas all other occupational roles, regardless of the specific characteristic of those roles, a priori, are evaluated as inferior, and as the followers of the social order. If this system works satisfactorily, leaders will be able to fulfill their obligations to spread morality throughout the society,

and the diverse elements that make up the groupings
of followers all will live in social harmony with
each other under the benevolent moral supervision of
the leaders.

And, by implication, conversely, insuring morality and harmony in the society requires insuring the
persistence of a particular grouping, the political
elite, which is dedicated to the spread of morality
as its occupational interest, and which has the
morally endowed social and physical rationale, legitimately, to enforce decisions on all other groupings in the system of social stratification.

In order to insure morality and harmony in the
society through means of the moral supervision of
followers, it is important that group (or class) security lie with the leaders alone. For, if the followers gain access to class security they might be
tempted to slight moral considerations in pursuit of
their class interests, to the point even of challenging the primacy of the moral authority and its
role in the social order, thus destroying the very
moral foundations of the social order. Control of
class security by the political elite implies that
the elite must monopolize all access to corporate
security* in the society and must determine the terms
of whatever security may exist for all the other
groupings in the society; all in the name of insuring
the triumph of morality in the social order. For
this reason, in order to obtain the necessary class
security to pursue legitimate class interests, all
follower classes must petition the political elite
for security. That security, first, is granted
only on grace and not as a corporate right, for it
may have to be removed at will if need be, by the
elite, if, in the judgment of the elite, this would
best serve the interests of morality in the society.

---

*   Corporate security refers to the ability, and
    legal recognition of the right of a grouping
    to organize itself as a distinct, independent
    unit, to limit its membership, to define its
    own rules, to pursue its own distinctive class
    interests, and to protect legally those inter-
    ests as it sees fit against potential opposi-
    tion from outside, competing, corporate group-
    ings.

That security, second, is offered on an individual basis rather than upon a class basis. For, to extend security on a class basis would be to extend a _principle_ which might grow into an irreversible (corporate) right among the potentially immoral; which theoretically, is unacceptable. Consequently, it may be said that non-elite class security is ephemeral and subject to the constant supervisory review and possible withdrawal by the political elite class which may not be sympathetic, on intellect-moral grounds, to the pursuit of particular class interests in particular ways; such as, for example, in the case of independent commercial and industrial classes.

The most efficacious way for members of the follower class to obtain enduring class security is to seek to obtain admission to the ranks of the privileged-intellect-moral elite class by accepting that class's class interests and style of life; that is, by becoming morally literate and/or joining the bureaucracy itself. But this can be accomplished only on an individual basis, upon the willingness of the elite to accept the candidate and by abandoning non-political class interests; that is, in effect, by becoming occupationally identical to the elite class. Alternately, the only possibilities to pursue independent class interests are afforded by association with foreigners (_if_ they are available to offer security), by migration (that is, by abandonment), or by counting on the overthrow of the social order (which may have no significant impact unless accompanied by some qualitative change in the doctrine of political morality). In all these cases, it is to be noted, individuals must go _outside_ their class, and even _outside_ the society, in order to obtain sufficient security to pursue their independent class interests _within_ the society. For, since all non-elite _classes_, _a priori_, are denied access to corporate security, it is not considered feasible for individuals to obtain the desired security within the existing system of social stratification in the society.

Such a system of social stratification is characterized by individual mobility rather than by social or group mobility. For, although movement is encouraged in the social scale, movement (especially moving upward into the arena of corporate security) is individual and is conditional upon

abandonment of present class roles and class interests and upon assumption of political, or politically allied,roles alone. Moving up in the scale
of social stratification, then, enhances the existing class interests and security of only the political elite. In the case of politically allied
roles, although such roles enjoy high status and
considerable class security, since that status
(and that security) is derived solely from and
dependent upon alliance with the political elite,
the status cannot connote access to independent
corporate security, which, a priori, only the
elite can enjoy.

Kinship: descent

Basic postulate:

Kinship: descent is characterized by the
forced division of strategic property among all
legitimate heirs in a way that no recipient receives anywhere near the accumulation of the previous generation.

Derivative statements:

Concentrations of economic power outside the
political control of the political authority smack
of immorality. Hence, if they are not properly
contained through controlled supervision or confiscation, they pose a threat to the primacy of moral-
political values in the society and to the pre-
eminent role of the political authority in the
social order. This very well may happen through
oversight, corruption, or the temporary inability
of the political authority to enforce its will.

But the political authority has an asset working for it; namely, the forced division of accumulated strategic property (and status) inter-
generationally in a way that no heir even can hope
to inherit anywhere near the property (or status)
which the benefactor had accumulated in his lifetime. This insures the relentless, fragmentary
diminution of private economic power (and status)
in time among all throughout the society.

Also, by providing all (legitimate) heirs
with the probability of receiving some property (or
status) from a benefactor, although what can be

offered may be depressing from the rational economic
standpoint, automatic pressure to accumulate property (and status) solely through one's own effort
outside the existing social order is diminished.

Finally, by providing something for everybody,
especially in the agricultural sector of the economy,
the system maximizes the number of potential (tax)
heads and hands who will provide the surpluses to be
placed at the disposal of the political authority to
enable it to carry out its moral supervisory role
over the social order.

Religion

Basic postulate:

Religion is characterized primarily by concern
with man's adjustment to this social order whose
rules are determined by, and administered by, an
intellectual-moral elite.

Derivative statements:

The primary concern of the predominant (orthodox) religion is to define man's social role and to
aid him in adjusting to the existing social order.
Because religion is socially oriented, it is concerned primarily with defining the rules of social
conduct which enable the individual to know what
to do correctly under various specific social circumstances. And since, religion primarily is concerned
with defining social rules, these rules are learned
by intellectual attention. And logically, the more
of these religiously sanctioned rules of social conduct one masters, the more one approaches religious
(and moral) perfection. In this way, intellect is
equated with religious perfection so that, if one
is religiously superior, one must be intellectually
superior, (that is more knowledgeable), and if one
is morally inferior, one must be intellectually
inferior. And since the concern of intellect, in
converse, came to be associated with the mastery
of the (moral) rules of social conduct, if one is
intellectually superior, one must be morally superior, and if one is intellectually inferior, one
must be morally inferior.

Since the orthodox religion primarily is concerned with social morality, it is allied closely
with the political authority, aiding and sanctifying

(that is, legitimizing) the right and obligation of
political authority to be the defender of moral-
social rectitude.

Because primarily it is concerned with social
morality, the predominant religion relegates individual religious interests to secondary consideration. But acknowledging the potential need for
such interests, it allows concern with these individual interests to be taken over by derivative,
specialized denominations within the orthodox
religion, or even by other religions. In this
sense, the predominant religion is tolerant of
alien religious ideas and of alien religions. But
in no case does the orthodox religion allow any
rival to challenge its monopolistic right to define
the significant moral-social codes and prescriptions
of the society or its right to be the exclusive defender of orthodox political authority. In this
sense, the orthodox religion is intolerant of alien
religious ideas and of alien religions.

The significance of the intimate association
between religion, (or morality in its diffused sense),
society, and political authority, is that, first, an
attack on one automatically is assumed to be an attack on all. Especially, those who advocate qualitative changes in the social order, automatically are
morally damned and subject to the wrath of the political authority which is the defender of moral rectitude in the society. And second, since intellect is
the means to obtain morality, and morality must be
learned, and both intellect and morality are associated with political authority, then, formal learning is both sufficient and necessary for the general
preparation for morally superior political elite
roles in the society.

Integration, Stability, and Legitimate Change

Basic postulate:

Integration, stability and legitimate change is
characterized by a monopoly of the sanction to determine an integrated and stable social order and any
legitimate changes in that social order in the hands
of an intellectual-moral political elite.

Derivative statements:

Since a legitimate social order must be responsive to the principles of intellect-morality, it can not be an expedient order. Since only the political elite has the ability to understand and be suitably ethically imbued, this elite alone has the constant right and responsibility to determine the nature of, and direct that inexpedient moral social order. And conversely, if this elite alone properly exercises this exclusive right, then, the social order is guaranteed to remain an inexpedient social order.

Consequently, whenever a problem appears in the social order, since the order a priori must be morally inexpedient, it is assumed that the difficulty cannot be due to any inherent defect in the fundamental nature of the social order. Rather, the problem, traditionally, has been attributed to specific individuals in positions of political responsibility who, through personal defect, are not measuring up to the standards of intellect-morality expected of them. And more recently, the problem has been attributed, as well, to certain procedural administrative maladjustments that require "modernization" and/or rectification.

Hence, the social order periodically must be purged of its structural impediments, human or material. These purges can be, and often are, very drastic. But no matter how thorough they are, these purges preclude the admissibility of possible qualitative changes in the moral-intellectual foundations of the integrated, stable, and legitimate social order. For, no matter what order of problem arises, intellect-morality is assumed essential for any integrated, stable, and legitimate social order.

THE MODEL AND IRANIAN SOCIETY RELATIVE TO THE PROBLEM OF DEVELOPMENT*

---

* The purpose of this section is to (re-)examine the case study in terms of the above model. Ideally, this should provide a summation of those aspects of the Iranian case material relevant to the problem of economic development. But since model analysis is, by definition, a highly selective process, quantitatively and qualitatively, it cannot be a substitute for a case study. Hence, the reader is advised to review the appropriate chapter of the case study, if he feels the argument presented in any particular section to follow requires more data for sake of clarity, or more evidence for sake of conviction.

Authority

The legitimacy of political authority in Iran derives from mastery of intellect-morality. Mastery of Iranian intellect-morality implies mastery of the moral essence of Iranian culture, as expressed in its written heritage of literature, language, and poetry. Consequently, dependence of political authority upon consideration of intellect-morality, implies, first, that mastery of intellect-morality is considered necessary and sufficient to make the kinds of decisions required to carry out political responsibility. Consequently, technicians, whose knowledge is derived from morally neutral, if not morally inferior, non-Iranian sources, must be subordinated to intellect-moral administrators whose mastery of morality is essential for the proper utilization of technical knowledge, even in purely technical situations. It is for this reason, that the technical shifts which have taken place in the Iranian social order, as for example the introduction of industrialization, have not been accompanied by a shift in the structure of authority. For based upon the ground rules of Iranian political authority, there seems to be no reason why intellect-moralists cannot continue to dominate the political order, and why potentially rationally oriented technicians should not continue to play secondary roles in the political order.

Since Iranian political authority is based on intellect-morality, and intellect-morality is derived from mastery of the essences of Iran-ality, second, the basis for political judgments and decisions can not be defined very concretely and hence, cannot be regularized or otherwise made calculable, especially to those outside the pale of the political apparatus.

Consequently, we may say that Iranian political decision making is unstable. Rules and regulations, if they ever are formalized, which often is not the case, mean little, for they are subject to individual variation and interpretation each and every time a decision is made. Such situations may arise in consequence of the fact that two individuals with different interpretations of morality, or even the same individual who appraises the moral dimension differ-may decide differently on two different ns involving the very same issues and/or the me participants.

Political decision making, then, is <u>capricious.</u> For it can be made by specific individuals without recourse to any prior, calculably defined standard by which to measure the decision. And the mere suggestion of using defined "rules" to insure regularity and predictability of political decisions is anti-ethical and anti-moral.

Iranian political decision making is <u>uncertain.</u> Because political decisions are based on consideration of morality, and formalized rules of enforcement may defeat the morality of decisions, political decisions may have to be enforced by the weight of morality, radiating out from decision-maker to the subject of the decision. This has been termed <u>rule</u> by <u>model</u>, for the decision-maker is a model in both the moral sense and in the initiative sense.

Political decision making is <u>confusing.</u> Since mastery of intellect-morality, rather than technical mastery, is the basis for determining who is entitled to make political decisions, then legitimately, all masters of intellect-morality equally are competent or incompetent, to make any and all political decisions. And, thus, since no objective technical standard exists to align roles with candidates for roles, overlapping jurisdiction, especially, but not exclusively in prestigeful roles, is left unresolved, if not actually encouraged.

Yet, regardless of all these administrative problems, which freely are admitted, the Iranian politician prefers to accept these problems as inevitable, rather than to surrender intellect-morality as the basis for political decision making. Consequently, those subject to political decision making outside the political orbit, as for example, commercialists and industrialists, must adjust their behavior accordingly. And such adjustment positively is detrimental to the establishment of a rational, self-generating economic system in Iran.

Since, in the absence of the theocratic authority of an <u>Imam</u>, by delegation, and/or by default, the pre-eminent locus of intellect-morality in Iranian society is to be found in the political apparatus, the political authority has assumed the role of political, moral-supervisor, and on occasion the moral-controller of the social actions of all non-political members of the society, including, of course, commercialists and industrialists. Consequently, regardless

of any technical or otherwise rational justification,
any attempt to evade political control is considered
prima facie evidence of immorality. And certainly,
active opposition to any policies of such a moral
order, is rebellion against morality itself. Especially is this true if the opposition has in mind
establishing an alternative to the intellect-moral
foundation of the social order, as would be the case
with those attempting to establish a rational, self-
generating economic system in Iranian society.

      Since intellect-morality is the basis for de-
fining and enforcing political action, and intellect-
morality normally is not found outside the political
orbit, the Iranian legal system is concerned primarily with what is important and useful to the political authority, and is dominated by the same kind of
political considerations as is the administration of
the political authority at large. And since, to re-
iterate, intellect-moral judgment is individual in
Iran, the defined codes tend to be treated with indifference by the populace. For they know that
although laws are on the books, the law-giver will
act according to his own predilections. Calculable
economic action under such a legal system, patently
is impossible.

      And finally, since the Iranian political order
is an intellectual-moral order, since those outside
the political order are without the pale of such
morality, and since, those within the political
apparatus in inferior positions have less morality,
Iranian political action is arbitrary, autocratic,
and authoritarian. For responsibility can be delegated to (moral) inferiors, but authority must not
be, or morality suffers. And so, because of the
moral necessity of substantively controlling inferiors, the political privileges of inferiors always
are reversible and are given out only on grace by
the political center. Local autonomy in Iran,
regardless of formal evidence to the contrary, is
unknown as a right, because the moral center has
the moral obligation to supervise and control what
is less moral, and that process cannot be fettered
by restrictive rules and intermediaries who might
impede the political order's maneuverability in
exercising that obligation. And since those who
are supervised and controlled, a priori, are less
intellectual and less moral than those at the center
who supervise and control, the moral supervisors-
controllers must assume the burden of politically

acting for those they supervise and control, for the
inferiors cannot be expected to assume properly this
moral and intellectual responsibility. This kind of
autocratic and authoritarian political action is not
"stable," in the sense that it reasonably can be predicted. For, since it is based on intellect-morality
its decisions never can be taken for granted beforehand by anyone in society, including admittedly, even
those who are responsible for making the decisions.
And predictability is the quintessence of a long-
range rational self-generating economic system.

The Economy

     The intrusion of intellect-morality into the
operation of the Iranian economy implies, first,
that economic action never must be left to its own
devices to maximize economic profit, for this, a
priori, is evil. Consequently, Iranian economic
actors are forced to include in their economic calculation a particular kind of non-economic element
that is not calculable, in the same sense that
purely economic means and ends are calculable. For,
by definition, this consideration is based on individual judgements outside the design of a rational
economic order, and varies in time and on occasion.
These intellect-moral judgements, not only may be
extraneous, they also may be contradictory to primarily rational economic judgements. For example,
an economic enterprise may be very profitable, but
it may be found wanting morally, and conversely, an
enterprise might be close to economic ruin, but it
may be judged a moral success. And, in like token,
purely economic "success" (profit, efficiency, etc.)
always may be challenged and purely economic
"failure" always may be justified, if that morality,
respectively, has been submerged to, or has
triumphed over economic evil. The willingness to
accept economic failure in the name of moral triumph
is of particular concern in Iran because it has been
used to justify (or at least condone) the waste, in
economic enterprises, and the indifference to rational
economic planning, all so typical of Iranian economic
endeavor, solely in the name of preserving the
Iranian intellect-moral way of life.

     The intrusion of intellect-morality in the oper-
ation of the Iranian economy, second, justifies a
particular kind of political supervision and control
over the economy. For the Iranian political authority, in the absence of the Imamate, has the preroga-

tive and responsibility of enforcing the requisite
(politically relevant) morality in the economy.
Consequently, the primary goal and policies of the
Iranian political authority in the economy are to
insure the triumph of morality and not necessarily
to assure economic profit, or economic efficiency.
And since judgement as to the morality of the
economy is defined exclusively by the moral-
intellectuality of the political authority, and
this is the measure of any decision to intervene
into the economy, and since intervention takes
place on such terms and on such occasions which can
not be calculated rationally by the actors in the
economy, this encourages the kind of economic activity in Iran that usually is associated with maximizing economic return in a milieu of politically
generated economic insecurity; namely, speculation
for high and fast profits, investment in land rather
than in productive economic enterprise, and recourse
to devious economic measures (such as political
bribery and corruption), to evade inevitable but in-
calculable political control or interference into
the actions of the economy.

Since rational economic profit, anywhere in the
economy may be considered non-moral, and subject to
supervision at any time by politicians, and conversely,
political profit, a priori, is always moral and acceptable, the intrusion of political morality into the
operation of the Iranian economy, third, has tended
to bring about an order of political profit that is
detrimental to the maximization of economic profit.
For economic action, whether it is based upon the
capital of the urban market or upon the surpluses
forceably or fraudulently bilked from the hapless peasants, is saddled with serving moral-political profit;
hence, the over-loaded bureaucratic or private payrolls to bribe potential political discontents, and
the choice of economic projects which enhance moral-
political prestige (such as the non-functional monuments found everywhere in the country), while productive economic enterprise wants for capital.

And finally, fourth, since economic morality is
defined by political individuals and not by economic
actors (importantly, even economic actors within the
public sector of the economy), and since that economic
morality is determined by the political authority's
definition of the threat of the economy to general
morality, and since this definition varies with individuals (and by logical extension, by time and cir-

cumstance), there cannot be any set of calculable ground rules as to the extent and quality of political regulation over the economy. Consequently, the legal relationship between authority and economy in Iran works always in the interest of the political authority and not necessarily at the same time, in the interest of the economy. But, ironically, since morality is determined on an individual basis, at the same time, individuals in the political authority always can be induced to change their mind, or at least reconsider and hence, delay, the imposition of economic decisions. This leaves the door open to individual negotiation, which although it may not always lead to corruption to avert a morally arbitrary decree, more often leads to the attempt of those imposed upon to weasel out of accepting political decisions as final. In either case, indecision arises in the Iranian economy, indecision over what the rules are, and whether or not these rules will be enforced. Examples of such indecision include indecision in the tax system, indecision in the government controlled credit system, indecision in economic planning and strategic economic policies, and indecision in the policy to emphasize the public sector or private sector or mixed economy in economic development. And it is this indecision, rather than how favorable or unfavorable an economic policy of the political authority is at the moment, that is the greatest enemy of long-range, rational, productive economic action. Yet that indecision is built into the very fabric of Iranian moral economics.

Occupation

Mastery, or alleged mastery of the knowledge contained in the Iranian heritage implies that one is a moral and superior man, and is entitled as a right to a position in the apparatus of political authority according to one's degree of mastery of that heritage. And conversely, it is the responsibility of those who master that heritage to seek careers and positions in the political apparatus. Consequently, the men of intellect-morality, who have mastered (or at least been exposed to) the Iranian traditional literary culture, constitute a distinctive productive, occupational grouping.

Not surprisingly, these government servants expect to be, and are, occupationally evaluated upon the basis of mastery of intellect-morality and are not evaluated upon the basis of any specific technical,

rational occupational worth or job performance. And
for this reason, even today, preparation for occupational roles, that is, education, primarily is concerned with the mastery of the traditional Iranian
literary heritage or its modern derivatives, where-
ever possible, rather than with the mastery of
rational scientific education.

       Only the men of intellect-morality associated
with political service (and the members of the
clergy are civil servants as they would be if the
Imamate was in existence) have the unqualified right
to pursue their own (independent) occupational
interest. Consequently, those outside the orbit of
political authority who, by definition, are divorced
from the aura of intellect-morality, are at an a
priori disadvantage in attempting to establish, protect and extend distinctive occupational interests.
For, the non-political interests have been forced to
align their occupational interests with the moral
interests of the political authority. Especially
has this been true of the commercial and industrial
interests. This alignment, unfortunately, has
served the political authority's economically non-
rational, wasteful inefficient use of the commercial-
industrial surpluses (e.g., in monument building), on
the one hand, and perhaps even more significant, has
encouraged the persistence of such non-rational, but
politically innocuous, occupational actions as speculation among the commercial and industrial economic
actors, on the other hand. For this reason, the
Iranian political authority has concluded that it
need not actually own the occupational means of the
commercial-industrial groupings to insure control of
the economy in its interest. For control of the
economy along political lines useful to itself, can,
and has been, achieved through the right of "moral"
intervention without actual ownership of the means
of the economy.

       These same principles of supervision and con-
trol also have been applied to such other occupational groupings of the society as farmers, laborers,
and the military. As well, none of these occupational
groupings have been able to rationalize their occupational actions to serve their own occupational best
interests. For by definition, this would be material,
selfish, and against the moral interests of the social
order, as defined by the Iranian political authority.
Especially is this true of farmers, but to some extent
it is true also of laborers, who are kept on a subsis-

tence level in a non-rationalized economy and at the
mercy of the policies and programs of political
authority to insure that farmers and laborers will
continue to provide the surpluses to sustain the
occupational interests of the members of the
intellectual-moral political apparatus. And, in
turn, by subordinating the Iranian military to non-
rational moral political control, the political
authority assures itself that the military will not
serve not only its own occupational interests, but
also will not serve the interests of such other
interests as any rising commercial-industrial economic force that might threaten to "break through" the
non-rational, morally-oriented occupational structure. In all these ways, the political authority is
assured not only of its own physical perpetuation,
but also of its ability to maintain sufficient access
to the economic benefices of the society without committing itself to rational economic development.

Stratification

The Iranian structure of social stratification
arbitrarily and constantly is bifurcated into an
elite class of superiors who possess intellect-
morality, and into a class of inferiors who are
divorced from possession of that morality. The
elite class a priori is associated with (political)
leadership, since politics is the means to insure
the validation and spread of morality in the society.
For inferiors to be considered morally acceptable,
they must subject themselves and their class interests to the scrutiny, supervision, and if necessary,
the control of the moral-political elite. By insisting on the constant necessity of moral supervision and control of the class interests of the non-
elite class(es), first, the political elite justifies denial of automatic access to (corporate) class
security to the non-political classes. Some degree
of (non-corporate) security, however, may be extended
on an individual, temporary basis, if it serves the
alleged moral interests of the political elite,
which, of course, is considered synonymous with the
moral interests of the society.

Second, supervision of control by the elite of
the class interests of the other elements of the
society, insures that, regardless of the potential readjustments or realighments in the specific composition of the non-elite class(es) all novel, non-
political groupings and their novel class interests

(as for example, industrialists) will be dominated
by a moral-political elite and its class interests.

And, finally, since the Iranian system of mobility, although very fluid for individuals, connotes
nothing as far as establishing corporate recognition
of class interests are concerned, without moral-
political approval, the political authority is able
to insure that non-political values will not become
paramount in the social order, if, under these circumstances, they ever will become paramount within
certain non-political elements in the social order.

The Iranian commercial-industrial groupings, as
other non-political interests in Iranian society,
suffer from all these stratification disabilities.
Most significantly, they have been denied the possibility of corporate recognition and protection of
their class interests on moral grounds. Especially
this is so if they ever are foolish enough to flirt
with the possibility of gaining recognition for
"selfish" (i.e., rational) economic values and
"selfish" economic actors. For this would threaten
to terminate the necessity of moral-political supervision and spoilage of the assets of this class, if
not threaten the whole rationally inefficient, but
morally efficient social order. And, by morally
precluding the possibility of class mobility in the
status hierarchy for commercial-industrialists, as
commercial-industrialists, the political authority
tempts individual economic talent and its material
assets to align with political interest if favorable social status and privilege ever is to be
achieved.

For all these reasons, the Iranian economy is
characterized by politically generated insecurity,
political plunder, individual economic actors begging for temporary favors on grace from economic non-
rationally oriented politicians, and speculative sub-
rosa economic activity--all in order to avoid the
heavy hand of the moral-political elite--rather
than by corporatively recognized and socially respected rational economic action.

Kinship: descent

The enforced fragmentation of economic power,
through the Islamic Iranian inheritance system,
helps further to reduce the possibility of the development of purely economically oriented economic

power. For whatever is accumulated in one lifetime
relentlessly and drastically is diminished inter-
generationally. In this way, the political authority, as a public corporate political entity (for its
members individually are subject to the same inheritance law), in its capacity as accumulator of surpluses for its moral supervisory role in the social
order, is insured that it alone will be able to accumulate substantial economic wealth and power. And
hence, the political authority is assured that, in
the long-term view, economic power is subordinated
to moral-political prerogatives and ends in the
society.

Also, in the short-term view, the political
authority insures political control of economic surpluses by offering the only means for individuals
who are economically talented to ameliorate their
losses through inheritance, by opening potentially
new avenues to economic accumulation. This is
achieved, however, only if the economically talented
individuals align their economic interests with
those of the polity by accepting, on grace, the primacy of moral-political values in economic action,
and by allowing moral-political access to the consequent economic material profit. Most recently, this
has been the case for those operating outside the
orbit of landed property; that is, for commercial
speculators who are favored with lucrative government contracts and loans which have insured high,
windfall profits.

Within the orbit of landed property, the
Iranian inheritance system, by providing always for
"room for one more," even with, and especially with,
land reform measures, insures the immobility and subsistence level of the farm labor force, while simultaneously assuring the political authority of expanded surpluses in the form of taxes, which it can
continue to use for moral-political, rather than for
rational-economic, ends.

Religion

The primary characteristic of Iranian religion
is the intimate association between the orthodox
religion, Shia Islam, and political authority, and
through the medium of political authority, the intimate association between religious values in general.
In Shia Islam, the religious leader (that is, Imam)
is considered to be an intermediary between God and

man and is considered to be free of sin. It has
come to be believed that the last religious leader
has delegated temporarily, albeit in theory, his temporal powers as the moral judge and disciplinarian
of the social order to the political authority, especially to the leader of the political authority, the
Shah. This symbolic delegation has provided the political authority, first, with a moral position, such
that an attack on it may be viewed by the political
authority as an attack on morality, and an attack on
morality may require the offensive action of the
political authority. But more significantly, second,
this delegation has provided the political authority
with a sanction to regulate and control the social
order in the name of the defender of <u>moral</u> rectitude.
And moral control of the social order, includes, of
course, moral control of the economic order. And
opposition, to that control, may be immoral, for it
is a defense of social, political, and religious immorality. Hence, the only feasible, morally-
desirable course is to adjust to the required rules
of the social order, rather than to oppose the prescription of what automatically is a moral order.
This ever present and morally unassailable threat of
political intervention, and in the name of protecting the morality of the social order, has generated
an economic insecurity which cannot be opposed on
economic grounds; that is, on grounds of efficiency
and economy. And this has encouraged speculation,
waste, and corruption with the full connivance and
even encouragement of political authority.

Although Iran, to a considerable extent, has
been "secularized," many of the religious values
underlying the social order including the economy,
also have been secularized and diffused, so that a
diminution of formal religion in Iran has not necessarily meant that once-religious values have been
diminished as well. This certainly has been true in
the case of educational values. For, although the
corpus of intellectual knowledge, once religious,
has been secularized, education still is associated
with the traditional Iranian culture to the extent,
that it is considered moral in and of itself, and
without doubt, morally superior to non-Iranian,
rational-scientific, technically specific, a-moral
education. As well, <u>all</u> education, Iranian <u>or</u>
foreign, continues to be placed primarily at the
service of the moral political order, in its capacity as the arm of knowledgeable morality in the
society. In this way, non-Iranian, rational, amoral

education remains the tool of the existing social
order, rather than a potential catalyst for the
introduction of rational, especially economically
rational goals (and to an extent, means) into the
social order.

Integration, Stability, and Legitimate Social Change

Since intellect-morality must be upheld as a
constant, no matter what specific structural
changes are proposed or introduced into the Iranian
social order, and the political authority, as the
guardian of morality, is the initiator and deter-
miner of those changes, the subordination of rational
economic interests to intellect-_moral_ political interests in any social change is assured.

And for the same reasons, when difficulties
and inadequacies in the social order, including the
economy, arise, a _priori_, the fundamental intellect-
moral nature of the social order cannot be at fault.
Consequently, the society, including the political
authority, resorts to purging "immoral" _individuals_,
and readjusting and formally changing _specific struc-
tures_ in order to meet a challenge, in which, perhaps, more drastic qualitative changes in the very
fundamental assumptions of the social order, including intellect-morality, may be required.

Even though all these assumptions have been
demonstrated, time and time again, to run counter
to the best interests of developing of a rational,
self-generating economy, no question can be raised
as to changing them; and the economy must "adjust"
accordingly (to pursue speculation and the like).

THE INTERACTION OF THE INSTITUTIONS OF A SOCIAL SYSTEM

Although the various (that is, seven) institutions have been treated throughout the present study
as analytically distinct, it has been assumed that
these discrete institutions interact in a system,
whether that system is conceived to be an abstract
model system or the concrete system of Iranian
society. This assumption implies that the institutions not only are compatible with each other, but
they also mutually reinforce each other. Specifically, in terms of the problem at hand (that is,
economic development) this means that, in the case

of Iranian society, all the institutions provide a facilitating structure and direct the interests of the society in general in a particular direction which is not conducive to economic development.

It is hoped that this has become apparent in the course of examining the case study and through the model explanations of this chapter. However, since the assumption that the problem of economic development is a problem of a whole society, as reflected in the fundamental goals, or basic values, of its institutional structure, is one of the key assumptions of the present study, it may be worthwhile to illustrate this point, by briefly running through a single theme among the problems of economic development, showing how the fundamental assumptions of each of the social institutions of Iranian society has contributed to that (problem) theme and in the same direction. A useful means to do this is to examine the theme of economic rationality.*

---

* Economic rationality connotes the acceptance of the goal of the maximization of economic efficiency and profit as being primary in the economy (see above, Chapter One, section "Some Technical Definitions"). According to this view, no economic system completely is rational, for, certainly, other than rational economic considerations, including political considerations, enter overtly or covertly into any economic decision. But this view does maintain that in a certain (model) kind of social system, as for example, in Iran, a situation exists in which, at best, rational economic procedures are adjusted or limited (that is, "contained") by certain fundamental institutional goals which are primary, the most significant of which is non-rational (political) morality. This latter situation has been termed by one observer, "substantive rationality," as contrasted with the "formal rationality" associated with that (model) kind of social system which accepts the goals of economic rationality as primary in the social order. (See Max Weber, The Theory of Social and Economic Organization, New York, 1947, passim.) Why this is so, and how this is justified in Iranian society, is the subject of the discussion of this section.

Iranian political authority fears and opposes economic rationality because economic rationality threatens to undermine the intellect-moral bases of economic decisions which legitimize its peculiar supervisory and intervening role in the economy. Consequently, the political authority has balked at developing, for example, a rational, legal system with defined rights, privileges, and obligations upon which those in the economy can calculate and pursue economic action with reasonable assurance. This has been especially detrimental to the kind of rational calculation necessary to establish and maintain long-range, self-generating enterprise (the institution of political authority).

Intellect-morality in Iran is infused into economic thought to produce moral economics, in contrast to rational economics. Rational economics is considered morally selfish and potentially evil, especially if one is a success at it. Consequently, moral economic action, which is indifferent to waste and inefficiency, encourages the pursuit of non-development economic goals such as land and commodity speculation as the only practical, pseudo-rational (that is, substantively rational) means to take advantage of the existing economic ground rules (the institution of the economy).

The members of groupings associated with economic action do not have the right to pursue, protect, and extend their occupational interests as they conceive those interests. Since the grouping which has that right is a particular kind of political elite, whose interests are not motivated primarily by rational, economic interests, economic rationality can but suffer (the occupation institution).

Because only bureaucrats-politicians have corporate privileges insuring the right and ability to pursue independent class interests, those who are primarily concerned with economic action in the society, (whether in the public or private sector of the economy) as a class, are dependent on a political class of administrators-politicians, as a class, for economic security. Consequently, economic actors, to be "successful," then, must subordinate rational economic interests to bureaucratic-politician, political interests. The very act of political subordination, moreover, deprives economic actors of even the possibility of using economic wherewithal to improve their social status as a class, and in doing so, establishing the legitimacy of such class values as the primacy of rational values, at least in the economy, if not in the total society (the stratification institution).

The forced division of property among all legitimate heirs over time helps dissipate any potential sources of independent economic power that may have escaped the watchful eye of the political authority. Consequently, any concentration of independent economic power that conceivably might be directed into rational channels, simply because it is free potentially of political control, inevitably, is dissipated inter-generationally (the institution of kinship: descent).

Since moral perfectibility can exist only by adjustment to the values and precepts of the existing social order, opposition to the existing social order, a priori, is moral heresy. Since the pursuit of rational economic goals is not a part of the rules of the existing social order, a priori, these goals are heterodox, and are unlikely to be accepted as orthodox unless the institutional values of the social order (and not merely its present specific structure) changes (the institution of religion).

Since legitimate social change implies only the purging of individuals, and perhaps, some structural "readjustments," but not the right to make qualitative changes in the basic moral foundations of the social order, even the right to contest for the right to "break through" to economic rationality, to say the least, is most difficult (institution of an integrated and stable social order, and legitimate change).

Clearly, then, introducing economic rationality into the Iranian economy logically, both undermines and, in turn, is dependent on undermining, the basic values underlying each of the institutions of the whole social system, and not merely undermining the basic values of the one institution of the economy alone. Or, to rephrase, it is the system of basic values underlying the whole institutional structure of the social system as a system that is the measure of the problem.

THE SIGNIFICANCE OF THE PROPOSED MODEL FOR THE STUDY OF IRANIAN DEVELOPMENTAL PROBLEMS

It is one of the basic premises of the present work that the <u>kind</u> of society which has been described in the case study, and which is being discussed to this point in the present chapter, <u>qualitatively</u> is different from the <u>kind</u> of society which <u>preceded</u> the modern developed societies in the West, and interestingly enough, also in Japan. One significant implication of this premise is that the present social structure of Iran is not to be considered as "feudal" or "semi-feudal."[1] This conception hardly is original with the author, and even those serious students of Iranian society and Iranian social history who still employ the label "feudal" have suggested that it might be better to indicate that Iranian "feudalism" is a "different kind of feudalism."[2] But the author, for one, prefers that the Gordion knot be cut and that the term "feudalism" be dropped completely.

Certainly, what a society is labeled, of itself, is of little logical consequence, <u>provided</u> consensus exists as to the denotation and connotation of the label. For a label, in addition to being a convenient short-cut sign for a term, also connotes a complex bundle of implicative ideas, <u>all</u> of whose components, may, or may not be, acceptable to all of the parties who are faced with the prospect of using the label. Consequently, consensus on one or more of the connotative components alone must not be assumed to imply total consensus on all the components; for the lack of consensus on one or more of the components may be (and, to suggest, in this case is) important. In addition, a label also may be a symbol or group of symbols which have come to be associated with certain judgements concerning the label and which also may or may not be accepted by everyone using the label; and this likewise may be (and in this case is) important. Unfortunately, all these confusions have come to be associated with the use of the term feudal (and semi-feudal).

Specifically, it is worth arguing that the existence of a predominantly agrarian economy with small villages, basically self-sufficient as far as the outside economy and other aspects of the social structure are concerned, dominated by landlords (often absentee), who live in a different world economically and socially from the peasants, and who are part of,

or allied with, the dominant political and social
class, is not necessarily indicative of feudalism,
although feudalism did have all of these features.[3]
Logically, one must say that these features are
necessary but not sufficient for feudalism, for they
also are necessary but not sufficient for another
type of agrarian society which is not feudal. For,
although these two systems share all of these
characteristics in common, there are other, and very
important, characteristics which are not shared in
common. For example, in the non-feudal system, in
contrast to feudalism, landlords do not live in
rural castles, but in cities; economic actors, and
others in the society are associated with a well-
developed money economy, instead of being associated
with a self-sufficient feudal economy; the lord's
access to the land comes from the grace of a strong
centralized ruler and not, in contrast to feudalism,
from an established, formally recognized principle
of mutually acknowledged rights, privileges, and
obligations between grantor and grantee (that is,
the "feudal contract"); and the lord's interest in
land is for fiscal benefit and not, as in feudalism,
for manpower to protect empirically limited and
fragmented economic and political power.[4] Consequently, since certain differences do exist between
the two kinds of systems, and since these differences may be more important than the similarities
for certain purposes, the differences warrant not
calling all agrarian societies "feudal." Certainly
this is so, if the term feudal automatically connotes to all that use it, that these differences
are to be ignored, which, logically, one can but
believe, if the term is used to cover the agrarian
structure of both kinds of systems.

     The question of acceptance or rejection of the
term "feudal," then, is not a pedantic battle over
labels, especially, for example, if the differences
between feudalism and non-feudal agrarianism bears
importantly on the question of why a society, here
Iranian society, has not developed, and what has to
be done to develop that society. For, if the
agrarian Iranian society is not viewed as feudal,
then, the important interpretation that agrarian
Iranian society is not the prior stage of the developed society which arose out of feudalism is possible. And consequently, Iran, by (giving the impression of) modernizing that society, while adhering
to the existing set of determinant circumstances,
will not necessarily simultaneously develop that

society. However, it then follows that the qualitative contrast between the order of determining circumstances, or model, of a non-feudal social order,
and the order of determining circumstances of a
feudal, later developed, social order, might suggest the order of changes necessary to develop the
Iranian economy (and society)--in so far as any
previous experience is a guide to the future. It is
now in order to present and discuss that alternative,
feudal-developed model.

THE ALTERNATE MODEL

Introduction:

To reiterate, the proposed model, has been
derived from the institutional characteristics of
the developed societies of both Western Europe and
of Japan.* One advantage of deriving the model
in part from the Japanese experience is that this
answers the legitimate criticism that most models
of developed societies are restricted to the
Western experience; and consequently, are culture
bound to the Western experience, and are not necessarily proper models for other than European,
especiallly Asian societies to follow. (See below,
Chapter Eleven). Consequently, in the course of
abstracting from the Japanese case as well as from
the Western European cases, the author hopes that
he has highlighted those conditions essential for
economic development without, at the same time,
being unduly dazzled by the particular patterned
means to the goals of the development, which have
varied between Japan and the West, and, presumably,
can vary in any particular social and cultural
situation, including the Iranian situation. It
might be mentioned that it is for this reason that
no attempt has been made to build a concrete body

---

* This model, with some important modifications,
  is a briefer presentation of the model proposed
  in the author's, The Origin of Modern Capitalism
  in Eastern Asia, (Hong Kong University Press,
  1958). The reader is referred to that study
  for a more detailed discussion of the model,
  and/or for the Japanese empirical case materials
  which illustrate the model.

of illustrations to this model representing the specific patterned means to achieve development in
Iranian society. For although this obviously is a
necessary next step, and a logical inevitability of
the present study, the author believes that this
lies outside the concern of the present study. In
part he believes this because he is convinced that
this dimension of the process of change may best be
left for the participants themselves to (help) formulate. For in this way Iranians can be satisfied
that they are preserving enough of the essentials
of their basic way of life while still acceding to
the imperatives of becoming a developed society; or
to put it another way, they will no longer have the
excuse that development necessarily will destroy the
essentials of the basic Iranian way of life, although
quite obviously, certain kinds of changes necessarily
will have to be considered.

Authority

The basic postulate:

Political authority is characterized by the
assumption that the right to authority is determined
(that is, validated) by a demonstrated superior pragmatic ability to successfully solve the existing
problem of order by administering and coordinating
the competing politically oriented groupings in the
society.

Derivative statements:

No a priori, constant sanction to political
authority exists, hence, no one political element
or political interest has the right to claim a
perpetual monopoly to authority. Rather, it is on
that political element that best can respond to the
political challenge, that the mantle of political
authority falls. And that response is the ability,
in pragmatic competition with political rivals, to
offer the most satisfactory means to coordinate
effectively the existing diverse, independent, or
at least semi-autonomous political elements in the
society, to maintain that coordination through cooperation, and to initiate constructive political
action as defined by the pragmatic political needs
of that particular society at that particular time.

In the process of establishing any specific
political system (or structure) of successful

coordination and administration of diverse elements
in the society, regardless of the amount of coercion
that is involved in that process, since that system
is, by definition, unstable, in the last analysis,
it is dependent on the assent of the elements involved. And in order to maintain that assent, the
rights, privileges, and obligations of the political
elements must be defined. All elements are expected
to live up to the terms of that definition, or the
carefully worked out structure of coordination
and administration will go asunder. Especially,
the geographic or "interest" autonomy and the maneuverability of these elements (their so-called "legal
rights") must be acknowledged formally to avoid
possible destruction of the system from within.
For, once again, in the absence of an a priori moral
right of control, force and coercion alone can
never retain a structure of authority, especially in
the face of an ever potential changing, pragmatic
political challenge which threatens to make obsolete
the assumed superiority and power of a particular
political structure. And since the specific structure is unstable, further, the structure has to be
left "open" by those in authority, to seize upon new
opportunities, if at all possible, and to allow for
potential new elements whose composition and role
might not be forseen, to be brought into the system
without destroying the system. And consequently,
allowance is made for the redress of political
grievances within the existing structure so that
the structure will not be destroyed necessarily by
every novel challenge within or without.

The response of the political authority to the
interests of the economy, by definition, can be no
different from its response to the interests of any
other element in the society. It may look upon the
economy as a useful, and perhaps even a vital element
to control, but economic interest must be treated as
any other potentially cooperative and potentially
coordinated element in the society. Specifically,
economic actors are assured, formally, of their
right to pursue (rational) economic objectives, and
of their right to respond readily to economic challenges in their own (economic) way. And especially,
economic actors are assured of a political milieu
in which they can calculate rationally their economic actions by the establishment by the political
authority of legally defined and enforced rights,
privileges, and obligations, concerning the relation-

ship between the political authority and themselves,
between other elements in the society and themselves,
and even among themselves. They are also assured of
the right to seek the kind of specific political
structure responsive to their economic needs (instead of the other way around), and to have their
own members, or individuals sympathetic to their
interests, participate in staffing the apparatus of
political authority, if this is considered necessary
to serve their economic interests. They are assured
of the right to seek redress for their economic
grievances, as they conceive economic grievances to
be, and within the existing political structure, if
at all possible. In brief, the political authority
assures the economy that, insofar as political
authority is able to assure it, economic goals will
be paramount in the economy and will not be thwarted
by other, non-economic goals or elements in the
society, and also that the political authority will
use its political prerogatives <u>positively</u> to facilitate the development of economic rationality in the
society.

The Economy

Basic postulate:

The economy is characterized by the assumption
that the maximization of rational economic profit
is the goal of economic action and that this goal
cannot be subordinated to any non-economic goal,
such as a political goal, in the social order.

Derivative statements:

The pursuit of economic profit is considered
to be legitimate, yet ethically-neutral of itself.
Consequently, the economy may be concerned primarily
with maximizing economic profit as a legitimate
right. And since the concept of what constitutes
the maximization of economic profit varies in time,
due at least to the changing nature of the technological forces operating in the economy, the basic
ideas as to how best to maximize economic profit also
vary in time. And, as well, as old ideas of maximizing economic profit are replaced with new ideas
better adapted to this end, the different elements
in particular social orders that are intimately associated with particular ways of maximizing this profit,
will change; rising and falling, and rising again

(and failing again) fragmenting, combining, and re-
combining, and refragmenting.

And, as the ideas they bear, the ultimate fortune of economic elements always is dependent upon
how well they meet the empirically changing challenge of maximizing economic profit at particular
periods of economic organization. For, as in the
case of economic ideas, the pre-eminence of any one
element in the economy at any one time, must be
based upon the pragmatic conclusion that that element offers the best means to serve the economy
efficiently and productively. Since this service,
by definition, is changeable, and hence, unstable,
no one element in the society, no matter how successful at a particular time, has any guarantee
that it will be able to continue to impose indefinitely upon that society, its views on how to organize the economy. Certainly, no one element a priori
can assume a moral right to control the economy in
perpetuity, any more than it can claim a moral right
to control the economy at the time that it is strug-
gling initially to assert the supremacy of its
(economic) ideas. And especially is all this true
of the political authority, which regardless of its
pre-eminent political role and power in the social
order, approaches the economy as another competitive element in the society. For political authority, as any other constituent element in the society,
is judged and is held accountable on the basis of
an objective contribution to the maximum rational
development of the economy.

The political authority, traditionally, has
best contributed to this maximum rational development of the economy by facilitating the cooperation
and coordination of the diverse elements in the
society interested in maximizing economic profit,
and in providing general security for the pursuit
of maximum profit. This has been achieved primarily
through the enforcement of political peace in the
economic environment and through the enforcement of
rational codified law. Rational codified law establishes the rules and procedures for the behavior
of all economic actors in the society including, of
course, the members of the political authority if
they too are economic actors of some sort. In this
way all economic actors are able to calculate rationally, and with reasonable assurance, the variables
of economic action as far as the individuals and
economic objects in the general society are concerned,

for regardless of the degree of government association with (or even intervention into) the economy,
the policy of political authority and its members
must be calculable in terms of rational economic
efficiency and economy, and the political authority
must be held accountable according to the legal
rules and regulations of the society, in the same
way as any other element in the economy. The measure of the polity's conformity to this principle
may be reflected in its tax laws, and in any other
such of its political laws regulating the economy,
on one hand, or in the (qualitative) way rather
than the (quantitative) amount with which it positively aids the economy with public credit and economic planning, on the other hand.

Consequently, regardless of the amount of
government association with the economy, the economy
may be said to be autonomous if its pursuit of maximizing economic profit is not confused with, or
impeded by, political profit, even when, and especially when, the political authority is heavily
involved in the economic process. For, it is only
in this way, that the choices of, and the operations
of, economic enterprise can be determined by rational
economic ends. And, it is only in this way, that
the economic sector of the society will have the
right to make the primary decisions as to the disposal of the economic surpluses of the society; certainly, at the least, in so far as disposal affects
the maximization of economic profit. Or to rephrase,
it is only in this way, those elements in the society
which are interested in cooperating in a particular
system of economic action will have the right to
control and use their surpluses in a way that the
pursuit of maximum economic profit is feasible.

If any element does not believe it is gaining
its proper share of maximum profit from a particular
scheme of economic action, it has the right to attempt to redress its grievances, for no element in
the society, least of all the political authority,
has the right, a priori, to monopolize the making of
these kinds of decisions. Hence, the structure of
the economy may be characterized as flexible and
"open." Consequently, new economic challenges such
as that posed by economic development, cannot be
thwarted arbitrarily by the a priori decision of any
one element in the society, especially the political
authority, to subordinate the maximum pursuit of

rational economic profit to existing economic procedures, or more significantly, to other, non-economic (especially political) considerations.

Occupation

Basic postulate:

Occupation is characterized by the assumption that all legitimate roles in the division of labor are of equal moral worth, although not all roles are privileged.

Derivative statements:

All legitimate roles in the division of labor, (that is, not prostitutes, for example) are considered occupationally moral (or in effect, amoral) and the occupational groupings in the society which are organized about these roles, likewise are considered moral (or in effect, amoral). Consequently, it has been considered legitimate (or moral) for all occupational groupings, on their own initiative, to claim, and if necessary contend, for the right of independent occupational action to pursue independent occupational interests and goals, as determined by the membership of the various occupational groupings themselves. Since this is accepted as a matter of course, regardless of specific social structures in existence at particular times, it is not necessary automatically for any particular occupational grouping to overturn the social structure in order to achieve these goals. For, since all legitimate roles are moral (or in effect, amoral), no one grouping has any ethical right, automatically, to deny the pursuit of occupational action to another grouping, although it might resist vehemently on pragmatic grounds. Consequently, the appearance of both novel occupational groupings and internal changes spanning novel occupational interests within existing occupational groupings can be expected to appear, in response to novel occupational opportunities and challenges arising out of significant changes in the social or technological order.

Consequently, even though the occupational interests and goals of specific occupational groupings, at specific times, in specific social structures, empirically, are deprivileged and unfulfilled, as for example the interests and goals of peasants under feudalism, since this is not _inevitable_ on any

preconceived standard, this situation conceivably
can be ameliorated with a shift in the occupational
structure arising out of new and effective responses
to new challenges in the technological and social
order. For this reason, leadership talent, when it
arises in particular occupational groupings, necessarily is not tempted to desert even the most deprivileged of occupational groupings. For any occupational grouping has, at least, the potentiality
of establishing its occupational interests, goals,
and privileges in the division of labor through a
change in the existing occupational structure which
that grouping's leadership itself can help to bring
about. For this reason, intellectual leadership
is dispersed throughout the occupational structure
and consequently, learning is but the practical,
technical tool of many diverse occupational groupings and not the natural monopolistic weapon of one
occupational grouping.

The commercial and industrial elements, as any
other elements in the society, have taken advantage
of all these generalized assumptions to sanction
the pursuit of, and eventually to win acceptance in
the society for, their specific occupational interests, goals, and privileges; goals, interests, and
privileges which included values and means conducive
to the development of a rational, self-generating
economic system.

Stratification

Basic postulate:

Stratification is characterized by the assumption that all legitimate roles in the division of
labor are able to assert and strive to win corporate
protection of occupational rights and privileges.

Derivative statements:

No a priori, evaluable constant exists for
determining a system of social stratification. Consequently, instability and the constant threat of
radical shifts in the specific hierarchy of social
stratification always exist, and no supposedly ideal
system of evaluation outlives any specific hierarchy
to which it is attached ideologically. For this
reason, the possibility that changes in the internal
composition of any existing class or the fragmentation and realignment of existing elements and exist-

ing classes, and even the appearance of novel classes based upon newly constituent elements, always
can occur. And these new classes have the right to
strive to win a favorable evaluable position within
the existing hierarchy of social stratification, or,
if they desire, in a new hierarchy of social stratification more to their liking. In doing so, these
new classes have the right to seek legitimization and
recognition of their corporate class identity, and,
consequently, of the right to pursue their corporate
class interests.

This system of social stratification then, is
flexible, certainly to the extent that it can be,
and is, responsive to changes in the division of
labor. For new corporate classes can and do appear
in response to novel occupational interests and
goals, and these novel corporate classes are in a
position legitimately to pursue corporate class
interests within the existing social order. Consequently, it may not be necessary to overturn the
fundamental (institutional) value foundations of
the social order in order to establish corporate
class recognition. A favorable position in an
existing hierarchy of social stratification, or
even a new, specific hierarchy of social stratification, is suitable, even though vehement resistance to all this can, and usually does, take place
on the pragmatic level.

Since the system of social stratification is
characterized by flexibility, instability, and the
constant potentiality of even radical shifting in
the existing specific status hierarchy, the possibility of the rise and fall of any class, and not
merely of individuals, always is present; even and
especially of the most cherished class, the class
at the apex of the status pyramid. In this way,
class mobility and not merely individual mobility
is acknowledged. And of equal importance, domination of the social order by the class interests of
one class at the apex of the hierarchy of social
stratification, if it can be achieved pragmatically,
is ephemeral.

For all these reasons, the commercial and industrial group is treated merely as another occupational group or class in the society. Consequently,
this group inherits the traditional right of all
classes and potential classes in the society to
attempt to establish its singular corporate class

identity and privileges and to pursue its singular
corporate class interests. It also inherits the
pragmatic right to win for itself and for its own
contribution to the division of labor as favorable
a status position in the hierarchy of social stratification as is possible, without any a priori assumption that what its class interests are or what it is
doing are any different in quality than are the
class interests and identities already established
in the social order.

Kinship: descent

Basic postulate:

Kinship: descent is characterized by the descent of strategic property through one heir, or the
separation of property and status.

Derivative statements:

The selection of a single heir, most characteristically, but not exclusively, the eldest male
descendant, to inherit the strategic property of the
predecessor, insures the transmission intact, inter-
generationally, of any economically significant
property accumulated in one lifetime, and assures
the possibility of the increasing growth of that
strategic property, generation after generation.
The significance of this is that, as one kind of
strategic property, landed property, gave way to
another, industrial capital, that property also
could be transmitted intact. Consequently, a strategic economic medium, industrial capital, could be
concentrated and maintained inter-generationally,
and legitimately, by an element in the society which
primarily was concerned with its accumulation and
use for potentially rational economic ends.

The selection of a single heir as inheritor
which dispossess all other descendants of strategic
property, here landed property, encourages mobility.
For it provides a core of property and status deprived individuals in all reaches of the social
order, who, in consequence, are willing to support
an alternative social order if it offers status and
economic security. This social order was to become
the modern developed society.

The developed society because it stresses specie,
makes it possible to divorce property and status with-

out diminishing opportunities to accumulate specie. For since specie in contrast to land is "unlimited" in a self-generating rational economic system, it is possible for all, and not merely the one favored heir, to obtain favorable status without any consequent deterrent to the necessary accumulation of specie.

Religion

Basic postulate:

Religion is characterized primarily by concern with man's inner, personal adjustment to another-worldly order, administered by a number of competing religious associations.

Derivative statements:

Since the religious problem of man is solved by administering to his personal interests, the solution of a particular religion at a particular period of interpretation might be found in accord with the belief system of the existing order, outside the belief system of the existing social order, and even in opposition to the belief system of the existing social order. Under these circumstances, religious practice, although not neglecting ritual by any means, cannot rely upon traditional knowledge associated with the existing prescriptions of the social order, which very well may not be considered applicable to the religious problems at particular times or at any time. And since the religious problem of man is open to changing interpretations, partly in response to the changing needs of man, a number of different solutions to the religious problems of man may be poised over time, and even simultaneously at any one time. Supporters of these various points of view, each are organized into potentially rival and competing sects whose power is measured by the attractiveness of their particular solution (religious message) at a particular time.

These sectarian religious orders may compete for independent political power, or ally themselves with the existing political order to serve their religious interests, and thus become established religions. But regardless of the closeness of this association, both the political authority and the religious order(s) keep their separate identity and

interests. For since either the message or the role
of the message of any religious order may change at
any time, the fact that a specific religion is established in one period of its history does not preclude the fact that it will not be established, not
be cooperative, and even be in open opposition to a
political authority or the whole social order in
another period of its history. And conceivably,
conversely, the religious message or the role of the
message may not change, but the political authority
(and the social order) may change.

Consequently, whatever is the specific reason,
and whichever is the cause, the alliance between
authority and religious order may break down at any
time over a conflict of divergent political and
religious interests. Because of this acknowledged
differentiation and potential divergence between
political and religious interests in the society,
even if these interests happen to go in the same
direction at one particular time, the political
authority is not anxious to intrude into or mediate
theological quarrels. In fact, even in the case of
an established religion, it balks at enforcing a
religious doctrine as an orthodox civil (that is,
political) doctrine. It does intervene readily,
however, if religious controversy threatens to
destroy the general peace or threaten its own purely
political prerogatives.

In viewing these religious values in a diffuse
form as general values of the society at large, it
might be said that the rise of novel solution
to man's problems above and apart from the existing
social order is considered logically possible and
ethically legitimate. And these novel solutions
legitimately may be defended in the market place of
ideas, because no one, least of all the political
authority, has a moral right to repress them automatically as evil, but must oppose these ideas compe-
titively or with a show of force against supporters,
which not only might fail, but which even might
destroy the avenger in the process.

Consequently, those who advocate the establishment of novel economic ideas, especially the idea
of a rational economic order in the social order,
can take advantage of the fact that those before
them, especially the members of religious orders,
already had established the legitimate right to pro-

pose any order of novel ideas in the society. Consequently, the problem of the establishment of the
ideal of a rational economic order in the social
order only is the problem of establishing that particular idea, and is not a problem of perpetually
striving to establish the very right to advocate
any novel, not alone economic idea which conceivably
could be judged a priori and eternally as immoral by
an established religion.

Integration, Stability, and Legitimate Social Change

Basic postulate:

Integration, stability, and legitimate social
change is characterized by the sanction to determine an integrated and stable social order and any
legitimate change in that social order in the hands
of that element which manifests the most effective
ability to solve the existing problem of social
order.

Derivative statements:

Since the social order by its very nature is
unstable and changing, no dogma that sanctions a
single exclusive solution to the problem of establishing and maintaining an integrated and stable
social order, a priori, either pragmatically is
feasible, or theoretically is acceptable. In consequence, the social order is characterized by the
rise and fall of specific novel sanctions whose
formulations and fortunes are based upon a practical
response to specific problems of the social order
at particular times. Hence, the cycle of aspiration,
consummation, and destruction of the establishment
of novel, integrated, stable, and legitimate social
orders goes on relentlessly.

The right to sanction an integrated, stable,
and legitimate social order, then, is both pragmatic, and ever-changing, with novel claims to that
right legitimately feasible and anticipated. Thus,
the right to propose a sanction to establish a
rational, self-generating economic system--and by
extension, a social order consistent with this sys-
tem--is no different qualitatively from other
similar proposals, economic or non-economic.

And the measure of success of that proposal, as any proposal, economic and non-economic,

is based on the calculable, practical efficacy of
the proposal in competition with other proposals,
as the most satisfactory solution to organizing the
economy, and by extension, meeting one of the challenges to organizing an integrated, stable, and
legitimate social order at a particular historical
moment of technological, economic, and social development in the society.

CHAPTER **11** THE MYTHS
OF
UNDERDEVELOPMENT

INTRODUCTION

This chapter will explore a number of myths of
(economic) underdevelopment theory and method which
concern directly both the case study and the analytic
models proposed in the previous chapter. Myths may
be defined as (a body of) concepts which are accepted,
a priori, as necessary and sufficient explanations
for certain beliefs and practices, so that no longer
is it considered needful to discuss critically the
origins and arguments of the concepts, which even
may have been forgotten. It is important to realize
that myths very well may be true. But regardless of
their truth value, if it is assumed that they are
true, whenever any problem arises in a situation
(practice) or theory (belief) in which myths serve
as explanation, then it is assumed automatically
that the myths cannot be the source of the problem;
and therein lies the danger. And perhaps even more
dangerous for the same reasons is to deny using
myths in theory, while implicitly employing them in
practice.

A major contention of the present study is that
the a priori acceptance of many prevalent myths of
underdevelopment theory and practice are among the
root causes of the difficulty of the underdevelopment
challenge. Consequently, in this chapter the acceptability of certain myths will be reopened for (re-)
consideration. The primary purpose of the discussion
is to underscore the importance of bringing out in
the open for fresh review many cherished hypotheses
of underdevelopment; in brief, to return the area of
too much of underdevelopment theory and practice
from myth to critical scientific review. In this review, no attempt will be made to "correct" the underdevelopment record, especially not to replace prevalent myths with new myths. For, although, in some
instances, a position may be taken in the course of
discussing certain myths, the purposes of this
chapter rather, only is to establish that it is important to appreciate the necessity of accepting nothing
on faith in existing underdevelopment theory, and not

to argue positively for a particular point of view.
This chapter, then, is a plea only for reconsideration of underdevelopment theory and methodology.

Because of this, because of the primary purpose
of the present study, and because of limitations of
space, then, this chapter cannot and will not be an
encyclopedic analysis of all the myths of underdevelopment.* But it is hoped that the ones which are
significant to the Iranian case study will be adequately discussed. This suggests a final caveat.
The myths are presented and discussed in the chapter from the point of view of the needs of the case
study. Consequently, it very well may be that the
true position of the individuals cited, or similar
individuals who uphold particular points of view,
have been simplified, or in some other way misrepre-
sented. It also very well may be true that these
individuals draw other than the conclusions drawn in
the discussions of this chapter from their analyses.
The only defense that the author can offer is that
the present discussions are trying to present the
"myths" as they actually have been used by theorists
or practitioners in the field, especially in Iran,
and/or as they apply to the focus of the present
study. Of course, this position may be challenged as
but another "myth" worthy of closer examination.

All this be it as it may, in any case, the
discussions, at the minimum should serve to place
the gauntlet on the table, and in doing so, inspire
others to either add to the existing list or at
least bear in mind that to question myths still is
the best refuge of problems both in analysis and in
action in this field.

---

*   A word on references or citations wherever they
    do occur in this chapter is in order. First, since
    the analysis is not encyclopedic, neither are the
    references. It is conceded that other references
    may be more typical or better representatives of
    particular points of view, or may be representative
    of other myths which are at least equally as impor-
    tant as the ones discussed in this chapter.

    Second, in general, a citation of myth-making
    or myth-using must not be construed as denigration
    of the work from which the citation has been made,
    --often, very much the contrary--but rather only a
    register of disappointment that the contributors
    used one or more myths as substitution for a fuller
    exposition of a point of view.

MYTHS OF UNILINEAR DEVELOPMENT

Unilinear Development Myths

The "Development Is Uniform" Myth

This myth argues that the process of development, if it does succeed in underdeveloped societies, will not (and even cannot) be very different than the process of development in existing developed societies. Due to the ready availability of advanced technology unknown in an earlier day, the process of development both might be shorter in length of time and the transition might be less painful. Local variation likewise, might produce some minor differences in specifics. But the basic process of change, especially the destruction of the old society and social adjustments to the new economic order will be cut out of the same cloth as has been observed in successful development in societies elsewhere. Consequently, the previous experience in development is important as a guide to inducing economic development in existing developing countries.[1]

The problem in this line of argument is that it blurs a number of discrete theses and makes them appear to be one thesis. That is, although, at first blush, a simple thesis, the argument in fact, is a complex package of theses which are of possible varying validity and utility. That the concepts and processes of economic development in any number of societies on the one hand, may share many features in common is of proven utility and at the same time scientifically is valid. For certainly from the point of view of the institutional sociologist or economist, it can be maintained that economic development (the rational, self-generating system) is a universal (model) system, with its own body of elements (that is, imperatives). Such a thesis has been most useful in the Iranian case study both for explaining the inadequacies of the existing Iranian economically underdeveloped system and for suggesting what might have to be done to initiate and maintain a system of true economic development. It has been most useful further to accept the thesis that development exacts a price, and that some economically underdeveloped societies, as Iranian society, are refusing to pay that price, and hence are not producing the rational economic system associated with

economic development.* But, be that as it may,
acceptance of these theses does not imply necessarily the acceptance of the thesis, that, even making
allowance for so-called local variations, the development process universally will be uniform. For it
is worth proposing that there may be qualitative
differences in what constitutes the process of development simply because the qualitative nature of the
economically underdeveloped societies may vary so
drastically. For this reason, and conversely (and
more significantly), being subjected to processes
similar to those experienced by the economically
developed societies need not imply, necessarily,
successful consummation of the development process
by economically underdeveloped societies. For the
same processes may have different roles to play in
potentially two kinds of societies, if the contemporary economically underdeveloped society is viewed
as qualitatively different from the pre-developed
period of the economically developed society, as
suggested in the contrasting model discussions of
the last chapter. For example, a program (process)
of agricultural, technical education which could be
and was used rationally in the budding economically
developing societies is not used rationally and does
not seem about to be used rationally in economically
underdeveloped Iran, for no other reason than that
education has two vitally different meanings (or
roles) in the two contexts, which go far beyond
consideration of "local variation." Consequently,
the history of the processes of development in the
existing economically developed societies necessarily
may not offer a model of what processes an economically underdeveloped society, such as Iran, has to
go through in order to develop. And failure of
foreign advisors, and foreign aid-givers especially
to appreciate this thesis, it is suggested, has been
one of the principal reasons for some of the disastrous failures of the development process on the
empirical level, as described in the case study.

The "Urbanization" Myth

This myth claims that growth in urbanization
is one barometer of increasing economic development,
because, at the least, it is one of the dislocations

---

* It is freely admitted that, as presented, these
  might be considered to be myths in turn, and
  hence worthy of intensive examination themselves.

accompanying the changeover to industrial development which stimulates the conversion of "traditional"
peasant roles to the urban worker and managerial
roles so necessary for economic development.

That this may not be true necessarily is suggested by the discussion of urbanization in the
Iranian case study. Large-scale urbanization is
not a new feature of Iranian life, and certainly,
it antedates economic development. Hence, urbanization in such an economically underdeveloped society
as Iran has not been correlated necessarily with
"increasing economic development." Rather, urbanization for millenniums has served non-development,
bureaucratic-service goals. Traditionally it is
associated with times of economic stagnation as
readily as with times of prosperity. It could be
argued it is even more associated with economic
stagnation than with development, because impoverished peasants are more stimulated at that time to
leave the farm for the city to seek hand-outs from
the service authority. Finally, conversely, economically developed societies, as for example, New
Zealand, are not highly urbanized percentage-wise,
while some underdeveloped societies, such as Iran,
are highly urbanized.

In sum, no necessary correlation between urbanization and economic development exists. Certainly,
at the least, more careful study of the process and
meaning of urbanization, especially Asian urbanization, is necessary, for numbers alone (that is,
"increasing urbanization") mean nothing in and of
themselves for the process of economic development.
To be asked rather are such questions as, what
order of urbanization is correlated with economic
development, and what kind is not? What kinds of
social and economic organization go on in an urban
center in economically developed societies, in contrast to economically underdeveloped societies?[2]

The "Westernization" Myth

This myth assumes that acquaintanceship with
the West on the economic, social or cultural level
necessarily will stimulate a desire for a change in
the social order, so that the process of development
will be both encouraged and facilitated. Exceptions
are acknowledged.

The exceptions are more significant than the
confirmations. Certainly as far as Iran is concerned,
individuals with high development-motivation but
with little Western contact are to be found in the
society. And, conversely, the absence of development-
motivation among those Iranians who identify themselves most closely with the developed West, is
notorious. For, as the case study attests, individuals who would smoke only American cigarettes, wear
only dress made in Europe, pride themselves on reading French or English, and outfit their wives in the
latest high fashions of Europe, are unimpressed with
changing the Asian-bureaucratic basis of Iranian
society or their peculiar social and economic roles
in that society, even when it is obvious that they
could make these conversions easily and successfully.
For this reason, perhaps the converse of the myth
could be argued; namely, that these individuals know
only too well what Westernization means, especially
what the consequences of economic development mean
to their social status and power, and, hence they are
determined to impede development in any way possible.
On the other hand, those who have no contact with
Westerners or western ideas are apt to be those who
have no stake in the existing system. Consequently,
they are more apt to be susceptible to the desire
for development even though, ironically, they are
apt to know less of the techniques of development
than do those who reject or subvert the economic
development process. Consequently, to assume that
the Western-associated elements in the society, then,
are, economically under-developed, and will see the
light, and fall in line, in the relentless unilinear
surge to economic development, is dubious indeed.
One can but conclude that the assumption that familiarity with the West breeds a desire for emulating
its economic development is not proven.[3]

Quantitative Development Myths

The "Stages of Growth" Myth

This myth usually is associated with the name
of W. W. Rostow and his book, The Stages of Economic
Growth, although the theory in various forms is
familiar to economists.[4] Very briefly, (and any
such summary does any complex theory a major injustice), the theory argues that the process of economic
development experienced by the developed societies,
since it has succeeded, may serve as a universal model

for economic development. The process from economic
underdevelopment to economic development has five
stages; namely, the traditional, pre-takeoff, take-
off, maturity, and high mass consumption stages.
The key stage in the process is the takeoff stage,
in which the traditional sources of resistance to
economic development fall away and growth becomes
the rule; society feeds on itself to produce, ultimately, the vital, self-generating aspect of economic development that has been made so much of in
the case study. Consequently, once the takeoff
stage is reached, the remaining stages are achieved,
inevitably, although in time. The underdeveloped
societies are said to be either in the first (or
traditional) or second (or pre-takeoff) stage of
development, but these societies can be brought
into the vital takeoff stage by means of financial
assistance and technical aid, which aim to increase
savings and productive investment, on the one hand,
and to create vital managerial and labor skills, on
the other hand. Since the development process that
is used as a model has been associated primarily
with democratic economic development in the West,
the whole theory has been viewed as a demonstrative
answer to the Communist solution of forced growth.
As such it has been described by some of its advo-
cates as an "anti-communist manifesto," or blueprint
for successful democratic economic development in
all societies.

     One can have no quarrel with either the statis-
tics or the generalizations of what has occurred in
the democratic West, even if it is only because some
historians and economists have quarreled about these
aspects of the theory, and, hence, at least in terms
of the aims set for this chapter in the introduction,
these aspects of the theory are not considered as
myths. But one may question, both logically, and on
the basis of empirical evidence, the thesis that
economically underdeveloped societies now are approaching, or entering, a pre-takeoff stage of economic
development, albeit fumbling in the attempt. For once
again, the preconditions for economic development
raised by Rostow in connection with the already economically developed societies, may not be identical to
the possible pre-conditions for economic development
in the contemporary underdeveloped societies. For
the Rostow thesis, in effect, compounds the previously
discussed unilinear myth with the closely related,
but logically distinct, myth that no qualitative distinction exists between the structures or goals of

the economies of pre-takeoff, developed societies
and contemporary economically underdeveloped societies.

Some consequences of reopening the question of
economic development pre-conditions, are as follows:
Although it may be argued that, for example, the
expansion of technical skills is a prerequisite to
economic development, conversely, it may not necessarily be argued that the introduction of technical
skills is an indication of even the possibility of
economic development. For the quantitative measurement of technical skills is exactly what it states;
no more, no less, merely a quantitative measurement
of technical skills. Consequently, although technical skills may be a necessary element in the development process, it is not a sufficient element. It is
not sufficient because the meaning of skills in the
economically developed societies of the West is not
the same in at least one type of underdeveloped
society, such as Iranian society, in which technical
skills are used for bureaucratic-administrative ends
and not for economic development ends. It is suggested that it is worth investigating whether this
characteristic also was true in the pre-takeoff
stages of the developed societies, and if it was not
(as the author believes), this may help to explain
why the introduction of any order of economic facilities into a social system with non-economic goals
does not, necessarily, provide the desired break-
through to economic development.

In sum, the pre-takeoff stage of the economically developed societies had characteristics (imperatives) within it that, even unintended, positively
facilitated the break-through to the takeoff stage,
these characteristics do not exist in such contemporary underdeveloped societies as Iran, and this has
significant bearing on understanding why the fortunes
of the economic development process have been different as between, say Japan, and say, Iran, comparative studies of "stages of growth" between such
developed and underdeveloped economies, notwithstanding.

The "Lag" Myth

An old myth in the social sciences which recently
has been associated intimately with the "stages of
growth" myth is the "lag" myth. The myth has both a

general and specific form. In the general form, it states that, if economic development is unilinear, and if a series of stages in the process of economic development exist, then, if the development process in a society is in a particular stage of consummation in the inevitable progression along the road to full development, then, consequently, the development process in that society is said to be in a lag relationship to the developed economy of another society with which it might be compared. In its specific form, the myth postulates that if at each stage of the universal process of economic growth, certain characteristic elements associated with that stage (alone?), can be identified, then, if some of these elements can not be identified as being present as yet, (thus impeding transition of the society to the next stage of economic development), then it is said that the missing element(s) lag in relation to the other elements already present in that stage.

As in the "stages of growth" myth, in both the general and specific form, the lag myth assumes that the particular stage of economic development of the economically developed society and the particular stage of the economic development of the economically underdeveloped society with which it is being compared, either are identical, or similar enough so that any differences cannot be due to any qualitative differences in the two models being used for comparison. Based upon the previous discussions of this chapter, and based upon the observations of the past chapter, it would seem at the least, that it is worthwhile considering that the two systems may not be qualitatively similar.

Consequently, arguing about the process of economic development in an economically developed society on the basis that if society "A" overcame problems, "B" can and will in time, may be misleading if "A" and "B" represent two qualitatively different kinds of societies; and certainly this is so if the argument is accepted a priori as a myth. Unfortunately, it is tempting too often for anyone responsible for, or involved in, planned change in an economically underdeveloped society as Iran to argue that, since society "A" overcame the problem of introducing element "X", and that since obviously the problem of introducing element "X", cannot be a problem of intelligence, certainly in time society "B" can make the change. And, hence, that element "X" may be considered to be in a state of lag in society "B" in relation to society "A".

A caution: Logically, it cannot be maintained
that element "X" now found in society "A" <u>cannot</u>
appear in society "B" for any reason whatsoever,
for it might very well appear for reasons other
than that associated with the argument. But in
that case, it can be maintained (to rephrase) that
"X" <u>may</u> appear in "B" without sharing the same
<u>meanings</u> that it has in "A", and, hence, the iden-
tity of existence in societies "A" and "B" is only
a ("physical") coincidence and is not due to the
same cause. As for example, in the Iranian case
study, mention was made of dams which might be
considered as practical economic tools in "A" in
terms of the developed society, but which were pure
bureaucratic conspicuous construction monuments in
society "B" (underdeveloped Iran).

Consequently, to carry the argument one step
further, the existence of element "X" in society
"A" and the absence of element "X" in society "B"
even though associative elements "Y" and "Z" may
exist in both societies "A" and "B", may not be
the case of a lag situation of element "X" in
relation to existing elements "Y" and "Z" in society "B" in comparison to the existence of all
three elements in society "A". For the situation
very well may be that in system "B" no role exists
for element "X" as is the case with elements "Y"
and "Z". As for example, in Iran, the presence of
technical schools and equipment does not mean that
merely because all these elements went together in
the economically developed societies, <u>rational</u>
technical education will be introduced into the
society. Consequently, to conclude, that "X" lags
with relation to "Y" and "Z" is not justified
because the roles of "Y" and "Z" in societies "A"
and "B" are not identical and the existence of "Y"
and "Z" in "A" is not due to the same reasons for
the existence of "Y" and "Z" in "B". Hence, a
<u>quantitative</u> comparative accounting of what traits
exist in society "A" in contrast to society "B" not
only may be of no significance, it even may be an
<u>obstacle</u> to the understanding of the process of
economic development in society "B". For it may be
more important to ask <u>why</u>, although traits "Y" and
"Z" are accepted both in "A" and "B", trait "X"
found in society "A" is not acceptable in society
"B", so that when "X" stubbornly resists all attempts

to be acceptable in society "B" and refuses to bail
us out of our theoretical dilemma by "unlagging," we
will not have been lulled to sleep, perhaps for too
long a time, to do anything constructive about the
problem.[6]*

The "It Takes Time" Myth

This myth is associated closely with the lag
myth of the previous section; in fact it might be
said that this myth is a temporal version of the
logical lag concept. For, it can be argued that
if an element (or trait) can be said to be in a
lag relationship with respect to other traits
already introduced into a society, in the process
of inevitable, unilinear economic development, it
may be assumed that sooner or later, but inevitably,
the introduction of that trait can be expected to
occur. But, "it (the introduction) takes time"
and one should be patient and tolerant. For change
always is difficult in traditional societies, especially in the area of ideas.[7]

This myth is a favorite among both the members
of societies with underdeveloped economies, and
among participants from donor societies who are
cooperating with societies supposedly in the process of economic development. This is so because
it serves the one cardinal role of all underdevelopment myths, namely to prevent having to face realistically the necessity of questioning the basic development assumptions, policies, and projects in these
societies. In Iran, most typically, it is argued

---

* If it can be demonstrated that societies "A" and
  "B" are identical for all purposes, then lag
  theory is both reliable and valuable. But since
  it is never known beforehand what future problem
  in the comparative analysis of societies "A"
  and "B" might better be served by concentrating
  on the differences between the two societies,
  one must always be prepared for such an eventu-
  ality. This does not mean that, on the other
  hand, all societies should be treated as unique;
  quite the contrary. This will be discussed
  further on in this chapter and in the following
  chapter.

that, if it took the United States "X" number of
years to develop, for example, its educational program, (true?), then how can Iran be expected to absorb a modern system of education in a mere few
years? Such an observation may be true, but it
also, possibly, may be but wishful thinking. The
possibility that this is false may become probability, if, as has been argued, the basic systems of
the economically developed societies in the pre-
developed period, qualitatively are different from
those now existent in the underdeveloped societies.
For, given the existing ground rules of Iranian
society, under a mythical mandate that economic
development "takes time," it is conceivable that
the observer may have to wait until proverbial "hell
freezes over" before the kinds of changes necessary
to create a self-generating economic development
will occur in Iranian society. And it cannot be
ignored, that, as has been suggested in the discussions of the previous section, even when certain
changes appear to occur, these changes do not have
the same effect that they have had in the economically developed societies. Hence, even to agree
that "in time" the changes may occur, is not to
agree that anything really significant has occurred,
because nothing really significant for economic
development may occur by such changes. Consequently,
further, to assume that time somehow must be an ally
of economic development is to misread the lesson of
history of economic development in the economically
developed societies. And unless, at least the possibility of this premise is accepted, the effort to
find out why it is that alleged trait "X" in contrast
to traits "Y" and "Z" cannot be introduced now, and
will have to wait twenty years, or a "generation"
from now (or whatever time, in this numbers game) to
be introduced, and even if introduced, somehow is
different from trait "X" in a developed society,
never will be made. And unless the effort is made,
Iranians, among others, will be encouraged even
further than they are now (if possible) to quote the
myth that change always has to be slow while they
continue to waste time in malingering and avoiding
making those painful decisions and changes which
true economic development requires.

The "Transitional Society" Myth

If economic development is unilinear and, is
inevitable, and the process takes time, then once
the process gets started, any element associated

with that process in the growth model of economically
developed societies that may be introduced successfully into the underdeveloped society, may be viewed
as indicative that the development process, indeed,
is taking place, and that the economically underdeveloped society, in fact, is an economically developing society in the pre-takeoff or "transitional"
phase of economic development. This phase often is
characterized as one in which a conflict between
material and spiritual values is paramount, and in
which bizarre combinations of "traditional" and
"developed" ways of doing things occur. In fact,
this phase of economic development even may be considered as synonomous with confusion and indecision,
as new ways of doing things are experimented with
and accepted or rejected.[8]

     This description of economic development refers
to a situation which perhaps is necessary but not
sufficient. That is, although great upheaval comes
inevitably in the painful process of economic development, great upheaval alone does not indicate that
economic development, either will or (conversely) is
taking place. Certainly Iran, as the case study
attests, is going through a period of great dislocation, but it is suggested, is not necessarily being
economically developed. As far as economic development is concerned, one might say that contemporary
Iran is "selectively" disorganized. Hence, an economically underdeveloped society, such as Iran, does
not become a transitional society (transitional to
an economically developed society, it is to be
assumed) by dint of how many, but what kind of
changes are being introduced. Consequently, a possible high positive quantitative correlation of
certain traits associated with the development process in a now economically developed society, and
the economic process of underdeveloped Iran may be
meaningless. Rather, it is worth knowing why
certain ideas, behavior patterns, or objects are
accepted and even few others are successfully rejected in an economically underdeveloped society, if
both series are supposed to be accepted at a particular stage of an alleged universal development model
and both series supposedly equally are disorganizing
to an existing, "traditional" society. For, perhaps,
the acceptance of certain characteristics and the
rejection of others is willful, conscious or not.
For, balking at acceptance of certain stimuli comes
readily when these stimuli threaten not some generalized, amorphous "tradition" (since presumably, all

innovation threatens tradition), but rather when
acceptance threatens the <u>specific</u> imperatives of the
system described in detail in the case study and in
analytic form in the previous chapter. This thesis,
in turn, also may help to explain the readiness of
such an economically underdeveloped society as Iran
to accept certain innovation associated with economic development on the <u>formal</u> level, (for prestige)
but to pervert that innovation on the operational
level if it threatens those same social ground
rules. Certainly, this is a possible explanation
as to why certain elements do not work out the way
they have worked out in economically developed
societies while other elements have.

Another thought: Yes, Iranian society very
well may be in a period of transition, but it need
not be a transition to an economically developed
society. All that the aforementioned dislocation
may imply is that Iran is in a transition of read-
justment to the imperatives of its <u>own</u> economic
system (as detailed in Chapter Three), selecting
and rejecting those changes which are useful to
this goal. Like the rat and the cheese in the trap,
the society is trying to get the benefits of the
cheese for its own goals, without springing what it
knows is a trap: the trap of economic development
and its demands on society, man, and resources which
it knows are associated with the organization of the
economically developed societies and which it rejects.

The "Gradual Progress" or "Isolated-trait Progress" Myth

This myth closely is related both to the "transition" and the "it takes time" myths. It assumes
that since development is inevitable, and that since
development can be assessed quantitatively against a
universal model of an economically developed society,*
then, any instance of change occurring in an economically underdeveloped society, which is prescribed
by (or at least is not contradicted by) the development model, is a step of varying significance up
that relentless path to a fully economically developed society. Consequently, since potentially each
individual change, no matter how insignificant or

----

*   Concerning the possible quantitative measurement
     of economic development, see below, item "The
     'Rate of Growth' Myth" and Chapter Twelve.

trivial, matters, at least in the long run, and
hence, is an indication of a progression of some
sort toward the inevitable goal of economic development, one must never despair. For at the least,
something is being accomplished, and after all, an
economic development process takes time to consummate.

One phase of the Iranian land reform program
may be cited as a concrete example of this myth.
It has been assumed that land reform will force
the indifferent, absentee landlord to accept the
vital new role of productive investor in commerce
and industry now that land speculation would be
closed to him. If the program encounters problems,
inevitably, they will be solved, but in any case,
at the least, land reform is an example of another
step in the right direction toward the gradual
development of a self-generating economic system in
Iranian society.

Unfortunately, this need not be, and probably
is not so. For, as has been argued in the case
study (see above, especially Chapter Six, section
"The Meaning of Land Reform") the conversion of the
economic basis of the old landlord class from country
to city will not insure that ex-landlords will act
any differently in their new environment than they
have in their old environment (and in fact as some
already have been acting for some time in the urban
environment), unless certain other measures, institutional measures, are taken; as for example, the
development of a system of security of an order to
encourage productive, long-term investment. Thus,
the notion that the mere physical and economic
migration of landlords and landlordism to an urban
environment will engender or insure the conversion
of landlord economic interests in a way that it
could be assumed that a change, even a gradual change,
is taking place toward the goal of economic development in Iran, because this is "logical" in terms of
the development model, cannot be supported. The
flow of funds from rural land investment to urban
speculative investment may be cited as concrete evidence to support this theoretical position.[9]

Consequently, it is suggested, once again, that
regardless of consideration of quantity, it is the
fact that it might be those very characteristics,
although perhaps few in number, that resist change
the most that may be the very significant ones, with-

out whose alterations, the process of true economic
development may be impossible. Hence, it is conceivable that particular changes although great in
number may indicate nothing more significant than
that change is taking place. Consequently, it would
seem that more attention must be devoted to defining
more exactly what these perhaps few, but crucial,
changes necessary for economic development might be,
so that if one is inclined to measurement, one can
use these key changes, rather than a meaningless
conjury of changes of any sort, as benchmarks for
determining "gradual" progress toward economic
development. For otherwise, an analysis of economic
development only spreads further the illusion that
something productive actually is being accomplished
"gradually" by the flurry of non-productive change
so typical of an economically underdeveloped society,
and that, perhaps more seriously, that the (few) key
problems of development can be and somehow will be
solved with the same techniques and (relative) ease
as the developmentally superficial, insignificant
and non-consequential problems already have been
solved.

The "Rate of Growth" Myth

This myth assumes that since economic development can be reckoned quantitatively, the rate of
economic growth is an important benchmark in determining how far along in the process of economic
development a society is, and especially whether
or not a particular society is on its way to the
critical takeoff stage.

It can be argued, and it has been argued by
some economists and other social scientists, that
a high rate of growth may be meaningless, either
positively or negatively, for determining the
existence or non-existence of a self-generating
system of economic development; that is, a distinction must be made between (quantitative) growth and
(qualitative) development.[10] For the quantitative
growth approach to development, or the "numbers
game" as it has come to be called by some economists,
can be (even deliberately) misleading, depending on
the base from which it is reckoned.[11] Also, and
perhaps, even more significant for the present study,
is the nature of what is being nurtured quantitatively by growth. For growth in consumption goods,
fancy living quarters, or statues of the Shah, no
matter how impressive quantitatively, of course,

cannot mean true economic development; that is, the
creation and maintenance of a rational, self-
generating economic system. Nor is it shown, on
the basis of the discussions of Chapter Three, by
such so-called development indicators as dams, unless
these indicators are accompanied by those certain
changes in Iran which insure that they will serve
primarily rational economic development goals.12

It is worthwhile mentioning in this context
that the growth rate in Japan in the early years
of its modernization (roughly, 1870-85) singularly
was unimpressive. But the base for a self-
generating economic system was being established
from which a rapid, true economic development was
to take place in the decades that followed. In
contrast, many underdeveloped societies, as Iran,
have impressive rates of growth, especially in
such meaningless growth indicators as monument
construction, but have no indicators that true
economic development is taking place. Interestingly, on the basis of the Japanese case, one
might even argue that the reverse of this myth
may not be valid; namely, that a low growth rate
is indicative of the existence of development
stagnation. Certainly, at the least, the whole
question of the necessary relationship, if any,
between growth and development must be reopened
for reconsideration.13

Underdevelopment Obstacle Myths

The "Internal Obstacles" Myth

Obstacle myths assert that since economic
development is an inevitable, universal, process,
when that process does not unfold in a regularized
quantitative progression as anticipated, then, this
may be attributed to the existence of obstacles.
Obstacles may be defined as temporary, obstructions
along existing paths (here, of economic processes).
Consequently, it is assumed that if the other
obstacles are eliminated, then, economic development,
inevitably, will take place.

Iranians have interpreted these obstacles
variously. Internally, these obstacles have allegedly
been due to a decline in Iranian moral fiber so that
only the worst and none of the virtues of the foreigner
are being copied. A lack of public responsibility

has replaced traditional negative attitudes toward
corruption; a fear to change the status quo has arisen.

Once again, all of these observations may be
true in and of themselves, and as such, may very
well be valid interpretations of the problems confronting economic development in Iran. But the implications of an obstacle approach to economic
development are worth (re-)considering. For, by
interpreting all problems as mere impediments to be
reformed or removed in some fashion, so that the
juggernaut of economic development can roll forward
relentlessly and inevitably, attention necessarily
is diverted from the possibility that it might be
the system that potentially is the source of difficulty and needs replacement if economic development
ever is to take place. This has been suggested in
the previous chapter (section "The Interaction of
the Institutions of a Social System"). Consequently,
the basic problem of economic development in societies such as Iran, unfortunately, may not be one
primarily of replacing the existing ways of doing
things in the existing economy, but rather is one of
facing up to the possibility that economic development may be incompatible qualitatively with the
tenaciously held basic values (or fundamental assumptions) of the whole social (institutional) order.
For true economic development is a goal and a value
system as much as it is a system of economic skills
and procedures. Therefore, although it is essential
to convince Iranians that a more efficient operation
of their economic system is conducive to economic
development, as many Iranians and many foreigners
believe, at the same time, this may not be at the
sufficient heart of the matter. For, as suggested
elsewhere, running the Iranian economic system as
"inefficiently" as it is run may not be an accident.
Not only does this confusion serve the purpose of
the Iranian social order very well, but also concern
with obstacles and replacement of individuals rather
than a replacement of existing goals--institutional
change, in fact--is integral to the very operation
of the system (see Chapter Eight, especially).
Hence, it is possible that unless goal or institutional replacement accompanies the conquest of
largely economic obstacles, little hope exists for
economic development (that is, once again, a rational,
self-generating economic order) in Iranian society,
although economic growth, especially buttressed with
foreign technical and material aid, very well may be
feasible.

Consequently, once again, it may not be resistance to change as such, but resistance to certain kinds of changes that ought to be the primary concern of any study of economic development problems. For it soon becomes obvious to any observer in an underdeveloped society such as Iran, that those changes which are most vehemently resisted are those that cannot be overcome merely by kicking out rascals from positions of authority or tearing down obstacle fences, but are those problems that must be solved outside the limits conceived of by the prevailing institutional structure. A more careful qualitative differentiation, then, must be made between the economic procedural problems (obstacles) and value problems of economic development, as far as the matter of resistance to development change in underdeveloped societies is concerned.

The "Imperialism" Myth

As in the previous section, this myth is predicated on the same assumption that if development is unilinear and quantitative, and if the existing social order is not developed, then the problem of development is one of overcoming certain obstacles. But if these obstacles persist perhaps they may be due to some hidden machinations from without the social order which in the past and/or even now are preventing the development process from being consummated. In this form, the obstacle myth is the imperialism myth, a myth very relevant both among the people of the underdeveloped world and also among those in the developed world who feel a sense of guilt for the economic role of their forefathers in these societies.

Iranians are firm believers in the imperialism myth. They believe that their country has very favorable conditions for development, for it has both abundant oil reserves and a favorable geographic position to encourage foreign competitive aid. But unfortunately, these favorable features have been a two-edged sword which also has worked to Iran's disadvantage. For it has encouraged the foreigner to interfere deviously into Iran's internal affairs to prevent her from developing to her full potential, so that the factors of geography and oil work fully to the foreigner's advantage. Since more than one outside power has been interested in Iran, Iran has escaped being annexed formally to any foreign power. But, on the other hand, Iran has not profited

materially from imperial control, because, unlike a
possession, she has not received the advantage of
the political stability of a colony, but has received
only the disadvantage of having her wealth plundered
amidst the internal confusion of big-power rivalry
and interference into Iranian internal affairs.
This is why some Iranians claim that, unlike the
people in certain other liberated former colonies,
Iranians are discouraged and discontented in that
they do not believe that it is possible to do anything constructive to change this kind of situation
which is beyond their control. This problem has
been going on for a long period of time, in fact
since the foreigner first came to Iran, but particularly since the arrival of the Europeans in the
sixteenth century. We were the equal of you in the
West when you first came to us, Iranians charge, but
we have fallen behind because we have been thwarted
deliberately, especially by the British in the more
recent period, in our attempt to keep up with the
advancing, developing West. But as soon as we can
throw off completely the yoke of imperialism, we can
and will be your equal. If we are not your equal,
even today, when imperialism supposedly is dead, it
is because you, who come to us and claim you are
helping us to develop, as for example, the United
States, really want us to support your way of doing
things, and to serve your interests. But you must
realize that you no longer can succeed in this, and
you will not succeed in any dealings with us, until,
or unless, you allow us to go on our own way, and
to use your support as we think best (the so-called
"no strings" aid). This argument, to be sure, is
not unique to Iran.

It hardly is worthwhile considering an alternative to, not alone arguing against, the thesis that
economically the colonial possessions of the then
developing West were organized to serve the best
interests of the parent country, and that radical
readjustments were, and still are necessary to convert these colonial economies to independent ones
serving primarily their own economic interests. But
the question of whether or not Iran, for example,
could and/or would have been able to achieve modern
economic development if imperialist control and interference into its economy had not occurred, although
one of those purely logical "if" questions, definitely
is not a fairylike question. For, since the myth persists, even today, it is of vital importance for purposes of the present study.

It is suggested that the answer to this question is no, as far as Iran is concerned. The answer is no, not because the Iranians biologically are inferior and hence incapable of developing their economy in contrast to superior Europeans (and Japanese!), or any other such non-scientific reasonings, but because the basic values of the institutional structure of Iranian society have prevented in the past, and continue to prevent today, the economic development of Iran, and too many Iranians are not that interested in changing those values.

It is worth examining, in turn, the various specific facets of this myth. First, the question of the presence or absence of imperialist control. Societies exist that excaped foreign control yet are underdeveloped, as for example, Thailand; and societies once colonies exist that are developed, as for example, Australia. And much to their ire, these underdeveloped ex-colonial societies have discovered that the mere existence of independence has not brought with it the realization of economic development or anything like development, only now the scapegoat of imperialism has vanished.[14] Consequently, the society creates a new (sub-)myth of a nefarious remote control economic imperialist-- in its Iranian version, the devious foreigner, especially the British--who will not remove his economic hooks to satisfy either ego or pocketbook. But it is very problematic that, say, for example, the oil company ever affected one way or the other, rural stagnation in Iran. For, it can be argued, based upon subsequent, purely Iranian practice, that the oil revenue would not have affected rural economic development, no matter how much of the oil revenue would have been made available to Iranians in the "imperialist" period of foreign control of Iran's oil. For the question of rural development, especially the question of rural development versus urban embellishment, is a question of the allocation and use of funds. And allocation of funds in Iran is not primarily a rational economic question, but an economically non-rational, moral-political question, indifferent to the issue of possible imperial divestiture of funds.

But if the mere absence or presence of imperialism, as such, has not determined that success or failure, respectively, of economic development in such an underdeveloped society as Iran, perhaps the

imperialist-colonialists, even by remote example,
deliberately, or through indifference, prevented the
efforts of locals to develop their economies? In
answer, it might be pointed out, first, that the
imperialists did perpetuate underdevelopment in
their colonies, but not only by what they prevented
the locals from achieving (which cannot be denied)
but also more important by what they positively did
to support the locals in what they wanted to do,
which, unfortunately, was not the development of the
(colonial) economy. Specifically, the imperialists
decided to work within and even buttress the existing
social order, because they soon realized that the
existing order was very successful in creating a
minimum of (political) friction and a maximum of
(economic) productivity among the broad masses of the
colonial peoples; and hence, that the system would
serve their own utilitarian political and economic
interests. Consequently, when they might have helped
to destroy the existing social system, in some cases
only by remaining neutral toward it and demonstrating
its inefficiency to meet even the basic challenges
of the early process of economic development in comparison with the colonials, the colonials contrariwise, provided an opportunity, under their auspices,
and even with their blessing, to modernize certain
features of the pre-colonial society which, in effect,
supported, rather than undermined, the colonial
societies' existing pre-colonial institutions and
values. Consequently, the colonialists, regardless
of the formal changes they wrought in their possessions, perpetuated the same social system so ill-
adapted to economic development, which had existed
in these societies in the pre-colonial period.

Especially significant was the recruitment and
training of a modern political bureaucracy as the
pre-eminent source of economic wealth and social
status in the colonies. In so doing, the imperialists either converted the old political elite into
this new political elite or established a political
elite where one did not exist before. This elite
formally was trained in all the modern operational
administrative techniques, but in truth, it was
wedded to the traditional Asian values of man and
political authority in relation to the economy and
the social order which always have been so inimical
to economic development. Quite obviously, to achieve
this end, the imperialist did not prevent the spread
of modern knowledge and western contact in the society;
quite the contrary (see above, section "The 'Westerni-

zation' Myth." For certainly, it spread education
widely among the very elite that now is most vocal
against imperialism. The imperialists sent these
individuals abroad and made its own educational
facilities fully available to them. And certainly,
there is no obstacle today for these individuals to
come and go as they please and to learn fully from
the West.[15] And yet, these individuals are not
successful in economic development, or for that
matter, by and large, even really interested in
true economic development, as far as one can see.
The question then becomes, why did these students
not use their Western education to oppose rather
than to support the traditional Asian social patterns of non-development, especially to become
other than moral-bureaucrats; to become revolutionaries not for the right to run their own moral-
bureaucracies, but for the right to either fill or
politically support the creation of those vital,
rational economic roles in society that they learned
in the West?[16] The answer, perhaps, lies in the
legacy of the colonialists, who, mistakenly, prided
themselves in leaving these political elites in
power in the Asian societies after personally edu-
cating them to take over when the colonials would
leave. Had the colonialists forsaken utilitarian
expediency and introduced the social legacy of their
own, liberalism, and, on the basis of this dogma,
attacked or at least, showed an indifference to the
traditional non-rational (that is, moral) bureaucratic political system it found upon annexation,
in favor of rationalization of the colonialists'
societies, (including the political structure), then,
perhaps, the history of underdeveloped Asia today
would be radically different from what it is.[17]

Consequently, the possibility that imperialism
is but another scapegoat in the long list of re-
fusals to face the realistic possibility that it may
be the social (institutional) structure itself that
is the root cause of the problem of economic development in Iran, at the least, is worthy of (re-)
consideration.

MYTHS OF TECHNOLOGY*

Myths Concerning the Technological
Bases of Development

The "Not Enough Trained People to do the Job" Myth

This myth asserts that no optimum limit exists in
the number of technologically trained individuals
that an underdeveloped economy can absorb and hence,
by implication, a shortage of trained individuals
is endemic to a developing economy such as Iran.

This myth is predicated on the two assumptions
that (1) individuals in an underdeveloped economy
are interested in, and are willing to accept intensive technological training that will equip them
occupationally and psychologically for rational
technological roles in that economy, and that (2)
the economy, in turn, is technologically oriented
to the extent that these trained individuals can,
and will be rationally utilized.

The myth immediately may be questioned on the
basis of the empirical evidence. First, as far as
the assumption concerning individuals is concerned,
although a dearth in all categories of technicians
obviously exists in Iran, as in all underdeveloped
societies, yet paradoxically a surplus of technicians simultaneously exists. But this paradox only
is apparent and not real. For Iran has a surplus of
technologists, because, it is acknowledged by both
Iranians and outside observers, existing technologists, all the way from doctors down to semi-skilled
workers, are not being utilized properly (that is,
rationally), and, that few of these individuals, or
those currently being technologically trained, seem
to have any particular incentive to practice their
specialty, or to practice it well (that is, rationally). But, because of this, ironically, Iran, by
definition, never can possibly have sufficient
technologists to fill even existing economic needs,
no matter how many technologists are or will be
available.   Iranian manpower surveys of existing

---

* "Technology" refers to the techniques of any of
   the practical arts of modern (economic) organization from the capacity to run a computing
   machine to the ability to lead villagers successfully to build a road.

technological utilization and technician shortages
are misleading, for they ignore evidence that existing trained manpower now is not being utilized properly.

Since the Iranian economy seems determined to
continue the present technologically non-rational,
but politically expedient system of recruiting,
training, and placing of potential technologists,
as discussed in the case study, the second assumption of the myth that the Iranian economy is now
or will be a stimulant to rational technological
utilization also is worth challenging.[18] For,
although no shortage of suggestions for rational
technological utilization exist, as various Iranian
proverbs say it so well,"By saying 'sugar' no one
can taste sweetness"[19] and, "A false lamp gives no
light"; that is, as in most such cases in Iran,
talk is one matter, and action is another (rule by
model at best). Consequently, the manpower surveys
which define shortages of technological futures, at
this stage of Iran's development are at best political daydreams. For, as yet, all the Shah's technologists and technological institutes have not been
able to begin to put together a rational-technological
order.

By way of conclusion, it must also be observed
that, while an underdeveloped society, as Iran, with
a mere handful of technologists, in fact, is overstaffed, developed societies, bulging with technicians, in fact, are understaffed in technicians, in
terms of the actual and realistic potential rational
utilization of technicians. And this, once again,
may be attributed to the contrast between the roles
of technology and the roles of technologists in the
two kinds of economies, and by implication, in turn,
to the social institutional determinants of those
roles in the two kinds of societies. The technological problem in Iran, then, is but another example of
the need to reconsider (Iranian) underdevelopment as
a qualitative rather than as a quantitative problem.

"Development is a Learning Process" Myth

This myth maintains that since technology is a
significant key to development, and since it is the
quantitative insufficiency of technology that is at
the root of the problem, consequently, this insufficiency can be overcome by a training program (that
is, by learning). For certainly, except for very

few industrial secrets, sufficient technological
information readily is available to enable Iran to
master the techniques of a modern technological
order. And since technologists are assumed to be
quantitatively produced through training, if the
training institutes are not successfully producing
such technologists, then most probably this is due
to either inadequate training or inadequate training
facilities. And if the technologists do not succeed
in their in-service responsibilities after training,
then this most probably is due to a personal inability to learn what is required.[20]

It is most apropos here to introduce the
question of the relationship of motivation to technological capability and effort. For if, as suggested in the case study, rational technological
roles are not prescribed in a society, because that
society is not committed to the development of a
self-generating rational economic system, yet it is
prestigeful to be called a technologist (the Iranian
engineer, or mohandes) as a mark of (largely political) equality with the modern societies, then, it is
not strange that the strong desire for a great number
of technologists does not connote any concomitant
desire for trained and job-motivated technologists.
For although one would be foolish to question the
assumption that trained technologists are in short
supply in the Iranian economy, or that technology
is mastered through learning, as in the case of
the arguments of the last section, it is worth
arguing that it is the role of technology in the
Iranian economy (and society) that determines how
successful technological training efforts will be.
Consequently, although it is true that in Iran, as
elsewhere, man wants to eat and live better, and is
attracted to technology and being a technologist, to
achieve this, these rational considerations in Iran
are subordinated to, and even perverted by, such non-
rational considerations as the validation of individual prestige and "face," to the extent that, little
or no learning, too often, goes on in the technological training centers, but all expect to be graduated
and to be placed in "important" jobs in which little
or no rational technological behavior will or can go
on.[21]

Another interesting question raised by the
learning process myth is that if technology is to
be transferred from the West where it was nurtured,
to Iran where it is needed, if technology is but

information, and if technology can be transferred by
a quantitative learning process, then is the technological learning process synonymous with imitation?
Technological imitation implies that reasonably
intelligent men, who are found everywhere, irrespective of race, economy, or culture, can be taught to
do any complex, technological job, if the technological content is made simple enough so that it can
be learned without the necessity of inculcating
more complex theoretical task understanding. Certainly, the modern Western system of training successfully low-level competent technicians to support high-level professionals is predicated on
this assumption. If this is reasonable, and certainly it appears to be, then, logically, is the
reverse of this also reasonable; namely that the
absence of efficient imitative learning, as in Iran,
is indicative of some intellectual inferiority?
More concretely, have, say, the Japanese, been successful to date because they are poor imitators,
because, in turn, they are of inferior intelligence?

Certainly Iranians, in contrast to Japanese in
a similar period of development in the nineteenth
century, seem to run into problems even of rote
copying of the most simple of necessary technological
tasks. For example, cases of the widespread abuse
among farmers of what can only be described as very
simple American seeding techniques frequently are
reported in Iran. This case illustrates what one
observer has termed "erring acculturation," or a
case in which the borrowing goes astray and the
changes go in directions that are different from the
intended aim, even in a direction harmful to the
participants. Progress is accepted, strongly so,
but the efforts are poor, and failure is blamed on
the source. For example, in this instance, it was
suggested that perhaps Americans deliberately were
providing inferior materials to humiliate the
Iranians. But most significantly, in erring acculturation the participants do not attempt to determine why they have erred, but hope for a miracle to
right wrongs, or in frustration, develop only envy
and seek a scapegoat (in this case, imperialism).[22]

But why is this so? The lack-of-intelligence
argument, certainly can be ruled out immediately on
scientific grounds. And, in any case, no one has
ever accused the Iranians of any lack of intellect.
But, significantly, this intellect is not harnessed

to the mastery of technology. What is being suggested, in fact, is only a social-psychological
truism; namely, that imitation is not a mechanistic
process that operates in a vacuum. Rather imitation
requires a socially determined talent; especially,
the willingness to accept imitation as an autonomous
process unto itself so that the only consideration
is that of imitative achievement. And this is not
so in Iran. Consequently, although Iranian education
specializes in rote-imitation, rather than creative,
or pseudo-creative, learning, since Iranian society
is not committed to rational technology, students in
low-level technological institutes, as well as their
more privileged brothers in the university, do not
seem to be able even to imitate simple technological
tasks. And since these same individuals have no
difficulty memorizing Iranian poetry one can but
suggest that it is not the method but the subject
matter that is causing the difficulty. It is that
subject matter which validates high status in the
moral-Iranian order (that is, poetry) which provides
an incentive to learn, and it is that content which
does not validate high status (that is, technology)
in an economically non-rational (or "moral") social
order that is difficult to learn. And this problem
is apt to continue, because, in Iran, technology and
technical learning are subordinated to moral considerations which, as discussed in the case study, dominate technology and technical learning in a way that
impedes the possibility of technology and technical
learning developing a rational autonomy of their own
which might challenge the moral imperatives of the
Iranian social order. And so, once again, it is the
(institutional) imperatives of the social order and the
problem of breaking through these imperatives, here
even on the level of so mundane a problem as simple
task-imitation, which should be (re-)considered in
the attempt to analyze and act upon the problems of
economic development in Iran.

Myths Concerning Technology and Ideas

"Technology Will Change Ideas" Myth

This myth asserts that, once economic development begins,* the development process itself will
destroy existing, especially social, obstacles to

---

* This may be a clever begging of the question, for
  "once it begins" very well may imply that technological development already had to be accepted
  on the idea level.

growth, and in turn will generate new social forms
compatible with the needs of a developed society.[23]
The myth does not ignore the weight of tradition,
especially the weight of traditional ideals which it
may claim are "psychological obstacles." But it
does maintain that human reason and the technological imperatives of development will overcome whatever resistance exists, and will provide the momen-
tum for establishing what is most rational in terms
of the new order; such as, for example, attitudes
toward discipline and changes in family structure
and family orientation.[24]

That this has not occurred, and is not occurring now in Iran, is attested by the case study.
Even the Iranians admit that technological innovation has not been able to inspire that kind of
orientation to develop what has come to be termed
"the ethic of industrialization." In fact, the
contrary seems to have occurred. For, as suggested
in the discussion of the previous section, in Iran
technology and technological roles both are used
positively to serve existing, largely non-technological instrumental ends; as for example, observed in
the case study, the lack of a technically-specific
and autonomous medical profession, in which some
doctors are not practicing medicine, and in which medical education is prostituted to Iranian concepts
of status by passing the incompetents simply because
they come from "good families." Quite obviously,
even in this supposedly most technically oriented.
highly rationalized and most ethically (morally)
indifferent aspect of modern technology, the rational
technological imperatives are subordinated to the
moral imperatives of the existing social order and
its ideational system; instead of, in converse, the
(medical) technology "breaking through" and forcing
rational ideational changes in (the) structure and
operation of the profession and in the society
at large.*

---

* It is important in this and similar discussions
  not to assume that the economically developed
  societies, as all societies, are unconcerned with
  the non-technological (or, so-called non-rational
  or substantive) consequences of technology on the
  society. For all societies create problems for
  the total maximization of the potential of the
  economy, and hence, logically, no society is
  maximally rational as far as the economy is

Certainly, it must be admitted that some ideational change has taken place in Iran. For example,
a modern medical profession does exist in Iran, and
some doctors, at the least, can pass master on any
of the most exacting standards of technological
professionalism. This, however, must not be construed as contradiction of the thesis of this section. For the key to the relationship between ideas
and technology in this case, as in any society, lies
in the fact that technology very well may change
ideas (and correlated social behavior), but only up
to the point where the fundamental values of the
social order are not being challenged. Significantly,
in the economically underdeveloped (Iranian) instance,
based on the discussions of the case study and of the
last chapter, these fundamental values are of a
qualitatively different order from those which facilitated (or, at the least, did not impede) the development process at a critical moment in the history of
the developed societies.* Consequently, perhaps the
myth that technological development when it comes
clamoring at the door, will out "no matter what," is
true only in that kind of social order which is willing to concede that technology ought to out in the
first instance. For, in Iran, in contrast, although
those in control of the social order may be goaded
into demonstrating their ability to do anything that
a technologically advanced society can do, in order
to vindicate themselves and/or the social system--
or as Iranians put it, "We could do it if we wanted
to" (and one can see enough evidence in Iran to
support this thesis)--at the same time, they are not
willing to commit the society to changing those
imperatives (ideas) of the social order which would

----

concerned. But it is one of the cardinal theses
of the present study that a qualitative distinction must be made between those societies in
which considerations (or fundamental goals)
positively prevent the achievement of a self-
generating, rational economic system and those
that only subtract in varying degrees, from maxi-
mal rationality in an already achieved or developing self-generating economy. Clearly, Iran represents the former kind of society. This matter
will be discussed further in the next chapter,
especially with reference to the Japanese case and
Asian communist economic development programs.

*   It is not surprising, then, that the myth of technological determinism was devised in the developed
society.

encourage the development of a <u>rational</u>, technological order. For this reason, the economic situation
undoubtedly is one of apparent ambiguity and contradiction to the (largely foreign) unitiated. But it
is possible to make sense of it by characterizing it
as one in which technology is subordinated to traditionalism. But that traditionalism is not of the
same order as the traditionalism of the economically
developed societies (as detailed in the model discussions of the previous chapter).25 Rather, this
traditionalism is a particular kind of traditionalism; for as the Shah himself has put it so well,
"Iran has to catch up with the technologically advanced West, so it must <u>adapt</u> to modern conditions
which are different from traditional ways, but Iran
must <u>adjust</u> the technological innovations to its
own system of ideas."26

In conclusion, this myth suggests that more
case research on the role of technology in economically non-rational societies at <u>various</u> levels of
technological development, definitely, is in order.

The "Ideas Will Create Technological Change" Myth

This myth is the converse of the previous myth.
It maintains that <u>if</u> a technologically oriented
system of ideas could be infused into the behavior
of the economic actors in an underdeveloped society,
then the "traditional" non-technologically oriented
order can be destroyed, and the process of development can begin and ultimately can be consummated.

The present study cannot have any quarrel with
a theory which assumes that ideas channel motivation
and change behavior and ultimately, change social
structures as well (a myth?). Nevertheless, the
study does have some misgivings about the one implication in this myth that suggests that the concept
of technological "incentive" ideas is transferrable
necessarily from the social system in which it was
nurtured (that is, the already developed society)
to another kind of social system (that is, the underdeveloped society) through the same process of transfer as other alien or material objects have been,
and are being transferred now. Consequently, when,
perhaps in converse to what has been paraphrased in
the closing paragraphs of the previous section, such
Iranians as the Shah state that Iran must, and can
develop a system of indigenous ideas compatible with
technology, and that this is possible because of the

364   THE SOCIOLOGY OF DEVELOPMENT

scholarly tradition of Iran, which has provided imaginative and adaptive processes in the past, these
individuals are saying something that requires more
careful scrutiny.[27] For, although they sponsor the
creation of technological ideas, they are suggesting that those technological ideas must be subordinated to certain "Iranian" moral, non-rational
considerations, even if those prevent the establishment of a rational, self-generating economic system
--in contrast to the Western sociological thesis
that certain ideas very well might both destroy
impeding non-rational considerations and even positively help to create the development of a rational
technology. It is for this reason, that Iranians
readily will accept ideas which underscore the
utility and the necessity of technology, as such,
while, at the same time, they hedge these ideas in
a particular way.

     This attitude toward technology helps to ex-
plain why it was that the Middle East, especially
during its Middle Ages, could have been a center
of advanced science, especially in the purest of
sciences, mathematics, and in the case of Iran in
particular, the world leader in science and technology, while recently, or so the conclusion goes,
there has been widespread scientific stagnation
throughout the area. For a closer look at that
science and technology demonstrates that much of
it was not placed at the rational service of the
economy as a neutral tool employed to raise the
well-being of the people, although it prospered
amazingly on the abstract, theoretical level.[28]
Certainly, this could not have been due to any
claimed failing of intellect, for one must assume,
without doubt, that the use of technological ideas
was as obvious to these geniuses of science as it
was to their Western counterparts. Rather this was
true because Middle Eastern society made its fateful
decision as to what the role of ideas and technology
would be, based not upon the belief, as a fundamental institutional assumption, as in the West, that
technological useful ideas would be supported "no
matter what," but upon the belief as a fundamental
institutional assumption, that certain other technologically non-rational, "moral" ideas would take
precedence over rational technological ideas in the
social order, even if those ideas impeded technological development in the economy. This deliberate
choice became most significant in the most recent
centuries, at the time when almost all technological

innovation became intimately associated with that
kind of Western, post-Renaissance social order which
threatened to destroy the moral basis of the Asian-
type social order. At this time, those in control
of the social order decided it might be wiser not to
tolerate locally any longer even the development of
rational science and technology on the theoretical
level; hence, scientific and technological stagnation.
And, in like spirit, when modern science and technology was re-introduced into the Middle East in the
Nineteenth and Twentieth centuries, often against
the will of the local political authorities, these
authorities were determined that these alien ideas
must be infiltrated with indigenous "moral considerations" in a way that autonomous technology and
science would be subordinated to the primary demands
of the Asian social order. And, as well, since
those in positions of authority tended to be the
ones who supplied the raw recruits for trainees in
the new technology, technological innovation by
those individuals could be assured not to stimulate
a desire to develop an autonomous (rational) technology. And so, as it is often put in Iran, technological values were "adapted to Iranian values and
needs," engendering the particular economically non-
developed technological order that has been documented in the case study.

    One of the signal lessons of the Iranian case,
then, might very well be that if ideas are to be
the means to provide the "break through" to advanced
technology and economic development, technological
change must be viewed not merely as commitment to
the material aspects of technological innovation
alone, (one idea) but must be viewed as an ideological commitment to a particular kind of technology,
specifically, a rational technology (another idea).
Consequently, the perennial chestnut as to whether
actions (technology) change ideas, whether ideas
change actions, or whether both ideas and actions
interact upon each other, has not been discussed.[29]
This has been deliberate because, it is suggested,
rather that it is both more meaningful, and more
fruitful, to (re-)consider the kinds of issues
raised in this and the previous section, in turn,
within each of these three possible relationships
between ideas and actions.*

---

* It is of some importance to state that the problem
   of the relationship between "culture," or specifically cultural ideas, and technology has not been

Myths Concerning Technological
Development and Outside Assistance

The "Capital Short" Myth

This myth asserts that a leading source of the
retardation of economic development has been a shortage of capital (resources) which, if made available,
could and would be invested productively, so that
economic development would be facilitated, if not
assured. In effect, this myth is another version
of the technological myth previously discussed in
section "The 'Not Enough Trained People to do the
Job' Myth" above.

Once again a myth has the germ of incontrover-
tible truth within it. For, according to most
economists, a shortage of capital is one way to
define an underdeveloped economy; an economy in
which income is low due to a lack of capital to
increase productivity, which, in turn, perpetuates
poverty, in a never-ending vicious circle of poverty
and capital shortage feeding on each other.[30] And
obviously, this is true in Iran. But at the same
time, it is worthwhile asking why, beyond the obvious
empirical fact that it isn't in hand, such a shortage
of productive capital exists in Iran. For, as these
same economists have pointed out, it is specifically
the low level of mobilization of existing capital
for productive purposes, regardless of the amount
that is or is not available, that is at the heart of
the problem of capital formation and economic development (in Iran).[31] For this reason, the lesson
of Japanese society, which started with a quantitatively modest accumulation of capital but with a
qualitatively high mobilization of that limited
capital (including, especially human resources)
should be most instructive to such a perennially
capital short society as economically underdeveloped
Iran.[32] For in contrast to Japan, it is obvious to
even the most casual observer on the spot in Iran,
that Iran has squandered, is squandering, and probably will continue to squander its available and

_____

raised in this or the previous sections. This
problem will be raised later in this chapter
(see below, sections "The 'Working in the Culture'
Myth (from the standpoint of the Western observer)"
and section "The 'Working in the Culture' Myth
(from the standpoint of the Iranian participant)."

potentially available, capital resources, including
its lucrative oil revenue and its under-utilized and
mis-utilized population, on essentially non-
productive purposes.

It has been estimated that perhaps <u>half</u> the
income of the society is used for non-essential
purposes.[33] True or not, the Iranian never claims
that capital has been short to support hordes of
admittedly, productively-useless bureaucrats who
might become revolutionaries if they were not assured of an income, to build statues to the Shah
in every town in Iran, while schools and school
teachers are scarce in villages, or to flood the
country with such status symbols as luxury automobiles for those who can afford them, while most
peasants cannot afford even a minimally satisfactory
diet.[34] The case study has suggested that it is not,
as Iranians prefer to believe, the result of ignorance, error, or venality. But rather it is the
result of the value imperatives of a kind of social
order which makes capital investment in monument
building important, and capital investment in rational
manpower utilization and project development, not important, and which makes the appertenances of economic
development important and a rational, self-generating
economic system not important.

Since, in Iran, capital is not being productively
utilized in an ever-hungry, expanding economy (the
self-generating economy), that economy may be embar-
rassed by an <u>oversupply</u> of capital, whenever it is
able to obtain a capital surplus; most probably
through foreign loans or gifts. And for the same
reason, capital surplus discourages, rather than encourages, thrift and savings, which further discourages productive and efficient investment of capital
(human and financial) resources; and another vicious
circle is established in an underdeveloped economy.[35]

It also is interesting to observe that there is
a steady leakage of human and monetary investment
capital from such underdeveloped countries as Iran
to the developed countries. This could be considered
as <u>prima facie</u> evidence of a shortage of capital.
But, simultaneously, it could be considered as evidence of a surplus of capital. For it may be indicative of the fact that poor usage internally of the
available capital is encouraging the export of this
"short" capital to those developed economies in which
it more profitably can be utilized; this in spite of

the fact that speculative profits can be obtained
readily from capital "invested" in Iran. In response, it has been suggested that if available
Iranian capital could be utilized productively,
then the trend would be reversed as lost capital
would be attracted back into Iran; or failing this,
at the least, if the remaining capital could be
utilized productively, then, capital would not flee
abroad so readily and this alone could increase the
supply of capital available internally for productive purposes.[36]   Perhaps so, but one must say
"could" because, given the fundamental (institutional) values of the Iranian social order, any
economic effort in Iran, by definition, always will
be short of capital. For like the beautiful woman
who loves new clothes, Iranian economy can squander
non-rationally <u>whatever</u> is invested in it, since it
is set up to do just that.

The "Give Us the Aid To Do the Job" Myth

This myth postulates that, since Iran is an
underdeveloped society and hence, is capital short,
then capital subsidization from outside the society,
which can make up the deficit, will insure that
Iranians, on their own, will be able to create a
self-generating economic system. Or, as Iranians
like to put it, "We are unable to develop because
we do not have the resources, much as a sick man
cannot get well because he cannot afford the doctor,
no matter how much he knows he needs the doctor.
If others will help us to pay the doctor, we will
get well."

As suggested in the discussions of the previous
section, most of the assumptions of this argument are
open to question. But those discussions do not necessarily bring the entire argument into dispute. For
even if domestic capital resources, controlled exclusively by Iranians, are ill-used, still, would it
not be possible for outsiders to supply capital
(which of course, includes capital goods and capital
know-how as well as people) which would be <u>earmarked</u>
specifically for productive use, and hence, <u>would</u>
serve as a catalyst for the development of a rational.
self-generating economic system in Iran? This is
the "aid with strings" argument (or myth). Although
this possibility has intrigued international investors bearing gifts and loans, and tremendous amounts
of capital have been introduced into Iran on this

basis, as yet, this foreign capital has not created
an environment in Iran conducive to the introduction
and development of the elusive, self-generating economic system.37

Perhaps, one reason why this is so, is that
"aid with strings" is not a simple policy to formulate or carry out. For no matter what kind of
"strings" a donor would like to attach, formally or
informally, to a capital aid program, no social system, least of all the Iranian social system, can
tolerate one set of ground rules for investing its
own internal capital and another set for investing
externally generated capital. For, since, as suggested in the previous section, the fundamental
values of Iranian society are committed to the
maintenance of an economy which serves ends not conducive to the development of rationality in the economy, then, acceptance of the principle of external
"aid with certain kinds of strings" will mean, in
effect, that Iran is sanctioning the possibility
that the aid program might lead to the development
of a rational economic system, to which it is not
only not committed, but to which, it is worth (re-)
considering, it is opposed. Consequently, Iranians
have balked at accepting aid with certain kinds of
strings, arguing that strings frustrate those
(Iranians) who know best how to use any loans or
gifts. And the donor, aroused by the Iranian reaction, has either placed too few strings on the
loan or gifts, or, more importantly, has placed the
wrong kind of strings on the aid. For example, regulations exist to reduce corruption and theft of
funds, but strings which effectively can reduce the
mal-investment of funds in a wasteful, non-productive
way (as the padded payrolls for political insurance)
are conspicuous by their absence. Significantly, and
unfortunately, this policy, not only has accomplished
nothing positive to aid the development of the
Iranian economy, it has further only convinced both
the Iranians and donors that strings are useless.
And, consequently, not surprisingly, the Iranians
have been able to continue to use aid to reinforce
the existing patterns of non-rational capital investment. This situation is to be contrasted with that
prevailing under the European Recovery Plan (The
Marshall Plan), for example, which worked successfully with modest expenditures, because the institutional imperatives of those societies insured that
the aid could be, and was used productively.

It seems apparent, to be the semantic pedant
for a moment, that what perpetually is in short
supply in Iran, and what Iranians really are pleading for by way of external subsidy, is not capital,
but money. For capital may be thought of as the
wherewithal for potentially productive investment,
to feed upon itself and ultimately to create a self-
generating economic system. But the Iranian wants
money, to be used either for direct consumption or
for other non-productive, especially purely politically profitable purposes. Or, as one observer put
it, "It is the difference between capital for development and money for aid." Hence, no amount of aid
money, as such, necessarily will change the basic
ends to which the money is being put, especially if
it is given "without strings" to be used to buy
political loyalty both by the donor and by the
Iranian political authority itself inside Iran.
Consequently, it might be worth considering that aid
provided under present ground rules, not only may
be useless, it may be worse than useless, because,
at the least it postpones any decision on the part
of the recipient to face up to the painful necessity
of reconsidering realistically his economic policies
in the light of failure to serve the minimum rational
economic needs of Iranian society, let alone the
failure to serve the needs of a rational, self-
generating economic system.[38]

POLITICAL MYTHS

The Strong Polity Myths

The "Political Solution" Myth

This maintains that political solutions are,
or should be, primary in the clearing up of all economic and social problems besetting an underdeveloped
society, especially the clearing up of the problem
of economic development.

The theoretical origins of this myth, especially
in Iran, are not hard to trace, especially in the
light of the model discussion of the previous chapter.
For the political order, in the absence of the
Imamate, as the arm of the moral-intellectual forces
in the society, has been assumed to have the primary
responsibility for supervising and even initiating
significant social and economic action in the society.
And, certainly, there is no reason to believe that

political authority should not continue to play this
role at present when the social and, particularly,
the economic problems confronting Iranian society
are so important and so grave.

This assumed dependence of the initiative for
significant social and economic action on political
decision-making has some interesting implications
for economic development. It implies, first, that
social and economic developmental problems not only
can be, but must be, solved primarily, if not exclusively, by resource to political action. Consequently, Iranians forever are suggesting the creation
of new government bureaus or expansion of the existing bureaucracy, as if these policies automatically
will aid the economy to solve its economic problems.
To suggest that these same individuals might enter
directly into the economy itself, either in the
public or private sector of that economy, and work
out economically useful solutions to primarily
rational economic ends, is considered ridiculous,
because, in doing so, these individuals not only
would enter into the world of dubious morality, but
also would become associated with empirically inferior means to accomplish their goals. For political authority, serving politically useful ends, a
priori, must be more effective economically for no
other reason that that it is political authority.
That these premises all are debatable empirically,
to say the least, have been demonstrated by the
evidence of the case study (especially Chapters Two
and Three). Consequently, it would seem that all of
the feverish Iranian politically-generated economic
activity, such as the constant changing of specific
regimes, the passing of new laws or rule by model
pronouncements, the periodic investigations of corruption and malingering, and the sponsorship of
monument building, all supposedly to economically
develop Iran, have done nothing substantial to
change economic ideas or to organize the society
and the economy in a way that, regardless of "progress," and "modernization" it can be said that Iran
now is dedicated seriously to economic development.39
Consequently, it seems reasonable to (re-)consider
the assumption that the association of any political
order with an economic problem, for better or worse,
is the way to solve that problem.

To carry the argument one step further, a second
implication of the dependence of economic development
on a political solution is that, it is assumed, in

Iranian thinking in any case, even if the present polity (or government) needs replacing, it is
the political authority in the existing (kind of)
social system that primarily is to be responsible
for achieving economic development. Hence, as it
usually has been phrased, the problem in an underdeveloped society, such as Iran, is, how do you get
the political order to commit itself to development?
It is suggested for (re-)consideration that the
question, as phrased, is misleading, although it
does hint at a crucial aspect of the problem of the
relationship between politics and economics in economic development. Rather, it is suggested that the
question be rephrased to read, "How do you get the
society to commit itself to economic development?"
In the rephrased question the political order becomes but one element, albeit, possibly a significant element, in the total social system.* For, as
has been suggested in the previous chapter (section
"The Significance of the Proposed Model for the
Study of Iranian Development Problems"), it is not
only the institution of political authority but all
the institutions of the social system as a coherent
interdependent operating system that contribute
positively or negatively (in Iran, negatively) to
the development of a self-generating economic system. Hence, perhaps political authority alone, no
matter what its attitude toward economic development, although it vitally affects the outcome, does
not affect completely the final solution. Consequently, political decisions, while important (and
even necessary) for economic development, are not
sufficient.

     The concrete significance of the above theo-
retical exercise for Iranian economic development,
is as follows: First, doubt is shed upon accepting, as inevitable, the Iranians' belief that the
significant economic and social problems of their
society must be concentrated within the preserve
of politics, so that both the political authority
and the members of the society expect economic
problems to wait upon political solutions; which,
whether forthcoming or not, logically relieve the
members of the society outside the orbit of the
political apparatus from responsibility for their

_____

*   The question of how significant is left for
    later discussions in this chapter.

solutions. Second, doubt is shed upon accepting the
Iranians' belief that the indecisions and contradictions in the Iranian economic order, which, in fact,
are the consequences of the interests and policies
of a political authority which places political considerations first at all times, are inevitable.[40]
Third, doubt is shed on accepting, as inevitable,
the Iranians' assumption that those problems in the
economy which are of no concern to political authority are unimportant, and, that, conversely, only
these problems which are unimportant economically
to political authority can be left to other than the
political authority to solve. Fourth, doubt is shed
upon accepting as inevitable the Iranians' assumption
that economic and social problems are of secondary
concern as compared to political problems, so that
it can be argued that what is good for political
authority must be good for society at large and the
economy in particular. And, fifth, finally, doubt
is shed on accepting as inevitable the Iranians'
assumptions that the economic order can not be
rationalized or must wait to be rationalized, because
rationality is inconsistent with a political authority's definition of political solutions to economic
problems.

The "Strong Polity" Myth

This myth asserts that a strong and usually,
but not exclusively, centralized political authority
is essential for economic development in an underdeveloped society, such as Iran; and that conversely,
an inability to develop an underdeveloped society is
due to a weak political authority.

Before actually discussing the myth, it might
be worthwhile to make three observations about it.
First, although closely interrelated with the political solution myth of the previous section, this
myth is not synonymous with it. For the former
myth may be accepted without accepting this myth
(but not vice-versa). Second, this myth assumes
that the problem of development is a quantitative
and not a qualitative one. For, implicitly, it is
the amount of political strength and the association of
that strength with the process of development, rather
than the kind of political authority or the kind of
association between politics and economics that is
considered to be crucial. And, finally, third, this
myth is predicated on the assumption that since the
political authority, albeit by default in Iran, has

the prime moral-service privilege or duty to serve
the development process, it will do so.

Although the myth, has certain philosophical
roots in the basic value system of the Iranian (or
Asian) social order, (to be discussed subsequently)
justification for accepting it, certainly in the
very recent period, seems also to stem from reaction
to the empirical situation in the underdeveloped
economies. To the foreign observer, on the one hand,
the present disarray of the Iranian economy implies
that the private sector of the economy is incapable
of organizing a rational economic system. Consequently, by default, the political authority must
shoulder this burden. It must "find a way" through
some priority system to concentrate resources and
make them available for development. It must provide the initiative to develop, irrespective of what
the private economic forces of the society can do or
can not do. It may stimulate the private economic
forces, and that will be all to the good, but it
should not be dependent upon them to initiate
development.[41] And since these kinds of economic
actions require a political authority that is able
to enforce certain painful but necessary (presumably
rational) decisions on the society, or at least on
the economic sector of the society, it is argued, a
political order strong enough to disregard, if need
be, public opinion and public pressures which resist
rationalization of the economy is essential. Strong
political authority also is essential because it can
evoke sufficient patriotic fervor to inspire a positive attack on the environment, thus making the task
of development less formidable, and insuring that
the economic changes will be more rapid and more
easily accepted.[42] If the political authority can
not meet these responsibilities successfully, then
the prospects for development are dim. Often cited
as justification for this point of view is the fact
that no society, in the twentieth century at least,
has developed rapidly without a strong polity with
an unchallenged monopoly of economic prerogatives.
As proof, the cases of Russia and Japan usually are
cited.[43]

Local observers in the economically underdeveloped societies, including Iran, on the other hand,
have accepted the myth readily on the same practical
grounds, but, perhaps more significantly, as previously suggested, also on grounds that it is consistent with traditional Asian political theory.

The political consideration is most apparent when
the converse of the myth is argued; namely, that
failure of development efforts have been due to a
lack of a strong polity. At this point in the discussion, it is in order to refer back to the second
observation on the myth in the opening remarks of
this section; namely, that a strong polity is a
quantitative conception. For the concept of the
lack of a strong polity in Iran does not necessarily include the possibility that it is the <u>kind</u>
of political authority that might be economically
impotent. Rather, it is only a <u>specific polity</u>
(that is, a specific regime or government) composed
of economically impotent individuals or economically
impotent organizations which, of course, can be
quantitatively reckoned for cathartic revolutionary
purposes, that are, and can be at fault (see above,
Chapter Nine). And so, if a specific economically
impotent regime that is weighed down (quantitatively)
with the economically impotent, is replaced with a
<u>strong</u> polity, composed of <u>strong</u> incorruptible men,
economic success is assured. For a strong polity
is the only potential force in the society strong
enough to initiate and consummate successful economic action, especially economic development.44

It may be observed that this myth is very hard
to question scientifically on empirical grounds.
For, on the one hand, it is accepted by Western observers on opportunistic <u>political</u> grounds, that
unless a strong polity of some sort is supported in
the economic field in underdeveloped societies, more
totalitarian methods, most probably Communist political methods, will be used. On the other hand,
locals to whom the myth is most pleasing <u>theoreti-
cally</u>, have a stock and logically potent answer to
any critique of the myth. Whenever discouraging
elements (foreign observers?) demonstrate empirically
that the polity in many underdeveloped societies is
as strong, or even stronger, than it is in the developing society of Russia, and that this "strength"
has not guaranteed economic success, to say the
least, anywhere in the economically underdeveloped
world, the members of the Iranian political authority,
very logically, insist that this is because these
societies used even a <u>stronger</u> polity, and with each
new failure, still stronger a polity, in order to
bring into line a stubborn reality that refuses to
recognize so obviously a correct theory.

Another facet: If the concept that political

strength is prerequisite to productive economic
action is accepted by the society at large, as under
Reza Shah in Iran, then it becomes axiomatic, conversely, that nothing much productively is possible
in periods of political weakness. In consequence,
the presence, or alleged presence, of a weak polity
can, and in Iran has, become the excuse for economic
inaction, not only by the polity, but also by the
general population, including the private sector of
the economy, as well. And, in a social order in
which a strong polity alternates with a weak polity,
as has been the case in Iran, whatever is accomplished or allegedly accomplished, during the period
of a strong polity, as under Reza Shah, logically
and empirically, can and does go asunder with the
removal of the strong man and his strong polity. At
the least, this indicates that even the (claimed)
accomplishments which have based on political
strength may be more apparent than real; especially
is this true in the case of economic organization
involving behavior and value change, in contrast
to monument building, which involves successful
action over the long haul--which is what really
counts in true economic development.

An interesting sub-myth of the strong polity
myth is the centralized polity myth for a decen-
tralized strong polity somehow seems to be a contradiction in terms of the political theorists and
practitioners of the underdeveloped world, including Iran. This is so because Asian political
authority, whenever possible, essentially is autocratic. Consequently, no matter how strong and
confident a polity may feel, it believes it can
not accept diffused authority and responsibility
without undermining the basic fabric of political
authority (see above, Chapter Two). It is fascinating to observe how the political leaders of
former colonial possessions who once had been adamant in extolling the virtues of their people to
be independent and to be the equal of any of the
developed countries (which cannot be denied),
somehow, once independence is achieved, have come
to believe that these same people now, suddenly,
are incapable of making their own independent
political decisions; and considering the accepted
relationship between economics and politics in
these societies, as discussed in Chapter Three of
the case study, making independent economic decisions as well. It is apparent that by "people" in
the colonial context, these political leaders had

been referring only to themselves (and this has been discussed in the case study, Chapters Two and Nine especially). And so, for better or worse, these political leaders have arrogated, as a monopoly, the right to make the significant economic decisions as political error, or even treason. This attitude has had the additional unfortunate consequence, too often, of making the political order rigid and defensive, and possibly, at critical times, indecisive. For to those in power, the halo of the perfect political authority must be defended at all costs, and to the opposition it must be destroyed at all costs. And since the economic order is caught in the middle of this political trap, it cannot help but suffer accordingly; to note, for reasons totally alien to rational economic considerations.

Consequently, in conclusion, rather than spend time considering how strong or how weak (quantitatively) a polity should be, it might be more fruitful to (re-)consider what kind of polity, strong or weak, is conducive to economic development. For, as hinted at in the course of the discussion, it is better to avoid considering this myth on its own terms. Unfortunately, to date, almost all discussion of this myth has been of the order of proving or disproving the myth, and significantly, predominantly, for purposes of political (ideological) interest, and not primarily for the purpose of furthering rational economic ends in the underdeveloped economies. This study will have much more to say on this matter in the next chapter.

The "Political Strength Will Lead to Economic Development" Myth

This myth asserts that political strength is equivalent to political security, which is equivalent to economic security, and that all of this is both necessary and sufficient for economic development. This myth, consequently, associates strength with security, and political strength and security with economic strength and security, so that political strength can be converted indubitably into economic development.45

By way of opening discussion on the myth, first may be cited the suggestion made by many observers that political strength may not be concident with political security. For example, strong totalitarian societies have not been able to provide security,

save for those few in absolute control of the security apparatus. In contrast, the vast majority in
the society, who are at the mercy of the arbitrary
and capricious policies of those in control, live in
fear and apathy. Iran, although not a totalitarian
society, suffers from the same political malaise of
totalitarianism. For, by monopolizing political
initiative and providing political security only
for those at the apex of the structure of political
authority, the political authority, including the
present polity, has not provided security even for
the lower echelons of its own apparatus. (See
above,Chapter Two·) The significance of this for
economic development is that, in such underdeveloped
societies as Iran, in which political authority and
economy intimately are intertwined, those in control
of the structure of political authority tend to
equate the measure of their own political security
with that of the social (and economic) strength of
the society as a whole. Yet, at the same time, it
is ironic, but also highly significant, that in
spite of a major concern with political strength,
the political order is weak and indecisive whenever
rational economic decisions must be made, a familiar
feature in all economically underdeveloped societies
where "strong" political orders abound or are the
ideal.46 In conclusion, therefore, the assumption
that political strength leads to economic strength,
let alone to economic development, at the least, is
open to considerable doubt.

     Since, the reverse of the myth; namely, that
economic development can be accomplished with a
weak polity, empirically has been true, at least
in the case of some of the already economically
developed societies, it is worth considering whether
or not the whole question (and answer) of political
strength and economic development as posed by the
myth may be meaningless, especially as far as economically underdeveloped Iran is concerned. For,
it very well may be that it is not the quantitative
strength or weakness of the political order that is
of primary concern for economic security, and ultimately for economic development; but that it is the
qualitative strength or weakness of that political
order that is crucial. Or to rephrase, it is how
the political order relates either strength or
weakness to the economy that determines the poten-
tial security and developmental destiny of the economic order. For, on the one hand, a strong polity
committed to economic development will aid the pro-

cess of development. A strong polity that is not
committed to economic development, especially one in
which economic considerations are subordinated to
political considerations, as in Iran, will have
serious problems of development. And, conversely,
a weak polity--weak in its relation to the economy,
that is--but committed to (or at least not opposed
to) economic development, will aid development by
its acts of omission, as economic actors take advantage of new opportunities and occupational interests. But a weak polity, if it is not committed
to economic development (even though it is unable
to enforce its decisions, and hence, intended or
not, creates politically generated insecurity in
the economy) in effect, discourages economic development. For, to recall the discussions of Chapter
Three, the ability to <u>threaten</u> interference is as
bad, or even worse than actual interference, since
it cannot be calculated rationally.[47]

Strength and security for economic development,
then, involves strength and security in the <u>economy</u>
of an order that rational economic decisions today,
tomorrow, and the day after tomorrow, can be made,
that ultimately will give rise to a self-generating
economic system. It is important to (re-)consider,
then, seriously the possibility that economic
strength and economic security, or the lack thereof,
may vary independently of the presence or absence of
security and strength in the political order.[48]
Although this position is not (politically) very
"realistic" in terms of <u>existing</u> Iranian political
assumptions, this not only theoretically is possible,
it also is empirically verifiable in the case of the
history of Iran, especially in the last few decades,
as against the history of the economically developed
societies.

The "Political Reform Will Lead to Economic Development" Myth

This myth is predicated on the assumption that
if a political apparatus is essential to initiating
and maintaining economic development, and if this
apparatus is not adequate at present to do the job
satisfactorily, then, the political apparatus must,
and can be reformed in a way that it adequately can
assume its present and future economic developmental
responsibilities.

It is by influence of this myth that so much

time and effort in economically underdeveloped societies have gone into formulating those proposals
for organizational changes (reforms) which supposedly
will rationalize the unwieldly, overstaffed, and ill-
motivated bureaucracies which are the curse of all
economically underdeveloped societies. Some of
those proposals include: (1) decentralization, to
allow for individuals responsibility and authority
on many different levels; (2) clear definition of
this individual responsibility and authority; (3)
diffusion of information throughout the political
apparatus, so that proposals (1) and (2) above,
intelligently, (that is, rationally) can be implemented; (4) promotion on merit; (5) adequate and
bona fide supervision, free of the suspicion of
spying and harassment; (6) recruitment based upon
economic needs and not upon support of a horde of
the monetarily hungry educated who feel that political authority owes them a guaranteed livelihood (7)
fiscal reform to insure the provision of funds primarily for operations; (8) commitment of funds in
accord with the personal desires of those in charge
of projects.[49]

        All are admirable proposals. But as suggested
by both the discussions of these proposals in the
case study, and by the arguments of the previous
chapter, these proposals strike at the very foundations of the Iranian political (and social)
order. These proposals, then, are not reasonable
to the members of that political order. Hence, in
contrast to the enthusiasm for formulating reforms
(on paper), executing reforms often are resisted
violently, much to the surprise of (especially
outside) reformers who consider these proposals as
modest, mild, and obviously in the "best interest"
of the Iranians.

        Perhaps, then, it is necessary to reopen
for consideration the whole question of what is
feasible and what is not feasible to "reform" in
such an economically underdeveloped society as Iran,
and, perhaps more significantly, implicitly, whether
or not economic development in an economically underdeveloped society as Iran can be considered a question of "reform" in the first instance. For any
discussion of this order of reform, as discussion of
obstacles (see section "The 'Internal Obstacles'
Myth" above), implies that the basic ground rules
(the fundamental institutional assumptions), especially the political ground rules of the society

will be retained, while adjustments will be made in
forms _within_ the limits established by those basic
ground rules. How modern administrative forms have
been perverted to serve traditional bureaucratic
ends, has been documented sufficiently in the case
study to save repetition here (see above, Chapter
Two).

     And certainly, as far as internal politics in
Iran are concerned, no significant element within
the present political order, including even the
National Front, the so-called political "radicals"
who advocate "reform," has suggested repudiation of
the accepted ground rules of Iranian society. The
Front formally has demanded the drastic reduction,
or even the elimination, of the armed forces, so
that the funds presently being used by the military
could be used rather for development programs.
Especially, these funds would be used to enlarge
the size and scope of the political apparatus, providing salaries for those followers of the Front
who are now unable to find political employment,
because bureaucratic funds are limited by military
expenditures, or because their political views are
distasteful to the present regime. Fundamentally,
what the Front is asking for, then, in distinction
to those who support the existing regime, is that
the present political power structure, which is
dependent on an army ("military security for
national security, including development") be
replaced with one which would be rooted in the
bureaucracy ("development for national strength").
Significantly, no spokesman of the Front has suggested reforming the bureaucratic apparatus along
the lines proposed earlier in this section. Rather,
the members of the Front, as other Iranian politicians, argue for a cathartic change of individuals,
so that "good people" (that is, their own followers)
will come to power, and, presumably, will busy themselves, more seriously than the members of the present bureaucracy are doing, with the formalities of
economic development.

     It is true that some outside and Iranian ob-
servers, especially economists, have not shared
local (political) optimism over the potential of
this kind of "reform." especially in the light of
its past ineffectiveness. But, at the same time,
these observers continue to see the fundamental
problem of economic development much as do the local politicians, as a problem of somehow _reforming_

the lack of interest, sincerity or ability of those
now in political power. And it is this, perhaps,
that is at the heart of the "reform" problem in
Iran. For as cogent as any observations about the
problems of the Iranian economy may be, and as
valuable as any "reform" suggestions arising out
of those observations (and those suggested in the
opening remarks of this section are very valuable),
such observations and suggestions, although necessary, are not sufficient to convey the full measure of what must be done to "reform" the kind of
economically underdeveloped society that is Iranian
society. For if the problem of economic development
was merely a problem of procedural reform of the ill-
used prerogatives of specific ill-motivated or venal
individuals, and not a problem of changing the very
basic imperatives of the social order, it is reasonable to assume that someone advocating "reform"
would have attempted to implement some developmentally relevant reforms some time in the past, even
if only as the means to achieve and maintain power.

No matter how distasteful it is to both outside theorists and to locals, then (re-)considera-
tion must be given to the possibility that something more serious than formal "reform" may be
needed to dislodge the difficulties standing in
the way of economic development in Iranian society.
At the least, it seems important to consider that
although the discrete proposals in any particular
"reform" package all may appear theoretically
(technically) to be of comparable difficulty to
achieve to the outside observer, in actual practice,
certain existing ways of doing things prove to be
so difficult to dislodge in comparison to other
ways of doing things, which are readily "reformable";
and that the measure of that difference may be explained in terms of the essential determinants
(goals) of the social order.*

Myths Concerning the Private Sector

The "Public Sector versus the Private Sector" Myth

The Public Sector myth asserts that the private
sector which now exists in the economically underdeveloped societies is incapable of engendering
economic development.50

---

* In this context, also see section " The 'Gradual
  Progress' or 'Isolated-Trait' Myth" above. .

This myth is defended both on theoretical and empirical grounds. The empirical argument is employed primarily, but not exclusively, by foreign observers to explain such facts, as, for example, the penchant for speculation and non-productive investment in the private sector of the Iranian economy.[51] It is for this reason that tax benefits, high tariffs against foreign competition, cheap loans, public services of all kinds, and other such incentives have not measurably improved the desire or ability of economic actors in the private sector to develop. In fact, such incentives only further intensify the desire not to develop, since further profits derived from non-productive economic action are now feasible, and hence, whatever new enterprise has been stimulated is organized and operated in other than an economically rational way; as for example, the cheap loan, wasteful expenditures, and fraud syndrome of the typical Iranian factory as detailed in the case study (see above, Chapter Two). Consequently, for all these reasons, logically, the private sector is both helpless and hopeless, and hence, the only remaining possibility is the public sector. Whether it likes it or not, then, by default, political authority must assume the responsibility. And, even without these inherent serious defects in the private sector, since the societies of the underdeveloped world are impatient to develop economically, so as to assert their equality with the West, (see above, Chapter Three, section "The Meaning of Economic Development"), the economies can not content themselves to wait for the private sector to muster the capital necessary for investment at the "take-off" level of development if and when that private sector sees fit, and is capable, to do so.[52]

Although the empirical argument essentially is non-Asian in origin, many Asian, especially Iranian politicians, enthusiastically have supported it. This is so, because the argument lends outside justification to their own theoretical predelection for upholding the primacy of the public sector in economic development through the doctrine of moral economics which proclaims that economic activity (including economic development) carried on without the orbit of the political (public) sector, morally is suspect.

It is now in order to introduce a hypothesis

that only has been implied previously in the case
study; namely, that the political order, acting upon
ideological conviction, has dominated the private
sector in a way that politically generated insecurity and failure to develop economically has characterized that sector of the economy. Political authority, then, turns about and uses this empirical
evidence of failure as <u>additional</u> vindication of
its rights to continue those dubious economic policies which helped create the stagnation in the private sector in the first instance. In this way, a
vicious circle feeding upon itself, to the detriment
of the private sector, is built up; a vicious circle
in which, to observe, the political authority can
argue that its position is justified on either
theoretical <u>or</u> empirical grounds, or both simultaneously. Consequently, perhaps, inadequate attention has been given to the possibility that if one
starts with the thesis that the private sector is
inadequate and is not likely to create the desired
conditions for economic development (which based on
the evidence of the case study, obviously, cannot be
denied in Iran) this does not imply <u>necessarily</u>
that political authority, for better or worse, is
the alternative for stimulating and operating the
process of economic development. Certainly, it is
true, as non-Westerners have suggested, and rightly
so, that out of its own experience in economic development, Western theorists have developed a thesis
which became a myth that nothing good economically
could be accomplished with public control of, or
even interference with the process of economic development. But non-Westerners have been reluctant to
admit their own penchant for accepting a reciprocal
myth; namely, that nothing productive economically
can be accomplished in the society without public
control over, or at least, without public interference
into the process of economic development. The Western
myth may be termed the Private Sector Myth: whereas
the Asian myth, of course, is the Public Sector Myth,
as defined in the opening paragraph of this section.

The Public Sector Myth closely is associated
with the previously discussed Strong Polity Myth, for
it implies that most anything in <u>economic</u> developmental action can be accomplished if only sufficient
power and prerogatives are provided the public sector
<u>political</u> apparatus. The Public Sector Myth also is
associated with the Reform Myth. For when it is demonstrated empirically that a political order is
hopelessly inept at economic development, which is

only too true in many such underdeveloped societies
as Iran, in which the polity has squandered its
superior access to organization and funds on monuments, palaces, sports stadiums, or statues of politicians, the public sector enthusiasts apologetically
mumble something about a need for "reform" in the
public sector to clear up the problem. Significantly, and why it is important to (re-)consider the
"public sector" theory as a myth, is that under
these conditions the public sector apologists refuse
to accept as feasible the same principle of "reform"
in the private sector, even though "reform," empirically has been demonstrated to be as much a failure
in the public as in the private sector of the economy.
Consequently, since, empirically, no evidence exists
that either the public or the private sector in Iran,
"reformed" or not, has been other than a failure in
creating a self-generating economic system, then,
there must be a built-in value judgment which automatically condemns the same order of economic actions in the private sector. And this value judgment is the Public Sector Myth.

It has been argued by some that this public
sector myth readily is acceptable because empirically, and through help of Marxist dogma, economic
theory which favors the private sector (capitalism)
has been associated too intimately in the minds of
the members of the underdeveloped societies with
colonialism and imperialism to be taken seriously.
For, since the underdeveloped world predominantly
is ex-colonial or has suffered from imperialism,
(as has Iran, the latter), private sector theory
automatically is suspect, if not considered automatically evil. But since the foreigners now have
surrendered the colonial burden so that it is an
indigenous element that presently controls the private sector, and since the foreigner most often now
works through the public and not through the private
sector in economically underdeveloped societies
(and even did so in the good-old capitalist-
imperialist days, regardless of preference for the
private sector back home), empirical evidence for
the myth seems to be on very shaky ground indeed.
Yet the myth can be and is being used as justification both to rationalize an existing situation, and
to further expand the public sector. It is worth
(re-)considering, then, that this cannot be a logical
reaction, or even an ideological reaction to an empirical situation. Rather, it is a social-ideological
reaction to the fundamental institutional imperatives

of the social order, which historically has favored
the public sector as the moral watchdog of the private economic order. And, now, that development is
in the air, it is being used to continue to justify
this long standing political policy.

It is for this same reason, that members of
the public sector in economically developed societies, especially in India, continually are amazed
whenever the private sector makes unanticipated
developmental advances. This is so, because, ideologically, (that is, in this case, morally) the
private sector cannot do so, therefore, it should
not do so. For the same reason, it is worth (re-)
considering that this is why even sincere individuals, especially sincere young people, deeply motivated to economically develop their societies, gravitate more often to the public sector than they do
to the private sector in the economically underdeveloped societies. For they assume that within the
political apparatus the best chance exists to serve
their own, and their society's basic aspirations.
The primary consequence is that this order of preference robs the private sector of potential talent,
which further seems to justify the primacy of the
public sector in economic development.

Theoretically, this preference for the public
sector should only disturb the dogmatists among the
supporters of the Public Sector Myth. But unfortunately, this preference has certain significant
negative empirical inferences. For, as discussed
in the case study (see above,Chapter Four), in associating with the political order, not surprisingly,
individuals are forced to accept the existing fundamental institutional values of that political order,
especially in its relation to the economy and this
implies, in a society such as Iran, that political
action may, and does, interfere positively with productive economic action in the public sector, as
well as in the private sector, of the economy.
Consequently, the hope that new blood and new ideas,
so necessary for creating a self-generating rational
economic system, will create such a system in the
public sector is stifled before it can get started.
And, consequently, to assume that those politicians
in control of the public sector's economic activities somehow will "reform" and come to the realization that a particular set of economic values and
priorities must be served if economic development
will take place, while it is being claimed that, at

the same time, no hope for such realization exists
as far as the private sector of the same society is
concerned, is neither logical nor feasible.[53]

What is being suggested, and this is the basic
conclusion of the discussion of the "private versus
public sector" myth, is that (re-)consideration at
least must be given to the thesis (for, hopefully,
this is not a myth) that perhaps since both the private and public sector are at fault, it is neither
the public nor the private sector as such that is
at fault. Rather it is the underlying social institutional imperatives operating in both sectors that
are at fault. Consequently, a particular kind of
social order, as that of Iran, which creates and
maintains economic difficulties in the public sector, no matter what the reason may be--ideology, venality, or ineptness--is apt to repeat these difficulties in the private sector, and for the same
reasons. And conversely, that if one sector (especially the public sector) succeeds, the other one
will, or could if allowed to, and if one has failed,
or is failing, the other is also. Certainly this
appears to be true in the economically underdeveloped society, Iran. Cited in evidence is the fact
that the same order of problems crop up in both
sectors; as for example, the fact that capital is
ill-invested in the public as readily as in the
private sector, and that the political authority
is not clearing away the same kind of economic problems in either sector.[54] Consequently, it is worth
(re-)considering that it is the specific inadequacies of the Iranian economy as a whole that one
should examine, rather than wasting time with arguments and counter-arguments on the alleged virtues of
either the public or private sector; as if the choice
of one or the other automatically assured economic
development. Much more will be said on this subject
in the next (concluding) chapter.

The "Private Sector that Exists in Iran" Myth

This myth asserts that in an economically underdeveloped society, as Iran, a private sector exists
that is, at the least, autonomous of the public sector. This private sector has control over economic
enterprises and market, which at the least parallel
those which exist in the public sector of the economy.
Consequently, individuals within the private sector
have both the ability and the responsibility to calculate with reasonable assurance their own economic

interests and are able to act to maximize those interests. The political authority may cooperate with
the private sector to aid it, or to regulate it, but
this is only to help it fulfill its responsibilities
to develop, without in any way impairing its basic
prerogatives.

     Importantly, the partisans of both the public
and private sector approach to economic development,
as described in the previous section, have accepted
this myth as a point of departure for their great
debate. For both sides accept the thesis that as
long as a society is not Communist, it must be
either capitalist or mixed, and hence, that, at the
least, an autonomous private sector exists in the
economy which the public sector serves as best it
can. The Iranians, in particular, have not been adverse to accepting this myth, since it justifies and
encourages foreign aid as part of the so-called
"peaceful competitive co-existence" rivalry between
the Communist and non-Communist world. For the private sector partisans have argued that if economic
development is successful in an economically underdeveloped society which is not committed to Communism,
as is the case in Iran, then, this will "prove" the
superiority of capitalism which stresses primarily
development in the private sector. If this effort
fails in Iran, presumably, the Communist solution
which demands a go at development through the public
sector alone, will be attempted. If this comes to
pass, and the Communists fail to live up to expectations, Iran will not be able to reintroduce private sector development, because Communism does not
permit societies to reverse the process of communi-
zation. Hence, Iran will remain Communist. This
will not only make Iran Communist, it will also
make capitalist-private sector economic development
theory more vulnerable to criticism throughout the
economically underdeveloped world. Hence, the non-
Communist developed world stands to gain or lose in
Iran, depending on how well the process of development does in that society. And, consequently, it
behooves the (private sector) developed societies
to do anything possible to support Iran's efforts
at economic development through primary stress on
the private sector.

     It may be observed, first, that this conception
of the "competitive co-existence struggle" is, at
the least, on dubious sociological grounds, for no
other reason than that it is extremely doubtful that

an autonomous private sector exists in Iran, and
hence, that the problem of private sector development is one of finding a way to make that sector
"responsible" and of otherwise inducing it to operate upon rational economic assumptions on its own.
For, an economic system is but an integral part of
a total social system, and the Iranian social system is not one, as in certain of the developed societies, in which true autonomy for decision-
making in the private sector is accepted. For as
discussed in the case study (see above, Chapters
Two and Three especially), the Iranian economic
system is characterized by the domination of a
political apparatus over the so-called private
sector in a way that economics always may be subordinated to politics, and economic action never
can be autonomous. Since it is not autonomous of
the kind of political order in which economically
non-rational political considerations are primary,
the private sector of the economy never is confident that it can calculate rationally in a way that
tomorrow can be predicted with reasonable certainty.
Hence it responds with the kinds of economic actions
that have not lead to development. Consequently,
the question of whether or not a private sector,
as such, exists in Iranian society means little, or
nothing.

This line of argument also suggests that (re-)
consideration be given to the kinds (and not only
to the extent) of roles which political authority
played in relationships with the private sectors
of the economies of the economically developed
societies. For whatever the extent of those roles,
it appears that, qualitatively, those roles were
different from the role of the polity in contemporary Iran. For, in the economically developed societies, the polities came to the economies to support the primacy of the autonomy of rational economic
values and not to control the economies in the name
of morality.

In conclusion, then, to assume because a society, as Iran, formally has a private sector, and
that society is non-Communist, and that, in consequence, the society is committed to the same autonomy of economic action as has occurred in the economically developed societies, and, that this is to
be damned or praised, according to one's ideological
conviction, is, at the least, a misleading way to

conceptualize the problem. For to assume so, as do
some Western observers who are at the same time
international donors (e.g., the International Bank),
is not conducive to economic development. For if
these individuals or agencies believe that, through
aid to the existing private sector, directly, or
through the local political authority, they can
persuade (or threaten) Iran's development process
to and through the "take-off" stimulant period,
because they have an autonomous private sector
potentially to work with, in effect, they only are
perpetuating the very causes of the problems these
efforts claim to be ameliorating; namely, the social
institutional determinants of unsatisfactory economic action in either the public or private sector
of the economy.55

SOCIOLOGICAL AND ANTHROPOLOGICAL MYTHS

The Myths of Social Structure

The "Elite-Innovator" Myth

This myth asserts that in order to consummate
national development, including economic development, it is vital to have a dedicated leadership of
competent, political decision-makers (termed
elites) who will have the responsibility, authority,
and capability to initiate and consummate that development. Without such elites, which often is the
case in economically underdeveloped societies, it
is argued that (a) the process of economic development will remain a hit-or-miss pattern of waste and
frustration which runs counter to the expressed
commitment to speed in these societies, and, that,
(b) the effort probably will not be able to "break
through" those formidable vested interests which
impede the development of a self-generating economic system.56

This concept is based, in part, upon a theory
of leadership that was old even among the ancient
Greeks; namely, that it is the creative minority
who alone can innovate effectively and speedily.57
It is assumed in this theory that, throughout human
history anywhere, most significant change has come
about, at best, with the passive cooperation of the
unsophisticated general population. For this reason,
because the West depended heavily upon mass participation in its economic development effort that devel-

opment took countless generations to institute, and
to some observers was not an especially efficient
process. Be that as it may, the need then for economic change was less urgent and involved, and hence,
the process of economic development could be more
leisurely and less orderly.[58] But this is impossible today. Consequently, in economically underdeveloped Iran only an elite which understands what
has to be done, can force through the order of
changes necessary to develop the economy, efficiently and quickly. The cases of Japan, and to some
extent, the Soviet Union, are cited as examples of
the new, more desirable elite-innovator economic
development process in contrast to, say, England
and the United States which are cited as examples
of the older, slower, and less efficient Western
elite-induced economic development process.[59]

     This myth appears to be based on the follow-
ing theoretical suppositions. It assumes, first,
that it is the quality of those in positions of
formal political leadership that is both necessary
and sufficient for economic development; second,
that it is mass ignorance which requires the use
of a (political) elite in the process of economic
development; and by implication, third, that the
economic development process can be speeded up by
improving the calibre of the existing (political)
elite or by "circulating" the existing elite so
that a new elite more capable or willing to carry
through the process of economic development is
brought to power.

     The empirical evidence in an economically
underdeveloped society such as Iran, appears to
substantiate the validity of these suppositions.
Certainly, the appalling backwardness of the population, especially the rural population, ignorant
of, and ill-motivated to learn, the techniques of
a developed economy is obvious to any observer.
And this situation seems to warrant that a competent, highly motivated, energetic political leadership should be at the helm to force the economy into
the twentieth century. And since Iranian society is
established on a hierarchial basis (see above,
Chapter Five) it is argued, why not take advantage
of rather than oppose this situation? For, if the
foreigner, in particular, can introduce the necessary
new technology and, if need be, support the emergence
of an elite which is not reluctant to try these new
techniques, that elite, in its role as political

opinion leader, will insure that the development
techniques will perculate down to the general population where they will be imitated; and hence, productive economic change will take place throughout
the society. For, it is argued, it is this kind of
elite, and only this kind of elite, which can overcome opposition in the more resistant, traditional
masses, especially the more backward peasant masses,
and not only to the techniques of economic development, but also to the ideas of economic develop-
ment.60

The idea of elite-innovation hardly is a novel
concept to Iranians. For, as has been noted in the
case study, the necessity of depending on political
elites who are morally and intellectually superior
to ignorant moral-inferiors to innovate in the
society is one of the fundamental institutional
assumptions of the Iranian social order. To these
political elites, economic development only is the
latest of a long series of decisions that have been
their exclusive responsibility by virtue of their
peculiar role in Iranian society. And so, if problems in elite effectiveness occur, undoubtedly, in
time, these problems can be worked out as similar
problems supposedly have been solved in the past.
For surely the corrupt and incompetent can be
purged (the cathartic revolution of Chapter Eight).
And then, good individuals (good for purposes of
economic development, supposedly) will be placed in
key positions in the political process. Especially
with a strong leader backing a wise political elite,
it is possible to do anything. It was for this
reason that the evil and jealous imperialists
removed the beloved Reza Shah, the maximum leader
of the Iranian people, who was honest, fearless,
and who was committed to economic change. For Reza
Shah forced the political elite, who, in turn,
forced the people to do what he wanted, which was to
develop the Iranian economy. Without the bad turn
of fate which led to the removal of Reza Shah, Iran
surely would be the equal of any developed society
of the West today. And for those, who with good
reason, are dubious of the validity of these assumptions, the singular answer is that no alternative
exists in terms of the existing Iranian ground rules
of innovation, whereby it is assumed that the masses
are inert, and some Iranian-style (political) elite
alone can bring those passive elements around to
accepting change --or as the proverb reads, "Only a
man from Mazdaran, can catch the Mazdaran deer." In

sum, the Iranian answer to criticism of the elitist argument is limited, even reluctantly, to the suggestion that the existing (political) elite, being a traditional elite, is neither motivated nor sufficiently competent to handle successfully the economic development process. And, consequently, at best, what Iran needs is a "new elite"; that is, a novel (political) elite not committed to the old order and the preservation of existing privileges, which, significantly, "traditionally" may date back no further than a few decades to the time of Reza Shah. In no case is the suggestion raised that perhaps other than political elites (that is, leaders drawn from the broad mass of the population), purely "economic elites," or even a different kind of political elite, may have anything to offer concerning the future development of the Iranian economy.

For this reason, it is worth (re-)considering that the conclusion of the Iranian elitist argument, fundamentally, is no different from the conclusion of the outside observer, including the Western-trained sociologist (which in fact was the viewpoint discussed in the opening paragraphs of the section), although the specific justification for accepting political elite-innovation, and the quality and characteristic of the elite, may vary as between the two interpretations. For whether the Westerner likes it or not, by supporting the general doctrine of political elite-innovation in Iranian society, he is, in effect, giving support to the specific Iranian political elite-innovation doctrine, even if not to a specific elite; a dogma which, as suggested by the case study and the subsequent discussions, has not led to, and is not likely to lead to, economic development.

It must not be assumed, that elites, including existing elites in such economically underdeveloped societies as Iran, per se are necessarily disinterested in economic development. For at the least, economic development is the means by which they hope to claim political equality with the big powers, a subject upon which elites in economically underdeveloped societies are so paranoid. But one problem is that the elites, which by definition, are political elites in such Asian societies as Iran, since they see themselves as the morally as well as the intellectually superiors in the society, assume that economic development must come exclusively from themselves and never from the ranks of those outside

their circle, even from non-politicians within the
public sector of the economy. Unlike in the economically developed societies (see Chapter Ten, section "The Alternative Model" above) these "outsiders,"
even if, and when, they could demonstrate, empirically, their economic utility, are not allowed to
innovate, because economic enthusiasm must never
get out of hand potentially to challenge political
interests and prerogatives. As long as political
and economic goals go in the same direction, as for
example, in the building of dams and roads, admittedly all may be well from the rational economic
standpoint. But it is another matter when economic
and political goals do not go in the same direction;
as for example, when it is a choice beween supporting
a rational bureaucracy, on the one hand, and using
the bureaucracy as an unemployment office for Iranian
patrimonial retainers, on the other hand. Given the
necessity of a choice in Iran, the answer obviously
is that the political goal, whether or not it is
conducive to the development of economic rationality,
wins out. Significantly, unless they have been keeping themselves conspicuously quiet, none of the current political alternative forces in Iranian society
see the choice as otherwise.

A significant consequence of this line of
reasoning on the prospects for economic development
in Iran is as follows: Iranian political elitists,
and too many Westerners who subscribe to this myth,
fantastically underestimate the capabilities of the
average Iranian, including the average peasant, to
play a significant, even innovative, role in economic development. For it is assumed that since
these ordinary individuals do not appear to have
either the ability or the motivation for economic
development, political elites are necessary for any
economic innovation. And, hence, by implication,
whenever economic developmental efforts, specifically political elite efforts fail, this is due to
the failings of the ordinary followers (rule by
model). It is worth (re-)considering, then, that
the failure of political elites to innovate and
carry the masses with them in their efforts to
force through economic change may not necessarily
be a reflection on the "stupid" masses. Rather, it
very well may be a reflection on the inability of
the political elites to appreciate that political
elite engendered innovation which does things for
people may be ineffective, no matter how much these
innovations appear to be needed, no matter how much

political pressure the elites have at their disposal,
and no matter how much the people themselves claim
to be waiting for the great elite political leaders
to guide them. This seems especially to be true in
the case of the great Iranian innovator, Reza Shah,
as mentioned earlier in this section, who forced
through many significant and economic changes by
means of accepted Iranian political elite innovator
techniques, but many of whose efforts did not survive his removal from the political scene. For
Iranian political elites, any elites, have refused
to accept the possibility of bringing the common
people into their confidence and to work with and
not for them. These political elites also have
refused to accept the possibility that the formal
leadership, as represented by themselves, may not
be coincident with the true leadership in the society, and hence, that they, the political elites,
may not exhaust the category of potential innovative
leadership in Iranian society. For acceptance of
these two theses would admit the possibility that
mere, ordinary people would be capable of innovating,
and would admit the possibility that elite innovators,
in order to remain the leaders of the society, would
have to prove their rational efficacy in each case,
and on a par with the natural leaders of the people.
And this could but lead to the possibility that the
a priori arrogation of the economic innovative roles
of the society by the existing moral political elite,
regardless of any empirical test of its rational
economic talents might be challenged. And this, in
turn, could lead to the possibility that confidence
in the whole political elitist structure of political authority might be shattered. It is for this
reason, that economic development programs in Iran,
which are supposed to encourage self-help, are perverted to political elite-innovator programs, in
which autonomous popular leadership which is interested and potential capable of economic innovation
is never allowed to develop its talents. Encour-
agingly, some Iranians do see this problem for what
it is. The attempt of India, albeit in a stumbling
way, to bring the public, especially that public
committed to the primacy of rational economic values,
into the process of economic development, has made
a limited impact in some quarters in Iran.61 But
whether anything will, or can, in the light of
Iranian institutional values, come of this light in
the economic darkness is only a moot question at this
time.

Clearly, a policy must be devised which will insure bringing the right <u>kind</u> of individuals into positions of political authority in the economically underdeveloped societies. But as clearly, such a policy cannot be based on continuing acceptance of the "elite-innovator" myth. Consequently, by way of conclusion, it might be suggested that the whole question of elite-innovation in economically underdeveloped societies is overdue for (re-)consideration, not only in terms of the "effectiveness" and the "motivation" of elites, but also more importantly, in terms of the relationship of elites to masses, especially in the struggle between potential non-elitist, primarily rational economic values and elitist moral-political values which are not conducive to the maximization of economic rationality.

The "Individualism-Collectivism" Myth

This myth actually is a combination of two discrete myths interacting with each other. One myth claims that individuals in such economically underdeveloped societies as Iran are too "individualistic," that is, self-seeking in their interpersonal relations. Consequently, it is necessary to mobilize these individuals into coordinated, collective units of some order that will submerge the tendencies of individuals to go their own way whenever possible. Only in this way, can the process of economic development, requiring large-scale, concerted effort and commitment, be implemented successfully, economically, and rapidly. The case of Japan usually is cited as evidence that this is a necessity in an economically underdeveloped society outside western Europe where individual responsibility is not widely accepted.[62]

The second, and apparently contradictory myth, claims that individuals in such economically underdeveloped societies as Iran, are too passive and too much subject to the collective pressure of the group. Hence, they tend to wait for economic development to "happen," especially to wait for a great man who will tell them what, when, and how to develop economically. And when the leadership is confused or ineffectual and no pressure is exerted, and when the ordinary individual has no personal initiative, as is the case now in Iran, then nothing much gets done. And so, unless one is willing to concede the use of Communist totalitarian methods, what is needed then, is more individualism and less collectivism.

In brief it is argued that, simultaneously, on
the one hand, that Iranians are too individualistic
and need some order of collective coercion to keep
them in line, while, on the other hand, that Iranians
are too much subject to collective coercion and need
more individualism to wake them up. Surely this must
be a logical inconsistency, for both claims cannot
be true, and so one or both claims must be false.

Resolution of the apparent contradiction in
these two interrelated myths lies in the appreciation
that the controversy is but a sham controversy, for
in fact, these two myths or sub-myths, are not true
contradictions of each other but are contraries.
This is so because, first, the terms, "individualism"
and "collectivism" as used in the two myths, are not
true logical equivalents, but rather are different
terms that only appear (formally) to be the same;
that is, they only are the same word, or sign, but
do not share the same connotations or symbols (see
above, Section "The 'Development is Uniform' Myth"
of this chapter). And second, this is so because,
as with most myths being discussed in this chapter,
simultaneously, both sub-myths are, at the same time,
true and false because in fact they both are half
true and half false. Therefore, it can be argued,
logically and empirically, that Iranians are both
not individualistic enough and not too collectivistic
enough, and at the very same time, it can be argued,
logically and empirically, Iranians are too individualistic and too collective, simply because the
terms do not have the same connotations in the two
premises of the myth. For in one context, it might
be argued that "individualism" refers primarily to a
sense of individual responsibility, reliance, and
initiative which is oriented to specific rational
economic goals, while "collectivism" (possibly) refers
to a sense of cooperation and a willingness to al-
lign self-interests with group interests for possibly
even greater personal gain in future. As matters
stand now, the average Iranian holds neither set of
values, and hence, both more individualism and more
collectivism is needed in Iranian interpersonal
relationships. Simultaneously, in the other context,
it might be argued that the Iranian tends to merge
into his group and plead passive irresponsibility
whenever the painful but necessary decisions associated with economic development have to be made.
At the same time the Iranian patterns his whole social interactional process either on protecting him-

self or in seeking his own immediate advantage, so
that no one can trust anyone else in the society,
even within the immediate individual family circle.
Hence, in this context, Iranian society needs both
less collectivism and less individualism.

This discussion has direct bearing as to
whether a Communist or non-Communist path to economic development is preferable. Clearly, each par-
tisan in the battle selects that aspect of the
myth which seemingly justifies its own position.
The Communists, on the one hand, claim that collectivism, that is, having a highly motivated elite
cajoling or forcing the Iranian "rope of sand" to
act, is the only practical solution for Iran's
economic development problem. On the other hand,
the Western partisans, especially the Americans,
claim that, without individual acceptance of collective responsibility, once the pressure is removed,
the rope returns to sand. They cite evidence that
this did happen when Reza Shah was removed from
power during World War II. They also point out
that even before the time of Reza Shah, resentment
and passive resistance has characterized collective
(largely authoritarian) economic action in Iran, and
that this has led inevitably to the economic wastage
that the Communists admit and deplore, but whose root
cause they refuse even to consider is due to collectivism of any kind, even non-Communist collectivism.
The Communists, in turn, have poked fun at the inept
Western-inspired local efforts to develop the Iranian
economy, based on the existing Iranian institutional
ground rules, which the West has mistakenly accepted
as incipient economic development potentially stimulating by individual initiative.

The often cited Japanese case is interesting
in the present context, but the case is not conclusive for either side of the argument. But it is
worth (re-)considering that the "collectivism" of
the Japanese may have had nothing to do with the
familiar ideal Asian conception of a masterful,
diabolical elite leading robots to productive economic efforts, as certain observers have suggested.
Rather, as implied by the discussion of the previous chapter, this collectivism may very well be
much more akin to the Western collectivism of individual responsibility (or commitment) for economic
action which was mobilized by a political authority
motivated to maximize economic rationality to serve
a productive economic development effort.[63] Regretfully, this possibility has not been explored at all

in the now extensive literature on the lessons of
the Japanese case for economic development. At the
least, the entire question of what is individualism
and what is collectivism, as far as economic development is concerned, must be opened for reconsideration.

The "Development is a Social Problem" Myth

This myth asserts that in a society such as
Iran, as it undergoes social change, as is inevitable in a process of economic development, a number
of social maladjustments occur. Although these maladjustments, inevitably, will work themselves out in
time, they do constitute problems for the time being.
These problems, however, can be ameliorated to a
great extent, and even helped along to resolution,
by a proper understanding of the general processes
of directed social change. This myth also may be
titled the "Social Work" myth, since these assumptions are compatible with the basic philosophy of
Western, especially American, social work.

Concretely, in terms of the way Iranians have
described their own situation, the myth asserts that
Iran is telescoping successfully economic changes
that took generations to achieve in the West. It is
this very rapidity of economic change that causes
the violent social dislocations and maladjustments
which arise when one part of the Iranian social system changes more rapidly than any other. But since
these maladjustments and imbalances are temporary,
they will subside as soon as Iran learns to adjust
to the demands of a modern, developed economy. And
if individuals can be helped to understand how to
overcome these problems, and if this painful trans-
formation period can be made with a minimum of personal and social disorganization, then, Iran surely
will advance more quickly and less painfully to the
ranks of the economically developed societies.

One cannot quarrel with the notion that Iran
is changing, and that the society is facing problems of personal and social disorganization of very
serious magnitude. Consequently, social workers,
both analytical and practical, can be of significant
service in that society's hour of need. In accepting the role of social work in the society, however,
one should be aware of the implicit major working
assumption of social work; namely, that because the
prime concerns are those of imbalance and disorgani-

zation, the fundamental institutional values of the
social system are accepted, either as positive, or
at least as neutral, so that a return to (social and
personal) integration, as soon as possible, is the
goal and is the measure of success. Hence, technical or formal adjustment to the existing social system, if it reduces or eliminates imbalance, automatically is considered to have positive value, while
that which threatens to disorganize personality or
society automatically has negative value, and is to
be overcome. And although it is true that new avenues of adjustment within the system may be proposed
to alleviate existing imbalance, the question of the
potential worth of the entire system of forms or
values, normally, never is considered. And thus,
unless overwhelming social and personal imbalance
occurs, questioning critically, or, in fact even
discussing, the over-all social system, or its
imperatives, is not considered significant, if it is
even considered legitimate.

Of course, one cannot dispute that social work
is a legitimate field of applied sociology. But it
is worth (re-)considering that, unfortunately, too
much of sociology devoted to applied planned social
change in economically underdeveloped areas is concerned almost exclusively with such social work
considerations as fostering good human relations and
adjusting individuals and social forms to potential
change under existing institutional ground rules,
rather than with the possibly more vital concerns of
the adequacies of the whole social system and its
characteristic institutional goals for economic development. In economic development programs sociologists have been placed in the rather peculiar role
of obstacle-course clearers for the economists.
Economists are expected to make up the blueprints
for economic change, while the sociologists are expected to conjure up the means to overcome the reluctance of the poor natives to succumb to economic
development, much and in the same manner as the
"applied" sociologist back home tries to make house-
wives buy a new brand of detergent.

It also is worth (re-)considering that the
social work approach to the sociology of change in
economically underdeveloped societies, has encouraged an extremist position among those who view the
social system itself, and not its inability to
"adjust" to changing needs, as the prime source

of underdevelopment difficulty. For, to too many
observers, only Marxists seem ready and willing to
challenge whole systems, while non-Marxists underdevelopment theorists toy with "reform" measures to
help existing systems to "adjust" to the "problems"
of a modern rational economic system, as if the
fundamental institutional assumptions of these social systems potentially were conducive to economic
development in the same way as the institutional
assumptions of the economically developed societies
were useful at a similar stage in their development
process.* For it is strongly suggested that non-
Marxists have the right, and one ventures to add
had better have the responsibility, to offer solutions to the problem of economic development in
economically underdeveloped societies which include
suggesting the rejection of certain of the fundamental institutional values of these societies, if
these values are incompatible with the goals of
economic development. For, unless this is so, the
foreign sociological advisor will continue to encourage the Iranian, for example, but to tinker
with his existing system, and to continue to believe
that some social gimmick miraculously will solve the
social aspects of the problem of economic development, at a time when the foreign advisor should be
forcing locals to fact up to the basic inadequacies
of social systems and to the necessity of thinking
about what has to be done about them. In sum, it

---

*   See above, Chapter Ten, section "The Alternative
     Model." See also, the critique by the American
     anthropologist, Sahlens, of Hoselitz's "Economic
     Growth Theory," American Anthropologist, Vol. 64,
     No. 5, Part I, pp. 1063-73. Significantly,
     Hoselitz denounced my non-Marxist critical ana-
     lysis of the fundamental institutional goals of
     an economically underdeveloped society (here
     traditional China) as of "no value." It was no
     value, in Hoselitz's estimation, perhaps, judging
     from that individual's writings, because it
     offered no concrete proposals of how to patch-
     reform an Asian social system which is not com-
     mitted to nor organized to develop economically.
     See his review of the author's 1958 study in
     The Annals of the Academy of Political Science,
     Vol. 322, March, 1959.

is worth (re-)considering that the non-Marxist institutional sociologist has something positive and
significant to offer to the process of economic
development in economically underdeveloped societies
along the lines explored in Chapters Ten to Twelve
inclusive, even though some of his proposals may be
drastic and make his social work colleagues shudder.
This, of course, is one of the very basic theses of
the present study.*

Myths of Social Interaction Between The Foreign Stimulator and the Local Innovator

The "Good Human Relations Implies Good Results" Myth

     This myth maintains that the ability to establish
and maintain good personal relationships among individuals is essential for the accomplishment of any
task involving these individuals; and, conversely,
that an inability to establish and maintain good
personal relationships among individuals insures
that nothing much can be accomplished involving
these individuals. For the essence of one individual being able to get something done which involves
the participation of other human beings lies in the
former's ability to handle these other people effectively, so that they can be made to do what he desires. And conversely, if the interpersonal relationships between an individual and others are poor,
then the first individual has very poor prospects of
influencing, or even working together productively,
with any of the other individuals in those relationships. This myth is accepted both by Westerners
working in Iran and Iranians themselves; but for
different reasons, as will be seen.

----

*   Whether or not the Iranian, for example, should
    accept economic development, if it means surren-
    dering the fundamental institutional values of
    his society, must be another question. For that
    question involves a value judgment and it is
    clearly presumptious, at the least, for an out-
    sider to that society to argue that a rational,
    self-generating economy is so great a value that
    all other values that run counter to it should be
    sacrificed. But asserting this does not imply
    that the institutional sociologist, among others,
    cannot assume the responsibility of making the
    issues involved clear to the Iranians, especially

That interpersonal relations, especially cooperative interpersonal relations, especially are bad in
Iran, no one can doubt (see above, Chapter Nine).
And that unproductive and unrewarding economic action
accompany these bad interpersonal relations, also no
one can doubt. Consequently, empirical support for
the converse of the myth seems to exist.

But acceptance of the converse of this myth does
not necessarily imply that the reverse of the myth
also is true; namely, that good relations will lead
to cooperative economic behavior, and hence, that
concern with good relations is one of the keys to
overcoming the problems of economic development in
such a society as Iran.* For, to recall (Chapter
Nine especially), all Iranians believe, on the one
hand, that they are experts in cultivating good
interpersonal relations, and that through flattery
and deviousness, they can get anyone to do anything.
But yet, on the other hand, because they are well
aware that deviousness may exist in all interpersonal relations, they are very wary of being played
for suckers. Hence, Iranians tend to find all
human relations, at the least, suspect, and tend,
automatically, to be suspicious of all overtures
for good interpersonal relations. They are fright-
ened by all interpersonal relations, but especially
"good" interpersonal relations, because they believe that if they accept good interpersonal relations with others, this may force upon them obligations, which in the uncertainties of Iranian society,
they may not want to incur. For if they are not
able to live up to the obligations when called upon
they will lose prestige (face). This is why Iranians
argue that if "A" is my friend, he should not impose
on me, by putting me in a potentially embarrassing
situation.

The ideal interpersonal situation, then, is to
obligate others, but not to obligate oneself; for
nothing ventured, nothing lost. To accomplish this,

---

if that sociologist is responsible, even margin-
ally, for the process of economic development in
Iranian society.

* Good relations, in the present context, of course,
must imply interpersonal relations which facilitate rational economic action.

whenever an Iranian does not want to do something
for others, which is a good part of the time, he
deliberately will create bad interpersonal relations,
so that others will not have the right to obligate
him and cause him anxiety, if he cannot fulfill his
obligations. Consequently, interpersonal relations
can be, and are broken readily whenever they are
believed to be an overburden to the parties involved.
And, consequently, depending on good interpersonal
relationships to get anything done (as, ironically,
the Iranians prefer), especially in the present
Iranian context, is self-defeating, especially for
those kinds of economic and social changes essential
for economic development, because those kinds of
changes cannot but be considered as "impositions"
to be avoided at all costs. And for this reason,
again given the ground rules of Iranian interpersonal relations, the original, tentatively accepted
counter-thesis of the myth that bad relations imply
that nothing can, or will get done, even may be open
to doubt. For, in Iranian terms, things can, and do
get done by a "strong man" forcing others, presumably strangers, against their will, to obligate themselves. For such an order of interpersonal relations
relieves the subordinate of any responsibility if
anything goes wrong.

     It also is worth noting, that even if good
relations determine good interpersonal actions,
logically (that is, in any specific context--here,
in the economically developed as well as in the
economically underdeveloped societies), all relations
in any web of interpersonal relationships are intran-
sitive. That is, if "A" can influence "B", and "B"
can influence "C", it does not follow necessarily
that "A" can influence "C" in sustaining the web of
good interpersonal relations. And, concretely,
certainly given the volatile nature of the Iranian
web of interpersonal relations, to attempt to build
a system of reliable (calculable interpersonal relationships in the society at large on the basis of
successful achievement in isolated, individual instances, is to doubly compound the building of
castles on sand.

     In sum, in any society, but especially in Iran,
the question of good or bad interpersonal relations
is a consideration independent of the question of
establishing productive economic action in the society. As elsewhere, at best, it is only a means
to accomplish the goal of productive economic action,

and not an end in itself that automatically insures
economic accomplishment. For nothing much can be
done by "influence" or lack of it, even in an inter-
personally related society, as in Iran, if parties
do not share fundamental goals. And, especially in
Iran, under such circumstances, one cannot expect
friends to do anything that they do not want to do,
and one can always dispense with obligations readily
oneself by claiming, or positively creating, "bad
relations" as rationalization, if need be. It is
for this reason, that when Iranians bicker among
themselves and especially with foreign advisors,
the conflict really is over the goals of economic
development and not over "difficulties in human
relations" which refer to means to facilitate the
accomplishment of goals. For obviously, there is
nothing much to be gained by trying amicably to
settle who is to sit where in a vehicle when the
participants are not sure as to where they want
to travel, although everyone may agree that they
want to go to some bountiful land that has the
appearance of the economically developed economy.

Unfortunately, foreigners, especially American
sociologists, even are more guilty of this kind of
misdirected energy than are locals. They busily
set up programs to encourage good human relations
which hopefully will facilitate economic change
and economic development in Iranian society. Yet,
quite clearly, as argued in Chapter Nine, if the
Iranian social system was able to provide individual security, which it seems it cannot or will not,
then good interpersonal relations would not be the
problem it is in that society. Consequently, it is
the social system that must be changed in order to
achieve good interpersonal relations in the society.
But in order to change the Iranian social system so
as to create interpersonal security, in effect, the
social system must be changed in other ways as well,
including, of course, those other aspects of vital
concern to developing a rational self-generating
economic system. Hence, applying the principle of
Occam's razor to eliminate the unnecessary element
in the argument, it is the Iranian social system
that must be changed to insure the general probability that good human relations will facilitate
economic development in Iran, and hence, once again,
it is the social system, or rather, certain fundamental institutional assumptions of that social
system that determine the probability of economic
development in Iran.

The "Ugly Foreigner" Myth

This myth affirms that one of the most significant problems impeding the development process in an
economically underdeveloped society as Iran, is the
inability of foreign advisors, who are highly skilled
in the know-how of development, to establish good
working, interpersonal relationships with local
"counterparts," so that these counterparts will
accept the advice offered and implement it. For it
has come to be appreciated that, unfortunately,
technical advice is not accepted readily in its own
right solely because it is assumed to be pragmatically useful to develop the economy; and this myth
is an attempt to provide an answer to the problem.
In one sense, this myth may be considered as but an
extension of the myth discussed in the previous section. For it emphasizes interpersonal relationships
as the root of all evil or virtue, especially that
interpersonal friction between advisor and advisee
leads inevitably to the rejection of development
innovation on the part of the advisee.

Quite clearly, those who accept this myth,
uncritically, underrate, if not ignore, the impact
of the Iranian institutional structure, while they
overrate the potential effectiveness of the manipu-
lative means of interpersonal interaction to induce
the kinds of changes in Iranian society conducive
to economic development; means, which, to reiterate,
the Iranians are far more clever at countermanding
than are the social dynamicists at selling, much in
the same style as Madison Avenue, U.S.A. sells soap.
Based on the discussions of the previous section, it
is worth (re-)considering that the recipient, as
personified by "counterparts in the development process," may be deliberately creating interpersonal
problems solely as a smoke screen for a lack of a commitment to economic development. For those responsible for the economic development effort must use
any excuse to avoid the onus of being labeled as
unwilling or incapable of establishing a self-
generating economic system, if for no other reason
than that development loans (in contrast to goal-
less aid) from the foreigner might be suspended.
Since Iranians, in turn, as explored earlier, (especially in Chapters Two and Nine), are not adverse to
excusing any difficulties on the basis of an alleged
failing in interpersonal relationships, and since
unfortunately the foreigner, in addition, is willing
to assume the burden of guilt for such difficulties,

this is most pleasing and useful to those Iranians who ever are willing to blame others and have others accept the blame for their own inadequacies; in this case, productive economic inadequacies.

At this point it is worth (re-)considering the question of the significance of the book, The Ugly American.64 Since it is not of direct concern to the present study, no comment is made on the general intrinsic value of the book, save to note that many general observations concerning American foreign economic policy made in the volume had to be made and that they were made well. However, on the other hand, in so far as certain ideas raised in the book directly concern the present study, especially the present section, it is worth (re-)considering that the book is a very misleading document. For the book never suggests that it might be the motives (the institutional goals) of either the foreigner or of the locals, that are the primary cause of the failure of economic development. Rather failure is placed at the threshold of the intrinsic ethical worth of individual, foreign rotten apples, local individuals, who in their heart wanted to do well but did not know how, or individual foreigners and locals, who, as the hero, The Ugly American, were outmaneuvered by evil, incompetent foreign (but apparently not local) bureaucrats. The Iranians, as other Asians, have read the book with great interest and thoroughly agree with its theme. They especially like the thesis that it is the foreigner, especially the American, with whom they have to interact (present company always excepted, of course) who fails to "understand" them or especially, does not treat them properly on the level of interpersonal relationships that is the root of all development evil.65

Iranians and Americans may not and often do not get along very well on the level of interpersonal relations. But, it is worth (re-)considering that this is not the cause but only the symptom of the development problem. For poor interpersonal relations may be due to the fact that the foreigner, regardless of tact, may have had to discuss certain economic facts of life that the Iranian does not wish to hear. For, the Iranian argues, if the foreigner is his friend, as he claims he is, then why does he impose on me? Or as an Iranian proverb puts it, "If you see evil, don't talk about it." To wit, here, the Iranian contemplates, "I know that this is so because I did it or I did not do it; and

I did it or did not do it because I must, given the
institutional imperatives of Iranian society; hence,
as my friend, don't remind me of my failings."[66]

Conversely, it is worth (re-)considering that
good interpersonal relations in Iran do not imply
that progress is being made toward initiating and
developing a self-generating economic system; and
in fact, that this might very well imply the contrary. For good interpersonal relations may exist
between foreigners and local counterparts, because
the Iranians are not being disturbed too alarmingly
by their foreign advisors, out of ignorance, or,
more often, what is (mythically) termed "political
necessity." And, in Iranian terms, acquiescence on
the part of the foreigner to existing patterns of
Iranian economic action is taken as approval of
those patterns, or of the effectiveness of the
Iranian dominant personality or cleverness to outwit the foreigner. This kind of "good interpersonal
relationship" which is, in reality, mutual avoidance,
is so typical of Iranian interpersonal relations
among Iranians themselves, is to be contrasted with
good working relationships in situations in which
productive, meaningful, working goals (here of economic development) are accepted and realistically
acted upon on both sides. Significantly, although
it is expected that good interpersonal relations
will exist under these conditions, conceivably, the
interpersonal relationships may be strained, much
as in a family that is meaningfully interacting (as
was the Ugly American and the ugly foreigner in the
book; see Chapter Ten), in contrast to the lack of
conflict in a family in which each member goes his
own way to the indifference of all other members.

In conclusion, then, it is worth (re-)consider-
ing that, rather than concern with good interpersonal
relations, it is worthwhile to ignore this myth and
try to ascertain what are effective interpersonal
relationships between advisor and advisee in those
work situations dedicated to accomplishment; and by
accomplishment, of course, is meant real productive
development accomplishment, and not monument building
to the personal glory of the Iranian counterpart,
supported by an indifferent or myth accepting advisor.

Anthropological Myths

The "Working in the Culture" Myth (From the Standpoint of the Western Observer)

This myth asserts that (1) solutions to problems in one concrete frame of reference cannot be depended upon necessarily to serve as solutions to problems in another frame of reference, and hence, that, (2) the appropriateness of a solution to a problem can be judged only on how well it works in its own frame of reference, unless it can be demonstrated that the solution is applicable empirically to any and all frames of reference, by study of the solutions in any number of different frames of reference (that is to say, that no arbitrary a priori abstract, judgment of appropriateness can exist); and hence, finally, that, (3) in the long run, it probably is more effective, and wiser, to preserve some continuity in the ground rules (patterns or values) of the existing frame of reference and to work out the problems by a reorganization of some order in the existing frame of reference, rather than to start afresh from a new and alien frame of reference which may prove to be inappropriate.[67]

This is one of those myths which can be accepted, to a great degree, in principle, but which one is apt to have misgivings about in many points of specificity, when applied on the practical level. For example, the first thesis of the myth (usually termed the thesis of cultural relativity); namely, that acceptance or rejection of the utility of a form or procedure (here for economic development) must be based upon how it works out in its own specific context (or frames of reference), here Iran, rather than be based upon the arbitrary judgement that it should work out the same way as it does in another context (here the economically developed societies of the West) has been of special value to the present study. But on the other hand, acceptance of this general principle, simultaneously, does not exclude the possibility that it is legitimate and fruitful also to design models of economically developed societies and economically underdeveloped societies, and to judge Iranian economic development performance against the former model, without necessarily implying that Iranian society "ought to be like" the economically developed society. For, although one can argue that a self-generating economic

system is incompatible with the basic institutional
imperatives of Iranian society, this does not imply
that Iran "ought to develop" in the same fashion as
the already economically developed societies (see
the discussions of the last chapter); or, in fact,
that Iran ought to develop at all. And, second,
although, as suggested in the discussions of the
previous chapters, significant differences exist in
the social systems (that is, economically underdeveloped Iran and any economically developed society), this does not preclude that certain similarities in material culture and even ideology between
Iran (as an economically underdeveloped society) and
an economically developed society simultaneously may
exist. Consequently, acceptance of the principles
of cultural relativity does not necessarily imply
that each society must be treated as unique and
incomparable whenever it is impossible to obtain
complete identity between all possible comparable
characteristics of two (or more) societies. Third,
to imply that each new society must be unique, and
hence, that the introduction of a trait (material
or value) from one frame of reference where it is
considered efficacious for economic development (as
in the economically developed society) into another
frame of reference (as in Iranian society) smacks
potentially of cultural imperialism or cultural
smugness, runs counter to the very rationale for
comparative studies--which, by definition, the study
cannot accept, as its myth. And, finally, acknowledging cultural uniqueness, especially that each
culture is a unique operating machine of unique
interdependent parts (that is, traits), and that
due consideration must be taken of this fact in suggesting change so that innovation will be accepted
(the theory of working in the culture), need not
imply, at the same time, that each innovation must
be reformulated in a way that it will be acceptable
to the system, and will not disrupt the system (the
theory of cultural continuity). For, what developmental innovations are accepted on these terms very
well may be accepted because they have been perverted
in a way that they will not contribute to economic
development.

By way of concrete illustration of the significance of these lines of argument, it is worth reopening for consideration the question of the
"imperialist myth" discussed earlier in this chapter
(see above section "The 'Imperialism' Myth"); specifically, in the present context, the question of

whether or not it was the imperialists <u>interfering</u>
<u>with</u> local economic action that prevented, say
Iran, from developing economically in the same
period that the West was economically developing.
To recall, it was suggested for (re-)consideration
that, contrary to the popular view, it was the negative legacy of imperialism; that is, that it was
the fact that the imperialists worked <u>with</u> the pre-
imperial social system to perpetuate certain features of the old order, that is of primary significance. To rephrase, in terms of the model interests of the present study, it might be said that
imperialism changed non-essentials and preserved
essentials as far as certain negative influences on
economic development are concerned, especially preservation of the existing political institutional
values and goals. Consequently, although many
behavioral patterns of the colonial societies changed
irrevocably, some even to approximate patterns of
those of the economically developed societies of the
West, as for example, a mobile labor force, a desire
for technology, and a money economy, yet, by only
<u>streamlining</u> the old bureaucracies, for example, so
that they became the civil service camp-followers
of the imperial powers, the imperialists in effect,
perpetuated the role of a moral-intellectual bureaucracy in the new society, and in the view of some
observers, provided this bureaucracy with a new
lease on life. Had the imperialists <u>not</u> decided
to work within the culture, especially had they
decided to introduce a rational bureaucracy in their
colonial possessions instead of "modernizing" and
hence, perpetuating the existing moral masters of
the economic order, this move would have had a radically different consequence on the present problem
of establishing a self-generating economic system in
the former colonial societies. Certainly, at least,
the ever failing policy of attempting to <u>convert</u> all
the existing bureaucracies into economic<u>ally rational</u>
bureaucracies would not be arising.

The expression "ever failing" was used in the
previous discussion because it is worth (re-)
considering that the constant reformulating of innovations which although, they are "modern," must be
made consistent with the prevailing institutional
goals, not only is not facilitating but in fact positively is <u>impeding</u> the development of the kind of
bureaucracy, for example, necessary for a self-
generating economic system. Some anthropologists
have argued that the familiar is more easily adapted

than the peripheral, and hence, in the short term, conversion is more easily accepted than is innovation; and, to recall, the story is that the economically underdeveloped societies are in a hurry to develop. But, it is worth (re-)considering that since economic development must be a long-term commitment, an entirely new pattern, and a new frame of reference, although harder to introduce, once accepted, are harder subsequently to pervert; in this instance, to serve an existing frame of reference (that is, an institutional system) which is not conducive to economic development. That clever innovator, the applied-anthropologist, who is forever called upon to find the means to get the "natives" to accept innovation, by relating the old frame of reference to the new frame of reference--in the present hypothetical case, getting the Iranians to accept a "modern" bureaucracy--may pat himself on the back, if successful. But in the long run, he may outsmart himself, because once the trait is incorporated into the old frame of reference, the subsequent problem of getting the pattern to work as an instrument of a rational economic system very well may be insurmountable. The problem, of course, is not a problem because the new pattern does not fit the culture but because it now does fit the culture only too well. In brief, working in the culture may defeat the very purpose for which presumably the anthropologist has been hired; that is, to facilitate innovation, because he is being forced by the existing institutional ground rules to have to work "within the culture," which may be the very hindrance and not the facilitator to productive innovation that he believes.

By way of introducing another consideration, it must be made clear that the previous arguments are not arguments against anthropology, or its great sophistication, as compared to the fantastic provincialism of much of Western, especially American, sociology and economics. But, nevertheless, it is a plea for the right of sociology and economics to build hypothetical models of imperatives for economic development which may be either indifferent to, or be opposed to, anthropological concerns of how unique cultural systems do and must operate. For although it is important to accept the thesis that there may be as many concrete specific paths (that is cultural patterned means) to economic development as there are unique cultures (and one thinks of the Japanese case as compared to the economically devel-

oped societies of the West here, and this supports
the cultural relativist's position), at the same
time, this does not preclude that certain fundamental goals of a society which relate to the possibility of introducing economic development may be
a matter that is indifferent to, and even obscured
by, the quest for any number of distinctive paths
to economic development. Hence, it should be legitimate to maintain, that certain institutional imperatives of Iranian society--which Iran shares
with other economically underdeveloped societies--
are incompatible with the goals of economic development, and hence that if Iran wants to develop
economically (and once again this is a matter for
the Iranians to decide), then Iran had better consider what the imperatives of an economically developed society might be--in effect, what all economically developed societies have in common irrespective of individual differences, as suggested
by the model discussions of the last chapter--
without simultaneously raising the ghost of being
accused of being a dogmatic moralist or a cultural
imperialist.68

    Part of the anthropological problem, certainly,
is that the anthropologist, as any disciplinarian,
is limited by his background and interests. To
date, the anthropologist has been little concerned
with the problem of converting certain complex
societies capable of economic development, and,
hence, is unaware of many of the institutional
problems discussed in the case study. Also, much
as the social worker, (see above, section "The
'Development is a Social Problem' Myth"), he has
conceived of his basic problem in the economically
underdeveloped societies, and, in turn, his basic
problem is conceived of by his employers in these
societies, as one of reducing tensions, and making
adjustments (patching) within the existing system
to facilitate the kinds of innovation already selected by others (presumably economists). Finally,
many anthropologists tend to see all innovation as
of equal potential importance and concern, for as
many anthropologists are fond to quote, "everyone
is an innovator." Although this approach is valuable
for certain purposes, it is worth (re-)considering
that it defeats solving the kinds of problems discussed in the present study. For example, it would
blur the attempt to differentiate qualitatively
between, say, monument building innovation and productive economic innovation. The failure of many

applied anthropologists to see these limitations on
their approach to economic development, has caused
them to be viewed as too conservative by their non-
anthropological colleagues, who are impatient to
get on with the job of planned social, including
economic change, in the face of Iranian passive resistance or perversion of potential productive economic change to serve the institutional goals
"within their culture." Discussion now turns to
this latter problem.

The "Working in the Culture" Myth (From the Stand-point of the Iranian Participant)

Iranians are committed to the myth that although
perhaps drastic changes in certain existing patterns
of daily behavior (that is, means) along "modern,"
usually Western, lines, may be necessary to achieve
economic development, economic development not
only must, but only can, come about in conformity
with the essence; that is, the fundamental goals of
Iranian society.

A typical concrete example of this myth would
be the argument that Iran is committed to economic
development but Iran never must change the essentials
of its sacred culture to do this. Consequently, if
need be, Iranians will conform their habits and traditions to the new way of life to modernize the
society, but they will never imitate blindly the
economically developed societies. Rather, they will
creatively select what is good from the developed
societies in order to initiate a distinctively
Iranian development process. Hence, forcing Iran
to choose between two development alternatives, that
of the East and that of the West, morally is wrong,
because these alternatives are but the unique solutions of two societies. Iranians must search for a
truly Iranian solution to their problems.[69]

Quite obviously, in this and similar arguments,
in spite of ample evidence to the contrary, Iranians
believe very firmly that economic development is
feasible, not only in spite of Iranian social goal
imperatives, but also only if the development process conforms to these imperatives; although they
admit to the necessity, to some extent, of accepting
certain selective changes, usually technical changes,
introduced from the economically developed societies.
Insofar as the question of economic development is
limited to discussion of the best means of introducing

certain changes vital to the initiation of a self-
generating economic system in Iran, the myth has a
germ of utility to it, for no other reason than,
as the anthropologists have demonstrated, and has
been discussed in the immediately previous section,
people live and act within the imperatives of their
own frame of references (cultural systems), and
these imperatives and Iranian sensibilities must be
understood and taken into account in any policy of
social, cultural, or economic action. But, on the
other hand, Iranians believe that because of this,
an economically underdeveloped society like Iran
is going to obtain a self-generating, rational
economic system without changing the goal imperatives that now exist in Iranian society, by giving
way only on specific selected patterns (most typically by accepting the appertenances of the economically developed society, such as modern airports).
Thus, Iranians are entitled to remain perpetually
mystified at their failure to develop economically,
as are the anthropologists or dynamic sociologists,
who respectively, are pledged to work "within the
culture" with them, helping them to adjust means
to existing goals, or alternately who are assuming
that means-innovation is going to serve as a
latent agent to lead "eventually" to goal innovation, and thus convert an existing situation of
economic non-development into a situation of economic development.[70]

CHAPTER **12** CONCLUSIONS:
UNDERDEVELOPMENT
RECONSIDERED*

RATIONALITY AND NON-RATIONALITY
IN IRANIAN ECONOMIC ACTION

The Non-Rational Characteristic
of the Iranian Social System

From the vantage point of the demands of self-
generating, developed economic system, the economy
of Iran as detailed in the case study cannot be
considered rational.** For although isolated aspects
of the Iranian economy, as for example, a modern
banking system, appear formally to resemble certain
aspects of a rational developed economy, under closer
scrutiny, in actual operation these aspects cannot
be considered economically rational. It is the central thesis of this study, as described throughout
the case study, but especially in Chapter Three,
that this primarily is due to the fact that economic
action in Iranian society a priori is subordinated
to the primacy of certain non-economic considerations, which are non-rational from the economic
standpoint, and hence, positively impede the development of rational economic action in Iranian
society. Although these non-economic considerations,
most typically, are political, the study has suggested, that, perhaps, it is better to view these
considerations as the very fundamental, transcending
assumption, values, or goals underlying each and all
of the (seven) institutions of Iranian society,
rather than as the values operative in the institutions of political authority or the economy alone.

----

* In this chapter, only the need to draw certain
  general conclusions from the discussions of the
  previous chapters remains; for obviously, specific
  conclusions have been drawn throughout the study
  from the very first chapter to, and especially,
  the last two chapters.

** For discussion of economic rationality, see
   Chapter One, and Chapter Ten, section "The Interaction of the Institutions of a Social System"
   above.

Consequently, it has been argued that any attempt to develop a rational economic system in Iran faces certain "built-in" difficulties which are fundamental to the very operating assumptions of the social system as an <u>integral</u> system. In this system, the values of a rational economic system not only are not <u>primary</u> in the values of the society, they also are <u>incompatible</u> with the fundamental goals of each and all of the institutions of this social system. It is the contention of this study, and it has been argued so in the text, that this cannot be attributed to a peculiarity of Iranian society at the present stage of its historical development. Rather, it has been suggested that the characteristic, economically non-rational, goals that have been embodied in the Iranian society of old, are now being embodied as well in so-called "modern way" of doing things. Consequently, it is worth (re-)considering that, as far as the process of economic development is considered, Iran is not necessarily a "transitional society" in the process of eliminating traditional ways of doing things in its inevitable march to modern economic rationality. And further, it is worth (re-)considering that there is no reason to assume that these fundamental values are not likely to continue to persist, and to prevent the development of a rational economic system, <u>unless</u> a choice is made by Iranians that the development of a rational economic system is more important than is the preservation of what, as far as the imperatives of a rational economic system are concerned, are the economically non-rational features of the Iranian social system.

The (Substantive) "Rationality" of the Iranian Social System

Although, as argued in the last section, the structure of the Iranian economy may be characterized as <u>non-rational</u> from the standpoint of the imparatives of a self-generating rational economic system, it might be argued, simultaneously, that the Iranian economy is rational from the standpoint of the role economics is expected to play in the existing Iranian social system as an integral system; for the operation of the economy <u>is</u> consistent with the goals and accepted operational procedures of that social system. Certainly, it is rational from the standpoint of the Iranian economic actors who, of course, make the day by day decisions <u>in</u> the system and <u>adjust</u> their economic behavior

according to the given goals and ground rules of the
economy. This is why the almost unbelievable confusion in the Iranian economy, that is so startling
to the outside observer, and which very well may be
accepted only grudgingly by the participants, still
makes "sense" to those participants. Consequently,
ironically, the introduction of a (formal-)rational
economy or a (formal-)rational system of economic
action into Iranian society in and of itself, would
be incongruous (objectively or logically), because
although "rational" in terms of the logical standards of a developed economy, it would be "non-rational"
in terms of the goals and values of Iranian society.[1]
For example, to recall a discussion of the case study,
Iranian society is resisting administrative rationalization because rationalization would destroy one of
the fundamental justifications that the political
authority has to make non-objective "moral" decisions
over the economy; for rationalization would open the
administrative flood gates to competent, technically
trained, rationally-oriented, non-morally imbued
administrators, instead of, as now, limiting the
selection primarily to often technically incompetent,
but a priori morally superior, and politically-
oriented masters of the culture. And so, the existing non-rational bureaucracy can but be the most
rational means to perpetuate the existing political
system of power and prerogatives, by insuring that
economically oriented action that might "spill over"
and encourage rational (from the economic viewpoint)
political action remains superfluous in the social
system. Viewed in this way, the Iranian social
system is fiendishly "rationally" un-rational. This
kind of instrumental rationality (alone) has been
termed substantive rationality by the sociologist
Max Weber, to distinguish it from the formal rationality discussed above, which assumes, as a goal, as
well as an instrumentality, the rational maximization
of economic efficiency and profit.*

     Hence, it is worth (re-)considering that any
attempt to introduce certain elements associated
with formal (objective) economic rationality in the
economically developed societies into the Iranian
economy, in the hopes that, by doing this, "eventually," formal rationalization of the Iranian economy

---

* For a fuller exploration of this, see Weber, M.,
  The Theory of Social and Economic Organization,
  op. cit., passim.

may be achieved, may be fruitless. For the Iranian economic (and social) goals are not similar to the economic (and social) goals of the economically developed society simply because it is argued that they are so, in that all "rational" men want (objectively) rational economic development.

It is also worth (re-)considering that, attempting to introduce formal rationality into the Iranian economy, is like trying to save a man dying of metastatized cancer by treating effects, and in one part of the body alone. For the supposed "inept confusion" of the Iranian economy is an integral part of the substantive rational ordering of a society whose goals demand commitment to doing things which are economically non-rational, not only in the economy, but also in all the institutions of the social system. The specifics of this have been discussed at length in the case study.

The Iranian Meaning of Economic Development

It is worthwhile at this point to review briefly the various interpretations of economic development in Iranian thinking, as compared to what development means, and what it does not mean, in terms of the introduction and maintenance of a rational self-generating economic system, which can be the only true measure of economic development.*

First, economic development is not, as Iranians believe, a scheme to get rich quick, and hence, (sudden) opulence is not indicative that a society is developed or developing economically. To discuss the obverse, first, it may be observed, that especially the early fruits of any economic enterprise must not be used for such as luxury consumer goods and monuments, but, rather, must be plowed back into the enterprise, if the enterprise is to establish and maintain a system of self-generation. As has been demonstrated in the case study, this principle almost is unknown in Iran,[2] and certainly, it is under negative sanction in the frantic struggle for personal and international "face." And conversely, Iranians often point to the great number of automobiles congesting the streets of Teheran

_____

* For a preliminary concrete discussion of this question, as conceptualized by the Iranians themselves, see above Chapter Three.

as a sign that Iran is developing. But these automobiles may be only the sign of someone else's economically developed society, which certain Iranians
have been able to acquire out of profits which have
not been made rationally, but, rather, have derived
from local speculation or international political
guile.

Second, economic development is not, as Iranians
believe, the proliferation of Western gadgets and
techniques haphazardly introduced into the existing
patterns of economic action. Rather, economic development depends upon a type of organization of human
beings, working with certain (formal) rational economic goals in mind, utilizing the material means
most (substantively) rational to achieve those goals.
Consequently, true economic development does not
favor the use of farm tractors, as employed in
northern Iran, where they are inefficient and only
throw more idle labor on the labor market, simply
because developed societies use such impressive
implements.[3]

Third, economic development is not synonymous
with social prestige, as Iranians believe, although
the fruits of an economically developed society
may be expended to this end. For, although the
economic ability, for example, to spend lavishly
and to protect and support the ineffectual, in at
least a minimum state of existence, simply because
those individuals are related by blood or friendship to those who have access to wealth, may enhance
prestige, this not only does not indicate that a
society is economically developed or developing,
since that ability may be based upon speculation,
but it also positively may prevent the development
of a rational, self-generating economic system, if
it reaches the point where it starves the system of
required capital in the formative stages of that
development.[4]

Fourth, economic development is not synonymous
with political prestige or power, nor is it the
means to obtain political prestige or power as
Iranians assert, although this might be a consequence of economic development. Much has been made
in the previous chapters of the premise that economic development cannot be motivated primarily by
political goals, for no other reason, than that
politics and economics each has its own set of primary rational determinants, and in a situation in

which one or the other set of determinants are in
conflict, the political will take precedence over
the economic, and the latter's rationality may suffer. The contest may be as simple as making a
choice between one kind of economic activity (arma-
ments) over another (internal communication).5 But
it also may mean, as in the case of Iran, the perpetuation of non-rationality in the economy solely
because it appears to serve only too well the political goals of prestige and power. For this is
what is at stake when Iranians build monuments
instead of an economically rational infrastructure,
in order to impress foreigners and peasants, and in
order to validate the existing power structure.6

Fifth, economic development is not, as Iranians
see it, a means to insure political control over the
population. It has been observed that some economic
development projects in underdeveloped areas seem
to have been selected over others, and set up the
way that they have, solely because they afford the
opportunity to inculcate the supposedly non-
disciplined general population (especially peasants)
with a sense of perpetual dependence upon the lar-
gesse of the political apparatus. Such projects
include those requiring large scale government organization (for example, irrigation projects),
government capital, and government technical services which can be withdrawn as a discipline meas-
ure.7 Through such projects the political order
hopes to "modernize" its political role of indis-
pensability along with the "modernization" of
the economy. Yes, the old system of political
and economic indifference to the fate of the masses,
especially the peasant, now is to be replaced with
"concern" for the masses, but such concern extends
only so far as it is accompanied by political control of the economy and of the masses. And, hence,
these primary considerations, because they are political and not economic, once again, may override
rational economic considerations at any time.

Economic development, sixth, does not mean
substituting foreign aid for the painful decision to
create a self-generating economy. A self-generating
economy connotes not only an economic system which
feeds upon itself ever increasingly to produce more
and more, but also an economic system in which the
source of the increase comes from within the system
itself. For only in a very limited sense can economic development ever be engendered from without.

Rather it must come primarily from within its own
system--its own particular enterprise system, its
own economic system, and its own social system.
In Iran this implies that a self-generating economy
will not come from advisors, but from Iranians,
that it will not come from foreign-bred enterprises,
but from Iranian trial and error, that it will not
come miraculously from imported funds, but from
capital which is derived from local productive investment.[8] In brief, a self-generating economy
will not come from what can be seduced out of others,
even if that knowledge ever will be put to use, which
is doubtful, for the simple reason that productive
economic action in Iran requires facing the fact
that the core institutional values and goals of
Iranian society must be changed by Iranians themselves before the establishment of a self-generating
economic system is feasible.

If economic development, then, is not any of
these six views, then, it is simply the acceptance
of the primacy of rational self-generating, economic
system as the economic goal (or value) of the society,
and the creation throughout the institutional structure of that society of those instrumental means
which are necessary to facilitate sufficiently (that
is, ideally, but not necessarily, to the maximum)
this goal.

The Significance of the Japanese Model For
Economic Development:
Traditionalism and Modernity

The economic development of Japan as a potential model for economically underdeveloped societies
to emulate has intrigued Iran as it has intrigued
other Asian societies. To many Iranians, Japan demonstrates that (1) other than Europeans can develop,
(2) that a society may retain its national traditions
without prostituting itself before Western glamour
in order to develop, (3) that a people can accomplish
anything by hard work, diligence, and the mobilization of native intelligence and creativity, and,
(4) that a society can succeed in developing without
having to submit to (foreign) economic domination.

Significantly, the conclusion many Iranians
draw from these implications is that through emulating Japan, the great conflict that the challenge of
development seems to present will be avoided. For,
in learning Japan's secret, Iran assuredly will not

have to change irrevocably its way of life (for the worse), but only will have to make some technological adjustments in order to develop. And thus, Iran can have the _fruit_ of development as it visualizes that fruit to be (specifically, as described in the previous section) without having to pay the price that the Westerners claim it must, to harvest that fruit. Or to state it more bluntly, Iran hopes that, by imitating the Japanese experiment, it can be considered as a developed society without having to undergo the painful process of development which it finds distasteful, yet which the Westerner claims is essential.

This study strongly agrees that the Japanese model is most significant for Iran, and that it should not be ignored, but it does not agree that it is significant in the way in which the Iranians claim it to be significant. Some of the confusion over the Japanese case surely lies in the fact that the model has been a success, and hence, has attracted all sorts of divergent admirers who have preferred to see only what they want to see in it to prove their own case. But certainly, it is worth (re-)considering that the Japanese case does not support the Iranian interpretation of the thesis that there are many ways to economic development, and that economic development need not destroy basic traditions. To wit, although many of the interpersonal relations of Japanese society are radically different from those of the economically developed societies of the West, especially the emphasis on collective rather than individual action; and although Japan has preserved its traditional culture to a great extent, certainly to a far greater degree than has the West; and although this "traditionalism" certainly has not prevented the emergence of a developed society (and some have argued that this even has _facilitated_ that development);[9] it is worth (re-)considering that all this still has not exhausted the lessons of the model. For it is worth (re-)considering, that, although Japan has preserved _its_ traditions to a great extent, this need not imply that _Iranian_ traditions can be preserved in like fashion in the process of its development. This can be said, then, not because it is assumed that traditionalism is the enemy of economic development (as Japan disproves), or that modernization is the ally of economic development (for a society can be modernized without being economically developed, provided others supply the money and technical skills

to do it, as Iran proves, but because, as suggested
in Chapter Ten, the Japanese model qualitatively
was different from Iran even in the traditional,
pre-development period.

It is worth (re-)considering, then, that the
question of "traditionalism" versus "modernism" at
best, is of secondary significance to the problem
of economic development. For traditionalism, at
best, may contain certain non-rational features
from the standpoint of maximum economic rationality;
but then, as discussed earlier, all social systems
do. But these features significantly, need not
negate the primary rationality of the economy, and
especially they need not negate those vital goals
of a society which are conducive to the development
of a rational economic system; and they do not in
the case of Japan. And, as well as argued in Chapter Ten, all this was true as much in the "traditional" period as in the "modern" period of Japan,
yet has not been, nor is now, true in the case of
Iran. Consequently, "modernization" and the introduction of a rational, self-generating economic
system meant something quite different in the
Japanese context and in the Iranian context. It
is for this reason that it was suggested for (re-)
consideration that Iran must change certain features
of its "traditional" and "modern" social order, if
it wishes to develop economically, not because these
features are "traditional" or because they are not
truly "modern," but because regardless of these considerations, they are incompatible with the imperatives of a rational economic system. And, by implication, how "traditional" or how "modern" Iranian
society and culture will be after that, as how
"traditional" or "modern" Japanese society is now,
is of no primary consequence to economic development
although it may be of possible academic and prestigeful importance. What is of primary consequence is
that in its eagerness to be considered "modern," it
has been the very superficial aspects of modernism
(or modernization) from the standpoint of a rational
economic system, that Iran has found acceptable and
has acted upon; namely, the new airport, the latest
Paris fashions, and the big cars. And so, what Iran
has not done while it has "modernized," is the measure of the failure of Iran to take seriously the
whole development model of Japan, no matter how much
it is intrigued by the prospect of being considered
like Japan, or emulating Japanese power or prestige.

THE STATE AND ECONOMIC DEVELOPMENT IN IRAN

The Existing State and Its Inadequacies

In most economically underdeveloped societies, it is assumed that the state must play the predominant, if not the exclusive role, in stimulating, planning, and executing the process of economic development. This assumption is accepted a priori by both academicians and politicians-civil servants of all political persuasion from the far left to the extreme right. To Communist partisans, on the one hand, the assumption implies that the existing state must be overthrown and replaced by a state committed to Communist development practices. And for non-Communists, on the other hand, the assumption implies that the existing state must be accepted, but the existing administrative apparatus must be reinforced and aligned with the more successful economic development program efforts of the economically developed societies; although those development efforts may or may not be intimately associated with the state in these societies.

The relationship between Communist state policy and Iranian economic development will be discussed in a later section (see below, section "The Public Sector and the Appeal of Socialism and Communism in Underdeveloped Societies, Including Iran"). This section will concentrate on consideration of the non-Communist state apparatus which exists in Iran today. The detailed description of that apparatus and its relation to economic development, has been treated in depth in the case study. Quite obviously, from the pragmatic standpoint, Iranian political authority, in its relationship to the economy, unfortunately, not only is not a facilitator, it even is a deterrent to economic development. For, most significantly, economic development, which requires economic rationality, if need be, depends on freedom from those very political considerations and political actions over the economy by which the kind of political authority that is Iranian authority, is preserved. For example, to recall an earlier discussion, while the politically generated labyrinth of confusion, division, and overlap of organizations, power and responsibility, insures against effective political opposition all the way from competing elites to underprivileged peasants, this kind of political environment is not conducive to the rational economic calculation so necessary for economic development. This is why,

although at least some Iranian politicians, do not
hate, or even are not indifferent to economic "progress," importantly, they are less than enthusiastic
about it, if and when, this means the possible end
of primacy of certain kinds of political assumptions
vis-a-vis the economy (and the society in general),
and not merely the specific political fortunes of
those temporarily in power; that is, on the occasion
when they must choose between preservation of the
primacy of certain fundamental institutional assumptions and goals of Iranian political authority (and
the social system in general) incompatible with economic development and acceptance of the goal of
economic development in the society.*

   Since in Iran today, the predominant role of
the state in and over the economy is accepted, and
it is the existing state and its role that is accepted, the question of the role of the state in
economic development (in contrast to a Communist
solution of overthrow of that state) is limited to
consideration of how to bring the existing state
apparatus more in line with economic rationality,
through reform of that state. It is possible that
reform of the existing state is attainable. But,
as suggested previously, especially in the last
chapter, in that political "reform" in Iran has
implied to date only the superficial formal changing of means, particularly the constant readjust-
ment of the unwieldy administrative apparatus, and
the replacement of particular individuals who have
fallen from grace either because they have been
judged incompetent or venal, "reform" will not lead
necessarily out of the present difficulties. For
given the persistence of the existing political
assumptions and goals in Iranian society, and the
characteristic way in which that political order
has chosen to solve its political problems, it seems
reasonable to assume that any changes contemplated
by the Iranian political apparatus now in power, or
among their alternatives, if, as seems to be the
case, they accept the same institutional political
assumptions and goals, will not provide differences
other than in faces or in superficial, formal organization. In contrast, if procedural changes are to
be other than "reform," they must include such

---

*   For further discussion of this matter, see below,
    section "The Commitment 'If' and the Commitment
    'No Matter What'."

changes as the introduction of administrative rationality, the coordination, elimination and duplication
of functions, integration of abstract planning with
the operating administration, and especially, the
training and motivation of civil-servants in elemen-
tal and advanced techniques of productive economic
action. But somehow these kinds of changes, in contrast to novel organizational flow charts, although
modest but significant, seem so very difficult for
Iranians to accomplish.[10] This appears to be true
although Iranians claim they are committed to political changes which will be productive for economic
development, and foreign advisors from all over the
world are available in (embarrassing) quantity to
advise in each and every technical step of any political, social, or economic reform program. And so,
can one say other than that it is no "accident" that,
although political interests and political institutions are the most elaborated of social institutions
in such underdeveloped societies as Iran, and politics is the favorite professional and recreational
pastime of youth, yet economics and the economy
somehow always are un(der)developed, this, in spite
of the constant lip-service to the desire to "catch
up" economically with the so-called advanced societies.

          Consequently, it is worth (re-)considering
that, if the state is assumed to have the vital
role in stimulating economic development, then
quite obviously, that state must have a radically
different relationship to the society in general,
and the economy in particular, than has the presently constituted one. For the Iranian state as
it is constituted today not only is not conducive
to the achievement of economic development, it is,
in fact, a primary obstacle to it. And the constant
administrative "reform" or the constant kicking out
of rascals from the sacred political temple, has not,
and to conjecture will not, solve the basic problems.
In fact, this kind of activity even is a deterrent
in itself to economic development, because it wastes
time and effort on fruitless busy-work, and offers
sterile hope to those who are reluctant to face the
painful necessity of having to change the fundamental institutional assumptions of Iranian society
(that were detailed in Chapter Ten).[11]

The State and the Private Sector:
The Vicious Circle

It is apparent to most observers that the private sector of the Iranian economy is as ill-suited to encouraging and sustaining economic development as is the public, or state, sector, as described in the previous section. And this is so, in spite of the fact that the private sector receives many special privileges, such as easy loans and export-import subsidies from the state in order to enhance its profits. For to recall the details of the case study, economic actors in the private sector are more apt to be speculators and to be investors in land, than they are apt to be entrepreneurs, especially industrial entrepreneurs.

There are two explanations for this, which, ironically, appear to be diametrically opposed to each other. One, the so-called private sector or "capitalist" interpretation, postulates that the private sector of the Iranian economy is weak because of state (that is, public sector) policy toward the private sector. For the political order, regardless of what it claims it is doing and why it is doing so, by its harassment tactics or omissions, (as detailed in the case study) is creating such basic insecurity for individual economic actors in the private sector, that they can only respond accordingly in order to make out, and even survive, economically. Consequently, when economic actors engage in those kinds of devious economic activities that insure economic success in such an economic milieu, but which are not conducive to developing a rational economic system, those actors are responding "rationally," but only substantively rationally, to the existing non-rational ground rules and goals established for the operation of the Iranian market (see above, section "The (Substantive) "Rationality" of the Iranian Social System"). And as long as the government threatens intervention into, and refuses to regularize its fiscal and legal relationship with, the private sector of the economy, this can be expected of that kind of private sector; for no one seriously can expect the members of the private sector deliberately to carry out economic actions which are to its economic disadvantage. Consequently, it is (substantively) rational to expect the members of the private sector rather to use the easy loan policy of the state to strive for a quick profit in luxury goods which can be hidden in the cellars of the bazaar, and to invest that profit immediately in land, which can be ravaged and taxed, but not destroyed. And it would be (substantively) non-rational to expect the members of the private sector to establish productive, especially industrial, enterprises which cannot be hidden or protected from political extortion, or from such non-rational harassments of the political authority as the constant pressure to increase personnel rosters, not out of any truly (formal) rational economic need, but solely to satisfy the purely political fears of the political authority of the restless unemployed. In sum, if the state is as interested in mobilizing the economy for economic development as it claims to be, it is surprisingly intent upon alienating productive activity in the private sector by its policies, yet it is so surprised when the private sector is not a productive element of the economy.[12]

The public sector partisans, which may include Marxists from right-wing Fabian Socialists to sectarian Communists, but which primarily consists of non-Marxists in economically underdeveloped societies, on the other hand, postulate that the initial discussion point must be realistic acceptance both of the existing unpromising situation in the private sector, and of the assumption that that sector is incapable of initiating, and to some, also of maintaining, economic development in the underdeveloped societies of today. For economic actors in the private sector, regardless of the reasons for their problems (some argue pragmatically, other attribute the situation to intrinsic capitalist incompetence), even when given the opportunity, have not carried out the kinds of economic activity conducive to the development of a rational, self-generating economic system, especially and particularly in the industrial sphere. Consequently, the state, at the minimum, must take the lead in the economy to plan, allocate, and use capital in such ways as to insure that the kind of economic activities that are essential to economic development will be accomplished. Especially is this true for the kinds of activities that the private sector is loath to accomplish everywhere, such as the development of infrastructure. But this is true also for any of the other essential activities that require long-term, low-profit investment, which can not attract the attention of the high-profit minded, private sector speculators. Beyond this point some controversy exists as to the exact role of the state in

the economy. The "right wing" argues that once the
impetus to economic development is established by
state policy and action, the existing enterprise
may be returned to private hands. Others, the
"centrists" argue, on pragmatic grounds that this
policy will fail because of the inherent incapacity
of the private sector which would have developed
the economy in the first instance, had it been able
to do so. Still others, the "radicals," on ideological grounds, suggest that the state has no
obligation to return the profit of any public property to a group of obvious failures, or more extremely, to a group which arbitrarily is inferior
a priori on moral grounds to those in the public
sector.13

      Although logically, at first blush, the public
sector and the private sector arguments appear obviously to be contradictory to each other, some
partisans have considered that it is possible to
argue that what both sectors claim has truth, and
that pragmatically this is the most useful way to
approach the problem of economic development. This
is the doctrine of the mixed economy, which accepts
pragmatically whatever theory and practice is considered desirable in either the public or private
sectors, and rejects whatever is considered detrimental, supposedly solely on the basis of rational
utility to economic development. But significantly,
the "mixed economy" approach has not been successful
in economically underdeveloped societies, especially
in Iran. It is worth (re-)considering that the
reason for that failure lies in the hypothesis that,
although, perhaps both of the claims of the public
and private sector partisans against each other may
be true, simultaneously, both claims may be false.
Both sides either are not aware of, or choose to
ignore, the fact that what each accuses the other
of in substance, if not in form, is true of themselves as well. Hence, as suggested in the discussions of the last chapter (see above, Chapter Eleven,
sections "The 'Public Sector versus the Private
Sector' Myth" and "The 'Ugly Foreigner' Myth"),
the problems in the two economic sectors are only
two different manifestations of the same underlying
problems, and of the imperatives of the institutional
structure of Iranian society in general. Hence, it
is not strange that both sectors should have the same
order of difficulty in developing the economy. Consequently, logically, and practically, a vicious

circle exists. Starting arbitrarily at any point,
it can be said, first, that the private sector is
ineffective as far as economic development is concerned, and this justifies public sector action.
But the public sector is not effective because it
is indifferent or incapable of establishing the
kind of system that would make its efforts effective. At the same time, it is not willing or
able to create the conditions which would enable
the private sector to be effective. Hence, the
private sector is ineffective. And so the vicious
circle goes on and on.

It is worth stating, however, that almost all
observers who agree with this view of the relationship between the state and the private sector suggest breaking that circle only through "reform" in
the public sector, not through "reform" in the private sector. For, in assuming that the state has
some role to play in economic development, somehow
it is also assumed that the state has the decisive
role to play; consequently, it is only the state
which can bring order to the private sector by
state intervention of some sort. Whether that
intervention is regulation or stimulation, depends
on whether one's political views are "left" or
"right." And so, even when it is grasped that
both sectors are suffering the same difficulties
simultaneously, it is worth (re-)considering that,
it is not grasped, at the same time, that both
sectors as well, are suffering from the same source
of difficulty; namely, the fundamental institutional
values of Iranian society in general.

The True Relationship of a Public Sector (State) and Private Sector in an Underdeveloped Economy

If a vicious circle of economic non-development
exists between the public sector in such an economically underdeveloped society as Iran, is the situation inevitable, and if not, what is to be done?

In the previous section it was suggested for
(re-)consideration that an economically productive
resolution of the problem of the relationship between the two sectors, as far as economically underdeveloped Iran is concerned, in any case, cannot be
made on the basis of arbitrarily selecting either
public or private sector to "reform" or on the
basis of the invention of some special hybrid combination of both sectors. It was also suggested for

(re-)consideration that perhaps one of the causes
of the problem of finding a satisfactory solution
has been that the wrong question has been asked.
It is worth (re-)considering that the right question to ask, is not how much public sector or how
much private sector exists or should exist in the
society, but rather what quality of (public sector
or state) exists and what kind of private sector
exists, and if the economy is to be mixed, what
quality of relationship between the two sectors
exists? As in the case of many of the other
problems of economic development previously discussed in this study, the problem of economic sectors, then, is a qualitative problem and not a
quantitative one.14 To rephrase, the question to
ask is what kind of political (state or public)
contributions can be made to the society (including
the economy) to help initiate and to sustain economic development, and what kind of individual contribution (in the private sector) can be made to the
same process? AND THE ALTERNATIVE MODEL OF THE
DEVELOPED SOCIETY IN CHAPTER TEN HAS BEEN DEVISED
WITH THIS CONSIDERATION IN MIND. Hence, although
the model has been devised out of the experience of
societies which have not had a very close association
of a political order with the economy, since it is
the qualitative relationship between state and economy that is important, the same quality of relationship between political authority and economy logically can be (and, in effect, must be) applied in
a society in which a close, even an interlocking
relationship between state and economy is assumed.

By way of illustration of the contrast between
the usual quantitative and the suggested qualitative
approach to the sector problem of economic development, one of the matters raised in the case study
now is briefly reviewed. All observers agree that,
in Iran, state fiscal policy toward the private
sector is not conducive to that sector developing a
self-generating rational economic system, for no
other reason than that it is impossible to calculate
with any degree of reasonable certainty from one
period to the next what tax policy, if any, will be
enforced. The quantitative presence or absence of
the state in this instance, is, at the most, peripheral to the problem, for less government, certainly,
would not remove the uncertainty of taxation. This
is because taxes, at least in theory, are as inevitable as death in all known societies, and, hence,
the possibility of collection always exists in any

society, even one with a weak state. At best,
diminishing the extent of the state might only diminish the ability of the state to collect the taxes
(which, in fact, already may be slight), but would
not diminish, one iota, the non-rationality of the
tax structure, or the ability of the private sector
to escape that non-rationality. And by like token,
increasing, quantitatively, the power of the state,
the Iranian (Asian) solution to all social problems,
would imply only increasing quantitatively the existing vacillating, politically determined pressures
on the economy, without in any way increasing the
calculability of the tax system.[15] This situation
may be contrasted with, say, the situation in the
United States, Sweden, or England, in which although
taxes are high, and collected, they are reasonably
calculable; and, hence, rational economic planning
in either the public or private sector is feasible.
Consequently, the quantitative presence or absence
of the Iranian state is indifferent to the qualitative problem of defining a fiscal program with
certainty in a way that the economic forces of the
society, regardless of sector, will be able to
calculate with reasonable assurance that what is
calculated will come to pass, not once by speculative luck, but over and over again. For only in
this way is a long-range, self-generating economic
system feasible in either sector.

The significance of a qualitative interpretation of the relationship between a public sector
and a private sector of an economy also can be
illustrated in the deliberate attempt to combine
both sectors in the "mixed economy" of the Public
Corporation. The Public Corporation is a device in
economically underdeveloped societies to combine
the rational-economic advantages of both public and
private sectors; specifically, the multiple-
initiative opportunities of an autonomous private
sector and the financial and political resources of
the public sector. Simultaneously, the Public
Corporation attempts to avoid the pitfalls of both
sectors, specifically the speculative interests,
weakness of talent, and the dearth of suitable
financial resources in the private sector, and petty
bureaucratic rigidity and over-regulation in the
public sector. Consequently, any Public Corporation
is set up under public regulation to do a specific
economic task (the state role) but is free to carry
out its own economic problems as it sees fit, provided the contribution is satisfactory, (presumably

to be judged on rational economic grounds; the private sector role).

Yet, significantly, the problems faced by the Public Corporation, in spite of the best of intentions, have proved to be of the same order as those found in the public and private sectors of the underdeveloped economies, as noted above; that is, in the economy in general, regardless of sector consideration. First, the special laws establishing the Public Corporations, as most laws in economically underdeveloped societies, are not apt to be enforced and to be countermanded by other laws. And, as suggested earlier, laws that may not be enforced, but remain on the books as potentially enforceable, generate confusion and uncertainty, which are the natural enemies of rational economic calculation. Second, political considerations of an order not conducive to rational economic calculation, which are supposed to be kept out of economic policies in the Corporation, soon creep in. Pressures are put on the Corporation to expand its labor force, required or not. The heads of the Corporation are forced into a back-biting competition with jealous old-line agencies who do not want their economic benefices reduced, or the economic order removed from their assumed so necessary, but incompetent and inconclusive, intervening hands, at the wrong place, and at the wrong time. Unfounded accusations and harassing "moral" bureaucratic investigations of Corporation policy lower morale and create the usual economic confusion and indecision, so characteristic of economically underdeveloped societies.17

Significantly, the usual reason offered to explain and help solve these problems is that a quantitative imbalance exists between the public sector and the private sector aspects of the Corporation's activities. This may very well be true. But it is worth (re-)considering that the problem also may be due to the incoherence, indecision, and confusion in the relationship between the public and private sector aspects of those activities, regardless of the question of balance. Consequently, once again, it is worth (re-)considering that it is the kind, or quality, of the relationship that exists between public sector and private sector in all economically underdeveloped societies, that, in part, is at the heart of certain problems between the public and private sectors of these economies.

The Public Sector and the Appeal of Socialism and Communism in Underdeveloped Societies, Including Iran

The discussion thus far has been approached from the vantage point that the economy might be either private, or mixed public and private. There remains the possibility, of course, that the economy might be solely public.

Iran has not chosen the public approach to economic development; hence, any conclusions concerning how a public economy would make out in Iran are pure conjecture. Although, admittedly, it is not logical to argue on this question, since total public control of the economy conceivably might be of a different qualitative order than is the present relationship between state and economy, at the same time, it is legitimate and worthwhile to point out once again, that the public sector of the economy that now exists in Iran is not any more successful than is the private sector in encouraging the development of a self-generating economic system. For those in charge of making economic decisions in public enterprises have the same ground rules to contend with as those making decisions in the private sector; and, hence, respond in the same substantively rational way in their economic actions as do their counterparts in the private sector—that is, "get what you are able, while you are able, in any way that you are able, for who knows what opportunities tomorrow will bring." Consequently, at the least, it is worth suggesting for (re-) consideration that it does not follow that the existence of total state control of the economy in Iran, as such, necessarily will make any appreciable difference on the nature of the economy.

With this as background, discussion now turns to the conjecture of what order a "socialist" state would be, if it came to Iran. Certainly, "socialism" is not an unusual doctrine in this part of the world. Certain states, such as Egypt and Iraq (as this is written), claim to be socialist societies in which the public sector is the overwhelming and even the exclusive economic force. However, this order of socialism is a far cry from the order of socialism which was nurtured in the economically developed societies of the West. For Asian socialism did not, as did Western socialism, grow out of the attempt to right the economic and social wrongs of the industrial

revolution which threatened to treat individuals as
chattel, and hence, stressed the social and economic
equalitarian problems of individuals within their
respective societies. Rather, Asian socialism has
been concerned with the political, social, and
economic inadequacies of Asian society which it is
believed are preventing Asian society from being
considered as the political equal of the developed
societies (of the West). Since economic development
has been judged to be the key to that equality,
Asian socialism has stressed economic development.
But since, it is _political_ equality of the society
that is sought, the specifics of economic development action have been inspired by whatever enhances
the prestige of the political apparatus in the eyes
of the people, and in the eyes of the people of
the economically developed societies. Consequently,
Asian socialism, save perhaps for those few influenced by the Fabian tradition, as is the case of
much of socialism in India, because of its concern
with political strength, although it talks in terms
of "economic development," tends to reject, as
inconsequential, the tenets of Western liberal and
pragmatic socialism, and to stress, rather, authoritarian _political_ doctrines and those economic development activities which aim to enhance the prestige
of the state.[18]   Therefore, and this must be only
(calculated) guessing, of course, nothing exists in
the value systems or goals of Iranian society to
reject Asian socialism, except possibly the fear of
losing Western, especially American aid; which, of
course, is only a passing consideration.[19]

     The key both to the acceptability and nature
of Asian socialism in Iran, and in other such economically underdeveloped societies which have not made
a similar decision, then, lies in the question of
how powerful political authority believes it must
become in relation to the economy, whenever it is
ready to consider seriously the possibility of introducing true economic development in the society.
Under such circumstances, a doctrine of Asian socialism cannot but be attractive to the kind of society,
as is Iranian society, which seeks to justify methods
which further enhance the prestige of the state,
without diminishing the goal of political control in
any way. For when Iranian political authority reluctantly comes to the conclusion that it must allow
some degree of rationality to enter the economy in
order to at least claim it is, in truth, achieving
some degree of economic development, it will have to

decide how much direct control of that economy is necessary to insure that that economic rationalization will not destroy more vital political prerogatives.

At present political authority can afford to play at economic development. Hence, it can afford to accept the lack of rationality and the ineptness of its political apparatus which successfully create sufficient confusion in the economy to achieve its political and economic objectives in the society. But this situation may not last. Suggested many times for (re-)consideration has been the hypothesis that at least a certain minimal degree of economic rationality is essential to achieving economic development and that the present political confusion and ineptitude is inimical to that development. And hence, if the course of events in Iranian society, for any number of reasons, finally will force the existing political authority, or any of its present serious alternatives, which is all one has to go on, to tighten up the rationality of the economy to insure some measure of success in the process of development, the Iranian polity simultaneously will be faced with the problem of insuring, by political control, that the consequent rationality will be prevented from "breaking through" to destroy the basic assumptions and goals of the other institutions of the society, as well as of the institution of political authority.

It is worth considering that Asian socialism, as such, will not necessarily bring full rationality, for conceivably the polity may "tolerate" only as much rationality as it believes it has to, in order to keep the economic systems moving and possibly preserve itself against open rebellion; and this is the case in most Asian socialist societies. If this policy fortuitously aids economic development; that is, if economic development and this kind of political maximization fortuitously go in the same direction, well and good,--but if they do not, it is economic development and not the "socialist" state that will suffer.

In turning now to the matter of the appeal of "extreme socialism" or Communism in Iran, it must be stated immediately that a disinterested observer is not in a position to provide a direct answer, since this never is public information in a society as nervous of its northern neighbor's traditional

imperialist designs on its country, as is Iran.
However, based upon implication alone, it is conceivable that it very well is attractive in some
quarters--distaste for anything Russian inspired
or associated nowtithstanding. For, it appears to
offer a solution to the problem of economic development that provides both the pleasure of eating
one's cake and having it too; that is, a chance to
develop economically not only by not diminishing
the role of the political apparatus over the economy
(and the society), but, in fact, by enhancing that
role. For, on the one hand, Communism sanctions,
simultaneously, an increase in the size and in the
power and prerogatives of the bureaucracy while
sanctioning a holy war against the traditional
rivals of the bureaucracy: the private sector of
the economy, and the non-bureaucratic classes. And
the political authority empirically and morally,
truly will be both essential and superior to other
elements of the society, instead of only claiming
to be so, as now, (by virtue of the doctrine of de-
facto Imamate delegation; see above, Chapter Seven).
And, on the other hand, in that no economic competitor to the state is envisioned, because the state
assumes monopolistic direction of the social actions
of the entire society, including the process of
economic development, the state fears no political
competitor. Hence, economic rationality theoretically need not suffer one iota, and thus maximum
development conceivably could take place.[20] For
more control means less political fear, means more
economic rationality, means more economic development, means more (to) control, and so on through the
argument in a perpetual circle.

But will Asian Communism lead to economic development in Iran? Again, one can only guess. But
it can be pointed out, that the principal Asian
society which has attempted a Communist solution to
economic development, the People's Republic of China,
is having excruciatingly painful economic difficulties. Although an impressive amount of economic
change for the better has been accomplished, its
efforts at this point have not created the foundations of a self-generating economic system, which is
the only true measure of economic development. And,
significantly, its economic development efforts do
not significantly compare more favorably with that
of India's "mixed economy," and certainly not with
certain other non-Communist Asian societies, such
as economically developed Japan, or even its erstwhile foe, developing Taiwan.

But beyond this cold war game of progress comparison between Communist and non-Communist societies, still another question is worth considering; namely, it is the strong state which is the byword of Communism, or is the commitment to development that eventually may result in the economic development of China; and can a distinction be made between these two ideas? This question, of course, only is the perennial question, once again, in a different form; to wit, is it the state, or is it the fundamental institutional assumptions of the society, including the state, (or political authority) that determines economic development? In attempting to answer the question, it is most interesting to point out that, in the People's Republic of China, after general peace and security were re-established in 1950-51, after over a decade of war and chaos, even under this, a Communist regime, much to the surprise and embarrassment of the polity, a spurt did occur, in productive economic activity in the private sector. And this effort continued until it was surpressed, quite frankly, for political reasons. This was so significantly, because the state provided general security for rational economic action in the economy proper, regardless of sector preference, and regardless of ideological commitment. But when the state insisted on enforcing a particular kind of ideology which espoused the primacy of politics over economics, as it desired, by destroying the private sector of the economy, at least this productive economic action suffered. Certainly, in this instance, it was a priori acceptance of a political assumption, of control of the economy by the state, without any accompanying commitment to formal economic rationality, that engendered political decisions not conducive to economic development. And, perhaps, it is this continuing order of decision-making that helps to explain, to some extent, why, in spite of total state control of the economy, China continues to be plagued by certain qualitative problems of economic development, in spite of often, but not always, impressive quantitative growth rates in the economy.

Consequently, the key question of state and economy, in a Communist society, is whether or not the imperative values of the society are such that in certain "showdown" situations, strategic to both the polity and economy, the state will, for whatever reason, adjust to the demands of economic development, or whether the reverse will be true. This

question must be posed not only in connection with
what has been, or is being accomplished, but also
in connection with what more could have been or
could be, accomplished if rational economic considerations (had) had primacy over political considerations, and not vice versa. This is especially true
in Communist societies, but it is not an issue
exclusive to those societies (as Communists like
to point out, but only in non-Communist societies).

In conclusion, then, it is worth (re-)consider-
ing that, given the long-standing rationale of political authority in Asia, regardless of specific
political ideological suasion (that is, regardless
of whether that rationale is Communist or non-
Communist), insofar as existing political values
and goals are allowed to continue to take primacy
over what should be rational economic goals and
economic decisions, the development of the economy,
will suffer accordingly. Insofar as purely economic
goals and hence, economic rationality are allowed
to predominate (not necessarily "be exclusive")
in economic decisions, the economy will profit and
will develop. And the question of whether only
Communism can achieve this goal, or whether Communism
is best able to achieve this goal by virtue of its
ability to provide the means to insure maximum security for the political apparatus (that is, the strong
state) so that it is unafraid of the effects of an
autonomous economy, especially a rational autonomous
economy, upon the society, is, of course, to pose
the question in Asian terms. For it assumes that
the Asian relationship between political goals and
economic goals is inevitable. As to whether or not,
beyond theoretical, ideological considerations, this
kind of relationship is inevitable, we do have empirical evidence upon which to base a decision; and to
this, we now turn.

The Japanese Model for Economic Development: The Strong State[21]

What does the Japanese development model imply
for the process of economic development in contemporary, underdeveloped Asian society? Is it an
example of a strong state which forced through economic development in the only way feasible for a
nineteenth century late-comer society; that is, for
a society which developed after the Western European
process, yet before the advent of Communism? And
hence, is it not the first example of a new kind of

state-propelled development which is mandatory for contemporary Asia, rather than an example of Western liberal, private-sector development? Many observers have argued so,[22] but this study dissents.

Once again, this study does not dissent on the question of the potentially useful role of state intervention into the economic development process. For, in fact, to clear the argument immediately of non-essential issues, it would be worthwhile for many Western theorists to acknowledge the role of the state throughout the economic development process in the West from the period of commercial mercantilism to the modern, pragmatic intervention of the welfare-state in the Twentieth Century.[23] Unfortunately, these theorists, by stressing the alleged absence of the state in Western economic development, in contrast to the presence of the state in non-Western economic activities, have confused what the study can only suggest, once again, for (re-)consideration is the real issue of state and the economy; namely, the qualitative nature of the role of the state in the economy, regardless of its quantitative presence or absence in that economy. And, as discussed in Chapter Ten, the Western and Japanese state was not, and is not now, qualitatively the Asian state. Significantly, to recall these discussions, the Western-Japanese state came and comes to the economy, not as the a priori ethical watchkeeper over the moral evil of the society as did and does the Asian state, but as one of a number of cooperative forces associating itself with the economic forces of that society.

Hence, in the West and in Japan, the political apparatus of the strong, centralized state accompanied the development of modern economic power, in a way that neither state nor economy was in a position a priori to dominate the other, but only to cooperate to mutual advantage. But in continental Asia, in contrast, the concept and reality of the strong state antedated the possible growth of a modern economy. Consequently, in Asia, the economy has had to accommodate itself to political authority, thus assuring primacy of political considerations in economic action. And, so political considerations which too often (though not always) were the antipathy of true economic development, came to impede the development process. But in contrast, although the Western state was no less involved in the economic development process, and economic development

did serve the interests of the centralized state as
in the East, yet the political apparatus in the West
was not in a position, if it ever was inclined, to
subordinate economics to politics in the strategic
"take-off" stages of economic development. And so,
when the state intervened into the economy, it
intervened as the friend of the economic court, in
a rational calculable way. Most significantly, it
accepted the primacy of rational economic values in
the economy as the intervening goal, although certainly, the specific motives for state intervention
varied with the specific political authority involved.

     The fact that Japan, in the initial period of
its modern, economic development (that is, 1868-
1900) looked upon the role of that development much
as does the economically underdeveloped world to
today, that is, as a weapon to fight for national
equality, indeed is interesting. But it is worth
(re-)considering that this fact does not imply
what the public sector partisans claim it implies.
For the Japanese polity did not assume that control of the economy was both necessary and sufficient for development, and hence, did not assume
that the perpetuation of state control over the
budding industrial expansion of that time was inevitable. And this was so because its economic goals
were rational, expedient goals--in effect, economic
development goals--and not the moral goals of continental Asian political authority, which assumes
that the private economic order is evil if the political order does not control or supervise it. Consequently, state control of that part of the economy
which did exist, primarily in the industrial sector,
lasted only from origin date (1868) until such time
as it no longer was considered rationally expedient
to continue that policy (usually given as 1880) althou
certainly the state continued to play an important
role in the development of the economy right down to
and including the present.

     It is not to be assumed that the study wishes
to minimize importance of this period of primarily
state control over the (industrial) economy, even
though little was accomplished materially as far as
economic growth was concerned. This may sound like
an argument contradicting itself. It only is, once
again, if one insists on stressing as significant
how little materially (that is, quantitatively) was
accomplished in this period, while ignoring what was

accomplished qualitatively in terms of the goals of economic development. For in this period, the polity helped to establish the vital structure and pattern of rationality in the economy, especially to help train the Japanese people, not only in the technical means to achieve development goals, but more significantly, in acceptance of rational development goals as their own personal goals. Consequently, and it cannot be overestimated, overemphasized, or repeated too often, the close association of the Japanese state with the prime centers of the incipient development process during this period in no way implied that political goals were to take primacy over rational economic goals. For it was the very determination of the polity to establish acceptance of the primacy of rational economic goals throughout the society that prompted the polity to establish its direct relationship with (at least) the (industrial section of the) economy in the first instance. And, consequently, once these goals had been achieved, and a situation arose in which it was no longer considered economically expedient to control exclusively the means of industrial production (in 1880), there was no "moral" obstacle to turning over voluntarily to private hands most of these public industrial enterprises that were publicly constructed and owned, if this seemed to be expedient from the standpoint of economic rationality. For significantly, the polity knew that these enterprises would be (re-) turned to a private economic sector in the kind of society in which rational economic goals were accepted as primary, as readily as they had been nurtured in the public sector, because the whole economy-- the whole society--accepted these fundamental institutional assumptions and goals; and hence, these enterprises were delivered over to an environment in which the process of economic development could not but succeed.

Consequently, it is worth (re-)considering that it was basic institutional values and goals characteristic of Japanese society (and here society includes the state and the economy, as usual) and not the strength of the state which determined the success of economic enterprises in Japan. For, significantly, these enterprises did not collapse or suffer retardation in development with the removal of the control of the "strong" state. And so, to rephrase the hypothesis: it was the kind of state and kind of association between the state and the economy in both the strong (1868-80) and weak (1880 on) private

sector phases of economic development, that determined the success of Japan's economic development
process. Certainly the result is indisputable;
Japan alone of Asian societies has developed a self-
generating economic system.

The question, then, is if Japan has been able
to do it, why hasn't continental Asia been able to
establish a self-generating economic system? To
recall an earlier discussion, the usual scapegoat
of imperialism is dubious because, for example,
Thailand has not economically developed. Certainly,
contrary to the prevailing Iranian myths, Iran has
been free enough from foreign domination to do what
Japan did, and certainly no such excuse for foreign
intervention holds for the past decade. It is worth
(re-)considering, then, that the answer lies, rather,
in the ultimate goals or values of the society, which
Japan shares with the West, but does not share with
continental Asian societies, in spite of many obvious
similarities in cultural and behavioral (interactional) patterns which Japan does share with continental Asia.*

---

* Regretfully this point cannot be developed fully
here. It can only be stated that Japan, although
an integral part of Asia culturally, not now, nor
at any time in its history, ever approximated the
social system of Asia. Rather, certain key aspects of its social system always have been start-
lingly similar to that of Western European society. And it is this characteristic difference
between Japan and continental Asia that may explain "why" Japan economically is developed, and
"why" its path to that development has been radically different from the proposals for economic
development in continental Asia, either in its
non-Communist form, as in Iran, or in its present
Communist form, as exemplified by development
efforts of the Peoples Republic of China, Democratic Republic of Vietnam (that is, North Vietnam)
and the People's Republic of Korea (that is, North
Korea). Reference is made to the author's
Origin of Modern Capitalism and Eastern Asia for
a full treatment of this thesis.

The real significance of the Japanese model, then, is that it can offer a successful path to economic development which is not incompatible culturally, or socially on the interpersonal, social behavioral level, with the Asian "way." And hence, the Japanese development effort is not a "Western process," incompatible with the Asian heritage. But at the same time, it does demonstrate that certain prime Asian values that are held with great tenacity, as revealed in the case study, most notably the primacy of "moral" political (that is, state) values over economic values, can be incompatible with economic development.24

SOME FURTHER OBSERVATIONS ON THE NATURE OF ECONOMIC DEVELOPMENT

The Commitment "If" and the Commitment "No Matter What"

By a commitment "if" is meant that, although economic development may be considered desirable, and, by and large, this undeniably is true of the economically underdeveloped societies of Asia, including Iranian society, economic development is desirable only if it does not challenge the primacy of certain basic social values in those societies. These values are the series of fundamental institutional preferences explored in detail throughout this study and presented systematically in Chapter Ten. In contrast, a commitment "no matter what" implies a qualitative change in these values, so that the economically underdeveloped societies are committed to the establishment and maintenance of rational, self-generating economic systems regardless of the consequences on the societies. Although a few, isolated individuals clearly see that if Iran ever is to develop a self-generating rational economic system, such a commitment is inevitable, or, perhaps, because they do, no commitment to economic development "no matter what" exists in Iranian society.

Specifically, in contrast to the commitment "if" the commitment "no matter what" implies, first, and foremost, that Iranians must want not at best a technological-gadget revolution in their society, but a scientific revolution as well. That is, they cannot want only the material technological products if and only if, the acquisition of these products do not destroy those few, but strategic institutional values discussed in the present study. They cannot reject the world of thought which forced man to face the unknown by observation, experimentation, questioning, and logic, and to employ that method to the social, especially economic order as well as in the laboratory, either as extraneous, or, more typically, as incompatible with the "Iranian way of life."[25] For, as any number of scientists have demonstrated, it was scientific changes and not merely the changes in technology that made the difference in the successful development of a rational, self-generating economic system in the economically developed societies.[26] They cannot rely alone on the technological know-how to put dams and airports on the ground, rejecting even the technological know-how to build them, if the foreigner is that eager to do the work. They cannot continue to claim that economic development is difficult in Iran because the technological innovations connected with economic development, occurred in the West only very recently, and that they will learn these techniques "in time"; and hence, that there is no cause to be impatient over Iran's lack of "progress." For if Iranians continue to do or claim all this, it is worth (re-)considering that Iranians do not understand one of the prerequisites of true economic development.[27]

Second, the commitment "no matter what" implies that Iranians cannot reserve the right to select the kind of development projects they consider "good," and to reject the kind of projects which they consider "bad," as if the process of economic development was a shopping tour in which individuals can reject consciously what they consider detrimental to the well being of the existing (institutional) value system. It especially implies, on the basis of the previous discussion, that Iranians do not have the privilege of rejecting the rational scientific method in formulating economic developmental goals and procedures; as for example, not rationalizing education or bureaucratic job specifications, solely because this runs counter to certain institutional goals.

Third, the commitment "no matter what" implies that Iranian society cannot continue to be unrealistic about the process of economic development; that is, to balk and malinger at painful decisions such as providing calculable security for economic action, while at the same time it yearns in fantasy for the material fruits of development. For this only postpones that day of reckoning when Iranians, all Iranians, must face up to their responsibilities to make those so necessary, painful decisions associated with the early stages of economic development. And certainly, the commitment "no matter what" implies further, that Iranians must not hope that foreign advisors will make those painful decisions, the scientifically painful ones especially, for Iranians, while, as suggested in the first discussion, Iranians only learn from them such technological gimmicks as are necessary to gain the fruits of development.

Fourth, the commitment "no matter what" implies that such notions as, that Iran must be true to its own goals and develop its spiritual side, that Iranian culture has provided leadership in the past so why should it not do so again, and that the Western concept of the "scientific man" is too materialistic and crude for Iranians to accept, must be discarded, once and for all, as substitutes for those necessary rational goals and procedures which alone provide realistic guides for solving current-day problems, especially the problem of economic development. It may be true that Iranian aesthetic culture was instrumental in Iran's ability to survive as a national identity before the repeated invasions of physical superiors, and it may have provided the Iranian contribution to the mainstream of world civilization, as claimed. But that cannot justify the comforting notion that Iran can gain the benefits of economic development without competing with the developed societies on their own "material" (i.e., economically rational) terms. The commitment "no matter what," as discussed earlier, does not imply that Iran has to adopt the specific behavioral patterns of the economically developed societies, even those of Japan, nor even that Iran has to accept economic development if it means "surrendering her sacred culture." But it does mean that when those certain features of that "sacred culture" which are incompatible with the prerequisites of an economically developed society arise, regardless of what Iranians would like to believe, a choice between the two sets of goals cannot be avoided; and, hence, Iranians must make a decision one way or the other, to preserve or not preserve those features of their sacred culture, and pay the price accordingly--economic non-development or economic development, respectively.

Fifth, and finally, even on the technological level itself, which is the most "neutral" facet of economic development, a commitment "no matter what" does not allow technology to be subordinated and perverted to considerations which are non-rational from the economic standpoint. This has been amply documented in the case study, especially in Chapter Three, and need not be repeated here.

To sum, the commitment "no matter what," in brief, implies rejection of the notion that Iran can develop a self-generating economic <u>system</u> by stumbling along with the institutional goals of the present social system. The choice, of course, is Iran's. No outsider can presume to make that choice. But it is worth (re-)considering that an observer does have a right to point out the implications of the choices, and why what is happening in the Iranian economy is happening; namely, the absence of true economic development in spite of great economic activity and even, at time, impressive growth rates.

Economic Development as an Institutional Sociological Question

A basic premise of the present study, often stated, is that the primary questions of economic development in an economically underdeveloped society must be social questions. This premise does not imply that the technical aspects of economic development should be down-graded, and, certainly the study has never implied that the political aspects of economic development should be slighted. But the premise does suggest that it is worth (re-)considering that, because it is a social milieu, for better or worse, that is intricately intertwined with <u>all</u> aspects of the economic development process, this milieu not only determines the peculiar way in which the process of economic development takes place, but also determines whether that development is <u>feasible</u> in the first instance. In the present study this social milieu has been portrayed as the underlying assumptions (values or goals) of each of the discrete institutions of any social system.

In concentrating on a social milieu of institutional goals and values, the study wishes to focus primary attention, first, on the conception of that milieu as an <u>integrated</u> system of institutional goals

and choices (values). Consequently, it is worth
(re-)considering that ad-hoc patching here and re-
vising there especially, but not exclusively in the
economy, rather than innovating meaningfully throughout the social system, logically may not have, and
empirically, does not have, any significance. By
patching rather than productively innovating is
meant, for example, throwing out the incompetent
and venal economic rascals, while ignoring the institutional roots engendering incompetence and rascality,
not only in the economy, but throughout the social
system. Certainly it would be comforting both to
those outsiders and locals who have invested time,
effort, and money to believe that by such patching
in the economy, sooner or later, something positive
will come of the Iranian economic development effort,
and to Iranians (and to some Western social scientists) to believe that Iranian institutional goals
and value choices can be preserved reasonably
intact while at least the fruits of economic development can be produced. But as with too many other
Iranian hopes, all this is but another flight into
fantasy, and substitution for making the hard choices
in facing up to the realities of economic development.

By concentrating on a social milieu of institutional goals and values, this study focuses primary
attention, second, upon that crucial environment in
which novel ideas, motivations, innovations, philosophers, motivators, and innovators, all play out
the ever exciting game of potential economic development. This premise does not deny the importance in
and of themselves of ideas, motivations, and innovations, and the role that the bearers of certain
kinds of social ideas and actions have in initiating
economic development. But it does postulate for
(re-)consideration that, unless the social milieu of
institutional goals and values (logically) accept as
possible these kinds of ideas, motivations, and innovators and role bearers associated with rationalizing
those aspects of the social system essential for
the establishment of a self-generating rational economic system, the "break-through" to economic development by development oriented philosophers, motivators,
and innovators, although not impossible, is improbable,
if not almost insurmountable.[28] The discussion of
Chapter Eight of such issues as what is legitimate
change and who inaugurates it, of what order, and in
what way, is innovation, including innovation of economic development, expected to take place, all have
been motivated with this argument in mind, and that

is why the study has assumed that these questions
are questions of institutional values, as much as
are the fundamental assumptions of political authority and of the economy (the integrated (institutional) social system, once again).

To be sure, a social milieu unfavorable to economic development can be overcome and can be made
favorable; certainly, this is the very rationale of
the present study. And conversely, the social milieu
alone, no matter how favorable to economic development, being "inert" cannot of itself produce economic
development. For regardless of theoretical potential,
it takes flesh and blood actors ready and able to
fight, figuratively or literally, for the initiation
of economic development, in order for development to
take place. But it is worth (re-)considering that
innovators with economic development motivations and
ideas will not necessarily "break-through" a so-
called "traditional," economically non-developed
society as is contemporary Iran, merely because actors with development ideas did so in the "traditional," later economically developed societies of
the West and of Japan. This statement is made on
the strength of the arguments in Chapter Ten that
the social milieu in the two instances represented
goals and structures of two qualitatively different
social orders, even and especially in their pre-
economic development "traditional" phases.

In this context, it is worth recalling that
social movements espousing ideologies potentially
conducive to motivating economic development interests among followers, have arisen from time to time
in continental Asia, as they have arisen, say, in
Japan. Of special interest to the present study
are the Bahai'i of Iran, which failed in the attempt
to economically innovate in the social milieu of
nineteenth century Iran.[29] And the reason this
movement, among others, failed, while those in
Japan succeeded, in sum, it is worth (re-)consider-
ing, is due to the qualitative difference in social
milieus as between the two kinds of institutional
social systems. For in a society such as Iran, individuals and ideas in social movements must not only
"break through" tradition, they must, in addition,
destroy the institutional goals and structure of the
social milieu which a priori have suggested that the
kind of "break through" necessary for economic development morally is reprehensible, if it ever can be

considered. This, at the least, is a far more formidable task than ever faced either "traditional"
Japan or Western society. And so, since most individuals follow the lines of least resistance and
accept the goals of their own social systems,
Iranians, because of the institutional goals of
their particular kind of social milieu, pursue
existing economic interests detrimental to economic
development. They do not attempt positively to
"break through" the traditional system of goals, and
establish an economic system conducive to their interests, as was feasible in terms of the institutional goals of the Japanese and Western "traditional" social milieu. In sum it might be said that
although the presence of development ideas, motivations, and individual motivators are necessary for
economic development, they are not sufficient for
economic development, as has been suggested by certain authors.[30] (The reverse of the argument, to
be sure, as conceded earlier in the paragraph, is
as true.)

By conceptualizing the problem of economic
development as primarily one of a social milieu of
institutional goals and values, rather than as a
social milieu of social forms, third, the study
wishes to focus attention on the necessity to make
changes which create qualitative distinctions and
not merely differences in Iranian social organization, if the prospects for economic development
are to be enhanced. For it is worth (re-)consider-
ing that most recent changes in Iranian society do
nothing substantially for economic development,
while they provide the comforting illusion that
this busy work somehow is helping development (the
quantitative myth; see above, Chapter Eleven),
because no serious attempt has been, or is being
made to challenge the fundamental goals or values
of the institutional structure of Iranian society.
Certainly Iran is "different" (more modern?) than
she was a decade ago, but, as far as economic
development is concerned, this implies nothing.
Yet, Iranians and foreign advisors still insist
on change within the Iranian institutional goal
system, as if somehow these changes will erode the
institutional goals in their favor. Perhaps, they
advocate this policy even when obviously they know
better, because changing institutional goals politically now is "impractical" in Iran, and solely is
feasible in the ideal dream world of the sociological
theorist. Perhaps; but if that is so, then it is

worth (re-)considering whose proposal is practical
and whose is impractical, as far as the potential
<u>achievement</u> of economic development in Iran is
concerned.

Economic Development and Industrialization

It is worth (re-)considering that one of the
key problems of developing the Iranian economy is
that Iranians do not understand what economic development is; to wit, a system that is both reasonably
able to maximize the economic potential of the
society and self-sufficient out of its own resources
and efforts. One of the more subtle confusions as
between what development is and what it is not, (not
only in Iran, it is worth noting) is that economic
development is considered to be equivalent to industrialization. That industrialization may be a significant part of the economic development process is
true enough, but that economic development is restricted to this, is a dangerous overstatement.

Certainly, constant Communist repetition of
this confusion only has further intensified confusion on this point in the economically underdeveloped
societies (not to speak of its effect on Western
economic theory). But Communist dogma alone cannot
account for the tenacity of this confusion. It is
worth (re-)considering that the appeal is of long-
standing duration and is a vital part of the institutional fabric of Asian societies. For, as suggested on many occasions earlier in this study,
industrialization is considered to be both the
symbol and the means for acquiring political and
national equality with the economically developed
West, as quickly and as painlessly as is possible.
Again, industrialization is concerned with the most-
up-to-date kinds of economic activities the political
apparatus traditionally has been concerned with;
namely, edifice or monument construction to demonstrate power, prestige, and "service" before the
people, and especially, where such activity matters;
namely, in the urban centers. And, finally, industrial activity is that kind of economic activity
which is easiest for the political center to supervise and control. For industrial enterprise depends
upon materials, and skills that the political apparatus can pre-empt, control, or at least supervise.
It is worth (re-)considering, therefore, that it is
for all these reasons (among others) that true agricultural development, in fact, if not in pious theory,

often is neglected in such underdeveloped societies as Iran. For, agriculture offers nothing that can be considered as a visual symbol of equality with the West (for, as the Iranian argues, "We already have it, and we are unequal to the West"). Although agriculture seems to work well enough for the purposes at hand (that is, to provide the surpluses to be placed at the disposal of the political apparatus as it sees fit), politicians agree that agriculture is harder to work in and control than is industrial activity, in that few of the predominantly urban politicians want even to visit it, let alone work with it.*

Not only is industrial enterprise confused with economic development, but industrialization also is confused with heavy industrialization. In the light of the discussion on the desirability of industrialization in general, the choice of heavy industrialization is but a logical consequence. For heavy industry is the symbol most closely associated with the developed societies, it is the most monumental symbol of prestige and power currently available, and it is the easiest of all economic activity to control. Consequently, small industry suffers as well as agriculture in the choice of development projects; but, of course, not to the same degree.

As suggested earlier in this discussion, the choice of building up industry over agriculture, and by implication, the choice of building up heavy industry over light industry, of course, is not limited to economically underdeveloped societies as Iran. For such conscious choices also characterize Communist proposals for economic development, regardless

---

* It must be mentioned that the Iranian political authority most recently has shown growing concern with agricultural development and productive land reform, especially in the now operative Third Plan.

The question, of course, is, contrary to past experience, whether or not such programs will be carried out, or even can be carried out. But at the least, the question is being discussed, which is a favorable sign for economic development.

of the "stage" of economic development that a particular Communist society, most notably, the Soviet
Union, happens to be in. Hence, not surprisingly,
all Communist societies, including the Soviet Union,
prefer that their economist development efforts be
judged on the basis of relative success in heavy
industry, as compared with their more modest successes in smaller industry, and certainly as compared with their monumental failures and even dis-
asters in agriculture. It is worth (re-)consider-
ing whether or not the failure in agriculture, and
the modest show in light industry, may not be attributed necessarily to ignorance or incapacity, as
claimed by the Communists (although this may be true
in some instances), but may be attributed rather to
deliberate political choices to neglect relatively
these sectors of the economy, on the basis of the
same kind of reasoning prevalent in such economically underdeveloped societies as Iran. Consequently, even if Communist heavy industrialization
programs succeed, at the least it is worth (re-)
considering such questions (or myths?) as whether
or not the economy really is developed, whether or
not an economy (and the social system in which it is
but one institution) has or can reach maximum, economic potentiality by exclusive emphasis upon heavy
industrial development, and hence, whether or not
such an economic development model apart from ideological (that is, political) considerations, economically is suitable for such economically underdeveloped societies as Iran. Unfortunately, as
hinted at earlier in this section, even non-
Communist theorists have tended to avoid bringing
up this matter even for discussion.

Entrepreneurship

One of the key indicators of economic development in any society is the development of entrepreneurship. Consequently, in what way a society conceives of, and utilizes potential economic entrepreneurship is a good indication of how serious it
is about developing a rational, self-generating
economic system.

It must be noted that the term "entrepreneurship" and not the term "entrepreneur" deliberately has
been used. An economic entrepreneur is a person
who assumes the risk and management of some economic
enterprise, and who has the capabilities and the
desire to do so. Economic entrepreneurship, in con-

trast, is the economic <u>system</u> by which individuals
are encouraged to be entrepreneurs. It is worth
aligning immediately this conceptual contrast with
an associated conceptual contrast; namely, a contrast between innovators and innovation. For innovators are motivated individuals, while innovation
is a <u>system</u> which encourages the possibility and
probability that those individuals will be able to
translate their motivations into productive social
(including economic) action.

It is worth (re-)considering first, that a contrast be made between entrepreneurs and entrepreneurship, because in an economically underdeveloped
society, such as Iranian society, entrepreneurs must
have sufficient physical and psychological security,
if they are properly to play their historical role
in the process of economic development. For although
entrepreneurs are necessary for economic development,
they are not sufficient to develop an economy; there
also must be entrepreneurship. Only the <u>security</u> of
entrepreneurship provides entrepreneurs and potential
entrepreneurs with the opportunity rationally to calculate means and ends with a reasonable assurance
that tomorrow will not be radically different from
today. Without security it is the clever and often
selfish men (speculators) taking advantage of fortuitous economic circumstances who come to the fore
in a changing economy. For example, to recall, economists have demonstrated that a polity that taxes
heavily but consistently is to be contrasted with
a polity that taxes higher lightly, but inconsis-
tently, or a polity which levies taxes by negotiation with the taxed; for the latter two (alternative)
policies encourage the speculators, who gamble on
either economic plenty or ruin, while the former
alone encourages entrepreneurs. Not strangely, the
latter two practices are common in such economically
underdeveloped countries as Iran, while the first is
found in the economically developed societies.

A second observation: It is only societies
which provide entrepreneurial <u>security</u> that allow
for the kind of <u>risk</u> associated with true, long-
range economic development. For no matter how much
technical knowledge is available, and how easily
funds are available, if potential entrepreneurs do
not know, within reasonable limits, what the policies
of the political apparatus will be tomorrow, and the
day after tomorrow, they cannot productively risk.

They only can speculate. Hence, to conclude, once
again, it is the society which encourages either
speculators or entrepreneurs to predominate among
the economic actors of that society.

A third suggestion for (re-)consideration is
that, without the acceptance of entrepreneurship
within a society, the efforts of entrepreneurs are
made excruciatingly difficult, and very well may
come to naught. For in a social system such as
Iran, in which entrepreneurship is not accepted,
"break through" entrepreneurial activity by entrepreneurs, not only is not encouraged or sanctioned,
it is not even considered permissible, in terms of
the institutional goals and values of the social
system. Once again, this does not make "break
through" impossible. But, if a society accepts
"break through-ness" as one of its core concepts,
as was the case in Western society in the pre-
developed phase of its social development, then the
problem and role of those who "break through"--
here, entrepreneurs--can become the pre-eminent concern, as is true in Western suggestions for achieving economic development. But in a society such
as Iran, concentration on concern with the "inert"
system of entrepreneurship, in which those who
"break through" must act out the drama of economic
development, cannot be avoided, for, unfortunately,
for entrepreneurs, Iranian society is not a neutral
bystander to entrepreneurial "break through" as was
the pre-developed, "traditional" societies of the
West and of Japan. It cannot be proved, but it is
worth (re-)considering, at least for further inquiry,
that there are sufficient entrepreneurs in Iranian
society and an adequate number of other individuals
who would become entrepreneurs to, at least, initiate
the economic development process, if that process
were reasonable and feasible in terms of the institutional goals and values of that society. But because
entrepreneurship is not accepted as possible, in
terms of the institutional goals and values of Iranian society, speculative and not entrepreneurial action is more natural (that is,is substantively rational), and the probability of entrepreneurs innovating (that is, breaking through) enough of a change
in the economy to facilitate entrepreneurial activity, in effect, implies changing the institutional
goals and values of the whole social system, which
is far more difficult and does not appear to be in
the offing in Iranian society today.

It is worthwhile at this point to recall for
review an earlier discussion; namely, the private
sector controversy (see above, Chapter Eleven). It
was suggested in that discussion that much of the
private versus the public sector argument is a sham
argument. Suggested now is that the question of
entrepreneurship within the private versus the public sector is a compounded sham argument. For it is
worth (re-)considering that the problem of entrepreneurship is not a sector problem but a total
society problem. And, hence, the notion that entrepreneurship and entrepreneurs must be limited exclusively to either sector, and that the lack of entrepreneurship and entrepreneurs in one sector is justification for believing that they must be, and can be
created in the other, is one of the prime illusions
of contemporary underdevelopment theory, policy, and
method. For, as suggested by the discussions of the
case study, it is worth (re-)considering that the
only way out of the problem of the general lack of
entrepreneurial talent and motivation in Iranian
society, is to establish entrepreneurship (such as
entrepreneurial security) in both the public and
private sectors, that is, in the society as a whole.
For then and only then, will non-speculative entrepreneurs appear not only in the private sector but
also in the public sector, and then and only then
will the entrepreneurial problems which plague both
sectors be eliminated. For, and this is the fourth
observation on entrepreneurship, as long as the
institutional values and goals of the social system
in general discourage the emergence of an entrepre-
neurially oriented economy, politicians with no
interest in economic rationality, will continue to
dominate the public sector of the economy and speculators will continue to dominate the private sector
of the economy.

A fifth thought for (re-)consideration: By
suggesting that the problem of economic development
is a lack of entrepreneurship in the social system,
and not merely an absence of entrepreneurs in the
private sector of the economy, the thesis that,
unless a public sector directed economic development
effort is accepted, economic development is left
only with the dubious possibility of "stimulating"
the existing commercialists in the private sector to
become entrepreneurs, is opened for (re-)considera-
tion. And, more significantly, simultaneously, the
argument (myth?) upon which this thesis rests; namely,

that it was a metamorphosis from commercial adventurer to productive entrepreneur in the economically developed societies that was instrumental in producing the vital enterprises of the new economic order, also is opened for (re-)consideration. The documentary evidence apparently is not conclusive as far as continental Europe is concerned. What is known of the English experience, however, suggests that, save possibly for certain Londoners, those who were instrumental in developing a rational, self-generating economic system in English society came from novel and diverse social and ecological (especially yeoman) backgrounds into "new (industrial) towns," and were not properly "stimulated" commercialists from the old commercial interests or towns. Certainly, in the case of Japan, it is very apparent that the new entrepreneurs did not come primarily from commercial sources, but rather were converts from agricultural and rural industrial pursuits.[31] Consequently, evidence that entrepreneurial "interest" among the commercialists of the private sector of an underdeveloped economy is lacking, and does not appear to be in the offing, which seems apparent in the case of Iran, does not necessarily imply that putting all one's economic development eggs in the public sector basket is the only alternative, if economic development ever is to be achieved. This especially is important in a society such as Iran, in which the public sector seems as incapable of developing true entrepreneurs as is the private sector. Rather the answer, once again, is that if entrepreneurs are not now appearing in the private sector of the Iranian economy, in spite of widespread technological capability and obvious "need" in that economy, it is because the inhibitor is the general system of institutional goals and values, and not the peculiar characteristics of the (commercial structure of) private sector of the Iranian economy alone, as important as those characteristics may be.

THE QUESTION OF FOREIGN AID AND FOREIGN ADVISORS

Introduction

Most studies of economic development in economically underdeveloped societies make much of foreign aid, both capital and human, as a potential facilitator of the development process. Certainly foreign aid cannot be ignored in Iran, and the study cannot ignore it, and has not ignored it, in many of its discussions. However, direct discussion of it deliberately has been left for the very last. For contrary to most economic development studies, this study does not propose to make much of foreign aid, simply because the study asserts that, contrary to the prevailing notion about foreign aid, certainly in the Iranian case, scholastically or materially, not much is or can be made of it. For, once again, given the major thesis of the study--that the present ground rules of economic action in Iran (the social milieu) are the major inhibitors of economic development--the goals and values of all the foreigner's capital and all the foreigner's advisors will not be able to put a rational self-generating economic system together simply because economic development will not take place, with or without the foreigner's aid, unless a radical change occurs in those goals and values. Then, foreign aid ideologically and materially speaking, is, at best, foreign charity.

Nevertheless, the general concept "foreign aid" does have some interesting and important implications for general development theory and practice, and it is these implications that the study proposes to discuss in the following sections. Under these terms, questions such as the nature and "value" of specific programs or methods, or the policies of specific aid donors, are peripheral. Consequently, it must be stated emphatically here and now, that no discussion is intended to be, and must not be interpreted as, a "critique" of any specific aid program or of any specific donor, since this would defeat the very purposes of the discussions from the outset.

The Iranian Motivation for Foreign Aid

The study on a number of occasions, has discussed the Iranian motivation for economic development. It now is in order to discuss why it is that the Iranian seeks foreign aid for that endeavor.

Long before any formal foreign aid program was instituted in Iran, early in the 1950's, an American, Arthur C. Millspaugh, who headed a mission to Iran from 1921-27, and again immediately after World War II, made the observation that Iranians were interested in foreign (friendship and) aid, primarily to obtain material property and to use the foreign poli-

tical presence as counterweight to the Russians,
while simultaneously, relieving the Iranians themselves of the bother of trying to find out how best
to cope with their own economic development problems.
The foreigners themselves, were treated as symbolic
pawns, to be kept in the background whenever any
successes were achieved, to insure that the Iranian
polity would get full credit and profit, yet to be
dragged out as scapegoats whenever insurmountable
problems, or popular unrest against bureaucratic
inefficiency and venality, inevitably arose.[32]

Although, it is indisputable that there have
been some modifications in the donor-recipient aid
relationship since that time, it also is indisputable that these observations are a very perceptive
summary of the existing aid problem in Iran. For
certainly, Iranians, as the members of many economically underdeveloped societies, view foreign aid
primarily as an "outside" source of material subsidy
to the existing pool of wealth, so that those in
positions of responsibility over the economy will
be relieved of the necessity of making their own
painful decisions as to how to provide these material extras associated with a modern economy solely
out of their own internal resources. And the most
"painful" of these decisions, to be sure, is the
choice between how strong is the goal of material
desires as compared to the goal of preserving the
imperatives of a non-rational economic order, which,
for example, insures dependence of the economy and
the society on a particular kind of economically non-
rational political order for even minimum security.
Such aid is popularly termed these days "aid-without
strings," in contrast to "aid-with-strings" which,
it is claimed, is provided as bait to serve the
donor(s)' covert interest in interfering into the
internal affairs of the recipient society.[33]

The Containment of Foreign Advisors

The second problem raised by the Millspaugh
thesis, as outlined in the previous section, is the
Iranian problem of "containing" the foreign advisors
who usually accompany the aid, supposedly to help
insure that the aid will be utilized properly--that
is, rationally--to serve economic development goals,
so that these advisors will not work to destroy the
institutional goals of the Iranian social fabric.

It is most important to appreciate that advisors, especially foreign advisors, have an already established role in Iranian (and Asian) society dating back many centuries, and therefore, are not a novelty to an Asian economically underdeveloped society. Hence, it is worth (re-)considering that one source of difficulty between advisors and their Iranian counterparts lies in the fact that the Iranians insist that the contemporary aid advisors accept their traditionally conceived role. But this often is not acceptable to the advisors, especially to those newly arrived advisors who are being introduced for the first time to the great game of overseasmanship, and who may take the challenge of developing the Iranian economy very seriously.

Because the nature of the traditional advisory role is so important, it is worth discussing that role in some detail. First, and foremost, that role specifies that foreign advisors must accept the fact that they are technicians, and as such, regardless of the knowledge they possess, they are never to act as administrators. Consequently, advisors are expected to restrict their advice to concrete, specific technical matters, and they are expressly prohibited from offering advice in the area of decision-making. Decision-making, in contrast, is reserved for the "moral" Iranian administrators, who are the acknowledged experts in the are of human relations of their own culture. At the least, under these ground rules, any attempt of the advisors to introduce objective (scientific) treatment of any phase of Iranian human relations, covertly, if not overtly, is considered unthinkable, and rejected automatically as inadmissible.

Second, the traditional advisory role specifies that the foreign advisor has to understand that he can never claim his position as a right, and, consequently, that he is to speak only when he is spoken to, and is not to volunteer opinions, especially in those areas in which the Iranian host does not want him to pry. Most especially, the advisors are expected to frame their advice within the institutional ground rules of the existing social system. For the advisor ever to claim, or even imply, that it is the ground rules of the existing social system that might be at the root of a problem, and not the lack of technical know-how, is an obvious display of arrogance and rigidity unbecoming the role of advisor.

The advisor, third, is never to suggest that his superior, the administrator, might be inefficient on technical grounds. For this only would be viewed as a clumsy attempt of technicians to try to take over control of the administration, and by foreign technicians at that. Although at first blush this conflict appears to be the same as the the familiar staff-line conflict found in Western bureaucratic organization, the analogy only is apparent. For there never has been any such conscious division in Iranian social organization, and any distinction that is made along these lines, is made upon separating moral superiors (administrators) from non-moral inferiors (technicians).[34]

In brief, Iranians have assimilated the contemporary foreign advisory role to the traditional advisory role of a specifically trained repository of technical information, which must serve the interests of and validate the prerogatives of the morally superior generalist, the administrator.[35] Unfortunately, for all concerned, some foreign advisors do not want to accept this specification of their role. Perhaps this is because of the difference in the role specifications of advisors as between Iranian society and certain foreign societies. But, perhaps, it is worth (re-)considering that this is because the advisors, once they become involved in "technical" advising, rightly ascertain that the real problems in their work lie elsewhere; elsewhere in the institutional goals of the society which Iranians prefer to wrap in the sacred, untouchable mantle of "administration." This unavoidable conflict in role specification is most apparent to those who work directly in the area of human relations, such as public administration and community development, but it also is faced by the so-called pure technician, such as the advisor on chicken breeding, who soon comes to appreciate that something beyond "know-how" is wrong when simple and obviously useful techniques are ignored, or wrongly applied by obviously intelligent Iranians.

Obviously something more than a simple problem of learning theory is involved here. For, in spite of the Iranian students' penchant for learning and the advisor's sincerity and effort, Iranians often make amazingly poor pupils under advisory circum- stances (individual exceptions always noted). They constantly press for subject matter not in the lecture or demonstration, for they seem ever suspicious

that they are not getting all the facts from the
advisor. They never seem to be able to see generalizing significance from one case to another, and
continually complain that the course is not "concrete
enough," or that the teacher is vague and incompetent.
For, to react otherwise, would be to admit that the
scientific, generalizing knowledge of the foreigner
has validity, and by implication, to admit that something might be wrong with continuing to employ the
Iranian moral generalizations as proper guide for
the administrative roles of Iranian society. But
since open rebellion is unthinkable, in that the
material aspects of the aid program might be affected
adversely by overt antagonism, students and advisors'
counterparts must "contain" the subject matter and
approach of the advisor through passive resistance.
And so the Iranians claim not to "understand" the
advice. And it is only when they are threatened
with sanctions that they suddenly begin to "understand." But that is as far as they will concede.
They never diminish their fears of, and resentments
against, conscientious advisors, by inattention,
bickering, and overt badgering.

In fairness to the Iranian position, it must
be conceded that if foreign technicians made administrative and policy decisions, even if it could be
assumed that foreign technicians would be able to
accomplish anything on their own, the programs would
most probably fail to survive the departure of the
technicians. Hence it can only be postulated, once
again, that, whether they like it or not, Iranians
must make all the necessary and painful decisions
themselves for economic development to take root
in Iranian society. But, on the other hand, it is
worth (re-)considering, more importantly, that
whether he has the opportunity or not, the advisor
must not accept the responsibility for administrative and policy decision-making, simply because as
Millspaugh warned decades ago, the Iranian knows
only too well that if the advisor is forced into
involvement in decision-making involving matters
which impinge upon the institutional goals of
Iranian society, nothing will be accomplished, while,
the Iranians, by saying "I told you so," simultaneously are relieved from shouldering the burden of
seeing to it themselves that these changes are
brought about in their society.36

Unfortunately, neither the frustrated advisors
nor the suspicious Iranian counterparts are willing

to openly face the problem of the (institutional)
role of the foreign advisor.[37] For to do so would
open the discussion to a host of other problems
concerning the very nature of the present ground
rules for aid and economic development efforts in
Iran, which neither side, for other than rational,
economic reasons, is willing to face. Both sides
prefer, rather, to interpret the foreign advisor
problem as one involving individual "misunderstand-
ings" in human relations between specific advisors
and specific advisees. And so, on the one hand, the
Iranians expect some technological miracle, or at
least some economic gain, from an aid program which
demands as an afterthought that they have to put up
with boorish, unsympathetic foreigners and their
unsolicited advice. When these unrealistic benefits
are not forthcoming, the Iranians blame the failure
on their advisor's "obvious" technical or social
ignorance of Iranian problems, especially a lack of
appreciation of the Iranian administrative facts of
life. The advisors, on the other hand, resent the
indifference of Iranian administrators toward basic
social problems and overconcern with the material
attributes of development, rather than concern with
true economic development. When their advice is not
taken, the advisors comfort themselves with the
pious hope that, in spite of all their trials and
tribulations, they must be getting something done
that some day may bear fruit. For after all, they
sigh, changing such an old and traditional country
as Iran "takes time." Those advisors who refuse to
delude themselves in this way become discouraged and
apathetic, and wait out the end of their tours of
duty as eagerly as do their resentful Iranian counterparts.[38] Under these circumstances, for all the
good advisors do, both sides agree, the advisors
might as well have stayed at home. And this is true,
given the ground rules of the advisory role in
Iranian society.

Foreign Misconceptions Concerning an Aid
Program: Means and Ends

Although this study takes the position that
Iranians must bear the primary responsibility for
not taking the measures necessary for developing
a self-generating rational economic system in their
society, foreign aid, contrary to its claimed intention, has helped contribute to Iran's difficulty, and
consequently, must share in the guilt for Iran's lack
of economic development. In this section, the philo-

sophy and method of foreign aid programs in Iran and why, on balance, these programs do more harm than good in the Iranian context will be discussed.

Already mentioned is that Iran, the recipient, prefers its aid either as "no-strings" funds, which is the ideal, or at the least as specific, concrete, technical aid. The various aid programs in Iran, since they are _aid_ programs by definition, have attempted to conform to this mandate. Consequently, whenever controversy arises concerning either policy or procedure in the aid programs, not surprisingly, discussion normally is limited to such technical considerations, as, for example, whether or not capital is more important than technical skills, and if skills are assumed to be important, what skills are required, and so forth.[39] And if certain projects are running into procedural difficulties, such questions as, for example, how to economize on individual projects that seem to be presenting unusual difficulties are brought up for review. Certainly, it cannot be argued that these questions do not reflect sound technical and economic judgments, and are in the best interests of an "aid-without-strings" philosophy which assures that "cultural imperialism" charges will never be raised against sensitive donors.

However, it is worth (re-)considering that, no matter how much monetary support and technical aid is provided the Iranian economy, for such admittedly worthwhile endeavors, unless certain basic changes in the institutional goals and values of Iranian society accompany such endeavors, Iran will not develop and sustain a self-generating economic system, which is the only true measure of economic development. Consequently, regardless of the economic changes now going on in Iran, and no one can deny that on the basis of such bench marks as material "growth" and the quantitative increase in education, the changes are impressive; whenever the aid subsidy is suspended, it is probable that whatever has been accomplished will stagnate, if not collapse. For given the (containing) ground rules for aid in Iran, aid _is_ not, and it is suggested, _cannot_ be the means to introduce a process of sustained, self-generating growth into Iran. It is and can be best only an end unto itself; that is, once again, a means to provide an economic wherewithal for Iranians to give the _impression_ of economic development, in order to bribe the economically

deprivileged into the belief that something useful
is about to be accomplished that will benefit them,
and to pay for the horde of patrimonial political
retainers, so that both groups will not become restless and challenge the stability of the existing
polity.*40

It is worth (re-)considering then, that the
basic problem of aid programs in Iran lies not in
the procedural nature of the aid, although admittedly corruption and inefficiency do not lend themselves readily to the proper utilization of aid benefits. Consequently, the study dissents from the familiar assumption that, when it is appreciated that
some order of drastic change in Iranian society is
necessary to facilitate economic development, then
these drastic changes can be made along with (that
is, as part of) the aid program, as merely another
"technical" problem; that the desire for aid, or
that the aid process itself, will be so overwhelming
as to stimulate acceptance of these significant
social changes; or finally, that the obstacles to
these changes are linked irrevocably to the specific
individuals or cliques (that is, elites) now in
power who will be removed, or will be reformed, in
the process of economic development. For it is questionable, especially in this case, that (material)
means will change (non-material)ends. In fact, in
this case, it is worth (re-)considering that ends
will pervert means in a way that aid not only will
not facilitate the process of economic development,
it also will only facilitate continuation of economic
non-development.

But perhaps even a more misleading misconcep-
tion concerning an aid program, since the misconcep-
tion is cherished both by foreigners and Iranians,
is the notion that good "human relations" between
donor and recipient will facilitate the achievement
of the aims of the aid program. The essence of why
this belief is a fallacy already has been discussed
(see above, Chapters Nine and Eleven). However, it
is worth bringing up the issue again here because

---

* This may very well be what some of the donors
  have in mind. But one must assume in the present discussion that, regardless of the reason
  that prompts them to extend the aid, the donors
  are interested in aiding true economic development in Iran.

this dogma particularly is insidious in the aid context, in that it further reinforces the unfounded
illusion on both sides that, through some public-
relations gimmick and through manipulating people,
in spite of radical differences in institutional
(economic) goals between donor and Iranian, the
goals of one can be imposed on the other. On the
one hand, the donor believes that if he makes friends
locally, he can gain confidence in his ability and
in his message, and hence, that he will be able to
make Iranians with whom he comes in contact at least
willing to consider, if not to accept, his bidding.
But the Iranian, on the other hand, believes that
his obviously superior understanding of human nature
will enable him to get what he wants; namely, to run
circles around the naive foreigner, while not endan-
gering the flow of aid to support the existing institutional goals of the economy. Consequently, at a
time when the foreigner is trying hard to be kind,
patient, deferential, willing to listen and learn,
and careful not to hurt Iranian sensibilities about
Iranian economic difficulties, and when he is eating
Iranian food and trying to fathom the mysteries of
Iranian Sufism, according to the command of "The
Ugly American," all in the hopes of creating trust
and friendship so that the Iranian will do as he
advises; the Iranian, simultaneously, is trying to
flatter the foreigner, and otherwise tolerate, as
best he can, what he considers a bumbling, incompetent boor who is insensitive to Iranian "ways," in
order that friendship likewise will be engendered,
but in this instance, so that the donor will not
impose on him, and especially that the foreigner
will not force him into a position that is incompatible with the recipient's best economic interests,
as he sees those interests (which are not economic development).41 Friendship between donor and recipient, then, not only is not necessarily a catalyst
to a successful aid program, it very well may be a
major obstacle to that program. In an answer to
certain charges against foreign aid made in the book,
The Ugly American, the (then) American International
Cooperation Administration (one donor in Iran)
claimed that if the charges were true, that is, for
example, if in India, the Chinese were in fact, more
popular than the Americans, this did not matter, because an aid program cannot be concerned with popularity, but only with getting the aid job done as pre-
scribed.42 This is a very significant point of view
to take, but unfortunately, as far as Iran is con-

cerned, it only is a point of view. For as far as
an outsider can ascertain, donor-aid officials of
all sorts, and of all nationalities, seem to be
spending most of their time "making friends," in the
hopes that this would bring the Iranians around to
doing something constructive as far as economic development is concerned.

Consequently, at the least, the discussions of
this section suggest that it is worth (re-)consider-
ing that if advisors, especially technical advisors,
are sent to do an aid job, which, for various reasons is restricted to means, the advisors, at the
least, inevitably will be put in the position of
having to fight for the opportunity to do their job,
in each and every case.43 For to be successful in
any specific instance (and, once again, by "success,"
the goals of economic development must be assumed),
whatever is done, no matter how modest, must affect
the institutional goals of a system which the
Iranians are determined to preserve at all cost.

Consequently, unless someone first fights for
and establishes successfully the right of opportunity
to challenge the institutional goals (ends) of
Iranian society, before the struggle to establish
proper means ever is broached, the advisor's work
not only may be useless, it may be less than useless.
For unless this is accomplished, the donor, in effect,
positively will encourage the recipient to believe
that means are all important, and, hence, that it is
possible to avoid facing up to those painful decisions necessary to initiate and maintain economic
development in Iranian society, simply because the
donor does not consider that goal considerations
(ends) are necessary, or even applicable in his decision to extend and maintain that aid. Iran's
"success" in economic development to date is the
empirical support for this position.

The True Role of the Donor In
a Foreign Aid Program

It is apparent that present aid philosophy and
tactics are not helping to establish a self-
generating, rational economic system in Iranian
society, and, in fact, may be helping to prevent it.
Nevertheless, the foreign aid situation is not hopeless, any more than the possibility of creating a
developed economy in Iran is hopeless. But, as in

the case of the general problem of economic development, certain realities must be faced.

First, and foremost, an aid program to make friends and an aid program to develop the economy must be separated logically and empirically. For although the two goals might go in the same direction, they might very well go in opposite directions, for no other reason than that economic development requires facing certain painful realities and making certain painful decisions that may cause friendship between donor and recipient, all the way from the Shah on down to the petty bureaucrat, to suffer. If friendship, (or as it usually is termed, "being liked") and a military alliance vis-a-vis an opponent in the cold war are the primary considerations in granting aid, while consideration of economic development, even if it is of interest, is of secondary consideration, then it appears that this must be acknowledged publicly, and realistically accepted. Certainly, an economic aid program which claims to be interested in economic development must never be what it appears to be in Iran: economic support of a social system which can only offer political and economic benefices to the restless not to create trouble, especially not to turn to a Communist "solution" to economic problems--all supposedly, in the mutual interest of donor and recipient. If this indeed is the case, or if friendship or military considerations are what truly are important, and pushing for economic development will interfere with these considerations, it is better formally to terminate the aid program and acknowledge that whatever material assistance is provided is a handout. For, at the least, then, the non-Communist solution to economic development will not be confused with support for continuation of the non-development now so characteristic of the Iranian economy.

Second, if the donor is as committed to economic development as he claims, then, he must be prepared to be committed in the same way as he expects the Iranians to be committed; that is, "no matter what." Especially, the donor must not look upon an aid program as an economic "holding operation" against more radical attempts to solve the problem of economic development, while at the same time, for some strange reason, expecting the Iranian voluntarily to take a position toward economic innovation that the donor is reluctant either to take himself or to induce the Iranian to take. Whether

appeasement, compromise, and refusal to take a stand
and stick to it, will make friends is a dubious sociological or political assumption. But certainly,
from the economic standpoint, this attitude can only
discourage and disillusion those few, but present
Iranians, who are trying sincerely to economically
develop Iranian society. For from only the donor
can these individuals hope to gain the support necessary to fight for rational economic principles.[44]
Consequently, the donor must be prepared for, and
ready to dismiss the typical Iranian personal accusations that attempt to cloud issues; as for example,
that the donor is an imperialist, and that the donor
is unimpressed with what is being done economically
in Iran.[45] Especially, the donor must be prepared
to terminate (and not only threaten to terminate)
economic aid selectively, or in an extreme case even
totally, if he is convinced that what is being done,
and how it is being done, qualitatively is not con-
tributing to the singular goal of creating a self-
generating rational economic system in Iranian society.[46]

It is worth presenting at this point a brief
review of the Chinese reaction to economic-aid
advice offered by a Nineteenth Century donor (the
English), for it is valid in the present discussion.
Apparently, although the role of the donor in an
Asian economy is a long-standing historical controversy, the story has not varied, because the issues
have not varied. First, the Chinese (politicians
and bureaucrats) accused the donor's representative
(an advisor) of making unacceptable threats, when
the advisor merely predicted that unless certain
measures (that is, social reform in institutional
goals) were taken, the Chinese would not succeed in
accomplishing what they claim they were eager to
accomplish; namely, economic development. For the
Chinese did not, and could not, conceive that the
donor's advice was given in good faith. For since
selfless advice from others in Chinese society was
not customary, how could such selfless advice be
possible from a mere foreigner? And in any case,
it was unthinkable that fundamental changes in institutions were necessary, for obviously only "adjustments" especially in methods and means were all that
was necessary to change the economy for the better.
Above all, the bureaucrats were infuriated with a
suggestion that the monopoly of initiating and
carrying on productive economic action in the society
by a group of self-proclaimed superior moral-

intellectuals, was neither the only way, nor, perhaps, the best way, to accomplish economic development. At best the bureaucrats conceded that perhaps the "interests" of the specific individuals of their group might have to change somewhat. But out of fear of difficulties with the stronger foreigners in general, the Chinese decided it was perhaps wise to tell the advisor that the proposals were either under serious consideration (indefinitely, of course), or were being carried out insofar as possible, while they would stall about attempting to ascertain how little of what was suggested safely could be carried out, or how the advice could be demonstrated as useless, without at the same time stimulating overt aggression from the advisor's mother country. It is this Nineteenth Century reaction to a particular foreign advisor which set the pattern for Chinese response to foreign "advice" and "aid" for almost one hundred years thereafter. And, in turn, in no case, for any number of reasons, did a donor take a stand and make aid conditional on developing a rational, economic system in Chinese society. In some periods the contrary was so obvious as to reach scandalous proportions. Of course, during that hundred years, much materially was accomplished in China through foreign aid, but significantly, a self-generating rational economic system did not develop. And finally in late 1949, the society gave up the ghost, certainly as far as the possibility of a liberal non-Communist solution to the problem of economic development was concerned. Perhaps even more significantly, when that same society moved to Taiwan after the fall of the mainland to the Communists, and when the principal donor in that particular situation did take a stand for economic development, forces within Chinese society were encouraged (or blackmailed; the means is a minor consideration in this case) to lay the foundation for what now may be the first economically developed society in Asia outside of Japan. The implication of this case study is clear. Most significantly, since full documentation of the Chinese failure to develop economically is available, there is no justification for the constant repetition of the same mistakes by donors in different (especially Asian) societies, such as Iran, out of the plea of ignorance or lack of experience.[47] Legis Neminem Excusat.

Third, the donor must see that it is not who is supported, but what is supported in Iranian

society, that is important. For if the donor, if he
is committed to economic development, has no stake
in those individuals now in control of the social
order, if they insist upon maintaining the same institutional goals in the society, then he may well
have no stake in any of the alternatives who come to
power and who retain those same goals. Certainly,
if he is a western donor he has no stake in the
Communist alternative. Consequently, if the donor
hopes to get something productive accomplished merely
by the expedient of making heads roll, he may very
well be disappointed no matter how "friendly" a particular group of individuals appear to be on the surface to the theory of economic development, expecially
if, by claiming support for the goal of economic development, they gain political support from the donor
to obtain or remain in power. Consequently, it is
more important to the success of Iranian economic
development for the donor to stand up for economically
productive programs, such as a rural community development program which aims at breaking out of the
sterile dependence on incompetent, ill-motivated
bureaucrats for initiating productive economic action
in rural Iran, than to make friends, say, with the
Minister of Interior, in the hopes that this will
enable the donor to get a development philosophy
accepted in Iranian society. This suggestion is
offered for (re-)consideration, even though it is
obvious that Iranians think of expediting change in
terms of changing personalities, or to give it some
thought, because the Iranians believe this. Also,
by standing up for programs associated with economic
development, instead of relying upon political manipulation of individuals, the donor offers a meaningful alternative to Communism, an alternative which
is a segment of a true "non-Communist manifesto."[48]
And by supporting this alternative, the donor demonstrates, not only that he believes that economic
development is not coincident with Communist political and economic action, but also that he appreciates
that the present goals of Iranian society which are
incompatible with economic development, never will
get anywhere save to waste more time, effort, and
material wealth; and that he is willing to support
a meaningful alternative. This is extremely important because the donor must appreciate, whether he
likes it or not, that by mere virtue of being a
donor, he is associated intimately with the economic
fortunes of Iranian society, as were the donors of
the previously mentioned pre-Communist Chinese
society. Consequently, whether the donor likes it

or not, he is being judged on how well the Iranian program is working out. This is true <u>regardless</u> of how little actual power the donor overtly is acknowledged to have to effect economic operations in the society. For, by accepting the present ground rules, or institutional goals of economic action, as inevitable, which only can result in repeated failure, because he doesn't want to be an "imperialist," the donor will be a part of that failure, and will not be absolved from guilt by association, any more than one in particular was in the China of 1949. It is worth (re-)considering that the answer to this dilemma, is to reject the trap either by fishing seriously in the Iranian economic lake or cutting bait economically. It must be appreciated that whether one is going to cut bait militarily, politically, and even charitably, at the same time as one cuts bait economically, <u>are other</u> questions, which, to suggest, are extraneous to the issue of economic aid; Iranian claims to the contrary, notwithstanding.

Consequently, fourth, the doctrine of "cultural pluralism" must be redefined in the foreign aid context. Certainly the donor must not attempt to force his own specific solutions (that is, <u>means</u>) to economic development on Iranian society, or on any other economically underdeveloped society, for that matter. For by doing so, the donor not only feeds into Communist charges of cultural imperialism (while simultaneously depriving himself of a weapon of counter-accusation against the Communist donor), but also, because on very practical grounds unless goal change accompanies pattern change, he cannot but alienate the sensitive Iranians, <u>without in any way necessarily affecting the success or failure of the Iranian economic development process</u>. Moreover, conversely, as cited many times in the present study in the case of Japan, preservation of many, indigenous, interpersonal and cultural patterns not only have not been incompatible with economic development, but to some observers actually have facilitated that process. But, in the Japanese case, a commitment to development <u>goals</u> also existed in the society, whereas, ironically, in Iran, as in many economically underdeveloped societies, the converse has been true. For many changes have occurred in Iranian interpersonal and cultural patterns, even in patterns which potentially could be construed as <u>means</u> facilitating economic development; but, significantly, no changes have occurred in the institutional goals of the Iranian social system.

Two implications: First, it is worth (re-)
considering that the donor must force himself to
turn his back on the "end of ideology," if not in
his own society, then as far as aid programs are
concerned.[49] That is, the donor must surrender the
notion that abstract, ideological goals (ends) "do
not really matter," but that it is only "practical"
concrete means that do, and especially the notion
that means can change ends. Second, it is worth
(re-)considering that perhaps non-Westerners who
are committed to economic development, such as the
Japanese, more successfully could contribute their
programs, techniques, and even personnel to economic
underdevelopment projects in such societies as Iran,
than can Westerners. If the donors sincerely are
interested in results, that is, economic development,
and not in political and military advantages through
economic aid programs, this is feasible and practical. For certainly individual Japanese now are
working very satisfactorily in Iran, and Japan, and
Japanese products and techniques, command respect,
and interest among other Iranians, who are less
sensitive to accepting things Japanese than they
are accepting things Western.

Aid to Iran, as to many economically underdeveloped economies, even if it eventually ends up
in the private sector of the economy, primarily is
channeled through the public sector. On Iranian
standards, to be sure, this policy is permissible
(legitimate), mandatory (moral) and useful to
insure continuing control over the economy and a
share of its benefices. Consequently, fifth, the
donor must face the fact that working through the
kind of political authority that exists in Iran
to help economically develop the society may be
defeating the very purpose of economic aid, for that
aid is sure to serve political ends which are not
conducive to economic development ends. At the
least, working through such a political authority
implies that the donor considers the question of
economic aid a political question, and hence, given
the Iranian political context, that he considers
rational economic values as not so important after
all.

Many Western donors, because of this situation,
have advised directly aiding the private sector, and
he who gives the aid commands attention, if not respect. But it is obvious to all Iranians that direct

aid to this sector, especially if it is accompanied
by mandatory foreign "advice," might challenge not
only the primacy of political authority over the
economy, but also the whole fabric of institutional
goals of both political authority and the economy,
and, by implication, of the social system as an
integral system. And so, not surprisingly, private
aid is denounced in some quarters as basically immoral, evidence of corruption, and as some sort of
plot abetted by wily foreigners for their own devious
ends.[50] The latter charge very well might be true.
But it is worth (re-)considering that, perhaps, it
should be true, if it means that this is the only
way to insure the proper use of aid for developmental ends.

But even if "leap-frogging" over the polity is
considered to be essential, if economic development
ever is to take place, accomplishment is another
matter. This is especially true because donors
either are reluctant, or are unable, to become involved in internal political problems, out of fear
of the "imperialist" bugaboo once again, and because
they believe they are forced to compromise with the
existing polity if any part of the aid program ever
is to be accepted. The disastrous results of this
policy for Iranian economic development have been
documented in the case study. Economically rational,
hard-headed, private (that is, "people to people")
programs between specific donors and specific recipients also exist in Iran, and these programs have
been suggested as, at least, one possible means to
avoid the pitfalls of government-to-government aid.
Certainly some problems are avoided in such programs,
but, at the least, once again, these programs must
work under existing social ground rules of economic
action, even if the polity is not involved formally
in their activities. And hence, the programs cannot
avoid the more serious, typical development problems,
because such problems are inherent in the institutional ground rules of the whole society.

This observation also suggests for (re-)
consideration that it may not be valid to argue
that it is a lack of interest on the part of donors
to "get out more with the people" that is the measure of project success or failure in an economically
underdeveloped society, as is suggested in The Ugly
American.[51] For, once again, regardless of the efficacy of these working contacts for political purposes

(that is, in "making friends"), the possibility of
economic development will not be enhanced one iota,
if the institutional goals of the society are not
altered. Hence, although there is little doubt that
the mass of the Iranian people, especially the much
underrated peasants, often are farther ahead in economic
development potential than is the horde of indecisive, incompetents which infest the polity, and
would be most receptive to the message of donor-
advisors, still they are unable to accomplish anything of substance on their own, because in terms of
the institutional goals of Iranian society, they are
positively or negatively prevented from taking part
in productive economic action even in their own
interests, while they are simultaneously enjoined
to wait in vain for the reluctant bureaucrats to do
what has to be done, or allow them to do what has to
be done.

However, even if the political goal of friendship is as important an aim of foreign aid as is
claimed by many, then it is worth (re-)considering
that true friendship, in contrast to temporary,
material bribery of inevitable turncoats, only
can be created by the donor standing up for true
economic development principles. This is because
only economic development principles, free of all
compromise, will produce economic development. And
then, and only then, will those committed to economic development, who in truth potentially are the
only true friends of the donor, because they alone
have the same ends for the society as does (or
should) the donor, come forth to embrace the donor.
If the donor continues to turn his back on these
potential friends, there will be no true friends of
the donor in these societies. For those who are
most disgusted with the Western donor in such economically underdeveloped societies as Iran, are
those who are in contact with the donor, and who see
him compromising with the acknowledged enemies of
economic development, allegedly "to get something
done." They have come to believe that what the donor
has to offer, that is, liberal economic development,
will not work in their own society, while at the
same time their appetite for something better has
been whetted by what they have learned from the
donor. It should be no surprise, then, to learn
that some of the bitterest enemies of the West in
high places in the Communist People's Republic of
China have been Western trained. And the West, once
again, may have the same dubious privilege of train-

ing in <u>means</u> the future Communist development leaders of <u>other</u> Asian societies, including Iran; simply
because the Western donor failed to stand on the
ideological-goal principles of what the donor really
has to offer an economically underdeveloped society,
out of some misguided notion that if the donor did
take an unpopular development stand in a particular
economically underdeveloped society, he would be
regarded as an overbearing imperialist, and not as
an understanding friend. It is worth noting, in
this context, that many Western donors were once on
friendly, even intimate terms with many of the very
Chinese Communist officials who now denounce the
West the loudest.52 And certainly, some of the
most violent critics of the West in Iran today are
Western-trained. And, it is worth (re-)considering
that this is so because the recipients feel betrayed
by donors who forever compromise on principle in
order to buy temporary "friendship" with aid to
existing social systems, which will not economically
develop, instead of fighting for true economic development in the economically underdeveloped societies
of the Asia of today.

FOOTNOTES

FOOTNOTES TO CHAPTER 1

1. J. H. Boeke, _Economics and Economic Policies of Dual Societies As Exemplified By Indonesia_ (New York: 1953), _passim_.

2. David Riesman _et. al._, _The Lonely Crowd_ (New York: 1955), p. 48; A. W. Stonier and D. C. Hague, _A Textbook of Economic Theory_ (London: 1953), p. 500.

3. G. P. Murdock, _Social Structure_ (New York: 1949), p. 127.

FOOTNOTES TO CHAPTER 2

1. Wayne Untereiner, "The Administrative Environment of Iran," (Stanford, no date), VI, 6-7. (Mimeographed.)

2. _Tehran Journal_, "What Is Wrong With Tehran Traffic?" October 29, 1959.

3. _Kayhan International_, Comment, February 25, 1961.

4. _Tehran Journal_, Home Press Editorials, "No One Is Exploited In Iran," June 22, 1960.

5. _Tehran Journal_, Home Press Editorials, "The Olympian Lesson," September 10, 1960; _Tehran Journal_, Editorials, "The Country Where They Achieved Their Victory," June 18, 1961.

6. A. K. S. Lambton, _Landlord and Peasant in Persia_ (Oxford: 1953), p. 136; Untereiner, _op. cit._, V, 56.

7. _Tehran Journal_, Home Press Editorials, "The Shah's Perspicacity," June 3, 1960.

8. _Tehran Journal_, "Government Has No Economic Plan, Charges Alam," June 19, 1960.

9. <u>Tehran Journal</u>, Home Press Editorials, "Government Account," June 24, 1960.

10. <u>Tehran Journal</u>, Home Press Editorials, "Political Struggle," June 21, 1960.

11. <u>Tehran Journal</u>, Editorials, "The Key is Always There," May 31, 1960; <u>Tehran Journal</u>, Home Press Editorials, "This Is What Was Expected," September 5, 1960.

12. <u>Tehran Journal</u>, Home Press Editorials, "The Third of Shahrivar," August 27, 1960.

13. <u>Tehran Journal</u>, Home Press Editorials, "National Integrity," December 15, 1960.

14. <u>Tehran Journal</u>, Editorials, "What The Others Are Saying," April 24, 1961.

15. <u>Ibid.</u>; <u>Tehran Journal</u>, Editorials, "The Shah is Above Responsibility," May 24, 1961.

16. <u>Tehran Journal</u>, Home Press Editorials, "Ignorant Friends" and "Show More Firmness," June 28, 1961.

17. <u>Tehran Journal</u>, Home Press Editorials, "There Is No Other Way," September 27, 1960; <u>Tehran Journal</u>, Home Press Editorials, "National Festivals," December 13, 1960; <u>Tehran Journal</u>, "Shah Stresses Vital Role of Cooperatives," July 3, 1960; General Department of Publications and Broadcasting, <u>Facts About Iran</u>, No. 99 (Tehran: 1961), pp. 3-4.

18. <u>Tehran Journal</u>, Home Press Editorials, "Elections," January 5, 1961.

19. <u>Facts About Iran</u>, No. 99, <u>op. cit.</u>, p. 2.

20. <u>Tehran Journal</u>, "Iran's Judiciary Asked to Help Save the Nation," May 18, 1961; <u>Tehran Journal</u>, "Justice Minister Vows to Fight Government Corruption," May 11, 1961.

21. <u>Tehran Journal</u>, "Text of Address by A. Alam on the Occasion of the 4th Anniversary of Mardom Party (II)," May 19, 1960.

22. <u>Tehran Journal</u>, "The Magic Key," July 18, 1960.

23. _Tehran Journal_, Home Press Editorials, "Political Struggle," June 21, 1960.

24. _Tehran Journal_, "H. I. M. Shah's Address to Senators, Deputies-Part II," April 25, 1960; _Tehran Journal_, "Shah Calls for Good Executive Machinery," July 27, 1960.

25. _Tehran Journal_, Editorials, "Activity in Election Market," June 21, 1960.

26. _Tehran Journal_, Home Press Editorials, "Education and the TV," February 21, 1960.

27. _Tehran Journal_, "Correct Atmosphere for Free Elections Essential: Premier," August 13, 1961.

28. _Tehran Journal_, Home Press Editorials, "Tribute to Mayor," December 4, 1960; _Tehran Journal_, Editorials, "Awaiting List of Candidates," July 11, 1960.

29. _Tehran Journal_, Home Press Editorials, "Ballots Must Be Secret and Free," July 27, 1960.

30. Department of Publication and Broadcasting, Office of Information, Tehran, Press Conferences [During 1337] (1958-59), p. 1 (hereafter cited as "Shah, Press, (1337)").

31. _Tehran Journal_, "H. I. M. Shah's Address to Senators, Deputies, Part II," April 25, 1960.

32. Untereiner, _op. cit._, VI, 14-15.

33. For the Middle East in general, see A. Bonne, _State and Economics In the Middle East_, 2nd ed. (London: 1955), p. 31.

34. Pahlavi, H. I. M. Mohammed Reza Shah, _Mission For My Country_ (New York: 1961), p. 97.

35. R. Bendix, "Industrialization, Ideologies and Social Structure," _American Sociological Review_, XXIV, 5 (October, 1959), 621.

36. _Tehran Journal_, "Too Much Expectation," March 12, 1960.

37. _Tehran Journal_, "Degrees Don't Help India's Idle," July 1, 1960.

38.   Shah, Press (1337), op. cit., p. 31.

39.   A. Millspaugh, Americans in Persia
(Washington: 1946), p. 89.

40.   Tehran Journal, Editorials, "Temporary
State Employees," January 5, 1961.

41.   Kayhan International, "Second Phase of
NIOC's Major Reorganization," May 29, 1961; Tehran
Journal, "Minister to Streamline Education Depart-
ment," November 29, 1960.

42.   Tehran Journal, "Derakhshesh Reorganizes
Education Ministry," May 27, 1961.

43.   Tehran Journal, "Ability Must Now Replace
Nepotism," July 9, 1960.

44.   Tehran Journal, Editorials, "Doctor Serves
Education," March 18, 1961.

45.   Tehran Journal, "Conspicuous Expenditure,"
November 9, 1959.

46.   For discussion of this problem in China,
see Mary C. Wright, The Last Stand of Chinese
Conservatism (Stanford: 1957), p. 145.

47.   For the Chinese version of this, see H. T.
Fei, China's Gentry (Chicago: 1953), p. 74.

48.   Tehran Journal, Home Press Editorials,
"It Is A Wrong System," November 26, 1959.

49.   Tehran Journal, Home Press Editorials,
"Tehran's Mayor-A Man of Action," October 11, 1960;
Tehran Journal, Editorials, "People's Expectations,"
April 21, 1961; Tehran Journal, Editorials, "The
People and Education," December 1, 1960.

50.   Tehran Journal, "Shah Says Per Capita
Income Could Be Raised to 1000 Dollars a Year,"
December 2, 1959.

51.   Tehran Journal, Home Press Editorials,
"Talk to the People," August 7, 1961.

52.   Tehran Journal, Home Press Editorials,
"Good Laws and Good Executives," August 30, 1960.

53. _Tehran Journal_, Home Press Editorials, "Rule by the People," November 28, 1960.

54. _Tehran Journal_, Home Press Editorials, "Germany Above All," August 13, 1961.

55. _Tehran Journal_, Home Press Editorials, "Opposition to the Present Government," June 20, 1961.

56. _Tehran Journal_, Home Press Editorials, "A New Incident," June 21, 1961.

57. _Tehran Journal_, Home Press Editorials, "The Smelting Plant," July 21, 1960.

58. _Tehran Journal_, Editorials, "Radical Changes in Elementary Education," April 6, 1961.

59. _Tehran Journal_, Comedies and Tragedies Retold, November 9, 1959.

60. _Tehran Journal_, Editorials, "Who is Responsible for the Suicide?" June 10, 1961.

61. _Tehran Journal_, Editorials, "Our Election Laws," February 8, 1960.

62. _Tehran Journal_, Home Press Editorials, "Banish the Embezzlers," August 24, 1960.

63. _Tehran Journal_, Editorials, "Teachers and the Education Ministry," July 16, 1961; also see below, Chapter Eleven, "Quantitative Development Myths."

64. Department of Publication and Broadcasting, Office of Information, Tehran, _Press Conferences of His Imperial Majesty, Mohammed Reza Shah Pahlavi of Iran_ [1338] (1959-60), p. 11 (hereafter cited as "Shah, Press, (1338)").

65. _Tehran Journal_, "'Wealthy Must Sacrifice More, Amini Asserts," June 20, 1961.

66. Untereiner, _op. cit._, pp. 9, 16.

67. _Tehran Journal_, Editorials, "The Shame of the City," January 7, 1960.

68. For a similar situation in China, see Wright, _op. cit._, p. 202.

69. A. H. Hanson, Public Enterprise and Economic Development (London: 1959), pp. 452-53.

70. Tehran Journal, "Discipline and Harshness," January 17, 1960.

71. Dorwin Cartwright and A. Zander, Group Dynamics, (New York: 1953), passim.

72. For a Chinese parallel, see K. C. Hsiao, Rural China, Imperial Control In the Nineteenth Century (Seattle: 1960), p. 170.

73. Tehran Journal, "Government Organs to be Checked by Inspectors," August 24, 1960.

74. Tehran Journal, "His Imperial Majesty's Press Conference (III)," December 3, 1959; Pahlavi, op. cit., pp. 176-77.

75. Tehran Journal, Home Press Editorials, "Freedom and Equality for All," August 8, 1960.

76. Shah, Press, (1338), op. cit., pp. 42-43.

77. Tehran Journal, "Decrease Noted in Public Complaints," August 17, 1960.

78. Untereiner, op. cit., VI, p. 16.

79. Reuben Levy, The Social Structure of Islam (Cambridge: 1957), pp. 370-87.

80. High Council of Stable Administrative Undersecretaries (Tehran, 1959), p. 13.

81. Bonne, op. cit., p. 44.

82. For a description and evaluation of a ruler on circuit in modern India, see A. Koestler, The Lotus and the Robot (New York: 1960), passim.

83. Tehran Journal, Editorials, "In the Midst of the People," May 3, 1960; Tehran Journal, "Cabinet Tour of Khorasan Continues," May 13, 1960.

99. _Tehran Journal,_ Home Press Editorials,
"People and Elections," December 17, 1960.

100. _Tehran Journal,_ Home Press Editorials,
"End of 19th Parliamentary Session," June 1, 1960.

101. _Tehran Journal,_ Editorials, "White or
Red Revolution," May 18, 1961.

102. For a similar concept in China, see
P. M. A. Linebarger, _The Political Doctrines of Sun
Yat-sen_ (Baltimore: 1937), pp. 89-96.

103. Lambton, _op. cit.,_ p. 193; Untereiner,
op. cit., VI, 18.

104. R. Levy. _op. cit.,_ pp. 263-66.

105. Untereiner, _op. cit.,_ VI, 18; A. T.
Olmstead, _History of the Persian Empire_ (Chicago:
1948), p. 120; Bonne, _op. cit.,_ pp. 23-24; for the
case of China, see Wright, _op. cit.,_ p. 138.

106. Bonne, _op. cit.,_ pp. 23-24.

107. _Tehran Journal,_ Editorials, "20th Year
of Reign," September 17, 1960.

108. _Tehran Journal,_ Home Press Editorials,
"Landlord-Tenant Law," July 25, 1960; _Tehran Journal,_
"Tehran Buses," March 27, 1960.

109. _Tehran Journal,_ Home Press Editorials,
"Chronic Ailment," May 26, 1960; _Tehran Journal,_
"Investigation," August 7, 1960; _Tehran Journal,_
Editorials, "Letter From the Court Minister," April
3, 1960.

110. _Tehran Journal,_ "Envelopes With Used
Stamps Lead Three to Court," August 11, 1960.

111. _Tehran Journal,_ Home Press Editorials,
"Chronic Ailment," May 26, 1960.

112. _Tehran Journal,_ Home Press Editorials,
"We Break Our Silence," June 13, 1960; _Tehran
Journal,_ Home Press Editorials, "Election Campaign,"
June 17, 1960.

84. <u>Tehran Journal</u>, "Cabinet Visits Fariman Plants," May 15, 1960; <u>Tehran Journal</u>, "Premier Eqbal, Ministers Return from Khorasan," May 22, 1960; <u>Tehran Journal</u>, "Cabinet to Tour Qazvin, Kashan, Khorasan Areas," April 22, 1960; <u>Tehran Journal</u>, Home Press Editorials, "Dr. Eqbal's School," May 23, 1960; <u>Tehran Journal</u>, Home Press Editorials, "Follow Dr. Eqbal's Example," November 25, 1959.

85. <u>Tehran Journal</u>, Home Press Editorials, "Well Done, Students," August 2, 1961.

86. <u>Tehran Journal</u>, "City of Tehran," February 23, 1960.

87. <u>Tehran Journal</u>, Home Press Editorials, "1000 Million Rials," November 16, 1960.

88. Pahlavi, <u>op. cit.</u>, p. 169.

89. <u>Tehran Journal</u>, Home Press Editorials, "The Problem of Tehran," November 15, 1959; <u>Tehran Journal</u>, Home Press Editorials, "At Kermanshah," November 20, 1959; <u>Tehran Journal</u>, "The Greater Tehran," July 21, 1960.

90. <u>Tehran Journal</u>, Comedies and Tragedies Retold, June 4, 1961.

91. Lambton, <u>op. cit.</u>, <u>passim</u>.

92. For a similar situation in China, see Hsiao, <u>op. cit.</u>, <u>passim</u>.

93. Lambton, <u>op. cit.</u>, pp. 175-76.

94. <u>Ibid.</u>, p. 291.

95. <u>Tehran Journal</u>, Home Press Editorials, "Public Support," October 20, 1960.

96. For the Middle East in general, see Bonne, <u>op. cit.</u>, Ch. XXX.

97. <u>Tehran Journal</u>, Home Press Editorials, "Are Elections Free?" June 17, 1960; <u>Tehran Journal</u>, Editorials, "The American Reporter," January 21, 1960.

98. Pahlavi, <u>op. cit.</u>, pp. 323-25.

113. For a similar situation in India, see
W. H. Wiser and Charlotte Wiser, Behind Mud Walls
(New York: 1951), pp. 169-170.

114. Kayhan International, "What About the
Foreigners?" July 16, 1961.

115. Tehran Journal, "Engineer Arrested on
Bribery Charges," May 11, 1960.

116. Tehran Journal, Editorials, "Justice
Ministry Again," August 1, 1961.

117. Tehran Journal, Home Press Editorials,
"Requirements for Election to Majlis," February 18,
1960; Tehran Journal, Home Press Editorials, "Korea
and Turkey," May 10, 1960; Tehran Journal, Home
Press Editorials, "The Mayor and the People,"
December 24, 1960.

FOOTNOTES TO CHAPTER 3

1. Tehran Journal,"'Achievements Attained Are
Proof of Resourcefulness of Nation,' says Shahanshah,"
December 22, 1959.

2. Pahlavi, op. cit., pp. 286-87.

3. Ibid., pp. 135-36.

4. Tehran Journal, "TIT Students Build Home-
made Casting Furnace," June 13, 1960.

5. Gustav Jahoda, White Man: A Study of the
Attitudes of Africans to Europeans in Ghana Before
Independence (New York: 1961), passim.

6. Tehran Journal, Home Press Editorials,
"Topic of the Day," December 2, 1959.

7. Tehran Journal, Home Press Editorials,
"Those Who Vote Against," March 13, 1960.

8. Tehran Journal, "Iran's Seven Year Plan to
Raise Living Standards," April 22, 1960.

9. Tehran Journal, Home Press Editorials, "U.S.
Aids," August 17, 1961.

10. <u>Tehran Journal</u>, Home Press Editorials, "Iran's Foreign Friends," August 12, 1961; <u>Tehran Journal</u>, Home Press Editorials, "Iran's Industrial Movement," March 9, 1960; <u>Tehran Journal</u>, "Third Plan Provides for Balanced Growth," October 13, 1960.

11. Pahlavi, <u>op. cit.</u>, pp. 177-78.

12. Untereiner, <u>op. cit.</u>, VIII, 5.

13. <u>Tehran Journal</u>, "Mahdavi Urges Hard Work to Improve Agriculture," September 22, 1960; <u>Tehran Journal</u>, "Small Industries to be Developed First," October 11, 1960; <u>Tehran Journal</u>, Iran Economic Commentaries, "Quick Yielding Projects," December 5, 1959; <u>Tehran Journal</u>, Iran Economic Commentaries, "Need for Small, Medium Industries Emphasized," February 16, 1960; <u>Tehran Journal</u>, Iran Economic Commentaries, "A New Approach to Industrialization," February 20, 1960.

14. <u>Tehran Journal</u>, "Kashani Describes Iran's Austerity Program to IMF," October 4, 1960.

15. <u>Tehran Journal</u>, Home Press Editorials, "Bandar Abbas," September 21, 1960.

16. <u>Tehran Journal</u>, Home Press Editorials, "Revival of a Memory," January 4, 1960.

17. <u>Tehran Journal</u>, Home Press Editorials, "The Steel Mill," November 8, 1960.

18. Fn. 16, <u>loc. cit</u>.

19. <u>Tehran Journal</u>, Editorials, "The Steel Dream," November 17, 1959.

20. Fn. 16, <u>loc. cit.</u>, <u>Tehran Journal</u>, Home Press Editorials, "Commerce and Industry," November 27, 1960.

21. <u>Tehran Journal</u>, "Smelting Industry in Its Final Stages," November 6, 1959; <u>Tehran Journal</u>, "Smelting Industry Highlighted," November 20, 1959.

22. Tehran Journal, "It Is Smelting Again,"
November 18, 1959; Tehran Journal, "Krupp's Partner-
ship," November 2, 1959; Tehran Journal, "Where to
Locate the Smelting Plant," November 1, 1959; Tehran
Journal, Iran Economic News, "Smelting Bill To Go
To Majlis," November 5, 1959.

23. Tehran Journal, "It is a Case of Foreign
Sabotage," November 3, 1959.

24. Tehran Journal, Home Press Editorials,
"The Steel Mill," November 8, 1960.

25. Olmstead, op. cit., passim.

26. Millspaugh, op. cit., pp. 31-32.

27. Ibid., p. 252; Pahlavi, op. cit., pp. 49-50.

28. Tehran Journal, "Cities or Villages,"
January 24, 1960; Tehran Journal, Editorial, "The New
City Park," October 11, 1960.

29. Kayhan International, "Big Dam's Dilemma,"
June 5, 1961.

30. Tehran Journal, the Panel, "Large or
Small Hotels," January 5, 1960.

31. Tehran Journal, Iran Economic Commentaries,
"Economic Aid Praised," December 31, 1959.

32. Norman Buchanan and Howard Ellis, Approaches
To Economic Development (New York: 1955), p. 65.

33. Ibid., p. 57.

34. Ibid., p. 64.

35. Tehran Journal, Home Press Editorials,
"Follow the Example of the Shahanshah," September
18, 1960; Tehran Journal, "Shahanshah Stops Palace
Project," September 10, 1960.

36. Tehran Journal, Local Press Reports, "New
Embassy Buildings in Foreign Countries," February 8,
1960.

37. Tehran Journal, the Panel, July 27, 1960.

38. Tehran Journal, "Monument to Vadar Shah,"
December 1, 1960.

39. Tehran Journal, "Municipal Office Building
for Sale; New Home Planned," March 29, 1960.

40. Tehran Journal, "Can Iran Organize for
Manpower Planning?" December 10, 1959.

41. Tehran Journal, "Smelting Factory,"
October 29, 1959.

42. For the Middle East in general, see Bonne,
op. cit., pp. 232-35.

43. Tehran Journal, Home Press Editorials,
"National Economy," November 5, 1960.

44. Pahlavi, op. cit., p. 165.

45. Tehran Journal, "Home Industries," September
17, 1960; Tehran Journal, "Why Iran Has Deficit
Budgets," November 9, 1959; Tehran Journal, "Mining
Companies to be Exempt from Taxes and Other Dues for
5 Years," December 28, 1959; Tehran Journal, Editorial,
"A Future for Agriculture," January 22, 1960.

46. Tehran Journal, Home Press Editorials,
"Does Tehran Have a Mayor?" August 13, 1961.

47. Tehran Journal, Home Press Editorials,
"Problem of the Day," November 26, 1959.

48. Tehran Journal, "The People First,"
October 25, 1960.

49. Tehran Journal, Home Press Editorials,
"Price Rise Alibis" and "Some Determination,"
October 19, 1960; Tehran Journal, Editorials, "The
Government Should Act," September 11, 1960.

50. Tehran Journal, Home Press Editorials,
"Start from the Bottom," October 23, 1960; Tehran
Journal, Home Press Editorials, "The Campaign Against
Rising Prices," October 16, 1960; Tehran Journal,
Editorials, "A Healthy Economy," July 23, 1961.

51. Tehran Journal, "Labor Minister Raps
Employers," June 3, 1961.

52. Pahlavi, op. cit., p. 279.

53. Tehran Journal, "His Imperial Majesty's Press Conference, November 28, 1959," December 1, 1959; Tehran Journal, Iran Economic Commentaries, "Investment in Mechanized Industries," November 21, 1959.

54. Millspaugh, op. cit., p. 82.

55. For an example elsewhere in Asia, see J. Halpern, "Government, Politics and Social Structure of Laos--A Study of Tradition and Innovation," (Los Angeles: University of California, 1961), p. 26. (Mimeographed.)

56. Tehran Journal, Editorials, "Misuse of the Trade Tax," September 28, 1960.

57. Tehran Journal, "A Thousand Houses for Civil Servants," July 5, 1961; Tehran Journal, "Teachers To Get New Govt. Houses," July 8, 1961; Tehran Journal, "New Houses for Civil Servants," April 22, 1961; Tehran Journal, "New Housing for Provincial Civil Servants," September 4, 1960; Tehran Journal, "4000 Apartments for Workers Ready," May 13, 1960; Tehran Journal, "Housing Body To Build Inexpensive Homes for Workers," April 22, 1960; Tehran Journal, "Shahr Ara Has Not Revised Conditions," September 26, 1959; Tehran Journal, "Shahr Ara Company Investors Protest Fresh Conditions," October 20, 1959; Tehran Journal, "Shahr Ara Co. Shareholders Approach Senator Massoudi," October 22, 1959.

58. Tehran Journal, "Eqbal Promises Added Facilities for Labor," June 23, 1960.

59. Tehran Journal, Editorials, "Visit to a Model Village," October 29, 1960.

60. Tehran Journal, "Alam Pledges Labor Control Over Insurance," July 20, 1960.

61. Shah, Press (1337), op. cit., p. 50.

62. Tehran Journal, the Panel, January 5, 1960.

63. Tehran Journal, "City Meat Shortage Temporary,' Declares Tehran Municipality," January 31, 1960.

72. Tehran Journal, Iran Economic News, "Ware-house Bill To Go to Majlis," April 6, 1960; Tehran Journal, Home Press Editorials, "Anti-profiteering," November 23, 1960; Tehran Journal, "City Takes Steps To Avert Meat, Charcoal Shortage," September 27, 1960; Tehran Journal, "Mayor Acts to Insure Winter Meat For City," January 7, 1961.

73. Tehran Journal, Home Press Editorials, "Anti-profiteering," November 23, 1960; Tehran Journal, the Panel, December 23, 1959; Tehran Journal, Letters to the Editor, December 6, 1959.

74. Tehran Journal, Home Press Editorials, "High Doctors' Fees," November 20, 1960.

75. For a similar situation in China, see Haiso, op. cit., p. 161.

76. Tehran Journal, "113 Unlicensed Bakeries Close," July 18, 1960; Tehran Journal, "Central Rice Office Plan," February 25, 1961.

77. Pahlavi, op. cit., Ch. 12; Tehran Journal, Home Press Editorials, "Agricultural Revival," November 22, 1960.

78. Tehran Journal, the Panel, April 21, 1960; Tehran Journal, Home Press Editorials, "Direct Taxes," February 7, 1960; Shah, Press (1337), op. cit., p. 39.

79. For the role of monopoly in the Middle East in general, see Bonne, op. cit., pp. 241-46.

80. Tehran Journal, "Senate Approves Five Govt. Bills," June 12, 1960.

81. Tehran Journal, "State Provisions Organi-zation Has Record Sale Figures," May 10, 1960; Tehran Journal, "Supply Dept. Provides Goal to Officials," October 11, 1960.

82. Tehran Journal, Home Press Editorials, "Assistance in Kind," January 24, 1960.

83. Tehran Journal, "Traders Complain of Low Tehran Market Condition," May 20, 1961.

64. _Tehran Journal_, "Mayor Acts To Avert Meat Crisis," May 29, 1961; _Tehran Journal_, "Butchers Warned Against Creating Meat Scarcity," October 23, 1959.

65. _Tehran Journal_, Iran Economic News, "Bank Melli Intends To Fight Rising Prices," December 29, 1959.

66. _Tehran Journal_, "Welfare Groups To Establish Drug Factory in Iran," June 5, 1960.

67. _Tehran Journal_, Home Press Editorials, "Problem of the Day," November 26, 1959.

68. _Tehran Journal_, "Business Leaders Pledge Support to Mayor Foroud," December 19, 1960; _Tehran Journal_, "Mayor, Merchants Council Discuss Rising Prices," January 9, 1961; _Tehran Journal_, "High Doctor Fees," November 20, 1960.

69. _Tehran Journal_, "Government Employees and the Coming Noruz," February 21, 1960.

70. _Tehran Journal_, Home Press Editorials, "Stop Profiteering," October 15, 1960; _Tehran Journal_, "Market Prices to be Broadcast," July 3, 1961; _Tehran Journal_, "Govt. City Ask Aid To Fight Profiteering," October 13, 1960; _Tehran Journal_, "Tehran Plans To Fix Prices On All Food Items," October 9, 1960; _Tehran Journal_, "Govt. Moves To Hit Profiteers" and "Sajjadi Defends Economic Policy Of Government," October 5, 1960; _Tehran Journal_, "Public Bath House Rates Raised by 2 Rls.," April 19, 1960; _Tehran Journal_, "New Rules To Control Tehran's Meat Shops," April 18, 1960; _Tehran Journal_, "Price of Ice Fixed in City," May 25, 1960; _Tehran Journal_, "30 Kiosks To Sell Ice At City Rates," May 30, 1960; _Tehran Journal_, "Shops To Display Price Lists of Goods On Sale," March 28, 1960; _Tehran Journal_, "Striking Force to Control Sale of Food," May 23, 1960; _Tehran Journal_, "Municipal Officers Supervise Slaughter, Distribution of Meat," April 25, 1960.

71. _Tehran Journal_, "Butchers Defied; Mutton Sold On Trucks, Vans," April 24, 1960; _Tehran Journal_, "First Open Market To Start Operation," May 17, 1960; _Tehran Journal_, "Mayor Determined To Tackle Meat Problem," January 19, 1960; _Tehran Journal_, "5 Open Markets To Run Under Municipal Control," June 1, 1960; _Tehran Journal_, Iran Economic News, "The Meat Problem," April 30, 1960.

84. <u>Tehran Journal</u>, "Iran Economy--More Comprehensive Development Plans," August 25, 1960.

85. <u>Tehran Journal</u>, "The Supermarket," April 13, 1960; <u>Tehran Journal</u>, "Iran Will Start New Foreign Purchase Org." and "Iranian Firm To Buy German Shares of Ferdowsi Store," September 5, 1960; <u>Tehran Journal</u>, "Ministry To Control Supermarket Affairs," May 4, 1960; <u>Tehran Journal</u>, "Supermarket Share Holders Special Meeting Called," April 13, 1960.

86. <u>Kayhan International</u>, "Bandar Pahlavi Chamber of Commerce Protests Municipal Export Tax," April 2, 1961.

87. <u>Kayhan International</u>, "Taxpayers' Concession Period Expires," February 9, 1961; <u>Tehran Journal</u>, Iran Economic News, "New Company Formations," May 10, 1960;

88. <u>Tehran Journal</u>, Editorials, "Isfahan's White Gold," October 10, 1960.

89. <u>Kayhan International</u>, "Guilds Income Tax Problems," June 11, 1961.

90. <u>Tehran Journal</u>, "Municipality To Get 10 Times More From Kiln Owners," April 14, 1960; <u>Tehran Journal</u>, "Municipality, Kiln Owners Reach Accord," April 8, 1960.

91. <u>Tehran Journal</u>, Iran Economic News, "584 Million Rials Paid By Farm Co-ops In Loans," July 22, 1960; <u>Tehran Journal</u>, Iran Economic News, "Tax Reforms," May 21, 1960; <u>Tehran Journal</u>, "Relief Offered for Payment of Big Income Tax," July 20, 1960; <u>Tehran Journal</u>, "Time Limit for Tax Payment to be Extended," July 24, 1960; <u>Tehran Journal</u>, "Abrogation of Tax Penalties," November 27, 1960; <u>Tehran Journal</u>, "Fresh Penalty Rebates Offered on Delayed Tax," May 11, 1960; <u>Tehran Journal</u>, "180 Million Is Income Tax Paid Up On Thursday," February 21, 1960.

92. <u>Tehran Journal</u>, Home Press Editorials, "Tax Collectors and Tax Payers," April 12, 1960.

93. <u>Tehran Journal</u>, Iran Economic Commentaries, "'Present Taxation Faulty,' says Minister," May 20, 1960.

94. *Tehran Journal*, Iran Economic Commentaries, "Tax Returns," July 2, 1960.

95. Millspaugh, *op. cit.*, pp. 33-34; *Tehran Journal*, Home Press Editorials, "Superfluous Formalities," May 20, 1960.

96. *Tehran Journal*, Home Press Editorials, "Equal Taxation," January 28, 1961; *Tehran Journal*, "Budget Debate--Deputy Asks Revision Of Tax Structure," April 25, 1961; *Tehran Journal*, "Trade Tax Rises Timely, Appropriate," September 12, 1960.

97. *Tehran Journal*, "'Revise Tax Law,' says Finance Min.," July 13, 1961; *Tehran Journal*, "More Money from Taxes," July 9, 1961.

98. *Tehran Journal*, Home Press Editorials, "We Should Collect More Direct Taxes," January 20, 1960.

99. *Tehran Journal*, Editorials, "Don't Bully The People," April 8, 1961; Lambton, *op. cit.*, pp. 144-64; Pahlavi, *op. cit.*, Ch. 8; for the Middle East in general, see Bonne, *op. cit.*, pp. 51ff.

100. See Bonne, *op. cit.*, p. 31.

101. Lambton, *op. cit.*, pp. 393-94.

102. Millspaugh, *op. cit.*, pp. 33-34.

103. *Kayhan International*, Comment, July 6, 1961.

104. *Tehran Journal*, Iran's Economic Problems, VII.4, "The Tax System," June 26, 1961; *Tehran Journal*, "The Role of the Tax System," December 13, 1959.

105. Millspaugh, *op. cit.*, *passim*.

106. *Tehran Journal*, "New Tax Laws Go Into Effect," July 15, 1960; *Tehran Journal*, "Income Tax to be Paid by July 22," June 21, 1960.

107. *Tehran Journal*, "Two Sections of Tax Department Disbanded," February 3, 1960.

108. Tehran Journal, "Red Tape, Formalities Eliminated in New Tax Laws Sent to Senate," May 17, 1960.

109. Tehran Journal, Iran Economic News, "Varsity Professors Examine, Develop Plans," May 16, 1960; Tehran Journal, Iran Economic News, "P.O. Receives 32.5 Mil. Dollars Oil Revenue," February 19, 1960.

110. Tehran Journal, Iran Economic Commentaries, "The Planned Budget and Manpower," May 28, 1960.

111. Tehran Journal, "Iranian Revenue," September 12, 1960; Tehran Journal, "Budget Surplus Claimed by Gov't.," October 2, 1960.

112. Tehran Journal, "Zargham Urges Curb on Govt. Expenditures," September 20, 1960.

113. Tehran Journal, Iran Economic News, "Govt. Owes Bank Melli 5,6000 Mil. Rials," August 15, 1960.

114. Tehran Journal, Iran Economic News, "P.O. Receives 32.5 Mil. Dollars Oil Revenue," February 18, 1960; Kayhan International, "Government To Pay Its Debts," July 16, 1961.

115. Tehran Journal, Home Press Editorials, "Budget Planning," February 19, 1961.

116. Tehran Journal, Editorials, "Cutting Out Non-essentials," April 19, 1961.

117. Tehran Journal, Iran Economic News, "19,000 Million Rials Recommended in Loans," May 15, 1960.

118. Tehran Journal, "Bank Melli has Pledged Loans Amounting to 5 Thousand Million Rials," February 25, 1960.

119. Tehran Journal, "Dr. Amini Urges Loan Priority To Province Students," May 31, 1961.

120. Tehran Journal, Iran Economic Commentaries, "An Untimely Discontinuation," January 23, 1960; Tehran Journal, Iran Economic News, "Sale of Agricultural Machinery Temporarily Stopped," January 19, 1960.

121. _Tehran Journal_, "Iran's Economic Conditions During 1960-61," May 16, 1961.

122. _Tehran Journal_, "New Council Will Coordinate Loans," November 12, 1960.

123. _Tehran Journal_, Home Press Editorials, "Only Confidence Can End Financial Crisis," August 10, 1961.

124. _Tehran Journal_, Iran Economic News, "Solution Sought To 'Small Loan' Problem," July 10, 1960; _Tehran Journal_, "Savings," January 26, 1960; _Tehran Journal_, "U.S. Mission Ends Tour With Calls On Officials," October 9, 1960.

125. _Tehran Journal_, Iran Economic News, "Interest Rate and Price Levels," August 16, 1960; _Tehran Journal_, Iran Economic Commentaries, "Interest Rate Declines," October 31, 1959; _Tehran Journal_, Iran Economic Commentaries, "High Interest Rate," October 24, 1959.

126. _Tehran Journal_, Iran Economic News, "Market Conditions," July 24, 1960.

127. _Tehran Journal_, Iran Economic News, "Industries More Than Compensate Tax Exemptions," August 8, 1960.

128. _Tehran Journal_, "Economic Forecast for 1339, Part I," April 5, 1960.

129. _Tehran Journal_, "Quantity of Money is Governed by Level of Savings," October 23, 1959; _Tehran Journal_, "Ways of Reducing Interest Rate," October 22, 1959; _Tehran Journal_, "Austria's Far-sighted Policies Promote Economic Stability," September 24, 1960; _Tehran Journal_, "Economic Lessons of Turkey and Austria," September 20, 1960.

130. _Tehran Journal_, "Industrial Bank To Commence Work from December 23," December 21, 1959; _Tehran Journal_, "U.S. Loan Agreement to Iranian Bank Signed," November 20, 1959; Pahlavi, _op. cit._, pp. 156-60.

131. _Tehran Journal_, "Announcement," December 19, 1960; _Tehran Journal_, "IMDBI Quarterly Report Shows Increased Profits," February 7, 1961; _Tehran Journal_, "Industrial Bank To Issue Loans," February 5, 1960.

132. Tehran Journal, Iran Economic News, "Industrial Loans Not Limited," November 17, 1959; Tehran Journal, Iran Economic News, "Industrial Investment Expands Rapidly," November 16, 1959; Tehran Journal, Iran Economic News, "Industrial Development Bank To Receive 600 Mil.," November 1, 1959; Tehran Journal, Iran Economic News, "Industrial Loans," May 25, 1960; Tehran Journal, Iran Economic News, "Bank Melli Has No More Funds for Industrial Loans," May 26, 1960; Tehran Journal, "An Anti-inflation Move," May 28, 1960; Tehran Journal, Iran Economic News, "Industrial Loans To Be Dealt With By IMDB," May 31, 1960; Tehran Journal, Iran Economic News, "1394 Mil. Rials Go To Industrial Bank," March 28, 1960; Tehran Journal, Iran Economic News, "Industrial Loans May Start In Two Months," March 29, 1960; Tehran Journal, Iran Economic Commentaries, "The Industrial and Mining Development Bank," April 1, 1960; Tehran Journal, Iran Economic News, "Openings of New Banks Will Not Be Permitted," December 28, 1959; Tehran Journal, "Announcement," March 29, 1961; Tehran Journal, "Protection Given To Industry Explained," August 7, 1960.

133. Tehran Journal, Iran Economic News, "Bank Melli Tightens Permanent Credits," October 27, 1959; Tehran Journal, Iran Economic Commentaries, "A Moral Suasion," October 24, 1959; Tehran Journal, Iran Economic News, "Banking Affairs To Be Regulated By Money, Credit Body," July 10, 1960; Tehran Journal, Iran Economic News, "B. Melli Controls Banks' Exch. Expend.," October 22, 1959; Tehran Journal, Iran Economic News, "Bank Melli Stops Bank Credits," August 30, 1960.

134. Tehran Journal, Home Press Editorials, "The Third of Sharivar," August 27, 1960; Tehran Journal, Local Press Reports, "Municipality and Deficit," February 4, 1960; Tehran Journal, Iran Economic Commentaries, "A Paradox," April 23, 1960; Tehran Journal, Comment, "The 1340 Budget Deficit," August 22, 1961.

135. Tehran Journal, Iran Economic Commentaries, "Ministry of Housing," June 25, 1960; Tehran Journal, "Credit and Inflation," November 22, 1959.

136. Tehran Journal, "So The People May Know," August 15, 1960.

137. _Tehran Journal_, Iran Economic News, "Bank
Melli Helps Out Four Traders," June 21, 1960; _Tehran
Journal_, Iran Economic News, "Commerce Minister
Promises To Help Iranian Traders," June 28, 1961;
Tehran Journal, "Bank Melli Saves 4 Merchants From
Bankruptcy," June 19, 1960; _Tehran Journal_, "3
Ministers, Bank Melli Governor Go to Esfahan," April
20, 1960; _Tehran Journal_, "Bank Melli To Grant 30
Million Rial Loan to Esfahan Factories," April 24,
1960; _Tehran Journal_, "Commerce Minister Promises
To Help Iranian Traders," June 28, 1961.

138. _Tehran Journal_, Iran Economic Commentaries, "The Bank Melli Iran Comes To The Rescue,"
June 25, 1960.

139. _Tehran Journal_, Iran Economic News,
"Market Reaction To Export Policy of Bank M.," July
31, 1960; _Tehran Journal_, Iran Economic Commentaries,
"Currency Stability," March 12, 1960; _Tehran Journal_,
Iran Economic News, "Traders Ask Speedier Grants of
Export Credit," December 7, 1959; _Tehran Journal_,
"Iran's Economic Problems, III," June 10, 1961;
Tehran Journal, "Industrial Expansion," July 29,
1960; _Tehran Journal_, "Credit Restrictions Pose
Major Threat To Iranian Finances," September 15,
1960; _Tehran Journal_, "Bazaar Welcomes Credit
Increase," August 16, 1961; _Tehran Journal_, "Govt.
Austerity--The Only Road to Stability," September 17,
1960.

140. _Tehran Journal_, Home Press Editorials,
"A Healthy Economy," September 7, 1960.

141. _Tehran Journal_, "Planning," August 29,
1960.

142. _Tehran Journal_, "Economic Planning,"
January 6, 1960.

143. _Tehran Journal_, Editorials, "Welcome, Mr.
Singh," July 21, 1960.

144. Fn. 142, _loc. cit_.

145. _Tehran Journal_, Home Press Editorials,
"Iran's Industrial Movement," March 9, 1960.

146. Fn. 142, _loc. cit_.

147. Tehran Journal, the Panel, June 13, 1960.

148. Tehran Journal, Home Press Editorials, "Shackles of Trivialities," August 16, 1961.

149. Tehran Journal, "P.O. Experts Report," June 24, 1960.

150. Homayoun Sahba and M.S. Meyers, "The Iranian Counterpart Role in Technical Development." Social science working paper. University of Tehran Faculty of Arts, and UNESCO, Tehran, n.d., p. 12. (Mimeographed.)

151. Tehran Journal, Iran Economic Commentaries, "The Economic Council Plans," October 31, 1959.

152. Lambton, op. cit., passim.

153. Kayhan International, Economic Comment, "Need for Planned Economy," January 21, 1961; Kayhan International, "Economic Cooperation Council to be Formed," August 10, 1961; Tehran Journal, Iran Economic News, "Factors Impeding Country's Progress," April 11, 1960.

154. Tehran Journal, Home Press Editorials, "Made in Iran," January 25, 1961.

155. Tehran Journal, "Cabinet Goals," September 4, 1960.

156. Tehran Journal, Home Press Editorials, "Unemployment Insurance," January 1, 1960.

157. Tehran Journal, "Need for Stable Economic Policies," December 30, 1959; Kayhan International, "We Must Have Real Political Power," June 5, 1961; Kayhan International, "No More Travel," June 10, 1961; Tehran Journal, Home Press Editorials, "Economic Stability," September 15, 1960; Tehran Journal, "Government's Program," April 6, 1961.

158. Hanson, op. cit., pp. 106-07.

159. General Department of Publications and Broadcasting, The Plan Organization of Iran; A Brief Summary of Activities, ("Facts About Iran," No. 88. Tehran: 1960), passim. Plan Organization, Division of Economic Affairs, Economic Bureau, Review of the Second Seven Year Program of Iran (Tehran, Iran: March 10, 1960), pp. 3-14. (Hereafter cited as "Review.")

160.   Review, op. cit., pp. 78-79; Tehran Journal, "Agr. Plans Have Had Little Effect," May 26, 1960; Tehran Journal, Iran Economic Commentaries, "The Third Plan," April 9, 1960; Tehran Journal, Iran Economic Commentaries, "Freedom From Want," February 13, 1960.

161.   Review, op. cit., pp. 15-16; Tehran Journal, Editorials, "Plan Organization's Life Extended," December 31, 1959; Tehran Journal, "Majlis Committee Revises Plan Organizations' Laws," December 30, 1959.

162.   Review, op. cit., p. 94.

163.   Tehran Journal, Local Press Reports, "Disagreement Between P.O. and Agriculture Ministry," March 3, 1960; Tehran Journal, Iran Economic Commentary, "Port Development," November 14, 1959; Tehran Journal, Iran Economic News, "1,000 Mil. Rials for Port Development," November 9, 1959; Tehran Journal, Iran Economic Commentaries, "Plan Organization Rejuvenates," January 2, 1960.

164.   Pahlavi, op. cit., p. 106.

165.   Ibid., p. 139; Tehran Journal, Iran Economic News, "Varsity Professors Examine Develop. Plans," May 16, 1960.

166.   Tehran Journal, Editorials, "The Heart of the Matter," July 11, 1960; Tehran Journal, Home Press Editorials, June 10, 1961.

167.   Review, op. cit., p. 17.

168.   Ibid., p. 16.

169.   Ibid., pp. 17, 26; Tehran Journal, the Panel, May 8, 1960.

170.   Review, op. cit., pp. 103-04, 107-08.

171.   Ibid., pp. 50-51.

172.   Ibid., pp. 71-74.

173.   Ibid., pp. 27, 31-32.

174.   Ibid., p. 51.

175. Ibid., pp. 46-47; Tehran Journal, Iran Economic News, "Supreme Economic Council to Study Labour Problems," February 3, 1960; Tehran Journal, Iran Economic Commentaries, "The State of Management in Iran," January 9, 1960.

176. Hanson, op. cit., p. 447.

177. Tehran Journal, Iran Economic Commentaries, "Interest Rate to Rise," May 14, 1960.

178. Review, op. cit., pp. 71-74.

179. Tehran Journal, Home Press Editorials, "Smelting Plant Enters Practical Phase," July 12, 1960.

180. Tehran Journal, Home Press Editorials, "Leaping Instead of Gliding," March 31, 1960.

181. Tehran Journal, Home Press Editorials, "Plans on Paper and in Practice," April 12, 1960. Tehran Journal, the Panel, May 22, 1960.

182. Koestler, op. cit., pp. 160-61.

183. Tehran Journal, the Panel, June 13, 1960.

184. Tehran Journal, the Panel, "Development Plans and the People," May 27, 1960; Tehran Journal, the Panel, March 16, 1960.

185. Review, op. cit., pp. 71-74, 102, 113.

186. Tehran Journal, Iran Economic News, "Development Plans Aim At Raising Living Standards; Nedayat," May 12, 1960; Tehran Journal, Iran Economic News, "Development Projects For Each Province," June 3, 1960.

187. Review, op. cit., p. 83.

188. Ibid., pp. 15-16.

189. Ibid., p. 44.

190. Ibid., p. 15.

191. Ibid., p. 33.

192.   Tehran Journal, Iran Economic News, "288 Mil. Rials For Studying Smelting Project," November 18, 1959.

193.   Review, op. cit., p. 12, 14.

194.   Tehran Journal, Home Press Editorials, "Dissolve the Plan Organization," July 10, 1961; Kayhan International, "Ebtehaj Answers..." and Tehran Journal, "Ebtehaj Replies to Aramesh's Criticism," April 2, 1961.

195.   Review, op. cit., pp. 17, 71-74; Tehran Journal, "The World Bank's Development Diplomacy," June 1, 1960.

196.   Review, op. cit., pp. 66-70.

197.   Ibid., p. 113.

198.   Tehran Journal, Home Press Editorials, "Plan Organization," October 6, 1960; Tehran Journal, "Plan Organization Reviews Contracts," March 27, 1961; Tehran Journal, "Second Plan Failure--Aramesh Tells Majlis," April 23, 1961; Tehran Journal, Home Press Editorials, "Oil Revenue," July 8, 1960.

199.   Tehran Journal, "German Industrialists, Plan Organization Leaders Hold Joint Conference," October 9, 1960; Review, op. cit., p. 3.

200.   Tehran Journal, "A Comparison of Consumption of Agricultural Products in 1337 and 1346," June 16, 1960.

201.   Review, op. cit., pp. 108-09.

202.   Ibid., p. 32; Tehran Journal, Home Press Editorials, "A Healthy Economy," September 7, 1960; Tehran Journal, "Review of the Second Plan," May 19, 1960; Tehran Journal, "The Second Versus the Third Development Plan of Iran, I," February 4, 1960; Tehran Journal,"'Campaign Against Poverty Final Aim of Development Plan,'says P.O. Minister," February 10, 1960.

203.   Review, op. cit., pp. 26-27.

204.   Ibid., pp. 71-74; Tehran Journal,"India's Economic Development," July 25, 1960.

205. Tehran Journal, Home Press Editorials, "Tehran's Rapidly Rising Population," November 12, 1960.

206. Tehran Journal, the Panel, "Large or Small Hotels?" January 5, 1960.

207. Tehran Journal, Local Press Reports, "Industrialists More Active in Tehran," January 15, 1960; Tehran Journal, Iran Economic News, "Industrial Loans So Far Recommended," December 30, 1959.

208. Tehran Journal, Iran Economic Commentaries, "Distribution of Industrial Loans," June 4, 1960.

209. Kayhan International, "The Building Industry; What of the Future?" March 1, 1960.

210. Tehran Journal, Editorials, "To the Capital," January 22, 1960.

211. Buchanan and Ellis, op. cit., p. 413; Tehran Journal, "Urbanism in the East," November 11, 1959.

212. Tehran Journal, "Tehran, the Center of Power," July 17, 1960; Tehran Journal, "People's Work in People's Hands," July 29, 1960.

213. Tehran Journal, Home Press Editorials, "Tehran's Rapidly Rising Population," October 13, 1960; Kayhan International, "Unemployment," June 12, 1961.

214. Tehran Journal, "Ways of Reducing Interest Rate," October 22, 1959.

215. Tehran Journal, Editorials, "If We Had a Sound Judicial Machinery," July 31, 1961.

216. Tehran Journal, Home Press Editorials, "Insured Blood-Money," October 25, 1959.

217. Tehran Journal, "300 Trucks, Tankers Held Up Near Qom," March 28, 1960; Tehran Journal, "Truck Owners Appeal to Dr. Eqbal," March 29, 1960; Tehran Journal, "Truck Owners May Strike If Requests Are Not Met," April 15, 1960; Tehran Journal, "Truckers Plan To Strike," May 14, 1961; Tehran Journal, "Truckers Union Calls Off Strike" and "Overweight Trucks to be Relicensed," May 20, 1961.

218. *Tehran Journal*, "The New Commerce Bill,"
June 8-19, 1960.

219. *Tehran Journal*, "Exports to Germany
Declining, Complain Iranian Merchants," March 31,
1960; *Tehran Journal*, "The Year Long Analysis,"
April 25, 1960.

220. *Tehran Journal*, "Duties of People and
Government," January 10, 1960.

221. *Tehran Journal*, Home Press Editorials,
"Economic Problems," November 12, 1960; *Tehran
Journal*, "Railway Committee Reviews Rate; Rates May
Rise," March 28, 1960.

222. *Tehran Journal*, Home Press Editorials,
"Stability," December 2, 1959.

223. Lambton, *op. cit.*, p. 192.

224. Buchanan and Ellis, *op. cit.*, p. 268.

225. *Review*, op. cit., p. 26.

226. *Tehran Journal*, Home Press Editorials,
"Buying U.S. Wheat," September 21, 1960; *Tehran
Journal*, "Exports and Agriculture," October 27,
1959.

227. *Tehran Journal,* Iran Economic News, "One
Third of Iran Arable,' says P.O.," April 3, 1960;
Tehran Journal, "Govt. Approves Deficit Budget,"
August 20, 1961.

228. For the systems in general, see Bart
Hoselitz, "Generative and Parasitic Cities,"
Economic Development and Cultural Change, III, No. 3,
(1955).

229. Lambton, *op. cit.*, pp. 279-280.

230. Agricultural Bank of Iran, *The Agricultural Bank of Iran In An Expanding Economy* (Tehran:
1961), p. 5.

231. *Tehran Journal*, "End of Feudalism in Iran,"
December 8, 1959.

232. Lambton, *op. cit.*, pp. 330-31.

233. Tehran Journal, Iran Economic News, "For-
ward Purchasing Impedes Agr. Progress," May 24, 1960;
Tehran Journal, Iran Economic News, "Forward Selling
Should Be Stopped," June 10, 1960; Tehran Journal,
"All About Melons," July 17, 1961.

234. Agricultural Bank of Iran, op. cit.,
p. 13.

235. Kenneth Parsons et. al., eds. Land
Tenure (Madison: 1957), pp. 280-82; Tehran Journal,
Iran Economic News, "Inflation," October 31, 1959.

236. Tehran Journal, Editorials, "Rumoured
Discriminations," November 16, 1959; Tehran Journal,
"Zahedi Announces Bank's Objectives," August 2, 1961;
Tehran Journal, Home Press Editorials, "The Vocife-
rous and the Quiet," November 17, 1959; Tehran Journal, Iran Economic News, "Agr, Credits Similar in
Iran and U.S.," May 19, 1960; Tehran Journal, Iran
Economic Commentaries, "Agricultural Credit," May 21,
1960; Tehran Journal, Iran Economic News, "Farm Co-
ops. Have Got 283,002,320 Rials From Bank," April 7,
1960.

237. Tehran Journal, Iran Economic Commentaries, "Credit and Cooperative Institute," November
14, 1959.

238. Kayhan International, "Deal First with
the Moneylenders," July 16, 1961; Kayhan International, "Letters to the Editor," June 5, 1961;
Agricultural Bank of Iran, op. cit.,pp. 6, 36.

239. Agricultural Bank of Iran, op. cit.,
p. 11; Tehran Journal, Home Press Editorials, "The
Spectre of New Land Speculation," November 17, 1960.

240. Tehran Journal, Local Press Reports,"Land
Grabbers Active Again," March 1, 1960; Tehran Journal,
the Panel, March 13, 1961; Tehran Journal, Letters
to the Editor, December 23, 1959; Tehran Journal, the
Panel, December 15, 1959.

241. Lambton, op. cit., passim.

242. Adapted from Lambton, op. cit.,pp. 244-53;
see also Pahlavi, op. cit., Ch. 9 and Agricultural
Bank of Iran, op. cit., p. 17.

243. Tehran Journal, Home Press Editorials,
"Land Reform Bill," March 1, 1960.

244. Pahlavi, op. cit., p. 200.

245. Agricultural Bank of Iran, op. cit.,
p. 11.

246. Tehran Journal, Editorials, "Campaign
Against the Cold War," May 13, 1961; Tehran Journal,
Iran Economic Commentaries, "Good News for Engineers,"
November 7, 1959; Tehran Journal, Iran Economic News,
"450 Mil. Rials for Engineers' Pay Scale," August 21,
1960; Tehran Journal, "Engineers Resent Delay in
Payment," July 15, 1960; Tehran Journal, "Teachers'
Bonus," March 20, 1961; Tehran Journal, Home Press
Editorials, "Government's Program," July 31, 1961;
Tehran Journal, "Govt. Acts To Pay Back Wages of
Civil Servants," June 3, 1961; Tehran Journal, Iran
Economic News, "5 Factors Determine Civil Service
Pay Scale," July 17, 1960; Tehran Journal, "Minimum
Govt. Wage Scale To Be 4000 Rls." January 20, 1960;
Tehran Journal, "Education Ministry Short of Funds
for Increments Payment," November 5, 1959; Tehran
Journal, "Engineers' Salary Scales Intimated to All
Ministries," April 8, 1960.

247. Tehran Journal, Editorials, "Unwarranted
Expenditure," February 11, 1960.

248. Tehran Journal, Editorials, "Bad Taste,"
July 5, 1961.

249. Tehran Journal, "Planning Sound Housing
Projects," August 24, 1960.

250. Tehran Journal, (advertisement) "From
Tonight: the Most Famous Oriental Belly Dancer...,"
July 29, 1961.

251. Tehran Journal, Home Press Editorials
"Economy," August 17, 1961.

252. Arthur W. Lewis, The Theory of Economic
Growth (London: 1955), p. 26; Tehran Journal,
"Conspicuous Expenditure," November 9, 1959.

253. Tehran Journal, "'Economic Difficulties
Not Feared,' Shah says," November 23, 1959; Tehran
Journal, Editorials, "Isfahan's White Gold," October
10, 1960; Tehran Journal, Iran Economic News, "New

Report on Isfahan Mills," May 30, 1960; Tehran Journal, Iran Economic Commentaries, "Montaz Textile Mill," June 25, 1960.

254. Tehran Journal, Iran Economic News, "Special Delegation To Report on Isfahan Textile Mills," March 7, 1960; Tehran Journal, Iran Economic News, "No Loan for Isfahan Textile Mills," March 9, 1960.

255. Tehran Journal, "Court Awards Factory to Workers," June 5, 1961.

256. George Frey & Associates, Market Survey of the Textile Industry of Iran (Tehran: 1959), IX, pp. 8-9. Kayhan International, "Iran's Textile Industry," June 10, 1961; Tehran Journal, Iran Economic News, "Protection of Infant Industries Urged," July 21, 1960.

257. Tehran Journal, Home Press Editorials, "Causes of Business Failures," September 26, 1960; Tehran Journal, "Welfare Groups To Establish Drug Factory in Iran," June 5, 1960.

258. Tehran Journal, Local Press Reports, "Embezzlement of Sherkat Vahed," February 8, 1960; Tehran Journal, "UBC Officials Had Planned Bankruptcy," June 6, 1961; Tehran Journal, "Meat Scandal Case Goes to Supreme Court," February 11, 1960; Tehran Journal, "Crowds Demonstrate Against Shin Company," November 26, 1959; Tehran Journal, "Power Supply Frauds Bared," March 2, 1961.

259. Tehran Journal, "Meat Scandal Trial Ends," July 31, 1961; Tehran Journal, "Forushgah Ferdousi," November 13, 1959; Tehran Journal, Comedies and Tragedies Retold, "Tehran," November 25, 1969.

260. Tehran Journal, "Iran's Economic Problems, V," June 14, 1961; Ibid., part VI, June 19, 1961; Tehran Journal, "Economic Planning in Iran," January 7, 1960; Tehran Journal, "Inflation and Economic Growth," June 13, 1960.

261. Hanson, op. cit., p. 184.

262. Tehran Journal, Iran Economic Commentaries, "Refrigerators," June 18, 1960; Kayhan International, "Big Dam's Dilemma," June 5, 1961; Tehran Journal, "80,000 kwts. of Electricity for

Tehran," July 31, 1961; Tehran Journal, Editorials, "Aptitude Rather Than Wealth," April 17, 1961.

263. Lewis, op. cit., pp. 203-04.

264. Tehran Journal, Home Press Editorials, "Govt's Basic Duty," October 31, 1960.

265. Lewis, op. cit., p. 227; Tehran Journal, Iran Economic News, "Land Prices Rose 20 to 50 Percent During Last Year," July 1, 1960.

266. Farmanfarmian, K.F., "Social Change and Economic Behavior in Iran," Social Science Seminar. Tehran: Univ. of Tehran Faculty of Arts and UNESCO, passim. (Mineographed.)

267. Tehran Journal, Comedies and Tragedies Retold, March 18, 1961; Tehran Journal, "Home Goods To Carry Persian Labels," April 4, 1960.

268. Millspaugh, op. cit., pp. 83-84.

269. Review, op. cit., pp. 9-14; Tehran Journal, Iran Economic News, "38 Mil. Rials Worth of Gifts Imported," January 19, 1960; Tehran Journal, Iran Economic News, "Private Investments in Industry Amounts to 18,416 Mil. Rials," January 13, 1960.

270. George Frey & Associates, op. cit., IPM 4, VII, p. 9; Shah, Press (1337), op. cit., pp. 28-29.

271. Tehran Journal, Home Press Editorials, "Make Medical Treatment Free," December 29, 1959; Tehran Journal, Iran Economic News, "The Warehouse Bill," May 14, 1960; Tehran Journal, "Miscellany," February 11, 1961.

272. Tehran Journal, "Amini Opens Campaign Against Waste of Labor," July 2, 1961.

273. Buchanan and Ellis, op. cit., p. 63, fn.; Tehran Journal, "Will The Third Plan Be Implemented?" October 18, 1960.

FOOTNOTES TO CHAPTER 4

1. Bertrand Russell, The History of Western Philosophy, and Its Connection With Political and Social Circumstances From the Earliest Times To the Present Day (New York: 1945), p. 111.

2. For this problem in China, see Fei, op. cit., pp. 73-74.

3. Tehran Journal, Editorials, "University Students," March 28, 1961.

4. Tehran Journal, Editorials, "Let the Colleges Open," February 7, 1961.

5. Untereiner, op. cit., VII, 1; Tehran Journal, the Panel, December 28, 1959.

6. Tehran Journal, Home Press Editorials, "Dear Students, We Have More To Tell You," January 14, 1960.

7. Tehran Journal, Editorials, "Students For Discussion," July 15, 1961.

8. Tehran Journal, "Labor Training Center Opens Near Rail Depot," December 11, 1960.

9. Hanson, op. cit., pp. 323, 372-73.

10. Tehran Journal, "Miscellany," June 18, 1961; Pahlavi, op. cit., Ch. 11.

11. Tehran Journal, Iran Economic News, "Statistics To Be Made of Iranian Experts," May 3, 1960.

12. Tehran Journal, Iran Economic Commentaries, "Non-professionals vs. Professionals," February 27, 1960.

13. Tehran Journal, Editorials, "People's Role in Education," October 19, 1960; Tehran Journal, "Students Set Their Terms," January 13, 1960.

14. Tehran Journal, Local Press Reports, "Best Mayor of the Year To Receive Prize," January 13, 1960.

15. Pahlavi, op. cit., Ch. 11.

16. Untereiner, op. cit., VII, 5; Tehran Journal, "Yakety-Yakety-Yak," July 27, 1960; Tehran Journal, "How To Start," February 4, 1960.

17. Levy, op. cit., passim.

18. Tehran Journal, Home Press Editorials, "Make Medical Treatment Free," December 29, 1960.

19. Untereiner, op. cit., VIII, 12; Tehran Journal, "Emerging Mediocrity," November 4, 1959.

20. Lambton, op. cit., pp. 278-82.

21. See Hsiao, op. cit., p. 254 for this in China.

22. Tehran Journal, Home Press Editorials, "Automation and Iran," December 22, 1960.

23. Pahlavi, op. cit., pp. 310-11.

24. Tehran Journal, the Panel, June 2, 1960.

25. Tehran Journal, "Iranian Army Will Revise Promotion, Retirement Rules," August 27, 1960; Tehran Journal, "Shah Expresses Gratitude To People for Big Support," October 29, 1959; Tehran Journal, "'Iranians Taking Over Aid Programs,' Brenn Says in Washington," November 1, 1959.

26. Lewis, op. cit., p. 326.

27. Tehran Journal, Iran Economic News, "Funds Allocated for Technical Shops," February 21, 1960; Tehran Journal, "Six Vocational Schools for City," October 13, 1960; Tehran Journal, "Budget Increase Urged by Min. of Education," December 31, 1960.

28. Buchanan and Ellis, op. cit., p. 85.

29. Pahlavi, op. cit., pp. 183-84.

30. Ibid., p. 239.

31. Levy, op. cit., pp. 334-35.

FOOTNOTES TO CHAPTER 5

1. Untereiner, op. cit., VI, 22; Tehran Journal, Home Press Editorials, "Youth Leaders Conference," July 17, 1960; Tehran Journal, Editorials, "Free Enterprise and Farming," October 23, 1960.

2. Bonne, op. cit., pp. 311-312.

3. Tehran Journal, "Economic Council To Debate Esfahan Factories Position," August 2, 1960; Tehran Journal, Home Press Editorials, "The New Deputies," February 26, 1961; for a similar problem in China, see Hsiao, op. cit., pp. 281-83.

4. Tehran Journal, Local Press Reports, "Control of Medical Practice," March 6, 1959; see also Hsiao, op. cit., pp. 255-58.

5. Tehran Journal, Home Press Editorials, "Political Parties," October 20, 1960.

6. Tehran Journal, Editorials, "Service for Iran's Students Abroad," November 21, 1960.

7. Tehran Journal, Home Press Editorials, "The Royal Speech," August 21, 1961.

8. Untereiner, op. cit., VI, 4.

9. Tehran Journal, Editorials, "Salary Discrimination," March 16, 1961.

10. Tehran Journal, Local Press Reports, "Salary Raise," January 31, 1960.

11. Untereiner, op. cit., VI, 21; Shah, Press, 1338, op. cit., pp. 27-29; Tehran Journal, "Meet the King's Minister of Agriculture," May 30, 1960.

12. Tehran Journal, "Teachers Now Draft Exempt," November 30, 1960.

13. Tehran Journal, Editorials, "Two More Letters," July 18, 1961.

14. Tehran Journal, "Forget About Government,"
January 25, 1960; Tehran Journal, "New System Neces-
sary," January 31, 1960; Tehran Journal, Editorials,
"Iranian Students Abroad," December 28, 1960; Tehran
Journal, Editorials, "It's a Good Idea!" December 29,
1960; for this same dilemma in China, see Y.C. Wang,
"Western Impact and Social Mobility in China,"
American Sociological Review, 6, (December, 1960),
845.

15. Kayhan International, Press Review,
"Asiaye Democrat," February 18, 1961; Tehran Journal,
"Problem After Problem," January 24, 1960.

16. Tehran Journal, Home Press Editorials,
"In Defense of the Students," January 18, 1960;
Tehran Journal, Home Press Editorials, "Who Was In
the Wrong?" January 15, 1960.

17. Tehran Journal, Editorials, "Birth of a
Varsity," August 15, 1960.

18. Tehran Journal, Home Press Editorials,
"Unemployment Danger Among High School Graduates,"
July 3, 1960; Tehran Journal, Iran Economic Commen-
taries, "Private Varsities," January 28, 1960.

19. Tehran Journal, Editorials, "Revised
Electoral Law," February 23, 1961.

20. Shah Press (1338), op. cit., pp. 51-52.

21. Tehran Journal, Editorials, "The Magic
Word," August 12, 1960.

22. For a similar situation in China, see
Wright, op. cit., pp. 92-93.

23. Tehran Journal, Home Press Editorials,
"The Story of Dr. Tayyebi," August 17, 1960.

24. Kayhan International, Supplement, "Down
to Earth," July 6, 1961.

25. Tehran Journal, Home Press Editorials,
June 18, 1960; Tehran Journal, Home Press Editorials,
"The People of Iran and Freedom of Elections," June
19, 1960.

26. Lambton, op. cit., p. 393.

27. For a general discussion of this problem, see K. Parsons et. al., op. cit., pp. 402-43.

28. For a discussion of this problem in China, see Fei, op. cit., pp. 132-36.

29. For a discussion of this in China, see Hsiao, op. cit., pp. 255-58.

30. Lambton, op. cit., p. 262.

31. Ibid., pp. 394-96.

32. Ibid., p. 264.

33. Tehran Journal, Home Press Editorials, "Majlis' Relativity," February 21, 1961.

34. Tehran Journal, Editorials, "An Inspiring Guest," November 9, 1959.

35. Lambton, op. cit., pp. 337-38.

36. Untereiner, op. cit., VI, 11; Tehran Journal, "Generals...," May 14, 1961.

37. Tehran Journal, "Increase in Workers' Wage Main Objective,' says Labour Minister," February 4, 1960.

38. Adapted from Bonne, op. cit. pp. 235-37; Tehran Journal, "Amini Vows To Continue Fight Against Graft," May 16, 1961.

39. Buchanan and Ellis, op. cit., p. 415.

40. Millspaugh, op. cit., p. 238.

41. Untereiner, op. cit., pp. 52-57.

42. Pahlavi, op. cit., p. 164.

43. See, for example, Bernard Barber, Social Stratification (New York: 1957), Ch. 16.

44. Buchanan and Ellis, op. cit., p. 32.

45. Lewis, op. cit., p. 48.

46. See, for example, Untereiner, op. cit., V, 54.

47. See any standard text on social stratification, as, e.g., Barber, op. cit., or E.E. Bergel, Social Stratification (New York: 1962), Chs. 1, 2.

48. Lewis, op. cit., p. 228.

49. Ibid., p. 232.

FOOTNOTES TO CHAPTER 6

1. Lambton, op. cit., p. 203.

2. Ibid., p. 200.

3. Ibid., p. 278.

4. Ibid., pp. 296-97.

5. Ibid., pp. 278-79, 282, 305.

6. Tehran Journal, "Law of Succession, Not Enough," January 14, 1960.

7. Lambton, op. cit., p. 259; R. Levy, op. cit., p. 70.

8. Norman Jacobs, "The Social Challenge of Land Reform in East Asia," Far Eastern Economic Review (Hong Kong), XXII, 8 (February 21, 1957), 234-37.

9. Tehran Journal, Home Press Editorials, December 13, 1959.

10. Hanson, op. cit., pp. 450-51.

11. Fn. 8, loc. cit.

FOOTNOTES TO CHAPTER 7

1. R. Levy, op. cit., p. 171.

2. H. A. R. Gibb and J. H. Kramers, Shorter Encyclopedia of Islam (Leiden: 1953), p. 534.

3. Dwight Donaldson, The Shi'ite Religion, A History of Islam In Persia and Irak (London: 1933), p. 37.

4. _Ibid._, p. 87.

5. _Tehran Journal_, Editorials, "The Duty of Parents," February 6, 1961.

6. Donaldson, _op. cit._, Ch. 33.

7. Untereiner, _op. cit._, VI, 4.

8. Lambton, _op. cit._, pp. 173-74.

9. Donaldson, _op. cit._, p. 63.

10. Lambton, _op. cit._, pp. 173-74.

11. _Ibid._, p. 238.

12. _Ibid._, Ch. XI.

13. Pahlavi, _op. cit._, p. 200.

14. Donaldson, _op. cit._, pp. 184-87.

15. Lambton, _op. cit._, p. 215.

16. Richard Gable, "Culture and Administration In Iran," _Middle East Journal_, (Autumn, 1959), 412.

17. Lambton, _op. cit._, pp. 194-95.

18. _Ibid._, p. xx.

19. Gibb and Kramers, _op. cit._, pp. 201-02.

20. R. Levy, _op. cit._, pp. 68-70.

21. Donaldson, _op. cit._, p. 67.

22. _Ibid._, pp. 47-48.

23. _Ibid._, _passim_; Gibb and Kramers, _op. cit._, pp. 164-66.

24. Donaldson, _op. cit._, XXIII-XXV; R. Levy, _op. cit._, p. 288.

25. R. Levy, _op. cit._, p. 373.

26. Pahlavi, _op. cit._, pp. 54-58.

27. Untereiner, _op. cit._, VI, 4.

28. Donaldson, op. cit., pp. xxi-xxiii.

29. Ibid., XXX; Levy, op. cit., pp. 209-11.

30. R. Levy, op. cit., pp. 181-82.

31. Shah, Press (1338), op. cit., pp. 30-31;
Tehran Journal, "Malayer Protests Foreign Radio
Attacks Against Iran," March 10, 1960; Tehran
Journal, "Iranians Demonstrate...," December 27, 1959;
Tehran Journal, "Najaf Religious Leaders Reportedly
Threaten Jehad," December 23, 1959; Tehran Journal,
Home Press Editorials, "From Jehad," August 5, 1960.

32. Bonne, op. cit., p. 325, Ch. XXXII.

33. Ibid., pp. 36-37.

34. Tehran Journal, "The Minister's Report,"
February 7, 1960.

35. Donaldson, op. cit., p. 291; Pahlavi, op.
cit., pp. 246-67.

36. Pahlavi, op. cit., pp. 227-29; Tehran
Journal, "For Men and for Women," April 13, 1960.

37. Clyde Kluckhohn, Mirror for Man (New York:
1957), p. 168.

38. Tehran Journal, Editorials, "The Now Ruz
Message," March 27, 1960; Tehran Journal, Editorials,
"It Shall Not Be," July 19, 1960.

39. Tehran Journal, Editorials, "Seven Days of
Mourning," April 5, 1961; Bonne, op. cit., XXXII;
Untereiner, op. cit., IV, 45.

40. Russell, op. cit., p. 427.

41. Tehran Journal, Editorials, "Provincial
Education," November 13, 1960.

42. Pahlavi, op. cit., pp. 238-42.

43. Tehran Journal, Editorials, "Let the
Colleges Open," February 7, 1961.

44. Tehran Journal, the Panel, December 6,
1959.

45.   _Tehran Journal_, Home Press Editorials,
"The Magic Spell," September 3, 1960.

46.   _Tehran Journal_, "Literary Academy To Be
Re-formed," June 20, 1960.

47.   _Tehran Journal_, Home Press Editorials,
"Farsi Language," January 19, 1961.

48.   Pahlavi, _op. cit._, pp. 238-39.

49.   Robert R. Merton, _Social Theory and Social
Structure_ (New York: 1957), part IV.

50.   _Tehran Journal_, Home Press Editorials,
"This Is Not the Way To Do Things," March 8, 1960.

51.   _Tehran Journal_, "Education Ministry and
Private Universities," February 25, 1960.

52.   Pahlavi, _op. cit._, pp. 244-45.

53.   _Tehran Journal_, Editorials, "Advice to
Students--Know Iran Before Going Abroad," September
7, 1960; _Tehran Journal_, Home Press Editorials,
"Private University, Colleges are Essential," March
10, 1960.

54.   _Tehran Journal_, "Iran's Loss of Non-
returning Students Highest," June 25, 1960.

55.   R. Levy, _op. cit._, VI, _passim_.

56.   Bonne, _op. cit._, p. 382.

57.   _Tehran Journal_, Home Press Editorials,
"What Is the Use Of...," February 16, 1960.

58.   _Tehran Journal_, Home Press Editorials, "At
the Press Association," July 20, 1961.

59.   _Tehran Journal_, Home Press Editorials, "Do
Foreigners Not Know?" August 19, 1960.

60.   _Tehran Journal_, Home Press Editorials,
"Better Propaganda," October 3, 1960.

61.   _Tehran Journal_, Home Press Editorials,
"How To Start Reforms," March 2, 1961.

FOOTNOTES TO CHAPTER 8

1. _Facts About Iran_, No. 99, _op. cit._, p. 5.

2. Pahlavi, _op. cit._, p. 328.

3. _Tehran Journal_, "Kassem Could Visit Iran," February 18, 1960.

4. _Tehran Journal_, Editorials, "Government's Mild Policy," July 30, 1961.

5. _Tehran Journal_, Home Press Editorials, "Hands of Foreign Agents Are Cut Off," July 19, 1960.

6. _Tehran Journal_, Editorials, "British Embassy Statement," July 10, 1961.

7. Derived from personal discussions with local citizens, Shiraz, September, 1960.

8. _Tehran Journal_, "Incentive to Farmers--Prize of 1,000 Rials," August 2, 1961; _Tehran Journal_, Local Press Reports, "Direct Taxes," January 31, 1960; _Tehran Journal_, "Fraud Detected In Tehran Municipal Books," August 12, 1961; _Tehran Journal_, "Investigations Continue in Gen. Kia's Case," August 13, 1961; _Kayhan International_, "Dud Cheques Galore," July 26, 1961; _Tehran Journal_, "24 Gilan Brigade Officers Arrested," July 19, 1960; _Tehran Journal_, "5 Brigadiers, 56 Colonels Under Trial," July 22, 1960; _Kayhan International_, "Zargham, Navici Interrogation by Tribunal," June 6, 1961; _Tehran Journal_, "Amini Promises To Fight Corruption...," April 21, 1961; _Tehran Journal_, "Fresh Charges Filed Against Gen. Zargham," June 1, 1961.

9. _Tehran Journal_, Editorials, "Land Reform," July 12, 1961.

10. _Tehran Journal_, "Iran Welcomes Amini Government's Reforms," June 8, 1961; _Tehran Journal_, Home Press Editorials, "Will Dr. Amini Succeed," July 16, 1961.

11. Karl Wittfogel, _Oriental Despotism_ (New Haven: 1957), _passim_.

12. _Kayhan International_, Press Review, -Bamshad, June 7, 1961.

13.   Untereiner, op. cit., VI, 25.

14.   Tehran Journal, "Amini Urges Administrative Overhaul," June 21, 1961; Tehran Journal, "Univ. Students Welcome Parliament Dissolution, Promise of Reforms," May 11, 1961.

15.   Tehran Journal, Home Press Editorials, "Troublemakers On The Political Scene," August 25, 1960.

16.   Pahlavi, op. cit., pp. 174-75.

17.   Tehran Journal, "'The Nation's Future in Hands of Youth,' Shah Tells Students," August 25, 1960.

18.   Tehran Journal, Editorials, "Khruschev's Warning to Iran," April 27, 1961.

19.   Tehran Journal, Editorials, "The Fanatic General," June 20, 1961.

20.   For a popular description of "tame-criticism," see Grace and Fred Hechinger, "In Criticism of Anti-criticism," New York Times, Magazine Section, (March 11, 1962), 28.

21.   Pahlavi, op. cit., p. 129.

FOOTNOTES TO CHAPTER 9

1.   Tehran Journal, Comedies and Tragedies Retold, "Tehran," February 2, 1960.

2.   Tehran Journal, "Ala Criticizes Foreign Press at I.A.S. Seminar," August 27, 1960.

3.   Tehran Journal, Comedies and Tragedies Retold, November 23, 1960; Tehran Journal, Iran Economic News, "Rumours Paralyze Tehran Market," June 8, 1960.

4.   Tehran Journal, the Panel, June 14, 1961; Tehran Journal, Comedies and Tragedies Retold, February 26, 1961.

5.   Tehran Journal, Comedies and Tragedies Retold, "Shahrara," May 11, 1961.

6. Untereiner, op. cit., IV, 25, 34.

7. Tehran Journal, Comedies and Tragedies Retold, April 23, 1961; Comedies and Tragedies Retold, May 27, 1961; Comedies and Tragedies Retold, December 31, 1960.

8. Tehran Journal, Comedies and Tragedies Retold, May 31, 1960.

9. Tehran Journal, Comedies and Tragedies Retold, August 7, 1960.

10. Tehran Journal, Comedies and Tragedies Retold, August 31, 1960.

11. Tehran Journal, Comedies and Tragedies Retold, February 7, 1961.

12. Tehran Journal, Comedies and Tragedies Retold, February 15, 1960.

13. Tehran Journal, "Father's Will Leads Two to Court Trial," July 17, 1960.

14. Untereiner, op. cit., IV, 30-31; Pahlavi, op. cit., pp. 247-48.

15. For a similar situation in India, see Koestler, op. cit., p. 154.

16. Tehran Journal, "Inshallah! or Manana!" July 1, 1960.

17. Bonne, op. cit., p. 327.

18. Tehran Journal, "Injured Denied Admission to City Hospitals," July 18, 1960.

19. Untereiner, op. cit., IV, 27-28.

20. Tehran Journal, "Old Matrix and New Industries," August 5, 1960.

21. Murdock, op. cit., pp. 273-74.

22. Tehran Journal, Comedies and Tragedies Retold, November 1, 1959.

23. Tehran Journal, Home Press Editorials, June 27, 1960.

24. *Tehran Journal*, Home Press Editorials, July 16, 1961.

25. *Tehran Journal*, Comedies and Tragedies Retold, February 17, 1960.

26. *Tehran Journal*, Comedies and Tragedies Retold,"Quchan," January 29, 1960.

27. Russell, *op. cit.*, p. 201.

28. *Tehran Journal*, Comedies and Tragedies Retold, January 4, 1960.

29. *Tehran Journal*, Comedies and Tragedies Retold, December 1, 1959.

30. *Tehran Journal*, the Panel, May 5, 1960.

31. *Tehran Journal*, Comedies and Tragedies Retold, May 8, 1960.

32. *Tehran Journal*, "Tehran," April 5, 1961.

33. *Tehran Journal*, Comedies and Tragedies Retold, March 31, 1960.; *Tehran Journal*, Comedies and Tragedies Retold, April 3, 1960.

34. *Kayhan International*, "Agricultural Policy in Economic Development," June 8, 1961.

35. *Tehran Journal*, the Panel, May 31, 1960.

36. *Tehran Journal*, "Woman's Death Case," January 7, 1961.

37. See S. M. Lipset, "Democracy and Working Class Authoritarianism," *American Sociological Review*, 4 (August, 1959), 492-93.

38. Pahlavi, *op. cit.*, p. 255.

39. Untereiner, *op. cit.*, IV, 25-26.

40. *Tehran Journal*, Editorials, "An Event of Significance," December 18, 1960.

41. *Tehran Journal*, Editorials, "The Sudden Calamity," April 26, 1960.

42. Untereiner, *op. cit.*, IV, 33.

43. *Tehran Journal*, "What is the Purpose of Education?" January 21, 1960.

44. Untereiner, *op. cit.*, IV, 2, 37.

45. Hanson, *op. cit.*, 6-7.

46. Untereiner, *op. cit.*, V, 56.

47. *Tehran Journal*, Comedies and Tragedies Retold, April 15, 1961; *Tehran Journal*, Comedies and Tragedies Retold, "Shirevan," May 27, 1961.

48. *Tehran Journal*, Comedies and Tragedies Retold, December 3, 1959.

49. *Tehran Journal*, Editorials, "The Student Who Murdered," October 20, 1960.

50. *Tehran Journal*, Home Press Editorials, "Let Us Be Fair," August 16, 1961.

51. Untereiner, *op. cit.*, IV, 30-33.

52. *Tehran Journal*, "Killer To Be Hanged Today," August 2, 1960.

53. *Tehran Journal*, Letters to the Editor, May 31, 1960.

54. *Tehran Journal*, Home Press Editorials, "The Farmers' Day," September 11, 1960.

55. Untereiner, *op. cit.*, IV, 32.

56. Gable, *op. cit.*, *passim*.

57. Untereiner, *op. cit.*, VI, 91; *Tehran Journal*, the Panel, September 23, 1960.

58. Untereiner, *op. cit.*, V, 53-54.

59. *Kayhan International*, Comment, July 6, 1961.

60. *Tehran Journal*, Comedies and Tragedies Retold, July 15, 1961.

61. Emile Burkheim, *Suicide* (New York: 1951), *passim*.

62. <u>Tehran Journal</u>, Iran Economic Commentaries, "The Steel Mill Contract Signed," July 2, 1960; <u>Tehran Journal</u>, Editorials, "Price Levels in 1340," April 29, 1961.

63. Pahlavi, <u>op. cit.</u>, Ch. 14.

64. Ssu-yu Teng and J. K. Fairbank, <u>China's Response to the West</u> (Cambridge: 1954), <u>passim.</u>

65. Riesman <u>et. al.</u>, <u>op. cit.</u>, pp. 278-79.

66. <u>Tehran Journal</u>, Home Press Editorials, "Let Us Keep Our Peace," August 8, 1961; <u>Tehran Journal</u>, Home Press Editorials, "From Audisheh Mardom," April 11, 1960.

67. Riesman <u>et. al.</u>, <u>op. cit.</u>, p. 33.

68. Lucy Mair, <u>Studies in Applied Anthropology</u>, (London, 1957), p. 72.

69. <u>Tehran Journal</u>, Comedies and Tragedies Retold, June 8, 1961.

70. <u>Tehran Journal</u>, Comedies and Tragedies Retold, June 1, 1960.

71. Untereiner, <u>op. cit.</u>, IV, 37.

72. <u>Tehran Journal</u>, "Honesty and Cooperation," April 21, 1960; <u>Tehran Journal</u>, "Social Obstacles Across Industrial Development," November 13, 1959.

73. <u>Tehran Journal</u>, "Police Officer Shoots Wife, Kills Himself," August 7, 1961.

FOOTNOTES TO CHAPTER 10

1. Norman Jacobs, <u>The Origin of Modern Capitalism and Eastern Asia</u> (Hong Kong: 1958) <u>passim</u>. (Hereafter cited as "Jacobs, Origin.")

2. Lambton, <u>op. cit.</u>, pp. 53-55; for an excellent discussion of Weber's contribution to this thesis, see Reinhard Bendix, <u>Max Weber, An Intellectual Portrait</u> (New York: 1962), pp. 360-69.

3. Bonne, <u>op. cit.</u>, pp. 382, 383; Buchanan and Ellis, <u>op. cit.</u>, pp. 407-08.

4. Bonne, <u>op. cit.</u>, pp. 122-26.

FOOTNOTES TO CHAPTER 11

1. Buchanan and Ellis, op. cit., p. 5.

2. UNESCO, Urbanization in Asia and the Far East (Calcutta: 1957), passim.

3. John Brush, "The Growth of Large Cities in India," Journal of Aisan Studies, XXI, 4 (August, 1962), 623.

4. Walt Whitman, Rostow, The Stages of Economic Growth (Cambridge: 1960), passim.

5. William F. Ogburn, Social Change (New York: 1922), passim.

6. Milbank Memorial Fund, Economic and Social Problems in Selected Underdeveloped Areas (New York: 1954), pp. 68-70.

7. Kluckhohn, op. cit., p. 51.

8. Lewis, op. cit., passim.

9. Hanson, op. cit., p. 67.

10. See the work of Fred W. Riggs, e.g., "Reflection and Development," (Honolulu: 1963). (Mimeographed for limited circulation.)

11. Choh-ming Li, Economic Development of Communist China (Berkeley: 1959).

12. Agricultural Bank of Iran, op. cit., p. 12.

13. Thomas C. Smith, Political Change and Industrial Development in Japan: Government Enterprise, 1868-80 (Stanford: 1955) and Henry Rosovsky, Capital Formation in Japan, 1868-1940 (New York: 1961).

14. Hanson, op. cit., p. 55; Tehran Journal, "Amini Bans Import of all Luxury Goods," June 5, 1961.

15. Compare Tehran Journal, Home Press Editorials, "Basis of Friendship," with Tehran Journal, the Panel, July 20, 1960; the Panel, July 26, 1960 and the Panel, July 31, 1960.

16.   Untereiner, op. cit., VIII, 12; Pahlavi, op. cit., p. 130-31; Tehran Journal, Editorials, "Visit of Queen Elizabeth," March 2, 1960; Tehran Journal, "Who Will Benefit by Dictatorship?" July 26, 1961; Tehran Journal, Home Press Editorials, "The New U.S. Ambassador," May 23, 1961; Tehran Journal, Home Press Editorials, "Confidence in Future," June 1, 1960; Tehran Journal, "Absolute Freedom Breeds Despotism," July 25, 1961.

17.   Compare Eric Stokes, The English Utilitarians and India (Oxford: 1959) with Frederick Clairmonte, Economic Liberalism and Underdevelopment (Bombay: 1960) and Hanson, op. cit., p. 212.

18.   For a similar controversy in China, see Wright, op. cit., p. 186.

19.   Tehran Journal, "Social, Administrative Reforms Necessary for Economic Growth," October 26, 1960.

20.   Hanson, op. cit., pp. 448-52.

21.   Ibid., p. 449.

22.   J. Van Ball, "Erring Acculturation," American Anthropologist, LXII, 1, (February,1960), 108-11.

23.   Lewis, op. cit., p. 143.

24.   For example, C. E. Ayres, Toward a Reasonable Society (Univ. of Texas Press, 1962) and Marion J. Levy, Jr., The Family Revolution in Modern China. (Cambridge: 1949).

25.   For this question in China, see Wright, op. cit., p. 196.

26.   Pahlavi, op. cit., pp. 132-33, 137.

27.   Ibid., p. 132.

28.   Buchanan and Ellis, op. cit., p. 407.

29.   Russell, op. cit., p. 620.

30.   Hanson, op. cit., pp. 24-25.

31.   Ibid., pp. 93-98.

32. Rosovsky, op. cit.; Smith, op. cit.

33. Tehran Journal, Home Press Editorials,
"Wasted Revenue," October 30, 1960; Tehran Journal,
"Iran's Resources and Needs," January 8, 1960.

34. Lewis, op. cit., p. 236.

35. Hanson, op. cit., p. 162.

36. Ibid., p. 62.

37. Buchanan and Ellis, op. cit., p. 407.

38. Arthur Krock, "Warning on Aid," New York
Times, News of the Week in Review, September 24,
1961.

39. Tehran Journal, "New York Tribune Cities
Problems Facing Dr. Amini," June 13, 1961.

40. Bonne, op. cit., p. 378.

41. Hanson, op. cit., pp. 70-71, 204, 422.

42. Ibid., p. 421.

43. Ibid., p. 149.

44. Tehran Journal, Home Press Editorials,
"Germany Above All," August 13, 1961.

45. Tehran Journal, Home Press Editorials,
"National Progress," January 24, 1960.

46. Buchanan and Ellis, op. cit., pp. 287, 289.

47. Hanson, op. cit., p. 51. For the pros-
pering of an economy during periods of unrest and
especially at that time in an Asian society, see,
for example, in the case of China, Wolfram Eberhard,
A History of China (Berkeley: 1955), passim.

48. Hanson, op. cit., pp. 51, 421.

49. Ibid., pp. 412-417.

50. Ibid., p. 54.

51. Ibid., pp. 296, 407-08; Review, op. cit.,
p. 33.

52. Hanson, op. cit., pp. 186-87.

53. Ibid., pp. 187-190.

54. Lewis, op. cit., p. 236.

55. Buchanan and Ellis, op. cit., p. 411; Hanson, op. cit., pp. 20, 147, 193, 322.

56. Robert K. Lamb, "Political Elites and the Process of Economic Development, in B. Hoselitz, The Progress of Underdeveloped Areas (Chicago: 1952), pp. 30-53.

57. Kayhan International, "Finding Free Enterprises--3," July 15, 1961.

58. Milbank Memorial Fund, op. cit., p. 181.

59. See, for example, Robert Bellah, Tokugawa Religion (Glencoe: 1957), especially Chapter VII.

60. Lewis, op. cit., p. 181; Hanson, op. cit., pp. 43-44.

61. Tehran Journal, "Development Plans," July 24, 1960.

62. Fn. 59, loc. cit.

63. Ibid; James Abeqqlen, The Japanese Factory, Aspects of its Social Organization (Glencoe: 1958), passim.

64. William J. Lederer and Eugene Burdick, The Ugly American (New York: 1958).

65. Peggy and Pierre Streit, "Remote Views of U.S. in a Remote Land," New York Times Magazine Section, (November 13, 1960), p. 43. The clever manipulation of a foreign press against itself is not a new technique in Asian political circles; for the 19th century China, see Wright, op. cit., p. 241.

66. Millspaugh, op. cit., pp. 143-44.

67. Kluckhohn, op. cit., pp. 38, 136.

68. Compare Hanson, op. cit., pp. 43-35 with G. W. Skinner, Chinese Society in Thailand (Ithaca: 1957), pp. 92-94.

69. Pahlavi, op. cit., pp. 13, 18, Ch. 7, and
p. 160; Tehran Journal, "Amini Stresses Need for
Order, Discipline," July 4, 1961; Tehran Journal,
"His Majesty Sends Message to Iranian Art Congress,"
April 27, 1960.

70. Untereiner, op. cit., IX, 3.

                    FOOTNOTES TO CHAPTER 12

1. Hanson, op. cit., pp. 270-71; Untereiner,
op. cit., II, 11-12, IX, 2.

2. Tehran Journal, "Improving Living Conditions," November 17, 1959.

3. For the same attitude by Lenin in the
Soviet Union, see Parsons et. al., op. cit.,
pp. 614-18.

4. Robert H. Lowie, Social Organization (New
York: 1948), p. 31.

5. Bonne, op. cit., p. 379.

6. Buchanan and Ellis, op. cit., p. 259.

7. Hanson, op. cit., p. 294.

8. Buchanan and Ellis, op. cit., p. 407.

9. Bellah, op. cit., passim.

10. Hanson, op. cit., p. 208.

11. Buchanan and Ellis, op. cit., pp. 81-82.

12. Lewis, op. cit., p. 391.

13. Hanson, op. cit., pp. 193, 322.

14. Lewis, op. cit., p. 376.

15. Hanson, op. cit., pp. 50-51.

16. Lewis, op. cit., pp. 349-50.

17. Hanson, op. cit., pp. 343-49.

18.   Untereiner, op. cit., VI, 5; Russell, op. cit., pp. 199-201; Saul Rose, Socialism in Southern Asia (London: 1959), passim.

19.   Tehran Journal, Editorials, "The State of Socialism," December 6, 1960.

20.   Lewis, op. cit., p. 382.

21.   For this chapter in general, see Smith, op. cit., and Jacobs, Origin, passim.

22.   Bellah, op. cit., VII; W. F. Wertheim, "Religion and Bureaucracy, and Economic Growth," paper delivered before the Fifth World Congress of Sociology, September, 1962, Washington D.C., and published in its transactions, Vol 4, Louvain, 1962.

23.   Lewis, op. cit., p. 376.

24.   Essentially this is my answer to Prof. Wertheim's paper (fn. 22, loc. cit.) which I presented at that Congress, entitled "Comments on W. F. Wertheim's "Religion, Bureaucracy and Economic Growth"; the comments are summarized in Archivas de Sociologie des Religions, XV, (Janvier-Juin 1963), 9-10

25.   Koestler, op. cit., p. 113; Lewis, op. cit., p. 166.

26.   Merton, op. cit., part IV.

27.   Pahlavi, op. cit., p. 135.

28.   Tehran Journal, "Germany's Economy," April 24, 1960.

29.   N. Jacobs, The Bahai'i of Iran and Pariah Entrepreneurship (Bloomington: 1964), passim.

30.   Bellah, op. cit., passim.

31.   I am indebted here to the work of the Japanese economist, Hisao Otsuka. See, for example, his paper "The Market Structure of Rural Industry in the Early States of the Development of Modern Capitalism," (Tokyo, 1962) and his many works in Japanese. This interpretation, to note, differs from the one I held in 1958 in my work, Origin, op. cit.

32. Millspaugh, op. cit., p. 135.

33. Tehran Journal, "Partnership for Development," December 1, 1960; Tehran Journal, Home Press Editorials, "We Shall Never Submit to Captivity," June 18, 1961.

34. For a description of this problem in "traditional" China, see Wright, op. cit., pp. 214-20.

35. Ibid., pp. 91-93.

36. Millspaugh, op. cit., p. 52.

37. Wright, op. cit., p. 202.

38. Millspaugh, op. cit., p. 138; Pahlavi, op. cit., pp. 298-304; Tehran Journal, "Meet the King's Minister of Agriculture," May 30, 1960.

39. Lewis, op. cit., pp. 19-20.

40. Buchanan and Ellis, op. cit., pp. 71-72.

41. Facts about Iran, No. 88, op. cit., pp. 3-14.

42. International Cooperation Administration, Reply to Criticism in the Ugly American (Washington: 1959), pp. 22-23.

43. Millspaugh, op. cit., p. 145.

44. Ibid., pp. 235-36.

45. Pahlavi, op. cit., Ch. 7, passim; Tehran Journal, Home Press Editorials, "Show More Firmness," June 28, 1961.

46. Wright, op. cit., pp. 265-67.

47. See, for example, Teng and Fairbank, op. cit., passim.

48. Rostow, op. cit., passim.

49. Daniel Bell, The End of Ideology; On the Exhaustion of Political Ideas in the Fifties (Glencoe: 1960), passim.

50.   Buchanan and Ellis, op. cit., pp. 71-72.

51.   Lederer and Burdick, op. cit., Chs. 14, 17, 18, 20, 22.

52.   Fei, op. cit., p. 14.

BIBLIOGRAPHY

BIBLIOGRAPHY

Abegglen, James. The Japanese Factory, Aspects Of Its
Social Organization. Glencoe: Free Press, 1958.

Agarwal, S. Narayan. Principles of Gandhian Planning.
Allahabad: Kitah Mahla, 1960.

"The Agricultural Bank of Iran In An Expanding Economy."
Tehran: Agricultural Bank of Iran, 1961.

Ayres, C. E. Toward a Reasonable Society. Austin:
University of Texas Press, 1962.

Barber, Bernard. Social Stratification. New York:
Harcourt, Brace & World, Inc., 1957.

Bell, Daniel. The End of Ideology: On the Exhaustion
Of Political Ideas In the Fifties. Glencoe: Free
Press, 1960.

Bellah, Robert. Tokugawa Religion. Glencoe: Free
Press, 1960.

Bendix, Reinhard. "Industrialization, Ideologies and
Social Structure," American Sociological Review,
XXIV, No. 5 (October, 1959).

_____. Max Weber, An Intellectual Portrait. New
York: Doubleday & Co., Inc., 1960.

Bergel, E. E. Social Stratification. New York:
McGraw-Hill, 1962.

Boeke, J. H. Economics and Economic Policies of Dual
Societies as Exemplified By Indonesia. New York:
Institute of Pacific Relations, 1953.

Bonne, Alfred. State and Economics in the Middle
East. 2nd ed. London: Kegan Paul, 1955.

Brush, John E. "The Growth of Large Cities In India,"
Journal of Asian Studies, XXI, No. 4 (August, 1962).

Buchanan, Norman and Ellis, Howard. Approaches to
Economic Development. New York: Twentieth Century
Fund, 1955.

Cartwright, Dorwin and Zander, A. Group Dynamics.
    New York: Harper & Row, 1953.

Clairmonte, Frederic. Economic Liberalism and
    Underdevelopment. London: Asia Publishing House,
    1960.

"Press Conferences of His Imperial Majesty Mohammed
    Reza Shah Pahlavi of Iran During 1337." Tehran:
    Department of Publications and Broadcasting, Office
    of Information, 1958-59.

"Press Conferences of His Imperial Majesty Mohammed
    Reza Shah Pahlavi of Iran During 1338." Tehran:
    Department of Publications and Broadcasting,
    Office of Information, 1959-60.

Donaldson, Dwight. The Shi'ite Religion, A History
    of Islam In Persia and Iraq. London: Luzac and
    Co., 1933.

Durkheim, Emile. Suicide, a Study In Sociology.
    Glencoe: Free Press, 1951.

Eberhard, Wolfram. A History of China. Berkeley:
    University of California Press, 1955.

Farmanfarmian, K. F. "Social Change and Economic
    Behavior In Iran." Social Science Seminar. Tehran:
    University of Tehran, Faculty of Arts, and UNESCO,
    1959. (Mimeographed.)

Fei, Hsiao-tung. China's Gentry. Chicago: University
    of Chicago Press, 1953.

Frey, George and Associates, Inc. "Market Survey of
    the Textile Industry In Iran." Teheran, 1959.

Gable, Richard. "Culture and Administration In Iran,"
    Middle East Journal (Autumn, 1959).

The Plan Organization of Iran, A Brief Economy of
    Activities. ("Facts About Iran," No. 88.) Tehran:
    General Department of Publications and Broadcasting,
    1960.

His Imperial Majesty's Remarks at No-Ruz Salam Cere-
    monies. ("Facts About Iran," No. 99.) Tehran:
    General Department of Publications and Broadcasting,
    1961.

Gibb, H. A. R. and Kramers, J. H.   Shorter Encyclopedia of Islam.   Leiden: E. J. Brill, 1953.

Halpern, Joel.   "Government, Politics and Social
Structure of Laos; A Study of Tradition and
Innovation."   University of California, Los Angeles,
1961.   (Mimeographed.)

Hanson, A. H.   Public Enterprise and Economic Development.   London: Routledge & K. Paul, 1959.

Hechinger, Grace and Hechinger, Fred.   "In Criticism
of Anti-Criticism," New York Times, Magazine Section,
March 11, 1962.

High Council of Stable Administrative Undersecretaries.   Tehran: 1959.

Hoselitz, Bert.   "Generative and Parasitic Cities,"
Economic Development and Cultural Change, III,
No. 3 (1955).

_____.   Review of "Origin of Modern Capitalism and
Eastern Asia" by N. Jacobs, The Annals of the
Academy of Political Science, CCCXXII (March, 1959).

Hsiao, Kung-chuan.   Rural China, Imperial Control in
the Nineteenth Century.   Seattle: University of
Washington Press, 1960.

"Reply to Criticism In the Ugly American." Washington:
International Cooperation Administration, 1959.

Jacobs, Norman.   "Comments on Wertheim, W. F., Religion,
Bureaucracy and Economic Growth."   Unpublished paper
delivered at Fifth World Congress of Sociology,
Washington, D.C., September, 1962.   Summarized (in
French) in Archives de Sociologie des Religions, XV,
(Janvier-Juin, 1963), 9-10.

_____.   The Origin of Modern Capitalism and Eastern
Asia.   Hong Kong: Hong Kong University Press, 1958.

_____.   "The Bahai'i of Iran and Pariah Entrepreneur-
ship."   Exploratory paper reproduced for limited circulation by the Study Group on Entrepreneurship,
IDRC, Indiana University, 1964.   (Mimeographed.)

_____. "The Social Basis of Capitalism: The Case of Iran." Paper delivered at Fifth World Congress of Sociology, Washington, D.C., September, 1962. Published (in French) in Archives de Sociologie des Religions, XV (Janvier-Juin, 1963) as "La Religion et le Developpement Economique: Le cas de l'Iran."

_____. "The Social Challenge of Land Reform in East Asia," Far Eastern Economic Review, (Hong Kong) XXII, No. 8 (February 21, 1957).

Jahoda, Gustav. White Man, A Study Of Attitudes to Europeans in Ghana Before Independence. New York: Oxford University Press, 1961.

Kayhan International (English language daily newspaper, Tehran). October, 1959.

Kluckhohn, Clyde. Mirror for Man. New York: Fawcett Publications, Inc., 1957.

_____, Murray, C. H. and Schneider, D. Personality in Nature, Society and Culture. New York: Alfred H. Knopf, 1956.

Koestler, Arthur. The Lotus and the Robot. New York: Macmillan & Co., 1960.

Krock, Arthur. "Warning on Aid," New York Times, News of the Week in Review, September 24, 1961.

Lamb, Robert K. "Political Elites and the Process of Economic Development," in The Progress of Under-developed Areas, edited by B. Hoselitz. Chicago: University of Chicago Press, 1952.

Lambton, A. K. S. Landlord and Peasant in Persia. Oxford: Royal Institute of International Affairs, 1953.

Lederer, William J. and Burdick, Eugene. The Ugly American. New York: W. W. Norton & Co., Inc., 1958.

Levy, Marion J. Jr. The Family Revolution in Modern China. Cambridge: Harvard University Press, 1949.

Levy, Reuben. The Social Structure of Islam. 2nd ed. Cambridge: Cambridge University Press, 1957.

Lewis, W. Arthur. The Theory of Economic Growth. London: Allen & Unwin, 1955.

Li, Choh-ming. Economic Development of Communist China. Berkeley: University of California Press, 1959.

Linebarger, Paul. The Political Doctrines of Sun Yat-sen. Baltimore: John's Hopkins Press, 1937.

Lipset, S.M. "Democracy and Working Class Authoritarianism," American Sociological Review, XXIV, No. 4 (August, 1959).

Lowie, Robert H. Social Organization. New York: Holt, Rinehart & Winston, 1948.

Mair, Lucy. Studies in Applied Anthropology. London: London School of Economics, 1957.

Merton, Robert K. Social Theory and Social Structure. 2nd ed. New York: Free Press, 1957.

Economic and Social Problems in Selected Underdeveloped Areas. New York: Milbank Memorial Fund, 1954.

Millspaugh, Arthur C. Americans in Persia. Washington: Brookings Institute, 1946.

Murdock, G. P. Social Structure. New York: Macmillan and Co., 1949.

Ogburn, William F. Social Change. New York: Viking Press, 1922.

Olmstead, A.T. History of the Persian Empire. Chicago: University of Chicago Press, 1948.

Otsuka, Hisao. "The Market Structure of Rural Industry in the Early Stages of Capitalism," Tokyo, n.d. (1962?). (Mimeographed.)

Pahlavi, His Imperial Majesty Mohammed Reza Shah, Shananshah of Iran. Mission for My Country. New York: McGraw-Hill Book Co., Inc., 1961.

Parsons, Kenneth H., Penn, R. and Raup, P. Land Tenure. Madison: University of Wisconsin Press, 1956.

Parsons, Talcott and Smelser, N. J. Economy and Society. Glencoe: Free Press, 1956.

Review of the Second Five Year Plan Program of Iran.
    Tehran: Plan Organization, Division of Economic
    Affairs (Economic Bureau), 1960.

Riesman, David, Glaser, N. and Denny. The Lonely
    Crowd. Garden City, New York: Doubleday & Co.,
    Inc., 1953.

Riggs, F. W. "Reflections on Development." Honolulu,
    1963. (Mimeographed for limited circulation.)

Rose, Saul. Socialism in Southern Asia. London:
    Oxford University Press, 1959.

Rosovsky, Henry. Capital Formation in Japan, 1868-
    1940. New York: Free Press, 1961.

Rostow, Walt Whitman. The Stages of Economic
    Growth. New York: Cambridge University Press,
    1960.

Russell, Bertrand. A History of Western Philosophy,
    and Its Connection With Political and Social Cir-
    cumstances From the Earliest Times to the Present
    Day. New York: Simon and Schuster, 1945.

Sahba, Homayoun and Meyers, M. S. "The Iranian Role
    in Technical Development." Social Science Seminar.
    Tehran: University of Tehran, Faculty of Arts,
    and UNESCO, 1959. (Mimeographed.)

Sahlins, Marshall. Review of "Economic Growth Theory,"
    B. Hoselitz, American Anthropologist, LXIV, No. 5,
    Part 1 (October, 1962).

Skinner, G. William. Chinese Society in Thailand.
    Ithaca: Cornell University Press, 1957.

Smith, Thomas C. Political Change and Industrial
    Development in Japan, 1868-80. Stanford: Stanford
    University Press, 1955.

Stokes, Eric. The English Utilitarians and India.
    Oxford: Oxford University Press, 1959.

Stonier, A. W. and Hague, Douglas C. A Textbook of
    Economic Theory. London and New York: Longmans,
    Green, 1953.

Streit, Peggy and Streit, Pierre. "Remote Views of
    the U.S. in a Remote Land," New York Times, Magazine
    Section, November 13, 1960.

Tehran Journal (English language daily newspaper),
October, 1959- September, 1961.

Teng, Ssu-yu and Fairbank, John. China's Response to
the West. Cambridge: Harvard University Press,
1954.

UNESCO, Urbanization in Asia and the Far East.
Calcutta, 1957.

Untereiner, Wayne. "The Administrative Environment
of Iran." Stanford: Stanford University Press, no
date (1958?). (Mimeographed.)

Van Baal, J. "Erring Acculturation," American
Anthropologist, IXII, No. 1 (February, 1960).

Wang, Y. C. "Western Impact and Social Mobility in
China," American Sociological Review, XXV, No. 6
(December, 1960).

Weber, Max. The Theory of Social and Economic
Organization. New York: Oxford University Press,
1947.

Wertheim, W. F. "Religion, Bureaucracy, and Economic
Growth," Transactions of the Fifth World Congress
of Sociology, IV, Louvain: International Sociological Association, 1964.

Wiser, William H. and C. V. Behind Mud Walls, New
York: Agricultural Missions, Inc., 1951.

Wittfogel, Karl. Oriental Depotism. New Haven: Yale
University Press, 1957.

Wright, Mary C. The Last Stand of Chinese Conservatism, The T'ung-chih Restoration, 1862-74. Stanford:
Stanford University Press, 1957.

ABOUT THE AUTHOR

Norman Jacobs is a sociologist and economist,
now serving as Fulbright Professor at the College of
Education, Bangkok, Thailand. His first-hand knowledge of the Middle and Far East began with his experience as Japanese language officer in the Philippines
during World War II and subsequent service on the
staff of the Supreme Commander for the Allied Powers.
He has taught at Taiwan Normal University, Taipei;
been a research scientist specializing in China at
the American University, Washington, D.C.; and was
Professor of Sociology at the University of Kansas.
He has lived in Iran for two years and traveled extensively throughout the area. He is the author of two
earlier books and numerous articles on Asian affairs.

Dr. Jacobs is a graduate of the College of
the City of New York and received his Ph.D. from
Harvard University. He is now in Bangkok on leave
as Professor of Sociology and Asian Studies, University of Illinois.